P9-DDR-080

INSPIRE / PLAN / DISCOVER / EXPERIENCE

ITALY

CONTENTS

DISCOVER 6

EXPERIENCE 48

NEED TO KNOW 534

Left: view over the Colosseum and Roman Forum at sunset; previous page: Matera at dusk

DISCOVER

Lake Orta, Piedmont

WELCOME TO
ITALY

Magnificent piazzas, turquoise seas and rolling hills – Italy has it all. And that's before you add iconic art, more UNESCO World Heritage Sites than anywhere else on earth, and the Italian knack for *la dolce vita*. Whatever your dream trip to Italy entails, this DK Eyewitness Travel Guide will prove the perfect travelling companion.

1 Flowers in bloom in Monti Sibillini National Park, Umbria.

2 Traditional Italian food.

3 A picturesque canal in Venice lined with boats.

Italy only became a country in 1870 – before that it was a turbulent collection of rival city states. Happily for the visitor, their conflicting allegiances and histories resulted in a variety of architecture and art not seen anywhere else in Europe. From the mighty architecture of ancient Rome and Pompeii to the pretty Teutonic mountain villages of the north, and from the lacy Gothic palazzi of Venice to the refined Renaissance churches of Florence, a tour along the Italian peninsula is a roller-coaster ride through European history.

The landscape, too, is incredibly diverse. Ski the spectacular slopes of the Dolomites or witness volcanic pyrotechnics on the summit of Mount Stromboli. Lose yourself in the wilderness of the maquis-clad Sardinian mountains or spot wild ibex in the rocky valleys of the Gran Paradiso national park. Bask on the unspoiled beaches of Puglia or sip vintage wine in the vineyard-cloaked hills of Tuscany. However you choose to experience its natural beauty, Italy will not disappoint.

Italy can easily overwhelm with the sheer number of unmissable cities, towns, villages, archaeological and natural sites that pepper the peninsula. We've picked out themes and planned itineraries to whet your appetite, broken the country down into easily navigable chapters, and created colourful, comprehensive maps to help you plan the perfect visit. Whether you're staying for a weekend, a week, or longer, this Eyewitness guide will ensure that you see the very best the country has to offer. Enjoy the book, and enjoy Italy.

3

SWITZERLAND

Maçon

Geneva

TRENTINO-
ALTO ADIGE
p128

LOMBARDY
AND THE LAKES
p162

Trento

THE VENET
AND FRIU
p102

Lyon

Aosta

NORTHERN ITALY

Brescia

Verona

VENICE
p58

MILAN
p142

Turin

FRANCE

Parma

EMILIA-
ROMAGNA
p424

Bologna

Gap

VALLE D'AOSTA
AND PIEDMONT
p180

Genoa

CENTRA
ITALY

Avignon

LIGURIA
p200

FLORENCE
p332

Nîmes

Monaco

Pisa

Marseille

*Ligurian
Sea*

Siena

Perugi

Toulon

TUSCANY
p366

Viterbo

Corsica

Sassari

SARDINIA
p526

Oristano

EXPLORE
ITALY

This guide divides Italy into
three distinct regions: northern
Italy *(p50)*, central Italy *(p214)*
and southern Italy *(p440)*.
These regions have been
divided into 20 colour-coded
sightseeing areas, as shown
on the map above.

Cagliari

*Mediterranean
Sea*

AUSTRIA

SLOVENIA

Udine

Ljubljana

Trieste

Zagreb

Rijecka

CROATIA

Zadar

EUROPE

North Sea

SWEDEN

DENMARK

UNITED KINGDOM

GERMANY

POLAND

CZECH REP.

FRANCE

SWITZ.

AUSTRIA

HUNGARY

CROATIA

ROMANIA

SERBIA

BULGARIA

ITALY

SPAIN

GREECE

ALGERIA

TUNISIA

Mediterranean Sea

Ancona

LE MARCHE
p414

Adriatic Sea

MBRIA
p400

Pescara

Dubrovnik

L'Aquila

ROME
p222

ABRUZZO, MOLISE AND PUGLIA
p476

Foggia

LAZIO
p320

Bari

Terracina

SOUTHERN ITALY

Brindisi

NAPLES
p448

Salerno

Potenza

Taranto

CAMPANIA
p462

Tyrrhenian Sea

BASILICATA AND CALABRIA
p490

Cosenza

Ionian Sea

Messina

Reggio di Calabria

Palermo

SICILY
p500

Catania

Agrigento

Syracuse

0 kilometres   100

0 miles   100

N

REASONS TO
LOVE ITALY

Evocative ruins, extravagant palaces, vineyards, strong espresso and freshly baked pizza: there are so many reasons to love Italy. Here, we pick some of our favourites.

1 THE APERITIVO

There's no better way to fill the hours before dinner. Designed to whet your appetite, this Italian tradition consists of a cool sparkling drink served with snacks ranging from olives to exquisite little antipasti.

CRUISING DOWN THE GRAND CANAL 2

Everyone should sail down Venice's great waterway at least once in their life. Take the slow boat, Vaporetto 1, and stand on the deck for the best views - not only of the lacy palace façades, but of life in a city in which everything happens by water.

3 PIZZA

Probably originating in Naples, pizza is, of course, now available all over Italy. Thick crusted in Naples, thin in Rome, sold by the slice, or folded over as a calzone, pizza comes in endless varieties. Wherever you eat it, you can be sure it will be fresh from the oven.

4 THE PASSEGGIATA

In every town, village and city in Italy, locals put on their finery and head out for an evening stroll. They might do a little window shopping or stop for an aperitivo, but the main purpose of the passeggiata is to see, be seen and bump into friends.

THE PALAZZO 5

From the Gothic façades of Venice to Renaissance townhouses, *palazzi* give Italian cities and towns much of their beauty. Built by royalty, nobility and wealthy merchants, many have been turned into museums and hotels.

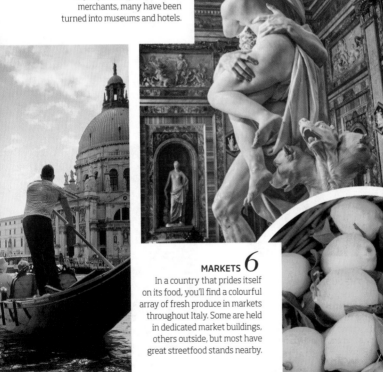

MARKETS 6

In a country that prides itself on its food, you'll find a colourful array of fresh produce in markets throughout Italy. Some are held in dedicated market buildings, others outside, but most have great streetfood stands nearby.

PIAZZA SAN PIETRO AT DAWN 7

Designed by Bernini, Piazza San Pietro is one of the most magnificent public spaces in the world. To see it at its best, get up at dawn and explore without the crowds.

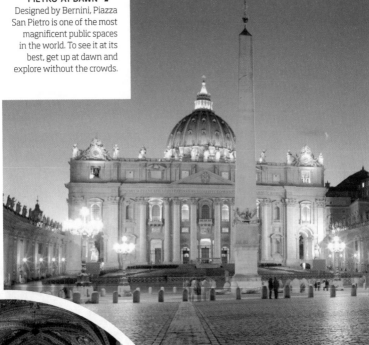

VESPAS 8

Launched in 1946 to meet the needs of a country crippled by war, the Vespa (wasp) became ubiquitous after Audrey Hepburn leapt on the back of one in *Roman Holiday* (1952).

9 THE DUOMO

The cathedrals (or duomos) of Italy are repositories for some of the world's greatest art. They cover every architectural style and era, from Byzantine to Baroque.

10 BEACHES

Italy has 7,600 km (4,722 miles) of shoreline, and its coast is one of the most varied in Europe, with sandy beaches, volcanic bays, dramatic cliffs and rocky coves.

THE PIAZZA 11

From intimate squares to grand open-air drawing rooms, Italy's piazzas are an essential feature of everyday life. Some are lined with pavement cafes, while others host daily markets.

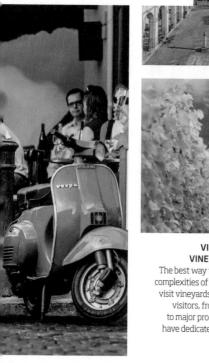

VISITING 12 VINEYARDS

The best way to appreciate the complexities of Italian wine is to visit vineyards. Many welcome visitors, from tiny wineries to major producers who may have dedicated tasting rooms.

2 WEEKS
A Grand Tour of Italy

Day 1

Morning Arrive in Venice from Marco Polo Airport by vaporetto and start to explore on foot. Allow time to get lost and indulge in a little people-watching over a coffee while working out a walking route to Piazza San Marco. When you get there, sit on the terrace of Caffè Florian for a drink.

Afternoon Walk towards the Ponte dell'Accademia to cross the Grand Canal (*p68*), zigzagging across Dorsoduro to lively Campo Santa Margherita (*p100*).

Evening Have dinner at a nearby restaurant, such as Osteria Alla Bifora Venezia (*Campo Santa Margherita 2930*).

Day 2

Morning Rise early for Mass at San Marco (*p72*) and drink in the atmosphere of the church. Weave north to the church of Santa Maria dei Miracoli (*p85*), then see the Giorgio Franchetti art collection in the Ca' d'Oro (*p84*). Take the gondola-ferry across to the Rialto (*p82*), and experience

the market bustle over *cicchetti* (snacks) in a typical bar, or *bacaro* (*p66*).

Afternoon Plot a route to Ca' Rezzonico (*p87*) for an evocative taste of aristocratic Venetian life, then dive into the art collections of the Accademia (*p90*) and Peggy Guggenheim (*p91*).

Evening Head to Campo San Giovanni dell'Orio and watch the world go by in the unpretentious Al Prosecco wine bar.

Day 3

Morning Catch an early-morning train to Florence. Start with the Duomo, Baptistry and Campanile (*p342*), climbing the latter for a crow's-eye view of the city. Circuit the Gothic Baptistry to see its east doors. Window-shop your way down Via Calzaiuoli to Piazza della Signoria (*p346*), dominated by the Palazzo Vecchio. Cross the medieval Ponte Vecchio (*p356*) for lunch on Piazza Santo Spirito (*p361*).

Afternoon Walk to the Cappella Brancacci (*p362*) then head back to the centre of

1 Florence's Duomo.
2 Campo dei Miracoli, Pisa.
3 Pizza on a Venetian canal.
4 *Gelato* outside Rome's Pantheon.
5 Ponte dell'Accademia, Venice.

town and visit the Uffizi *(p344)*, which is at its least crowded after 4:30pm.

Evening Wind down with an aperitivo at Procacci 1885 on Via Tornabuoni.

Day 4

Morning Head to the Bargello *(p354)*, a former prison now housing Renaissance sculptures. Devote the rest of the morning to ethereal frescoes by Fra Angelico in the convent of San Marco *(p353)*.

Afternoon See Michelangelo's *David* at the Accademia *(p348)*, then take the bus to the delicate church of San Miniato al Monte *(p362)*, for splendid views.

Evening Walk downhill into town, ending up at the Ponte Vecchio, with time for an aperitivo along the Arno before dinner.

Day 5

Morning Make a day trip to Pisa *(p378)*. Instead of heading straight to the Campo dei Miracoli *(p380)*, take in the atmosphere slowly, with a visit to the market on arcaded Piazza Vettovaglie – a good place

to have lunch – and a walk along the languid Arno, lined with *palazzi*.

Afternoon Explore the various sights on the Campo dei Miracoli and climb the famous Leaning Tower.

Evening Head back to Florence for dinner at Il Latini *(Via dei Palchetti 6R)*.

Day 6

Morning Catch the Frecciarossa (high-speed train) to Rome, heading straight for Piazza Navona *(p258)* for ice cream. Visit the Pantheon *(p260)* nearby and then cross the Ponte Sisto to lively Trastevere *(p283)* for lunch in one of its trattorias.

Afternoon Catch a tram to the Colosseum *(p242)*, then walk past the Roman Forum *(p246)* and Imperial Forum to the virtually-recreated villa of a wealthy patrician family at Palazzo Valentini *(p251)*. Visit the Capitoline Museums *(p250)*, and do not miss the bird's-eye view of the Forum from the museum café's terrace.

Evening Walk into the former Jewish ghetto *(p264)* for an aperitivo, then have dinner in a traditional kosher restaurant.

Day 7

Morning Get up early to see St Peter's *(p286)* for Mass without the crowds then visit the Vatican Museums and Sistine Chapel *(p288)*. Have lunch in a trattoria on Borgo Pio.

Afternoon Catch a tram to the Villa Borghese park, followed by visits to the Museo e Galleria Borghese *(p314)* and the Etruscan finds at Villa Giulia *(p316)*.

Evening Have a drink on the stylish terrace of the Caffé delle Arti at Galleria Nazionale d'Arte Moderna, then take a tram to San Lorenzo for traditional Roman fare at Il Pommidoro *(Piazza dei Sanniti 44/46)*.

Day 8

Morning Spend the morning at Ostia Antica *(p326)*, returning in time for lunch in a trattoria in Testaccio.

Afternoon Head to Piazza del Popolo and Santa Maria del Popolo *(p278)*, then explore the streets around the Piazza di Spagna *(p272)* and climb the Spanish Steps.

Evening Experience first-class seafood at Il Simposio *(p298)*, and then walk back to the centre via the Trevi Fountain *(p274)*, perhaps indulging in a final *gelato* at San Crispino *(Via della Panetteria 42)*.

Day 9

Morning Catch the Frecciarossa to Naples and make a beeline for Spaccanapoli *(p461)*. About halfway along is Via San Gregorio Armeno, lined with shops and workshops. See the Gothic Duomo, then stop for pizza at Da Michele *(p454)*.

Afternoon Explore the wonderful collection of ancient finds at the Museo Archeologico Nazionale *(p452)*.

Evening Go to the Chiaia neighbourhood for a sundowner by the sea and dinner at Da Dora *(Via Ferdinando Palasciano 30)*.

Day 10

Morning Take a hydrofoil to Capri *(p472)*. Explore the narrow alleys of the Marina Grande, and shop on Via Camerelle, before heading to the Blue Grotto *(p473)*.

Afternoon Take the funicular up to the upper part of town for a drink or lunch on

① Staircase, Vatican Museums.
② Historic streets of Naples.
③ Café on the island of Capri.
④ Catania waterfront, Sicily.
⑤ Aperitivo in a piazza in Rome.
⑥ Galleria Borghese, Rome.

Piazza Umberto I. Then take a walk across the island to Villa Jovis.

Evening Have a sundowner and dinner before taking the last hydrofoil to Naples.

Day 11

Morning Fly to Catania in Sicily, and take an 80-minute bus ride to Siracusa *(p510)*, heading straight for its historic centre, Ortigia *(p512)*. Admire the Duomo then walk up to the lively morning market for lunch at the Fratelli Burgio *(p513)*.

Afternoon Stroll down the Lungomare Levante, pausing for a swim at the Forte Vigliena rocks, then visit the Palazzo Bellomo *(p513)*.

Evening Walk down to Fontana Aretusa and along the Lungomare Alfio, stopping for an aperitivo in a pavement café.

Day 12

Morning Take the electric minibus to the archaeological zone *(p510)*, home to Sicily's best preserved Ancient Greek theatre.

Afternoon Explore the collection of the

Museo Archeologico Regionale, then relax and swim at the nearby Zen Lido.

Evening Return to Ortigia for authentic country cooking at A Putia *(Via Roma 8)*.

Day 13

Morning It is worth hiring a car to make the most of your last full day. Admire the architecture of Noto and have a *gelato* from Caffè Sicilia *(Corso Vittorio Emanuele 125)*.

Afternoon Either drive up to the ruins of Noto Antica *(p525)*, and follow the path into the ravine, or discover the Roman mosaics at the little known Villa Romana del Tellaro. Afterwards, talk a walk through the coastal nature reserve of Vendicari.

Evening Back in Ortigia, dine on inspired versions of Sicilian cuisine at Hotel Gutkowski *(Lungomare Elio Vittorini 26)*.

Day 14

Morning Admire the façade of Ortigia's Duomo as you breakfast at the lovely Bar del Duomo *(Piazza Duomo 18/19)*, then head back to Catania for a flight home.

Val Camonica Rock Carvings (1,000–400 BC)

The extraordinary rock carvings of the Val Camonica in Lombardy *(p175)* were created by people who settled the valley during the Neolithic period (known to the Romans as Camuni), leaving behind extraordinary drawings of hunting scenes and a map.
Where to see it now: *Val Camonica, Lombardy*

Rock carving showing hunters and their horses at Val Camonica, Lombardy

UNEARTHING ITALY'S
ANCIENT PAST

From Etruscan painted tombs to prehistoric finds, Italy is one of the most astonishing destinations on earth for anyone interested in archaeology. Sicily and Southern Italy, once Magna Graecia, hold many ancient Greek ruins, while lovers of Roman civilisation should target Rome, Pompeii and Herculaneum.

Tomb of the Leopards (c.500 BC)

Italy's first major civilisation, the Etruscans left behind necropolises full of frescoes, sculpture and ceramics that testify to the sophistication of their culture. This tomb is decorated with feast scenes *(p237)*.
Where to see it now: *Tarquinia, Lazio*

Dancing Faun Sculpture, Pompeii (79 AD)

The Romans emerged to conquer the peninsula – and eventually most of Europe – with their language, military organization and laws. For wealthy Romans life was good, with slaves to take care of manual labour, and cities such as Pompeii *(p466)* filled with theatres, villas and art, including this Dancing Faun.
Where to see it now: *Museo Archeologico Nazionale, Naples*

→

Dancing Faun sculpture from the House of the Faun in Pompeii

Ancient Greek Vase from Akragas (Agrigento), (around 430 BC)

In the 8th century BC, Greeks began to settle in Sicily and southern Italy. Several of the great intellectuals of Classical Greece, including Empedocles and Archimedes, were in fact Sicilian, and by the 4th century Siracusa was the most powerful city in the region. This 430 BC vase, showing the gods Haephestus and Dionysus drinking wine, is evidence of the area's wealth.
Where to see it now: *Museo Regionale Archeologico, Agrigento* (p520)

↑ Greek vase depicting Haephestus and Dionysus from the Valley of the Temples, Agrigento

Giants of Sardinia with Spiral Eyes (around 1,100 BC)

Created by the mysterious Nuraghic civilisation, an entire stone army of giants with spiral eyes appears to have guarded the Mont'e Prama necropolis. Their significance is unknown, but their weapons suggest they had different military "roles".
Where to see it now: *Mont'e Prama, Sardinia*

→

↑ Colourful Etruscan fresco at the Tomb of the Leopards, Lazio

Head of one of the Giants of Mont'e Prama, with its trademark spiral eyes

Sistine Chapel Ceiling

Initially reluctant to accept the commission from Pope Julius II in 1508, as he had little experience in fresco, Michelangelo worked on the Sistine Chapel ceiling for four years, creating 366 figures. Under pressure from the pope, Michelangelo had to work quickly – sometimes leaving behind hogs' hairs from his brushes. *The Creation of Adam* was painted over the course of three days, and the white of his eye is simply unpainted plaster.

Where to find it:
The Vatican, Rome (p292)

→

The Creation of Adam, one of nine stories from the Bible on the Sistine Chapel ceiling

Did You Know?

Throughout Italy, entry to state-run museums is free on the first Sunday of each month.

ITALY'S RENAISSANCE
MASTERPIECES

The 14th to 16th centuries saw an explosion of the arts in Italy. Rome was the power-centre of the Christian Church, and the rest of the peninsula was ruled by a collection of competing city states. Cardinals, merchants and aristocrats alike flaunted their wealth and power through the patronage of artists, architects and thinkers.

David

Perhaps the most famous sculpture in the whole world, Michelangelo's colossal statue of the young biblical hero David is perhaps the quintessential Renaissance work, clearly exhibiting the influence of Classical Greek and Roman art. The choice of subject was popular in Renaissance Florence, with David representing Florence as a warning to the Goliath of Rome.

Where to find it: *Galleria dell' Accademia, Florence* (p348)

←

Michelangelo's *David* at the Galleria dell'Accademia in Florence

The Birth of Venus

Botticelli's painting of the Roman goddess of beauty was influenced by Neo-Platonism, which held that the contemplation of physical beauty led to an understanding of spiritual beauty.
Where to find it: *Uffizi, Florence* (p344)

←

Detail of *The Birth of Venus* (c.1483-86) by Sandro Botticelli

The Last Supper

The fragile condition of Da Vinci's masterpiece is a result of him painting onto dry, rather than wet plaster (as was usual for frescoes). He did this to allow time to create more detail and subtlety in the work.
Where to find it: *Santa Maria delle Grazie, Milan* (p154)

Leonardo's *The Last Supper* (c.1494-7) in Santa Maria delle Grazie

San Marco, Venice

An exotic fusion of Classical, Romanesque and Gothic architecture, San Marco *(p72)* clearly reflects the Eastern traditions of Byzantium both in terms of its structure – it is built on a Greek (even-armed) cross-plan with turban-like domes – and its lavish interior, which is covered by more than 4 sq km (1.5 sq miles) of glinting gold-backed mosaics and ornate marble carvings.

Gilded mosaics adorning the dome of Basilica di San Marco in Venice

ITALY'S INCREDIBLE
ARCHITECTURE

There is nowhere better than Italy to experience the glories of European architecture. Roman buildings borrowed heavily from Ancient Greek temples (still seen in Sicily), while in later centuries Norman, Arabic and Byzantine invaders coloured Italy's Romanesque and Gothic buildings. Classical ideals returned to infuse the country's Renaissance and Baroque buildings.

STYLISTIC TERMS

Romanesque
An early medieval style that adapted Roman techniques such as the rounded arch.

Gothic
Characterized by the use of the pointed arch, Gothic architecture sought to build taller, lighter buildings.

Renaissance
A rediscovery of the Classical architectural ideals of ancient Greece and Rome in the 14th to 17th centuries.

Baroque
This ornate, theatrical style was used in the Counter-Reformation.

Colosseum, Rome

The Colosseum *(p242)* makes great use of the rounded arch, an architectural innovation the Romans used to build stronger, taller structures. Each tier of arches represents one of three Classical orders – hefty, unadorned Doric on the first level, scrolled Ionic on the second and acanthus-leaf-inspired Corinthian on the top.

→

The Colosseum in Rome, with its three tiers of arcades

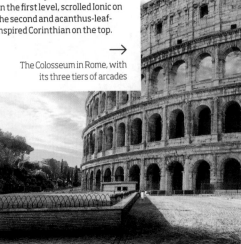

Leaning Tower of Pisa

The rounded arches that typify the Romanesque style had their origins in ancient Roman basilicas, and re-emerged from the Dark Ages in buildings such as the Leaning Tower of Pisa *(p380)*. Interiors were usually simple, like those of their Roman predecessors, making great play of stone, geometry and light, elements clearly visible in Pisa's famous landmark. The lean here was not intentional: it results from the tower having been built on soft land made up of clay, sand and shell.

→

Pisa's iconic Leaning Tower with the cathedral and baptistery behind

Palazzo Ducale, Venice

The pointed arches and intricate stonework of Gothic architecture were imported into Italy from France by the Cistercian order. Adopted by palace architects in Venice, it is exemplified in the delicate lacy stone embroidery of the Palazzo Ducale *(p76)*. Here, the style is combined with Byzantine and Moorish influences.

←

Colonnaded loggia at the Palazzo Ducale in Venice, looking out towards the island of San Giorgio Maggiore

Bramante's Tempietto, Rome

Bramante's masterpiece at San Pietro Montorio in Rome *(p299)* is the embodiment of the Renaissance ideals of order, precision and symmetry. It is also an example of the era's fascination with geometry, believed to reflect the perfection of God.

→

Bramante's Tempietto in the courtyard of San Pietro Montorio in Rome

Did You Know?

Very little Etruscan architecture survives, probably because most buildings were made from wood.

◁ **Puglia and Sicily**

Puglia is one of Italy's biggest producers of fresh produce, while Sicily's long history of invasions is reflected in its rich and varied cuisine.

What to eat: Arancini *(stuffed deep-fried rice balls)* at Savia (Catania, Sicily), burrata *(buffalo cheese with a creamy centre)*, and cannoli at Roscaglione (Palermo, Sicily).

What to drink: *Salice Salentino and Etna Rossa wines, and Malvasia and Passito di Pantelleria dessert wines.*

▷ **Rome and Lazio**

The traditional cuisine in this central region is based on cheap cuts of meat and offal, along with simple pasta dishes.

What to eat: Carciofi alla giudia *(deep-fried artichokes)* at Piperno (Rome), spaghetti carbonara at Lo Zozzone (p263) and pizza bianca sandwiches *(cooked pizza base, sliced and stuffed)* at Da Danilo (Rome).

What to drink: *Frascati wine.*

ITALY FOR
FOODIES

The gastronomic traditions of Italy are a vibrant mosaic, with specialities differing from one town to the next. Although famous for its wines, craft beers are enjoying a renaissance, and aperitivo drinks remain popular.

◁ **Venice and the Veneto**

Fish and seafood dominate, while a fondness for sweet-sour sauces is a legacy of Venice's Oriental trade.

What to eat: Cicchetti e ombre *(traditional canapés, best served with wine)* at Bar Puppa (p85), bigoli in salsa *(whole-wheat pasta with onion and salt-cured fish)* at Cantina Do Spade (Venice), and risotto al nero di seppie *(squid-ink risotto)* at Osteria al Portego (Venice).

What to drink: *Prosecco, Aperol spritz and Valpolicella.*

◁ Florence and Tuscany

Rich bean soups, toasted bread topped with chicken liver pâté, and steaks from prized Chianina cattle dominate here.

What to eat: Ribollita *(bread and vege-table soup)* at Il Latini *(p371)*, Chianina steak at Trattoria Mario *(Florence)* and crostini at Fiaschetteria Nuvoli *(Florence).*

What to drink: *Chianti, Brunello di Montalcino, Vernaccia di San Gimignano and Vin Santo dessert wine.*

◁ Naples and Campania

This region is home to the classic Mediterranean diet, based on vegetables, tomatoes and olive oil.

What to eat: Mozzarella di bufala *(soft cheese made from buffalos' milk)*, pizza Margherita at Da Michele *(p454)* and sfogliatelle *(shell-shaped filled pastries)* at Pasticceria Andrea Pansa *(Amalfi).*

What to drink: *Aglianico and Greco di Tufo.*

TOP 3 TIPS FOR DINING IN ITALY

Stand for Coffee
Standing at the bar for a coffee is usually about half the price of sitting at a table for one.

Menu Fisso
Fixed-price menus, including a glass of wine and water, can be extremely good value.

Aperitivo
When ordering a drink it may be offered as an "aperitivo". This will be more expensive but it will include antipasti, or items that can be selected from a buffet.

△ Milan and Northwest Italy

Risotto, truffles and polenta are popular inland, while coastal Liguria is famous for its seafood, olive oil and basil.

What to eat: *Pesto pasta at Il Genovese (Genoa), risotto at Trattoria Masuelli San Marco (Milan) and cacciucco (seafood casserole) at Trattoria Da Galileo (Livorno).*

What to drink: *Barolo and Barberesco wine, and Campari.*

Val d'Orcia, Tuscany

Perhaps the most beautiful valley in Tuscany, the rolling cypress-spiked hills of Val d'Orcia to the south of Siena appear in the backgrounds of many Renaissance paintings. Lush and green in spring, crisp and golden in summer, this valley is captivating at any time of the year. Explore its sinuous country roads and pause in its exquisite towns.

←

Sunset over the picturesque hills of Val d'Orcia

ITALY FOR
NATURAL
WONDERS

From erupting volcanoes to magnificent coastal scenery, Italy is rich in breathtaking natural wonders. Experience them by driving, hiking, sailing, skiing or simply lazing on a beach.

Mount Etna

Standing at 3,350 m (10,990 ft), Etna *(p522)* is the highest active volcano in Europe, and is in an almost constant state of activity. Lying between Catania and Messina, it is most easily explored by cable car. It is at its most magical in winter, when the peak is covered in snow.

Smoke rising from the crater of snow-covered Mount Etna ↓

HIKING IN ITALY

Hiking holidays in Italy are becoming increasingly popular, with Tuscany, Umbria, Liguria, the Italian Lakes, Sicily and the Dolomites as the main targets. Hikers may find trails less clearly waymarked than in the UK or USA. CAI and other local walking groups often advertise guided walks, which are open to visitors.

Dolomites

The jagged, snow-covered peaks of the Dolomites *(p132)* form the northeastern border between Italy and Austria. Drive the Great Dolomites Road, tackle the challenging Vie Ferrate climbing route or ski some of the 1,200 km (740 miles) of fabulous slopes from its majestically-sited winter resorts, such as Cortina d'Ampezzo. Hiking, cycling, BASE jumping, para- gliding and hang gliding are also popular pastimes here during the warmer months.

$\rightarrow$

Hikers enjoying views offered by the Dolomites in the summer

Grotte di Frasassi

The spectacular limestone formations of the Grotte di Frasassi *(p421)* in Marche, discovered in 1971, comprise one of the largest cave- systems in Europe – over 15 km (9 miles) have been explored. The public can tour a 1.5-km (1-mile) route, enhanced by theatrical lighting.

$\leftarrow$

The dramatic subterranean landscape of the Grotte di Frasassi

Scala dei Turchi, Agrigento

Eroded by sea and wind into a magnifi- cent natural white staircase, the marl cliffs of Scala dei Turchi *(p520)*, on the south coast of Sicily, descend into a crystalline turquoise sea and beaches of glinting quartz. The beach is ideal for a swim after visiting Agrigento's Valley of the Temples.

$\rightarrow$

The unique, white Scala dei Turchi cliffs in southern Sicily

Sardinia

The island of Sardinia *(p526)*, off Italy's west coast, is widely acknowledged to have the best beaches in the country. There are hundreds of them, including the sparkling white quartz beaches found on the Sinis Peninsula, the silky golden sweeps of the Costa Rei and the dramatic coves of Cala Gonone. The Maddalena Peninsula and Costa Smeralda, on the northeast tip of Sardinia, are home to the island's chicest holiday resorts, with Caribbean-blue seas and a vast number of picturesque white beaches and coves.

→

The white-quartz
San Giovanni di Sinis
beach, Sardinia

ITALY'S BREATHTAKING
BEACHES

Italy has some fantastic beaches, especially in the south and on the islands of Elba, Sicily and Sardinia. Most beaches have sections given over to lidos with ranks of loungers and parasols rented by the day or week, but there are always small areas of *spiaggia libera* (literally "free beach") dotted about.

CALABRIAN DISCOVERY

An area better known to the Italians than to foreigner visitors, the Tyrrhenian coast of Calabria and Basilicata has a little string of beautiful sandy beaches around the picturesque village of Tropea, which is dramatically fused to a white cliff above a pristine sea. There is another lovely stretch of coastline either side of the former fishing village of Maratea, to the south of Potenza.

Tuscan Coast and Islands

The white beaches and crystal-clear waters of the Monte Argentario *(p399)* are enchanting, but true beach aficionados should head to the tiny island of Giglio, where the coastline is peppered with sandy coves, or Elba *(p393)*, which has over 150 beaches, ranging from broad sweeps of sand to shingly coves.

→

Sunset at Capo d'Enfola,
near Portoferraio on
Elba Island

Sicily and Islands

From the white shingle coves of the Zingaro nature reserve in the east to the long golden sweep of Cefalù in the north, and from the dramatic black lava bays of the Aeolian islands to the endless shifting dunes of Sampieri and Vendicari, Sicily's beaches are some of the most varied in Italy *(p500)*. Those seeking seclusion during the incredibly busy summer season should head for beaches that are accessible only by footpath or rent a boat and anchor off one of the more remote stretches of coast here.

Vibrant blue water and white sand at Guidaloca beach on Sicily's north coast

TOP 5 CITY BEACH ESCAPES

Lido, Venice
Easily reached by vaporetto, the beaches and campsites offer an alternative to Venice.

Ostia, Rome
Connected to Rome by train, the long sandy beach of Ostia is packed with busy lidos.

Rimini, Ravenna
The endless sandy ribbons of the Adriatic coast are hugely popular, offering easy escapes from Ravenna.

Plemmirio, Siracusa
City buses head out regularly to the beach resorts of Arenella and Fontane Bianche.

Mondello, Palermo
The sandy beach of Mondello, easily reached by city bus, makes a great escape.

Puglia

The beaches of Puglia's Adriatic coast are mainland Italy's most beautiful. The best are to be found around the craggy indented shoreline of the Gargano Peninsula *(p485)*, near the town of Otranto, and along the arid coast of the Salento Peninsula, which forms the very tip of Italy's "heel".

↑ Crowded beach on the Salento Peninsula in Puglia

Dress the Part for a Local Festival

Carnevale is celebrated all over Italy, with children dressing up to take part in processions or just to wander the town with their parents. The most famous celebrations are in Venice in the weeks leading up to Lent, when children and adults wear elaborate Venetian masks. The carnival can trace its roots back to 1162, though its modern incarnation dates from 1979. In Siena, medieval costumes are traditionally worn for the dramatic Palio horse race, which tears around the Piazza del Campo twice a year – on 2nd July and 16th August.

↑ Masked revellers parading through the streets at the Venice Carnevale

ITALY FOR
FAMILIES

Did You Know?

Italians rarely eat dinner before 9pm. Consider having lunch as your main family meal.

Italy's broad mix of child-friendly attractions and activities means that you will never be short of ways to keep your kids entertained. Families are at the centre of Italian life so children will receive a warm welcome wherever they go, while an increasing number of museums and sites have dedicated tours for younger visitors.

Travel Back in Time

Italy's museums are always searching for new ways to entertain youngsters. Virtual reality installations and headsets at some sights (including the Palazzo Valentini and the Baths of Caracalla) do a great job of bringing history to life. The Vatican Museums' audio guide for children is so good that adults might wish to opt for it as well, while the Roman Gladiator Museum gives kids the chance to dress up as gladiators and learn to fight for a day.

←

Children admiring exhibits in the Vatican Museums, which offer an excellent audio guide

↑ Statue of Orcus, god of the underworld, at the Bomarzo Monster Park

Tour the Bomarzo Monster Park

Created in the 16th century by an eccentric duke, Bomarzo is the original theme park *(p325)*. Located in northern Lazio, it is scattered with grotesque statues of monsters, including a 6-m-(20-ft-) high screaming face, a life-sized elephant crushing a Roman soldier and an enormous giant ripping a man in two.

Make Pizza and Gelato

Fancy having a budding chef in the family? Pizza and ice-cream-making classes for kids are becoming increasingly popular, especially in major cities. Italian Connection *(www. italian-connection.co.uk)* specializes in creating tailor-made experiences for families with children.

→ A lesson in making pizza, everyone's favourite Italian dish

TOP 5 BUDGET TIPS FOR FAMILIES

Free Travel
Children under a certain age or height can often travel for free. Check transport websites *(p540)* for details.

Family Passes
Save with family travel and museum passes in Rome, Florence and other major art cities.

Free Beaches
Look out for the *spiaggia libera* (free beach) signs.

Picnic Lunches
Italy is full of great delicatessens that let children pick their own sandwich fillings and charge a fraction of the price found in cafés. Most towns also have drinking water fountains and taps.

Hop-On, Hop-Off Tour Buses
In big cities these can be a cost-effective way to see as many sites as possible and keep tantrums to a minimum.

Festival at Baths of Caracalla

Experiencing great, crowd-pleasing ballets, operas and musical performances against a backdrop of the deftly illuminated ruins of Rome's Baths of Caracalla is unforgettable. Recent guest performers have included the Tokyo Ballet, Roberto Bolle, Ennio Morricone and Björk.
When to go: *mid-Jun, Jul & Aug*

Outdoor concert in the ruins of the Baths of Caracalla in Rome

ITALY'S SPECTACULAR
SHOWS

Whether you want to see opera performed in one of Europe's most incredible spaces, to experience cutting-edge fashion, or to admire some of the world's best contemporary art, Italy is the perfect destination for anyone who loves an extravaganza.

TOP 5 MUSIC FESTIVALS

Umbria Jazz
Italy's largest Jazz festival, held in July.

Pistoia Blues
This annual blues, folk and rock festival attracts a varied line-up to Pistoia every July.

La Foce
Summer chamber music festival in Tuscany.

Maggio Musicale
Renowned classical concerts and opera held in Florence each May.

I-days
Big names perform at this music festival in Milan every June.

Opera at the Verona Arena

Verona's Roman Arena is one of the most spectacular opera venues in the world, hosting an annual summer festival. The arena is also used for pop concerts. Bob Dylan, Bruce Springsteen, Pink Floyd and Adele have all performed here.
When to go: *Jun–Aug*

Venice Art Biennale

Founded in 1895, the Art Biennale is an international arts festival with a proud tradition of embracing controversy. It takes place in odd-numbered years, in the famous purpose-built pavilions of the Giardini park, the Arsenale, and in other locations across the city. Linked with the Art Biennale is the annual Venice Film Festival and the Biennale of Architecture, which is held in even-numbered years.
When to go: *May–Nov*

$\rightarrow$

Support by Lorenzo Quinn at the 2017 Venice Art Biennale

San Remo Music Festival

Held to select the artist to represent Italy in the Eurovision Song Contest, San Remo is full of schmaltz and razzamattazz, with all songs performed to a live audience. The night is watched on TV by over half the nation.
When to go: *Feb*

$\leftarrow$

Italian singer Eva Pevarello performing at the San Remo Music Festival

Milan Fashion Week

Founded in 1958, Milan's Fashion Week is widely considered to be the most glamorous of the Big Four (the others are New York, Paris and London). The shows are held in venues across the city twice a year. Few shows are open to the general public, but usually at least some are held outside.
When to go: *Feb or Sep*

$\leftarrow$

Performance of Puccini's opera *Madame Butterfly* at Verona Arena

$\rightarrow$

Walking the catwalk at a show during Milan Fashion Week

The Godfather, Sicily

Several scenes from Francis Ford Coppola's Mafia-inspired *Godfather* movies were filmed in the remote Sicilian hilltop villages of Savoca and Forza d'Agro, between Messina and Taormina *(p522)*. Afficionados can sit at the table at Bar Vitelli in Savoca, where Al Pacino's character, Michael Corleone, sat and asked the *padrone* for his daughter Apollonia's hand in marriage. Another location to visit is the Chiesa Madre in the piazza where the two were married.

Did You Know?

Al Pacino's grandparents were born in Corleone, where the family came from in the *Godfather* novel and films.

→

Bar Vitelli in Savoca; Marlon Brando as Vito Corleone in *The Godfather* (inset)

ITALY FOR
INSPIRATION

Not only has Italy produced many writers of international acclaim, but it has inspired foreign novelists from E M Forster to contemporary crime writers such as Dan Brown. Shakespeare based many of his plays on Italian stories, and Italy has provided the backdrop for countless classic films.

A Florentine Room with a View

E M Forster's novel – and the 1985 Merchant Ivory film starring Helena Bonham Carter – explores the impact of sensuous Italy on the stiff conventions of Edwardian English travellers. The famous "room" with its view of the Arno is actually Room 414 of the Hotel degli Orafi, while the piazza where Lucy is filmed fainting after witnessing a fight is the Piazza della Signoria *(p346)*. Lucy and Emerson have their first kiss in the hills of Fiesole, overlooking Florence.

←

Film poster from the 1985 adaptation of E M Forster's *A Room with a View*

↑ Tom Hanks in the film adaptation of *Angels and Demons*

Angels and Demons in Rome

Plotted around the murders of four Cardinals in four locations in Rome – St Peter's Square, Santa Maria della Vittoria, Santa Maria del Popolo, and Piazza Navona – Dan Brown's novel makes an exciting guide to the city *(p222)*.

↑ The Chiesa di San Giorgio dei Greci, featured in the Inspector Brunetti novels

TOP 5 ITALIAN AUTHORS

1. Petrarch
This 14th-century poet refined the sonnet.

2. Dante
The Divine Comedy (1320) was one of the first major works in Italian rather than Latin.

3. Carlo Collodi
Collodi first wrote *The Adventures of Pinocchio* as a serial for a paper.

4. Umberto Eco
Eco is most famous for his historical novel *The Name of the Rose*.

5. Italo Calvino
Widely translated author of engaging and imaginative fables.

Inspector Brunetti's Venice

Fans of author Donna Leon's charismatic Commissario can discover Venice with Toni Sepeda's brilliant book *Brunetti's Venice*, which uses extracts from the crime novels to guide readers around the *calles, campi, palazzi* and fictional crime scenes, giving some fascinating insights into life in the city *(p58)*.

Greek Theatre, Taormina

Perched on a hillside, pretty Taormina offers mesmerising views of Mount Etna and the glistening sea below. Visit the splendid Greek Theatre (p522) and photograph the ruins at sunset, making sure to capture snowy Etna and the sparkling blue waters of the Mediterranean to the east – the view is surreal.

The view down to the sea from the top of Taormina's Greek Theatre

ITALY FOR
PHOTOGRAPHERS

Each and every one of Italy's regions has its own distinctive physical and cultural identity, offering photographers boundless opportunities for capturing the country's many facets. While the crowds are flocking to Venice and Rome, these spots offer an alternative to Italy's most touristy places.

Venaria Reale, Turin

With its intricate decorations and striking black-and-white floor design, the spectacular Great Gallery of Turin's sumptuous Venaria Reale has 44 windows and 22 eyelets on the ceiling, creating incredible contrasts between light and shade. Visit in the late afternoon on a summer's day and use a wide-angle lens to obtain an impressive shot.

 INSIDER TIP
Sunrise Shot
Wake up early in the morning to shoot in a warm and soft light and do not forget a tripod to stabilise the camera when light is low.

Galleria Vittorio Emanuele II, Milan

Dominated by an impressive iron-and-glass dome, Milan's opulent Galleria Vittorio Emanuele II *(p147)* is embellished with marble, stuccoes and mosaics. Stand below the dome and point the camera up to capture one of Italy's most impressive buildings.

→

The vast glass roof of the Galleria Vittorio Emanuele II

Sassi, Matera

In the early morning, the low-lying sun bathes Matera's cavernous dwellings in gentle golden hues. Head to the Sassi *(p494)* and give photos a surreal perspective by putting the camera on the floor. This creates a different point of view of the messy hotchpotch of buildings that form this fascinating troglodyte settlement.

←

The jumble of buildings that make up the Sassi in Matera

Castello di Vezio, Lake Como

For unobstructed Lake Como views, climb up to the Castello di Vezio, a perfectly positioned medieval military outpost. Check the website for events before you visit *(www. castellodivezio.it)*. Once a year volunteers in outfits pose as eerie ghost-like statues around the grounds.

↑ The ever-photogenic Great Gallery of the Venaria Reale, Turin

→

View over Lake Como from the Castello di Vezio

A YEAR IN
ITALY

JANUARY

Capodanno (1 Jan) New Year's Day is celebrated throughout Italy with lively firework displays and free concerts.

△ **La Befana** (6 Jan) Children receive stockings of gifts from La Befana, the Christmas witch.

FEBRUARY

△ **Carnevale** (3–5 Jan) National festival featuring feasts and fancy-dress processions (notably in Viareggio and Oristano), and masked balls in Venice.

Sagra della Mandorle in Fiore (first week) Agrigento, Sicily. Almond blossom celebration among the ancient Greek temples.

MAY

Festa di San Domenico Abate (first Thu) Cocullo, Abruzzo. Extraordinary procession with a statue of St Dominic covered with live snakes.

△ **Rome Masters** (second week May) Rome. Prestigious clay-court tennis tournament.

Maggio Musicale (May–Jun) Florence. Arts festival, including music, drama and dance.

Giro d'Italia (May–Jun) Nationwide international cycle race, which takes place over several stages.

JUNE

△ **Calcio Storico** (24 Jun & two other days in Jun) Florence. Authentically violent football in 16th-century costumes.

Venice Art Biennale (Jun–Sep) Venice. The world's biggest exhibition of contemporary art. Held in odd-numbered years.

SEPTEMBER

Giostra del Saracino (first Sun) Arezzo, Umbria. Joust of the Saracen and knights.

Regata Storica (first Sun) Venice. Procession of historic boats and a colourful gondola race.

△ **Italian Grand Prix** (early Sep) Monza. The Italian stage of the Formula One World Championship.

San Gennaro (Sep 19) Naples. Neapolitans wait with baited breath to see if the blood of San Gennaro liquefies, bringing good fortune.

OCTOBER

△ **Sagra dell'Uva** (dates vary) Grape harvests all over Italy, with lively festivals including dancing and food.

Fiera del Tartufo (Oct–Nov) Alba, Piedmont. Various events are held to celebrate the harvest of the famous white truffle.

MARCH

△ **Dolomiti Ski Jazz Festival** (mid-Mar) Trentino-Alto Adige. Jazz on the ski-slopes.

Su e Zo Per I Ponti (Sun, varies) Venice. A friendly 12-km (7-mile) walk for charity along the city's streets, squares and bridges.

Ciliegi in Fiore (31 Mar–8 Apr) Vignola. Blooming Cherry Trees Festival.

APRIL

△ **Holy Week** (Easter Week) Easter celebrations across the country, with Pope's Easter blessing in Rome, fireworks in Florence, and re-enactments of The Passion in the South and Sicily.

Festa di San Marco (25 Apr) Venice. Gondola race in honour of St Mark.

JULY

Corsa del Palio (2 Jul) Siena. Tuscany's most famous event presents a medieval flag-waving horse race.

△ **Opera Festival** (Jul & Aug) Verona, Veneto and Baths of Caracalla, Rome. Renowned artists perform at historic venues.

AUGUST

Ferragosto (Aug 15) Throughout Italy. Public holiday celebrated with open-air concerts, dances and fireworks.

Settimane Musicali di Stresa (late Aug– end Sep) Stresa, Lombardy. Four weeks of concerts and recitals.

△ **Venice Film Festival** (late Aug/Sep) Venice Lido. Italy's most prestigious film festival.

NOVEMBER

△ **Festa della Salute** (21 Nov) Venice. Feast giving thanks to the Virgin Mary for deliverance from the plague.

DECEMBER

Festa di Sant'Ambrogio (early Dec) Milan. Official opening of La Scala Opera season.

△ **Christmas Fair** (mid-Dec) Fairs through Italy sell crib figures, traditional decorations and other crafts.

Christmas Day, St Peters (25 Dec) St Peter's, Rome. Blessing by the pope.

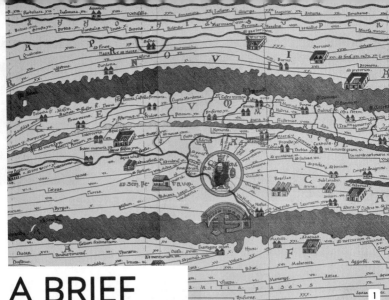

A BRIEF
HISTORY

Italy's history is one of discord and division. The only time Italy was united prior to the 19th century was under the Romans. For centuries, popes, emperors and warring states battled it out or fought against foreign invaders. The goal of a unified Italy was achieved in 1870.

The Age of the Etruscans

The Etruscans were Italy's first major civilization. Their origin is a mystery, as is their language, but from the 9th century BC they spread through central Italy, their chief rivals being the Greeks in the south. In the 6th century Etruscan kings ruled Rome, the city that would ultimately eclipse them.

From Republic to Empire

From the scores of tribes inhabiting ancient Italy, the Romans emerged to conquer the peninsula and impose their language, customs and laws on the other regions. Rome's success was due

1 Medieval map of the Roman Empire.

2 Temple of Hercules Victor in the Forum Boarium, Rome.

3 Detail from Trajan's Column, Rome.

4 Mosaic of Emperor Justinian in San Vitale, Ravenna.

Timeline of Events

753 BC

Legendary date of the founding of Rome by demi-god brothers, Romulus and Remus

509 BC

Last Etruscan king, Tarquinius Superbus, expelled from Rome; establishment of Roman Republic

450 BC

Roman law codified in the Twelve Tables, purportedly based on a study of Greek legislature

265 BC

After an attempted slave revolt, the last Etruscan city, Volsinii, is razed to the ground by Romans; the inhabitants migrate and establish New Volsinii

to superb skill in military and civil organization. The State was a republic ruled by two consuls but, as the extent of Rome's conquests grew, power passed to generals such as Julius Caesar. Caesar's heirs became the first Roman emperors.

The Golden Age of Rome

From the age of Augustus to the reign of Trajan, Rome's power grew until her empire stretched from Britain to the Red Sea. Despite the extravagance of emperors such as Nero, taxes and booty from military campaigns continually refilled the Imperial coffers, and Roman citizens enjoyed great wealth.

The Splitting of the Empire

A turning point in the history of the Roman Empire came with Emperor Constantine's decision to build a new capital at Constantinople (Byzantium). By the 5th century the Empire was split into two and Germanic invaders began migrating southwards. The Eastern Empire retained nominal control over parts of Italy from Ravenna, which became the most powerful city of the age, while Rome was reduced to ruins.

TOP 4 **PLACES TO SEE ROMAN ITALY**

Pantheon
Perfectly preserved temple *(see p144)*.

Pompeii
A city frozen in time by volcanic ash *(see p242)*.

Colosseum
Vast gladiatorial stadium *(see p135)*.

Hadrian's Villa
Emperor Hadrian's rural retreat *(see p152)*.

146 BC

Carthage falls to the Roman Republic in the Third Punic War; the city is redeveloped as Roman Carthage, the empire's major city in Africa

79 AD

Eruption of Vesuvius destroys Pompeii and preserves its remains under a blanket of ash

44 BC

Tensions between Julius Caesar and the Senate lead to his assassination and the breakdown of the Republic

161–80 AD

Reign of Marcus Aurelius; his death in 180 AD is considered the beginning of the eventual Fall of the Western Roman Empire

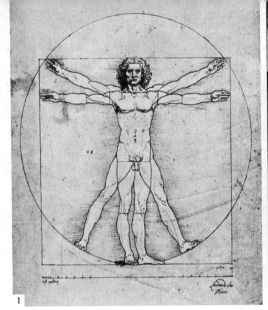

The Rise of Venice

Medieval Italy saw waves of foreign invaders joining the power-struggle between popes and emperors. In the confusion, many northern cities asserted their independence from feudal overlords. The most powerful was Venice, which grew rich through trade with the East and by shipping Crusaders to fight the Saracens in the Holy Land.

The Late Middle Ages

Old feuds between pope and emperor thrived throughout the 14th century, kept alive by two warring factions – the Guelphs, who backed the papacy, and the Ghibellines, who favoured Imperial power. Cities used the political chaos to consolidate their strength, building protective walls and towers and creating fortified public buildings such as the Palazzo Vecchio in Florence, Palazzo Pubblico in Siena and the Palazzo dei Priori in Viterbo. It was against this turbulent backdrop that a great new age in painting was inspired by artists such as Duccio and Giotto, while the Florentine poets Dante and Petrarch laid the foundations of Italian literature.

1. Leonardo Da Vinci's *Renaissance Man*.

2. Marco Polo departing from Venice.

3. Coronation of Charles V.

4. Guelfs fighting the Ghibellines.

Did You Know?

The word Renaissance is a French word meaning "rebirth". It wasn't applied to the 15th century until the 1830s.

Timeline of Events

1204

Sacking of Constantinople in the 4th Crusade sees the power of Byzantium crushed

1228

Gregory IX excommunicates Holy Roman Emperor Frederick II; the rivalry between the Guelphs and the Ghibellines gains traction

1320

Dante completes the *Divine Comedy*, reserving hell's worst punishments for corrupt popes

1378–1415

Period of Schism, with rival popes and antipopes in Rome and Avignon threatening the stability of Europe

1434

Super-wealthy banker and art patron Cosimo de' Medici comes to power in Florence

3

4

The Renaissance

Fifteenth-century Italy saw a flowering of the arts and scholarship unmatched in Europe since the Classical age. Architects turned to ancient Greek and Roman models for inspiration, while painting, with its new grasp of perspective and anatomy, produced a generation of artists that included such giants as Leonardo da Vinci, Raphael and Michelangelo. Patronage for this "rebirth" came from wealthy ruling dynasties, initiated by the Medici of Florence, with the papacy following their lead.

The Counter-Reformation

After the Sack of Rome by Imperial forces in 1527, Italy was at the mercy of Charles V, Holy Roman Emperor and King of Spain. In response to the growing threat from Protestantism, a series of reforms, known as the Counter-Reformation and backed by the Inquisition, imposed rigid orthodoxy. New religious orders, such as the Jesuits, were set up to take the battle for men's souls overseas. The missionary spirit of the age inspired the dramatic forms of the Baroque, designed to conquer through awe and emotion.

TRIAL OF GALILEO

The great astronomer Galileo was frequently in trouble with the Inquisition. After being summoned to Rome for promoting heresy in 1633, he was forced to deny that the Earth and planets moved round the sun and was put under house arrest for the rest of his life.

1436
Brunelleschi completes dome of Florence cathedral commissioned by the Medici

1475
Birth of Michelangelo

1503
Giuliano della Rovere elected Pope Julius II, the most powerful of the Renaissance popes

1542
Inquisition established in Rome

1545–63
Council of Trent sets out agenda of Counter-Reformation

The Grand Tour

In the late 18th century Italy, with its great art treasures and Classical ruins, became Europe's first great tourist destination. Young English aristocrats visited Rome, Florence and Venice as part of the Grand Tour, while artists and poets sought inspiration in Rome's glorious past. In 1800, Napoleon, who conquered and briefly united Italy, threatened to destroy the old order, but in 1815 the status quo was restored.

The Risorgimento

The word "Risorgimento" (resurgence) describes the five decades of struggle for liberation from foreign rule, culminating in the unification of Italy in 1870. In 1848, patriots rose up against the Austrians in Milan and Venice, the Bourbons in Naples, the South and Sicily, and the pope in Rome, where a republic was declared. Garibaldi valiantly defended the republic, but the uprisings were all too localized. By 1859, the movement was better organized, with Vittorio Emanuele II at its head. Two years saw the conquest of all but Venice and Rome, both of which fell within a decade.

↑ Vittorio Emanuele II, the first king of a united Italy since the 6th century

Timeline of Events

1936
Italy conquers Abyssinia; pact with Germany, forming anti-Communist "Axis"

1960
Olympic Games and first official Paralympic Games held in Rome

1870
Rome falls to royalist troops and is made capital of new kingdom of Italy

1922
Fascists march on Rome; Mussolini invited to form government

1943
Allies land in Sicily; Italy signs armistice and new Badoglio government declares war on Germany

Fascism and World War II

Fascism under Mussolini (1922–43) promised the Italians greatness, but delivered only humiliation, as Italy entered World War II on the side of Nazi Germany, switching to the Allies after the successful invasion of Sicily by British and American troops.

After the war, Italy's economic recovery was powered by great factories in the North, such as Fiat. Despite a series of unstable coalitions, terrorist outrages in the 1970s and political corruption scandals of the 1990s (involving numerous government ministers and officials), the latter half of the 20th century was boomtime in Italy, with many families enjoying a standard of living that would have been unthinkable a generation before.

Italy Today

In June 2018, Italy swore in what is Western Europe's first populist government. The country still struggles under the weight of an incredibly complicated legal system, huge public debt, high unemployment and has an economy which has been stagnant for the last decade.

1 Adolf Hitler and Benito Mussolini. ↑

2 An 18th-century depiction of a gallery packed with art from Italy.

3 The Italian Senate in session.

4 The Fiat Factory in Turin in 1965.

1990

World Cup in Italy

1997

Earthquake in Assisi, severely damaging Giotto frescoes

2009

Earthquake in Abruzzo kills 314 and almost destroys town of L'Aquil

2011

Silvio Berlusconi resigns. Technical government under Mario Monti

2013

Pope Francis elected

EXPERIENCE

Piazza Navona in Rome

NORTHERN ITALY

Piazza San Marco at sunset

EXPLORE
NORTHERN ITALY

This section divides northern Italy
into seven colour-coded sightseeing
areas, as shown on the map below.
Find out more about each area
on the following pages.

SWITZERLAND

Locarno · Bellinzona · Sondri

Lake
Maggiore

Verbania

Lake
Como

Aosta · VALLE
D'AOSTA

Varese · Como · Lecco

Biella

Bergamo

Ivrea

Rho · Monza

Novara

Bresc

VALLE D'AOSTA
AND PIEDMONT
p180

Vercelli

MILAN
p142

LOMBARDY
p164

Susa

Lodi

Pavia

Cremona

Turin

Moncalieri

Pinerolo

Asti

Alessandria

Piacenza

PIEDMONT

Tortona

Fiorenzuola
d'Arda

Alba

Par

Fossano

Acqui Terme

Cuneo

LIGURIA
p200

Genoa

Savona

Portofino

Sestri
Levante

FRANCE

Albenga

La Spezia

Mas

Imperia

Monaco · San Remo

Antibes

Pis

*Ligurian
Sea*

Livorno

0 kilometres   50

0 miles   50

N
↑

Worgl

Landeck

Innsbruck

AUSTRIA

St Michel im
Lungau

Malles Venosta

Brunico

Merano

Bressanone

Spittal an
der Drau

Bolzano

Cortina d'Ampezzo

Villach

TRENTINO-
ALTO ADIGE
p128

Tolmezzo

FRIULI-
VENEZIA
GIULIA

SLOVENIA

Trento

Belluno

Rovereto

Vittorio Veneto

Udine

Pordenone

Gorizia

Lake
Garda

THE VENETO
AND FRIULI
p102

Aquileia

Monfalcone

rmione

Vicenza

Treviso

Trieste

Verona

Mestre

Padua

CROATIA

VENETO

VENICE
p58

Mantua

Chioggia

Rovigo

Po

Rovinj

Ferrara

Pula

Reggio nell'
Emilia

Comacchio

*Adriatic
Sea*

Modena

Bologna

EMILIA-
ROMAGNA

Ravenna

Imola

Forli

ucca

Prato

ITALY

Arno

Florence

Bibbiena

TUSCANY

olterra

Arezzo

Siena

ampiglia
larittima

GETTING TO KNOW
NORTHERN ITALY

The economic powerhouse of the peninsular, northern Italy also encompasses an immense variety of landscapes, from the Alps, Dolomites and Italian Lakes, to the world-famous vineyards of Piedmont and the dramatic coast of Liguria. City-wise, Venice is the main focus, but historic towns such as Padua, Verona, Mantua and Trieste and bustling cities like Milan, Turin and Genoa also have their delights.

PAGE 58

VENICE

This improbable canal city of lacy Gothic palaces built on mudbanks amid the tidal waters of the Adriatic is totally unique. Once a powerful commercial and naval force in the Mediterranean, Venice has found a new role in the modern age. Her palazzi have become museums, shops, hotels and apartments, while her convents have been turned into centres for art restoration. These days there is barely an off-season, though visiting in winter, and taking the little alleyways that lead off the well-beaten tourist track, give a good chance of finding pockets of this magical city that still escape the crowds.

Best for
Getting lost and not caring

Home to
San Marco and the Doge's Palace

Experience
An ombra (glass of white wine) and cicchetti (bar snacks) in one of the traditional bars of the Rialto market

THE VENETO AND FRIULI

Encompassing the natural beauty of the Dolomites and the rolling Euganean hills – along with magnificent ancient cities such as Verona, Vicenza and Padua – the Veneto is a region of extraordinary contrasts. Here, you can easily combine sightseeing with mountain hiking, skiing or wine-tasting in the region's many vineyards. Friuli-Venezia-Giulia is one of Italy's lesser-visited regions, producing some of Italy's finest white wines.

Best for
Romantic getaways and experiencing the unique east-meets-west atmosphere of Trieste

Home to
Juliet's Balcony in Verona and the Giotto-frescoed Scrovegni Chapel in Padua

Experience
An open-air opera performance at the Arena in Verona

TRENTINO-ALTO ADIGE

Dominated by the majestic peaks of the Dolomites, Italian-speaking Trentino and German-speaking Alto Adige (or Südtirol) make up Italy's northernmost region. Bordering Austria and Switzerland, it has long been a battle zone, witnessed by the string of medieval castles protecting the Adige valley. These days its dramatic mountains and unspoilt lakes, rivers, woodland and pastures make the region one of the best in Italy for skiing, hiking and mountain climbing.

Best for
Outdoor adventures in the Dolomites and indulging in the region's spas

Home to
The dramatic Vie Ferrate and the ski resort of Madonna di Campiglio

Experience
Craft beers created in Trento's many independent breweries

→

PAGE 142

MILAN

Italy's fashion capital, Milan is a slick, affluent and fast-moving international city. With a fabulous historic centre, dominated by Italy's most magnificent Gothic cathedral, it is the birthplace of numerous world-famous works of art, including Leonardo's *The Last Supper*, and is home to the renowned Teatro alla Scala opera company. Shopping is superb, the quality of places to eat and drink is world-class, and the regeneration of industrial buildings and formerly run-down parts of the city, such as the Navigli canal area, are providing ever-more places to drink and party.

Best for
Shopping and chic bars

Home to
Leonardo's The Last Supper *and the Castello Sforzesco.*

Experience
The buzzing nightlife of the Navigli canals

PAGE 162

LOMBARDY AND THE LAKES

Fringed by the Alps and carved out by glaciers, the Italian lakes are surrounded by pretty lakeside villages, exuberant villas and magnificent gardens. Of the three major lakes, only Como lies entirely within Lombardy – Maggiore shares a border with Piedmont and Garda with the Veneto. The historic cities of Bergamo, Pavia, Cremona and Mantua offer another aspect to the region, while the trails and peaks of the Parco Nazionale dello Stelvio provide perfect wild escapes.

Best for
Beautiful lakeside landscapes and watersports

Home to
Lake Como, Lake Garda and Mantua

Experience
A violin recital in Cremona

PAGE 180

VALLE D'AOSTA AND PIEDMONT

Abutting France, and bordered by the Alps, Valle d'Aosta and Piedmont were ruled by the royal House of Savoy until the 18th century, and the influence of French culture remains in the region's food and dialect. Valle d'Aosta is a largely rural region, a series of pretty Alpine valleys headed by dramatic peaks that offer some world-class skiing. Piedmont stretches from the industrial Po plain, dominated by the capital, Turin, to the rolling vineyards of Barolo and Le Langhe.

Best for
Skiing and mountain scenery

Home to
The Slow Food movement, Parco del Gran Paradiso and Turin

Experience
A truffle hunt or wine-tasting in the Barolo vineyards

PAGE 200

LIGURIA

Nestling at the foot of vine-covered mountains, Liguria has one of the prettiest and most dramatic coastlines in Italy, where pastel-coloured houses bask in the Mediterranean sun of the clement microclimate. The most attractive stretch of coast is the Riviera di Levante, to the south of the bustling regional capital and port of Genoa (Genova), and between Camogli and the five towns of the Cinque Terre. To the north of Genoa, the Riviera di Ponente is a thin strip of coastal plain stretching across to the French border that includes big resorts such as Sanremo.

Best for
Swimming, hiking and coastal walks

Home to
The pastel-painted coastal villages of Camogli and the Cinque Terre

Experience
Skinny twists of Ligurian trofie pasta smothered in freshly made pesto

Gondolas moored in the Grand Canal

VENICE

Lying in the extreme northeast of Italy, Venice, gateway to the Orient, became an independent Byzantine province in the 10th century. Exclusive trading links with the East and victory in the Crusade of 1204 brought wealth and power, which were only gradually eroded by European and Turkish rivals. Today, Venice's ties are with the local Veneto region that stretches from the flat river plains to the Dolomites.

Venice is one of the few cities in the world that can be truly described as unique. It survives against all the odds, built on a series of low mudbanks amid the tidal waters of the Adriatic, and regularly subject to floods. During the Middle Ages, under the leadership of successive doges (chief magistrates), Venice expanded its power and influence throughout the Mediterranean to Constantinople (modern Istanbul). Its immense wealth was celebrated in art and architecture throughout the city.

The riches of St Mark's alone bear witness to Venice's position as a world power from the 12th to 14th centuries. After slowly losing ground to the new states of Europe, however, it fell to Napoleon in 1797. Finally, Venice joined the Kingdom of Italy in 1866, so bringing unity to the country for the first time in its history.

Little of the essential fabric of Venice has altered in 200 years. The city's sounds are still those of footsteps and the cries of boatmen. The only engines are those of barges delivering supplies or water-buses ferrying passengers between stops. The same well-worn streets are still trodden. More than 20 million visitors a year succumb to the magic of this improbable place whose "streets are full of water" and where the glories of the past are evident at every turn.

VENICE

Must Sees
1. Basilica di San Marco
2. Palazzo Ducale
3. Santa Maria Gloriosa dei Frari
4. Rialto

Experience More
5. Madonna dell'Orto
6. Ca' d'Oro
7. San Giovanni Grisostomo
8. Santa Maria dei Miracoli
9. San Polo
10. Scuola Grande di San Rocco
11. Ca' Rezzonico
12. San Nicolo dei Mendicoli
13. San Sebastiano
14. Santa Maria della Salute
15. Punta della Dogana
16. Accademia
17. Peggy Guggenheim Collection
18. Santo Stefano
19. Torre dell'Orologio
20. Campanile
21. Museo Correr
22. San Zaccaria
23. Santa Maria Formosa
24. Santi Giovanni e Paolo
25. Statue of Colleoni
26. Scuola di San Giorgio degli Schiavoni
27. Arsenale
28. Torcello
29. Giudecca
30. San Giorgio Maggiore
31. Murano
32. Burano

Eat
1. Osteria Alla Ciurma
2. Alla Palanca
3. Osteria Santa Marina
4. La Zucca
5. Trattoria dalla Marisa

Drink
6. Bar Puppa
7. Tappa Obbligatoria
8. Osteria ai Osti
9. Skyline Rooftop Bar
10. Harry's Dolci

Shop
11. Ca' Macana
12. Papier Mache Venezia
13. Maschere di Guerrino Lovato

The Islands

✈ Aeroporto di Venezia Marco Polo

Canale Osellino

Laguna Veneto

Torcello 28

Mazzorbo 32

Burano

Murano 31

Lazzaretto Nuovo

Sant' Erasmo

Area of main Venice map

Tronchetto

🚉 VENICE

San Michele

Vignole

Certosa

Santa Maria delle Grazie

San Servolo

Lido

0 km   3

0 miles   3

Canale delle Fondamenta Nuove

Sant'Alvise

CAMPO DI SANT'ALVISE

FMTA DI Sant'Alvise

CAMPIELLO PIAVE

🚉 Orto

Madonna dell'Orto 5

FMTA MADONNA DELL'ORTO

FMTA DELLA SENSA

Palazzo Mastelli

CAMPO DEI MORI

Sacca della Misericordia

FMTA D. ORMESINI

Museo Ebraico

RIO TERRA FARSETTI

FOND. DELLA MISERICORDIA

Santa Maria della Misericordia

Canale di Misericordia

FONDAMENTA NUOVE

Gesuiti

CAMPO DEI GESUITI

🚉 Fondamente Nove

PO LEONARDO

CAMPO DELLA MADDALENA

STRADA NOVA

Rio di Noale

Rio di S. Caterina

CAMPO SAN MARCUOLA

🚉 San Marcuola

Rio di San Marcuola

RIO TERRA D. MADDALENA

CAMPO SAN FELICE

🚉 Ospedale

Ospedale Civile

FOND. DEI MENDICANTI

FONDAMENTA NUOVE

Fondaco dei Turchi

🚉 San Stae

CAMPO SAN STAE

STRADA NOVA

Ca' d'Oro 6

🚉 Ca' d'Oro 7

CAMPO DEI SANTI APOSTOLI

Rio dei Santi Apostoli

CAMPIELLO WIDMAN

Statue of Colleoni 25

🚉 Celestia

Santi Giovanni e Paolo 24

San Francesco della Vigna

MPO SAN DEGOLA

Palazzo Mocenigo

CAMPO S. GIACOMO DELL'ORIO

CAMPO SAN CASSIANO

C. DELLA CHIESA

Rialto Mercato D. PESCHERIA

Santa Maria dei Miracoli 8

CAMPO S. MARIA NOVA

CAMPO SS. GIOVANNI E PAOLO

BARBARIA DELLE TOLE

CALLE CAPPUCCINE

F. DI SAN LORENZO

San Lorenzo

CAMPO D. CELESTIA

SAN POLO

RIOTERRA SECONDO

San Giovanni Grisostomo 7

San Polo 9

🚉 San Silvestro

RUGA VECCHIA S. GIOVANNI

🚉 Rialto 4

CAMPO S. BARTOLOMEO

🚉 Rialto

CAMPO SAN SILVESTRO

RIVA DEL CARBON

CAMPO S. MARINA

3

CAMPO SAN MARINA

12

CASTELLO

Rio di San Giovanni Laterano

CAMPO SS. GIOVANNI E PAOLO

CAMPO S. TERNITA

S. LORENZO

Scuola di San Giorgio degli Schiavoni 26

Arsenale 27

Arsenale Vecchio

PO STIN

Sant'Aponal

CAMPO SAN POLO

CAMPO SAN POLO

San Salvatore

MERCERIA

San Zulian

Santa Maria Formosa 23

RUGA GIUFFA

SAL. DEI GRECI

CAMPO BANDIERA E MORO

San Giovanni in Bragora

CAMPO ARSENALE

🚉 Arsenale

RIVA CA' DI DIO

San Toma

CAMPO S. TOMA

🚉 Sant'Angelo

Museo Fortuny

CAMPO MANIN

Scala Contarini del Bovolo

CALLE DEI FABBRI

SPADARIA

MERCERIA

SAL. SAN LIO

Torre dell'Orologio 19

Campanile 20

Basilica di San Marco 1

PIAZZA SAN MARCO

Palazzo Ducale

SAL SAN LIO

22 San Zaccaria

CAMPO S. ZACCARIA

🚉 San Zaccaria

RIVA DEGLI SCHIAVONI

CAMPO SAN BIAGIO

SAN MARCO

SAL SAN SAMUELE

🚉 San Samuele

CAMPO SANTO STEFANO

Santo Stefano 18

Teatro La Fenice

CAMPO S. FANTIN

Museo Correr 21

i

🚉 San Marco-Vallaresso

🚉 San Marco-Giardinetti

CALLE LARGA XXII MARZO

CAMPO SAN MOISE

🚉 Rezzonico

CAMPO SANTO STEFANO

CAMPO SAN MAURIZIO

Accademia

CAMPO SAN VIDAL

Ponte dell'Accademia

🚉 Giglio

🚉 Salute

16 Accademia

CAMPO SAN VIO

Peggy Guggenheim Collection 17

Santa Maria della Salute 14

RIO TERRA D. CATECUMENI

Punta della Dogana 15

Bacino di San Marco

Canale di San Marco

CAMPO SAN GIORGIO

🚉 San Giorgio

San Giorgio Maggiore 30

A ZATTERE GESUATI

FMTA ZATTERE ALLO SPIRITO SANTO

RIO TERRA D. AI SALONI

🚉 Spirito Santo

Hotel Cipriani

VENICE

della

Giudecca

🚉 Palanca

Ponte Lungo

FONDAMENTA SAN GIACOMO

Redentore

FONDAMENTA DELLA CROCE

C. D. ZITELLE

Zitelle

FONDAMENTA D. ZITELLE

Le Zitelle

29 Giudecca

LA GIUDECCA

0 metres   400

0 yards   400

N

D   E   F

→

1 Gondola ride under the Rialto Bridge.

2 Glass blowing in Murano.

3 Pastel-coloured houses lining the canal in Burano.

4 Coffee at Caffè Florian.

2 DAYS
A Weekend in Venice

Day 1

Morning Start the day at the bustling Rialto Market *(p82)*, stopping for mid-morning *cicchetti* (bar snacks) and prosecco in one of the market's wine bars. Afterwards, take a vaporetto along the Grand Canal. Not only is this one of the best (and fastest) ways to get around Venice, it's also one of the cheapest – a boon when staying in one of the world's most expensive cities. Line 1 zips you to San Marco in 25 minutes, and from there it's a short walk to Basilica di San Marco *(p72)*. English guided tours run daily at 11am, 2:30pm and 4pm, though it's best to see the mosaics in the morning light. Don't miss the Treasury, home to jewels, reliquaries, and Byzantine and Islamic art from the Crusades. Next, head to the adjacent Palazzo Ducale *(p76)* for paintings by Titian, Tintoretto and Veronese and a glimpse at the opulent Doge's restored apartments.

Afternoon After a hearty lunch, explore the district of San Polo *(p86)*, Venice's smallest *sestiere*, before heading to the magnificent Gothic Santa Maria Gloriosa dei Frari *(p80)* to see the Titian's glorious *Assumption of the Virgin*.

Evening Finish the day with a campari spritz aperitivo in the ever-lively Campo Santa Margherita *(p100)*.

Day 2

Morning After breakfast, make for the Dorsoduro *sestiere* and visit the Ca' Rezzonico *(p87)*, a palace-turned-museum that traces the history of 18th-century Venice. Move on to the Accademia *(p90)*, which houses pre-19th-century art, then complete the triumvirate at the Peggy Guggenheim Collection *(p91)*, home to an exceptional selection of modern paintings and sculptures. Grab an espresso at the Guggenheim café before beginning a picturesque zig-zag across the city to Fondamente Nuove, where vaporetti depart for the northern section of the lagoon. On the way, stop at Venetian Renaissance church Santa Maria dei Miracoli *(p85)*, and then go for a bowl of spaghetti with clams at the canalside trattoria Da Rioba *(Fondamenta de la Misericordia 2553)* in Cannareggio.

Afternoon Stomach full, take the *traghetto* (ferry) to the small but pretty island of Torcello *(p96)*, where the church of Santa Maria Assunta houses some of the city's most stunning mosaics. Look out for depictions of angels, devils, beasts and hell-fire in the *Universal Judgment*, which covers the west wall.

Evening Head to Locanda Cipriani *(p66)* for dinner, and soak up the jaw-slackening views over Venice on the way.

Parco delle Rimembranze

Away from Venice's crowded streets, this public park on the Island of Sant'Elena is a haven of tranquillity and greenery. The park is dedicated to the Venetian soldiers who died in World War II. Paths twist between the trees and around benches and statues of notable figures. It is the perfect place to relax in the open air and enjoy views of the lagoon.

←

View across the lagoon from the Parco delle Rimembranze

VENICE'S
QUIET PLACES

A trip to Venice wouldn't be complete without ticking off some of the biggest sights. But, just a few steps away from the tightly-packed tourist groups, you'll find some astonishingly peaceful places. From ancient churches to quiet gardens, these tranquil spots can be explored at leisure.

San Lazzaro degli Armeni

Named after St Lazarus, the patron saint of lepers, this small island in the lagoon was occupied by an Armenian monk in the 18th century, who constructed a monastery, church and library, all nestled among idyllic gardens. Today, monks give visitors guided tours of the serene complex.

→

San Lazzaro degli Armeni island

💬 INSIDER TIP
Dodge the Cruises

Cruises tend to bring the biggest crowds to Venice. Check ship schedules online (*www.ports.cruisett.com*) and visit on quieter days.

Palazzo Grimani

Originally the residence of the Venetian doge Antonio Grimani, Palazzo Grimani combines Tuscan and Roman features with traditional Venetian architecture. The interior is beautifully decorated with outstanding stuccowork, soaring ceilings, and frescoes by Mannerist artists such as Francesco Salviati, Francesco Menzocchi and Federico Zuccari.

→

The sculpture gallery in Palazzo Grimani

Palazzo Mocenigo

Palazzo Mocenigo, formerly home to one of the city's oldest families, provides a rare opportunity to visit an impeccably preserved palazzo. The Museo del Tessuto, inside the building, showcases 16th- and 17th-century refined fabrics and elegant costumes, beautifully embellished with embroidery and lace.

←

Costumes on display in the Museo del Tessuto, Palazzo Mocenigo

Chiesa di Santo Stefano

Campo Santo Stefano is usually filled with tourists enjoying a drink or bite to eat in the many cafés leading up to Ponte dell'Accademia, but the hushed interior of the square's namesake 14th-century church is a peaceful antidote to the hustle and bustle outside.

→

The nave of the Chiesa di Santo Stefano

Bacari

Unique to Venice, *bacari* are bars where locals go for aperitivo and *chicchetti* (small plates of tapas-like bites). Venetians tend to head to their local *bacari* for drinks after work, or for a pre-dinner cocktail with friends.
Venice's finest *bacari*: *Al Bottegon* (Fondamenta Nani 992), *Ai DiVini* (Fondamenta Trapolin 5905) *and Osteria al Squero* (Dorsoduro 943–4).

←

A waiter preparing plates of *chicchetti* in one of Venice's *bacari*

VENICE FOR
FOODIES

Not far from Piazza San Marco lie a handful of neighbourhood trattorias, where locals huddle over plates of spaghetti. Stop by one of the city's ubiquitous *gelaterie* for an afternoon pick-me-up, or head to the outer *sestieri* (districts) for buzzy *bacari* (bars) serving Campari spritz and snacks.

RIALTO MARKET

Live like a Venetian and head to the daily Rialto market, where colourful stalls lining the Grand Canal in San Polo are piled high with fresh fruit and vegetables. Next door is the Pescaria fish market; in the morning, fishermen sell the day's catch of octopus, squid, soft-shelled crabs and swordfish. Come lunchtime, the fishermen cook whatever has not been sold, turning out plates of freshly fried fish and bowls of piping hot seafood risotto for only a few euros each. Make sure you don't leave your visit too late – few stalls are left in the afternoon.

Fine Dining

There are numerous fine dining options in Venice, a favourite destination of the rich and famous. There is often a strict dress code, so check when booking.
Venice's fine-dining hotspots: *Locanda Cipriani* (Piazza Santa Fosca, Torcello), *Antica Osteria Cera* (Via Marghera 24) *and Venissa* (Fondamenta di Santa Caterina 3).

Bars

Not to be mistaken with the Anglo Saxon term for bar, these coffee-serving bars are where Venetians go for their breakfast coffee and brioche (sweet croissant). If visiting before 11am, order a creamy cappuccino; any time after that calls for either an espresso or a macchiato (an espresso with an added spoonful of steamed milk). **Venice's best bars:** *Bar Puppa* (p85), *Bar Pasticceria di Chiusso Pierino* (Salizzada dei Greci 3306), *Tonolo* (Calle S. Pantalon 3764).

↓ Coffee and romance next to the canals in Venice

↑ Venetian *gelato* on a sunny day by the canal

Gelaterie

Gelato is a way of life in Venice, with locals meeting for ice cream at any time of the day. **Venice's greatest *gelaterie*:** *Grom gelato* (Campo San Barnaba), *Boutique del Gelato* (Salizzada San Lio 5727) and *Gelateria Nico* (Fodamenta Zattere al Ponte Longo 922).

Trattorias and Osterias

Venetian trattorias are small, family-run establishments with short menus, while osterias traditionally focus on wines, with a few dishes on a daily-changing menu. **Venice's top trattorias and osterias:** *La Vedova* (Calle Cà d'Oro 3912), *Osteria Ai Osti* (p85) and *Alla Ciurma* (Calle Galiazza 406/A).

← Venissa, one of Venice's many fine-dining establishments

→ Chairs outside an osteria on a colourful Venetian street

THE GRAND CANAL

SANTA LUCIA
TO THE RIALTO

The best way to view the Grand Canal as it winds through the heart of the city is from a vaporetto, or waterbus. Two lines travel the length of the canal. The palaces lining the waterway were built over a span of five centuries and present a panoramic survey of the city's history.

Shaped like a back-to-front "S", the Grand Canal snakes through the heart of Venice, connecting its various districts. From the earliest times it was a key trade and transport route, which is why the city's wealthy families built their palaces along its banks. The most spectacular palazzo on this stretch of the canal is the Gothic Ca' d'Oro, whose façade once glittered with gold. Santa Lucia, the city's railway station, links the city with the mainland.

View of the Ponte ↑
degli Scalzi and San
Geremia beyond

0 metres   100   N
0 yards   100   ↑

Canale di
Cannaregio

The San Marcuola
church was rebuilt in
the 18th century, but
the new façade was
never completed.

San Geremia houses
the relics of St Lucy.

The Palazzo Labia ballroom was
decorated by Giambattista
Tiepolo with scenes from the
life of Cleopatra.

Ferrovia

Riva di Biasio

The Fondaco dei Turchi,
the former Turkish
warehouse, is now the
Natural History Museum.

Ponte degli Scalzi

The 18th-century domed church
of San Simeone Piccolo is based
on the Pantheon in Rome.

→

The Baroque façade of
San Stae, richly decorated
with statues

↑ Sculptures inside the magnificent Ca' d'Oro palace

THE GONDOLAS OF VENICE

The gondola has been a part of Venice since the 11th century. With its slim hull and flat underside, the craft is perfectly adapted to negotiating narrow, shallow canals. There is a slight leftward curve to the prow, which counteracts the force of the oar, preventing the gondola from going round in circles.

In 1562 it was decreed that all gondolas should be black, to stop people making an ostentatious show of their wealth. For special occasions they are decorated with flowers.

The German composer Richard Wagner died at the Palazzo Vendramin Calergi in 1883.

The Ca' d'Oro, with its delicate Gothic tracery, is one of the finest Venetian palaces.

Graceful Veneto-Byzantine and Gothic arches feature on the Palazzo Sagredo façade.

The façade of San Stae is richly adorned with statues.

The Baroque palace Ca' Pesaro today houses a gallery of modern art.

The Pescheria has been the site of a busy fish market for six centuries.

The Rialto Bridge ↓

↑ Aerial view of the Grand Canal from Santa Lucia to the Rialto

THE GRAND CANAL
THE RIALTO TO SAN MARCO

After passing the Rialto, the canal doubles back on itself along a stretch known as La Volta (the bend). It then widens out and the views become more spectacular approaching San Marco. Façades may have faded and foundations battered with the tides, but the canal remains spectacularly beautiful.

The area around the Rialto Bridge is the oldest and busiest quarter of the city. Traditionally a centre of trade, crowded quaysides and colourful food markets still border the canal. Past the splendid curve known as La Volta, the view along the final stretch of the Grand Canal is one of the finest in Venice. Near the mouth rises the magnificent church of La Salute with busy St Mark's Basin beyond.

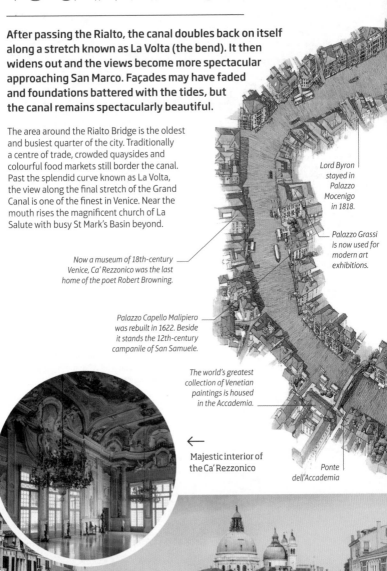

Lord Byron stayed in Palazzo Mocenigo in 1818.

Palazzo Grassi is now used for modern art exhibitions.

Now a museum of 18th-century Venice, Ca' Rezzonico was the last home of the poet Robert Browning.

Palazzo Capello Malipiero was rebuilt in 1622. Beside it stands the 12th-century campanile of San Samuele.

The world's greatest collection of Venetian paintings is housed in the Accademia.

← Majestic interior of the Ca' Rezzonico

Ponte dell'Accademia

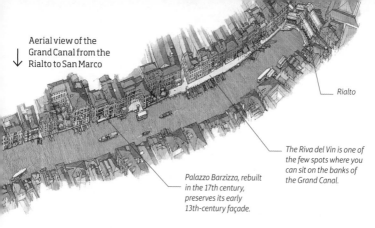

Aerial view of the Grand Canal from the Rialto to San Marco

Rialto

The Riva del Vin is one of the few spots where you can sit on the banks of the Grand Canal.

Palazzo Barzizza, rebuilt in the 17th century, preserves its early 13th-century façade.

📷 **PICTURE PERFECT**
Grand Canal

For an iconic shot of the Grand Canal there's no better place than the Ponte dell'Accademia. Get in position about half an hour before sunset and point your camera lens towards San Marco and Santa Maria della Salute.

↑ Crowds crossing the canal on the Ponte dell'Accademia

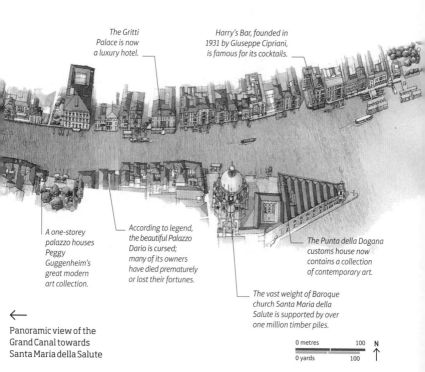

The Gritti Palace is now a luxury hotel.

Harry's Bar, founded in 1931 by Giuseppe Cipriani, is famous for its cocktails.

A one-storey palazzo houses Peggy Guggenheim's great modern art collection.

According to legend, the beautiful Palazzo Dario is cursed; many of its owners have died prematurely or lost their fortunes.

The Punta della Dogana customs house now contains a collection of contemporary art.

The vast weight of Baroque church Santa Maria della Salute is supported by over one million timber piles.

← Panoramic view of the Grand Canal towards Santa Maria della Salute

| 0 metres | 100 |
| 0 yards | 100 |

N ↑

BASILICA DI SAN MARCO

📍 E3 🏛 Piazza San Marco 🚊 San Marco 🕐 9:45am–5pm Mon–Sat, 2–4pm Sun
🌐 basilicasanmarco.it

Dark, mysterious and enriched with the spoils of conquest, Venice's famous Basilica blends the architectural and decorative styles of East and West to create one of Europe's greatest buildings. Inside, this Byzantine extravaganza is embellished with golden mosaics, icons and ornate marble carvings.

Exterior of St Mark's

Built on a Greek cross plan and crowned with five huge domes, St Marks owes its almost Oriental splendour to countless treasures from the Republic's overseas empire. Among these are copies of the famous bronze horses brought from Constantinople in 1204, and a wealth of columns, bas-reliefs and coloured marbles studded across the main façade. Mosaics from different epochs adorn the five doorways, while the main portal is framed by some of Italy's loveliest Romanesque carving (1240–65). Initially built in the 9th century, this is the third church to stand on the site.

↑ Romanesque carvings surrounding the arches of the main portal

> St Mark's owes its almost Oriental splendour to countless treasures from the Republic's overseas empire.

← Façada and campanile of the Basilica, seen from Piazza San Marco

Timeline

828–978
△ A church is built to house relics of St Mark, stolen from Alexandria. It burns down in 976 and is rebuilt in 978

978–1117
△ The church is replaced by a grand basilica, "the House of St Mark", reflecting Venice's growing power

1117–c.1300
△ 4,240 sq m (45,622 sq ft) of gleaming golden mosaics are added to the domes, walls and floors of the Basilica

1807
△ The doge's private chapel until 1807, San Marco succeeds San Pietro di Castello as the cathedral of Venice

↑ Ornate coloured marble panels on the exterior of the Basilica

Inside the Basilica

St Mark's magnificent interior is clad with dazzling mosaics, which begin in the narthex, or atrium, of the Basilica, and culminate in the glittering panels of the Pentecost and Ascension domes. The Genesis Cupola in the atrium has a stunning scene of the Creation of the World described in concentric circles. The *pavimento*, or floor, is also patterned with mosaics in marble and glass. Steps from the atrium lead to the Museo Marciano, home to the Basilica's famous horses. Other treasures include the jewel-encrusted Pala d'Oro, the Nicopeia icon and the precious hoards of silver, gold and glassware in the Treasury.

Statues of St Mark and angels, which crown the central arch, are additions from the early 15th century.

The Pentecost Dome was probably the first dome to be decorated with mosaics.

The four horses of St Mark are replicas of the gilded bronze originals, now protected inside the Basilica's museum.

> St Mark's magnificent interior is clad with dazzling mosaics, which culminate in the glittering panels of the Pentecost and Ascension domes.

→

Stunning mosaic of Christ in Glory in the vast Ascension Dome

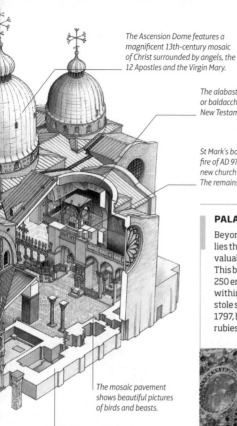

The Ascension Dome features a magnificent 13th-century mosaic of Christ surrounded by angels, the 12 Apostles and the Virgin Mary.

The alabaster columns of the altar canopy, or baldacchino, are adorned with New Testament scenes.

St Mark's body, believed lost in the fire of AD 976, reappeared when the new church was consecrated in 1094. The remains are housed in the altar.

The mosaic pavement shows beautiful pictures of birds and beasts.

The Treasury is a repository of precious artifacts from both Italy and Constantinople.

PALA D'ORO

Beyond the Cappella di San Clemente lies the entrance to San Marco's most valuable treasure: the Pala d'Oro. This bejewelled altarpiece consists of 250 enamel paintings on gold, enclosed within a gilded silver frame. Napoleon stole some of the precious stones in 1797, but the screen still gleams with rubies, pearls and sapphires.

Mosaics

The earliest of the Basilica's gleaming mosaics date from the 12th century, and were the work of specialists from the East. Their delicate techniques were soon adopted by Venetian craftsmen, who gradually took over the Basilica's decoration, combining Byzantine inspiration with Western influences. During the 16th century, many sketches by Tintoretto, Titian, Veronese and other artists were reproduced in mosaic.

Museo Marciano

Look out for signposts to the "Loggia dei Cavalli", which lead you up to the museum. Here, the gallery offers a splendid view into the Basilica. The star exhibits are gilded bronze horses, stolen from the top of Constantinople's Hippodrome (ancient racecourse) in 1204.

←

Gilded bronze horses housed in the Museo Marciano

2 (icons)

PALAZZO DUCALE

Q E3 **A** Piazza San Marco 1 **San Marco** **8:30am–5:30pm daily (Apr–Oct: to 7pm);** last adm: 1 hour before closing **1 Jan, 25 Dec** **w** visitmuve.it

A magnificent combination of Byzantine, Gothic and Renaissance architecture, the Palazzo Ducale (Doge's Palace) was the official residence of the 120 doges who ruled Venice from 697 to 1797. Artists such as Titian, Tintoretto and Bellini vied with each other to embellish the palace with painting and sculpture, not to mention architects Antonio Rizzo and Pietro Lombardo, the latter responsible for the ornate western façade.

The Palazzo Ducale was founded in the 9th century, when a fortress-like structure stood on this spot. The present palace owes its external appearance to the building work of the 14th and early 15th centuries, despite a string of fires in the 1500s. The designers broke with tradition by perching the bulk of the pink Verona marble palace on lace-like Istrian stone arcades, with a portico supported by columns below. The result is a light and airy masterpiece of Gothic architecture.

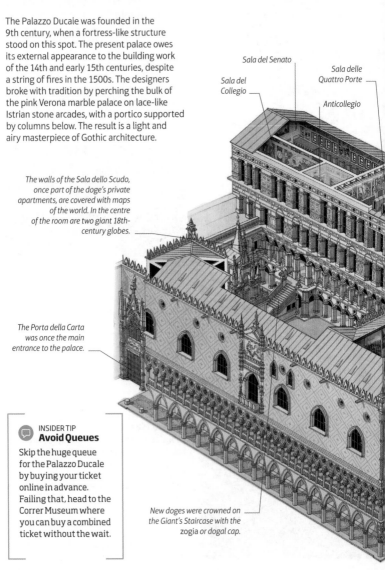

Sala del Senato

Sala delle Quattro Porte

Sala del Collegio

Anticollegio

The walls of the Sala dello Scudo, once part of the doge's private apartments, are covered with maps of the world. In the centre of the room are two giant 18th-century globes.

The Porta della Carta was once the main entrance to the palace.

New doges were crowned on the Giant's Staircase with the zogia or dogal cap.

> **INSIDER TIP**
> **Avoid Queues**
>
> Skip the huge queue for the Palazzo Ducale by buying your ticket online in advance. Failing that, head to the Correr Museum where you can buy a combined ticket without the wait.

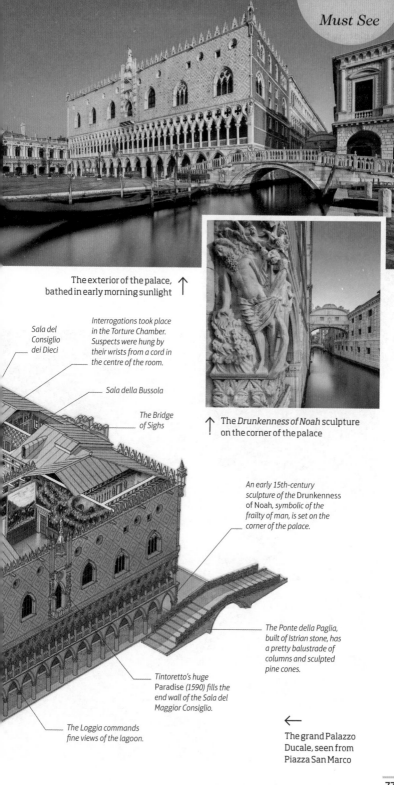

The exterior of the palace, bathed in early morning sunlight ↑

Sala del Consiglio dei Dieci

Interrogations took place in the Torture Chamber. Suspects were hung by their wrists from a cord in the centre of the room.

Sala della Bussola

The Bridge of Sighs

↑ The *Drunkenness of Noah* sculpture on the corner of the palace

An early 15th-century sculpture of the *Drunkenness of Noah,* symbolic of the frailty of man, is set on the corner of the palace.

The Ponte della Paglia, built of Istrian stone, has a pretty balustrade of columns and sculpted pine cones.

Tintoretto's huge *Paradise (1590)* fills the end wall of the Sala del Maggior Consiglio.

The Loggia commands fine views of the lagoon.

← The grand Palazzo Ducale, seen from Piazza San Marco

Exploring the Palazzo Ducale

A tour of the Palazzo Ducale takes visitors through a succession of richly decorated chambers and halls, arranged over four floors, culminating with the Bridge of Sighs, which links the palace to the prisons. The Secret Itineraries tour gives access to parts of the palace normally out of bounds, including the prison cell from which Casanova escaped.

State Apartments and Council Chambers

The doge's private State Apartments on the second floor were built after the fire of 1483. Looted under the orders of Napoleon, they are bare of furnishings, but the lavish ceilings and colossal carved chimneypieces in some of the rooms give an idea of the doges' lifestyle. The Sala dello Scudo, or map room, contains maps and charts, while the picture gallery features some incongruous wooden demoniac panels by Hieronymous Bosch.

The Scala d'Oro ("golden staircase") leads to the third floor and its Council Chambers. In the Sala del Consiglio dei Dieci, the awesomely powerful Council of Ten, set up in 1310, would meet to investigate and prosecute crimes concerning the security of the state. Napoleon pilfered some of the Veroneses from the ceiling

←

Veronese's *Rape of Europa* in the Anticollegio chamber

→

The magnificent Sala del Maggior Consiglio, featuring Tintoretto's *Paradise*

WHO COULD JOIN THE GREAT COUNCIL?

By the mid-16th century the Great Council had around 2,000 members. Any Venetian of high birth over 25 years old was entitled to a seat - with the exception of those married to a commoner. From 1646, those from merchant or professional classes with 100,000 ducats to spare could purchase their way in.

but two of the finest found their way back here in 1920: *Age and Youth* and *Juno Offering the Ducal Crown to Venice* (both 1553–4).

The magnificent Anticollegio chamber was the waiting room for those meeting with the Council. The end walls are decorated with mythological scenes by Tintoretto: *Vulcan's Forge, Mercury and the Graces, Bacchus and Ariadne* and *Minerva Dismissing Mars*, all

↑ Dank corridor leading to cells in the palace prisons

painted in 1578. Veronese's masterly *Rape of Europa* (1580), opposite the window, is one of the most eye-catching works in the palace.

In the Sala della Bussola were lions' heads, where citizens could post anonymous bills denouncing others for their crimes, real or imaginary. The wooden door in this room leads to the rooms of the Heads of the Ten, the State Inquisitors' Room and thence to the torture chamber and prisons.

The star attraction of the palace is the monumental Sala del Maggior Consiglio. It was here that the Great Council convened to vote on constitutional questions, to pass laws and elect the top officials of the Serene Republic. Tintoretto's huge *Paradise* (1587–90) occupies the eastern wall. Measuring 7.45 by 24.65 m (25 by 81 ft), it is one of the largest oil paintings in the world. A frieze along the walls illustrates 76 doges by Tintoretto's pupils. The portrait covered by a curtain is of Marin Falier, beheaded for treason in 1355.

Prisons

The Bridge of Sighs links the palace to what were known as the New Prisons, built between 1556 and 1595. Situated at the top of the palace, just below the leaded roof, are the *piombi* cells (*piombo* means lead). These cells are hardly inviting but prisoners here were far more comfortable than the criminals left to fester in the *pozzi* – the dark dank dungeons at ground level. The windowless cells of these ancient prisons are still covered with the graffiti of the convicts.

Did You Know?
—
Notorious womanizer Casanova escaped from the palace prisons through a hole in the roof of his cell.

SANTA MARIA GLORIOSA DEI FRARI

C3 **Campo dei Frari** **San Tomà** **9am–6pm Mon–Sat, 1–6pm Sun & religious hols** **1 Jan, 25 Dec & during Mass** **chorusvenezia.org**

More commonly known as the Frari (a corruption of *frati*, meaning "brothers"), this vast Gothic church dwarfs the eastern area of San Polo. The airy interior is striking for the sheer size and quality of its works of art, including masterpieces by Titian and Giovanni Bellini, a statue by Donatello and several grandiose tombs.

The first church on this site was built by Franciscan friars in 1250–1338, but was replaced by a much larger building in the 15th century. The labyrinthine monastery and courtyards adjoining the church have been home to Venice's State Archives since the fall of the Republic. Its 300 rooms are loaded with precious records documenting the history of Venice right back to the 9th century.

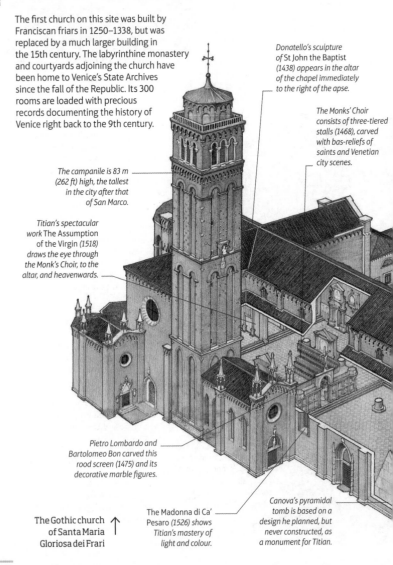

Donatello's sculpture of St John the Baptist (1438) appears in the altar of the chapel immediately to the right of the apse.

The Monks' Choir consists of three-tiered stalls (1468), carved with bas-reliefs of saints and Venetian city scenes.

The campanile is 83 m (262 ft) high, the tallest in the city after that of San Marco.

Titian's spectacular work The Assumption of the Virgin (1518) draws the eye through the Monk's Choir, to the altar, and heavenwards.

Pietro Lombardo and Bartolomeo Bon carved this rood screen (1475) and its decorative marble figures.

The Gothic church of Santa Maria Gloriosa dei Frari ↑

The Madonna di Ca' Pesaro (1526) shows Titian's mastery of light and colour.

Canova's pyramidal tomb is based on a design he planned, but never constructed, as a monument for Titian.

1 The entrance to Santa Maria Gloriosa dei Frari faces the Rio del Frari canal.

2 Titian's famous *Assumption of the Virgin* dominates the apse.

3 The sacristy's altarpiece, *Madonna and Child* (1488), by Bellini, is one of Venice's most beautiful Renaissance paintings.

4 The church's former monastery houses Venice's State Archives.

Courtyard and former monastery

④

RIALTO

◉ E3 🚋 Rialto

The commercial hub of Venice, the Rialto takes its name from *rivo alto* (high bank) and was one of the first areas of Venice to be inhabited. A financial and then a market district, it remains one of the city's busiest and most bustling areas. Locals and visitors alike jostle among the colourful stalls of the Erberia (fruit and vegetable market) and Pescheria (fish market), while crowds gather on the famous Rialto Bridge, browsing for souvenirs or taking a break to watch the swirl of activity on the Grand Canal below.

→

Gondola boats bobbing on the Grand Canal, with the Rialto bridge in the background

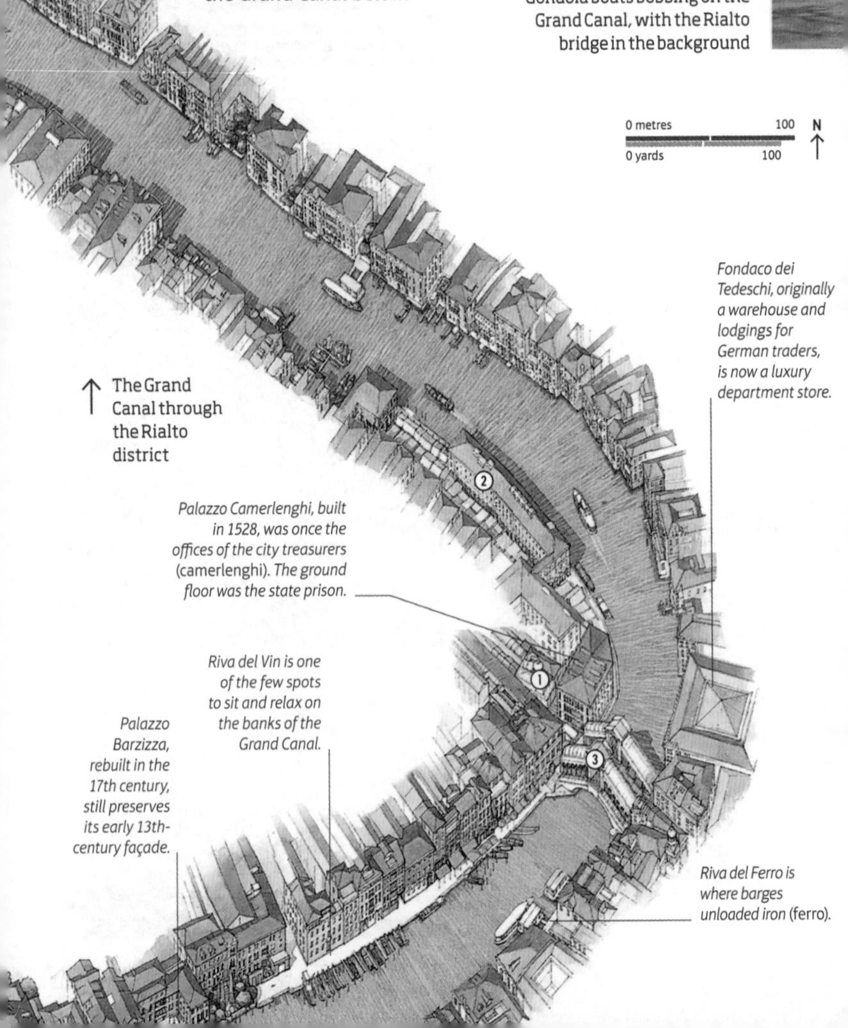

0 metres   100   N

0 yards   100   ↑

Fondaco dei Tedeschi, originally a warehouse and lodgings for German traders, is now a luxury department store.

↑ The Grand Canal through the Rialto district

Palazzo Camerlenghi, built in 1528, was once the offices of the city treasurers (camerlenghi). The ground floor was the state prison.

Riva del Vin is one of the few spots to sit and relax on the banks of the Grand Canal.

Palazzo Barzizza, rebuilt in the 17th century, still preserves its early 13th-century façade.

Riva del Ferro is where barges unloaded iron (ferro).

Did You Know?

An early wooden Rialto Bridge collapsed under the weight of a wedding party in 1444.

 ①

San Giacomo di Rialto

 Campo San Giacomo, San Polo 📞 041 522 47 45 🕐 9:30am–noon & 4–5pm Mon–Sat, 11am–noon Sun 🚫 During Mass

The first church to be built on this site was allegedly founded in the 5th century, making it the oldest church in Venice. The present building dates from between the 11th and 12th centuries, while major restoration work took place in 1601. The original Gothic portico and huge 15th-centruy 24-hour clock on its façade are the church's most striking features.

The crouching stone figure on the far side of the square is the so-called Gobbo (hunchback) of the Rialto. In the 16th century this was a welcome sight for minor offenders who were forced to run the gauntlet from Piazza San Marco to this square at the Rialto.

②

Rialto Markets

📍 San Polo 🕐 Dawn–12:30pm Mon–Sat (fruit and vegetable market); dawn–12:30pm Tue–Sat (fish market)

Venetians have come to the Erberia fruit and vegetable market to buy fresh produce for hundreds of years. Heavily laden barges arrive at dawn and offload their crates on to the quayside by the Grand Canal. Local produce includes red *radicchio* from Treviso, and succulent asparagus and baby artichokes from the islands of Sant'Erasmo and Vignole. In the adjoining Pescheria fish market are sole, sardines, skate, squid, crabs, clams and other species of seafood and fish for sale.

 ③

Rialto Bridge

Very few visitors leave Venice without crossing the iconic Rialto Bridge. The oldest of the four crossings over the Grand Canal, it is a wonderful place to watch the constant activity of boats on the water below. Stone bridges were built in Venice as early as the 12th century, but it was not until 1588, after the collapse, decay or sabotage of earlier wooden structures, that a competition was held for the design of a new Rialto bridge to be built in stone. Andrea Palladio, Jacopo Sansovino and Michelangelo were among the eminent contenders, but after months of deliberation it was the aptly named Antonio da Ponte who won the commission. Work was completed on the 48-m (157-ft) bridge in 1591. Until 1854, when the Accademia Bridge was constructed, the Rialto Bridge remained the only means of crossing the Grand Canal on foot.

 INSIDER TIP:
Rialto Market

To see the market in full, bustling swing, visitors must arrive early in the morning - by noon the vendors are already starting to pack up.

EXPERIENCE MORE

5

Madonna dell'Orto

📍 D1 🏛 Campo Madonna dell'Orto 🚤 Madonna dell'Orto ⏰ 10am–5pm Mon–Sat, noon–5pm Sun & pub hols 🚫 1 Jan, 25 Dec 🌐 madonnadellorto.org

This lovely Gothic church, founded in the mid-14th century, was dedicated to St Christopher, patron saint of travellers, to protect the boatmen who ferried passengers to the islands in the northern lagoon. A 15th-century statue of the saint, restored by the Venice in Peril fund, stands above the main portal. The dedication was changed and the church reconstructed in the early 15th century, after the discovery, in a nearby vegetable garden (*orto*), of a statue of the Virgin Mary said to have miraculous powers.

The interior is large and uncluttered. On the right is a magnificent painting by Cima da Conegliano, *St John the Baptist and Other Saints* (c.1493). The vacant space in the chapel opposite belongs to Giovanni Bellini's *Madonna with Child* (c.1478), stolen in 1993 for the third time.

The church's greatest remaining treasures are the works of art by Tintoretto, including the *Presentation of the Virgin in the Temple*, in the right nave. The most dramatic of his works are the towering masterpieces that decorate the chancel (1562–4). On the right wall is the *Last Judgment*, whose turbulent content caused John Ruskin's wife, Effie, to flee the church in horror. In *The Adoration of the Golden Calf* on the left wall, the figure carrying the calf, fourth from the left, is believed to be a portrait of the artist, who was a parishioner of the church.

6

Ca' d'Oro

📍 D2 🏛 Calle Ca' d'Oro 🚤 Ca' d'Oro ⏰ 8:15am–2pm Mon, 8:15–7:15pm Tue–Sat & 9am–7pm Sun 🚫 1 Jan, 1 May, 25 Dec 🌐 cadoro.org

In 1420 Marino Contarini, a wealthy patrician, commissioned the building of what he hoped would be the city's most magnificent palace. The building's intricate carving was entrusted to a team of Venetian and Lombard craftsmen, while the façade was adorned with the most expensive decorative finishes, including gold leaf, vermilion and ultramarine. Over the years the palace was extensively remodelled, and by the 18th century it was in

> **On the right wall is the *Last Judgment*, whose turbulent content caused John Ruskin's wife, Effie, to flee the church in horror.**

↑ Glorious sunset over the Grand Canal and the Ca' d'Oro

DRINK

Bar Puppa

Best for local *cicchetti* (tapas) and glasses of house red and white.

📍E2 🚪Calle della Spezier 4800
📞041 476 14 54

Tappa Obbligatoria

Stop by for an Aperol spritz, a slice of pizza and some excellent people-watching.

📍D2 🚪Fondamenta Trapolin 3947
📞041 241 37 42

Osteria ai Osti

Local wines, prosecco by the glass and fish dishes are the items to order here.

📍E2 🚪Corte dei Pali già Testori, Calle S Felice 3849
📞041 520 79 93 🕐Sun

a state of semi-dereliction. In 1846 it was bought by the Russian Prince Troubetzkoy for the famous ballerina Marie Taglioni. Under her direction the palace suffered barbaric restoration, losing, among other things, its staircase and much of its original stonework. It was finally rescued by Baron Giorgio Franchetti, a wealthy patron of the arts, who bequeathed both the building and his private art collection to the state in 1915.

Pride of place on the first of the gallery's two floors goes to Andrea Mantegna's *St Sebastian* (1506), the artist's last work. Elsewhere, the floor's main exhibits are ranged around the *portego* (entrance hall). This is largely dominated by the vivid 15th-century *Double Portrait* (c.1493) by the sculptor Tullio

Lombardo and Sansovino's lunette of the *Madonna and Child* (c.1530). Rooms leading off the *portego* to the right contain numerous bronzes and medallions, with some examples by Pisanello and Gentile Bellini. Paintings here also include the famous *Madonna of the Beautiful Eyes*, attributed to Giovanni Bellini, a *Madonna and Child*, attributed to Alvise Vivarini (both late 15th century), and Carpaccio's *Annunciation* (c.1504). A room to the left of the *portego* contains non-Venetian paintings, notably a *Flagellation* by Luca Signorelli (c.1480). A lovely staircase leads to the second floor, which opens with a room hung with tapestries. It has bronzes by Alessandro Vittoria and paintings by Titian and Van Dyck. The *portego* displays frescoes (c.1532) by Pordenone from the cloister of Santo Stefano, while an anteroom contains damaged frescoes by Titian taken from the Fondaco dei Tedeschi.

7

San Giovanni Grisostomo

📍E3 🚪Campo San Giovanni Grisostomo
📞041 523 52 93 🚉Rialto
🕐8:15am–12:15pm & 3–7pm daily 🕐During Mass

This terracotta-coloured church is located near to the Rialto. Built between 1479 and 1504, it is a lovely Renaissance design, the last work of Mauro Coducci.

Inside, the light meter illuminates Giovanni Bellini's *St Jerome with Saints Christopher and Augustine* (1513) above the first altar on the right. This was most probably Bellini's last painting, executed when he was in his eighties.

Over the high altar hangs Sebastiano del Piombo's *St John Chrysostom and Six Saints* (1509–11).

↑ Tintoretto's *Presentation of the Virgin in the Temple*, Madonna dell'Orto

8

Santa Maria dei Miracoli

📍E3 🚪Campo dei Miracoli
🚉Rialto or Fondamenta Nuove 🕐10:30am–4:20pm Mon-Sat 🕐1 Jan, 25 Dec
🌐chorusvenezia.org

This exquisite masterpiece of the early Renaissance is the church where many Venetians like to get married.

Santa Maria dei Miracoli was built in 1481–9 by the architect Pietro Lombardo to enshrine *The Virgin and Child* (1408), a painting believed to have miraculous powers. The picture, by Niccolò di Pietro, still hangs above the altar.

The interior, embellished by pink, white and grey marble, is crowned by a barrel-vaulted ceiling (1528) with portraits of saints and prophets. The balustrade, between the nave and the chancel, is decorated by Tullio Lombardo's carved figures of Archangel Gabriel, St Francis, the Virgin and St Clare.

The screen around the high altar and the medallions of the Evangelists in the cupola spandrels are also Lombardo's work. Above the main door, the choir gallery was used by the nuns from the neighbouring convent, who entered the church through an overhead gallery.

9

San Polo

D3 **Campo San Polo**
San Silvestro
**10:30am–4:30pm
Mon–Sat** **1 Jan, 25 Dec**
chorusvenezia.org

This church is worth visiting for the Gothic portal and the Romanesque lions at the foot of the 14th-century campanile.

Inside, follow the signs for the *Via Crucis del Tiepolo* – 14 pictures of the Stations of the Cross (1749) by the painter Giandomenico Tiepolo; many of these works include vivid portraits of 18th-century Venetian life. The church also has paintings by Veronese and Palma il Giovane (the Younger), and a dramatic *Last Supper* by Tintoretto.

10

Scuola Grande di San Rocco

E3 **Campo San Rocco**
San Tomà **9:30am–
5:30pm daily** **1 Jan, 25 Dec**
scuolagrandesanrocco.it

Founded in honour of San Rocco (St Roch), a saint who

dedicated his life to helping the sick, the Scuola started out as a charitable confraternity. Construction began in 1515 under Bartolomeo Bon and was continued by Scarpagnino until his death in 1549. The work was financed by donations from Venetians keen to invoke San Rocco's protection and the Scuola quickly became one of the wealthiest in Venice. In 1564 its members decided to commission Tintoretto to decorate its walls and ceilings.

The ground-floor cycle was executed in 1582–7, when Tintoretto was in his sixties, and consists of eight large paintings illustrating, among others, the life of Mary. The series starts with the *Annunciation* and ends with the *Assumption*.

The tranquil scenes of *The Flight into Egypt*, *St Mary Magdalene* and *St Mary of Egypt* are remarkable for their serenity. This is portrayed most lucidly by the repentant hermit's isolated spiritual contemplation in *St Mary of Egypt*. In all three paintings, the landscapes are rendered with noticeably rapid strokes, and are an important part of the final composition.

Scarpagnino's great staircase (1544–6), its upper flight decorated with two vast paintings commemorating the plague of 1630, leads to the Upper Hall. Here, biblical subjects decorate the ceiling and walls, painted by Tintoretto from 1575 to 1581.

The ceiling paintings portray scenes from the Old Testament. The three large and dynamic square paintings in the centre show episodes from the Book of Exodus: *Moses Strikes Water from the Rock*; *The Miracle of the Bronze Serpent*; and *The Fall of Manna in the Desert*. These all allude to the charitable aims of the Scuola in alleviating thirst, sickness and hunger. All three paintings are crowded compositions displaying much violent movement.

The vast wall paintings in the hall feature episodes from the New Testament, linking with the ceiling paintings. Two of the most striking are *The Temptation of Christ*, which shows a handsome young Satan offering Christ two loaves of bread, and *The Adoration of the Shepherds*. Like *The Temptation of Christ*, *The Adoration* is composed in two halves, with a female

figure, shepherds and an ox below, and the Holy Family and onlookers above.

The splendid carvings below the paintings were added in the 17th century by sculptor Francesco Pianta. The figures are allegorical and include (near the altar) a caricature of Tintoretto with his palette and brushes, representing Painting. The easel painting *Christ Carrying the Cross* was once attributed to Giorgione, though many believe it to be by Titian.

Near the entrance to the Sala dell'Albergo is the *Annunciation* by Titian. The Sala dell'Albergo itself holds the most breathtaking of Tintoretto's works – the *Crucifixion* (1565). Henry James remarked of this painting: "No single picture contains more of human life; there is everything in it, including the most exquisite beauty." Tintoretto began the cycle of paintings in this room in 1564, when he won the commission with the ceiling painting *San Rocco in Glory*. On the wall opposite the *Crucifixion* are paintings of episodes from the Passion: *Christ before Pilate; The Crowning with Thorns;* and *The Ascent to Calvary*.

← The monumental Upper Hall in the Scuola Grande di San Rocco

Closely associated with the celebrated Scuola is the church of the same name, **San Rocco**. Designed by the sculptor and architect Bartolomeo Bon in 1489 and largely rebuilt in 1725, the exterior suffers from a mixture of styles. Inside, the chancel is decorated with a series of paintings by Tintoretto depicting scenes from the life of San Rocco.

San Rocco

⌂ Campo San Rocco 🖀 041 523 48 64 🚊 San Tomà ⏲ 9:30am–5:30pm daily (to 12:30pm 1 Jan, Easter Sun & 25 Dec)

Ca' Rezzonico

📍 D4 ⌂ Fondamenta Rezzonico 3136 🚊 Ca' Rezzonico ⏲ 10am–5pm Wed–Mon (Apr–Dec: to 6pm); last adm: 1 hour before closing 🚫 1 Jan, 25 Dec 🌐 visitmuve.it

This palazzo houses the museum of 18th-century Venice, its rooms furnished with frescoes, paintings and period pieces taken from other palaces or museums. Building began with Longhena (architect of Santa Maria della Salute) in 1667, but the funds of the Bon family, who commissioned it, ran dry before the second floor was started. In 1712 the unfinished palace was bought by the Rezzonico family of Genoa, who spent a large portion of their fortune on its completion.

The Rezzonico family sold it on, in 1888, to the famous poet Robert Browning and his son, Pen. The outstanding attraction in the palace today is Giorgio Massari's ballroom, which occupies the entire breadth of the building. It is adorned with gilded chandeliers, carved furniture by Andrea Brustolon and a ceiling with *trompe l'oeil* frescoes. Other rooms have frescoes by Giambattista Tiepolo, including his lively *Nuptial Allegory* (1758), and one by his son, Giandomenico, originally in his villa at Zianigo. There are paintings by Longhi, Guardi and – rare in Venice – Canaletto. On the top floor is a reconstructed 18th-century apothecary's shop and the Pinacoteca Martini.

CARNEVALE

The Venetian gift for intrigue comes into its own during Carnevale, a vibrant, playful festival preceding the abstinence of Lent. Masks and costumes play a key role in this anonymous world; social divisions are dissolved, participants delight in playing practical jokes, and anything goes. The tradition of Carnevale in Venice began in the 11th century and reached its peak in popularity and outrageousness in the 18th century.

12

San Nicolò dei Mendicoli

 B4 ⌂ Campo San Nicolò ☎ 041 275 03 82 🚊 San Basilio ◷ 10am–noon & 3–5:30pm Mon–Sat, 9am–noon Sun & public hols

Contrasting with the remote and run-down area which surrounds it, this church still remains one of the most charming in Venice. Founded in the 7th century, it has been rebuilt extensively over the years. The little porch on the north flank was built in the 15th century and once sheltered the beggars, or *mendicanti*, who gave the church its name.

Thanks to the Venice in Peril fund, in the 1970s the church underwent one of the most comprehensive restoration programmes since the floods of 1966. Flooding had become such a problem that the priest often ferried himself around the church in a small wicker boat. The floor, which was 30 cm (1 ft) below the level of the canals, was rebuilt and raised slightly to prevent more flood damage. The roofs and lower walls were reconstructed, and the paintings and statues restored.

The interior is delightfully embellished, particularly the nave with its 16th-century gilded wooden statues.

These include the figure of San Nicolò himself. On the upper walls is a series of paintings of the life of Christ (c.1553) by Alvise dal Friso and other pupils of Veronese.

Outside, a small column supports a stone lion, in a humbler echo of the Column of San Marco in the Piazzetta.

---

13 ⊛

San Sebastiano

 C4 ⌂ Campo San Sebastiano 🚊 San Basilio ◷ 10:30am–4:20pm Mon–Sat ◷ 1 Jan, 15 Aug, 25 Dec 🌐 chorusvenezia.org

This 16th-century church features one of the most colourful and homogeneous interiors in the whole of Venice. Much of its splendour is down to Veronese who, from 1555 to 1560 and again in the 1570s, was commissioned to decorate the sacristy ceiling, the nave ceiling, the frieze, the east end of the choir, the high altar, the doors of the organ panels and the chancel.

The paintings feature radiant colours and rich costumes. Those on the sacristy ceiling depict the *Coronation of the Virgin* and the *Four Evangelists*.

Of the other paintings, the finest are the three that tell the story of Esther, Queen

↑ Veronese ceiling painting in the church of San Sebastiano

of Xerxes I of Persia, famous for securing the deliverance of the Jewish people.

Veronese is buried here. His tomb is in front of the paved chapel to the left of the chancel.

---

14 ⊛

Santa Maria della Salute

 D4-E4 ⌂ Campo della Salute 🚊 Salute ◷ 9:30am–noon & 3–5:30pm daily (main church); 10am–noon & 3–5pm Mon–Sat (sacristy) ◷ Mornings on religious holidays 🌐 basilicasalute venezia.it

This great Baroque church standing at the entrance of the Grand Canal is one of the most imposing Venetian landmarks. Henry James likened it to "some great lady on the threshold of her salon".

Santa Maria della Salute was built in thanksgiving for the city's deliverance from the plague epidemic of 1630; hence the name *Salute*, which means "health and salvation".

Every 21 November, in celebration of the occasion, worshippers light candles and approach across a temporary bridge, resting on boats, which spans the mouth of the Grand Canal.

A BIT OF SPRITZ

The spritz is ubiquitous all over Italy, and no more so than in the Veneto, where the drink originated in the 1800s. The two most popular versions are made with either Aperol or Campari, depending on preference. The spirit is mixed with prosecco or sparkling water and white wine, and usually served with an olive or orange slice.

Baldassare Longhena started the church in 1630 at the age of 32, and worked on it for the rest of his life. It was completed in 1687, five years after his death.

The interior consists of a large octagonal space below the cupola and six chapels radiating from the ambulatory. The large domed chancel and grandiose high altar dominate the view from the main door.

The altar's sculptural group by Giusto Le Corte represents the Virgin and Child giving protection to Venice from the plague. The best of the paintings are in the sacristy to the left of the altar: Titian's early altarpiece *St Mark Enthroned with Saints Cosmas, Damian, Roch and Sebastian* (1511–12) and his dramatic ceiling paintings *Cain and Abel*, *The Sacrifice of Abraham and Isaac* and *David and Goliath* (1540–9). *The Wedding at Cana* (1551) on the wall opposite the entrance is by Jacopo Tintoretto.

15

Punta della Dogana

◘ E4 **▲** Campo della Salute **🚏** Salute **◷** 10am–7pm Wed-Mon (ticket counter closes at 6pm) **🗓** 25 Dec **ⓦ** palazzograssi.it

Formerly a customs house, where cargo ships were inspected before they entered Venice, the magnificent 17th-century Punta della Dogana was restored by the Japanese architect Tadao Ando and opened in 2009 as a contemporary art gallery. Together with the Palazzo Grassi, it houses the French billionaire François Pinault's large collection of contemporary art. It contains important works, including pieces by Jeff Koons, Takashi Murakami and British artists Rachel Whiteread and the Chapman Brothers. The building also has fantastic views towards St Mark's, San Giorgio and the two main canals of Venice.

SHOP

Here are the best places to buy Carnevale masks.

Ca' Macana

A wide range of masks, as well as in-store mask-making workshops.

◘ C4 **▲** Calle de le Botteghe 3172 **ⓦ** camacana.com

Papier Mache Venezia

This is where locals buy their Carnevale masks.

◘ E3 **▲** Castello 5174/B/517 **ⓦ** papier mache.it

Maschere di Guerrino Lovato

This boutique has supplied masks to films such as *Eyes Wide Shut*.

◘ C4 **▲** Canal Dorsoduro 3063 **ⓦ** maskedart.com

↑ Santa Maria della Salute, at the entrance to the Grand Canal

16

Accademia

D4 **Campo della Carità 1050** **Accademia** **8:15am-7:15pm Tue-Sun, 8:15-2pm Mon** **galllerie accademia.org**

Housing the largest collection of Venetian art in existence, the Accademia occupies three former religious buildings. The basis of the collection was the Accademia di Belle Arti, founded in 1750 by painter Giovanni Battisa Piazetta. In 1807 Napoleon moved the collection to its current premises, enriching it with artworks removed from churches and monasteries.

Spanning five centuries, the paintings and altarpieces in the museum provide a complete spectrum of the Venetian school, from the Byzantine period through the Renaissance to the Baroque and the Rococo. Perhaps the highlight of the collection is Giorgione's famous *Tempest* (c.1507). In this enigmatic landscape, Giorgione was probably indulging in his imagination rather than portraying a specific subject.

The International Gothic collection shows the influence of Byzantine art on the early Venetian painters. Paolo Veneziano, the true founder of the Venetian school, displays a blend of both Western and Eastern influences in his sumptuous *Coronation of the Virgin* (1325). The linear rhythms are unmistakably Gothic, yet the glowing gold background and overall effect are distinctly Byzantine.

←

Bellini's *Madonna and Child,* a star exhibit at the Accademia

Highlights of the Renaissance collection include Giovanni Bellini's *Madonna and Child between St John the Baptist and a Saint* (c.1504), Andrea Mantegna's *St George* (c.1460), Paolo Veronese's monumental *Feast in the House of the Levi* (1573) and Titian's haunting final painting, the *Pietà* (1575–6). Other must-see works include a view of Venice by Canaletto (dated 1763) and Vittore Carpaccio's ensemble of nine large wall paintings chronicling the tragic story of St Ursula (1495–1500).

17

Peggy Guggenheim Collection

D4 **Palazzo Venier dei Leoni** **Accademia** **10am-6pm Wed-Mon** **25 Dec** **guggenheim-venice.it**

In 1949 the 18th-century Palazzo Venier dei Leoni was bought as a home by the American millionairess Peggy Guggenheim (1898–1979), a collector, dealer and patron of the arts who befriended, and

> **Light-filled rooms and the large modern canvases provide a striking contrast to the Renaissance paintings in most Venetian churches and museums.**

then furthered the careers of, many innovative abstract and Surrealist artists. One was Max Ernst, who became her second husband.

The Guggenheim is the best place in the city to see 20th-century art. Light-filled rooms and the large modern canvases provide a striking contrast to the Renaissance paintings in most Venetian churches and museums. The collection consists of 200 fine paintings and sculptures, each representing the 20th century's most influential modern art movements.

The dining room has notable Cubist works of art, including *The Poet* by Pablo Picasso, and an entire room is devoted to Jackson Pollock, who was "discovered" by Guggenheim.

Other artists represented are Braque, Chagall, de Chirico, Dalí, Duchamp, Léger, Kandinsky, Klee, Mondrian, Miró, Malevich, Rothko, Bacon and Magritte, whose Surreal *Empire of Light* (1953–4) shows a night scene of a darkened house in a wooded setting with a bright day sky above. The sculpture collection, which includes Constantin Brancusi's elegant *Maiastra* (1912), is laid out in the house and the picturesque paved garden.

Marino Marini's *Angelo della Città* (Angel of the Citadel, 1948), on the terrace overlooking the Grand Canal, is perhaps the most provocative piece. This shows a prominently displayed man sitting on a horse, erect in all respects.

There are presentations about Peggy Guggenheim and her collection given in several languages every day, and the museum holds special art workshops for children each Sunday.

Santo Stefano

📍 D4 **🏛 Campo Santo Stefano** **🚤 Accademia or Sant'Angelo** **🕐 10:30am–4:30pm Mon-Sat** **🚫 1 Jan, Easter Sun, 15 Aug, 25 Dec** **🌐 chorusvenezia.org**

Deconsecrated six times on account of the blood spilled within its walls, Santo Stefano – one of Venice's most beautiful churches – is now remarkably serene. Built in the 1300s, and altered in the 15th century, it has a carved portal by Bartolomeo Bon, and a campanile with a typical Venetian tilt. The interior has a splendid ship's keel ceiling with carved tie-beams, and the sacristy is crammed with valuable paintings.

←

Gallery filled with priceless works of art at the Accademia

EAT

Osteria Alla Ciurma
Locals come to this cosy osteria for the fried *cicchetti* (tapas) and Venetian wines.

📍 D3 **🏛 Calle Galiazza 406/A** **📞 340 686 3561** **🚫 Sun**

Alla Palanca
This unassuming café does a great tagliatelle with *funghi porcini* (dried mushrooms).

📍 D5 **🏛 Giudecca 448** **📞 041 528 7719** **🚫 D & Sun**

Osteria Santa Marina
A splurge-worthy local restaurant offering an excellent seafood-based tasting menu.

📍 E3 **🏛 Campo Santa Marina 5911** **🚫 Sun** **🌐 osteria disantamarina.com**

La Zucca
Head to this family-run osteria for vegetarian takes on Italian classics, like courgette and almond lasagne.

📍 D2 **🏛 Santa Croce 1762** **🚫 Sun** **🌐 lazucca.it**

Trattoria dalla Marisa
Don't expect a menu here; rather, it's plates of whatever the chef has made that day.

📍 C2 **🏛 Cannaregio 652** **📞 041 720 211**

↑ The Campanile, dominating the whole of the lagoon

INSIDER TIP
Feeding Fines

Pigeons were once the unofficial mascots of Venice, with around 40,000 reportedly living in and around Piazza San Marco. In 2008 Venice's then-mayor brought in a law that banned pigeon feeding. Any tourists caught feeding the birds today could face a fine of up to €700.

19

Torre dell'Orologio

Q E3 **Q** Piazza San Marco **🚊** San Marco **🕓** 1 Jan, 25 Dec **w** visitmuve.it

This richly decorated clock tower on the north side of the piazza was built in the late 15th century, and Mauro Coducci is thought to have worked on the design. With its display of the phases of the moon and zodiac signs, the clock face was designed with seafarers in mind. According to legend, once the clock was completed, the two inventors had their eyes gouged out to prevent them from ever creating a replica.

On the upper level, the winged lion of St Mark stands against a star-spangled blue backdrop. At the very top, two huge bronze figures, known as the *Mori*, or Moors, strike the bell on the hour.

Guided tours to visit the clock tower must be booked in advance; they depart from the Museo Correr ticket office.

20

Campanile

Q E3 **Q** Piazza San Marco **🚊** San Marco **🕓** Daily; Apr: 9am-4:45pm; May-Aug: 8:30am-8:45pm; Sep: 8:30am-7:45pm; Oct-Mar: 9:30am-4:45pm **w** basilicasanmarco.it

From the top of San Marco's campanile, high above the piazza, visitors can enjoy views of the city, the lagoon and, visibility permitting, the peaks of the Alps. It was from here that Galileo demonstrated his telescope to Doge Leonardo Donà in 1609. To do so he would have climbed the internal ramp, but access today is via a lift.

The first tower, completed in 1173, was built as a lighthouse to assist navigators in the lagoon. It took on a less benevolent role in the Middle Ages, when offenders were imprisoned – and in some cases left to die – in a cage hung near its summit. In July 1902, with little warning, the tower collapsed. The only casualties were the Loggetta at the foot of the tower and the custodian's cat. Donations flooded in, and in 1903 the foundation stone was laid for a new campanile *"dov'era e com'era"* ("where it was and as it was"). The new tower opened on 25 April (the Feast of St Mark), 1912.

21

Museo Correr

Q E3-E4 **Q** Procuratie Nuove; entrance in Ala Napoleonica **🚊** San Marco **🕓** 10am-5pm daily (Apr-Oct: to 7pm) **🕓** 1 Jan, 25 Dec **w** visitmuve.it

Teodoro Correr bequeathed his extensive collection of works of art to Venice in 1830, thus forming the core of the city's fine civic museum.

Its first rooms form a suitably Neo-Classical backdrop for early statues by Antonio Canova (1757–1822). The rest of the floor covers the history of the Venetian

Republic, with maps, coins, armour and a host of doge-related exhibits.

The second floor contains a picture collection second only to that of the Accademia. The paintings, hung chronologically, trace the evolution of Venetian painting, and show the influence of Ferrarese, Paduan and Flemish artists.

The gallery's most famous works are by Carpaccio: *Portrait of a Young Man in a Red Hat* (c.1490) and *Two Venetian Ladies* (c.1507). The latter is traditionally, but probably incorrectly, known as *The Courtesans* because of the ladies' provocative low-cut dresses. The Museo del Risorgimento on the same floor looks at the history of Venice until unification with Italy in 1866.

22
San Zaccaria

☉F3 ⌂Campo San Zaccaria ☏041 522 12 57 ☷San Zaccaria ◷10am–noon & 4–6pm Mon–Sat; 4–6pm Sun & public hols

Set in a quiet square just a stone's throw from the busy ferry terminals, the church of San Zaccaria is a successful blend of Flamboyant Gothic and Classical Renaissance styles. Founded in the 9th century, it was rebuilt between 1444 and 1515. Antonio Gambello began the façade in Gothic style and, when he died in 1481, Mauro Coducci added all the Classical detail.

Every Easter the doge came to San Zaccaria – a custom that started as an expression of gratitude to the nuns, who had relinquished part of their garden so that Piazza San Marco could be enlarged.

The interior's artistic highlight is Giovanni Bellini's serene and

sumptuously coloured *Madonna and Child with Four Saints* (1505) in the north aisle. A door off the right nave leads to the Chapel of St Athanasius, which in turn leads to the Chapel of San Tarasio. The chapel contains vault frescoes (1442) by Andrea del Castagno, and polyptychs (1443–4) by Antonio Vivarini and Giovanni d'Alemagna.

23
Santa Maria Formosa

☉E3 ⌂Campo Santa Maria Formosa ☷Rialto ◷10:30am–4:20pm Mon–Sat ☒1 Jan, Easter Sun, 15 Aug, 25 Dec ⓦchorus venezia.org

Designed by Mauro Coducci in 1492, this church is most unusual in having two main façades – one overlooks the *campo*, the other the canal. The bell tower or campanile, added in 1688, is noted for the grotesque face at its base.

Two paintings stand out in the interior: a triptych (1473) by Bartolomeo Vivarini and Palma il Vecchio's *St Barbara* (c.1510).

Torre dell' Orologio, with its winged lion sculpture (inset) ↓

Imposing towers and wooden bridge at the Arsenale ↑

Santi Giovanni e Paolo

📍 E3 🏛 Campo Santi Giovanni e Paolo 🚊 Fondamente Nuove or Ospedale Civile 🕐 9am–6pm daily 🌐 basilicasanti giovanniepaolo.it

Known colloquially as San Zanipolo, Santi Giovanni e Paolo vies with the Frari as the city's greatest Gothic church. Located in the Castello area, it is slightly off the tourist track, meaning it is often very quiet. Built by the Dominicans in the 14th century, the church is

↑ One of the stone lions guarding the entrance to Venice's Arsenale

striking for its vast scale and architectural austerity. Known as the Pantheon of Venice, it houses monuments to no fewer than 25 doges. Among these are several fine works of art, executed by the Lombardi family and other leading sculptors.

On arrival, visitors enter through a doorway decorated with Byzantine reliefs and carvings by celebrated Italian sculptor Bartolomeo Bon. The doorway is thought to be one of Venice's earliest Renaissance architectural works. The commanding bronze statue at the opposite end of the church is a monument to Doge Sebastiano Venier, who was Commander of the Fleet at Lepanto. A few steps away lies the tomb of Andrea Vendramin. Created by Pietro Lombardo in 1476–8, it takes the form of a Roman triumphal arch.

Highlights of the church include the Baroque high altar and the 16th-century frescoes attributed to Palma il Giovane. The tomb of Nicolò Marcello, a Renaissance tribute to Doge

HIDDEN GEM
Venice FC

For a local experience, book tickets to a Venice FC match, held from January to May at Stadio Pierluigi Penzo. Tickets are available from the club's website (www. veneziafc.club).

Nicolò Marcello by Pietro Lombardo, is another must-see masterpiece. Giovanni Bellini created the church's polyptych (1465), which shows St Vincent Ferrer, a Spanish cleric, flanked by St Sebastian and St Christopher. Nearby lies the tomb of Pietro Mocenigo, which commemorates the doge's military pursuits when he was Grand Captain of the Venetian forces.

Further up on the right of the church is the grand Cappella di San Domenico, containing St Catherine of Siena's foot in a precious reliquary. Giovanni Battista Piazzetta frescoed the ceiling of this chapel. His Glory of St Dominic displays a mastery of colour, perspective and foreshortening that is said to have had a profound influence on the young Tiepolo.

Statue of Colleoni

◊ E3 ◊ Campo Santi Giovanni e Paolo ◊ Ospedale Civile

Bartolomeo Colleoni, the famous commander of mercenaries, left his fortune to the Republic on condition that his statue was placed in front of San Marco. A prominent statue in the piazza would have broken with precedent, so the Senate cunningly had Colleoni raised before the Scuola di San Marco instead of the basilica. A touchstone of early Renaissance sculpture, the equestrian statue of the proud warrior (1481–8) is by the Florentine Andrea Verrocchio, but was cast in bronze after his death by Alessandro Leopardi. The statue has a strong sense of power and movement.

Scuola di San Giorgio degli Schiavoni

◊ F3 ◊ Calle Furlani, Castello 3959a ◊ 041 522 88 28 ◊ San Zaccaria ◊ 1:30–5:30pm Mon, 9:30am–5:30pm Tue–Sat, 9:30am–1:30pm Sun ◊ 1 Jan, 1 May, 25 Dec and other religious hols

This small gem houses some of Vittore Carpaccio's finest paintings, commissioned by the Schiavoni (or Dalmatian Slav) community in Venice.

The Scuola was established in 1451 and rebuilt in 1551. It has changed very little since.

→

Carpaccio's *Calling of St Matthew*, Scuola di San Giorgio degli Schiavoni

---

> **By the 16th century it had become the greatest naval shipyard in the world, capable of constructing a whole galley in 24 hours, using an assembly-line system.**

The exquisite frieze, executed between 1502 and 1508, shows scenes from the lives of patron saints St George, St Tryphone and St Jerome. Each episode of the narrative cycle is remarkable for its vivid colouring, minute detail and historic record of Venetian life. Outstanding among them are *St George Slaying the Dragon* and *St Jerome Leading the Tamed Lion to the Monastery*.

Arsenale

◊ F3 ◊ Arsenale

The Arsenale was founded in the 12th century. By the 16th century it had become the greatest naval shipyard in the world, capable of constructing a whole galley in 24 hours, using an assembly-line system. Surrounded by crenellated walls, it was like a city within a city. Today the site is used as an exhibition space by the Biennale. Its impressive 15th-century gateway, twin towers and guardian lions can be viewed from the *campo* or bridge outside. The gateway was built by Antonio Gambello and is often cited as Venice's first Renaissance construction.

Around the corner, in Campo San Biago, the **Museo Storico Navale** charts Venetian naval history from the heyday of the Arsenale to the present. Exhibits include friezes from famous galleys of the past and a replica of the *Bucintoro*, the doge's ceremonial barge.

Museo Storico Navale
◊ ◊ Campo San Biagio ◊ 8:45am–4:30pm daily ◊ public hols ◊ visitmuve.it

28

Torcello

🚩 1F 🚢 12 from Fondamenta Nuove, then 9 from Burano

Established between the 5th and 6th centuries, Torcello was once a thriving colony with palaces, churches and a population that is said to have reached 20,000. But with the rise of Venice, the island went into decline. Today, the population is just 60, and all that remains of this once-bustling island are the Byzantine cathedral of Santa Maria Assunta, the church of Santa Fosca and the memory of its former glory.

Founded in 639 but radically restructured in 1008, **Santa Maria Assunta** retains its Romanesque form and arcaded 9th-century portico. The cathedral's campanile offers spectacular views. Inside, are breathtaking 12th- and 13th-century Doomsday Mosaics, which depict scenes of devils, angels, wild beasts and fires. The iconostasis is made up of exquisite marble panels showing peacocks drinking from the fountain of eternal life.

Alongside the cathedral is **Santa Fosca**, an elegant church based on a Greek cross design, encircled by a five-sided portico with columns and carved capitals.

The **Museo dell'Estuario**, in adjoining Gothic buildings, houses archaeological finds from the island and priceless treasures from the church.

Santa Maria Assunta

♿ 🅿 **☎** 041 73 01 19
🕐 10:30am–4:30pm daily (Mar–Oct: to 5:30pm)
🚫 1 Jan, 25 Dec

Santa Fosca

🕐 For masses only

Museo dell'Estuario

♿ 🅿 Campo San Biagio
🕐 10:30am–5pm Tue–Sun (Mar–Oct: to 5:30pm) 🚫 Pub hols 🌐 museodi torcello. provincia.venezia.it

Did You Know?

Daphne du Maurier came up with the plot for *Don't Look Now* during a visit to Torcello.

29

Giudecca

🚩 D5 🚢 2, 4.1 or 4.2

In the days of the Republic, the island of Giudecca was a pleasure ground of palaces and gardens. Today it is very much a suburb of the city, its narrow alleys flanked by apartments, its squares overgrown and its palazzi neglected. Many of its old factories have been converted into modern housing. However, the long, wide quayside skirting the city side of the island makes a very pleasant promenade and provides stunning views of Venice across the water. The name Giudecca, once thought to have referred to the Jews, or *giudei*, who lived here in the 13th century, is more likely to

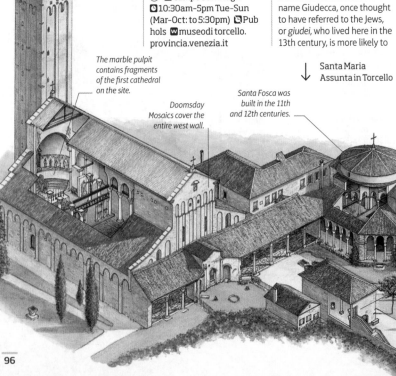

The campanile has great views over the lagoon.

The marble pulpit contains fragments of the first cathedral on the site.

Doomsday Mosaics cover the entire west wall.

Santa Fosca was built in the 11th and 12th centuries.

↓ Santa Maria Assunta in Torcello

↑ Palladio's church of San Giorgio Maggiore, on the island of the same name

have originated from the word *giudicati*, meaning "the judged". This referred to troublesome aristocrats who, as early as the 9th century, were banished to the island.

Hotel Cipriani, among the most luxurious places to stay in Venice, is discreetly located at the tip of the island. At the western end of Giudecca looms the massive Neo-Gothic Molino Stucky, a former flour mill that is now home to Venice's Hilton hotel.

Giudecca's main monument is Palladio's church of **Il Redentore** (The Redeemer). It was built in 1577–92 in thanksgiving for the end of the 1576 plague, which wiped out a third of the city's population. The Classical interior of the church presents a marked contrast to the ornate and elaborate style of most Venetian

The Museo dell'Estuario contains archaeological finds.

churches. The main paintings, by Paolo Veronese and Alvise Vivarini, are in the sacristy to the right of the choir.

Il Redentore

⊘ 🏛 Campo Redentore 🚏 Redentore ⏰ 10am–4:30pm Mon–Sat 🚫 1 Jan, 25 Dec 🌐 chorusvenezia.org

30 ⊘

San Giorgio Maggiore

📍 F4 📞 041 522 78 27 🚏 San Giorgio ⏰ 9:30am–12:30pm & 2:30–5:30pm daily (4:30pm in winter)

Appearing like a stage set across the water from the Piazzetta is the little island of San Giorgio Maggiore. The church and monastery, built between 1566 and 1610, are among architect Andrea Palladio's greatest achievements. The church's temple front and the spacious interior, with its perfect proportions, are typically Palladian.

On the chancel walls of San Giorgio Maggiore are two fine paintings by Tintoretto: *The Last Supper* and *Gathering of the Manna* (both 1594). In the Chapel of the Dead is his last work, *The Deposition* (1592–4), which was finished by his son Domenico.

The top of the campanile affords superb views of the

DRINK

Skyline Rooftop Bar
Skyline has a decidedly Miami vibe – think plush couches, white stools and, come nightfall, moody purple lighting. The views over Venice are the bar's main draw, but the cocktails aren't bad either.

📍 C4 🏛 Molino Stucky, Via Giudecca 810 🌐 hilton.com

Harry's Dolci
Part of the esteemed Cipriani chain, which first opened Harry's Bar in Venice in 1931. Expect white tablecloths, waiters in bow ties, panama hat-clad guests and Bellinis served on the quayside terrace.

📍 C5 🏛 Fondamenta S Biagio 773 🌐 cipriani.com

city and lagoon. You can see the monastery cloisters below, now part of the **Fondazione Cini**, a cultural centre that hosts international exhibitions and events.

Fondazione Cini

⊘ ⊘ ⏰ 10am–4pm Sat & Sun (Apr–Sep: to 5pm) 🌐 cini.it

㉛

Murano

⬤ F1 🚢 **4.1, 4.2 or 12 from Fondamenta Nuove; 3 from Piazzale Roma**

Much like Venice, Murano comprises a cluster of small islands connected by bridges. It has been the centre of the glassmaking industry since 1291, when the furnaces and glass craftsmen were moved here from the city, prompted by the risk of fire to the buildings and the unpleasant effects of the smoke.

Historically, Murano owes its prosperity entirely to glass. In the 15th and 16th centuries it was Europe's principal glass-producing centre. Murano's glass artisans were granted unprecedented privileges, but for those who left the island to find businesses elsewhere there were severe penalties – even death. Although a few of Murano's palazzi bear the hallmarks of its former splendour, and its basilica still survives, most tourists visit for the glass alone. Some are enticed by offers of free trips from factory touts in San Marco; others go by excursion launch or independently on the public *vaporetti*.

Some of the factories are now derelict, but glass is still produced in vast quantities. Among the plethora of kitsch (including imports from the Far East) are some wonderful pieces, and it pays to seek out the top glass factories. Many furnaces, however, close at the weekend.

MURANO GLASS

A main attraction of a trip to Murano is a demonstration of the glass-blowing technique. Visitors can watch while a glass-blower takes a blob of molten paste on the end of an iron rod and, by twisting, turning and blowing, transforms it into a vase, bird, lion, wine goblet or similar work of art. The display is followed by a tour of the showroom and some pressure from the salespeople. There is no obligation to buy, however.

↑ Vibrant colours in a Murano glass sphere

Museo del Vetro

Ⓐ Ⓑ ⬤ **Palazzo Giustinian, Fondamenta Giustinian** 🕙 **10am–6pm daily (Nov–Mar: to 5pm)** 🚫 **1 Jan, 1 May, 25 Dec** 🌐 **museovetro. visitmuve.it**

This glass museum houses a splendid collection of antique pieces. Its prize exhibit is the Barovier wedding cup (1470–80), with enamelwork by Angelo Barovier. There is also a section on modern glass.

↑ Glass baubles in one of Murano's factories

↑ Colourful fishermen's houses lining the waterways of Burano

Basilica dei Santi Maria e Donato

🏠 Fondamenta Giustinian
📞 041 73 90 56 🕐 9am–noon & 3:30–7pm daily (Nov–Mar: to 6pm)
🚫 Sun am

The undisputed architectural highlight of the island of Murano is the Basilica dei Santi Maria e Donato, whose magnificent colonnaded apse is reflected in the waters of the San Donato canal. Despite some heavy-handed restoration undertaken in the 19th century, this 12th-century church still retains much of its original beauty. Visitors should note the Veneto-Byzantine columns and Gothic ship's keel roof. An enchantingly evocative mosaic portrait of the Madonna, portrayed standing alone against a gold background, decorates the apse. The church's floor, or *pavimento*, dating from 1140, is equally beautiful. With its medieval mosaics of geometric figures, exotic birds, mythical creatures and inexplicable symbols, it incorporates fragments of ancient glass from the island's foundries into its imagery.

32 (M)

Burano

📍 F1 🚌 12 from Fondamenta Nuove; 14 from San Zaccaria via Lido and Punta Sabbioni

Its canals fringed with brightly painted houses, Burano is the most colourful of the lagoon islands and can be recognized from a distance by the tilting tower of its church.

The main thoroughfare, Via Baldassare Galuppi, features traditional lace and linen stalls, plus open-air trattorias serving fresh fish.

Museo del Merletto

🏠 Piazza Baldassare Galuppi 187 🕐 10am–6pm Tue–Sun (Nov–Mar: to 5pm)
🚫 1 Jan, 25 Dec 🌐 visit muve.it

The people of Burano are fishermen and lacemakers by tradition. You can still see fishermen scraping their boats or mending nets, but today lacemakers are rare. In the 16th century, the local lace was the most sought after in Europe. After a slump in the 18th century, the industry revived and a lacemaking school was set up here in 1872. You can watch authentic Burano lace being made at the school, now a museum, which displays fine examples of antique lace.

SHOP

Here are the best places to buy Murano glassware.

Davide Penso

Watch a master craftsman create (affordable) necklaces and earrings by shaping portions of coloured glass over a flame.

📍 F1 🏠 Fondamenta Riva Longa 48, Murano
🌐 davidepenso.com

L'ISOLA – The Carlo Moretti Showroom

Founded by brothers Carlo and Giovanni, this glass factory creates exquisite homewares in vibrant patterns and colours.

📍 D3 🏠 Calle de le Botteghe 2970, Venice
🌐 lisola.com

Marina e Susanna Sent

The Sent sisters create glass jewellery and sculptures using traditional techniques passed down through their glassmaking family for generations.

📍 F1 🏠 Fondamenta Serenella 20, Murano
🌐 marinaesusanna sent.com

A SHORT WALK
DORSODURO

Distance 1.3 km (0.8 miles) **Nearest Vaporetto** Ca' Rezzonico
Time 15 minutes

Lively Campo Santo Margherita is at the heart of the *sestiere* of Dorsoduro. The square bustles with activity, particularly in the morning, when the market stalls are open, and in the evening when it is the haunt of students from nearby Ca' Foscari, now part of the University of Venice. The surrounding streets contain several spectacular buildings, most notably Ca' Rezzonico and the Scuola Grande dei Carmini, which has decorations by Tiepolo. Of the area's waterways, the delightful Rio San Barnaba is best appreciated from the Ponte dei Pugni, near the barge selling fruit and vegetables – itself a time-honoured Venetian sight. To discover the quieter part of the *sestiere*, travel east of the Peggy Guggenheim Collection for shaded squares and picturesque residences.

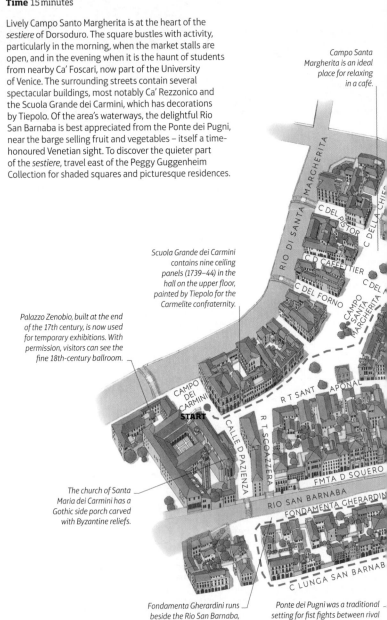

Campo Santa Margherita is an ideal place for relaxing in a café.

Scuola Grande dei Carmini contains nine ceiling panels (1739–44) in the hall on the upper floor, painted by Tiepolo for the Carmelite confraternity.

Palazzo Zenobio, built at the end of the 17th century, is now used for temporary exhibitions. With permission, visitors can see the fine 18th-century ballroom.

The church of Santa Maria dei Carmini has a Gothic side porch carved with Byzantine reliefs.

Fondamenta Gherardini runs beside the Rio San Barnaba, one of the prettiest canals in the sestiere.

Ponte dei Pugni was a traditional setting for fist fights between rival factions. They were finally banned in 1705 for being too violent.

↑ Barges lining the canal
by Campo San Barnaba

Locator Map
For more detail see p60

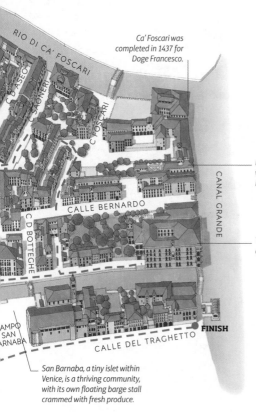

Did You Know?

Dorsoduro is built on solid
subsoil, unlike much of
Venice. This accounts
for its name, meaning
"hard backbone".

*Ca' Foscari was
completed in 1437 for
Doge Francesco.*

*Palazzo Giustinian
was home to Wagner
in 1858.*

*The ballroom of Ca' Rezzonico
covers the width of the palazzo.*

FINISH

*San Barnaba, a tiny islet within
Venice, is a thriving community,
with its own floating barge stall
crammed with fresh produce.*

0 metres	75
0 yards	75

N ↑

THE VENETO AND FRIULI

The Veneto's sheer variety makes it one of Italy's most fascinating regions to explore. The cities of Verona, Padua and Vicenza are all noted for their outstanding architecture, churches and museums. Villas in the rural hinterland are gorgeously frescoed with scenes from ancient mythology. The lagoon has busy fishing ports and beach resorts, while to the north lie the majestic Dolomites, with their Alpine beauty and excellent hiking facilities.

The Romans built frontier posts on this fertile land of silt deposits, and these survive today as the cities of Vicenza, Padua, Verona and Treviso. Strategically placed at the hub of the empire's road network, the cities prospered under Roman rule, but suffered in the wave of Germanic invasions of the 5th century AD.

The region's fortunes revived under the benign rule of the Venetian empire. The medieval cities of the Veneto lay on important trade routes such as the Serenissima, the road connecting the flourishing port cities of Venice and Genoa, and the Brenner Pass, used by commercial travellers crossing the Alps from northern Europe. Wealth from agriculture, commerce and the spoils of war paid for the beautification of these cities through the building of Renaissance palaces and public buildings, many designed by the Veneto's great architect, Andrea Palladio.

Today the Veneto is a thriving wine exporter, textile producer and agricultural centre, and Friuli is a focus for new technology while remaining largely agricultural. Both regions are popular tourist destinations, despite lying a little in the shadow of Venice, and boast an abundant and enchanting variety of attractions.

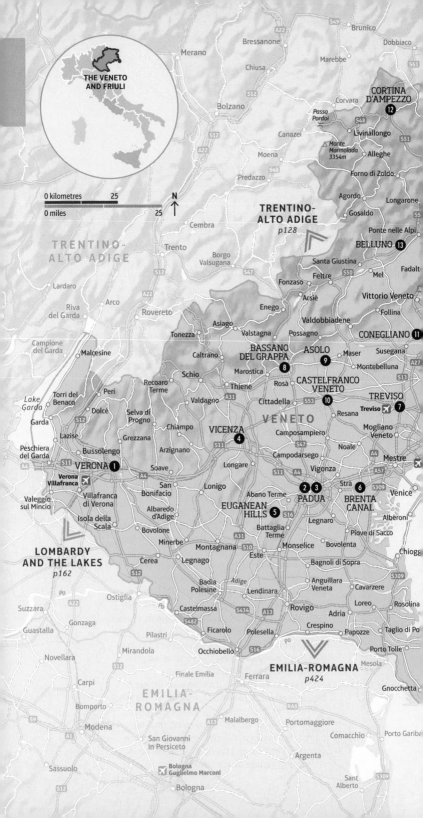

THE VENETO AND FRIULI

Must Sees

1 Verona
2 Padua
3 Cappella degli Scrovegni, Padua
4 Vicenza

Experience More

5 Euganean Hills
6 Brenta Canal
7 Treviso
8 Bassano del Grappa
9 Asolo

10 Castelfranco Veneto
11 Conegliano
12 Cortina d'Ampezzo
13 Belluno
14 Udine
15 Aquileia
16 Gorizia
17 Cividale del Friuli
18 Grado
19 Carso
20 Trieste

←

1 Vineyards in the Veneto's prosecco hills.

2 Harvesting the grapes.

3 Cured meat and cheese.

4 Bottle of Valdobbiadene prosecco and panettone.

2 DAYS
A Prosecco Tour of Veneto

Day 1

Morning Begin the tour in Valdobbiadene with a mid-morning glass of prosecco at Bar Alpino *(Via Mazzolini 14, Valdobbiadene)*, then move on to the restored farmhouse Osteria Senz'Oste *(Str. delle Treziese, Valdobbiadene)* for a simple self-service picnic-style lunch of bread, cured meats and olives in the grounds.

Afternoon A visit to Nino Franco vineyard *(Via Garibaldi 147, 31049 Valdobbiadene)*, one of the country's most esteemed prosecco producers, is a must but make sure you have called in advance to book your place. After a tour and on-site tasting, move on to the ever-chic Bisol vineyard *(Via Follo 33, Santo Stefano di Valdobbiadene)* for further fizz tastings in their cool stone cellar.

Evening Check in to the utterly charming wine property Hotel Villa del Poggio *(Via dei Pascoli, 8/a, San Pietro di Feletto)*, then journey high into the heart of prosecco country to Locanda da Marinelli *(Via Castella, 5, Farra di Soligo)* for beautifully presented plates of hyperlocal cuisine, matched with regional wines.

Day 2

Morning After a lazy hotel breakfast make for the Carpenè Malvolti vineyard *(Via Antonio Carpenè, 1, Conegliano)*, one of the region's oldest family-run prosecco houses, in the centre of Conegliano. Next up, visit Zardetto vineyard, tucked away in the Conegliano hills *(Via Martiri delle Foibe, Scomigo)*, to see how they use modern techniques to create one of the most esteemed proseccos on the market.

Afternoon Book a table at the informal, family-run Trattoria Ristoro Fos de Marai *(Via Santo Stefano, 20, Valdobbiadene, closed Mon D & Tue)*. The speciality here is meat cooked on an open grill and served with accompanying bitter greens at tables overlooking the vines.

Evening Head to Relais Dolce Vita *(Str. Masare, 4, Valdobbiadene)*, a quaint, family-run farmhouse with a swimming pool and extraordinary views over the prosecco hills. Owners Monica and Renato are very kind and generous, and will organize tours or day trips for you, book restaurants, or simply tell you about the region over a glass of wine.

↑ View over the River Adige towards the Duomo's bell tower

1

VERONA

🅰 C2 ✈ Villafranca 14 km (9 miles) SW 🚉🚌 Piazzale 25 Aprile 🅸 Via degli Alpini 9; www.turismoverona.eu

Verona is a vibrant trading centre, the largest city in the Veneto region (followed by Venice) and one of the most prosperous in northern Italy. Its ancient centre boasts many magnificent Roman ruins and fine palazzi built of *rosso di Verona*, the local pink-tinged limestone.

San Zeno Maggiore

🅰 Piazza San Zeno ⏰ Mar-Oct: 8:30am-6pm Mon-Sat, 12:30-6pm Sun; Nov-Feb: 10am-1pm 1:30-5pm Mon-Sat, 12:30-5pm Sun 🚫 For mass 🖥 chieseverona.it

San Zeno, built in 1120–38 to house the shrine of Verona's patron saint, is the most ornate Romanesque church in northern Italy. The façade is adorned with an impressive rose window, marble reliefs and a porch canopy. The fascinating 11th- and 12th-century bronze door panels are also particular highlights. A squat tower just to the north of San Zeno is said to cover the tomb of King Pepin of Italy (777–810).

Castelvecchio

🅰 Corso Castelvecchio 2 📞 045 80 62 611 ⏰ Dec-Oct: 1:30-7:30pm Mon, 8:30am-7:30pm Tue-Sun; last adm: 45 mins before closing 🚫 1 Jan, 25 & 26 Dec 🖥 museodicastelvecchio. comune.verona.it

This impressive castle, built by Cangrande II between 1355 and 1375, houses one of the finest art galleries in the area outside Venice. The section on medieval and Renaissance art illustrates the influence of northern art on local painters. A walkway offers views of the Ponte Scaligero, a medieval bridge that leads to the Arsenal, fronted by gardens.

3

Arena

🅰 Piazza Brà ⏰ 8:30am-7:30pm Tue-Sun (Jun-Sep: daily) 🚫 1 Jan, 25 Dec; Jun-Aug: from mid-afternoon on performance days; Oct-May: Mon 🖥 arena.it

Completed in AD 30, this is the world's third-largest Roman amphitheatre, after Rome's Colosseum and the amphitheatre at Santa Maria Capua Vetere, near Naples. It could hold almost the entire population of Roman Verona, and visitors would come from across the Veneto to watch gladiatorial combats. Since then, the arena has seen executions, fairs, bullfights and opera productions.

4

San Lorenzo

🅰 Corso Cavour 28 📞 045 805 00 00 ⏰ Daily 🚫 During mass

San Lorenzo is one of Verona's lesser-known churches, but is one of the city's most beautiful. Built in 1117 on the remains of a Paleo-Christian basilica, the Romanesque exterior, with alternate strips of stone and

Timeline

1301
Dante is welcomed to the Scaligeri court, and dedicates the final part of his epic *Divine Comedy* to the ruler Cangrande I.

1866
▽ The Veneto is reunited with Italy.

1263
△ The Scaligeri family begins their 124-year rule of Verona. They use ruthless tactics to rise to power but once established, the family brings peace to the city.

1387
Verona falls to the Visconti of Milan, and then a succession of outsiders - Venice, France, and Austria - rule the city.

1597
△ Shakespeare sets *Romeo and Juliet* in Verona.

---

bricks, is typical of Veronese churches. The bell tower dates from the 15th century and inside there are 13th-century frescoes. The church has two unusual cylindrical towers.

---

⑤ 🗺️

Duomo

🏠 Piazza Duomo ⏰ Daily (pm only Sun) 🌐 chiese verona.it

Verona's cathedral was begun in 1139 and is fronted by a magnificent Romanesque portal carved by Nicolò, one of the two master masons responsible for the façade of San Zeno Maggiore. Here he sculpted the figures of Oliver and Roland, two of Charlemagne's knights. The highlight of the interior is Titian's lovely *Assumption* (1535–40). Outside is a Romanesque cloister in which the excavated ruins of earlier churches are visible. The 8th-century baptistry San Giovanni in Fonte (St John of the Spring) was built from Roman masonry; the marble font was carved in 1220.

↑ The western façade of Verona's Duomo, carved by Nicolò

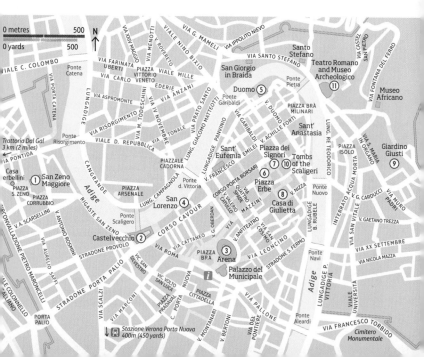

Piazza Erbe

Piazza Erbe is named after the city's old herb market. Today's stalls, shaded by umbrellas, sell everything from herb-flavoured roast suckling pig in bread rolls to succulent fresh-picked fruit. At the northern end of the square is the Baroque Palazzo Maffei (1668), surmounted by statues. On the west side is the Casa dei Mercanti, a largely 17th-century building that dates originally from 1301. Opposite, frescoes are still visible above the cafés.

Piazza dei Signori

🏛 Torre dei Lamberti
📞 045 927 30 27 ⏰ 10am-7pm daily

In the centre of this elegant square is a 19th-century statue of Dante, whose gaze seems fixed on the forbidding 14th-century Palazzo del Capitano, the former home of Verona's military commanders. Beside it is the equally intimidating Palazzo della Ragione, the palace of Reason, now the city's law courts. Stunning views of the Alps can be enjoyed from atop the 84-m (275-ft) Torre dei Lamberti, which rises from the western side of the courtyard.

Casa di Giulietta

🏛 Via Cappello 23 ⏰ Daily (pm only Mon)

The tragic story of Romeo and Juliet, two lovers from rival families, has inspired countless dramas, films and ballets. At the Casa di Giulietta (Juliet's House), Romeo is said to have climbed to Juliet's balcony; in reality this is a restored 13th-century inn. Today, crowds throng to see the simple façade and stand on the small marble balcony. The run-down Casa di Romeo is a few streets away, in Via Arche Scaligeri. The so-called Tomba di Giulietta is in a crypt below the cloister of San Francesco al Corso on Via del Pontiere.

EAT

Casa Perbellini

Dining at this intimate, Michelin-starred trattoria is like stepping into a friend's kitchen - and that is exactly what the owners are after. The open kitchen is more a theatre stage than a food preparation area, and guests can interact with the chefs as they work.

🏛 Piazza San Zeno, 16
🚫 Mon & Sun

💲💲💲

Trattoria Dal Gal

This welcoming neighbourhood local does plates of freshly made pastas matched with local wines. Choose from five daily-changing pasta dishes, then head straight for a dessert degustation, which can feature anything from tiramisu to fresh strawberries and sorbet.

🏛 Via Don Gregorio Segala, 39
🚫 Mon & Sun D

💲💲💲

Giardino Giusti

🏛 Via Giardino Giusti 2
📞 045 803 40 29 ⏰ Apr-Sep: 9am-8pm daily (Oct-Mar: to 7pm) 🚫 25 Dec

This Renaissance garden was laid out in 1580. As with other gardens of the period, there is a deliberate juxtaposition of

Passers-by admire the central fountain in Piazza Erbe

↑ Visitors taking a photo on the famous balcony at Casa di Giulietta

← The lower garden of the beautiful Giardino Giusti

Today's stalls, shaded by umbrellas, sell everything from herb-flavoured roast suckling pig in bread rolls to succulent fresh-picked fruit.

nature and artifice: the formal lower garden contrasts with the wilder woods above. John Evelyn, the English author and diarist, thought this the finest garden in Europe.

 ⑩

Tombs of the Scaligeri

⌂ Via Arche Scaligeri

Beside the entrance to the tiny Romanesque church of Santa Maria Antica, once the parish church of the powerful Scaligeri family, lie a profusion of bizarre tombs of the former rulers of Verona. Perhaps the most notable is the tomb of Cangrande I (died 1329) near the entrance – the sarcophagus is surmounted by an equestrian statue of the ruler, a copy of the original which is now in Castelvecchio (p108).

⑪

Teatro Romano and Museo Archeologico

⌂ Regaste Redentore 2
☎ 045 800 03 60 **⌚ 1:30–7:30pm Mon (all day on pub hols), 8:30am–7:30pm Tue–Sun ⌚ Early on performance days, 1 Jan, 25 & 26 Dec**

This Roman theatre was built in the 1st century BC; little survives of the stage, but the seating area is largely intact. It offers great views over Verona. A lift carries visitors up to the monastery above, now an archaeological museum. The exhibits around the cloister and in the monks' cells include mosaics, pottery and glass.

TOP 5 ROMANTIC THINGS TO DO

Verona in Love
Sign up to the citywide Verona in Love festival in February *(www. dolcementeinlove.com)*.

Wine tasting
Hire a bicycle, pack a picnic, and go wine tasting in the emerald hills around Verona.

River Adige
Take a sunset stroll along the River Adige.

Giardino Giusti
Get lost among the statues, grottoes and clipped mazes of the Giardino Giusti.

Trattoria Dal Gal
Enjoy a romantic candlelit dinner at the Trattoria Dal Gal.

↑ Statues lining the lake in Padua's Piazza Prato della Valle

❷

PADUA

🅐 D2 🚌 Piazza Boschetti 🚉 𝒊 Piazzale della Stazione; www.turismopadova.it

Padua (Padova) is a university town with an illustrious academic history. Rich in art and architecture, it has two particularly outstanding sights. The magnificent Cappella degli Scrovegni (p114), north of the city centre, is famous for Giotto's lyrical frescoes, and forms part of the complex incorporating the Eremitani church and museums. The Basilica di Sant'Antonio is one of the most popular pilgrimage destinations in Italy.

①

Duomo and Baptistry

🅐 Piazza Duomo 🕽 049 65 69 14 🕒 10am–6pm daily 🚫 1 Jan, Easter, 25 Dec

The Duomo was built in 1552 to designs partly drawn up by Michelangelo, on the site of an earlier 14th-century cathedral. Beside it stands a domed baptistry (c.1200). The interior is decorated with frescoes by Giusto de' Menabuoi. Dating from around 1378, they depict episodes from the Bible, including the Creation and the Crucifixion.

↑ Fresco of Christ by Giusto de' Menabuoi in Padua's Duomo

②

Palazzo della Ragione

🅐 Piazza delle Erbe (via the town hall) 🕽 049 820 50 06 🕒 9am–7pm Tue–Sun (Nov–Jan: to 6pm) 🚫 1 Jan, 1 May, 25 & 26 Dec

The "Palace of Reason" was built in 1218 to serve as Padua's law court and council chamber. The vast main hall was originally decorated with frescoes by Giotto, but fire destroyed his work in 1420. Frescoes painted by Nicola Miretto now cover its walls.

③

Chiesa degli Eremitani and Museo Civico Eremitani

🅐 Piazza Eremitani 8 🕒 Daily (chapel); Tue–Sun (museum) 🚫 1 Jan, 1 May, 25 & 26 Dec 🌐 turismo padova.it

The Eremitani church, built from 1276 to 1306, contains magnificent roof and wall tombs and frescoes (1454–7) by Andrea Mantegna. The Museo Civico Eremitani holds a collection of rare Roman

EAT

Belle Parti

Tradition reigns at Belle Parti, from the candlelit white-clothed tables to the suited waiters. The sommelier is on hand to match every dish with local wines.

🏠 Via Belle Parti 11
🕐 Sun

💲💲💲

Osteria Dal Capo

The menu here truly delights, with seasonal dishes such as lasagne with radicchio, or black tagliatelle with chestnuts and pumpkin.

🏠 Via Obizzi 2 🕐 Sun & Mon

💲💲💲

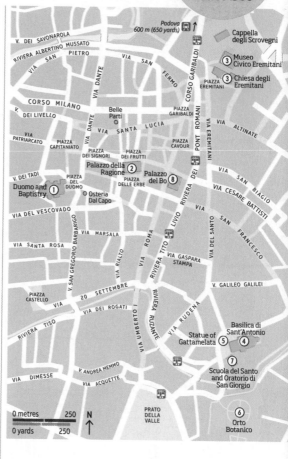

medallions, a set of Venetian coinage, an archaeological section and an art gallery.

---

④

Basilica di Sant'Antonio

🏠 Piazza del Santo 📞 049 822 56 52 🕐 7am-7:30pm daily

This exotic church, with its Byzantine domes and minaret-like spires, is also known as Il Santo. It was built from 1232 to house the remains of St Anthony of Padua. Inside, the high altar features Donatello's magnificent reliefs (1444-5) on the miracles of St Anthony.

---

⑤

Statue of Gattamelata

Beside the entrance to the Basilica stands a great work of the Renaissance: a statue of the soldier Gattamelata by artist Donatello, made in 1452.

---

⑥

Orto Botanico

🏠 Via Orto Botanico 15
🕐 Tue-Sun (Apr-May: daily)
🕐 1 Jan, 25 Dec 🌐 ortobotanicopd.it

Padua's botanical garden is one of the oldest in Europe (1545). The gardens were used to grow Italy's first lilac trees, sunflowers and potatoes.

---

⑦ 🖼️

Scuola del Santo and Oratorio di San Giorgio

🏠 Piazza del Santo 11
📞 049 822 56 52 🕐 Daily

Five frescoes, including the earliest documented paintings

by Titian, are to be found here, including two scenes from the life of St Anthony, painted in 1511. The works in the San Giorgio oratory are by Altichiero da Zevio and Jacopo Avenzo, painted in 1378–84.

---

⑧ 🖼️ 🖼️

Palazzo del Bo

🏠 Via VIII Febbraio 2 🕐 For guided tours only (Mon-Sat) 🌐 unipd.it

The historic main university building originally housed the medical faculty, renowned throughout Europe. Guided tours include Galileo's pulpit and the oldest surviving medical lecture theatre in the world, built in 1594.

Giotto's frescoes
covering the walls of
the Scrovegni Chapel ↑

Must See

3

CAPPELLA DEGLI SCROVEGNI, PADUA

🅐D2 🅐Piazza Eremitani 🚍To Piazzale Boschetti ⏰9am-7pm daily; advance booking compulsory 🗓Pub hols 🌐cappelladegliscrovegni.it

Enrico Scrovegni built this chapel in 1303, hoping thereby to spare his dead father, a usurer, from the eternal damnation in hell described by the poet Dante in his *Inferno*. The interior of the chapel is covered with beautiful frescoes of scenes from the life of Christ, painted by Giotto between 1303 and 1305. As works of great narrative force, they exerted a powerful influence on the development of European art.

Giotto's Frescoes

The Florentine artist Giotto (1266–1337) is regarded as the father of the Renaissance, the great revival in the Classical traditions of Western art. His frescoes in this chapel – with their sense of pictorial space, naturalism and narrative drama – mark a decisive break with the Byzantine tradition of the preceding 1,000 years. In such scenes as *Lament over the Dead Christ* figures are naturalistic and three-dimensional, not stylized, and emotions are clearly expressed. Although Giotto was considered a great artist in his lifetime, few of the works attributed to him are fully documented. The frescoes in the Scrovegni Chapel are rare exceptions where his authorship is in no doubt.

↑ Exterior of the Cappella degli Scrovegni

← Giotto's *Mary is Presented at the Temple*

VISITING THE CHAPEL

It is compulsory to book your visit on the website in advance as there are strict limits on the number of visitors allowed in to the Scrovegni Chapel at any one time. Before entering, visitors must spend 15 minutes in a decontamination chamber, where an explanatory film on the chapel and its famous frescoes is provided. The visit itself is restricted to 15 minutes.

↑ Figures expressing grief in Giotto's *Lament over the Dead Christ*

 4

VICENZA

 C2 🚗🚌 Piazza Stazione ℹ️ Piazza Matteotti 12; www.vicenzae.org

Vicenza is known as the adoptive city of Andrea Palladio (1508–80), who started out as a stonemason and became one of the most influential architects of all time. One of the wealthiest cities in the Veneto, Vicenza is celebrated the world over for its splendid and varied architecture, which shows the extraordinary evolution of Palladio's distinctive style. It also offers a dazzling array of elegant shops and cafés to visit.

① Piazza dei Signori

This square at the heart of Vicenza is dominated by the **Palazzo della Ragione**, its balustrade bristling with statues of Greek and Roman gods. Often referred to as the Basilica, the building is now an exhibition space. Beside it stands the 12th-century Torre di Piazza. The Loggia del Capitaniato, to the northwest, was built by Palladio in 1571.

Palazzo della Ragione
⊘ 🏛️ Piazza dei Signori 📞 04 44 22 28 11 🕐 For exhibitions, concerts and guided tours only (call for timings)

② Teatro Olimpico

🏛️ Piazza Matteotti 11 🕐 9am–5pm Tue–Sun (last entry: 4:30pm) 🚫 during performances, 1 Jan, 25 Dec 🌐 teatrolimpicovicenza.it

Palladio began work on the Teatro Olimpico, Europe's oldest surviving indoor theatre In 1579, but died the following year. His pupil Vicenzo Scamozzi took over

the project, designing the scenery for the first production in 1585. Using wood and plaster painted to look like marble, he created the illusion of streets receding to a distant horizon through *trompe l'oeil* effects.

③ Museo Civico

🏛️ Piazza Matteotti 37–39 📞 0444 32 50 71 🕐 10am–5pm Tue–Sun 🌐 musei civicivicenza.it

This museum is housed in Palazzo Chiericati, which was built by Palladio. Among the

→ The intricate stage design at the Teatro Olimpico

←

Palazzo della Ragione and the Torre di Piazza in Piazza dei Signori

Gothic altarpieces from Vicenza churches on display here is Hans Memling's *Crucifixion* (1468–70).

---

④

Santa Corona

🏛 Contrà Santa Corona ☎ 0444 22 28 11 🕐 Tue-Sun 🚪 Noon–3pm, Easter Sun

This Gothic church was built in 1261 to house a thorn donated by Louis IX of France, and said to be from Christ's Crown of Thorns. Notable paintings include Giovanni Bellini's *Baptism of Christ* (c.1500) and the *Adoration of the Magi* (1573) by Paolo Veronese.

---

⑤

Monte Berico

🏛 Viale X Giugno 87 ☎ 0444 55 94 11 🕐 Daily (only pm Sun)

Monte Berico is the cypress-clad hill to which wealthy residents once escaped in the heat of summer to enjoy the cooler air and pastoral charms of their country estates.

The domed basilica on top of the hill is dedicated to the Virgin who is said to have appeared here during the 1426–8 plague to announce that Vicenza would be spared.

---

⑥

San Lorenzo

🏛 Piazza San Lorenzo 🕐 7am–noon & 3:30–7pm daily

The portal of this church is a fine example of Gothic stone carving, decorated with the figures of the Virgin and Child, and St Francis and St Clare.

---

⑦

Villa Valmarana ai Nani

🏛 Via dei Nani 8 ☎ 0444 32 18 03 🕐 10am–6pm 🌐 villavalmarana.com

The wall alongside the Villa Valmarana, built in 1688 by Antonio Muttoni, is topped by figures of dwarfs (*nani*), which give the building its name.

Inside, the walls are covered with frescoes by Tiepolo, in which the gods float about on clouds watching scenes from the epics of Homer and Virgil. In the separate Foresteria (guesthouse) are 18th-century frescoes painted by Tiepolo's son Giandomenico.

⑧

La Rotonda

🏛 Via Rotonda 45 ☎ 0444 32 17 93 🕐 Wed & Sat (villa); Tue–Sun (garden) 🌐 villa larotonda.it

With its perfectly regular, symmetrical forms, this villa, also known as the Villa Capra Valmarana, is the epitome of Palladio's architecture. The design, consisting of a dome rising above a cube, received immediate acclaim for the way it blends perfectly with its surroundings.

The villa, built in 1550–52 has inspired many copies in cities as far away as London, St Petersberg and Delhi.

> **PALLADIO**
>
> Andrea Palladio was perhaps the most sought-after architect of the 16th century. Inspired by the treatises of ancient authors such as Vitruvius and Virgil, Palladio designed elegant palaces and villas for his clients that harked back to the Classical Golden Age. His own architectural treatise *The Four Books of Architecture* gained him widespread international recognition.

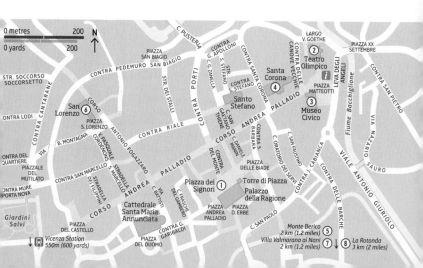

❺ Euganean Hills

🅰C2 🄵🄢🚌To Terme Euganee, Montegrotto Terme 🚹 **Viale Stazione 60, Montegrotto Terme; www.turismopadova.it**

The conical Euganean Hills, remnants of long-extinct volcanoes, rise abruptly out of the surrounding plain. Hot-water springs bubble up at Abano Terme and Montegrotto Terme, where scores of establishments offer thermal treatments, ranging from mudbaths to immersion in the hot sulphurated waters.

Abbazia di Praglia

🛐 🄰 **Via Abbazia di Praglia 16, Bresseo di Teolo** 🄾Tue-Sun (pm only) 🔒**Religious holidays** 🆆**praglia.it**

The Benedictine monastery at Praglia, 6 km (4 miles) west of Abano Terme, is a peaceful haven in the hills where the monks grow herbs and restore manuscripts. They lead guided tours of parts of the abbey and the church (1490–1548), noted for its beautiful cloisters. There are also carved stalls in both the choir and the refectory, and paintings and frescoes by Zelotti, a 16th-century painter from Verona.

Casa di Petrarca

🛐📷 🄰 **Via Valleselle 4, Arquà Petrarca** 📞**042971 8292** 🄾Tue-Sun (also Mon if pub hol) 🔒**Public hols**

The picturesque town of Arquà Petrarca, on the southern edge of the Euganean Hills, is named after Francesco Petrarca (1304–74). This medieval poet, known in English as Petrarch, spent the final years of his life here, in a house frescoed with scenes from his lyrical poems, overlooking a landscape of olive groves and vineyards. He lies buried in a simple sarco-phagus in front of the church.

> ### Did You Know?
>
> A 30-minute train ride away, Treviso is a great base for exploring Venice - without the expensive hotels.

Villa Barbarigo

🛐📷 🄰 **Via Diana 2, Valsanzibio** 🄾**Feb-Nov: daily** 🆆**valsanzibio giardino.it**

This 18th-century villa to the north of Arquà has fine Baroque gardens. Planned by Antonio Barbarigo in 1669, they are a grandiose mix of statuary, fountains, a maze, formal parterres, lakes and avenues of cypress trees.

---

❻ Brenta Canal

🅰D2 🄰Padua & Venice 🄵🄢Venezia Santa Lucia, Padua 🚌To Mira, Dolo & Strà

Over the centuries, in order to prevent the Venetian lagoon silting up, the rivers flowing into it were diverted. The River Brenta was canalized in two sections: the older branch, between Padua and Fusina (just west of Venice), dates back to the 1500s and flows for 36 km (22 miles). Its potential as a transport route was quickly realized and fine villas were built along its length. Many of these elegant buildings can still be admired today – the S11 road runs alongside most of the canal's length – and several of them are open to the public.

The 18th-century **Villa Pisani** at Strà has an extravagant frescoed ceiling by Tiepolo. The **Barchessa Valmarana** at Mira boasts 18th-century decorations. In the village of Malcontenta is **Villa Foscari**, or Villa Malcontenta, one of

---

STAY

Maison Matilda

This hotel in a 19th-century palazzo has six individually designed rooms. The "Charming" room has parquet floors and a four-poster bed. An all-day breakfast is served in a peaceful courtyard.

🄰**Via Jacopo Riccati, Treviso** 🆆**maison matilda.com**

€€€

→ Charming wooden bridge across the River Sile in Treviso

Palladio's loveliest villas. It was built in 1560 and the interior features frescoes by Zelotti.

Villa Pisani

⊛⊛⊛ 🏠 Via Pisani, Strà
🕐 Tue-Sun 🛑 1 Jan, 1 May, 25 Dec 🌐 villapisani. beniculturali.it

Barchessa Valmarana

⊛ 🏠 Via Valmarana 11, Mira
🕐 10am-4:30pm Tue-Sun (Mar-Oct: to 6pm)
🌐 villavalmarana.net

Villa Foscari

⊛ 🏠 Via dei Turisti 9, Malcontenta 🕐 Tue & Sat am 🛑 Nov-Mar
🌐 lamalcontenta.com

7
Treviso

🅰 D2 🚍🚆 Via Fiumicelli 30, Piazza Borsa; www. visittreviso.it

A good place to start a tour of the fortified city of Treviso is Calmaggiore. The street links the 13th-century Palazzo dei Trecento town hall with the Duomo, which was founded in the 1100s but rebuilt several times. Inside the Duomo, Titian's *Annunciation* (1570) vies for attention with the striking *Adoration of the Magi* fresco (1520) by Il Pordenone. More paintings by Titian and other Renaissance artists may be seen in the **Museo Civico**.

Open mornings from Tuesday to Saturday, the city's bustling fish market is held on a picturesque island in the middle of Treviso's River Sile.

The church of **San Nicolò**, by the 16th-century city wall, contains interesting frescoes, including, on a wall of the chapterhouse, the first ever depiction of spectacles in art.

Museo Civico

⊛ 🏠 Chiesa Santa Caterina, Piazzetta Mario Botter 1
🕐 Tue-Sun 🛑 Public hols
🌐 museicivicitreviso.it

Chiesa di San Nicolò

🏠 Via San Nicolò 📞 0422 54 86 26 🕐 Daily

→
A boat moored by a small pier on a canal in Treviso

DRINK

Bar Beltrame

Piazza bars aren't to everyone's taste, but Bar Beltrame is so charming that it's impossible not to stop by. Wicker seats are crowded under cool stone arches, where stylish locals gather in the evening for a Campari spritz or glass of prosecco. Mini-sandwiches and bowls of crisps are complimentary.

🏠 Piazza dei Signori, Treviso 📞 0422 54 07 89 🕐 Thu

8

Bassano del Grappa

▲D1 ▲Vicenza FS▬
**🛈 Largo Corona d'Italia 35;
www.bassanodelgrappa.
com**

This peaceful town lies at the foot of Monte Grappa. The River Brenta is straddled by the graceful Ponte degli Alpini, designed in 1569 by Palladio. It is built of timber to allow it to flex when hit by the spring meltwaters. Bassano is well known for its majolica products (decorated and glazed earthenware), some of which are on display in the **Palazzo Sturm**. The town is also synonymous with the popular Italian clear spirit known as *grappa*. It is produced from the lees *(graspa)* left over from wine production. Information about the process, and also about the impact of World War I in the area, is given in the **Museo degli Alpini**.

Palazzo Sturm
♻ ▲Via Schiavonetti
🕒Mon & Wed-Sat
🅆museibassano.it

Museo degli Alpini
🄯🄯 ▲Via Angarano 2
🕒Tue-Sun 🅆musei
bassano.it

 9

Asolo

▲D1 ▲Treviso ▬
**🛈 Piazza Garibaldi 73;
Tue-Sun; www.asolo.it**

This tiny walled town was once ruled by Queen Caterina Cornaro (1454–1510), the Venetian wife of the King of Cyprus, who poisoned her husband so that Venice would gain Cyprus. Cardinal Pietro Bembo, a poet, coined the verb *asolare* to describe the bittersweet life of enforced idleness she endured in exile here. Among others who fell in love with the place was poet Robert Browning, who named a volume of poems *Asolanda* (1889) after Asolo.

At Maser, 10 km (6 miles) east of the town, stands the magnificent **Villa Barbaro**. It was designed by Palladio in about 1555, in conjunction with the artist Veronese, and perfectly blends symmetry and light, airy rooms with sumptuous *trompe l'oeil* frescoes.

Villa Barbaro
♻ ▲Maser 🕒Apr-Oct:
11am-5pm Tue-Sun; Nov-
Mar: 11am-5pm Sat, Sun &
pub hols 🕒1 Jan, Easter Sun,
25 Dec 🅆villadimaser.it

 10

Castelfranco Veneto

▲D2 ▲Treviso FS▬
**🛈 Via Riccati 14; 0423
49 50 00; Tue-Sat am**

The historic core of this town lies within well-preserved walls. The **Casa di Giorgione**, said to be the birthplace of the painter Giorgione (1478–1511), houses a museum devoted to his life. Giorgione innovatively used landscape to create mood, as can be seen in his most famous work, the broodingly mysterious and evocative *Tempest (p90)*.

About 8 km (5 miles) northeast of the town, at Fanzolo, lies the pretty **Villa Emo** (c.1555). Designed by Palladio, it is a typical

←

Bassano del Grappa's Ponte degli Alpini, designed by Andrea Palladio

↑ Cypress-clad hills around the walled town of Asolo

example of his work: a cube flanked by two symmetrical wings. Inside there are lavish frescoes by Zelotti.

Casa di Giorgione

⊛ ⌂ Piazza San Liberale ⊙ Tue–Sun ⊗ Public hols ⊠ museocasagiorgione.it

Villa Emo

⊛ ⊙ ⌂ Via Stazione 5, Fanzolo ⊙ Daily ⊗ 1 Jan, 25 & 31 Dec ⊠ villaemo.org

Conegliano

⌂ D1 ⌂ Treviso ⊟⊟ 🛈 Via XX Settembre 61; 0438 212 30

Conegliano lies among prosecco-producing vineyards, and winemakers from all over Italy learn their craft at Conegliano's renowned wine school. Via XX Settembre, the

arcaded main street, is lined with fine 15th- to 18th-century palazzi, many in the Venetian Gothic style or decorated with fading frescoes. The Duomo contains the town's one great work of art, an altarpiece painted by local artist Cima da Conegliano (1460–1518) depicting the *Virgin and Child with Saints* (1493).

Reproductions of Cima's most famous works are on show in the **Casa di Cima**, the artist's birthplace. The detailed landscapes in the background of his paintings were based on the hills around the town; the same views can still be seen from the gardens surrounding the ruined battlements and towers of the 10th-century Castelvecchio (old castle).

Casa di Cima

⊛ ⌂ Via Cima 24 ☎ 0438 224 94 ⊙ Sat & Sun, pm only and during temporary exhibitions

---

THE DOLOMITE ROAD

The Strada delle Dolomiti, or Dolomite Road, is a feat of highway construction. It enters the Veneto region via the Passo Pordoi, which at 2,239 m (7,346 ft), is the most scenic of all the Dolomite passes. From here the route follows the winding S48 for another 35 km (22 miles) east to the resort of Cortina d'Ampezzo.

There are plenty of stopping places along the route where it is possible to pause and enjoy the spectacular views. In many of the ski resorts, cable cars will carry visitors up to Alpine refuges (some with cafés attached) that are open from mid-June to mid-September. These refuges mark the start of a series of signposted walks.

---

⑫ Cortina d'Ampezzo

🗺D1 🚆Belluno 🚌
ℹ Corso Italia 81;
www.infodolomiti.it

Italy's top ski resort is well supplied with restaurants and bars. Cortina is set amid the dramatic scenery of the Dolomites, which explains part of its attraction: all around, crags and spires thrust their distinctive weather-beaten shapes above the trees. Cortina has better-than-average sports facilities, thanks to hosting the 1956 Winter Olympics. In addition to downhill and cross-country skiing, there is also a ski jump and a bobsleigh run, as well as an Olympic ice stadium, swimming pools, tennis courts and riding facilities.

During the summer months, Cortina becomes an excellent base for walkers. Useful information on trails and guided walks is available from the tourist office or, during the summer, from the tour guides' office opposite.

STAY

Here are some of the best mid-range hotels in Cortina d'Ampezzo.

Villa Blu Cortina
Mountain chic at its best, with caramel Alpine-style furniture, plush carpets and great mountain views.

🏠Località Verocai 73
🌐hotelvillablu
cortina.it

€€€

Hotel Ambra Cortina
This hotel has 24 quaint Alpine rooms with wooden hues and floral drapes, some with whirlpools, spas and four-poster beds.

🏠Via XXIX Maggio 28
🌐hotelambracortina.it

€€€

Panda
A charming family-run hotel, Panda has simple but comfortable rooms. Those on the Balcony Floor have private terraces, and there's a self-contained apartment on the top floor.

🏠Via Roma 64
🌐cortinahotelpanda.it

€€€

⑬ Belluno

🗺D1 🚍🚌 ℹPiazza
Duomo 2; www.info
dolomiti.it

Picturesque Belluno serves as a bridge between the two different parts of the Veneto, with the flat plains to the south and the Dolomite peaks to the north. Both are encapsulated in the views to be seen from the 12th-century Porta Rugo at the southern end of Via Mezzaterra, the main street of the old town. More spectacular still are the views from the bell tower of the 16th-century Duomo (subsequently rebuilt). The nearby Baptistry houses a font cover with the figure of John the Baptist carved by Andrea Brustolon (1662–1732). Brustolon's works also grace the churches of San Pietro (on Via San Pietro) and Santo Stefano (Piazza Santo Stefano). North of Piazza del Duomo stands the elegant Palazzo dei Rettori (1491) – once home to the town's Venetian rulers – and the 12th-century Torre Civica, all that now survives of a medieval castle.

⟶

Snowy slopes around the fashionable resort of Cortina d'Ampezzo

The **Museo Civico** contains paintings by Bartolomeo Montagna (1450–1523) and Sebastiano Ricci (1659–1734), and a notable archaeological section. North of the museum is Belluno's finest square, the Piazza del Mercato, with its arcaded Renaissance palaces and its fountain of 1410.

South of Belluno are the picturesque ski resorts of the Alpe del Nevegal; in the summer a chairlift operates from Faverghera up the flank of the mountain to a height of 1,600 m (5,250 ft), offering extensive views.

Museo Civico
⊘⊘🕐 🏠Piazza Duomo 16
🕐Tue, Wed, Fri & Sat am
🌐museo.comune.belluno.it

WHERE TO GO IN CORTINA

Cortina is one of Italy's most fashionable resorts. Away from the slopes, days here are spent shopping on the town's main drag, Corso Italia, followed by cocktails at Bar Arnika *(Corso Italia 983)* or a local prosecco at wine bar Enoteca *(Via del Mercato 5)*. Anyone wanting something a bit more substantial will love wine-and-cured-meats bar Dok Dall'Ava LP 26 *(Largo delle Poste 26)*. The best city-centre après-ski happens at Birreria Hacker Pschorr *(Via Stazione 7)*, followed by dancing at VIP club *(Corso Italia 207)*.

$\longrightarrow$

Dramatic backdrop of the Dolomites in the charming ski resort of Cortina d'Ampezzo

⑭

Udine

🅰D1 🚆 𝐢 Piazza I
Maggio 7; www.turismo
fvg.it

Udine is a city of varied and
surprising architecture. In the
central Piazza della Libertà, the
Loggia del Lionello (1448–56),
built of pink stone in Venetian
Gothic style, stands beside
the Art Deco Caffè Contarena.
Opposite, the Renaissance
symmetry of the Porticato di
San Giovanni is interrupted by
the Torre dell'Orologio (Clock
Tower, 1527), crowned by two
bronze Moors that strike every
hour. Note also the fountain of
1542, the two 18th-century
statues, and the column
supporting the Lion of St Mark.

Beyond the Arco Bollani, a
gateway designed by Palladio
in 1556, steps lead up to a
26-m (85-ft) hill that offers
sweeping views over the city.
On the hill is the 16th-century
castle, now the **Musei Civici
e Galleria di Storia e Arte
Antica**, which houses fine art
and archaeology collections.

Southeast of Piazza
Matteotti, at the end of Via
Savorgnana (where a small
market is held), stands the
Oratorio della Purità, and the
Duomo with its octagonal bell
tower. Both contain important
paintings and frescoes by
Giambattista Tiepolo (1696–
1770). More of Tiepolo's work
can be seen in the **Museo
Diocesano e Galleria Tiepolo**,
formerly the Palazzo
Arcivescovile, which the artist
decorated with frescoes.

Outside Codroipo, 24 km
(15 miles) west, rises the
imposing **Villa Manin**. A road
passes through its grounds,
so it can be seen even when
the house – once the retreat
of Ludovico Manin, the last
doge of Venice (1725–1802) –
and its gardens are closed.

Musei Civici e Galleria di
Storia e Arte Antica

⊗ 🅰 Castello di Udine
📞 0432 27 15 91 🕐 Tue–Sun
📅 1 Jan, Easter, 1 May, 25 Dec

Museo Diocesano e
Galleria Tiepolo

🖐⊗ 🅰 Piazza Patriarcato 1
📞 0432 29 80 56 🕐 Wed–Mon
📅 1 Jan, Easter, 25 Dec

Villa Manin

⊗ 🅰 Piazza del Doge,
Passariano 📞 0432 82 12 10
🕐 Tue–Sun for exhibitions
only 📅 1 Jan, 25 Dec

EAT

Rosenbar

This family-run place
offers a great seasonal
tasting menu. In summer
you can eat on a terrace.

🅰 Via Duca d'Aosta 96,
Gorizia 🌐 rosenbar.it

€€€

Al Piave

A homely trattoria
serving local dishes such
as stewed beef. Excellent
local wine list.

🅰 Via Cormons 6, Gorizia
🌐 trattoriaalpiave.it

€€€

Ca di Pieri

A popular eatery
specializing in simple
dishes such as gnocchi
and minestrone, plus
crepes with apricot jam.

🅰 Via Piero Antonio
Codelli 5, Gorizia
📞 0481 53 33 08

€€€

↑ A Venetian Gothic loggia in
Udine, a city known for its
eclectic architecture

SYMBOLISM IN EARLY CHRISTIAN ART

Christians were persecuted until AD 313, when their religion was granted official status by Constantine the Great. Prior to this they had developed a language of symbols – like the fish, or ICHTHUS (an acronym for Iesous CHristos THeou Uios Soter – Jesus Christ, Son of God, Saviour, in ancient Greek) to express their beliefs. Many of these symbols can be seen in the mosaics and marble tomb chests of Aquileia.

⓯ Aquileia

🅐D2 🚌 𝑖 Via Julia Augusta; www.turismo fvg.it

Aquileia, now little more than a village but encircled by the ruins of palatial villas, baths, temples and market buildings, provides a poignant reminder of the lost splendour of the Roman Empire.

It was here that Emperor Augustus received Herod the Great, King of Judea, in 10 BC, and it was here, too, in AD 381, that the early Christian church held a major council to settle doctrinal issues. In the 5th century, however, the town was abandoned following several sackings.

On a group of low islands in the Adriatic lagoon, attached to the mainland by a narrow causeway, Grado grew into a port for Aquileia in the 2nd century and was used as a haven during the barbarian invasions. Today, it is a popular seaside resort. At the centre of the old town is the Duomo, which contains 6th-century frescoes in the apse. Nearby, in the church of Santa Maria delle Grazie, there are more 6th-century mosaics.

Basilica

⊛ 🏛 Piazza Capitolo
📞 0431 91 97 19 🕐 Daily
🕐 During Mass

The Basilica was founded in about AD 313 and much of the original structure still survives, including the floor mosaics of the nave and Cripta degli Scavi below. The designs mix biblical stories and scenes from everyday life. There is a lively portrayal of the tale of Jonah, who was swallowed by a sea monster.

Museo Archeologico Nazionale

⊛ 🏛 Via Roma 1 🕐 Tue-Sun 🌐 museoarcheologico aquileia.beniculturali.it

Mosaics and stone carvings from the 1st to 3rd centuries are on display here, along with glass, amber and a collection of flies, beautifully worked in gold, that formed the adornment of a Roman matron's veil.

Museo Paleocristiano

🏛 Località Monastero
📞 0431 911 31 🕐 8:30am-1:45pm Tue-Sun

This museum, which stands not far from Aquileia's ancient harbour beside the once navigable River Natissa, focuses on the development of art during the early Christian era.

⓰ Gorizia

🅐E1 🚌🚆 𝑖 Corso Italia 9; www.turismofvg.it

Gorizia was at the centre of fierce fighting during both world wars and was split in two by the 1947 Treaty of Paris, leaving part in Italy, part in Yugoslavia (now Slovenia).

The Museo Provinciale della Grande Guerra (Museum of the Great War), in the basement of the **Museo Provinciale di Storia e Arte**, has videos, photographs, and mock-ups of trenches, latrines and gun emplacements showing the waste, squalor and heroism of war.

On a mound nearby rises the castle, encircled by 16th-century fortifications. From here there are views over the town.

Southwest of Gorizia, scenic country roads pass through the foothills of the Carso (p126), a limestone plateau gouged with tunnels, caves and underground rivers.

Museo Provinciale di Storia e Arte

⊛ 🏛 Borgo Castello 13
📞 0481 53 39 26 🕐 Tue-Sun
🕐 25 Dec

EAT

Al Bagatto

Come here for the exceptional seafood-based tasting menu. Sophisticated, beautifully presented dishes are served in an intimate, refined dining room.

🏠 Via Luigi Cadorna 7, Trieste ⓦ albagatto.it

€€€

Scabar

The menu here is exceptional, with all ingredients sourced locally. Nab a table on the terrace and order the ravioli with prawns, followed by the grilled catch of the day.

🏠 Via Erta di Sant'Anna 63, Trieste ⓦ scabar.it

€€€

---

⑰

Cividale del Friuli

🅐D1 FS🚌 𝐢 Piazza Paolo Diacono 10; www.cividale.net

A gate in the medieval walls of Cividale leads to the dramatic ravine of the River Natisone, which is spanned by the Ponte del Diavolo (Devil's Bridge). Above the river's north bank is the **Tempietto Longobardo** (Lombardic Chapel), an 8th-century church decorated with reliefs of saints, modelled in stucco. The town's history is traced in the excellent **Museo Archeologico Nazionale**, which contains the excavated remains of buildings from a Roman town, and a collection of Lombardic items including jewellery, ivory and weapons.

Next door is the Duomo, rebuilt in 1453 after a fire, with its beautiful silver altarpiece (13th century). The **Museo Cristiano**, off the south aisle, contains sculptures from the original church, like the altar donated by Ratchis, the Lombardic Duke of Friuli and later King of Italy (737–44), which is finely carved with scenes from the Life of Christ.

Tempietto Longobardo

⊗ 🏠 Via Monastero Maggiore 34 📞 0432 70 08 67 🕒 Daily

↑ Cividale del Friuli, surrounded by forested mountains

Museo Archeologico Nazionale

⊗ 🏠 Palazzo dei Provveditori Veneti, Piazza del Duomo 13 📞 0432 70 07 00 🕒 Daily (am only Mon) 🔒 1 Jan, 1 May, 25 Dec

Museo Cristiano

⊗ 🏠 Via Condotti 1 🕒 Wed-Sun 🔒 1 Jan, 25 Dec ⓦ mucris.it

---

⑱

Grado

🅐D2 🏠 Gorizia 🚉 𝐢 Via della Vittoria 4; www.grado-tourism.com

An important port during the Roman Empire, this lagoon city became part of Austria in 1815, returning to Italy only after World War II. Today Grado is a pleasant resort, with clean beaches and a lively city centre. The Basilica of Sant'Eufemia features beautifully preserved 6th-century mosaics.

Grado is also a popular spa destination, and it offers outdoor activities such as tennis, sailing and golf.

⑲

Carso

🅐D1

A limestone plateau cutting a swathe through northeastern Italy, the Carso region is utterly unique. Its features include a cliffside series of villages with some of the oldest and largest caves in the world, as well as forests, gorges, lakes, rivers and views to the Adriatic – all of them drawing keen hikers and cyclists to the region.

There are 100 settlements in the Carso, some of which can be reached from Trieste in just 25 minutes, thanks to regular bus services.

Heading north from Italy, country roads stretch into the Slovenian hills, passing churches, wineries, rivers and farmhouses.

20

Trieste

E2 FS

i Via dell'Orologio 1;
www.turismofvg.it

Trieste is an atmospheric city with a long, bustling harbour lined with handsome buildings and lapped by the waves of the Adriatic Sea.

From Villa Opicina, just to the north, there are sweeping views over the city, its bay and the coast of Slovenia.

Acquario Marino

Molo Pescheria 2, Riva Nazario Sauro 1 04030 6201 9am–5pm Thu–Tue (May–Sep: to 7pm)

This small aquarium contains examples of the fascinating marine life in the Adriatic. On the upper floor is a vivarium filled with local and exotic reptiles and amphibians.

Castello di San Giusto

Piazza Cattedrale 3 040 30 93 62 10am– 5pm Tue–Sun (May–Sep: to 7pm)

Up above the harbour stands a hilltop castle built by Trieste's Venetian governors from 1368. It is set on a terrace that offers views over the Gulf of

Trieste. The castle houses two museums containing Roman mosaics and a collection of weapons and armour.

Basilica Paleocristiana

Via Madonna del Mare 11 040 426 14 11 10am– noon Wed

Beside the Castello di San Giusto lie the substantial ruins of the Roman Basilica (or law court) built around AD 100. Note the stone magistrates' bench and throne.

Duomo

Piazza Cattedrale 2 040 322 45 75 Daily

Trieste's Duomo is built on the site of a 5th-century Christian basilica and two 9th-century churches. The churches were merged in the 14th century, leaving the cathedral with two apses and an asymmetrical façade. Highlights include the Gothic rose window, the bell tower (which incorporates Romanesque debris from the earlier buildings), and the two 13th-century Venetian-style apse mosaics.

Museo di Storia ed Arte e Orto Lapidario

Pza della Cattedrale 1 040 31 05 00 Tue–Sun (Nov–Mar: daily)

This archaeological collection documents Trieste's trade links with ancient Greece.

Grotta del Gigante

Borgo Grotta Gigante 42a 040 32 73 12 Tue–Sun (Jul & Aug: daily)

Beyond the city lies this huge cavern filled with a series of tall stalagmites that resemble organ pipes in their formation.

Castello di Miramare

Viale Miramare, Grignano 040 22 41 43 Daily

At Grignano, 8 km (5 miles) northwest of the city, stands this castle set in lush gardens. It was built as a summer retreat by the Archduke Maximilian in 1856–60, a few years before he was assassinated in Mexico.

→

The 19th-century Castello di Miramare, at Grignano, near Trieste

Elegant buildings ↑
lining the lively
harbour of Trieste

TRENTINO-ALTO ADIGE

The Italian-speaking Trentino – named after Trento, the regional capital – and the German-speaking Alto Adige or Südtirol (South Tyrol, the region bordering the upper reaches of the River Adige) differ dramatically in culture. However, they do share one feature in common: the majestic Dolomites, covered in snow for three months of every year and carpeted with exquisite Alpine plants for another three.

The region's mountains have been cut by glaciers into a series of deep, broad valleys. Travellers have passed up and down these valleys for generations – as confirmed by the extraordinary discovery of a 5,000-year-old man's body in 1991, found emerging from the surface of a melting glacier in Alto Adige. The frozen corpse wore leather boots, stuffed with hay for warmth, and was armed with an ice pick.

The paths once trodden by Neolithic man became major road networks under the Romans, when many of the region's cities were founded. By the Middle Ages, Alto Adige had established its very own distinctive culture under the Counts of Tyrol, whose land (later appropriated by the Habsburgs) straddled both sides of today's Italy-Austria border. The Tyrolean nobility built the castles that still line the valleys and the mountain passes, in order to protect travellers from brigands.

Another ancient legacy is the tradition of hospitality, found in the numerous guesthouses along the valleys. Many of these are built in the distinctive Tyrolean style, with beautiful timber balconies for making the most of the winter sun, and overhanging roof eaves to keep snow at a distance. Offering marvellous views, they make the ideal base from which to enjoy the region's mountain footpaths and ski slopes.

TRENTINO-ALTO ADIGE

Experience

Skiing

Skiing in the Dolomites means gorgeous powdery slopes and some of the world's chicest resorts. Stop in for apres-ski food at quaint restaurants offering hearty plates of dumplings, before retiring to one of the many cosy mountain huts dotted across the region.
When to go: *Dec–Apr*

→
Skiier on the slopes at the Madonna di Campiglio resort

THE DOLOMITES FOR
THRILLSEEKERS

A striking mountain range in northeastern Italy, the Dolomites are home to bubbling springs, thick tangles of forest, cool lakes and swathes of lush green fields. It's the perfect place for some adrenaline-pumping outdoor activities.

Via Ferrata

These well-marked climbing and scrambling routes are suitable for both beginners and experienced climbers. Following the metal rungs, steel cables, and cliff-top bridges, you can take the same route the military did during World War II, including the Pordoi pass.
When to go: *Apr–Sep*

Scramblers on a small suspension bridge on the Via Ferrata ↑

Hot-Air Ballooning

One of the best ways to see the Dolomites is from a hot-air balloon. South Tyrol, in particular, is popular with balloon enthusiasts. The Dolomites Hot Air Balloon Festival runs every January in Dobbiaco.
When to go: *Jan*

→

Balloonists enjoying spectacular views of the Dolomites

Horseriding

Tackling the Dolomites' steep cliffs, high mountain plateaus and hair-raising ledges is a breeze when you're riding one of the region's local mountain horses. Riding holidays and organized treks are run throughout the year, taking advantage of the area's 300 annual days of sunshine.
When to go: *Best Apr–Oct*

←

Horses roaming the land at the foot of the Dolomites

TOP 3 SPAS IN THE DOLOMITES

Alpina Dolomites Lodge
📍 D1 🏠 Compatsch 62/3, Alpe di Siusi 🌐 alpina dolomites.it
Modern chic spa hotel focusing on beauty, health and fitness.

Chalet Grumer Suites & Spa
📍 C1 🏠 Via Grumeregg 4, Soprabolzano 🌐 chalet grumer.it
A secluded luxury spa chalet with private hot tubs and a rustic spa.

Hohenwart
📍 C1 🏠 Via Verdines 5, Scena 🌐 hohenwart.com
A slick hotel offering a state-of-the-art spa and great sports facilities.

↑ Thrillseeker at the Adrenaline Centre Adventure Park

Tree Parks

Both the Adrenalin Centre Adventure Park in Ronco and the Adventure Park in Colfosco offer vertical challenges, fantastic outdoor adventures and tree-climbing activities for children and adults of all ages. There are special play areas reserved for the tiniest tots.
When to go: *Apr–Oct*

Cable car amid the dramatic mountain scenery of Madonna di Campiglio

EXPERIENCE

① Madonna di Campiglio

 C1 🚌 **𝒊** Via Pradalago 4; www.campigliodolomiti.it

Madonna di Campiglio is the chief resort in the Val Meledrio. Nestling between the Brenta and Adamello groups of peaks, it makes the perfect base for walking or skiing amid the magnificent mountain terrain. Cableways radiate out from the town in every direction, giving easy access to the peaks.

The church at Pinzolo, 14 km (9 miles) south, has a well-preserved fresco depicting a *Dance of Death* (1539). The inevitable march of the figures, both rich and poor, is underlined by a text written in local dialect.

North of Pinzolo, the road west from Carisolo leads to the verdant and popular, yet unspoiled, Val Genova. About 4 km (2 miles) along the valley is the spectacular Cascate di Nardis, a waterfall that plunges down 90 m (300 ft). The two masses of rock at the bottom are said to be the forms of petrified demons.

② Malles Venosta

Mals Im Vinschgau

 C1 **FS** 🚌 **𝒊** Via San Benedetto 1; www. vinschgau.net

Malles Venosta sits in high border country, close to Switzerland and Austria, and was a customs point during the Middle Ages. The town has several Gothic churches, whose spires and towers give an appealing skyline, mirroring the jagged peaks that rise all around. The oldest is the tiny church of San Benedetto, a 9th-century Carolingian building on Via San Benedetto, with frescoes of its patrons.

The medieval **Castel Coira** (Churburg) rises at Sluderno (Schluderns), 4 km (2 miles) southeast of Malles. It contains an excellent collection of weapons and armour.

CANEDERLI

Canederli are dumplings, traditionally made from stale bread, milk, eggs and flour. The name comes from the German word for dumplings, *knödel*, and they are served as a first course or in soups. *Canederli* can be flavoured with parsley, cheese, ham and spinach, and they are a common dish at most restaurants in Trentino-Alto Adige/Südtirol. They can also be purchased at local delis and supermarkets.

Clinging to the mountainside above the town of Burgusio (Burgeis), 5 km (3 miles) north of Malles, is the Benedictine **Abbazia di Monte Maria** (Marienberg), founded in the 12th century but enlarged in the 18th and 19th centuries. The church's crypt shelters an outstanding series of 12th-century frescoes.

The glorious medieval town of Glorenza lies just 2 km (1 mile) south of Malles.

Castel Coira

⊛⊛ Churburg, Sluderno 【0473 61 51 13 ☐20 Mar-Oct: Tue-Sun (& Mon if public hol)

Abbazia di Monte Maria

⊛⊛ 【0473 83 13 06 (abbey); 0473 84 39 80 (museum) ☐mid-Mar-Oct: Mon-Sat; Nov-mid-Mar: groups by appt only ☒Public hols

3

Merano
Meran

C1 🚌 ✈ **i** Corso della Libertà 45; www.meran.eu

Merano is an attractive spa town popular with Austrians, Germans and Italians. On Corso della Libertà, a street of smart shops and hotels, stands the Kurhaus or Spa Hall built in 1914, now a concert venue. Furnished in period style, the 15th-century **Castello Principesco** was home to the Habsburg Archduke Sigismund.

Inviting gardens line the River Passirio, which winds its way through the town. The Passeggiata Lungo Passirio d'Inverno (Winter Walk) follows the north bank to the Roman bridge, Ponte Romano; the Passeggiata d'Estate (Summer Walk) on the south bank leads to the medieval Ponte Passirio.

The romantic 12th-century **Castel Tirolo** lies 4 km (2 miles) to the north of Merano. It hosts a fascinating museum of Tyrolean history.

↑ One of Merano's two beautiful promenades, skirting the River Passirio

The grounds of **Castel Trauttmansdorff** house a lovely botanical garden.

Castello Principesco

⊛⊛ Via Galilei 【329018 63 90 ☐Tue-Sun & public hols ☒7 Jan-Easter

Castel Tirolo

⊛⊛⊛ Via Castello 24, Tirolo ☐Mid Mar-10 Dec: Tue-Sun ☒schlosstirol.it

Castel Trauttmansdorff

⊛⊛⊛ Via S Valentino 51a ☐1 Apr-15 Nov: daily ☒trauttmansdorff.it

4 ⊛⊛⊛⊛

Castello di Avio

C1 Via Castello, Sabbionara d'Avio 【0464 68 44 53 🚌🚉To Avio, then 3-km (2-mile) walk ☐Mar-Sep: 10am-6pm Wed-Sun (also Tue in Aug); Oct-Nov: 10am-5pm Wed-Sun; Mon & Tue if public hol ☒3rd week of Nov-Feb

Castles line the Adige Valley to the Brenner Pass, but few are as accessible as the Castello di Avio. It was founded in the 11th century, extended in the 13th, and today offers far-reaching views. Among the many frescoes is a fantastic series depicting 13th-century battle scenes in the Casa delle Guardie (Sentry House).

SLEEP

Here are some of the best ski chalets in Madonna di Campiglio.

Chalet Laura Lodge Hotel

This splurge-worthy ski lodge has easy access to the ski lifts and hiking trails, and a great spa.

Via Pradalago 21 ☒chaletlaura.it

€€€

DV Chalet Boutique Hotel and Spa

Spa-hotel with Alpine-style rooms, a Turkish bath and hot tubs.

Via Castelletto Inferiore 10 ☒dv chalet.it

€€€

Hotel Chalet del Sogno

Rooms here come with private terraces. There's also a cutting-edge spa.

Via Spinale 37b ☒hotelchalet delsognocampiglio.com

€€€

Chalet dei Pini

Four great apartments with direct access to the slopes.

Via Campanil Basso 24 ☒chaletdeipini.com

€€€

Hotel Milano

A quaint three-star hotel that offers a decent half-board rate.

Piazza Righi 10 ☒campigliohotel milano.it

€€€

WALK IN CEMBRA

A walk through the terraced slopes of the wine-producing town of Cembra takes you past pretty flower-filled villages and across scenic valleys. Some 6 km (4 miles) east of Cembra stand the Piramidi di Segonzano, a rare series of erosion pillars, some over 30 m (100 ft) high, each topped by a rock. Views encompass Cembra Valley and the Dolomites beyond.

5

Rovereto

🅰C1 🚉 ℹ️ Via M Del Ben 5; www.visitrovereto.it

Rovereto was at the centre of fierce fighting during World War I, after which the Venetian castle (built in 1416) that dominates the town was transformed into the **Museo Storico Italiano della Guerra**, a war museum. Near the museum entrance, stairs lead out on to the castle roof for a view of the imposing Ossario del Castel Dante.

Some distance away is the Campana dei Caduti (Bell of the Fallen), which was cast from melted-down cannons at the end of World War II; it is rung daily at sunset.

Below the war museum is the **Museo Civico**, with its collections on archaeology, art, natural history and folklore. The Mario Botta-designed **Museo di Arte**

> The builders maintained architectural harmony by ignoring Gothic and Renaissance styles entirely.

Contemporanea di Trento e Rovereto (MART) showcases 20th-century Italian art. A second site, in Via Portici, holds Italian Futurist art.

A little over 8 km (5 miles) north of Rovereto is **Castel Beseno**. This vast castle was built and rebuilt from the 12th to the 18th century to guard the junction of the three valleys.

Just 5 km (3 miles) south of Rovereto, the main road passes through a valley littered with massive boulders: these are known as Lavini di Marco or Ruina Dantesca, because they are mentioned in Dante's *Inferno* (XII, 4–9). Fossilized dinosaur footprints have been discovered there.

Museo Storico Italiano della Guerra

✒️ 🏛 Via Castelbarco 7 ⏰ Tue–Sun 🔒 Public hols 🌐 museodellaguerra.it

Museo Civico

✒️ 🏛 Borgo Santa Caterina 41 ⏰ Tue–Sun 🔒 1 Jan, 5 Aug, 1 Nov, 25 Dec 🌐 fondazionemcr.it

MART

✒️🕙☕♿ 🏛 Corso Bettini 43 (main museum); Via Portici 38 (Casa d'Arte Futurista Depero) ⏰ Tue–Sun (Mon if public hol) 🌐 mart.trento.it

Castel Beseno

✒️ 🏛 Besenello ⏰ Mar–Oct: Tue–Sun (Mon if public hol); Nov–Feb: Sat & Sun 🌐 buonconsiglio.it

6

Trento

🅰C1 🚉 ℹ️ Piazza Duomo 24; www.discover trento.it

Trento, the capital of the region to which it gave its name, has a fine cathedral, a castle and streets lined with Renaissance mansions. Trento is noted as the venue for the Council of Trent (1545–63), set up by the Catholic Church to consider reforms that might encourage breakaway groups like the German Protestants to return to the fold. The reforms were only partly successful.

The Duomo was begun in Romanesque style in the 1200s. It took three centuries to complete, in 1515, but the builders maintained architectural harmony by ignoring Gothic and Renaissance styles entirely. The result is a church of unusual integrity. Trento's

→

Hiking in the Val di Fiemme, near Cavalese

Roman name, Tridentum, is commemorated in the figure of Neptune, who stands at the top of the 18th-century fountain in Piazza Duomo. Immediately to the west of Trento a scenic round trip along a winding road leads up the north flank of Monte Bondone and back, via Vezzano, down the western slopes. The views along the route are magnificent, in particular from Vaneze and Vason. East of Trento, Pergine marks the start of the Val Sugana, a broad valley with lakes. In the hills north of Lake Levico lies the spa town of Levico Terme, distinguished by elegant Neo-Classical buildings set amid beautifully wooded parkland.

Museo Diocesano Tridentino

◈ 🏛 Piazza Duomo 18
🕐 Wed-Mon 🗓 6 Jan, Easter, 26 Jun, 15 Aug, 1 Nov, 25 Dec
🌐 museodiocesano tridentino.it

This museum is housed in the Palazzo Pretorio, an imposing medieval building on Piazza Duomo. Its contents include early ivory reliquaries, Flemish tapestries and paintings depicting the Council of Trent.

Castello del Buonconsiglio

◈ 🏛 Via Bernardo Clesio 5 🕐 Tue-Sun (Jul & Aug: daily) 🗓 25 Dec
🌐 buon consiglio.it

This large castle, built in the 1200s and later enlarged with additional buildings, is part of the defences of the town. The southern section of the castle consists of the magnificent Magno Palazzo (1530), built for the ruling prince-bishops of Trento, who were given extensive powers by the Holy Roman Emperor to foster loyalty to the pope. The lavish decoration (including frescoes of virile satyrs and nymphs by Gerolamo Romanino, 1531–2) speaks of huge wealth and a luxurious lifestyle. The palazzo houses the Museo Provinciale, with paintings, ceramics and 15th-century wood carvings, and prehistoric, Etruscan and Roman items.

---

❼ Cavalese

🄰C1 🚌 ℹ️ Via Fratelli Bronzetti 60; www. visitfiemme.it

Cavalese is the chief town in the Val di Fiemme, a pretty region of flower-filled pastures, wooded valleys and Tyrolean architecture. At the centre of the town stands the **Palazzo della Magnifica Comunità**. Originally built in the 1200s, this was the seat of the medieval governing council which ruled the area as a semi-autonomous region. Today the panelled interiors contain medieval paintings by local artists and an archaeology collection. Most visitors come for the excellent summer and winter resort facilities, and to climb, by cable car, to the 2,229-m (7,311-ft) top of Alpe Cermis, the mountain that rises to the south of the town.

At Predazzo, about 13 km (8 miles) east, the **Museo Geologico delle Dolomiti** explains the local geology.

Palazzo della Magnifica Comunità

◈◈ 🏛 Piazza Cesare Battisti 2 🕐 Tue-Sun (mid-Sep-Nov & Jan-Jun by appt)
🌐 palazzomagnifica.eu

Museo Geologico delle Dolomiti

◈ 🏛 Piazza SS Filippo e Giacomo 1 🕐 10am-6pm Tue-Sun 🌐 muse.it

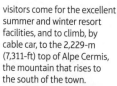

DRINK

Scrigno del Duomo

Every evening from 6pm this osteria serves one of the best aperitivi in Trento: plates of local cured meats and cheese, mini-sandwiches, quiches and dumplings, paired with excellent local red, white and rosé wines by the glass.

🄰C1 🏛 Piazza del Duomo 29, Trento 🌐 scrigno delduomo.com

Antica Birreria Pedavena

This enormous German-style brewery serves jugs of their own beer, plus a decent selection of craft ales and beers.

🄰C1 🏛 Piazza di Fiera 13, Trento 🌐 birreriapedavena.com

Spectacular scenery
in the Dolomites
near Canazei

Duomo

 Piazza Duomo ☎ 0471 97
86 76 🕙 10am-noon & 2-5pm
Mon-Sat

Museo Archeologico

🕙 Via Museo 43
🕙 Tue-Sun (Jul, Aug & Dec:
daily) 🌐 iceman.it

---

⑨

Canazei

🅐 D1 🚌 ℹ Piazza Marconi
5; www.fassa.com

Canazei is a good base for
exploring the Dolomites. In
summer, chairlifts climb to
viewpoints where the beauty
of the encircling mountains
can be appreciated to the
full. The most popular pano-
ramas are from Pecol and
Col dei Rossi, reached by
the Belvedere cableway from
Via Pareda in Canazei: the
cliffs of the Sella group are
visible to the north, with
Sasso Lungo to the west

TOP 3 BOLZANO DISHES

Canederli

In Bolzano these hearty
bread dumplings are
often mixed with
cheese and speck, a
type of smoked ham.
Find it at: Restaurant
Mauriz Keller (Strada
Rezia 32, Ortisei). The
cheese and spinach
version is fantastic.

Apple strudel

A real speciality of the
region. Expect flaky
pastry, sweet apples,
pine nuts and dollops
of whipped cream.
Find it at: Restaurant
Oberspeiser (Klaus at
Terlan 15, Terlano) or
Café Lintner (Via
Leonardo da Vinci 8).

Goulash

This spicy, meaty
Hungarian soup is
exceptionally popular
in Bolzano, no doubt
thanks to its cool winter
climes. The Italians
serve it with lashings
of runny polenta.
Find it at: Wirtshaus
Vögele (Via Johann
Wolfgang von Goethe
3, Bolzano).

⑧

Bolzano

Bozen

🅐 C1 🚆🚌 ℹ Piazza
Walther 8; www.bolzano-
bozen.it

Bolzano, the capital of the
Alto Adige, is the gateway
between the Italian-speaking
Trentino region and the
German-speaking Alto Adige,
or Südtirol, and has a marked
Tyrolean atmosphere.

The old centre, Piazza
Walther, is dominated by the
imposing 15th-century Gothic
Duomo, with its multicoloured
mosaic-patterned roof and
elaborate spire. The "wine
door" inside the Duomo is
carved with figures at work
among vines and reflects the
importance of wine to the
local economy.

In the middle of Piazza
Walther is a statue of Walther
von der Vogelweide, the 13th-
century troubadour – born,
according to legend, in this
area. North of the square, the
streets are lined with houses
adorned with intricate gables,
balconies and oriel windows.

The modern **Museo
Archeologico** houses
impressive finds from the
Stone Age, the Bronze Age, the
Iron Age, Roman times and the
time of Charlemagne. A key
exhibit is Ötzi, the famous
5,000-year-old "Iceman".

and Marmolada, the highest of the Dolomites at 3,343 m (10,965 ft), to the south.

At Vigo di Fassa, 13 km (8 miles) southwest, the **Museo Ladino** focuses on the Ladin-speaking people of some of the valleys. Ladin – a Rhaeto-Romance language – is taught in local schools, and traditions thrive.

Museo Ladino

 Località San Giovanni, Vigo di Fassa ⏲ 3-7pm Tue-Sat (Jun-mid-Sep: daily) 🚫 1 Jan, 1 May, 1-9 Jun, Nov, 25 Dec 🌐 istladin.net

---

Ortisei

Sankt Ulrich

🅰 C1 🚌 ℹ Via Rezia 1; www.valgardena.it

Ortisei is the prosperous main resort for the Val Gardena, and a major centre for wood carving; examples of local craftsmanship may be seen in local shops and in the **Museo della Val Gardena** (which also focuses on local archaeology).

To the south is the Alpe di Siusi (Seiser Alm) region, noted for Alpine meadows and onion-domed churches. The best way to explore this area is by cableway from Ortisei: to the northeast,

LANGUAGES IN ALTO ADIGE

Most residents in the autonomous region of Alto Adige/Südtirol speak German, followed by Italian, with a small sector of the population classing Ladin as their native dialect. The different languages reflect two different cultures that have lived side by side since the area – once part of the Austro-Hungarian Empire – became part of Italy after World War I. Road signs, train stations and restaurant menus feature both Italian and German. Schools teach the syllabus in two languages, and being bilingual is usually required for employment in the area.

a cable car runs to 2,518-m- (8,260-ft-) high Monte Seceda, and walks from here lead into the Odle Dolomites.

Museo della Val Gardena

Via Rezia 83 ⏲ Dec-Mar: Tue-Fri; mid-May-Oct: Mon-Fri (Jul & Aug: Mon-Sat); 26 Dec-6 Jan: daily 🚫 31 Dec, 1 Jan 🌐 museumgherdeina.it

---

⑪ San Martino di Castrozza

🅰 C1 🚌 ℹ Via Passo Rolle 165; www.sanmartino.com

The resort of San Martino occupies one of the most scenic and accessible valleys in the southern Dolomites, making it very popular with walkers and skiers. Cable cars rise to the peak of Alpe Tognola (2,163 m/7,095 ft), southwest of the town, and up the Cima della Rosetta (2,609 m/8,557 ft) to the east. Both offer views of the Pale di San Martino peaks, a stirring sight as the massive rock peaks, split by glaciers, rise above a sea of green meadows and woodland. San Martino is almost entirely surrounded by forest, which once supplied the Venetian Republic with timber for ships. The forest is now protected, and it is possible to see Alpine flowers, birds and other wildlife with relative ease.

Pretty Ortisei, with a Tyrolean onion-domed bell tower ↓

⓬ Brunico
Bruneck

🅰 D1 FS 🚌 🛈 Piazza Municipio 7; www.bruneck.com

Overlooked by an imposing medieval castle, this attractive town retains 14th-century fortifications and a network of narrow streets. The church of St Ursula holds a series of outstanding mid-15th-century altar reliefs of the Nativity. The **Museo Etnografico di Teodone** offers displays of traditional agricultural life and local costumes; this folklore museum also provides an opportunity to visit a 16th-century farmhouse and barn.

Museo Etnografico di Teodone
 🚗 🛈 🚹 Via Duca di Teodone 24, Teodone 🕐 Easter-Oct: Tue-Sat, Sun & pub hols pm (Aug: also Mon) 🔲 volks kundemuseum.it

---

⓭ Bressanone
Brixen

🅰 D1 FS 🚌 🛈 Viale Ratisbona 9; www.brixen.org

The narrow medieval alleys of Bressanone cluster

↑ Players of the Alpine horn in the historic centre of Brunico

around the cathedral and the palace of the prince-bishops who ruled the town for much of its history.

The **Duomo** was rebuilt in the 18th century but retains its 12th-century cloister, which is decorated with superb 15th-century frescoes. The lavish interiors of Palazzo Vescovile, the bishops' Renaissance palace, house the **Museo Diocesano**. It contains precious items from the Middle Ages, as well as the **Museo dei Presepi**, with its collection of wooden crib figures that are carved locally.

At Velturno (Feldthurns), just 8 km (5 miles) to the southwest, stands the Renaissance **Castello di Velturno**, the summer retreat of the rulers of Bressanone, noted for its frescoed rooms. A little over 3 km (2 miles) north of Bressanone lies the **Abbazia di Novacella**, a picturesque group of

TOP 4
🅰 SPAS IN THE TRENTINO-ALTO ADIGE

Hotel Monchalet
🅰 C1 🏠 Via Paul Grohmann 97, Ortisei 🔲 montchalet.it
Guests move from the sauna to the pool to the Turkish baths. The in-house spa offers massages and beauty treatments, and there's a meditation room, too.

Preidlhof Dolce Vita Spa and Resort
🅰 C1 🏠 Via San Zeno 13, Naturno 🔲 preidlhof.it
Hemmed in by the Merano mountains, this adults-only wellness hotel features a medi-spa offering a range of therapies, health checks and dietary analysis.

San Luis Bolzano
🅰 C1 🏠 Via Verano 5, Avelengo, Bolzano 🔲 sanluis-hotel.com
This exclusive retreat features chic chalets and treehouses, plus lake hydromassage, saunas, steam rooms and swimming pools.

Hotel Cyprianerhof Similde Spa
🅰 C1 🏠 St-Zyprian 69, Tires, Bolzano 🔲 cyprianerhof.com
Tucked beneath the Dolomites, this place runs an exercise and relaxation programme incorporating barefoot hiking and yoga, followed by time in their state-of-the-art relaxation room with hay beds and a crushed-ice grotto.

← The richly decorated, colourful cloister of Bressanone Duomo

↑ The Torre dei Dodici in Vipiteno, with snowy peaks in the background

fortified monastic buildings with outstanding cloister frescoes. Further north up the valley, at Rio di Pusteria (Mühlbach), the remains of a 16th-century fortified barrier can be seen to the east of the town. The barrier funnelled ancient travellers through the customs post that divided Tyrol from the Görz district.

High above Rio di Pusteria, to the southeast, looms the massive outline of the **Castel Rodengo** (Rodeneck). The castle contains wonderful 13th-century frescoes showing battle scenes, the Last Judgment and courtly episodes from the *Iwein* romance by Hartmann von Aue, the medieval poet.

Duomo

🏠 Piazza Palazzo Vescovile 1
🕐 6am–noon & 3–6pm daily
🚫 To visitors during mass
🌐 bz-bx.net

> **The castle contains wonderful 13th-century frescoes showing battle scenes, the Last Judgment and courtly episodes from the *Iwein* romance.**

Museo Diocesano & Museo dei Presepi

🏠 Piazza Palazzo Vescovile 2 🕐 10am–5pm Tue–Sun 🚫 8 Jan–mid-Mar, Nov, 24 & 25 Dec 🌐 hofburg.it

Castello di Velturno

🏠 Velturno 🕐 Mid-Mar–mid-Nov: Tue–Sun 🌐 castelvelturno.it

Abbazia di Novacella

🏠 Via Abbazia 1/2b, Varna 📞 0472 83 61 89 🕐 Mon–Sat 🚫 Pub hols

Castel Rodengo

🏠 Rodengo 📞 0472 45 40 56 🕐 Mid-May–mid-Oct: Sun–Fri

14
Vipiteno
Sterzing

🅰 C1 🚇 ℹ Piazza Città 3; 0472 76 53 25

Surrounded by mineral-rich valleys, Vipiteno is very Tyrolean in feel. On Via Città Nuova, a street lined with

Did You Know?

Italian doctors often prescribe stays at the medi-spas in this region to treat persistent ailments.

fine mansions, rise the Gothic **Palazzo Comunale**, containing Renaissance sculpture and paintings, and the Torre dei Dodici clock tower, the symbol of the town. Wood carvings in the **Museo Multscher** are the work of Hans Multscher; this Bavarian sculptor came to Vipiteno in 1456–8 to carve the altar for the parish church, which lies just south of the town.

To the west, the charming Val di Racines includes waterfalls and a natural rock bridge.

Palazzo Comunale

🏠 Via Città Nuova 21
📞 0472 72 37 00
🕐 Mon–Fri 🚫 Fri pm & public hols

Museo Multscher

🏠 Via della Commenda 11
📞 0472 76 64 64 🕐 Apr–Oct: Tue–Sat 🚫 Public hols

MILAN

Italy's economic powerhouse, a bustling city of finance and industry, media empires and fashion houses, Milan has an impressive cultural heritage. The buildings in the historic centre are perhaps more varied than in any other Italian city and the museums and galleries are among Italy's best.

The city was founded in the early 4th century BC when the Gallic Insubre tribes settled in the area where the Duomo now stands. It later became a flourishing commercial centre and was made the capital of the Western Empire by the Romans. Emperor Constantine, holding court here in 313, made Christianity the official religion, setting a new course for European history.

The 5th and 6th centuries marked a period of decline for Milan. After being invaded by numerous barbarian forces, the region was dissolved into a network of city-states. The 12th century saw the rise of the Lombard League, a band of forceful separatists founded to counter the imperialism of German emperors. Power was seized by the region's great families, most notably the Sforza family, which ruled from the 14th to the 16th centuries and commissioned many of the city's greatest palaces, churches and artworks. Ludovico "Il Moro" Sforza ushered in the Renaissance to Milan, inviting the likes of Leonardo da Vinci to his court, but ceded control to the French in 1499.

In the following centuries, the city repeatedly changed hands, eventually coming under Austrian control in 1706. The Milanese revolted in the Cinque Giornate, a five-day riot that triggered the end of foreign rule. King Vittorio Emanuale II, King of Sardinia, took control in 1858 and sent General Garibaldi to conquer the rest of the peninsula, forming the new kingdom of Italy.

MILAN

Must Sees

1 Duomo

2 Castello Sforzesco and Parco Simpione

3 Pinacoteca di Brera

4 Leonardo da Vinci's Last Supper

Experience More

5 Museo Poldi-Pezzoli

6 Teatro alla Scala

7 Palazzo Reale

8 Villa Belgiojoso Bonaparte and Galleria d'Arte Moderna (GAM)

9 Pinacoteca Ambrosiana

10 San Satiro

11 Navigli

12 Civico Museo Archeologico

13 Armani Silos

14 San Lorenzo Maggiore

15 MUDEC

16 Sant'Ambrogio

17 Museo Nazionale della Scienza

18 Fondazione Prada

Drink

1 Rita & Cocktails

2 Mag Café

3 Ugo

4 Morgante Cocktail and Soul

5 La Vineria

Stay

6 Camperio House

7 Hotel Viu

8 The Yard Milano

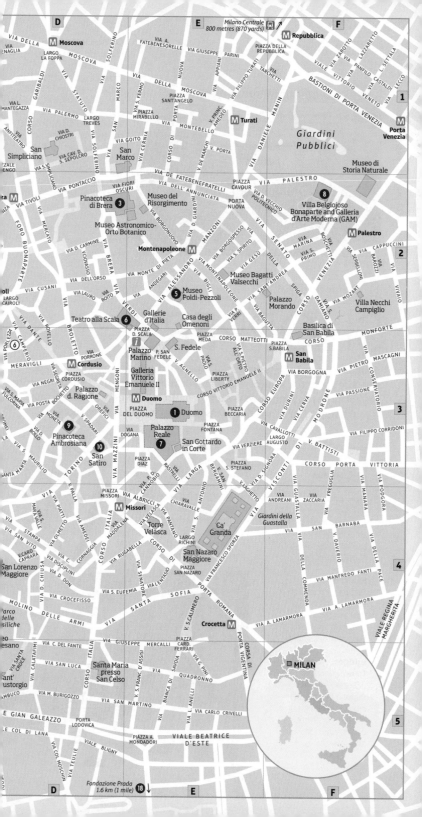

Corso Como 10

The world's first concept store, Corso Como 10 is something of an institution. While the rest of Corso Como is not much to look at, this high-end superstore features a wonderful combination of creative fashion and designer books, plus beautifully decorated restaurants and a boutique hotel. Don't miss the art gallery, and take time for a coffee in the peaceful café garden.

←

The café garden at Corso Como 10

MILAN FOR
SHOPPERS

Shopping is practically a professional pastime in Milan, Italy's fashion and sartorial epicentre. A major textile production hub since the 19th century, the city today has boutiques, chains and department stores to suit every taste. If you're staying for a short time, these are the city's must-shop spots.

TOP 3 SHOPS IN MILAN

Blow out:
Biffi (Corso Genova 6)
A cool, curated space stocking designers such as Alexander Wang, Marni and more.

Mid-range:
Dictionary (Corso di Porta Ticinese 46)
Cool, contemporary clothes from young European designers.

Budget:
Fiera di Sinigaglia (Ripa di Porta Ticinese)
Popular flea market stocked with vintage clothes, furniture, books, vinyl records, and accessories.

Galleria Vittoria Emanuele II

This ornate shopping arcade was designed by the architect Giuseppe Mengoni in 1865, and is filled with stylish shops and cafés. The floors are decorated with mosaics of the signs of the zodiac; tourists may be seen stepping on the genitals of Taurus the Bull, said to bring luck.

Via Montenapoleone

Milan's most upscale – and most expensive – street, Via Montenapoleone makes up part of the city's Quadrilatero della Moda fashion district. You'll find high-end Italian designer clothes, jewellery and shoe stores. Take time to soak up the atmosphere, spot the luxury sportscars, and explore the shops. If you are in need of refreshment, there are plenty of upmarket bars, restaurants and cafés (the best is Caffè Cova) to choose from.

→

Window-shoppers outside Versace on Via Montenapoleone

Corso Buenos Aires

This major shopping street specializes in prêt-à-porter, and is home to more than 350 shops – the highest concentration in Europe. Both sides of this 1.5-km (1-mile) street are packed with international stores such as H&M, Zara, Nike, plus Italian brands including Liu Jo, Furla and Boggi.

←

Tram on Corso Buenos Aires, home to highstreet chains

Corso di Porta Ticinese

This shopping street runs from Colonne di San Lorenzo to Piazza XXIV Maggio. A good place to find clothes and accessories by young designers, it's also popular with Milanese looking for jewellery boutiques, vintage stores and record shops.

→

Shoppers exploring Corso di Porta Ticinese in the evening

↑ Stunning interior of the Galleria Vittoria Emanuele II

① 🏛️ Ⓜ

DUOMO

📍 E3 🏛️ Piazza Duomo Ⓜ 1, 3 🚋 1, 2, 3, 12, 14, 15, 16, 24, 27
🕐 8am–7pm daily (main cathedral); 10am–6pm Thu–Tue (museum); 9am–6pm daily (baptistry); May–mid-Sep: 9am–10pm daily; mid-Sep–Apr: 9am–7pm daily (roof terraces)
🌐 duomomilano.it

Milan's massive Duomo has a forest of soaring marble spires dating back to 1386. In sheer figures it is impressive: it's the largest Gothic cathedral in the world, it has more than 3,500 exterior statues and it is supported by 52 massive columns inside.

From its inception to the finishing touches, Milan's cathedral took almost 430 years to complete. Construction began in 1386, with the city's bishop, Antonio da Saluzzo, as its patron. Duke Gian Galeazzo Visconti invited Lombard, German and French architects to supervise the works and insisted they use Candoglia marble, which was transported from Lake Maggiore along the Navigli canals. The official seal AUF (ad usum fabricae), stamped on the slabs, exempted them from customs duty. Over the centuries, some of Italy's best sculptors and architects worked on the cathedral, including Leonardo da Vinci. The cathedral was consecrated in 1418, yet remained unfinished until the 19th century, when Napoleon, who was crowned King of Italy here, had the façade completed. Its bronze doors were only fitted in 1965.

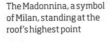

→ The lofty nave, supported by a thicket of 52 pilasters

← The Madonnina, a symbol of Milan, standing at the roof's highest point

ROOF TERRACES

The view of the city from the roof terraces is simply unforgettable. Take in a bird's-eye view of the city and the cathedral's remarkable Gothic crown of spires, gargoyles, statues and tracery.

↑ Intricate Gothic façade
of Milan's Duomo

② 🔄 🚫 🎒

CASTELLO SFORZESCO AND PARCO SIMPIONE

📍 C2 🏛 Piazza Castello Ⓜ Cairoli-Cadorna, 2 Lanza-Cadorna 🚋 1, 4 🚌 50, 57, 61, 94
🕐 7am-6pm daily (Castello); 9am-5:30pm Tue-Sun (Musei Civici) 🚫 1 Jan, Easter, Easter Mon, 1 May, 25 Dec 🌐 milanocastello.it

The Sforza dukes of Milan ruled over one of the most cultured Renaissance courts in Europe from this complex of fortresses, castles and towers. Since 1896, the Castello Sforzesco has housed the Civic Museums, with a vast collection of art and decorative arts. The Parco Simpione, the old ducal hunting reserve, surrounds the castle.

Francesco Sforza, who became lord of Milan in 1450, and his son Lodovico il Moro made the Sforza castle the home of one of the most magnificent courts in Renaissance Italy, graced by Bramante and Leonardo da Vinci. Later, however, under Spanish, Austrian and French occupation the Castello went into decline and was used as barracks. Today, the Corte Ducale is home to the Raccolte di Arte Antica and the art and sculpture gallery, as well as the furniture collection, while the Rocchetta holds decorative arts and the Trivulzio Tapestries.

↑ Ornate frescoed ceiling in the Raccolte di Arte Antica

← Visitors enjoying a stroll in the Parco Sempione, the park surrounding the Castello Sforzesco

Furniture Collection and Pinacoteca

From 15th-century court furniture to 20th-century pieces by important designers such as Giò Ponti and Ettore Sottsass, the furniture collection showcases Milanese design through the ages.

The art gallery houses works from the mid-15th to the 18th centuries, with works by Mantegna, Antonello da Messina, Giovanni Bellimi, Filippo Lippi, Titian, Tintoretto and Canaletto.

Applied Art Collection

The Rocchetta is perhaps best known for displaying Bramantino's splendid Trivulzio Tapestries. Other attractions here include a selection of old musical instruments, an array of medieval gold jewellery, and a large collection of fine Italian and European glass, ceramics, majolica and porcelain.

In the basement of the Corte Ducale are prehistoric and Egyptian displays featuring cult funarary objects, including a fascinating tomb from c.640 BC.

← Fountain lit up in the evening in front of the Castello Sforzesco

Raccolte d'Arte Antica

The collection of Ancient Art is arranged in broadly chronological order in rooms facing the Corte Ducale, while the 14th-century Pusterla dei Fabbri postern, rebuilt after being demolished in 1900, features 4th- to 6th-century sculpture.

Perhaps the highlight of this section is Michelangelo's masterpiece, the *Rondanini Pietà*. The artist was working on this until a few days before his death in 1564. Other star attractions include Agostino Busti's funerary monument to Gaston de Foix, which commemorates the death of the young captain on the battlefield in 1512, and the Sala delle Asse (1498), a room painted by Leonardo to look like an outdoor pergola.

Parco Sempione

This vast park occupies only a part of the old Visconti ducal garden and hunting reserve. The present-day layout was the work of Emilio Alemagna, who in 1890–93 designed it along the lines of an English garden.

Standing among the trees are monuments to Napoleon III, De Chirico's Metaphysical construction *Mysterious Baths*, a sulphur water fountain near the Arena and the Torre del Parco, a 108-m (354-ft) tower made of steel tubes in 1932 after a design by Giò Ponti.

TRIVULZIO TAPESTRIES

Named after General Gian Giacomo Trivulzio, who commissioned them in 1503, the stunning tapestries in the large Sala della Balla (ballroom) were designed by Bramantino. The 12 scenes in the cycle represent the 12 months of the year. The Trivulzio coat of arms (featuring a mermaid breaking a file on a diamond) frame each tapestry, along with an image of the sun and the relevant zodiac sign.

Sculpture of *Napoleon as Mars the Peacemaker* in the courtyard of the museum ↑

3

PINACOTECA DI BRERA

📍D2 🏛Via Brera 28 Ⓜ Lanza, Monte napoleone & Duomo 🚌61 🕐8:30am– 7:15pm Tue-Sun (last adm: 45 min before closing) 🚫1 Jan, 1 May, 25 Dec 🌐pinacotecabrera.org

The Brera holds one of Italy's most important art collections, featuring masterpieces by leading Italian artists from the 13th to the 20th centuries, including Raphael, Mantegna, Piero della Francesca and Caravaggio. The collection is unique among the country's major art galleries in that it isn't founded on the riches of the church or a noble family, but on the policies of Napoleon.

The museum is housed in the imposing 17th-century Palazzo di Brera, a grand palace built as a Jesuit college and later used as an art academy. In the early 19th century, Napoleon augmented the academy's collection with works stolen from churches across the region, opening a picture gallery here in 1809. Over the next two centuries, the collection grew to take in some of the finest examples of Italian Renaissance and Baroque painting.

13th–15th-Century Italian Painting

Rooms 2–4 feature frescoes from the *Oratory at Mocchirolo*, painted by an unknown Lombard master in around 1365–70. Other highlights include Ambrogio Lorenzetti's *Madonna and Child* and *Christ the Judge* by Giovanni da Milano.

↑ Gallery of Renaissance paintings in the Pinacoteca di Brera

GALLERY GUIDE

The collection is displayed in 38 rooms, and was first built up by paintings from churches, later from acquisitions. The paintings are also grouped together by schools of painting (Venetian, Tuscan, Lombard, etc). Not all the exhibits are permanently on view – this is due to restoration work and research. The Sala della Passione on the ground floor is used for temporary exhibitions.

Did You Know?

Next to the museum, just off Piazzetta di Brera, is a pretty botanical garden, a welcome retreat after gallery gazing.

↑ Francesco Hayez's patriotic and sentimental painting *The Kiss*

15th-16th-Century Italian Painting

The Venetian section (rooms 5–9) features works by 15th- and 16th-century artists active in the Veneto, including Giovanni and Gentile Bellini, Carpaccio, Titian and Veronese. Mantegna's *Dead Christ* (c.1480), a piece striking for its intense light and bold foreshortening, is a star attraction.

A large collection of 15th- to 16th-century Lombard paintings is exhibited in rooms 15, 18 and 19, including works by Bergognone, Luini, Bramantino and Vincenzo Foppa.

Rooms 20–23 illustrate artistic movements in the regions of Emilia and Marche. The Ferrara school is represented by leading artists Cosmè Tura, Francesco del Cossa and Ercole de' Roberti. In Room 24 is Raphael's altarpiece *The Marriage of the Virgin* (1504). Some scholars say the young man breaking the staff in the background to this painting is a self-portrait of the artist. Piero della Francesco's *Montefeltro Altarpiece* (c.1475) is in the same room. The egg suspended from the shell in this striking masterpiece is a symbol of the Immaculate Conception.

17th-18th-Century Italian, Flemish and Dutch Painting

Among the non-Italian artists featured in rooms 31–32 are Rubens, Van Dyck, Rembrandt, El Greco and Brueghel the Elder. In room 37 is Francesco Hayez's *The Kiss* (1859), a frequently reproduced work epitomizing the optimism that prevailed after Italy's unification.

Jesi Collection

The 72 works of modern work donated by Emilio and Maria Jesi in 1976 and 1984 are on show in room 10. The collection, mostly by Italian artists, covers the 1910–40 period.

↑ Leonardo's *Last Supper* fresco in the refectory of Santa Maria delle Grazie

4

LEONARDO DA VINCI'S LAST SUPPER

📍 B3 🏛 Santa Maria delle Grazie refectory, Piazza Santa Maria delle Grazie 2 Ⓜ 1, 2 Cadorna 🚃 16 🚌 18 ⏰ 8:15am–6:45pm Tue–Sun 🚫 Pub hols, 1 May, 15 Aug 🌐 cenacolo vinciano.org

This masterpiece was painted for Lodovico il Moro in the refectory of Santa Maria delle Grazie in 1495–7. Leonardo depicts the moment just after Christ has uttered the words, "One of you will betray me". The artist captures the stunned reactions of his disciples in a remarkably realistic and vivid representation of the Last Supper.

↑ Exterior of Santa Maria delle Grazie, where the *Last Supper* can be seen

Leonardo depicts Jesus composed in the centre, and all the disciples around the table shocked and protesting except Judas (fifth from the left) who drops his bread and recoils in guilty horror. Leonardo is reported to have wandered Milan in search of faces to use for the Apostles, and many of the sketches he produced survive in the Royal Library in Windsor, England. The painting is famous for the gesturing hands of the Apostles, so expressive that critics have said they "speak".

The fragility of the blotchy and faded image means that visits are limited to 15 minutes, but it is amazing there is anything left at all. Leonardo painted in tempera rather than the standard, longer-lasting fresco technique in which pigment is mixed with the plaster, and

↑ Judas cartoon, Royal Library, Windsor, UK

←

Donato Montorfano's *Crucifixion*, on the opposite wall of the refectory

the painting started to deteriorate almost immediately. Later, a door was knocked through the bottom part of the picture, then Napoleon's troops used the wall for target practice and, in 1943, the rest of the monastery was destroyed by a bomb.

On the opposite wall of the refectory is Donato Montorfano's fresco of the *Crucifixion*, commissioned by the Dominican monks in 1495. In this dense composition the despairing Mary Magdalene hugs the cross while the soldiers on the right throw dice for Christ's robe. On either side of the work, under the cross, Leonardo added the portraits – now almost invisible – of Lodovico il Moro, his wife Beatrice and their children, which he signed and dated.

THE RESTORATION

It was not the humidity but the method used by Leonardo, *tempera forte*, that caused the immediate deterioration of the *Last Supper*. As early as 1550 the art historian Vasari called it "a dazzling blotch" and regarded it as a lost work. There have been many attempts to restore the *Last Supper*, but in retouching the picture further damage was often done. The seventh restoration ended in spring 1999: it lacks the vibrancy of the original, but it is at least authentic.

EXPERIENCE MORE

↑ Pollaiuolo's *Portrait of a Young Woman*, in the Museo Poldi-Pezzoli

Museo Poldi-Pezzoli

📍E2 🏛Via Alessandro Manzoni 12 🕐10am-6pm Wed-Mon 🔒Public hols 🌐museopoldipezzoli.it

Giacomo Poldi-Pezzoli was a wealthy nobleman who, on his death in 1879, bequeathed his magnificent art collection to the state. Its most famous painting is the 15th-century Renaissance *Portrait of a Young Woman* by Antonio Pollaiuolo, though there are also works by Piero della Francesca, Botticelli and Mantegna, among others.

Teatro alla Scala

📍D2-E2 🏛Piazza della Scala 🌐teatroallascala.org

This Neo-Classical theatre opened in 1778 and is one of the world's most prestigious opera houses. It has one of the largest stages in Europe and hosts sumptuous productions. Two hours before each performance the box office sells tickets at discount prices.

Located within the theatre, the **Museo Teatrale** houses sets and costumes of past productions and theatrical items dating back to Roman times. There is also a good view of the auditorium, with its gilded box galleries and huge chandelier.

Museo Teatrale
🏛Largo Ghiringhelli 1 (Piazza Scala) 🕐9am-5:30pm daily 🌐museoscala.org

Palazzo Reale

📍E3 🏛Piazza del Duomo 🕐2:30-7:30 Mon; 9:30am-7:30pm Tue, Wed, Fri & Sun; 9:30-10:30pm Thu & Sat 🌐palazzorealemilano.it

The former royal palace, for centuries home to the Visconti and other rulers of Milan, houses the Museo della Reggia. It displays the sumptuous interiors of the building and showcases the four historic phases of the palace, including the Neo-Classical era and the Restoration. The palace is also regularly used as a venue for prestigious temporary art exhibitions.

The building abutting the Palazzo Reale to the west (the Arengario) now houses a modern art museum, the **Museo del Novecento**. Works by international artists such as Braque, Kandinsky, Klee,

→ A room in the Museo Teatrale, located within the Scala Theatre

↑ Eclectic mix of old and new at the Museo Poldi-Pezzoli

Léger, Matisse, Mondrian and Picasso can be found alongside pieces by Italy's foremost 20th-century artists.

Museo del Novecento
📍 Via Marconi 1
🌐 museodelnovecento.org

Villa Belgiojoso Bonaparte and Galleria d'Arte Moderna (GAM)

📍 F2 📍 Via Palestro 16
🕐 9am–5:30pm Tue–Sun
🌐 gam-milano.com

Milan's 19th-century and modern art collections are housed in a Neo-Classical villa built by Leopold Pollack

> **HIDDEN GEM**
> **Villa Necchi Campiglio**
>
> This Art Deco villa-turned-museum *(Via Mozart 14)* was the setting for the 2009 film *I Am Love*. You can see one-off artworks and wander the gardens for a glimpse of aristocratic life in the 1930s.

↑ Staircase at the Villa Belgiojoso Bonaparte and Gallerie d'Arte Moderna

in 1790 for Count Ludovico Barbiano di Belgiojoso. It was lived in by Napoleon in 1802 and later by Marshal Radetzky. The villa houses 19th-century Italian art, showing all the major art movements, as well as the Grassi and Vismara collections of 19th- and 20th-century Italian and inter-national artists. Of particular note are works by Giorgio Morandi (1890–1964), Carlo Carrà (1881–1966), Modigliani (1884–1920) and De Chirico (1888–1978). Non-Italian artists include Van Gogh, Cézanne, Gauguin, Picasso, Matisse, Klee and Kandinsky.

STAY

Camperio House
This is a stylish, private, self-catering residence with an on-site restaurant, elegant Italian furnishings and ever-helpful staff.

📍 D3 📍 Via Manfredo Camperio 9
🌐 camperio.com

€€€

Hotel Viu
This chic hotel is set in an ecofriendly building covered with foliage. There are minimalist rooms and a stunning rooftop swimming pool.

📍 C1 📍 Via Aristotile Fioravanti 6
🌐 hotelviumilan.com

€€€

The Yard Milano
Boutique hipster hotel packed with objets d'art, plus 32 well-decorated suites.

📍 C5 📍 Piazza XXIV Maggio 8 🌐 the yardmilano.com

€€€

↑ Bars and cafés lining the Naviglio Grande canal at dusk

Pinacoteca Ambrosiana

D3 **Piazza Pio XI 2**
10am-6pm Tue-Sun
ambrosiana.eu

The Ambrosiana is home to Cardinal Federico Borromeo's magnificent library of 36,000 manuscripts. These include a 5th-century illustrated *Iliad*, early manuscripts of Dante's *Divine Comedy* (1353) and the *Atlantic Codex* (1478–1519) by Leonardo da Vinci. In order to exhibit as much of the *Atlantic Codex* as possible, the pages on show are changed every three months.

The building also houses an art gallery, bequeathed by Borromeo in 1618. The collection ranges from 14th-century pieces to works of the early 19th century. Among the canvases are *Portrait of a Musician* by Leonardo, the *Madonna of the Canopy* by Botticelli (15th century), a cartoon version of Raphael's Vatican fresco, *The School of Athens* (16th century) and Caravaggio's *Fruit Basket*. There is also a strong collection of Venetian art, with paintings by Giorgione, Titian, Bassano and Tiepolo, and panel paintings by the late 15th-century Lombard painter Bergognone.

San Satiro

D3 **Via Speronari 3**
02 87 46 83 **9:30am-5:30pm Tue-Sat, 2-5:30pm Sun & public hols**

Santa Maria presso San Satiro church is one of the most beautiful Renaissance buildings in Milan. It was built on the site of a 9th-century sanctuary, little of which remains apart from the Cappella della Pietà, beside an 11th-century bell tower.

The interior seems to be in the shape of a Greek cross, but this is an illusion created by *trompe-l'oeil* effects, since space restrictions led Bramante to choose a T-shaped plan. Above the altar is a 13th-century fresco. An octagonal baptistry lies off the right aisle. The church's façade was finished in the 19th century.

Navigli

C5 **Corso Magenta 15**
02 88 44 52 08 **1, 2 Cadorna** **16, 27** **50, 58, 94** **9am-5:30pm Tue-Sun**

Developed around a 90-km- (55-mile-) long series of artificial canals built between the 12th and 16th century, Milan's Navigli (canal) neighbourhood is one of the city's buzziest places. The area was historically designed to support Milan's growing trade routes, and it aimed to encourage the transport of merchandise such as marble to the city, from the Ticino and Adda rivers.

Despite being in construction from the 12th century, it wasn't until Leonardo da Vinci joined the project to design a new series of dams that the canal project really took hold. Leonardo then designed a second system of canals linking the Valtellina area with Milan, bringing further trade to the city, which was then Italy's industrial centre.

Today the Navigli area runs from Naviglio Pavese

to Naviglio Grande, with a plethora of boutiques, cafés, restaurants and bars running alongside the waterways. It's one of Milan's most popular nightlife spots and is best visited in the early evening, when bars fling open their doors and welcome locals for aperitivo hour. There is very good furniture shopping in the area, too, with Italian artisans still working from small studios along the river. On the last Sunday of every month, a huge outdoor flea market takes place on Naviglio Grande.

Civico Museo Archeologico

📍 C3 🏛 Corso Magenta 15 📞 02 88 44 52 08 Ⓜ 1, 2 Cadorna 🚋 16, 27 🚌 50, 58, 94 🕐 9am–5:30pm Tue–Sun

At the entrance to this museum is a model of Roman Milan, which illustrates urban planning and architecture in Milan from the 1st to the 4th century AD. The exhibition begins in a hall on the right, containing clay objects and Roman sculpture. At the end of this room is a huge fragment of a torso of Hercules and 3rd-century-AD floor mosaics. Also in this room are two of the most important works in the museum: the Parabiago Patera and the Diatreta Cup.

← The brushed-concrete minimalist look of the Armani Silos

↑ The Parabiago Patera, in the Civico Museo Archeologico

The Patera is a gilded silver plate with a relief of the goddess Cybele (4th century AD). The Diatreta Cup, which dates from the same period, is a single piece of coloured glass, with finely wrought, intricate decoration.

Armani Silos

📍 A5 🏛 Corso Magenta 15 📞 02 88 44 52 08 Ⓜ 1, 2 Cadorna 🚋 16, 27 🚌 50, 58, 94 🕐 9am–5:30pm Tue–Sun

Fashion-art museum Armani Silos offers a glimpse into the inimitable style created by the iconic Italian brand Armani. It runs across four floors in a former grain store, and visitors can view hundreds of outfits and accessories spanning Armani's collections from 1980 to today, under the themes of daywear, exoticism, colour schemes and light. The building is decidedly minimalist, with a pared-back design aesthetic: black ceilings, brushed-concrete floors and plenty of light. Visitors can also take a look at Armani's workstations, with an archive of around 2,000 garment and accessory images, and prints of the most iconic Armani photo shoots of all time.

DRINK

Rita & Cocktails
An intimate neighbourhood locale doling out creative cocktails served in jam jars. Get there by 6pm for an aperitivo before it gets too busy.

📍 B5 🏛 Via Angelo Fumagalli 1 📞 02 837 28 65

Mag Café
This popular bar is crammed with goodies – from coffee cups on the walls to wrought-iron lanterns and a bicycle hanging from the ceiling. Excellent cocktails, but it gets packed at happy hour.

📍 B5 🏛 Ripa di Porta Ticinese 43 🌐 mimag.it

Ugo
The bartenders at Ugo, one of the Navigli's best cocktail bars, magic up a mean *Negroni sbagliato*.

📍 B5-C5 🏛 Via Corsico 12 🚫 Mon 🌐 ugobar.it

Morgante Cocktail and Soul
This bar, in a private garden, offers potent Martinis and snacks.

📍 C5 🏛 Vicolo Privato Lavandai 2 🚫 Mon 🌐 morgante cocktail.com

La Vineria
Choose from the long wine list here, and pair with charcuterie plates piled high with salami, *prosciutto di Parma* and local cheeses.

📍 B5 🏛 Via Casale 4 🌐 la-vineria.it

14

San Lorenzo Maggiore

D4 **Corso di Porta Ticinese 39** **8am-6:30pm Mon-Sat, 9am-7pm Sun (church); 9am-6:30pm daily (Cappella di Sant'Aquilino)** **sanlorenzomaggiore.com**

This church contains a vast collection of Roman and early Christian remains. The octagonal basilica was built in the 4th century, above what was probably a Roman amphitheatre, and rebuilt in the 12th and 16th centuries.

In front of the church stands a row of 16 Roman columns and a statue of Emperor Constantine. Fine 4th-century mosaics adorn the Cappella di Sant'Aquilino, a Romanesque chapel with two early Christian sarcophagi. Other Roman architectural elements of this church are in a chamber below the chapel.

15

MUDEC

A5 **Via Tortona 56** **9:30am-7:30pm daily (Thu & Sat: to 10:30pm)** **mudec.it**

Milan's art and culture museum, MUDEC (a contraction of Museo delle Culture di Milano) is set in the heart of the city's design district, on Via Tortona. It focuses on cultures of the world and their relationship with the city of Milan while also promoting local cultural activities. Inside, the permanent collection features everyday objects such as textiles and musical instruments donated to the city's missionaries, scholars and explorers during their travels in the Middle East, Asia and Africa. Check the website for an ever-changing series of excellent, innovative temporary exhibitions.

SALONE DEL MOBILE

Every April, the best-known names in design descend on Milan for the Salone del Mobile, the biggest furniture trade fair in the world. While the fair is held slightly outside of Milan, in Rho, there are always exciting associated events - such as design talks, drinks and furniture shows - happening in the centre each night.

16

Sant'Ambrogio

C5 **Piazza Sant' Ambrogio 15** **10am-noon & 2:30-6pm Mon-Sat, 3-5pm Sun** **basilicasant ambrogio.it**

Sant'Ambrogio, or St Ambrose, Milan's patron saint and its bishop in the 4th century, was so eloquent that bees were said to fly into his mouth, attracted by his honeyed tongue. This is the basilica that he began in AD 379, though today most of it is 10th-century Romanesque. A gateway leads to the bronze doors of the entrance, flanked by two bell towers. Inside, note the fine rib vaulting and pulpit, as well as the 9th-century altar, which is decorated with gold, silver and gems. In a chapel off the south aisle, fine mosaics line a stunning cupola. In the crypt lies the tomb of Sant'Ambrogio himself.

Above the portico, **Sant' Ambrogio Museum** contains a fascinating collection of architectural fragments, tapestries and paintings relating to the church and its history.

←

Statue of Constantine in front of the church of San Lorenzo Maggiore

Sant'Ambrogio Museum
📞 0286 450 895 🕐 10am-noon & 2:30-5:30pm Mon-Sat, 3-5pm Sun

17 Museo Nazionale della Scienza

📍 B3 🏛 Via San Vittore 21
🕐 9:30am-5pm Tue-Sun
(Sat & Sun: to 6:30pm)
🌐 museoscienza.org

The largest science and technology museum in Italy, the Museo Nazione della Scienza covers transport, energy and communication, as well as art and science based on Leonardo da Vinci's work. Visitors get a glimpse into Italy's rich entrepreneurial and artisanal roots by way of some fascinating one-off objects.

Upon entering the museum, visitors are greeted by Italian military aircraft replicas, including a Farman 1909, plus modern aircraft such as the powerful Italian fighter jet the Fiat G.91. Train lovers can explore vintage railway façades and learn about Lombardy's public-transport history, while the submarine section looks at the Toti submarine S-506, built following World War II.

The Leonardo da Vinci section looks at completed versions of the artist's drawings, including the armoured fighting vehicle known as Leonardo's Tank and a spinning machine.

The cinema and photography rooms show how the claw device used for motion-picture film grew out of a sewing machine needle conceived by Singer in 1851. Among the exhibits in the fascinating television and telephone section is a pantelegraph, an early ancestor of the fax machine.

Elsewhere there are musical instruments dating from the 1600s onwards, and there is a fascinating 17th-century lute-makers workshop on display, too. Children will love the i.lab area, which allows hands-on interaction and participation.

↑ An astronaut's spacesuit in the Museo Nazionale della Scienza

↑ The colonnaded courtyard of the basilica of Sant'Ambrogio

18 Fondazione Prada

📍 E5 🏛 Largo Isarco 2
🕐 10am-7pm Wed-Mon
(Fri-Sun: to 8pm)
🌐 fondazioneprada.org

Set in a former grain distillery, this chic contemporary art museum is the brainchild of Prada duo Miuccia Prada and Patrizio Bertelli, who sought to bring a permanent cultural space to the city. The exhibitions here focus on literature, cinema, music, philosophy, art and science – but they also look at the ways in which these various disciplines interact.

Permanent exhibitions include the Processo Grottesco (a virtual-reality recreation of a Maiorcan grotto) and a room featuring works by artists Robert Gober and Louise Bourgeois. The museum's bar, Bar Luce, was designed by US film director Wes Anderson, who worked with the building's architectural details to create a space inspired by the 1950s and 60s, complete with vintage-style pinball machines.

LOMBARDY AND THE LAKES

Appreciated by the ancient Romans for their beautiful location and mild climate, the lakes of northern Italy – most of which are in Lombardy – are deservedly renowned for the fascinating and unique combination of magnificent scenery and historic and artistic heritage.

Besides Lake Maggiore, Lake Como and Lake Garda, there are smaller and less well-known bodies of water such as the lakes of Varese, Iseo and Idro. All are the result of glaciation in the Pleistocene era, which enlarged clefts already in the terrain. The lake shores were inhabited during the prehistoric period and were later colonized by the Romans, as can be seen in the grid street plans of many towns and in the villas at Lake Garda. Many churches, sanctuaries and castles were built here in the Middle Ages.

In the winter the shores of the lakes can be battered by winds from Central Europe, but the climate remains quite mild thanks to the water. Typical Mediterranean vegetation can be seen everywhere: vineyards, olive trees, oleanders and palm trees. The many splendid villa gardens along the lakes' shores enhance the environment.

In the 18th century a visit to the lake region was one of the stages on the Grand Tour, the trip to Europe considered essential for the education of young people of good birth. These shores were also favourites with writers, musicians and artists such as Goethe, Stendhal, Byron, Nietzsche, Toscanini, Hesse, Klee and Hemingway. The numerous vantage points, connected to the shore by funiculars, narrow-gauge trains and cable cars, offer truly spectacular views over the landscape.

LOMBARDY AND THE LAKES

Must Sees

1. Lake Como
2. Lake Garda
3. Certosa di Pavia

Experience More

4. Lake Maggiore
5. Monza
6. Bergamo
7. Lake Iseo
8. Val Camonica
9. Parco Nazionale dello Stelvio
10. Brescia
11. Mantua
12. Sabbioneta
13. Cremona
14. Pavia

❶
LAKE COMO

🅰 B1 🚊 Como, Lecco 🛈 Piazza Cavour 17, Como; www.lakecomo.it

Set in an idyllic landscape of mountains and rugged hillsides, Lake Como has for centuries attracted visitors who come here to go boating, for walks in the hills, or for relaxation and inspiration. The northern stretches, in particular, are shrouded in an almost eerie calm. The long and narrow lake, shaped into a wishbone by glacial erosion, offers fine views up to the Alps and down to the towns of Como and Lecco.

① Bellagio

This delightful resort on the cusp of the lake's two arms has everything: a harbourside arcade of cafés, sumptuous gardens surrounding stately villas, steep medieval alleys and hotels, restaurants and shops in all price ranges.

② Varenna

Less touristy than Bellagio, Verenna has a pretty waterfront promenade, two small churches with medieval frescoes and two spectacular villas with gardens to wander around. A 20-minute walk away is the medieval Vezio castle, which offers stunning panoramic views of the lake.

③ Villa Carlotta

🏠 Via Regina Teodolinda 2b Tremezzo ⏰ Mid-Mar-Sep: 9am-7:30pm daily; Oct: 9:30am-6:30pm daily 🌐 villacarlotta.it

Lake Como is famous for its extravagant villas, but while some gardens are open, few of the buildings themselves can be visited. At Villa Carlotta, however, it is possible to visit the exquisite landscaped gardens as well as the sumptuous late-Baroque villa.

④ Santa Maria del Tiglio

🏠 Piazza XI Febbraio 📞 034 48 52 61 ⏰ Opening times vary, call ahead

This church in Gravedona is the most famous Lombard Romanesque construction in the Alto Lario region. Its main features are the black-and-white striped stone walls and the unusual octagonal bell tower set into its façade.

↑ The landscaped gardens of Villa Carlotta with Lake Como behind

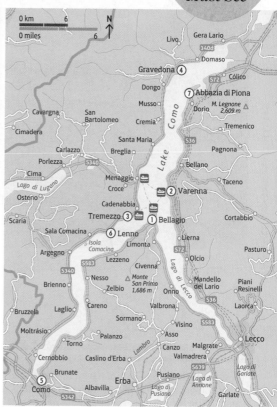

←

Lake Como with the town of Gravedona in the foreground

EAT

Napule e'
A lakeside eatery, Napule e' does excellent pizzas and an even better seafood linguine.

Via Luigi Dottesio 22
napulelago.com

$ $ $

Cascina Respaù
Set in the hills above Como, this farmhouse serves a changing menu of dishes such as risotto and pastas washed down with local wines.

Via Santi Brigida e Respaù
031 52 36 62

$ $ $

⑤

Como

The town that gave its name to the lake boasts a fine **Duomo** in mixed Gothic and Renaissance styles, with carvings on its façade. From the harbour, visitors can take a **funicular** to the small hillside village of Brunate to take in stunning views over the lake.

Duomo
Piazza del Duomo 031 26 52 44 7am-noon & 3-7pm daily

Brunate Funicular
Piazza A De Gasperi 031 30 36 08 Every 15 min 6am-10:30pm daily

⑥

Villa Balbianello

Lenno 034 45 61 10
Mid-Mar-mid-Nov: 10am-6pm Thu-Tue

The statue-lined balustrades fringed with flowers that outline the gardens of this 1784 villa have caught the eye of many a film director.

⑦

Abbazia di Piona

Via Abbazia di Piona 55
0341 94 03 31 9am-noon & 2:30-6pm daily

At the tip of the Ogliasca Peninsula sits this Benedictine abbey. Founded in the 9th century, the abbey features some lovely Romanesque carvings. The monks distil and sell potent liqueur, too.

> **INSIDER TIP**
> **Flea Market**
>
> Each Saturday in Como's Piazza San Fedele, the Mercato dell'Artigianato e Antiquariato sets up its stalls selling vintage clothing, art, furniture and homewares.

↑ Malcesine's waterfront and medieval castle, overlooking Lake Garda

②

LAKE GARDA

🅰 C2 🚉 Peschiera del Garda, Desenzano del Garda 🚌🚋 To all towns 🚹 Viale Marconi 8, Sirmione; 030 91 61 14

The largest and easternmost of the Italian lakes, Lake Garda borders three regions: Trentino to the north, Lombardy to the west and south, and the Veneto to the south and east. The sporting facilities, many sights and splendid scenery of snow-capped mountains help make the lake a favourite summer playground.

①

Gardone Riviera

This pleasant tourist resort is home to **Il Vittoriale**, an over-the-top Art Deco villa built for the poet and writer Gabriele D'Annunzio. Nearby is the **Giardino Botanico Hruska**, a small set of botanical gardens sitting on a terraced hillside.

Il Vittoriale

 🏠 Via Vittoriale 12 📞 0365 296 511 🕐 Apr-Sep: 9:30am-7pm Tue-Sun; Oct-Mar: 9am-1pm & 2-5pm Tue-Sun

Giardino Botanico Hruska

🏠 Via Roma 2 📞 0365 203 47 🕐 Mid-Mar-mid-Oct: 9am-6pm daily

②

Isola del Garda

🕐 For guided tours May-Oct: Tue & Thu (book in advance) 🌐 isoladelgarda.com

Garda's largest island once supported a monastery that attracted the great medieval saints: Bernardino of Siena, Francis of Assisi and Anthony of Padua. The monastery was destroyed by Napoleon and replaced with a Neo-Gothic villa with luxuriant gardens.

③

Desenzano del Garda

This is one the liveliest and most popular towns on Lake Garda. The **Villa Romana**, built in the 4th century, has beautiful polychrome floor mosaics.

Villa Romana

 🏠 Via Crocefisso 2 📞 039 14 35 47 🕐 8:30am-5pm Tue-Sun (to 7pm Mar-mid-Oct)

④

Sirmione

A fascinating 13th-century castle, the Rocca Scaligera, dominates the town of Sirmione. At the tip of the peninsula lies the **Grotte di Catullo**, the ruins of a villa thought to be the residence of the Roman poet Catullus.

Grotte di Catullo

 🏠 Via Catullo 📞 030 91 61 57 🕐 8:30am-4:30pm Tue-Sat (Jun-Sep: to 7pm), 8:30am-noon Sun

---

🔍 HIDDEN GEM
Camaldolese Hermitage

The Camaldolese Hermitage, near Garda, offers panoramic views of the lake, but visitors must respect the sacred nature of the place.

DRINK

Villa Calicantus

Bardolino has long been famous for its light red wine, and this little winery in the Bardolino hills produces some of the best in the region. Booking is essential.

📍 **Via Concordia 13, Bardolino** 🚫 **Sun & Mon** 🌐 **villacalicantus.it**

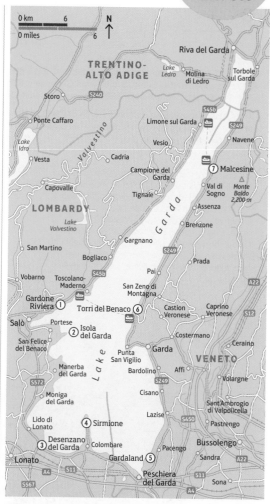

⑤

Gardaland

📍 **Via Derna 4** 🚫 **Nov–Mar** 🌐 **gardaland.it**

This popular theme park features roller coasters, carnival rides, a water park, a jungle safari and medieval shows.

---

⑥

Torri del Benaco

This little town was the capital of Lake Garda in the 14th century and important enough for Verona's Scaligeri family to build one of their castles here. Prehistoric rock carvings can be seen on trails on the nearby mountainside.

---

⑦

Malcesine

One of the most fascinating towns along the lake shore, Malcesine stands on a stretch of impervious rock, hence the name, *mala silex* (inaccessible rock). Its historic buildings are clustered below a medieval castle. A cable car climbs to the summit of Monte Baldo, offering far-reaching views.

→

View over Lake Garda from the Rocca Scaligera castle in Sirmione

3 🏛️ 🗺️

CERTOSA DI PAVIA

△B2 🏠 Viale del Monumento 4, Pavia 📞 0382 92 56 13 🚌 from Pavia & Milan
🚉 Certosa, followed by 1 km (0.5 mile) walk 🕐 Apr-Sep: 8:30am-noon & 2:30-6pm
Tue-Sun; Oct-Mar: 9am-noon & 2:30-5pm Tue-Sun; last adm: 30 mins before closing

The Charterhouse, 8 km (5 miles) north of Pavia, is the pinnacle of Renaissance
architecture in Lombardy, a gloriously decorated Carthusian church and
monastery built over 200 years.

Conceived as a monument to Gian Galeazzo Visconti,
the Milanese ruler who founded the complex in 1396,
the monastery and church were created by the great
15th-century craftsman Giovanni Antonio Amadeo,
among others. The church was intended to be a kind
of mausoleum housing the tombs of the Visconti
family. The monastery gives a fascinating insight into
the daily lives of Carthusian monks, who still live
here under a strict vow of silence.

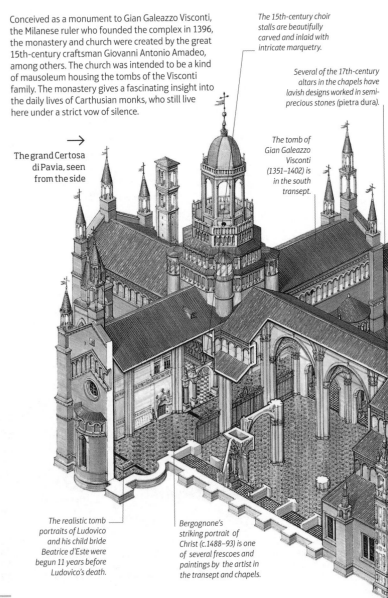

*The 15th-century choir
stalls are beautifully
carved and inlaid with
intricate marquetry.*

*Several of the 17th-century
altars in the chapels have
lavish designs worked in semi-
precious stones (pietra dura).*

*The tomb of
Gian Galeazzo
Visconti
(1351–1402) is
in the south
transept.*

→
The grand Certosa
di Pavia, seen
from the side

*The realistic tomb
portraits of Ludovico
and his child bride
Beatrice d'Este were
begun 11 years before
Ludovico's death.*

*Bergognone's
striking portrait of
Christ (c.1488–93) is
one of several frescoes
and paintings by the artist in
the transept and chapels.*

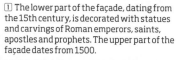

1 The lower part of the façade, dating from the 15th century, is decorated with statues and carvings of Roman emperors, saints, apostles and prophets. The upper part of the façade dates from 1500.

2 This delightful arcaded Small Cloister, with fine terracotta ornamentation, contains a small garden, planted in formal designs.

3 The ceiling of the church is made up of a series of intricately decorated ribbed vaults.

The New Sacristy is painted with colourful ceiling frescoes.

The monks' cells are attractive two-storey cottages with their own private gardens.

PERUGINO'S ALTARPIECE

The church's six-panelled altarpiece was painted by Perugino in 1499 but now only one panel - that depicting *God the Father* (below) - is original; it is flanked by two paintings by Bergognone. The three original lower panels of Perugino's polyptych are on display in the National Gallery in London.

EXPERIENCE MORE

4

Lake Maggiore

🅰 B1 🅰 Verbania 🚆🚌
🚌 Stresa, Verbania, Baveno
& the islands ℹ Piazza
Marconi 16, Stresa; www.
distrettolaghi.it

Lake Maggiore, the second-
largest Italian lake after Lake
Garda, is a long expanse of
water nestling right against
the mountains and stretching
into Alpine Switzerland. The
gently sloping shores are
dotted with camellias, azaleas
and verbena – from which
the ancient lake derived its
Roman name, Verbanus.

A huge copper statue of
Cardinal San Carlo Borromeo,
the chief patron of the lake,
stands in Arona, the town
where he was born in 1538.
It is possible to climb inside
the statue and look out over
the lake through his eyes and
ears. Arona also has a ruined
castle and a chapel dedicated
to the Borromeo family.

Further up the western
coast of the lake is Stresa,
the chief resort and main
jumping-off point for visits to
the islands; the town boasts
many grand hotels, handsome
villas and pleasant gardens.
Behind Stresa, a cable-car ride
away, rises Monte Mottarone,
a snow-capped peak offering
spectacular panoramic views
of the surrounding mountains,
including Monte Rosa.

Did You Know?

Ernest Hemingway, a fan
of Lake Maggiore, spent
time here to recover
from his injuries
in World War I.

↑ A handsome cloister
clinging to the rock
face on Lake Maggiore

The Borromean islands, at
the centre of the lake near
Stresa, are small jewels of
natural beauty augmented
by artificial grottoes,
architectural follies and
landscaped gardens. The
Isola Bella is home to the
17th-century **Palazzo
Borromeo** and its splendid
gardens, while Isola Madre

 Islands in beautiful Lake Maggiore, ringed by forested mountains

is largely given over to a botanical garden. The only island inhabited all year round is Isola dei Pescatori, with a population of 50. The private Isola di San Giovanni is the smallest of the isles, with a villa that once belonged to the great conductor Arturo Toscanini (1867–1957).

The lake becomes quieter towards the Swiss border, but continues to be lined with attractive villas. The **Villa Taranto**, located on the outskirts of Verbania, is home to one of Italy's finest botanic gardens.

About 3 km (2 miles) west of Cannobio, a market town near Switzerland, is the dramatic gorge and tumbling waterfall of Orrido di Sant'Anna, which can be reached by boat.

Palazzo Borromeo
⌖ 🏠 Isola Bella 🚢 From Stresa ⏰ Early Mar-Oct: 9am-5:30pm daily 🌐 isoleborromee.it

Villa Taranto
⌖ 🏠 Via Vittorio Veneto 111, Verbania, Pallanza 📞 0323 40 45 55 ⏰ Mid-Mar-Oct: daily

5

Monza
🅰 B2 🏠 Monza 🚇
ℹ Piazza Carducci 2; 039 32 32 22

These days Monza is mostly famous for its Formula One **Autodromo**, which lies inside a vast park that also has an elegant Rococo hunting lodge, the Villa Reale, and a golf course. At one time, however, Monza was one of the most important towns in Lombardy. Theodolinda, the 6th-century Lombard queen, built its first cathedral and bequeathed her treasure to the town.

In the town centre is the **Duomo**, with its green and white 14th-century façade and beautiful 15th-century frescoes portraying Theodolinda's life. Behind the high altar is the Iron Crown, said to have once belonged to Emperor Constantine. It is named after a small iron strip running around the inside of the crown, supposedly beaten from one of the nails used for the Crucifixion. More local treasures in the Duomo include a silver hen standing over seven tiny chicks – which symbolize Lombardy and the seven provinces it ruled – and a relic said to be John the Baptist's tooth.

Autodromo
⌖ 🏠 Parco di Monza ⏰ Daily 🚫 Public hols 🌐 monzanet.it

Duomo
⌖ 🏠 Piazza Duomo ⏰ 9am-6pm Tue-Sun (Museo e Tesoro del Duomo) 🌐 museoduomomonza.it

STAY

Relais San Lorenzo
Contemporary rooms and a Finnish spa make up this chic property in Bergamo's centre.

🏠 Piazza Lorenzo Mascheroni 9, Bergamo 🌐 relaisanlorenzo.com

€€€

Gombithotel
This design hotel near Bergamo's cathedral offers smart, modern rooms with views over the medieval district.

🏠 Via Mario Lupo 6, Bergamo 🌐 gombithotel.com

€€€

Petronilla Hotel
Guests enjoy minimalist rooms, contemporary art and a good restaurant in this chic Bergamo hotel.

🏠 Via San Lazzaro 4, Bergamo 🌐 petronillahotel.com

€€€

Hotel Splendid
Stunning views of the lake and great amenities set this hotel apart.

🏠 Via Sempione 12, Baveno 🌐 hotel splendid.com

€€€

Hotel Villa e Palazzo Aminta
Gorgeous villa complete with chandeliers and lavish furnishings.

🏠 Via Sempione Nord 123, Stresa 🌐 villa-aminta.it

€€€

Sunrise over the charming old town of Bergamo Alta ↑

6

Bergamo

🅰B1 FS 🚆 ℹ Via Gombito 13; www.visitbergamo.net

Bergamo owes much of its artistic inspiration and architectural splendour to the influence of Venice, which ruled it from the 15th to the late 18th century. The town is divided into two distinct parts: Bergamo Alta, crowning the hill with its cluster of attractive medieval and Renaissance buildings, and the more modern Bergamo Bassa below.

The jewel of the upper town is Piazza Vecchia, containing one of the most appealing architectural ensembles in the region. Its buildings include the 12th-century Torre del Comune, with its fine clock and curfew bell that rings daily at 10pm; the late 16th-century Biblioteca Civica; and the attractive 12th-century

> For walkers, the area offers excellent hiking, and access to remote areas populated by ibexes, marmots, chamois and eagles.

Palazzo della Ragione, or law courts, adorned with a bas-relief of the Lion of Venice.

The arcades of the Palazzo della Ragione lead to Piazza del Duomo. The square is dominated by the Cappella Colleoni, a chapel built in 1476 to house the tomb of Bergamo's famous political leader, Bartolomeo Colleoni. It is flanked by two 14th-century buildings: an octagonal baptistry and the porch leading to the Romanesque basilica of Santa Maria Maggiore. The Neo-Classical basilica's austere exterior contrasts with its Baroque interior, which contains the tomb of Bergamo-born composer Gaetano Donizetti (1797–1848).

The collection from the Galleria dell'Accademia Carrara, a major picture gallery with works by Venetian masters and local artists, as well as masterpieces from the rest of Italy, is housed temporarily in **Palazzo della Ragione** while the building is being restored. It includes 15th- and 16th-century works by Pisanello, Crivelli, Mantegna, Giovanni Bellini, Botticelli, Titian, Raphael and Perugino, 18th-century canvases by Tiepolo, Guardi and Canaletto, and paintings by Holbein, Dürer, Brueghel and Velázquez.

Palazzo della Ragione

◈ 🏛 Città Alta 📞 035 39 96 77 🕐 Jun-Sep: 10am-9pm Tue-Sun (to 11pm Sat); Oct-May: 9:30am-5:30pm Tue-Fri, 10am-6pm Sat & Sun

---

TOP **3** | **FRANCIACORTA WINERIES**

Tenuta Montenisa
🅰C2 🏛 Via Papa Paolo VI 62, Cazzago San Martino
🌐 tenutamontenisa.it
Book ahead for guided tours and tastings with sweeping views over the rolling vineyards and red rooftops of the region.

Ca' del Bosco
🅰C2 🏛 Via Albano Zanella 13, Erbusco 🌐 cadelbosco. com
Tour the vineyards and cellar at this leading Franciacorta producer.

Villa Crespia
🅰C2 🏛 Via Valli 31, Adro
📞 030 745 10 51
Visit the farmhouse of this smaller producer for a look at their award-winning winery, and enjoy tastings in the cellar.

Lake Iseo

C1 **Bergamo & Brescia** **Iseo** **Lungolago Marconi 2, Iseo; www. lagodiseo.org**

This small glaciated lake is surrounded by tall mountains and waterfalls and boasts a mini-mountain of its own, in the form of the island of Monte Isola. Along the shores of the lake are a clutch of fishing villages such as Sale Marasino and Iseo itself. From Marone, on the east bank of the lake, a road leads to the village of Cislano, about 5 km (3 miles) away. Here, extraordinary spire-like rock formations rise from the ground, each topped by a boulder. These distinctive erosion pillars, one of the strangest natural wonders in Lombardy, are known as the "Fairies of the Forest".

Val Camonica

C1 **Brescia** **Capo di Ponte** **Via Briscioli 42, Capo di Ponte; www. proloco.capo-di-ponte.bs it**

This broad valley formed by a glacier is the setting for an extraordinary series of pre-historic rock carvings. These form an astonishing outdoor mural from Lake Iseo to Capo di Ponte and beyond, and the valley is a UNESCO cultural protection zone. More than 180,000 engravings from the Neolithic era until early Roman times have been found; the best are in the **Parco Nazionale delle Incisioni Rupestri**. Do not miss the Naquane rock, carved with nearly 1,000 figures from the Ice Age.

Parco Nazionale delle Incisioni Rupestri

Capo di Ponte 8am-4pm Tue-Sat, 8:30am-1pm Sun & pub hols 1 Jan, 1 May, 25 Dec parcoincisioni. capodiponte.beniculturali.it

Parco Nazionale dello Stelvio

C1 **Trento, Bolzano, Sondrio & Brescia** **From Bormio to Santa Caterina Valfurva & Madonna dei Monti** **Piazza del Municipio 4, Peio (Trento); www.stelviopark.it**

The Stelvio, Italy's largest national park, is the gateway from Lombardy to the glacier-strewn Dolomite mountains stretching into Trentino-Alto Adige. The glaciers are dotted with more than 50 lakes, and dominated by craggy peaks such as Gran Zebrù, Cevedale and Ortles – the tallest mountain here is 3,905 m (12,811 ft).

For walkers, the area offers excellent hiking, and access to remote areas populated by ibexes, marmots, chamois and eagles.

The only real population centre in the Lombardy part of the park is at Bormio, which boasts plenty of winter and summer sports facilities, and is a good base from which to explore the area. The town's **Giardino Botanico Alpino Rezia**, a 1 km (half a mile) walk

FRANCIACORTA

Set between Milan and Verona, Franciacorta is one of Italy's best-known winemaking regions – and its delicious namesake sparkling wine is fast gaining popularity. Unlike prosecco, which is made in large vats, Franciacorta is produced in a similar way to Champagne, with secondary fermentation taking place in the bottle. Like Champagne, Franciacorta is made using chardonnay or pinot noir grapes, but thanks to the region's warmer climate, the end result is a complex, more refined flavour. The Franciacorta wine trail, known in Italy as Strada del Vino Franciacorta, travels from Brescia through Franciacorta, cutting a swathe through olive groves and vineyards.

from the centre, displays some of the species of mountain plants found in the region.

Giardino Botanico Alpino Rezia

Via Sertorelli, Loc Rovinaccia, Bormio Jun-Sep: Mon-Fri Noon-2pm ortobotanicoitalia.it

→ Village of Peschiera on Lake Iseo

⑩ Brescia

🅰C2 🇫🇸🚌 🛈 Via Musei 32; 030 374 96 16

Lombardy's second city has a rich artistic heritage, ranging from Roman temples to the triumphalist Mussolini-era architecture of Piazza Vittoriale. The major sights include the Roman ruins around Piazza del Foro, consisting of the **Tempio Capitolino** (a temple incorporating the Museo di Santa Giulia, Brescia's main gallery) and a theatre. The **Pinacoteca Civica Tosio Martinengo** has masterpieces by Raphael, Lorenzo Lotto and Tintoretto.

The 11th-century **Duomo Vecchio** and 17th-century **Duomo Nuovo** are also star attractions. One of the relics in the Duomo Vecchio is the banner from the *Carroccio*, or sacred ox cart, which served as a symbol for the medieval Lega Lombarda.

Piazza della Loggia, where the market is held, is named after the Renaissance loggia, built in Palladian style. The 18th-century church of San Nazaro e San Celso on Via Bronzoni contains an altarpiece by Titian.

Tempio Capitolino
⊘ 🅰 Via Musei 57a 🅲 030 240 06 40 🕒 Tue, Thu & Sun 🌐 bresciamusei.com

Pinacoteca Civica Tosio Martinengo
🅰 Via Martinengo da Barcol 🅲 030 377 49 99 🕒 Tue–Sun

Duomo Vecchio & Nuovo
🅰 Piazza Paolo VI 🅲 030 375 70 37 🕒 9am–noon & 3–6pm Tue–Sat, 9–10:45am & 3–7pm Sun

---

⑪ Mantua

🅰C2 🇫🇸🚌 🛈 Piazza Andrea Mantegna 6; www.turismo.mantova.it

Mantua (Mantova in Italian) is a striking place of fine squares and aristocratic architecture, bordered on three sides by lakes formed by the River Mincio. The climate can be humid as a consequence, but the city more than makes up for it with its cultural history: it was the birthplace of the poet Virgil and the playground of the Gonzaga dukes for three centuries. Mantua was also the refuge where Shakespeare sent Romeo into exile from Verona, and the setting for Verdi's opera *Rigoletto*. These links are all celebrated in street names, signposts and monuments around the town. The theatrical connections are enhanced by the 18th-century Teatro Accademico Bibiena, on Via Accademia, which Mozart's father claimed was the finest he had ever seen.

The historic centre of Mantua is focused on three attractive main squares: Piazza delle Erbe; Piazza Broletto, named after the 13th-century

> **Mantua was also the refuge where Shakespeare sent Romeo into exile from Verona, and the setting for Verdi's opera *Rigoletto*.**

building adorned with a statue of the poet Virgil; and the cobbled Piazza Sordello. On one side of Piazza Sordello stands the Duomo, with an 18th-century façade and fine interior stuccoes by Giulio Romano (c.1492–1546); on another side is the forbidding façade of the Palazzo Bonacolsi, with its tall prison tower. Piazza delle Erbe is dominated by the Basilica di Sant'Andrea (15th century), designed largely by Leon Battista Alberti, the early Renaissance architect and theorist, and now flanked by an arcade of shops.

The square is also notable for the appealing 11th-century Rotonda di San Lorenzo, and the part-13th-century Palazzo della Ragione with its 15th-century clock tower.

Palazzo Ducale
⊛ ⊛ ☐ Piazza Sordello 40 ☐ 8:15am–7:15pm Tue–Sun (last adm: 6pm) ☐ 1 Jan, 1 May, 25 Dec ⓦ ducalemantova.org

The vast, 500-room home of the Gonzaga family covers the northeastern corner of the town and incorporates Castello San Giorgio (a 14th-century fortress), a basilica and the palace proper.

Works of art include a series of 15th-century frescoes by Pisanello, retelling episodes from the Arthurian legends; a large 17th-century portrait by Rubens of the ducal family in the Salone degli Arcieri; and – most absorbing of all – the frescoes by Mantegna in the Camera degli Sposi (1465–74). These portray Lodovico Gonzaga and members of his family and court in all their magnificence. The entire room is decorated with images of people, animals and fantastic landscapes, and completed by a light-hearted trompe-l'oeil ceiling of *putti* and a blue sky. Book ahead if you intend to visit the Camera degli Sposi.

Palazzo Tè
⊛ ☐ Viale Tè ☐ 1–6:30pm Mon, 9am–6:30pm Tue–Sun ☐ 25 Dec ⓦ palazzote.it

At the other end of town stands the early 16th-century Palazzo Tè, built by Giulio Romano for the Gonzaga family as a base from which they could go horse riding. Here, the artworks conspire with the architecture to produce striking effects: in the Sala dei Giganti, for instance, the frescoed Titans seem to be tearing down the very pillars of the room. Also remarkable is the Sala di Amore e Psiche, decorated with erotic scenes from Apuleius' *Golden Ass* and said to celebrate Federico II's love for his mistress. Other rooms are lavishly painted with horses and signs of the zodiac.

Mantua's old centre, seen from across one of the lakes that surround the city

12

Sabbioneta

C2 Mantua From Mantua Piazza d'Armi 1; www.iatsabbioneta.org

Sabbioneta is the result of a delightful experiment in the theory of Renaissance architecture. It was built by Vespasiano Gonzaga Colonna (1531–91) as an ideal city, and within its hexagonal walls is a perfect gridwork arrangement of streets and buildings designed on a human scale. The finest buildings include the splendid Teatro All'Antica designed by Scamozzi, the Palazzo Ducale, and the frescoed Palazzo del Giardino, which may be visited as part of a tour of the town.

13

Cremona

C2 Piazza del Comune 5; www.turismo. comune.cremona.it

Set in the Po Valley, the pretty city of Cremona is a major economic centre for agricultural production in the region. It is also famous for its rich musical heritage, thanks to former inhabitants such as the composer Claudio Monteverdi (1567–1643) and the violin-makers Andrea Amati (1505–77) and Antonio Stradivari, known as Stradivarius (1644–1737). The city's historic centre is dominated by the beautiful Piazza del Comune.

Cremona's main attraction is the exuberant part-Romanesque **Duomo**, and its bell tower – said to be the tallest medieval tower in Italy – known as the **Torrazzo**; the two are linked by a Renaissance loggia. The wonderful façade is dominated by the large 13th-century rose window and by a number of intricate touches, including a small portico with statues of the Virgin and saints. Inside, the Duomo is decorated with magnificent early 16th-century frescoes and Flemish tapestries, as well as paintings in the side chapels. The top of the Torrazzo tower offers sweeping views over the city. Outside the Duomo, note the pulpit where itinerant preachers, including San Bernardino of Siena, would address the crowd.

> ### Did You Know?
>
> Cremona is famous for *torrone*, a nougat eaten at Christmas time.

Next to the Duomo stands an octagonal 12th-century baptistry. On the other side of the piazza you can see the arcades of the late 13th-century Loggia dei Militi, where the town's lords once met. The Loggia is now a war memorial.

The **Palazzo del Comune** (town hall) is the other major building on the square. It was rebuilt in the 1200s.

The **Museo Civico**, in a 16th-century palazzo, houses the Pinacoteca, containing paintings, wood carvings, the cathedral's treasure and ceramics. The **Museo del Violino** has a large display of important historic instruments, including the Stradivari family collection of violins and masterpieces by Amati and Guarnieri. It also tells the history of the

←
The eight-sided baptistry near the Duomo in Cremona

ANTONIO STRADIVARI AND HIS VIOLINS

Cremona has been synonymous with violin-making since the 1530s, when Andrea Amati's instruments became sought after at royal courts all over Europe. However, it was Antonio Stradivari, or Stradivarius, who raised the level of violin crafts-manship to genius. Stopping-off points on a Stradivarius tour of Cremona are the Museo del Violino, the Palazzo del Comune and his tombstone in the public gardens in Piazza Roma.

violin and the importance of Cremona in the history of violin-making.

On the eastern outskirts of the town, on the road to Casalmaggiore, lies the Renaissance church of San Sigismondo (closed at lunchtime). It was here in a small chapel that Francesco Sforza married Bianca Visconti in 1441. The interior is decorated with 16th-century paintings, altarpieces and frescoes by artists of the Cremona school (Campi family, Gatti and Boccaccino).

Duomo & Torrazzo

⊛ 🏛 Piazza del Comune 📞 0372 4071 🕐 10am-12:30pm & 2:30-5:40pm daily 🚫 Public hols

Palazzo del Comune

🏛 Piazza del Comune 📞 0372 40 72 91 🕐 10am-5pm daily 🚫 For meetings, public hols

Museo Civico

⊛ 🏛 Via Ugolani Dati 4 📞 0372 40 77 70 🕐 10am-5pm Tue-Sun 🚫 Public hols

Museo del Violino

⊛ 🏛 Piazza Marconi 5 🕐 10am-6pm Tue-Sun 🚫 Public hols 🌐 museodel violino.org

---

🏷14 Pavia

🅰B2 🚉🚌 ℹ Palazzo del Broletto, Piazza della Vittoria; www.turismo. provincia.pv.it

During Pavia's golden age, the city was the Lombards' capital, and later witnessed coronations of Charlemagne and Frederick Barbarossa. Even after it lost its status to Milan in 1359, Pavia remained an important city, and great Romanesque churches, tall towers and other monuments still reflect this.

As well as the Charterhouse (Certosa) *(p170)*, there is the sandstone **Basilica di San Michele** off Corso Garibaldi. The building was founded in the 7th century but largely rebuilt in the 12th. Its façade is decorated with symbols and friezes of fantastic animals, and inside there are intricate carvings on the columns.

In the town centre, around Piazza della Vittoria, are such ancient monuments as the medieval Broletto (town hall), with its 16th-century façade, and the **Duomo**, begun in 1488 and worked on in turn by Giovanni Antonio Amadeo, Leonardo and Bramante.

The dome was added in the 1880s. The 11th-century tower that stood next to it collapsed suddenly in 1989.

Crossing the river is the Ponte Coperto, a Renaissance covered bridge with a consecrated chapel halfway along it.

Pavia is also the site of one of Europe's oldest (1361) universities, now residing around a series of Neo-Classical courtyards off Strada Nuova. This road continues north to the 14th-century castle, now home to the **Museo Civico**.

Northwest of Piazza Castello is the 12th-century church, **San Pietro in Ciel d'Oro**. It no longer boasts the fine gilded ceiling after which it is named, but does still contain a magnificent shrine to St Augustine, whose bones were allegedly brought to Pavia in the 8th century.

Basilica di San Michele

🏛 Piazza S Michele 📞 0382 26063 🕐 7am-noon & 3-7pm

Duomo

🏛 Piazza del Duomo 📞 0382 386511 🕐 9am-noon & 3-7pm

Museo Civico

⊛ 🏛 Castello Visconteo, Viale XI Febbraio 35 🌐 museicivici.pavia.it

San Pietro in Ciel d'Oro

🏛 Piazza S Pietro in Ciel d'Oro 🕐 7am-noon & 3-7pm

↑ Tall towers in Pavia, reminders of the city's status in ancient times

Snowy scene in Druogno, near Domodossola

VALLE D'AOSTA AND PIEDMONT

Piedmont and the neighbouring Valle d'Aosta are – apart from Turin and its cultural splendours – essentially countryside. To the north lie the Alps, with ski resorts such as Courmayeur, and the wild stretches of the Parco Nazionale del Gran Paradiso. To the south lie the vineyard-clad hills around Barolo, and seemingly endless fields of grain and rice, used in the local dish, risotto.

The northwest is also rich in culture. From the 11th century to the 18th, both the verdant Valle d'Aosta and Piedmont were part of the French-speaking principality of Savoy and enjoyed the influences of both sides of the Alpine divide. Even today, French and dialectal variants are still spoken in the remote valleys of Piedmont and in much of the Valle d'Aosta. It was only under Duke Emanuele Filiberto in the 16th century that the region was brought definitively into the Italian sphere of influence; and later it was to play the key role in the Risorgimento, the ambitious movement that united Italy under a king from Piedmont. The vestiges of this history are to be found in the medieval castles of the Valle d'Aosta and the clusters of chapels known as *sacri monti* (sacred mountains) built into the foothills of the Alps. The most impressive architecture in the northwest is undoubtedly to be found in Turin, a much underrated and surprisingly elegant Baroque city which boasts, among other things, one of the best Egyptian museums in the world.

Piedmont is also known for its industry – Fiat in Turin, Olivetti in Ivrea, Ferrero in Alba – but it has not forgotten its agricultural roots, and food and drink play an important role in the life of the region: the hills of southern Piedmont produce many of the great Italian red wines.

VALLE D'AOSTA AND PIEDMONT

Must Sees
1 Parco Nazionale Gran Paradiso
2 Turin

Experience More
3 Domodossola
4 Lake Orta
5 Varallo
6 Aosta
7 Sacra di San Michele
8 Avigliana
9 Vercelli
10 Novara
11 Asti
12 Alba
13 Bossea Caves
14 Garessio
15 Le Langhe
16 Cuneo

LOMBARDY
AND THE LAKES
p162

LIGURIA
p200

VALLE D'AOSTA
AND PIEDMONT

←

1 Vineyards near Alba.

2 Wine tasting.

3 Tagliatelle with truffle.

4 Local cheeses.

2 DAYS

A Gastronomic Tour of Piedmont

Day 1

Morning At family-run Ca del Baio *(Via Ferrere Sottano 33, Treiso)*, visitors can sample organic wines such as Barbaresco and Nebbiolo. Tastings last a couple of hours and fees are waived if you purchase a bottle of wine.

Afternoon Head to the pretty town of Alba *(p198)*, famed for its white truffles. Truffle season runs from September to January, with the International Truffle Festival taking place in October and November. Alba's dining scene is one of the best in Italy; most restaurants offer truffle-based dishes, paired with local wines and chocolate-based desserts.

Evening Book a table at Osteria del Boccondivino *(Via Mendicità Istruita 14, Bra)*, which is part of Bra's Slow Food Movement. Ask for the truffle-based tasting menu, then bed down at the simple but charming Hotel La Corte Albertina *(Via Amedeo di Savoia 8, Bra)*.

Day 2

Morning Grab a coffee and a still-warm custard-filled pastry at Bar Pasticceria Converso *(Via Vittorio Emanuele II 199, Bra)*, then drive to Marchesi di Barolo *(Via Roma 1, Barola)*. This traditional estate has been run by five generations of the same family for more than 200 years. Book ahead for tastings and a tour of the cellars.

Afternoon From here, head to peaceful Piemontese family-run farmhouse, Cascina Meriame *(Meriame, 1, Serralunga d'Alba)* and sample some excellent wines, ranging from Dolcetto d'Alba to Barbera d'Alba from Nebbiolo d'Alba to Barolo. Every stage of their wine production is done by hand, including plucking grapes on the 14-hectare property, pressing, fermentation and bottling.

Evening Visitors can stay on-site at the winery and dine at Michelin-starred Guido *(Via Alba, 15, Fontanafredda, Serralunga d'Alba)* nearby.

Cervinia

Italian ski bunnies head to Cervinia, in the Aosta Valley, for its buzzy après ski, panoramic ski-lifts and 350 km (217 miles) of pistes, which are good for beginner to advanced skiers. It's not the prettiest of resorts, but thanks to its high altitude, it is possible to ski the slopes here until May. It also offers glacier skiing and snow-boarding in the summer months to help tide you over until the season starts again in November.

←

Skiers enjoying an après-ski in Cervinia

ALPINE
SKI RESORTS

Six Italian regions touch the Alps: Aosta Valley, Piedmont, Lombardy, the Veneto, Trentino, Alto Adige and Friuli Venezia-Giulia. In winter, the mountain peaks are covered with snow, making the area popular with skiers. Come spring, hiking trails cut a swathe through lush green mountain fields to remote villages.

CASTLES AND FORTS

Valle d'Aosta is known for its medieval castles and forts, with many people travelling to the region specifically to visit them. Perhaps the best known is Fènis Castle, which is admired for its architecturally symmetrical towers and turrets. The 14th-century Verres Castle in the Aosta Valley is a striking example of architecture from the Middle Ages, while 19th-century Fort Bard Museum hosts regular art exhibitions and theatre performances.

Corvara

Tucked among snow-dusted mountain peaks, this pretty Alpine resort in South Tyrol is best for skiing and cycling holidays. Hotels are welcoming and generally family-run, and there is an excellent selection of mountain restaurants.

Cortina d'Ampezzo

The host of the 2021 Alpine Ski World Championships, Cortina *(p122)* is one of the world's chicest ski resorts. It is best for intermediate to advanced skiers looking for a smart, stylish place to speed down the slopes. It's the sort of place where you'll find the jet-set mingling with the locals at quiet wine bars before retreating to chic hotels. During the summer months, the resort becomes an excellent base for walkers.

→

Professional skier performing a jump at Cortina d'Ampezzo

Did You Know?

The Alps are Europe's youngest mountain range, formed a mere 65 million years ago.

Champoluc

Part of the "three valleys" Monterosa region, Champoluc is one of Italy's best-kept secrets. There are very good red runs, fabulous off-piste terrain and welcoming, uncrowded beginners' slopes, too. Hotels are family-run, and there's a charming, rather than rowdy, après-ski scene.

←

Pretty mountain scenery at Champoluc

Courmayeur

This stylish alpine resort offers excellent on- and off-piste skiing, along with a spirited après-ski scene (lifts run until midnight) and great mountain restaurants. Quaint boutiques and delicatessens line the main street, and there's a wide variety of very good hotels.

↑ The Alpine village of Corvara during the summer

→

Chalets with panoramic views at Courmayeur ski resort

Did You Know?

The park was made a royal hunting reserve in 1856 specifically to save the ibex from extinction.

PARCO NAZIONALE GRAN PARADISO

A1 **Piemonte and Valle d'Aosta** **Aosta & Pont Canavese** **From Aosta or Pont Canavese to the different valleys** **Parco Nazionale del Gran Paradiso visitor centre, Villaggio Minatori; www.pngp.it**

A breathtaking wilderness of dramatic mountains and lush meadows, the Gran Paradiso is Italy's foremost national park, created in 1922 from part of a former royal hunting reserve of the House of Savoy.

The park is mainly a summer resort for walkers due to its unspoiled scenery, rare wildlife and unusual Alpine flowers, though there is also cross-country skiing during the winter months. It is home to the endangered ibex, as well as numerous chamois, marmots, ptarmigans and golden eagles. One of the main towns in the park is Cogne, beyond which is the hamlet of Lillaz. From here it is possible to walk through

←

Giardino Botanico Alpino Paradisia at Valnontey

←
Bridge over a torrent in Cogne, set against the picturesque backdrop of the Aosta Valley

> **It is possible to walk through a stone garden - an open-air museum explaining the rocks in the area - and up to the Cascata di Lillaz, a fantastic waterfall.**

→
Dramatic rocky scenery surrounding the waterfall near the hamlet of Lillaz

a stone garden – an open-air museum explaining the rocks in the area – and up to the Cascata di Lillaz, a fantastic waterfall. At Valnontey, the other main town in the park, is the **Giardino Botanico Alpino Paradisia**, an Alpine botanical garden with a network of paths and grassy slopes set against the craggy backdrop of the mountains. Other highlights include the Castello di Aymavilles, an 18th-century castle framed by medieval corner towers, and the Val di Rhêmes-Notre-Dame, a broad valley offering magnificent scenery.

Giardino Botanico Alpino Paradisia
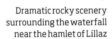 Frazione Valnontey 📞0165 749 264
🕙10am–5:30pm daily

IBEX

The endangered Alpine ibex is a species of wild goat that lives largely above the tree line of the Parco Nazionale Gran Paradiso. Ibexes tend to live in herds of around 10 to 20 individuals. The males, identifiable by their long curved horns, only join with female herds during breeding season, which starts in late autumn. Groups are often seen around Col Lauson at dawn and dusk, and also around Pont. Sightings are particularly common during the summer months.

2

TURIN

 A2 ✈ Caselle 15 km (9 miles) N 🚉 Porta Nuova, Piazza Carlo Felice; Porta Susa, Piazza XVIII Dicembre 🚌 Corso Vittorio Emanuele II 131 ℹ Piazza Castello/Via Garibaldi; www.turismotorino.org

Mention Turin (Torino) and most people will think of industry and prosperity. It is certainly an economic powerhouse but it is also a town of grace and charm, with the Alps in the background, rolling hills close to the city centre, the River Po running through it, long tree-lined streets of Baroque architecture, elegant arcades of shops and excellent museums. Turin is also, of course, home to the famous Turin Shroud, the Fiat car company and the Juventus football team.

① Duomo

🏠 Via XX Settembre 87/Piazza San Giovanni
☎ 011 436 15 40 ⏰ Daily
🕐 12:30-3pm

The cathedral, built between 1491 and 1498 and dedicated to St John the Baptist, is the only example of Renaissance architecture in Turin. The sober square bell tower, which predates the rest of the church by 20 years, stands in refreshing contrast to Turin's sumptuous Baroque buildings; its top was designed by Filippo Juvarra in 1720. Inside, the Duomo is heavy with statuary and paintings. On the right side of the church is the Cappella della Sacra Sindone (Chapel of the Holy Shroud), which is incorporated into the Palazzo Reale (p193). The chapel is a remarkable feat, designed by Guarino Guarini (1624–83), with an extraordinary mesh-like cupola; the exterior is equally eccentric.

Palazzo Madama

🏠 Piazza Castello 10
⏰ 10am-6pm Wed-Mon (to 7pm Sun); last adm: 1 hour before closing 🌐 palazzo madamatorino.it

Turin's main square once featured a medieval castle, which incorporated elements of the original Roman city walls. The castle was later enlarged and remodelled, and a new façade by Filippo Juvarra was added at the request of a royal widow in the 18th century. The castle was renamed Palazzo Madama and sits in the centre of the square with a stately façade. The interior, with its grand staircase and first floor, both designed by Juvarra, houses the Museo Civico d'Arte Antica.

This collection contains numerous treasures ranging from the Graeco-Roman era to the 19th century. The display includes *Portrait of an Unknown Man* by Antonello da Messina (15th-century) and reproductions of the Duc de Berry's Book of Hours, dating from around 1420. Furniture, glass, jewellery and textiles are also on display.

↑ The 19th-century Mole Antonelliana, dominating Turin's skyline

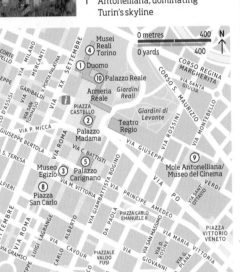

0 metres 400
0 yards 400
N

VIA CORTE D'APPELLO · **VIA MILANO** · **VIA MERCANTI** · **V. PORTA PALATINA** · **VIA XX SETTEMBRE**

VIA GIUSEPPE

Musei Reali Torino ④
① Duomo
⑩ Palazzo Reale

CORSO REGINA MARGHERITA
CORSO S. GIULIA

VIA GARIBALDI · **VIA SAN TOMMASO**

Armeria Reale
Giardini Reali

ℹ️ PIAZZA CASTELLO

Giardini di Levante

CORSO S. MAURIZIO

VIA SAN FRANCESCO D'ASSISI · **VIA GIUSEPPE BERTOLA** · **VIA P. MICCA**

VIA ROMA

Palazzo ②
Madama

Teatro Regio

VIA C. BATTISTI

VIA ROSSINI · VIA MONTEBELLO

VIA S. TERESA

VIA GIUSEPPE

Museo ③
Egizio

Palazzo ⑤
Carignano

Mole Antonelliana/ ⑨
Museo del Cinema

VIA V. ALFIERI

VIA M. VITTORIA

VIA GIAMBATTISTA BOGINO

VIA PRINCIPE AMEDEO

VIA PO · VIA SANT'OTTAVIO · VIA VERDI

⑧
Piazza San Carlo

DA PAOLA

PIAZZA CARLO EMANUELE II

VIA XX SETTEMBRE · **VIA ROMA** · **VIA GRAMSCI** · **VIA GIUSEPPE LUIGI LAGRANGE** · **VIA CARLO ALBERTO** · **VIA CAVOUR**

VIA SAN MASSIMO

VIA MARIA VITTORIA

PIAZZA VITTORIO VENETO

PIAZZALE VALDO FUSI

VIA GIOVANNI GIOLITTI

PIAZZA MARIA TERESA

🚉 Stazione Porta Nuova

PIAZZA CARLO FELICE

PIAZZA BODONI

VIA SAN FRANCESCO

VIA ACCADEMIA ALBERTINA

PIAZZA CAVOUR

VIA CAVOUR

CORSO VITTORIO EMANUELE II

VIA SAN MASSIMO DEI

VIA G.

VIA FRATELLI CALANDRA

MILLE

MAZZINI

CORSO CAIROLI

VIA NIZZA · **VIA SALUZZO** · **VIA GOITO** · **VIA SANT'ANSELMO** · **VIA B. GALLIARI**

Parco del Valentino ⑥

Ponte Umberto I

C. MONCALIERI

PO

↙ ⑦ *Pinacoteca Giovanni e Marella Agnelli* 3.5km (2 miles)

The sober square bell tower, which pre-dates the rest of the church by 20 years, stands in refreshing contrast to Turin's sumptuous Baroque buildings.

Timeline

1st century BC
Turin is settled by the Romans.

15th century
▶ University of Turin is established.

1536
▶ Emanuele Filiberto of Savoy moves his capital to Turin.

1861–5
Turin becomes the first capital of the newly unified Italy.

1899
▶ The Agnelli family creates the car company Fiat (Fabbrica Italiana Automobili Torino).

1993
▶ Turin football team Juventus wins the UEFA cup for the third time.

↑ Palazzo Madama, home to the Museo Civico d'Arte Antica

191

③
Museo Egizio

📍 Via Accademia delle Scienze 6 🕐 9am-2pm Mon, 9am-6:30pm Tue-Sat 🌐 museoegizio.it

Turin owes its magnificent Egyptian Museum to the collection of Piedmont-born Bernardo Drovetti, who was stationed in Egypt as French Consul General at the time of the Napoleonic Wars. The items on display are arranged in chronological order, from 4000 BC to AD 700.

The ground floor hosts statues in rooms decorated by the Oscar-winning set designer Dante Ferretti, plus the reconstruction of the 15th-century-BC Rock Temple of Ellesija.

On the first floor is the Coffin Gallery, featuring very fine coffins, such as the 14th-century-BC Tomb of Kha and Merit, complete with the food, tools and ornaments buried with them for the afterlife.

The Papyrus Room holds a collection of enormous interest to scholars: one document, the Royal Papyrus, lists all the pharaohs up to the 17th dynasty, with their dates. The museum holds three different versions of the Book of the Dead, including the oldest known copy. On the second floor are artifacts from the Old Kingdom to the New Kingdom.

④
Musei Reali Torino

📍 Via XX Settembre 86 🕐 9am-7:30pm Tue-Sun; last adm: 6pm 🌐 musei reali.beniculturali.it

The collection of artworks that make up the Galleria Sabauda was originally started in the mid- to late 1400s, and it has been expanded over the centuries by the Savoy family.

The artworks are exhibited on four floors in chronological order, from medieval times to the 1700s, in large, bright rooms with self-explanatory labels and multimedia aids.

Among works of particular interest from the Italian schools are Antonio and Paolo Pollaiolo's 15th-century *Tobias and the Archangel Raphael*, the *Ritratto di Gentiluomo* by Bronzino and a *Madonna con Bambino* by Beato Angelico. Mantegna, Bellini and Veronese are among the other Italian artists represented here. Dutch and Flemish works include important paintings such as Jan Van Eyck's *St Francis* (15th century) and Rembrandt's *Old Man Sleeping* (17th century), as well as several portraits by Van Dyck. The fourth floor hosts the Gualino Collection, which contains Roman archaeological finds, Oriental artworks and a *Venere* (Venus) by Botticelli.

⑤
Palazzo Carignano

📍 Via Accademia delle Scienze 5 🕐 10am-6pm Tue-Sun (last adm: 5pm) 🌐 museorisorgimento torino.it

This Baroque palazzo is not only Guarini's masterpiece; it is arguably the finest building in Turin, with its magnificent brick façade and ornate rotunda. It was built in 1679 for the Carignano family – an offshoot of the main House of Savoy and ancestors of the Italian kings – but came into its own in the 1800s. Italy's first king, Vittorio Emanuele II, was born here in 1820.

The palazzo is now home to the Museo Nazionale del Risorgimento Italiano, which, through paintings and a collection of artifacts, tells the story of Italy's unification. It introduces Mazzini, Cavour and Garibaldi – key figures in the Risorgimento.

---

⑥
Parco del Valentino

📍 Corso Massimo d'Azeglio 🕐 9am-7pm daily (Borgo Medioevale); 10am-6pm Tue-Sun (castle); mid-Apr-mid-Oct: 9am-noon Mon-Fri, 3-7pm Sat, 10am-1pm, 3-7pm Sun (Orto Botanico) 🌐 parcovalentino.it

This park contains the Borgo Medioevale, a complex of medieval buildings that was built for the General Italian exhibition of 1884. The edifices show different constructions and designs, based on traditional regional houses and castles.

The Orto Botanico, beside the castle, is an impressive botanical garden.

←

Kha and his wife Merit adoring Osiris, from the Tomb of Kha, Museo Egizio

←

Statue of Duke Emanuele Filiberto in the centre of Piazza San Carlo

and houses the National Cinema Museum, which is widely believed to be the world's tallest museum.

⑩
Palazzo Reale/ Polo Reale

🏛 Piazzetta Reale
🕐 8:30am-7:30pm Tue-Sun; last adm: 6:20pm
🌐 museireali.beniculturali.it/palazzo-reale/

Behind this palace's austere façade, designed by Amedeo di Castellamonte, lie richly decorated state apartments; the ceilings were painted by Morello, Miel and Seyter in the 17th century. The splendid furnishings date from the 17th to the 19th centuries; they include the Chinese Cabinet, the Alcove Room, the lavish Throne Room, and the Scala delle Forbici, or Scissor Stairs, created by Juvarra in 1720.

Pinacoteca Giovanni e Marella Agnelli

🏛 Lingotto, Via Nizza 230/130 🕐 10am-7pm Tue-Sun (last adm: 6:15pm)
🌐 pinacoteca-agnelli.it

Located on the roof of the former Fiat factory (which has been redesigned by architect Renzo Piano), this museum displays art dating from between the 18th and 20th centuries, including works by Picasso, Matisse and Manet.

---

⑧
Piazza San Carlo

The ensemble of Baroque architecture on this square has earned it the nickname "Turin's drawing room". At its southern end are the twin churches of Santa Cristina and San Carlo; both were built in the 1630s, though the former has a Baroque façade, designed by Juvarra in the 18th century. At the centre of the square stands a 19th-century statue of Duke Emanuele

Filiberto. The work, by Carlo Marocchetti, has become an emblem of the city. The Galleria San Federico, in the northwestern corner, is a stylish shopping arcade.

---

⑨
Mole Antonelliana/ Museo del Cinema

🏛 Via Montebello 20 ☎ 011 813 85 60/61 🕐 9am-8pm Wed-Mon (to 11pm Sat); last adm: 1 hour before closing
🌐 museocinema.it

This building is an unmissably tall landmark on Turin's skyline. It looks like a glorified lightning conductor: indeed, in 1953 an electrical storm damaged the top, which was replaced. The 167-m (550-ft) Mole, by Alessandro Antonelli (1798–1888), was meant to be a synagogue. On completion in 1889, the city left it for years without a use before it eventually housed the Risorgimento museum between 1908 and 1938. Today, the building provides panoramic views from its lift

THE HOLY SHROUD

The most famous - and the most dubious - holy relic of them all is kept in the Duomo. The shroud, said to be the winding-sheet in which Christ was wrapped after His crucifixion, owes its fame to the fact that it bears the imprint of a crucified man.

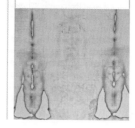

Pretty Isola San Giulio, sitting in the middle of Lake Orta ↑

EXPERIENCE MORE

❸
Domodossola

🅰B1 🚋Verbania 🚊🚌
ℹ️Piazza Matteotti 24;
www.prodomodossola.it

At the centre of this mountain town of Roman origin lies the Piazza Mercato, or market square, framed by attractive arcades and houses from the 15th and 16th centuries. Pretty villages to the north include Crodo, with its cold-water mineral spas, and Baceno, where a 14th- to 16th-century church contains fine frescoes and wood carvings.

❹
Lake Orta

🅰B1

Tiny Lake Orta snakes through mountains and woodlands. Orta San Giulio, a medieval village on a peninsula on the eastern coast, is known for Sacro Monte, a UNESCO-listed place of pilgrimage and worship on a hill overlooking the water. In the centre of the lake, Isola San Giulio, accessible by boat, is home to the 12th-century Basilica di San Giulio. There are good hiking routes around the lake.

❺
Varallo

🅰B1 🚋Vercelli 🚊🚌
ℹ️Corso Roma 38; www.
atlvalsesiavercelli.it

The small town of Varallo is home to the remarkable **Santa Maria delle Grazie**. This late 15th-century church is notable for its beautiful frescoed wall depicting the *Life of Christ* and *trompe l'oeil* architectural elements, painted by Gaudenzio Ferrari (1484–1546).

A long stairway behind the church climbs up to the Sacro Monte, a religious community built at an altitude of about 610 m (2,000 ft) under the patronage of the Archbishop of Milan, San Carlo Borromeo.

The Basilica dell'Assunta is a riot of Baroque architecture. Dotted around it are over 40 chapels with statues and painted figures positioned in front of frescoed backdrops painted by Gaudenzio Ferrari, Tanzio da Varallo and others.

Santa Maria delle Grazie
📍Piazza Ferrari ⏰Daily
🌐sacromontedivarallo.com

ALPINE TOWNS

The smaller towns of the Val d'Aosta region are popular with Italians during the summer months for their lakes and cycling paths. Come winter, they draw skiers and snowboarders from around the world. Outside Turin, the town of Cuneo is popular with locals for its pretty medieval centre and proximity to the ski slopes. Similarly, the Alpine villages of Sestriere and Bardonecchia come alive in winter, as do the resorts of Courmayeur and Cervinia. Further off the beaten track is Macugnaga, a small mountain village popular with hikers and mountaineers.

6

Aosta

A1 FS □ **i** Piazza Porta Pretoria 3; www.lovevda.it

Surrounded by mountains, the town of Aosta combines ancient culture and spectacular scenery. The Romans captured it from the Gauls in 25 BC, and Aosta is still dotted with fine Roman architecture built in honour of Emperor Augustus – indeed the town was once called Augusta Praetoria. The centre still consists of a grid of large squares.

EAT

Edera

Locals come here for the excellent seasonal fish and meat menu.

B1 Via Bersani 15, Orta San Giulio **w** ristoranteedera orta.com

€€€

Pizzeria La Campana

Crisp-based pizzas with simple toppings in a casual environment.

B1 Via Giovanetti 43, Orta San Giulio **□** 0322 90 211

€€€

Taverna Antico Agnello

Enjoy dishes such as pasta with rabbit ragout, and duck breast.

B1 Via Solaroli 5, Miasino **w** ristorante anticoagnello.com

€€€

Roman Ruins

□ Via Baillage (Roman Theatre), Piazza Papa Giovanni XXIII (Roman Forum) **□** Daily

In Roman times, entry to Aosta was through the Arch of Augustus, a triumphal arch now marred by a roof added in the 18th century. Ahead stands the Porta Pretoria, its double row of stone arches flanked by a medieval tower. Also worth a look is the 20-m- (65-ft-) high façade of the Roman Theatre. A little to the north is the amphitheatre, although this is almost completely buried apart from three columns. In the old town lies the Roman Forum, or marketplace.

Cattedrale

□ Piazza Papa Giovanni XXIII **□** 0165 40 413 **□** Daily; 3–5pm Sat & Sun (Museo del Tesoro) **□** For mass

This relatively modest shrine to St John the Baptist has a Gothic interior with floor mosaics and finely carved 15th-century choir stalls. Next door, the Museo del Tesoro contains a rich collection of statuettes and reliquaries.

Sant'Orso

□ Via Sant'Orso **□** Daily

East of the town walls is this medieval church complex. Sant'Orso itself has a Gothic façade. The interior has 11th-

↑ Painted statues in a biblical scene decorating a chapel at the Sacro Monte

century frescoes and a crypt holding the tomb of St Orso, patron saint of Aosta.

Castello di Fénis

□ Fénis **□** 0165 76 42 63 **□** Daily **□** Oct–Mar: Mon, 1 Jan, 25 Dec

Just 12 km east of Aosta, this castle has a well-preserved interior with frescoes and wooden galleries.

Castello di Issogne

□ Issogne **□** 0125 92 93 73 **□** Daily **□** Oct–Mar: Mon

This picturesque medieval castle is located 38 km (23 miles) to the southeast of Aosta. Decorative motifs here include a fountain with a centrepiece in the shape of a pomegranate tree.

→ Roman ruins in Aosta, with the dramatic background of the Alps

7

Sacra di San Michele

🅰A2 🏠Strada Sacra San Michele 🚍May-Sep: Sun pm from Avigliana & Turin 🕐9:30am-12:30pm & 2:30-5pm Tue-Sun (mid-Mar-mid-Oct: to 6pm) 🌐sacradi sanmichele.com

This abbey complex is perched halfway up Monte Pirchiriano, at 962 m (3,156 ft). Its monastic community was founded around AD 1000. During its prime, the abbey attracted pilgrims on their way to Rome, and as a result it grew enormously powerful. It was subsequently looted several times, before falling into decline and eventually being suppressed in 1662.

The sanctuary is reached by climbing 154 steep steps hewn out of the rock. At the top of this stairway, known as the Scalone dei Morti (Stairway of the Dead), is the Romanesque Porta dello Zodiaco, a doorway carved with creatures and symbols relating to the signs of the zodiac. The church itself dates from the 12th–13th centuries. The interior houses 15th- and 16th-century paintings and frescoes, and a 16th-century triptych by the Piedmontese artist Defendente Ferrari.

8

Avigliana

🅰A2 🏠Turin 🚉🚍 ℹCorso Laghi 389; www.turismo avigliana.it

Perched beside two glacier-fed lakes and encircled by tall mountains, Avigliana looks breathtakingly beautiful. It is overlooked by the ruins of a castle, which was once the home of the Counts of Savoy.

The medieval houses here are largely unspoiled, particularly in the two main piazzas, Santa Maria and Conte Rosso. The church of San Giovanni (13th–14th century) contains early 16th-century paintings by Defendente Ferrari.

9

Vercelli

🅰B2 🚉🚍 ℹViale Garibaldi 90; www.atlvalsesia vercelli.it

Set in a vast plain of paddy fields, Vercelli is the rice capital of Europe. The town also developed its own school of painting in the 1500s. The **Museo Borgogna** is the best place to admire the town's Renaissance masterpieces.

The city's main architectural treasure is the 13th-century Basilica di Sant'Andrea, said to be the first example of Italian architecture to be influenced by the Gothic style of northern France – note the vaulted nave and flying buttresses. Overall, however, the Basilica, built from 1219 to 1227, remains a stunning achievement in Romanesque architecture. The façade changes colour halfway up, the blue-grey of the lower part turning to red and white in the twin towers. Off the north side is a 13th-century cloister framed by arcades.

The church of **San Cristoforo** houses frescoes and a fine *Madonna degli Aranci* (both c.1529) by Gaudenzio Ferrari.

Museo Borgogna

 🏠Via A Borgogna 4/6 🕐Tue-Fri pm, Sat am (Mar-mid-May also pm), Sun am & pm 🌐museoborgogna.it

San Cristoforo

🏠Via S Cristoforo 5 📞0161 25 80 00 🕐Daily

⑩ Novara

A B2 **FS** 🚌 **ℹ** Baluardo Quintino Sella 40; www.turismonovara.it

Novara's arcaded streets, squares and historic buildings exude a quiet affluence. Many of the main buildings – like the Renaissance courtyard of the Broletto (town hall), with its graceful 15th-century red-brick arcades and covered stairway – stand around Piazza della Repubblica.

Across the piazza is the **Duomo**, rebuilt in around 1865 in Neo-Classical style. It contains Renaissance paintings of the Vercelli school and Flemish tapestries, as well as the remains of an earlier sanctuary on this site: these include the frescoed 12th-century chapel of San Siro and the 15th-century cloisters. The octagonal **Baptistry** next door is painted with medieval scenes of the Apocalypse. The **Museo della Canonica del Duomo**, beside the Duomo, has tombstones and inscriptions from the Roman and early Christian eras.

The forbidding abbey complex of Sacra di San Michele

DOUJA D'OR ASTI

On the second Sunday of September, Asti comes alive with a foodie festival that lasts three days and is said to be one of the truest representations of gastronomic country life in Italy. Farmers and producers from the province serve their best dishes and wines, including polenta, truffles, roasted meats and pastas. It's one of the region's most popular festivals, so it's advisable to book accommodation early.

A few streets away stands the **Basilica di San Gaudenzio**. It is crowned by an elongated four-tiered dome and spire. Designed by Alessandro Antonelli, it is reminiscent of his Mole Antonelliana in Turin *(p193)*. At the top of the spire, which is 121 m (400 ft) high, is a statue of San Gaudenzio himself. Inside, the late 16th-century church contains a fine collection of Renaissance and Baroque paintings by artists from Piedmont. These include a notable 17th-century battle scene by Tanzio da Varallo and a 16th-century altarpiece by Gaudenzio Ferrari.

Duomo & Baptistry

A Piazza della Repubblica **☎** 0321 66 16 35 **🕐** 9:30am-noon & 3-5:30pm Sat & Sun

Museo della Canonica del Duomo

A Vicolo della Canonica 9 **🕐** 3-6pm Sat & Sun **W** novariae.it

Basilica di San Gaudenzio

A Via S Gaudenzio 22 **☎** 0321 62 98 94 **🕐** 8am-noon & 2:30-7pm daily

⑪ Asti

A B2 **FS** 🚌 **ℹ** Piazza Alfieri 34; www.astiturismo.it

Renowned for its *spumante* (sparkling) wine, Asti is a noble city of medieval towers and elegant churches.

On the triangular Piazza Alfieri a statue commemorates the local poet and dramatist

↑ A bust of the 18th-century poet Vittorio Alfieri, born in Asti

Vittorio Alfieri (1749–1803). Corso Alfieri runs the entire length of the old city centre. At its eastern end stands the 15th-century church of San Pietro in Consavia, with its terracotta decoration, 17th-century frescoes and attractive cloister. Beside it is the circular Romanesque Baptistry dating from the 10th to the 12th centuries.

West of Piazza Alfieri is the Collegiata di San Secondo (13th–15th century), which houses a Renaissance polyptych by Gandolfino d'Asti and 15th-century frescoes. The area around the western section of Corso Alfieri contains a few of the medieval towers for which the town was once famous. The nearby 14th-century Gothic Duomo holds 18th-century frescoes, and two 12th- to 13th-century carvings on the west corner of the transept.

❶❷ Alba

🅰 A2 🏛 Comune Cuneo
ℹ️ Piazza Risorgimento 2;
www.langheroero.it

Piemonte's gastronomic capital, Alba is the home of Ferrero, Italy's most famous chocolate export, and of the precious white truffle. Grape lovers come to the region for the excellent Barbera d'Alba and Barolo wines. The town itself is charming, with cobbled streets leading to medieval buildings and palaces. The main drag of Via Cavour takes visitors to Piazza del Duomo, and the striking 11th-century Gothic Cathedral of San Lorenzo. From there, many choose to climb the Sineo, Bonino and Artesiano towers, with spectacular views over the city. Via Vittorio Emanuele snakes past local restaurants and cafés before arriving at the 15th-century Do House on Via Calissano, decorated with imprinted terracotta friezes.

Some excellent artwork can be found in the city, namely at the town hall, where the Caravaggio-style *Piccolo Concerto* by Mattia Preti stands, as well as a spectacular altarpiece by the avant-garde artist Pinot Gallizio. In nearby Piazza Savona, restaurants and bars do a roaring trade at lunch and in the evening, when locals gather for a pre-dinner cocktail under the arches.

TRUFFLES

Alba's white truffle is among the world's most valuable fungi, often selling for thousands of euros at auction. These truffles are foraged in the woods around Alba, with dogs trained to sniff them out. The town's biggest event is the annual White Truffle Fair (October-November).

❶❸ Bossea Caves

🅰 A2 🏛 Località Bossea,
Comune Frabosa Soprana
🚉 Mondovì 🚌 From
Mondovì 🕐 Daily for
guided tours only
🌐 grottadibossea.com

Some 25 km (16 miles) south of Mondovì, near the end of a scenic route that follows the valley of the Torrente Corsaglia up into the Maritime Alps, are the caves of Bossea, some of the finest in Italy. The series of caves contains remarkable stalactite columns and shapes that have formed over many hundreds of thousands of years. Guided tours lead through different chambers – some of them surprisingly vast – following the underground rivers and lakes. The fascinating skeleton of a prehistoric bear

called *Ursus spelaeus*, which was discovered here, is also on display.

Bring a sweater – the temperature rarely rises above 9°C (50°F).

❶❹ Garessio

🅰 A3 🏛 Comune Cuneo
🚉🚌 ℹ️ Corso Statuto 1;
www.garessio.net

One of the most attractive resorts of the Maritime Alps, Garessio is little more than a sprinkling of houses spread out over the hills, surrounded by woods of chestnut trees. It is also a very popular spa destination.

According to legend, the waters here have miraculous powers: in about AD 980 an octogenarian nobleman found

↑ Low sun in an autumnal landscape in the hills of Le Langhe

instant relief from his circulatory problems by drinking the mineral-rich water. Since then, the waters have been drunk for their remedial properties – linked in particular with the relief of diuretic and digestive problems – and for their refreshing taste.

The town of Ormea, 12 km (7 miles) southwest, is known for its ruined 11th-century castle, its church with late 14th-century Gothic frescoes and its attractive houses.

Le Langhe

 A2

Piedmont's Langhe hills are best known for their wines, cheese and white truffles, making it a gastronome's paradise. The region is listed by UNESCO as a World Heritage Site, thanks to unique winemaking traditions that combine historical methods with modern machinery. Hiking is popular here, thanks

The red rooftops of the town of Alba, famous for its truffles

to Le Langhe's rolling hills, topped with medieval towns such as Alba, Serralunga, Morra and Verduno.

Cuneo

 A2 FS🚌 𝒊 Via Amedeo II 8a; www.cuneoholiday. com

Cuneo in Italian means "wedge-shaped", and this perfectly describes the sliver of land that this town occupies at the confluence of two rivers, the Gesso and the Stura di Demonte. In early November the town hosts the regional cheese fair, with unusual local cheese varieties.

Cuneo centres on a large square, Piazza Galimberti, with its old arcades, where traders come to hawk their wares every Tuesday. Much of the town was rebuilt in the 18th and 19th centuries, providing Cuneo with wide, tree-lined boulevards, though the impressive viaduct that takes the railway line into town dates from the 1930s. The 18th-century church of Santa Croce has a pretty concave façade, designed by Francesco Gallo.

EAT

Restaurant Larossa
Expect a new spin on Piedmontese cuisine, including truffles, at this restaurant.

⌂ Via Don Giacomo Alberione 10d, Alba
🖥 ristorantelarossa.com

€€€

Osteria dei Sognatori
Head to this local spot for roasted and stewed meats, fresh vegetables and truffle pasta.

⌂ Via Macrino 8, Alba
📞 333 787 9230

€€€

La Piola
A small, buzzy bistro with a weekly changing menu of dishes made from local produce. Truffles regularly feature in the fare.

⌂ Piazza Risorgimento 4, Alba 🖥 lapiola-alba.it

€€€

LIGURIA

Backed by steep hillsides glittering with olive trees, Liguria looks out over the Tyrrhenian Sea. For centuries maritime trade was a mainstay, bringing sugar, salt and fish – the flavours of the region's cuisine – to the coast, along with prosperity. West of the bustling city of Genoa are sandy beaches, while the southeast offers walks between picturesque Cinque Terre fishing villages.

Genoa has a long history as a seafaring power, achieving greatness first as a trading post with ancient Greece and Phoenicia and, later, as the capital of a small commercial empire that at one stage eclipsed even Venice. The great sea admiral Andrea Doria came from Genoa, as did the 15th-century explorer Christopher Columbus.

Genoa's rise began in the 12th century, when it succeeded in beating the Saracen pirates that plagued the Ligurian coast. Thereafter, the maritime republic prospered, profiting from the Crusades to set up trading posts in the Middle East and marshalling its naval might to humble its rivals. The golden age lasted from the 16th to the mid-17th century. Factionalism among the ruling aristocracy and foreign conquest, by the French in 1668 and the Austrians in 1734, led to the region's decline. It was only in the early 19th century, with unification fervour spreading thanks to native son Giuseppe Mazzini and the revolutionary Garibaldi, that Liguria recaptured a glimpse of its former prominence.

Today, sheltered by the steep slopes that rise from the sea, faded, elegant mansions lie along the coast, particularly in Sanremo, where aristocrats came to spend the winter at the end of the 19th century.

FRANCE

Ligurian
Sea

VALLE D'AOSTA
AND PIEDMONT
p180

PIEDMONT

GROTTE DI
TOIRANO **10**

9 ALBENGA

8 CERVO

DOLCEACQUA

5

BUSSANA
VECCHIA

7

6 SAN REMO

3 **4**

BALZI
ROSSI

VILLA
HANBURY

LIGURIA

Sardinia,
Tunisia

LIGURIA

Must Sees
1 Genoa
2 Cinque Terre

Experience More
3 Balzi Rossi
4 Villa Hanbury
5 Dolceacqua
6 San Remo
7 Bussana Vecchia
8 Cervo
9 Albenga
10 Grotte di Toirano
11 Camogli
12 Portofino Peninsula
13 Rapallo
14 Portovenere
15 Lerici

The impressive fountain on Piazza de Ferrari in the heart of Genoa ↑

GENOA

🅰B2 ✈Cristoforo Colombo 6 km (4 miles) W 🚉Stazione Principe, Piazza Acquaverde ⛴Stazione Marittima, Ponte dei Mille ℹAeroporto Cristoforo Colombo; www.visitgenoa.it

There is something refreshingly rough-edged about Genoa (Genova in Italian), Italy's most important commercial port. In contrast to the genteel resorts along the neighbouring coast, the narrow streets of the old town have a gritty industrial feel to them. With its natural harbour and the mountains to protect it, Genoa rose to prominence as a sea-based power. The palazzi of Via Balbi and Via Garibaldi, and the paintings and sculptures dotted around the city in churches and museums, are among the finest in northwestern Italy.

① 🖉

San Lorenzo (Duomo)

🏛Piazza San Lorenzo
📞010 247 18 31 🕐Daily

The Duomo, with its black-and-white-striped exterior, blends many architectural styles, from the 12th-century Romanesque side portal of San Giovanni to the Baroque touches of some of its chapels.

The most sumptuous of the chapels is dedicated to St John the Baptist, patron saint of the city; it includes a 13th-century sarcophagus that once held the venerated saint's relics.

Steps lead down from the sacristy to the **Museo del Tesoro di San Lorenzo**. It houses such treasures as a glass dish said to have been used at the Last Supper, and the plate on which the head of John the Baptist was allegedly served up to Salome.

Museo del Tesoro di San Lorenzo

📞010 254 12 50 🕐9am-noon & 3-6pm Mon-Sat

② 🖉 🍴 🛍

The Port

The port is the heart of Genoa and the origin of its power as a seafaring city state in the 11th and 12th centuries. A workaday place, it is ringed by roads and 1960s buildings.

Among the vestiges of its medieval glory is the Lanterna lighthouse (restored in 1543) near the Stazione Marittima. Fires would be lit at the top of the Lanterna to guide ships into port. Today, regeneration of the port is in part due to the Renzo Piano-designed conference centre and the **Aquarium**, one of the largest in Europe and teeming with diverse marine life.

Aquarium

🏛Ponte Spinola 🕐Mar-Jun & Sep-Oct: 9am-8pm Mon-Fri, 8:30am-9pm Sat-Sun & pub hols; Jul-Aug: 8:30am-10pm; 🔗acquariodigenova.it

🔍 HIDDEN GEM
Sant'Andrea

The pretty 12th-century cloisters standing in this garden are all that remain of the convent that once stood here.

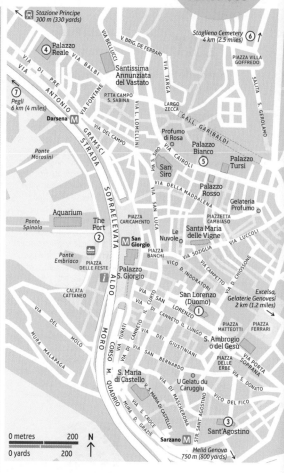

STAY

Meliá Genova

This five-star hotel has bright and airy rooms and suites decorated in subdued, neutral hues. There are in-room tea- and coffee-making facilities, and the bathrooms are spacious.

⌂ Via Corsica 4
🌐 melia.com

€€€

Le Nuvole

Set in a 16th-century palace decorated with 17th-century frescoes, Le Nuvole has been meticulously restored to its former glory. Rooms are chic and contemporary, with big, airy windows designed to let in plenty of light. Breakfast is very good, and there is a free afternoon buffet and cocktail hour every day.

⌂ Piazza delle Vigne 6
🌐 hotellenuvole.it

€€€

③
Sant'Agostino

⌂ Piazza Sarzano 35

This Gothic church was begun in 1260, but destroyed in World War II. It is now deconsecrated and all that remains of the original building is the Gothic bell tower, decorated with coloured tiles. The monastery, of which the church was once a part, was also bombed. What remained were two ruined cloisters – one of which forms the only triangular building in Genoa. The cloisters have been converted into the **Museo di Architettura e Scultura Ligure**, which houses the city's collection of architectural

pieces, some dating back to the Roman era, along with fragments of sculpture and frescoes – all salvaged from Genoa's other destroyed churches. The finest piece is a fragment from the tomb of Margaret of Brabant, who died in 1311. She was the wife of Emperor Henry VII, who invaded Italy in 1310. Carved by Giovanni Pisano around 1313, the sculptures from her tomb were restored in 1987.

Museo di Architettura e Scultura Ligure

♿ 📞 010 251 12 63 🕐 10 Oct–26 Mar: 9:30am–6:30pm Tue–Sun; 27 Mar–9 Oct: 9am–7pm Tue–Fri, 10am–7:30pm Sat & Sun 🚫 Pub hols

EAT

Here are the best *gelaterie* in Genoa.

Gelateria Profumo

The decor is old-fashioned and so are the flavours but that's part of the magic. Make sure you try the pistachio and *crema* flavours.

 Vico Superiore del Ferro 14 🗓 Sun & Mon

€€€

Profumo di Rosa

At ice-cream shop, Rosa prepares all the *gelato* herself. *Fragola* (strawberry) is the most popular flavour.

 Via Cairoli 13 🗓 Sun

€€€

Excelsa

This *gelateria* does *gelato* in tiny dessert cups, with interesting flavour combinations such as salted caramel and peanuts.

 Via Oreste de Gaspari 12-14

€€€

U Gelatu du Caruggiu

Whipped cream and nuts will be added to every order here.

 Via di San Bernardo 🗓 Mon

€€€

Gelaterie Genovesi

Sorbets are the best pick here: choose from lemon, strawberry, raspberry or chocolate.

 Corso Sardegna 1 🗓 Sat

€€€

Palazzo Reale

📍 Via Balbi 10 🕐 9am-7pm Tue-Fri, 1:30-7pm Sat & Sun; last adm: 30 mins before closing 🗓 1 Jan, 1 May, 25 Dec 🌐 palazzoreale genova.beniculturali.it

Used by members of the House of Savoy royal family from the 17th century onwards, this austere-looking residence has a highly ornate Rococo interior – most notably in its ballroom and its Hall of Mirrors. Among the collection of old master paintings is a *Crucifixion* by Van Dyck. The pretty garden, which slopes down towards the old port, includes an intriguing cobble-stone mosaic around the central fountain, depicting houses and animals.

Opposite the palace is the old university (1634), which was designed by Bartolomeo Bianco, as was much of Via Balbi. The large building brilliantly overcomes Genoa's hilly topography, and is constructed on four levels.

Palazzo Bianco

📍 Via Garibaldi 11 📞 010 557 21 93 🕐 10 Oct-26 Mar: 9am-6:30pm Tue-Fri, 8:30am-6:30pm Sat & Sun; 27 Mar-9 Oct: 9am-7pm Tue-Fri, 10am-7:30pm Sat & Sun 🗓 25 Dec

The Palazzo Bianco is situated on Genoa's most beautiful street, Via Garibaldi, where there are numerous fine 16th-century mansions and palazzi. It houses the city's best collection of paintings, including wonderful works by Filippino Lippi, Veronese and Caravaggio, as well as pieces by Dutch and Flemish masters Rubens, Van Dyck and Memling. Paintings by local Genoese artists such as Luca Cambiaso, Bernardo Strozzi and Domenico Piola are also on display. At No. 9 Via Garibaldi, **Palazzo Tursi** hosts the Lord Mayor's boardrooms, as well as an extension of the Palazzo Bianco Gallery. Across the street in the **Palazzo Rosso** is another great art

CHRISTOPHER COLUMBUS IN GENOA

The name of Cristoforo Colombo, or Christopher Columbus, as English speakers know him, is in evidence all over Genoa. A statue of the explorer of the New World greets those emerging into Piazza Acquaverde from Porta Principe railway station and various public buildings bear his name. In 17th-century Palazzo Belimbau, built on top of the old city walls, is a series of frescoes by the local artist Tavarone celebrating the explorer's life, and three of his letters are in the Sala del Sindaco in Palazzo Tursi (the city hall) on Via Garibaldi. It is not certain whether Columbus (c.1451–1506) was born in Genoa, in Savona, 15 km (9 miles) to the west, or even outside Italy. However, city registers mention his father and various family homes within the city. The small ivy-clad house adjacent to Porta Soprana may have been Columbus's childhood home.

collection, featuring works by Caravaggio and Dürer, as well as ceramics and furniture.

Palazzo Tursi
⊗ 【 010 557 21 93
🕒 As for Palazzo Bianco

Palazzo Rosso
⊗ 【 010 275 91 85
🕒 As for Palazzo Bianco

←

Cobblestone mosaic around the fountain at the Palazzo Reale

Staglieno Cemetery

🏛 Piazzale Resasco, Staglieno 【 010 87 01 84
🕒 7:30am–5pm daily
🚫 Public hols

Established in 1844, this grandiose cemetery is situated just over the hills northeast of Genoa along the Bisagno River, and is so large that it has its own bus system. The cemetery's tombs and monuments make up an eerie city of miniature cathedrals, Art Nouveau palaces and Egyptian temples. Its most famous resident is Giuseppe Mazzini, the Genoese revolutionary who died near Pisa in 1872.

Pegli

Until World War II, the town of Pegli, 6 km (4 miles) west of the city centre, was a popular weekend retreat for rich Genoese. Now it forms part of the city, but maintains an air of tranquillity thanks mainly to its picturesque public parks and its two famous villas: the **Villa Durazzo-Pallavicini** and the **Villa Doria Centurione, Museo Navale**.

The 19th-century Villa Durazzo-Pallavicini houses an archaeological museum relating the pre-Roman history of the Ligurian coast. The villa's 19th-century garden is landscaped with romantic grottoes, pavilions and fountains. It also has a small botanical garden that contains a number of interesting specimens.

The 16th-century Villa Doria Centurione is now a naval history museum celebrating Genoa's glorious maritime past. Among the exhibits on display here are compasses, astrolabes, globes, model ships and a portrait of Columbus, ascribed to Ghirlandaio, probably dating from 1525.

Villa Durazzo-Pallavicini
🏛 Via Pallavicini 11, Pegli
【 010 698 10 48 🕒 9am–7pm Tue–Fri (from 10am Sat & Sun) 🚫 Pub hols

Villa Doria Centurione, Museo Navale
🏛 Piazza Bonavino 7, Pegli
【 010 696 98 85 🕒 9am–1:30pm Tue–Fri (6pm Sat, 1pm Sun) 🚫 Pub hols

↑ Pastel-coloured houses perched on the cliffside at Monterosso al Mare

❷

CINQUE TERRE

🅰B3 🚊La Spezia, Lerici & Porto Venere 🚉To all towns
🌐parconazionale5terre.it

The Cinque Terre are five villages – Monterosso al Mare, Vernazza, Corniglia, Manarola and Riomaggiore – located along the rocky coastline of the Riviera di Levante. Clinging dramatically to the steep cliffs, these villages are linked only by an ancient footpath known as the Sentiero Azzurro (Blue Path), which offers some spectacular views of the rocky coastline and terraced vineyards that produce the local dry white wines. The footpath also provides access to secluded beaches. The best way to visit the villages is by boat or by train.

① Monterosso al Mare

The largest of the five Cinque Terre villages, Monterosso al Mare, is situated to the northwest and overlooks a wide bay with its own sandy beach. Picturesque streets are lined with lemon trees and olive groves, and lead to a centre divided in two: the new development, Fegina, with bustling hotels and restaurants; and the old village of Monterosso, with narrow cobbled streets and pastel-coloured houses.

② Vernazza

The fishing village of Vernazza is a warren of quaint, cobbled streets linked by *arpaie* (steep steps). Founded around 1000 AD, the village straddles a large rocky promontory. The main throughfare, Via Roma, stretches from the tiny harbour (Cinque Terre's only natural port) to Piazza Marconi, with plenty of cafés, bars and restaurants dotted along the way. Head further inland and wander up Vernazza's *caruggi* (narrow lanes) for sea views.

③ Corniglia

Perched at the pinnacle of rocky terraces and hemmed in by vineyards, Corniglia seems untouched by the passage of time. From the train station it is best to take a shuttle bus in, or, if you're feeling fit, head for the 377-step stairway that leads to the centre.

④ Manarola

Linked by the famous Via dell'Amore (Lovers' Lane) to Riomaggiore, a 15-minute walk away, Manarola is idyllic in every sense of the word. The oldest village of the

> 💬 INSIDER TIP
> **Best Time to Visit the Villages**
>
> The best time to visit the Cinque Terre for hiking and swimming is from mid-April to mid-October. Avoid August, when hotel prices sky-rocket and the hiking trails and beaches become very crowded.

STAY

Hotel Porto Roca
A charming hotel with
an infinity pool, sea
views and an excellent
on-site restaurant.

🏠 Via Corone 1,
Monterosso al Mare
🌐 portoroca.it

$$$

La Mala
A lovely family-run
B&B with stunning
seaside views.

🏠 Via San Giovanni
Battista 29, Vernazza
🌐 lamala.it

$$$

Cinqueterre Residence
One of the more
upmarket Cinque Terre
hotels. Rooms come
with a hot tub and
a free minibar.

🏠 Via de Batte 67,
Riomaggiore 🌐 cinque
terre residence.it

$$$

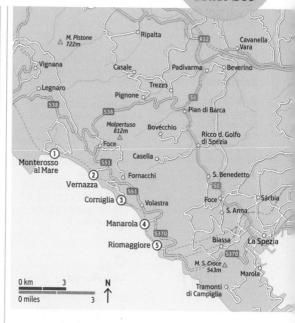

Cinque Terre, it thrives on winemaking, tourism and fishing – which means the seafood restaurants here are some of the best in Italy. The hamlet is divided by a road that was once a stream, Il Ponte, which connects the central church of San Lorenzo with the marina. Close by are hiking trails that cut through pretty vineyards with views down to the sea.

⑤ Riomaggiore

The pretty pastel-coloured houses of Riomaggiore cling to cliffs overlooking curved bays where colourful fishing boats bob on the water. The best known of the Cinque Terre villages, visitors flock here for its tiny beaches, excellent fish restaurants and buzzy bars.

↑ Sunbathers preparing for a swim off the coast of Corniglia

EXPERIENCE MORE

3
Balzi Rossi

 A3 Imperia
Ventimiglia & Menton
From Ventimiglia to Ponte San Luigi, then a 10-min walk soprintendenza. liguria.beniculturali.it

An unassuming promontory is the setting for some of the most important caves in northern Italy. Guided tours lead through the pre-Iron Age dwellings, which contain excavated burial sites where the dead were adorned with seashells. The **Museo Nazionale dei Balzi Rossi** contains tools, weapons and stone-etched female figures dating from 100,000 years ago.

Museo Nazionale dei Balzi Rossi
 Via Balzi Rossi 9
0184 381 13 8:30am-7:30pm Tue-Sun 1 Jan, 1 May, 25 Dec

4
Villa Hanbury

 A3 Corso Monte Carlo 43, Località La Mortola
Ventimiglia From Ventimiglia 9:30am-5pm (mid-Jun-mid-Sep: to 6pm; mid-Oct-Feb: to 4pm) daily Mon Nov-Feb giardinihanbury.com

In 1867, the English botanist Sir Thomas Hanbury and his brother bought this seaside villa on a promontory. They took full advantage of the exceptionally mild Ligurian climate to establish a garden of exotic plants.

The collection, gathered by Hanbury on trips to Africa and Asia, has grown to number more than 3,000 varieties of tropical flora, including rubber trees, palms and wild cacti.

5
Dolceacqua

A3 Imperia
Via Barberis Colomba 3; www.dolceacqua.it

This pretty village, 8 km (5 miles) north of Ventimiglia, is built on either side of the River Nervia, its two halves joined by an arching 33-m (108-ft) medieval stone bridge. The highlight is the ruined 12th- to 15th-century castle, inhabited for a while in the 16th century by the powerful Doria family from Genoa. The two square towers at the front dominate the village. The terraced vineyards in the surrounding hills produce grapes for a robust red wine known as Rossese or vino di Dolceacqua.

6
San Remo

A3 Imperia
Corso degli Inglesi 14; www.lamialiguria.it

San Remo is a pleasant resort of faded elegance. The composer Tchaikovsky, Alfred Nobel (the father of modern explosives) and the nonsense poet Edward Lear all stayed in the stuccoed mansions of the palm-lined seafront avenue, the Corso Imperatrice. The focus of the town, then as now, is the Casino. A little further down the Corso stands the ornate Russian Orthodox church of San Borilio.

The old town, La Pigna (fir cone), is a huddle of narrow lanes with medieval houses and pastel-coloured shutters.

EAT

Here are two of the best *gelaterie* in San Remo.

Gelateria Profumo
Serves excellent traditional *gelato*.

Vico Superiore del Ferro 14

$ $ $

Profumo di Rosa
Rosa prepares all the *gelato* herself – hazelnut is the most popular flavour.

Via Cairoli 13

$ $ $

Exotic plants in the elegant Villa Hanbury gardens, founded by an English botanist

↑ Sunset over the village of Cervo, on a hillside overlooking the sea

A coach service goes from San Remo to San Romolo, a small village 786 m (2,579 ft) above sea level that offers beautiful views of the area.

A delightful wholesale flower market is held in Valle Armea *(5–7am, Oct–Jun, www. sanremoflowermarket.it)*, while the Italian Song Festival takes place here in February.

 7

Bussana Vecchia

🗺 A3 🚉 Imperia, off San Remo-Arma di Taggia road

Bussana Vecchia is a marvellously atmospheric ghost town. In February 1887 an earthquake shook the village, reducing its Baroque church and surrounding houses to ruins. (One survivor, Giovanni Torre del Merlo, went on to invent the ice-cream cone.)

The town was rebuilt closer to the sea and since then the original village has been taken over by artists, who have restored some interiors, providing a venue for summer concerts and exhibitions.

 8

Cervo

🗺 A3 🚉 Imperia 🚆🚌
ℹ Piazza Santa Caterina 2; www.cervo.com

Cervo is a pretty seafront village with a narrow complex of streets and houses rising dramatically up from the shingle beach. At the top of the village stands the concave Baroque façade of San Giovanni Battista. Chamber orchestra performances are held in front of the church in July and August. The church is also known as the *"dei corallini"*, after the coral fishing that once brought prosperity to the local people.

 9

Albenga

🗺 A3 🚉 Savona 🚆🚌
ℹ Piazza del Popolo 11; www.lamialiguria.it

Until the Middle Ages, the Roman port of Albium Ingaunum played an important role. The sea, however, gradually moved further out, leaving the town, now called Albenga, stranded on the Centa River. Most striking now is its Romanesque brick architecture, in particular the three 13th-century towers clustered around the cathedral of San Michele. To the south is an intriguing 5th-century **Baptistry** with a ten-sided exterior and octagonal interior. Inside, the original 5th-century blue-and-white mosaics of doves represent the 12 Apostles.

In a 14th-century palace on Piazza San Michele is the **Museo Navale Romano**, founded in 1950 following the salvage of a Roman ship that had sunk in the 1st century BC. The museum contains ancient amphorae as well as exhibits salvaged from more recent shipwrecks.

Baptistry
♿ 🏛 Piazza San Michele
📞 347 808 58 11 🕐 Tue–Sun (Oct–Apr: groups only Sun)
🚫 1 Jan, Easter, 25 Dec

Museo Navale Romano
♿ 🏛 Piazza San Michele 12
📞 0182 51215 🕐 Tue–Sun
🚫 1 Jan, Easter, 25 Dec

Fascinating geological formations in the Grotte di Toirano ↑

Grotte di Toirano

A3 Via alle Grotte, Toirano From Albenga to Borghetto Santo Spirito To Borghetto Santo Spirito or Loano 9:30am–12:30pm & 2–4:30pm daily 25 Dec–1 Jan toiranogrotte.it

Beneath the medieval town of Toirano lies a series of caves housing relics of Paleolithic life dating from 100,000 years ago.

The Grotta di Santa Lucia reveals the full beauty of the yellow and grey stalactites and stalagmites formed here over millennia.

The **Museo Etnografico della Val Varatella**, in the 16th-century stables of the Palazzo del Marchese, has a collection of agricultural and domestic tools.

Museo Etnografico della Val Varatella

Via G Polla, Toirano 0182 98 99 68 10am–1pm & 3–6pm daily

Camogli

B2 Genoa Via XX Settembre 33; www.camogliturismo.it

Built on a pine-wooded slope, Camogli is a fishing village where seashells adorn the pastel-painted house walls.

Near the pebble beach and fishing port is the medieval Castello della Dragonara.

Camogli celebrates its famous Blessing of the Fish festival on the second Sunday of May. Sardines are fried in a huge pan and distributed free to everyone.

Portofino Peninsula

B2–B3 Genoa Portofino Via Roma 35; www.parcoportofino.com

Portofino is Italy's most exclusive resort and harbour town, crammed with the yachts of the wealthy. You can reach it by road (although cars are not allowed into the village), or by boat, from the resort of Santa Margherita Ligure. Above the town are the church of San Giorgio, containing relics said to be those of the dragon-slayer, and a castle.

On the other side of the peninsula, which you have to reach on foot (a 2-hour walk) or by boat, is the **Abbazia di San Fruttuoso**, named after a 3rd-century saint whose followers were shipwrecked here and, according to legend, protected by three lions. The white abbey buildings, set among pines and olive trees, date mostly from the 11th century, although the imposing Torre dei Doria was added some 500 years later.

Experienced divers can sign up for excursions to try to locate the Cristo degli Abissi, a bronze statue of Christ that sits 17-m (55-ft) deep on the sea bed near San Fruttuoso and is said to protect sailors.

Abbazia di San Fruttuoso

San Fruttuoso 0185 77 27 03 Mar–Oct: daily; Nov–Jan: Tue–Sun

Rapallo

B2 Genoa Lungomare Vittorio Veneto 7; www.lamia liguria.it

Historians know Rapallo as the place where two post-World War I treaties were signed, while film buffs might recognize it from the 1954 movie *The Barefoot Contessa*, which was shot here. Rapallo was also a haven for writers such as D H Lawrence and Ezra Pound. The palm-lined esplanade ends in a 16th-century castle. A cable car from

Did You Know?

The Grotte de Toirano once provided shelter for cave bears during hibernation.

the centre of the town leads to the 16th-century **Santuario di Montallegro**, which houses a Byzantine icon said to possess miraculous powers.

Santuario di Montallegro

 Montallegro 📞 0185 23 90 00 🕐 Daily 🕐 Noon–2:30pm

Portovenere

🅰 B3 🚉 La Spezia 🚌🚌
ℹ Piazza Bastreri 7; www. prolocoportovenere.it

Portovenere is one of the most romantic villages on the Ligurian coast, with its cluster of narrow streets lined with pastel-coloured houses. In the upper part of the village is the 12th-century church of San Lorenzo. A sculpture over the doorway here depicts the martyrdom of the saint who was roasted alive on a grill. On the stone promontory that curls out into the sea is the small, black-and-white, 13th-century church of San Pietro.

Lerici

🅰 B3 🚉 La Spezia 🚌🚌
ℹ Via Biagini 6, Località Venere Azzurra; www. parconazionale5terre.it

The popular resort of Lerici sits on the edge of a beautiful bay overlooked by pastel-coloured houses. The forbidding medieval **Castello di Lerici** (13th century) was built by the Pisans and later passed to the Genoese. Today it houses a museum of geopaleontology and hosts art exhibitions and concerts.

The village of San Terenzo, across the bay, is where the poet Shelley spent his last years. It was from his home, the Casa Magni, that he set out in 1822 on a voyage to meet Leigh Hunt in Livorno. Tragically, he was shipwrecked near Viareggio and drowned.

Castello di Lerici

♿ 🚉 Piazza San Giorgio 🕐 Tue–Sun 🕐 9–26 Dec 🌐 castellodilerici.it

STAY

Hotel San Terenzo
Rooms here come with balconies and sea views. Guests can rent boats, plus there are good ferry links to the Cinque Terre.

🏠 Via S Biaggini 42, San Terenzo
🌐 hotelsanterenzo.it

€€€

B&B La Matta Gatta
The rooms at this simple-but-chic family-run B&B a short walk from the beach have huge windows and stunning sea views.

🏠 La Sare 21, Lerici
📞 334 293 7377

€€€

↑ The picturesque village of Portovenere, with colourful houses and a busy marina

CENTRAL ITALY

Vineyard-cloaked hills in Tuscany

EXPLORE
CENTRAL ITALY

This section divides central Italy into seven colour-coded sightseeing areas, as shown on the map above. Find out more about each area on the following pages.

GETTING TO KNOW
CENTRAL ITALY

Stretching from the Adriatic to the Tyrrhenian Sea, and from the mists of the Po Valley to the Mediterranean, this is Italy's heartland. Rome and Florence - connected by frequent fast trains - are the main targets, closely followed by the hill towns of Tuscany and Umbria. There are, however, plenty of opportunities to leave the crowds behind, exploring the forgotten villages of Le Marche or walking in the Apennine Mountains.

PAGE 222

ROME

Rome is an exuberant, noisy metropolis, where layers of history form an extraordinary stage for everyday life in a contemporary European capital. Yet in many ways, Rome remains a neighbourly city where the life of the community continues alongside its ancient monuments, medieval churches and picturesque piazzas. As well as sightseeing, Rome is a fabulous destination for more hedonistic pursuits, with a beguiling array of designer boutiques, tempting delicatessens, and wonderful places to eat, ranging from pavement cafés to chic, voguish restaurants.

Best for
Stumbling across amazing ancient sites by chance

Home to
The Colosseum and the Vatican

Experience
Opera at the Baths of Caracalla and Mass in St Peter's

PAGE 320

LAZIO

Lying between the Apennines and the Tyrrhenian sea, Lazio is a varied region of volcanic lakes, hot springs, mountains, ravines, vineyards and olive groves. The Etruscans, who flourished in the region in the 7th century BC, left behind cities and cemeteries, while traces of ancient Rome include Emperor Hadrian's magnificent villa at Tivoli, and the ruins of Ostia Antica. Lakes Bracciano, Bolsena and Albano are great for swimming and sailing; wine-lovers can tour the *cantinas* of the Castelli Romani; while the best beaches are on the shores of the Monte Circeo national park.

Best for
Days out and escapes from Rome

Home to
Bomarzo Monster Park, Tivoli and incredible volcanic lakes

Experience
Lunch on the shores of Lake Bracciano

PAGE 332

FLORENCE

Created in a whirlwind of artistic energy that can still be felt more than 500 years later, Florence is an exquisite monument to the Renaissance, the artistic and intellectual reawakening of the 15th century. But it is no museum piece: it is a lively place with bustling shops and markets, spirited street performers and a plethora of tempting *gelaterie*, markets, restaurants and cafés. With a compact historic centre bisected by the river Arno, it is an easy city to explore on foot. The north bank of the river is packed with art and architectural highlights, while to the south lies the more lived-in Oltrarno, with Ponte Vecchio connecting the two.

Best for
Sightseeing on foot, with plenty of coffee breaks

Home to
The Uffizi, the Duomo and Ponte Vecchio

Experience
Panoramic views of the city from San Miniato

→

PAGE 366

TUSCANY

Famed for its art, history, wine and evocative landscapes, Tuscany offers the quintessential Italian experience, with its picturesque medieval hill-towns and vine-grooved hills. The towns of Siena, Pisa, Lucca, Cortona and Arezzo contain some of Italy's most familiar art treasures, while villages such as San Gimignano, with its iconic towers, or Pienza, a tiny Renaissance jewel, sit at the heart of the landscapes for which the region is renowned. The main targets for wine-lovers wanting to tour the region's wineries are Chianti, Montalcino and Montepulciano.

Best for
Rural scenery and picturesque hill-towns

Home to
Siena, the Leaning Tower of Pisa and Chianti wine

Experience
Wine-tasting in the ancient cellars of Montepulciano

PAGE 400

UMBRIA

With a profusion of exquisite medieval hill-towns surrounded by gentle pastures and high mountain wilderness, Umbria has been dubbed the "Green Heart of Italy". Famous for its truffles, mushrooms and cured meats, the region is a great destination for foodies. Walkers flock here for landscapes ranging from the eerie wastes of the Piano Grande to the mountainous splendours of Monti Sibillini national park. Assisi – birthplace of Saint Francis – and Spoleto are Umbria's loveliest towns, but there are many other gems, including Orvieto, Gubbio, Spello, Montefalco and Todi.

Best for
Hill-towns, food, country walks

Home to
Assisi, Spoleto and Lake Trasimeno

Experience
Truffle hunting and white-water rafting in the Valnerina

PAGE 414

LE MARCHE

The beach resorts of Le Marche buzz with activity all summer long, but the region's inland treasures remain almost undiscovered. Most of the countryside is a pretty mixture of woods and rolling hills peppered with fascinating little towns and villages. The cultural highlights are found in the walled city of Urbino – home to the Palazzo Ducale, the most famous court in Renaissance Italy – and medieval Ascoli Piceno, while the indented coast of the Conero Peninsula provides respite from the uninterrupted sandy beaches that fringe the region's shoreline.

Best for
Driving around remote hill-towns

Home to
Urbino and the Conero Peninsula

Experience
Macerata opera festival or coffee spiked with anice liqueur in Ascoli Piceno

PAGE 424

EMILIA-ROMAGNA

Stretching from the Adriatic coast inland across the hills and plains of the Po Valley, Emilia-Romagna marks the watershed between the cold north of the Alps and the hot Mediterranean south. The region is famous for its rich cuisine, and makes the perfect destination for foodies. Bologna, the regional capital, is a thriving medieval university city, while Modena is home to one of Italy's finest Romanesque cathedrals. Ravenna is perhaps Emilia-Romana's most extraordinary town, its churches glittering with mosaics.

Best for
Dining out and packing your suitcase with gastronomic delights to take home

Home to
The mosaics of Ravenna, long sandy beaches and historic towns filled with art

Experience
A plate of spaghetti Bolognese in Bologna

ROME

The Tiber at Sunset

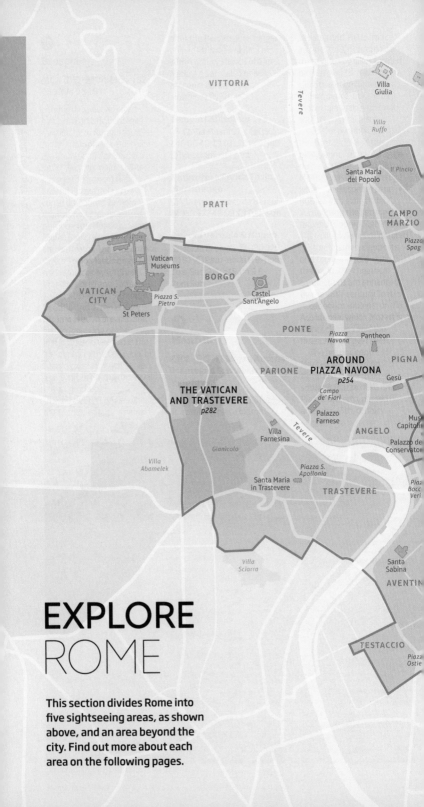

VITTORIA

Villa
Giulia

Tevere

Villa
Ruffo

Santa Maria
del Popolo

Il Pincio

PRATI

CAMPO
MARZIO

Piazza
Spag

Vatican
Museums

BORGO

VATICAN
CITY

Piazza S.
Pietro

Castel
Sant'Angelo

St Peters

PONTE

Piazza
Navona

Pantheon

PIGNA

AROUND
PIAZZA NAVONA
p254

PARIONE

Gesù

Campo
de' Fiori

THE VATICAN
AND TRASTEVERE
p282

Palazzo
Farnese

Mus
Capitoli

Villa
Farnesina

Tevere

ANGELO

Palazzo de
Conservato

Gianicolo

Villa
Abamelek

Piazza S.
Apollonia

Piaz
Bocc
Veri

Santa Maria
in Trastevere

TRASTEVERE

Villa
Sciarra

Santa
Sabina

AVENTIN

EXPLORE
ROME

TESTACCIO

Piaz
Ostie

This section divides Rome into
five sightseeing areas, as shown
above, and an area beyond the
city. Find out more about each
area on the following pages.

ITALY

Galleria
Nazionale d'Arte
Moderna

Villa
Borghese

Museo e Galleria
Borghese

LUDOVISI

Trinità dei
Monti

SALLUSTIANO

Piazza
Barberini

CASTRO
PRETORIO

Piazza della
Repubblica

REVI

NORTHEAST ROME
p268

evi
ountain

MONTI

Santa Maria
Maggiore

Cimitero
Monumentale
del Verano

Mercati
Traianei

azzo
ovo

Parco di
Traiano

ESQUILINO

SAN
LORENZO

Roman
Forum

Domus
Aurea

THE
ANCIENT
CENTRE
p238

Colosseum

San
Clemente

LATERAN

PALATINE

Parco
del Celio

Pza. S. Giovanni
In Laterano

Parco del
co Massimo

Santo Stefano
Rotondo

San Giovanni
in Laterano

RIPA

AVENTINE
AND LATERAN
p300

Villa
Celimontana

azza
nia

CELIO

Parco di
Porta Capena

Parco
Egerio

Parco
San Sebastiana

GARBATELLA

0 metres   800
0 yards   800

N
↑

GETTING TO KNOW
ROME

Rome's *centro storico*, cradled within a great loop of the Tiber River, is a maze of cobbled streets and piazzas studded with fountains, palaces and churches. Peppering the city are the toothy remains of ancient Rome, shaded by green swathes of umbrella pines. Across the river, the dome of St Peter's dominates the horizon, rising high above Vatican City and the mellow façades and intimate piazzas of Trastevere.

THE ANCIENT CENTRE

PAGE 238

Mussolini's Via dei Fori Imperiali slices above the ruins of the temples and basilicas that once formed the centre of political, commercial and judicial life in ancient Rome. By day, the area is filled with souvenir stands and coachloads of tourists following umbrella-toting guides around the Roman Forum, Colosseum and Capitoline Museums. The Forum is far quieter and more atmospheric at night, when the tour groups have left and the monuments are illuminated. Crowds are easier to avoid at all times in the green, pine-shaded expanses of the Palatine Hill.

Best for
Exploring the fascinating ruins of Ancient Rome

Home to
The Roman Forum, the Palatine and the Colosseum

Experience
Views of the Roman Forum from the terrace of the Caffè Capitolino

AROUND PIAZZA NAVONA

An extravagant Baroque oval dominated by the towering obelisk and cascading waters of Bernini's Four Rivers fountain, Piazza Navona is the social heart of Rome. An outdoor salon fringed with expensive pavement cafés, it is packed morning to night with buskers, mime-artists and street vendors. The tangle of narrow cobbled streets surrounding the square is home to extraordinary churches and palaces, enticing *gelaterie* and a string of busy cafés and restaurants.

Best for
People-watching in Piazza Navona

Home to
The Pantheon and the Gesù

Experience
Gelati from San Crispino or Grom

NORTHEAST ROME

The streets around Piazza di Spagna are studded with designer clothes and shoe boutiques, bijou cosmetics shops, art galleries, antiques shops and upmarket delicatessens. It is an area in which to wander and window-shop between some leisurely sightseeing. Via del Corso is full of chain stores, and at peak shopping times it transforms into a human river. Nearby are the Trevi Fountain, the imposing church of Santa Maria del Maggiore, and the trendy Monti district, great for street food and alternative fashion shops.

Best for
Shopping

Home to
Piazza di Spagna, Santa Maria del Maggiore and the Trevi Fountain

Experience
Lunch or a drink in Piazza Madonna dei Monti

→

PAGE 282

THE VATICAN AND TRASTEVERE

Home to St Peter's, the Sistine Chapel and the eclectic collections of the Vatican Museums, the Vatican is a must for both pilgrims and art lovers. The surrounding area is full of streets lined with souvenir shops and hawkers flogging Sistine Chapel T-shirts and plaster Pietàs. Nearby are the picturesque and higgledy-piggledy cobbled streets of Trastevere, where Piazza San Cosimato hosts a daily produce market, and shrines to the Madonna still protect the area's piazzas.

Best for
World-famous art and sculpture

Home to
St Peter's, the Vatican Museums and Castel Sant'Angelo

Experience
A Papal Audience on Piazza San Pietro

PAGE 300

AVENTINE AND LATERAN

Rising above the Tiber to the southwest of the Palatine, the twin-peaked Aventine Hill is a lush, leafy residential area with a handful of early Christian churches scattered among its secluded private villas. Although it is in the centre of Rome it is remarkably peaceful. Traditionally a working-class area, the adjacent Lateran retains an unpretentious feel. Its modern avenues open out onto beautiful churches and it is home to the huge Via Sannio clothes and shoes market.

Best for
Strolling through leafy parks

Home to
San Giovanni in Laterano and San Clemente

Experience
The spooky Mithraeum, hidden below the church of San Clemente

BEYOND THE CENTRE

Rome has a small, compact centre – you can walk across from one side to the other in only a couple of hours – and keen walkers can easily cover some of the city's peripheral sights on foot. Ranging from Roman catacombs to 21st-century MAXXI, and from the sumptuous Villa Borghese estate to the futuristic suburb of EUR, delving outside the centre not only brings you to sights off the beaten tourist track, but into residential neighbourhoods where you can get a real sense of everyday life in Rome.

Best for
Escaping the crowds and discovering Rome's hidden gems

Home to
Villa Giulia, Villa Borghese, MAXXI and EUR

Experience
A classical or jazz concert at the Auditorium Parco della Musica

→

1 The Colosseum

2 Fresco at the Museo Nazionale Romano

3 Nuns in Piazza San Pietro

4 Enoteca Ferrara, Trastevere

3 DAYS
A Long Weekend in Rome

Day 1
Morning For an unforgettable experience, get up at dawn to see Piazza San Pietro almost empty, and enter St Peter's *(p286)* along with nuns, priests and pilgrims when it opens at 7am. The spiral steps that wind up to the cupola open at 8am, and having the amazing views to yourself is magical. Speed your entry into the Vatican Museums by booking a slot in advance on the website *(p289)*, and take in the glories of the Cortile della Pigna over breakfast in its café. With twelve museums and 7 km (4 miles) of corridors, there is too much to see in a single visit so select your highlights. Have lunch in the pizzeria outside the Carriage Pavilion.

Afternoon Take a bracing walk up the Janiculum Hill, with its great views over the city, winding down past the Tempietto *(p297)* into Trastevere *(p283)*.

Evening Enjoy a well-earned aperitivo in Piazza Santa Maria in Trastevere, followed by dinner at Enoteca Ferrara *(p295)*.

Day 2
Morning Explore the Colosseum *(p242)*, then walk to the entrance to the Palatine *(p248)* on Via di San Gregorio (which tends to be less busy than the main Forum entrance to the site). Do not miss the Flavian Palace or the surviving section of the Cryptoporticus tunnel. Head down to the Roman Forum, and spot the coins fused to the pavement of the Basilica Aemilia and the chequerboards in the steps of Basilica Julia *(p246)*. Treat yourself to lunch at La Bottega del Caffè, on Piazza Madonna dei Monti.

Afternoon Stroll up past the quirky boutiques of Via dei Serpenti to Trajan's Forum and Markets *(p250)*, an ancient Roman shopping mall, and admire the digitally reconstructed Roman villas below Palazzo Valentini. Afterwards see exquisite frescoes from a country villa belonging to Emperor Augustus' wife, Livia, at the Museo Nazionale Romano *(p281)*. You can book ahead to see some of the villa's other surviving frescoes in situ on the Palatine.

Evening Reflect on your busy day and collapse over a fine glass of wine at the Trimani Il Wine Bar *(Via Cernaia 37/b)*.

Day 3
Morning Start with a leisurely caffè latte and *cornetto* at the Antico Caffè Vitti on pretty Piazza San Lorenzo in Lucina, then head across Piazza del Parlamento to Piazza del Montecitorio, where you can watch the politicians, lobby correspondents and protestors coming and going from the parliament building. Zigzag down to the Pantheon *(p260)*, taking in little Piazza delle Coppelle and Piazza Capranica. See Caravaggio canvases in the church of San Luigi dei Francesi and the courtyard of Sant'Ivo alla Sapienza *(p262)*, then cross Piazza Navona to lunch at the Chiostro Bramante Bistrot *(Arco della Pace 5)*.

Afternoon Enjoy the antiques shops along Via dei Coronari, then meander down Via Giulia to Campo de' Fiori *(p264)*, and into the Jewish Ghetto.

Evening Grab an aperitivo at one of the cafés on Via del Portico d'Ottavia and dinner at Piperno *(Via Monte dè Cenci 9)*.

◁ Contemporary Dining

Rome has no shortage of chic places to eat with creative twists on traditional food. The emphasis is on carefully sourced ingredients cooked to perfection. **Rome's supreme modern restaurants:** *Casa Coppelle* (Piazza delle Coppelle 49), *Casa e Bottega* (Via Tor di Millina 34A) and *Glass Hostaria* (Vicolo Dè Cinque 58).

▷ Aperitivi and Wine Bars

Although the aperitivo is a northern tradition, the Romans have adopted it as their own. At the very least you'll be presented with crisps, olives and peanuts to accompany your drinks, but the best places will offer a buffet feast of beautifully crafted mini antipasti. In wine bars, order Frascati, Chianti Classico or Torre Ercolana. **Rome's best bars:** *VinAllegro* (Piazza Giuditta Tavani Arquati 114), *Momart Cafè* (Viale Ventuno Aprile 19) *and* '*Gusto* (Piazza Imperatore Augusto 9).

ROME FOR
FOODIES

In Rome, eating out can bring both joy and entertainment. The city's best food and drink isn't confined to its Michelin-starred restaurants: food-lovers can find much to rave about in its cafés, pizzerias and *gelaterie*.

◁ Creamy Gelato

Gourmet ice creams made with organic ingredients have taken Rome by storm. You'll find an array of artisan flavours, some made with centuries-old methods and recipes. **Rome's top gelaterie:** *Grom* (Via della Maddalena 30A), *Giolitti* (Via degli Uffici del Vicario 40) *and Gelarmony* (Via Marcantonio Colonna 34).

◁ Pizza and Focaccia

A slice of pizza fresh from the oven (*pizza a taglio*), and hot focaccia dripping with Ligurian olive oil and rosemary count among the great gastronomic experiences of Rome.

Rome's finest snacks: *Antico Forno Roscioli* (Via dei Chiavari 34), *Forno Campo de' Fiori* (Piazza Campo De' Fiori 22), *La Renella* (Via del Moro 15).

◁ Traditional Roman Dishes

The traditional food of Rome has its origins in working-class areas such as Testaccio, and is based on cheap cuts of meat and offal. The Jewish community of the Ghetto also influenced local cuisine with dishes such as *carciofi alla giudia* (deep-fried artichokes) and *filetti di baccalà* (deep-fried fillets of salt cod).

First-rate Roman eateries: *Da Armando al Pantheon* (Salita De' Crescenzi 31) *and Felice a Testaccio* (Via Mastro Giorgio 29).

COFFEE GUIDE

Caffè: A short, strong single shot of coffee, popularly known as an espresso abroad

Caffè Lungo: Slightly longer and weaker than a caffè – the water is allowed to run through for longer

Caffè Macchiato: Caffè with a dash of frothy milk

Latte Macchiato: Hot milk with a dash of coffee

Caffè Corretto: Caffè with a splash of alcohol such as grappa or *anice*

Caffè Marocchino: Caffè with chocolate powder and a little frothy milk

△ Exceptional Coffee

Coffee was first brought to Italy by traders in the 16th century and, though initially regarded as sinful, it was given the stamp of approval after Pope Clement VIII declared "this devil's drink is delicious". Rome was very quickly converted – and some of the world's best coffee can now be found in its cafés.

Where to find it: *Bar Cappuccino* (Via Arenula 50), *Caffè Sant'Eustachio* (p267) *and La Tazza d'Oro* (Via degli Orfani 84).

Magnificent Music and Ballet Shows

Since it opened in 2002, the Auditorium Parco della Musica has become a much-loved focus of Rome's music scene, hosting classical music, jazz and pop concerts, along with exhibitions and other cultural events. Many of Rome's churches are also used for classical concerts, while Teatro Olimpico *(Piazza Gentile da Fabriano 17)* is the city's principal venue for modern dance.

Ballet performance at the Auditorium Parco della Musica

ROME
AFTER DARK

In the summer, Rome's ancient sites, parks, and piazzas become outdoor theatres, while throughout the year there is a packed programme at the Auditorium Parco della Musica. International jazz musicians have long been drawn to Rome's festivals, and pop acts frequently perform in the city's stadia.

Do as the Romans Do

One of the most enjoyable things to do in Rome at night is to stroll the lively streets of the historic centre as part of the *passeggiata (p11)*. A number of shops around Piazza Navona stay open late, while Piazza Navona itself becomes a magnet for mime artists and other street performers.

ROMAESTATE

Rome's packed season of summer cultural events is organized under the umbrella of RomaEstate *(www. estate-romana.it)*. There are pop-up cafés and bars on banks of the Tiber – a very atmospheric place to spend an evening. Venues throughout the city also host performances and outdoor cinema screenings

Awesome Street Festivals

Rome has a tradition of street celebrations, many with their origins in religious festivals, others born of left-wing politics. New Year is ushered in with fireworks at the Colosseum and a free concert on Via dei Fori Imperiali, while Chinese New Year sees a spectacular procession down the Spanish Steps. Organized by trades unions, the free pop concerts on 1 May and 24 June in Piazza San Giovanni are a Rome institution.

→

New Year fireworks display outside the Colosseum

Outstanding Opera

The opera scene in Rome may not be as famous as in Milan or Naples, but world-class singers do perform here. A highlight is the sheer spectacle of the summer open-air opera performances at the Baths of Caracalla – the setting among the ruins is hard to beat (www.operaroma.it).

←

Opera performance at the Baths of Caracella

Razzama-jazz

Alexanderplatz (Via Ostia 9), Casa del Jazz (Viale di Porta Ardeatina 55) and Big Mama (Viccolo San Francesco a Ripa 18) are legendary jazz clubs. Summer sees several jazz festivals, including Villa Celimontana Jazz, held in the Villa Celimontana park. The main event of the year, the Rome Jazz Festival, is in November.

→

Charles Lloyd performing at a summer jazz festival in Rome

↑ Lively Piazza di Spagna bustling with crowds during the *passeggiata*

▽ Cinecitta si Mostra

Tour the legendary film studios to see costumes worn by Elizabeth Taylor in *Cleopatra* (1963), props from *Gladiator* (2000) and some spectacular film sets, including a street set created for the Martin Scorcese film *Gangs of New York* (2002) *(p319).*

△ Catacombs of Priscilla

Instead of joining the throngs in the catacombs on the Via Appia Antica, head for these rarely visited catacombs on Via Salaria *(www.catacombepriscilla. com),* run by Benedictine Sisters who give visitors a fascinating personal tour. Highlights include the earliest known image of the Madonna and Child.

ROME'S HIDDEN
SECRETS

Rome is so crammed with world-famous sights that visitors often feel unable to stray from popular tourist spots and packed itineraries. But the city's best-kept secrets are never far away if you know the right places to look.

▽ Roman Art Nouveau

To see part of Rome that few people imagine - let alone experience - head to the little cluster of upscale streets between Piazza Buenos Aires and Via Tagliamento, and discover a perfectly preserved Art Nouveau quarter of fantastic villas and fairytale palaces created by architect Gino Coppodè in the early 20th century.

Did You Know?

Legend has it that the Beatles bathed in the Fontana delle Rane *(below)* after a night out in 1965.

△ Italian Craft Beer

Italy may be famous for its wine, but it also produces excellent craft beer. Seek out Open Baladin *(Via degli Specchi 6)*, which has over 40 draft craft brews, or Birra Più *(Via del Pigneto 105)*, which is packed with vintage Italian beers.

▷ Eritrean Food

Italy's links with its former colony, Eritrea, ensure Rome has a handful of incredible authentic Ethiopian eateries. Feast on fiery vegetable and pulse dishes at Mesob *(Via Prenestina 118)* or sample wonderfully seasoned dishes with honeyed and spiced wine at Enqutatash *(Viale della Stazione Prenestina 55)*.

◁ Take a Food Tour of Testaccio

Cucina romana (ancient Roman cuisine) originated in the streets around Testaccio's slaughterhouse (now an art gallery), and the area remains famous throughout Rome for its butchers and trattorias, which specialize in offal and dishes made from offal. Once a gutsy working-class neighbourhood, Testaccio has now become one of Rome's trendiest spots. Explore the steet food stalls, market (p309), food shops and traditional trattorias here on your own, or take a 4-hour street food tour which includes lots of opportunities to eat *(www.eatingitaly foodtours.com)*.

ROME: THE ANCIENT CENTRE

The Capitol, the southern summit of the Capitoline Hill, was the symbolic centre of the Roman world and home to the city's three most important temples. These were dedicated to the god Jupiter Optimus Maximus, protector of Rome, Minerva, goddess of wisdom and war, and Juno Moneta, a guardian goddess. Below the Capitol lies the Forum, once the focus of political, social, legal and commercial life; the Imperial Fora, built when Rome's population grew; and the Colosseum, the centre of entertainment. Overlooking the Forum is the Palatine Hill, where Romulus is said to have founded Rome in the 8th century BC and where emperors made their home for over 400 years.

This part of the city has always been a study of contrasts. In Roman times the emperors' palaces on the Palatine were located just a stone's throw from the docks where roustabouts heaved goods imported from around the world. Today, the area is again an enclave of smart houses and greenery, studded with hidden art treasures and some of the world's finest ancient monuments and priceless archaeological finds.

ROME: THE ANCIENT CENTRE

Must Sees
1 The Colosseum
2 Capitoline Hill
3 Roman Forum
4 Palatine

Experience More
5 Trajan's Forum and Markets
6 Capitoline Museums
7 Forum of Augustus
8 Forum of Caesar
9 Arch of Constantine
10 Mamertine Prison
11 Santa Maria in Aracoeli
12 Palazzo Valentini

Eat
1 Caffè Capitolino

Drink
2 American Bar

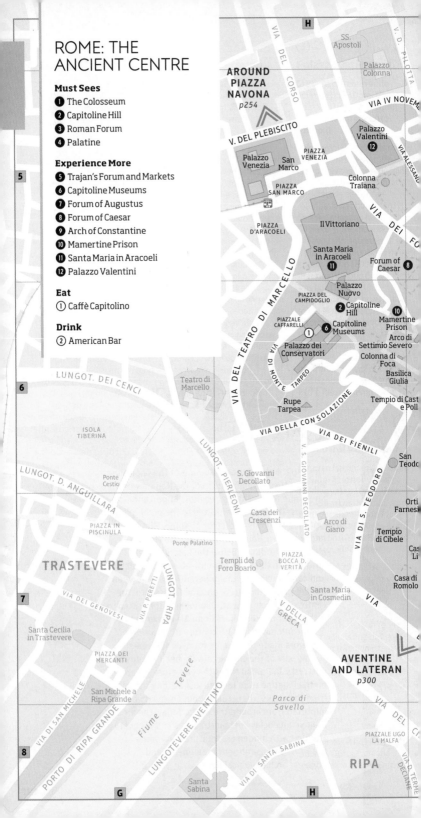

AROUND PIAZZA NAVONA
p254

SS. Apostoli
Palazzo Colonna
V. D. PILOTTA
VIA DEL CORSO
VIA IV NOVEMBRE
V. DEL PLEBISCITO
Palazzo Valentini 12
VIA ALESSAND
Palazzo Venezia
San Marco
PIAZZA VENEZIA
PIAZZA SAN MARCO
Colonna Traiana
VIA DEI FO
PIAZZA D'ARACOELI
Il Vittoriano
Forum of Caesar 8
Santa Maria in Aracoeli 11
Palazzo Nuovo
Mamertine Prison 10
PIAZZA DEL CAMPIDOGLIO
Capitoline Hill 2
VIA DEL TEATRO DI MARCELLO
PIAZZALE CAFFARELLI
Capitoline Museums 6
Arco di Settimio Severo
1
Colonna di Foca
Palazzo dei Conservatori
Basilica Giulia
VIA DI MONTE TARPEO
Tempio di Cast e Poll
LUNGOT. DEI CENCI
Teatro di Marcello
Rupe Tarpea
VIA DELLA CONSOLAZIONE
VIA DEI FIENILI
ISOLA TIBERINA
San Teodo
LUNGOT. D. ANGUILLARA
Ponte Cestio
LUNGOT. PIERLEONI
S. Giovanni Decollato
V. S. GIOVANNI DECOLLATO
Orti Farnesi
Casa dei Crescenzi
Arco di Giano
VIA DI S. TEODORO
Tempio di Cibele
Cas Li
Ponte Palatino
TRASTEVERE
LUNGOT. RIPA
Templi del Foro Boario
PIAZZA BOCCA D. VERITA
Casa di Romolo
VIA DEI GENOVESI
VIA P. PERETTI
Santa Maria in Cosmedin
V DELLA GRECA
VIA
Santa Cecilia in Trastevere
PIAZZA DEI MERCANTI
Tevere
AVENTINE AND LATERAN
p300
San Michele a Ripa Grande
VIA DI SAN MICHELE
Fiume
Parco di Savello
LUNGOTEVERE AVENTINO
PORTO DI RIPA GRANDE
PIAZZALE UGO LA MALFA
VIA DEL CA
VIA SANTA SABINA
RIPA
Santa Sabina
VIA DI SANTA SABINA
VIA D. TERME DECIANE

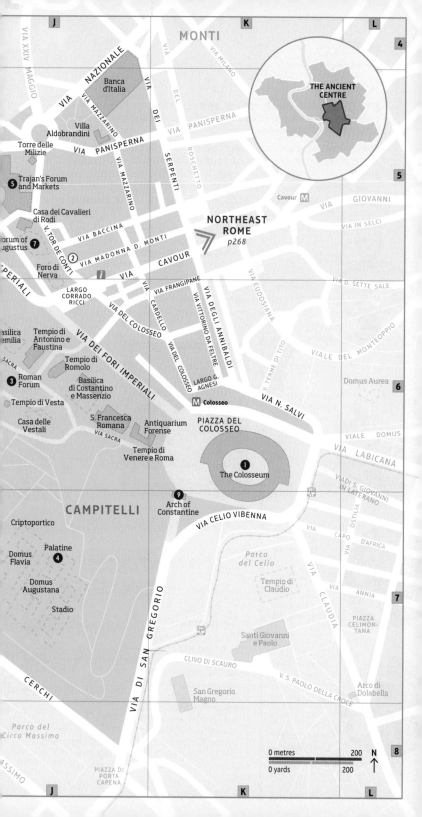

MONTI

VIA XXIV MAGGIO

VIA NAZIONALE

Banca d'Italia

Villa Aldobrandini

Torre delle Milizie

❺ Trajan's Forum and Markets

Casa dei Cavalieri di Rodi

Forum of Augustus ❼

Foro di Nerva

IMPERIALI

VIA MAZZARINO

VIA PANISPERNA

VIA DEI SERPENTI

VIA DEL BOSCHETTO

VIA PANISPERNA

Cavour Ⓜ

VIA GIOVANNI

VIA IN SELCI

NORTHEAST ROME
p268

VIA MAZZARINO

V. TOR DE CONTI

VIA BACCINA

② VIA MADONNA D. MONTI

VIA CAVOUR

LARGO CORRADO RICCI

VIA FRANGIPANE

VIA CARDELLO

VIA DEL COLOSSEO

VIA VITTORINO DA FELTRE

VIA DEGLI ANNIBALDI

VIA EUDOSIANA

VIA D. SETTE SALE

VIALE DEL MONTEOPPIO

SACRA

Basilica Emilia

Tempio di Antonino e Faustina

Tempio di Romolo

❸ Roman Forum

Tempio di Vesta

Casa delle Vestali

Basilica di Costantino e Massenzio

S. Francesca Romana

VIA SACRA

Antiquarium Forense

Tempio di Venere e Roma

VIA DEI FORI IMPERIALI

V. TERME DI TITO

LARGO G. AGNESI

Ⓜ Colosseo

VIA N. SALVI

Domus Aurea

VIALE DOMUS

VIA LABICANA

PIAZZA DEL COLOSSEO

❶ The Colosseum

VIA DI S. GIOVANNI IN LATERANO

CAMPITELLI

Criptoportico

Domus Flavia

Palatine ❹

Domus Augustana

Stadio

❾ Arch of Constantine

VIA CELIO VIBENNA

VIA DI SAN GREGORIO

Parco del Celio

Tempio di Claudio

VIA CLAUDIA

CAPO VIA D'AFRICA

OSTILIA

ANNIA

PIAZZA CELIMONTANA

CERCHI

CLIVO DI SCAURO

Santi Giovanni e Paolo

San Gregorio Magno

V. S. PAOLO DELLA CROCE

Arco di Dolabella

Parco del Circo Massimo

MASSIMO

PIAZZA DI PORTA CAPENA

0 metres 200
0 yards 200

N

THE ANCIENT CENTRE

COLOSSEUM

K6 ⌂ Piazza del Colosseo 1 🚌 75, 81, 85, 87, 117, 673, 810 🚊 Tram 3 to Piazza del Colosseo 🕐 8:30am-approx 1 hour before sunset daily (last adm: 1 hour before closing) 🚫 1 Jan, 25 Dec 🌐 coopculture.it

Rome's greatest amphitheatre was commissioned by the Emperor Vespasian in AD 72. Deadly gladiatorial combats and wild animal fights were staged by the emperor and wealthy citizens, largely to gain popularity. Slaughter was on a huge scale: at the inaugural games in AD 80, over 9,000 wild animals were killed. The Colosseum could hold up to 55,000 people, who were seated according to rank.

The Colosseum was built to a practical design, with its 80 arched entrances allowing easy access to the spectators, but it is also a building of great beauty. The drawing here shows how it looked at the time of its opening in AD 80. It was one of several similar amphitheatres built in the Roman Empire – other surviving examples are at El Djem in North Africa, Nîmes and Arles in France, and Verona in northern Italy. Despite being damaged over the years by neglect and theft, the Roman Colosseum remains a majestic sight.

Timeline

72
◀ Emperor Vespasian begins work on the Colosseum

80
Vespasian's son, Titus, stages the inaugural festival here

404
◀ Gladiatorial combats are banned

442
Building damaged in an earthquake

523
◀ Wild animal fights are banned

1200s
Frangipane family turns Colosseum into a fortress

1312
◀ Emperor Henry VII gives Colosseum to the people of Rome

↑ An arched corridor in the Colosseum

The velarium was a huge awning which shaded spectators from the sun.

Stone plundered from the façade during the Renaissance was used to build several palaces and bridges, and also parts of St Peter's.

💬 INSIDER TIP
Roma Pass

Holders of a Roma Pass gain direct entry via a special turnstile. The quietest time to visit is early morning - arrive at least 30 minutes before the scheduled opening time. Beware "gladiators" who charge tourists for photos.

→ Illustration of the Colosseum as it was in AD 80

The interior of the Colosseum as it looks today ↓

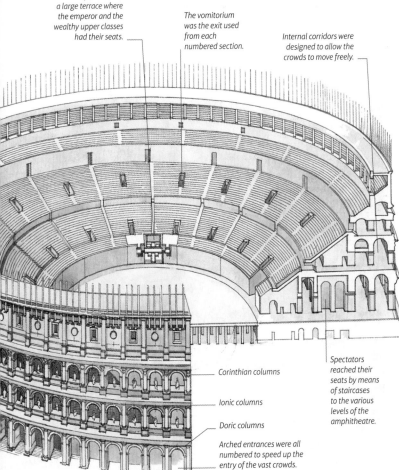

The podium was a large terrace where the emperor and the wealthy upper classes had their seats.

The vomitorium was the exit used from each numbered section.

Internal corridors were designed to allow the crowds to move freely.

Corinthian columns

Ionic columns

Doric columns

Arched entrances were all numbered to speed up the entry of the vast crowds.

Spectators reached their seats by means of staircases to the various levels of the amphitheatre.

CAPITOLINE HILL

📍H6 🏛Piazza del Campidoglio 🚌40, 63, 70, 81, 87 & other routes through Piazza Venezia

One of the seven hills of Rome, the Capitoline Hill was first the fortified centre of ancient Rome and later home to its most important temples. The broad flight of steps leading up the hill and the Piazza del Campidoglio at its head were designed in the 16th century by Michelangelo.

The Piazza del Campidoglio is flanked by Palazzo Nuovo and Palazzo dei Conservatori, which house the Capitoline Museums *(p250)* with their fine collections of sculpture and paintings. It is well worth walking behind the museums to the Tarpeian Rock, for a superb view of the Forum lying below. At the centre of the piazza is a gilded bronze statue of Marcus Aurelius, the original of which is in the Capitoline Museums. Legend has it that when the last gold leaf flakes off the statue the world will end. Another major highlight of the area is the Victor Emmanuel Monument, which was begun in 1885 and inaugurated in 1911 in honour of Victor Emmanuel II, the first king of unified Italy.

↑ Hall of the Philosophers in Palazzo Nuovo at the Capitoline Museums

→ The imposing Vittorio Emanuele II Monument

Did You Know?

The nearby Roman Ghetto and the trendy Monti district are home to a great selection of cafés and bars.

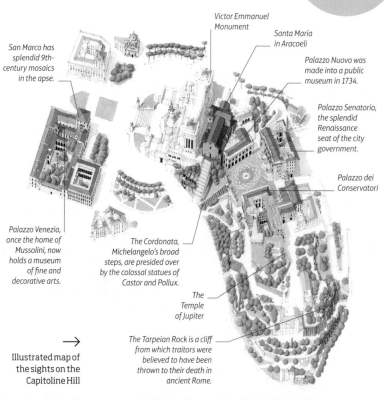

Victor Emmanuel Monument

Santa Maria in Aracoeli

San Marco has splendid 9th-century mosaics in the apse.

Palazzo Nuovo was made into a public museum in 1734.

Palazzo Senatorio, the splendid Renaissance seat of the city government.

Palazzo dei Conservatori

Palazzo Venezia, once the home of Mussolini, now holds a museum of fine and decorative arts.

The Cordonata, Michelangelo's broad steps, are presided over by the colossal statues of Castor and Pollux.

The Temple of Jupiter

→ Illustrated map of the sights on the Capitoline Hill

The Tarpeian Rock is a cliff from which traitors were believed to have been thrown to their death in ancient Rome.

↑ The geometric paving and palace façades of the Piazza del Campidoglio

Sun rising over the dramatic ruins of the Roman Forum ↑

3 ⟨⟩ ⟨⟩ ⟨⟩

ROMAN FORUM

📍J6 🏠 Via della Salara Vecchia 5/6 (main entrance) 🚌85, 87, 117, 175, 186, 810 Ⓜ Colosseo 🚊3 📞06 39 96 77 00 🕐8:30am–1 hour before sunset 🚫1 Jan, 25 Dec

Gazing on the picturesque ruins today, you would hardly guess that the Forum was the symbol of civic pride for 1,000 years. Its beginning, more than 3,000 years ago, was as a cemetery for the village on the Palatine Hill. When the marshy land was drained in the 6th century BC, the Forum took on a more central role.

In the early days of the Republic, the Forum was a chaotic place, containing food stalls and brothels as well as temples and the Senate House. By the 2nd century BC, Rome controlled not only Italy, but also Greece, Spain and North Africa, and the need for a more dignified centre arose. Food stalls and street hawkers were replaced by business centres, monuments and law courts. As the population expanded, the Forum became too small. However, it remained the ceremonial centre of the city under the Empire, with emperors renovating old buildings, erecting new temples and monuments, and celebrating military victories here. To appreciate the layout of the Forum before attempting to wander through its confusing patchwork of ruined temples, triumphal arches and basilicas, it is best to view the whole area from the Capitoline Hill above.

↑ Arch of Septimius Severus, a triumphal arch celebrating military victories

THE VESTAL VIRGINS

The cult of Vesta, the goddess of fire, dates back to at least the 8th century BC. Romulus and Remus were allegedly born of the Vestal priestess Rhea and the god Mars. Six virgins kept the sacred flame of Vesta burning in her circular temple. The girls, who came from noble families, were selected when they were between 6 and 10 years old, and served for 30 years. They had high status and financial security, but were buried alive if they lost their virginity and whipped by the high priest if the sacred flame died out. Although they were permitted to marry after finishing their service, few did so.

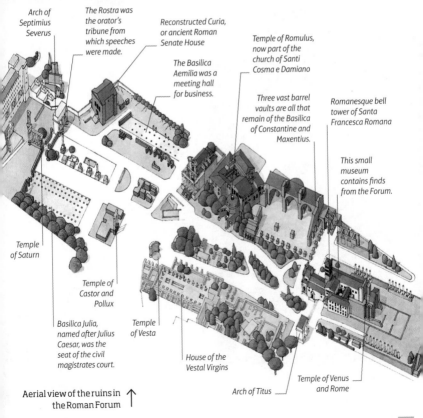

Arch of Septimius Severus

The Rostra was the orator's tribune from which speeches were made.

Reconstructed Curia, or ancient Roman Senate House

The Basilica Aemilia was a meeting hall for business.

Temple of Romulus, now part of the church of Santi Cosma e Damiano

Three vast barrel vaults are all that remain of the Basilica of Constantine and Maxentius.

Romanesque bell tower of Santa Francesca Romana

This small museum contains finds from the Forum.

Temple of Saturn

Temple of Castor and Pollux

Basilica Julia, named after Julius Caesar, was the seat of the civil magistrates court.

Temple of Vesta

House of the Vestal Virgins

Arch of Titus

Temple of Venus and Rome

Aerial view of the ruins in the Roman Forum ↑

4 ⊘ ⊘ 🖐

PALATINE

📍J7 🏛Via di San Gregorio 30 ☎06 39 96 77 00 🚌75, 80, 81, 175, 673, 850
Ⓜ Colosseo 🚃3 ⏰8:30am–1 hour before sunset 🚫1 Jan, 25 Dec

Shaded on its lower slopes with pines, and scattered in spring with wild flowers, the Palatine is the most pleasant and relaxing of Rome's ancient sites. Once the residence of emperors and aristocrats, the ruins range from the simple house in which Augustus is thought to have lived, to the Domus Flavia and Domus Augustana, the public and private wings of a luxurious palace built by Domitian at the end of the 1st century AD.

Most European languages derive their word for palace from the name of this hill. All-important in the history of early Rome, first as its birthplace and then as the site of its leaders' houses, it became the home of the glitterati of the late Republic and the Imperial family. Today the remains of elaborate fountains, colourful marble floors, fine stone carvings, columns, stuccoes and frescoes can be seen within the magnificent walls of the Imperial palaces.

↑ The Palatine Hill, seen from inside an arch of the Colosseum

A History of the Palatine Hill

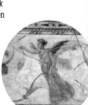

The Founding

According to legend the twins Romulus and Remus were brought up on the Palatine by a wolf. Here Romulus, having killed his brother, is said to have founded the village that was destined to become Rome. Traces of mud huts dating back to the 8th century BC have been found here, lending archaeological support to the legend.

The Republic

By the 1st century BC the Palatine was Rome's most desirable address, home to the leading citizens of the Republic. Its residents, including the erotic poet Catullus and the orator Cicero, were notoriously indulgent, their villas magnificent with doors of ivory, floors of bronze and frescoed walls.

The Empire

Augustus was born on the Palatine in 63 BC, and lived there after becoming emperor. The hill was therefore an obvious choice of abode for all future emperors. Domitian's palace, the Domus Flavia, and its private quarters, the Domus Augustana, remained the official residence of emperors for more than 300 years.

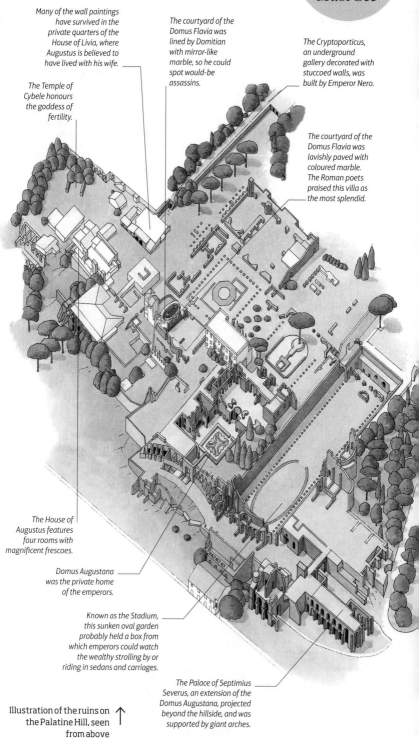

Many of the wall paintings have survived in the private quarters of the House of Livia, where Augustus is believed to have lived with his wife.

The Temple of Cybele honours the goddess of fertility.

The courtyard of the Domus Flavia was lined by Domitian with mirror-like marble, so he could spot would-be assassins.

The Cryptoporticus, an underground gallery decorated with stuccoed walls, was built by Emperor Nero.

The courtyard of the Domus Flavia was lavishly paved with coloured marble. The Roman poets praised this villa as the most splendid.

The House of Augustus features four rooms with magnificent frescoes.

Domus Augustana was the private home of the emperors.

Known as the Stadium, this sunken oval garden probably held a box from which emperors could watch the wealthy strolling by or riding in sedans and carriages.

The Palace of Septimius Severus, an extension of the Domus Augustana, projected beyond the hillside, and was supported by giant arches.

Illustration of the ruins on the Palatine Hill, seen from above ↑

EXPERIENCE MORE

5

Trajan's Forum and Markets

J5 **Via dei Fori Imperiali (Forum); Via IV Novembre (Markets)** **06 06 08** **9:30am-7:30pm daily (last adm: 6:30pm)**

Originally considered among the wonders of the Classical world, Trajan's Forum and Markets now show only a hint of their former splendour.

Trajan began to build his forum in AD 107 to commemorate his final conquest of Dacia (present-day Romania) after campaigns in AD 101–2 and 105–6. It was his most ambitious project yet, with a vast colonnaded open space centring on an equestrian statue of the emperor, a huge basilica and two big libraries. Dominating the ruins today

is Trajan's Column, which originally stood between the two libraries. Spiralling up its 30-m- (98-ft-) high stem are minutely detailed scenes from the Dacian campaigns, beginning with the Romans preparing for war and ending with the Dacians being ousted from their homeland. The subtly modelled reliefs were designed to be seen from viewing platforms on the libraries, and are consequently difficult to interpret from ground level. If you want to examine the scenes in detail, seek out the casts in the Museo della Civiltà Romana *(p319)*.

The market complex, which is situated directly behind the Forum, was begun slightly earlier. Like the Forum, it was probably designed by Apollodorus of Damascus, and was the ancient Roman equivalent of the shopping

> ## Did You Know?
>
> Palazzo Valentini runs screenings of a brilliant animation of the bas-reliefs of Trajan's Column. Book in advance.

centre. There were around 150 shops selling everything from oriental silks and spices to fruit, fresh fish and flowers. It was also here that the *annone*, or corn dole, was distributed. This was a free ration of corn given to Roman men, a practice which was introduced in the Republic by politicians who wanted to buy votes and prevent unrest during periods of famine. The markets now host contemporary art exhibitions.

6

Capitoline Museums

H6 **Piazza del Campidoglio** **40, 63, 70, 81, 87 & many other routes through Piazza Venezia** **9:30am-7:30pm daily** **1 Jan, 1 May, 25 Dec** **museicapitolini.org**

There has been a collection of Classical sculptures on the Capitoline Hill since Pope Sixtus IV, a patron of the arts and sciences, donated a group of bronze statues to the city in 1471. Paintings, as well as sculpture, are now housed in two palaces designed by Michelangelo: Palazzo Nuovo and Palazzo dei Conservatori.

The former contains a fine selection of Greek and Roman sculptures. Star exhibits include the *Discobolus*, a Greek statue showing the twisted form of a discus thrower (later transformed by an 18th-century sculptor into a wounded warrior), and

↑ The imposing complex of Trajan's Forum, built in the early 2nd century

← Antique statuary
adorning the halls of the
Capitoline Museums

Caravaggio, Van Dyck and
Titian. Highlights here include
Caravaggio's sensual and
highly unorthodox portrait
of a young *St John the Baptist*
caressing a sheep (1595–6),
Bernini's bust of the mythological, snake-haired monster
Medusa (1640s) and Pietro
da Cortona's *The Rape of the
Sabine Women* (1629), a
glamorization of the mass
abduction of Sabine women
by the Romans.

Forum of Augustus

◉ J6 **⌂** Piazza del Grillo 1
☎ 06 06 08 **🚌** 87, 186
◷ To the public, but
viewable from above

The Forum of Augustus, which
once stretched from the foot
of sleazy Suburra to the edge
of Caesar's Forum, was built to
celebrate Augustus's victory in
41 BC over Brutus and Cassius,
the assassins of Julius Caesar.
Consequentially, the temple
in its centre was dedicated to
Mars the Avenger. The temple,
with its cracked steps and four
Corinthian columns, is easily
identified. Originally it had
a statue of Mars that looked
very like Augustus, but in case
anyone failed to notice the
resemblance, a colossal statue
of the emperor himself was
placed against the wall of
the Suburra quarter.

EAT

Caffè Capitolino
The big draw of this
café-restaurant on
the top floor of the
Capitoline Museums
is its vast terrace, with
a panoramic view that
takes in rooftops and
assorted ruins. Go for
superior coffee and cake
rather than a full meal.

◉ H6 **⌂** Piazzale
Caffarelli 4 **🖳** musei
capitolini.org/it/oltre_
il_museo/cafeteria

famous Greek sculptor
Praxiteles, including his *Faun*
and *Venus of Cnidus*. Other
highlights include the *Mosaic
of the Doves*, a 1st-century-AD
mosaic that once decorated
the floor of Hadrian's Villa at
Tivoli *(p328)*, and the Hall of
the Philosophers, featuring
Roman copies of busts of
Greek politicians, scientists
and poets that once adorned
the homes of wealthy Romans.

The Palazzo dei Conservatori
was the seat of the city's
magistrates during the late
Middle Ages. Its frescoed halls
are still used occasionally for
political meetings, and the
ground floor houses the
municipal registry office.
Much of the palazzo is given
over to sculpture, including
the iconic bronze she-wolf
suckling the baby twins
Romulus and Remus, frag-
ments of a huge statue of
Constantine, and the *Spinario*,
a charming 1st-century-BC
bronze sculpture of a boy
trying to remove a thorn from
his foot. The art galleries on
the second floor hold works
by Veronese, Tintoretto,

the *Dying Galatian*, a Roman
sculpture of a wounded Celtic
soldier that has been
frequently copied by artists
since its rediscovery in the
17th century. There are also
antique copies of works by the

 HIDDEN GEM
**Villa
Aldobrandini**

High above Via IV
Novembre is this walled
garden planted with
palms and orange trees,
with plenty of benches
for a quiet picnic.

Ruins of temples and scattered columns at the Forum of Caesar

8
Forum of Caesar

 J5 ⬛ Clivo Argentario
📞 06 06 08 🚌 80, 85, 87, 175, 186, 810 🕐 To research scholars by appointment only

The first of Rome's Imperial fora was built by Julius Caesar to relieve congestion in the Roman Forum when Rome's population boomed. He spent a fortune buying up and demolishing houses on the site. Pride of place went to a temple dedicated in 46 BC to Venus Genetrix (Venus the Ancestor), as Caesar claimed to be descended from the goddess. The temple contained statues of Caesar and Cleopatra as well as of Venus, but all that remains today is a platform and three Corinthian columns. The forum was once enclosed by a double colonnade, under which was sheltered a row of shops. However, this burned down in AD 80 and was rebuilt by Domitian and Trajan. The latter also added the Basilica Argentaria – which became an important financial exchange – as well as shops and a heated public lavatory.

9
Arch of Constantine

 K7 ⬛ Between Via di San Gregorio & Piazza del Colosseo 🚌 75, 85, 87, 175, 673, 810 🚋 3 Ⓜ Colosseo

This arch was built in AD 315 to mark Constantine's victory three years before over his co-emperor Maxentius at the Battle of the Milvian Bridge. Constantine attributed the victory to a vision of Christ, but there is nothing Christian about the arch: most of the reliefs were scavenged from earlier pagan monuments.

10
Mamertine Prison

 H6 ⬛ Clivo Argentario 1
📞 06 69 89 63 75 🚌 80, 85, 87, 175, 186 🕐 8:30am–4:30pm daily

Below the 16th-century church of San Giuseppe dei Falegnami is a dank dungeon in which, according

← The Arch of Constantine, one of Imperial Rome's last monuments

to Christian legend, St Peter and St Paul were imprisoned. They are said to have caused a spring to bubble up into the cell, and to have used the water to baptize two prison guards. The prison was in an old cistern with access to the city's main sewer (the Cloaca Maxima). The lower cell was used for executions, and corpses were thrown into the sewer. However, the inmates, who received no food, often died of starvation.

Santa Maria in Aracoeli

Q H5 **A** Scala dell'Arce Capitolina 14 **C** 06 69 76 38 39 **E** 63, 70, 81 **O** 9am–6:30pm daily (9:30am–5:30pm in winter)

This church stands on the site of the temple of Juno on the northern summit of the Capitoline Hill, and dates back to at least the 6th century. The church is famous for its ornate gilded ceiling and a very fine series of frescoes by Pinturicchio, dating from the 1480s. They depict scenes from the life of San Bernardino of Siena. The miracle-working *Santo Bambino* figure, stolen in 1994, has been replaced by a replica.

Palazzo Valentini

Q H5 **E** Via IV Novembre 119a **O** 9:30am–6:30pm Wed-Mon **W** palazzo valentini.it

During maintenance work in the basement of Palazzo Valentini in 2005, the remains of two houses belonging to

a leading patrician family of Imperial Rome were discovered. Elegant living rooms, courtyards, a kitchen and a private baths complex were revealed, complete with fascinating traces of their original decorations.

Using digital technology, light and sound effects, film and projections, the houses have been "reconstructed", creating a virtual-reality museum that brings ancient Rome vividly to life. Tours take visitors through the rooms. It is an incredible experience – as you watch, mosaic floors, marble decorations, statues and frescoed walls are restored to their former glory, while sound effects are used to recreate an earthquake that buckled the floors in AD 38.

→

Pinturicchio's frescoes in the church of Santa Maria in Aracoeli

DRINK

American Bar
Nestled in greenery and offering stunning views of the Imperial Forums, this old-time rooftop bar is a lovely spot for a cocktail in the summer. There's also a smart restaurant attached, if you want to make a night of it.

Q J5 **A** Hotel Forum, Via Tor de' Conti 25 **W** hotelforum.com

ROME: AROUND PIAZZA NAVONA

The area around Piazza Navona, known as the *centro storico*, has been inhabited for at least 2,000 years. Piazza Navona stands above an ancient stadium; the Pantheon has been a temple since AD 27; and the ruins of the Curia of Pompey remain in the Area Sacra di Largo Argentina. The area's heyday began in the 15th century, when the papacy returned to Rome. Throughout the 16th, 17th and 18th centuries, princes, popes and cardinals settled here, as did the artists and artisans they commissioned to build and adorn lavish palaces, churches and fountains.

The area showcases Baroque Rome in all its glory, with curvaceous architecture and elaborate fountains by the era's two greatest architects, Bernini and Borromini, and churches filled with works by Caravaggio and Rubens. These days Piazza Navona is a centre of Roman nightlife, but the area's artistic heritage lives on in the workshops of craftsmen and antiques restorers, while some of its ancient buildings, such as the Theatre of Marcellus in the Ghetto, have been converted into exclusive flats.

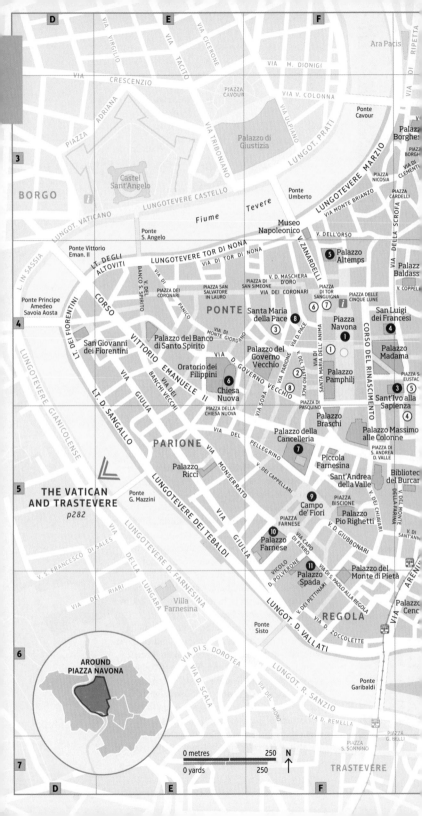

ROME: AROUND PIAZZA NAVONA

Must Sees

1 Piazza Navona
2 The Pantheon

Experience More

3 Sant'Ivo alla Sapienza
4 San Luigi dei Francesi
5 Palazzo Altemps
6 Chiesa Nuova
7 Palazzo della Cancelleria
8 Santa Maria della Pace
9 Campo de' Fiori
10 Palazzo Farnese
11 Palazzo Spada
12 Ghetto and Tiber Island
13 Area Sacra di Largo Argentina
14 Gesù
15 Palazzo Doria Pamphilj
16 Santa Maria sopra Minerva
17 Sant'Ignazio di Loyola
18 Piazza Colonna
19 Piazza di Montecitorio
20 La Maddalena

Eat

1 Tre Scalini
2 Lo Zozzone
3 Osteria del Pegno
4 Casa Bleve

Drink

5 Caffè Sant'Eustachio

Stay

6 Hotel Raphael

Shop

7 Antica Libreria Cascianelli
8 Delfina Delettrez

↑ The Baroque fountains and elegant buildings of bustling Piazza Navona

❶

PIAZZA NAVONA

📍F4 🚌46, 62, 64, 70, 81, 87, 116, 492, 628

No other piazza in Rome can rival the theatricality of Piazza Navona. The luxurious cafés are the social centre of the city, and day and night there is always something going on in the pedestrian area around the three flamboyant Baroque fountains.

Piazza Navona is dominated by the Egyptian obelisk, cascading waters and gleaming marble figures of Bernini's Fontana dei Quattro Fiumi (1651), which features representations of the four great rivers of the time (the Nile, the Plate, the Ganges and the Danube). Bernini also sculpted a Moor wrestling a dolphin at the centre of the Fontana del Moro to the south of

the square. At the north of the square is the 19th-century Fontana di Nettuno, showing the sea god Neptune struggling with a sea monster. Looming over the centre of the square is Sant'Agnese in Agone, a church dedicated to a virgin martyred on the site in AD 304 for refusing to marry a pagan. Borromini designed the church's startling concave façade (1652–7).

1500–1600

Rome's city market is transferred from the Campidoglio to Piazza Navona.

1655–1866

Every August, the fountains are plugged and the piazza flooded. The lower classes swim while the aristocrats watch from their carriages.

Timeline

1–100 AD

△ A stadium is built for athletic contests (*agones*), chariot races and other sports. Piazza Navona is later built to follow the shape of this stadium.

1644–55

△ Pope Innocent X, whose family palazzo is on the piazza, commissions a new church, palace and fountain for the square.

1869

Rome's city market moves to the nearby Campo de' Fiori.

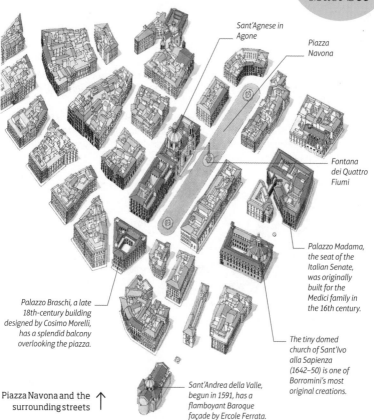

Sant'Agnese in Agone

Piazza Navona

Fontana dei Quattro Fiumi

Palazzo Madama, the seat of the Italian Senate, was originally built for the Medici family in the 16th century.

The tiny domed church of Sant'Ivo alla Sapienza (1642–50) is one of Borromini's most original creations.

Palazzo Braschi, a late 18th-century building designed by Cosimo Morelli, has a splendid balcony overlooking the piazza.

Sant'Andrea della Valle, begun in 1591, has a flamboyant Baroque façade by Ercole Ferrata.

Piazza Navona and the surrounding streets ↑

① Bernini's elaborate Fontana dei Quattro Fiumi forms the centrepiece of Piazza Navona.

② The square is lined with art stalls in the daytime, while buskers and mime artists perform after dark.

③ Dotted around Piazza Navona are numerous places to dine al fresco.

THE LEGEND OF THE FOUNTAIN

The rivalry between Bernini and Borromini has given rise to the legend that the veiled head of the river Nile in the Fontana dei Quattro Fiumi was Bernini's way of conveying his disgust at Borromini's façade for Sant'Agnese in Agone, while the figure of the river Plate, with his arm upraised, expresses Bernini's fear that the church is so badly constructed it might collapse. In fact, the fountain was completed a year before construction on the church began.

2 ⓂⓈ

PANTHEON

📍G4 🏛Piazza della Rotonda 🚌116 and routes along Via del Corso, Corso Vittorio Emanuele II & Corso del Rinascimento 🕐9am–7:30pm Mon–Sat, 9am–6pm Sun, 9am–1pm public hols 🚫1 Jan, 1 May, 25 Dec 🌐pantheonroma.com

With its awe-inspiring domed interior, the Pantheon – the Roman temple of "all the gods" – is the best-preserved ancient building in Rome. Unlike many other Roman structures that fell into disrepair, it became a church in the 7th century, ensuring its continued use and conservation.

↑ The Pantheon's immense portico, built on the foundations of Agrippa's temple

Inside the Pantheon

The interior of the church is dominated by the vast hemispherical dome, which has both a height and diameter of 43.3 m (142 ft). The hole at the top of the dome, the oculus, provides the only light source; we owe this marvel of engineering to the emperor Hadrian, who designed the structure (AD 118–125) to replace an earlier temple built by Marcus Agrippa, son-in-law of Augustus. The shrines that line the wall of the Pantheon range from the Tomb of Raphael to those of the kings of Italy.

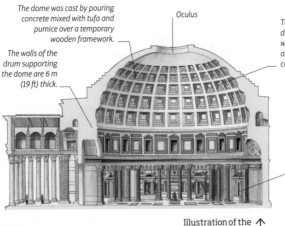

The dome was cast by pouring concrete mixed with tufa and pumice over a temporary wooden framework.

Oculus

The hollow coffers in the dome help to reduce its weight. Many Renaissance and Baroque architects copied this technique.

The walls of the drum supporting the dome are 6 m (19 ft) thick.

The Tomb of Raphael rests below a Madonna *sculpture by Lorenzetto (1520).*

Illustration of the Pantheon ↑

Timeline

27–25 BC
△ Marcus Agrippa builds first Pantheon.

118–25
Hadrian builds new Pantheon.

609
▽ Pope Boniface IV consecrates Pantheon as church of Santa Maria ad Martyres.

663
Byzantine Emperor Constans II strips gilded tiles from the roof.

1309–77
While the papal seat is in Avignon, Pantheon is used as a poultry market.

1632
△ Urban VIII melts bronze from portico for the baldacchino in St Peter's.

Did You Know?
—
The Pantheon's dome remains the largest unreinforced concrete dome in the world.

Oculus and coffered ↑
interior of the
Pantheon's dome

Ornate Baroque interior of the church of San Luigi dei Francesi

5

Palazzo Altemps

⚲F4 ⌂Via di Sant' Apollinare 46 ☎06 39 96 77 00 🚌70, 81, 87, 115, 280, 628 🕐9am-7:45pm Tue–Sun 🚫1 Jan, 25 Dec

An extraordinary collection of Classical sculpture is housed in this branch of the Museo Nazionale Romano *(p281)*. Restored as a museum during the 1990s, the palazzo was originally built for Girolamo Riario, nephew of Pope Sixtus IV in 1480. In the popular uprising that followed the pope's death in 1484, the building was sacked and Girolamo fled the city. In 1568 Cardinal Marco Sittico Altemps bought the palazzo; it was renovated in the 1570s by Martino Longhi the Elder, who added the obelisk-crowned belvedere and marble unicorn.

The Altemps family were avid collectors; the courtyard and its staircase are lined with ancient sculptures, which complement the Ludovisi sculptures. One of the highlights is the marble statue *Galata's Suicide*, a copy of the original in the Salone del Camino. On the first floor is the Greek, 5th-century-BC Ludovisi Throne, with a panel depicting Aphrodite.

6

Chiesa Nuova

⚲E4 ⌂Via del Governo Vecchio 134 ☎06 687 52 89 🚌46, 64 🕐7:30am–noon & 4:30-7pm daily

San Filippo Neri commissioned this church in 1575 to replace the dilapidated one given to his Order by Pope Gregory XIII. Neri required his followers to humble themselves, and

EXPERIENCE MORE

3

Sant'Ivo alla Sapienza

⚲G4 ⌂Corso del Rinascimento 40 ☎06 06 08 (tourist information) 🚌30, 70, 81, 87, 116, 186, 492, 628 🕐9am-noon Sun

Hidden in the courtyard of Palazzo della Sapienza, seat of the old University of Rome, Sant'Ivo's spiral belfry is nevertheless a distinctive landmark on Rome's skyline. Built by Borromini in 1642–60, the church is astonishingly complex, an ingenious combination of concave and convex surfaces. The work spanned the reigns of three popes, and incorporated in the design are their emblems: Urban VIII's bee, Innocent X's dove and olive branch, and the star and hills of Alexander VII.

4

San Luigi dei Francesi

⚲F4 ⌂Piazza di San Luigi de' Francesi 5 ☎06 68 82 71 🚌70, 81, 87, 116, 186, 492, 628 🕐Opening times vary, check website 🌐saintlouis-rome.net

The French national church in Rome, San Luigi is a 16th-century building that is best known for three magnificent canvases by Caravaggio in the Cerasi chapel. Painted between 1597 and 1602, these were Caravaggio's first significant religious works: *The Calling of St Matthew*, *Martyrdom of St Matthew* and *St Matthew and the Angel*. The first version of this last was initially rejected because it depicted the saint as an old man with dirty feet.

he set aristocratic young men to work as labourers on the church.

Against his wishes, the nave, apse and dome were richly frescoed after his death by Pietro da Cortona. There are three paintings by Rubens around the altar. The first versions were rejected, so Rubens repainted them on slate, placing the originals above his mother's tomb.

 7

Palazzo della Cancelleria

F5 Piazza della Cancelleria **06 69 88 75 66** 46, 62, 64, 116, 916 **7:30am–8pm Mon–Sat, 9:30am–7:30pm Sun & hols**

A supreme example of early Renaissance architecture, this palazzo, begun in 1485, was allegedly financed by the gambling proceeds of Raffaele Riario, Pope Sixtus I's nephew.

In 1478 Riario was involved in the Pazzi conspiracy against the Medici, and when Giovanni de' Medici became Pope Leo XIII in 1513, he took belated revenge, turning the palace into the papal chancellery.

 8

Santa Maria della Pace

F4 Vicolo del Arco della Pace 5 70, 81, 87, 116, 492, 628 **9–11:45am Mon, Wed & Sat**

Named by Pope Sixtus IV to celebrate the peace he hoped to bring to Italy, this church dates from the 1480s and contains a beautiful fresco by Raphael. Bramante's refined cloister was added in 1504, while the façade was designed in 1656 by Pietro da Cortona.

One of three Rubens paintings near the altar in the Chiesa Nuova ↓

EAT

Tre Scalini

This terrace café is famous for its *tartufo* – dark-chocolate ice cream studded with shards of bitter chocolate and served with a wafer and smear of whipped cream.

F4 Piazza Navona 28 Wed **06 68 80 19 96**

€€€

Lo Zozzone

A Roman institution, this homely place on a cobbled side street near Piazza Navona serves *pizza bianca* stuffed with an array of fillings from mozzarella to artichoke.

F4 Via del Teatro Pace **06 68 80 85 75**

€€€

Osteria del Pegno

This romantic restaurant offers a menu of perfectly executed Italian dishes. Complimentary limoncello and homemade biscuits round off a meal nicely.

F4 Vicolo Montevecchio 8 **06 68 80 70 25**

€€€

Casa Bleve

In a grand vaulted dining room, this *enoteca*-restaurant has an impressive wine list and gourmet offerings.

G4 Via del Teatro Valle 48 casa bleve.com

€€€

⑨ Campo de' Fiori

♥ F5 **🚌 116 & routes to Corso Vittorio Emanuele II**

Campo de' Fiori (Field of Flowers) was one of the liveliest and roughest areas of medieval and Renaissance Rome. Cardinals and nobles mingled with fishmongers and foreigners in the piazza's market; Caravaggio killed his opponent after losing a game of tennis on the square; and the goldsmith Cellini murdered a business rival nearby. Today, the area continues to be a hub of secular activity, with a colourful morning market (Monday to Saturday), and numerous bars and trattorias.

In the Renaissance the piazza was surrounded by inns, many of which were owned by the 15th-century courtesan Vannozza Catanei, mistress of Pope Alexander VI.

The square was also a place of execution. The statue in its centre is the philosopher Giordano Bruno, burned at the stake for heresy on this spot in 1600 for suggesting the earth moved around the sun.

⑩ Palazzo Farnese

♥ F5 **🏛 Piazza Farnese**
🚌 23, 116, 280 & routes to Corso Vittorio Emanuele II
🌐 inventerrome.com

Originally constructed for Cardinal Alessandro Farnese, who became Pope Paul III in 1534, this palazzo was started by Antonio da Sangallo the Younger, and continued after his death by Michelangelo.

The palace, now the French Embassy, can be seen only as part of a private tour.

⑪   Palazzo Spada

♥ F5 **🏛 Piazza Capo di Ferro 13** **📞 06 683 24 09** **🚌 23, 116, 280 & routes to Largo di Torre Argentina**
🕐 8:30am–7:30pm daily
🚫 1 Jan, 25 Dec

A stucco extravaganza studded with reliefs of illustrious Romans, this palazzo was built in 1550, but bought in 1637 by Cardinal Bernardino Spada. A keen patron of the arts, Spada commissioned Borromini to create an illusionistic tunnel that appears four times longer than it is. The cardinal's art collection, in the Galleria Spada, includes works by Guercino, Dürer and Artemisia Gentileschi.

⑫ Ghetto and Tiber Island

♥ G6 **🚌 23, 63, 280, 780 & routes to Largo di Torre Argentina**

The first Jews came to Rome as traders in the 2nd century BC and were greatly appreciated for their financial and medical skills during the Roman Empire. Persecution began in the 16th century, when Pope Paul IV forced all of the Jews to live within a walled enclosure, an area later to form the hub of the present-day Ghetto.

Today Via del Portico d'Ottavia, the district's main street, leads to Rome's central synagogue. Ponte Fabricio links the Ghetto with Tiber Island, a centre of healing since 293 BC, when a Temple to Aesculapius was founded. The island is now home to a hospital.

STAY

Hotel Raphael

This historic vine-covered hotel offers modern-luxe rooms designed by architect Richard Meier, as well as more traditional options. There's also a good vegetarian restaurant and a stunning rooftop bar.

♥ F4 **🏛 Largo Febo 2**
🌐 raphaelhotel.com

€€€

Stalls selling colourful fruit and vegetables at the Campo de' Fiori market ↑

→ Lush gardens on Tiber Island, now home to a hospital

 13

Area Sacra di Largo Argentina

📍 G5 📌 Largo di Torre Argentina 🚌 40, 46, 62, 64, 70, 81, 87, 186, 492 🕐 To the public

The remains of four temples were discovered here in the 1920s. Dating from the Republican era, they are among the oldest in Rome, and are known as temples A, B, C and D. The oldest (temple C) dates from the early 3rd century BC. It was placed on a high platform preceded by an altar and is typical of Italic temple plans. Temple A is from the 3rd century BC, but in medieval times the small church of San Nicola di Cesarini was built over its podium. The column stumps to the north belonged to a great portico, known as the Hecatostylum (portico of 100 columns). Behind temples B and C, near Via di Torre Argentina, are the remains of a great platform of tufa blocks. These have been identified as part of the Curia of Pompey, a building where the Senate met, and where Julius Caesar was assassinated by Brutus, Cassius and their followers on 15 March 44 BC.

 14

Gesù

📍 G5 📌 Piazza del Gesù 📞 06 69 70 01 🚌 H, 46, 62, 64, 70, 81, 87, 186, 492, 628 & other routes 🕐 7am–12:30pm & 4-7:45pm daily

Built between 1568 and 1584, the Gesù was Rome's first Jesuit church. The Jesuit order was founded in 1537 by a Basque soldier, Ignatius Loyola, who became a Christian after

SHOP

Antica Libreria Cascianelli

Located opposite the Hotel Raphael, this wonderful shop (in business since 1837) is an Aladdin's cave of antiquarian books, vintage posters, postcards and maps, as well as antiques. It's a very rewarding place for a browse.

📍 F4 📌 Largo Febo 14 📞 328 785 0288 🕐 Sun am

Delfina Delettrez

A scion of the Fendi dynasty, Delettrez is a jeweller whose bold and distinctive creations are beautifully arrayed in this sparkling little boutique made to resemble a jewellery box.

📍 F4 📌 Via del Governo Vecchio 67 🕐 Sun & Mon am 🌐 delfinadelettrez.com

Did You Know?

Michelangelo offered to design the Gesù church for free, but died before it reached the planning stages.

being wounded in battle. The order was heavily engaged in missionary activity.

The much-imitated design of the Gesù typifies Counter-Reformation architecture, with a large nave with side pulpits for preaching to crowds, and a main altar as the centrepiece for the Mass. The illusionistic decoration on the nave ceiling and dome was added by Il Baciccia in the 17th century.

The nave depicts the *Triumph of the Name of Jesus* and its message is clear: faithful, Catholic worshippers will be joyfully uplifted to Heaven while Protestants and heretics are flung into the fires of Hell. The message is reiterated in the Cappella di Sant'Ignazio, a rich display of lapis lazuli, silver and gold. The Baroque marble by Legros, *Triumph of Faith over Idolatry*, shows a female "Religion" trampling on the head of the serpent Idolatry, while in Théudon's *Barbarians Adoring the Faith*, an angel aims a kick towards a decrepit old barbarian couple entangled with a snake.

Palazzo Doria Pamphilj

📍 H5 🏛 Via del Corso 305
🚍 64, 81, 119, 492 🕐 9am–7pm daily 🚫 1 Jan, Easter Sun, 1 May, 25 Dec
🌐 doriapamphilj.it

Palazzo Doria Pamphilj is a vast edifice whose oldest parts date from 1435. When the Pamphilj family took over in 1647 they built a new wing, a splendid chapel and a theatre.

The family art collection has over 400 paintings dating from the 15th to 18th centuries, including a portrait of Pope Innocent X by Velázquez and works by Titian, Guercino, Caravaggio and Claude Lorrain. The opulent rooms of the private apartments retain many of their original furnishings, including Brussels and Gobelins tapestries, Murano chandeliers and a gilded crib.

16
Santa Maria sopra Minerva

📍 G4 🏛 Piazza della Minerva 42 ☎ 06 679 39 26
🚍 116 & many other routes
🕐 10:30am–12:30pm & 2–7pm daily

One of Rome's rare Gothic buildings, this church was built in the 13th century over what were thought to be the ruins of a Temple of Minerva. It was a stronghold of the Dominicans, who produced some of the Church's most infamous inquisitors and tried the scientist Galileo

→

Marble sculpture in the church of Santa Maria sopra Minerva

in the adjoining monastery. Inside, the church has a superb collection of art and sculpture, ranging from 13th-century Cosmatesque tombs to a bust by Bernini. Highlights include Antoniazzo Romano's *Annunciation* (featuring Cardinal Juan de Torquemada, uncle of the vicious Spanish Inquisitor), and the Carafa Chapel's frescoes by Filippino Lippi.

In the Aldobrandini Chapel are the tombs of the 16th-century Medici popes, Leo X and his cousin Clement VII, and near the steps of the choir is a stocky *Risen Christ*, begun by Michelangelo.

The church also contains the tombs of many famous Italians, such as St Catherine of Siena who died in 1380, and Fra Angelico, the Dominican friar and painter, who died in 1455. Outside, Bernini's spectacular sculpture of an elephant holds an obelisk on its back.

17
Sant'Ignazio di Loyola

📍 G4 🏛 Piazza di Sant' Ignazio ☎ 06 679 44 06
🚍 117, 119, 492 🕐 7:30am–7pm Mon–Sat, 9am–7pm Sun

This church was built by Pope Gregory XV in 1626 in honour of St gnatius of Loyola, founder of the Society of Jesus (Jesuits) and the man who most

embodied the zeal of the Counter-Reformation. Along with the Gesù (p265), Sant'Ignazio forms the nucleus of the Jesuit area of Rome. It is one of the city's most extravagant Baroque churches and its vast interior is plated with precious stones, marble, stucco and gilt, creating a thrilling sense of theatre. The church has a Latin-cross plan, with an apse and many side chapels.

A cupola was planned but never built, as the nuns from a nearby convent objected that it would obscure the view from their roof garden. Instead the space was filled by a perspective painting of a dome on a flat disc.

Even more striking is the illusionistic ceiling created by the Jesuit artist Andrea Pozzo in 1685, a propagandist extravaganza extolling the success of Jesuit missionaries throughout the world. Above four women, representing Asia, Europe, America and Africa, lithe angels and beautiful youths are sucked into a heaven of fluffy clouds.

↑ Night time in Piazza di Montecitorio, with its Egyptian obelisk

 18

Piazza Colonna

◉H4 🚌116, 117, 492

Home to Palazzo Chigi, official residence of the prime minister, Piazza Colonna is dominated by the Column of Marcus Aurelius. This was erected after the death of Marcus Aurelius in AD 180 to commemorate his victories over the barbarian tribes of the Danube. It is an imitation of Trajan's Column *(p250)*, but the style of the relief sculptures is different. The wars of Marcus Aurelius are rendered with simplified pictures in stronger relief – Classical proportions have been sacrificed for clarity.

 19

Piazza di Montecitorio

◉G4 📞06 676 01 🚌116 **◷**1st Sun of month (except Jul–early Sep)

The obelisk in the centre of Piazza di Montecitorio formed the spine of a giant sundial brought back from Egypt by Augustus. It vanished in the 9th century, and was rediscovered under medieval houses during the reign of Julius II (1503–13).

The piazza is dominated by the Palazzo di Montecitorio, designed by Bernini and completed in 1697, after his death, by Carlo Fontana. It has been the seat of Italy's Chamber of Deputies since the late 19th century.

 20

La Maddalena

◉G4 **⌂**Piazza della Maddalena 53 📞06 899 281 🚌116 & many other routes **◷**8:30–11:30am Mon–Fri & Sun, 9–11:30am Sat, 5–6pm daily

Situated in a small piazza near the Pantheon, the Maddalena's façade, constructed in 1735, epitomizes the dynamism of the late Baroque. Its curves recall Borromini's San Carlo alle Quattro Fontane *(p279)*. The façade has been restored, despite the protests of Neo-Classicists who dismissed its painted stucco as icing sugar.

The diminutive dimensions of the church did not deter 17th- and 18th-century decorators from filling the interior with paintings and ornaments from the floor to the top of the elegant cupola.

DRINK

Caffè Sant'Eustachio
Many Romans believe that this tiny bar serves the city's best coffee – hence the hordes of locals that throng it from morning till late. There's a tempting selection of coffee-flavoured cakes too.

◉G4
⌂Via Sant'Eustachio 82 **ⓦ**santeustachio ilcaffe.com

ROME: NORTHEAST

This area stretches from the exclusive shopping streets around Piazza di Spagna to the Esquiline Hill, a once bourgeois but now run-down area full of early Christian churches, their interiors mosaicked like jewellery boxes. The Piazza di Spagna and Piazza del Popolo district grew up in the 16th century, when the increase in the influx of pilgrims was such that a road was built to channel them as quickly as possible to the Vatican. About the same time, the Quirinal Hill became the site of a papal palace. When Rome became capital of Italy in 1870, Via Veneto grew into a lavish residential area, and the Esquiline was covered with apartments for the new civil servants.

One of the busiest parts of the city, Northeast Rome offers plenty of opportunities for window-shopping, sightseeing and dining. The city's most fashionable *passeggiata* unfolds down the length of the Via del Corso, while tourists flock to Rome's most famous fountain, the Trevi. The trendy Monti district offers an array of hip shops, restaurants and bars, and Rome's most multicultural quarter, the Esquiline, is the city's best spot for ethnic dining options.

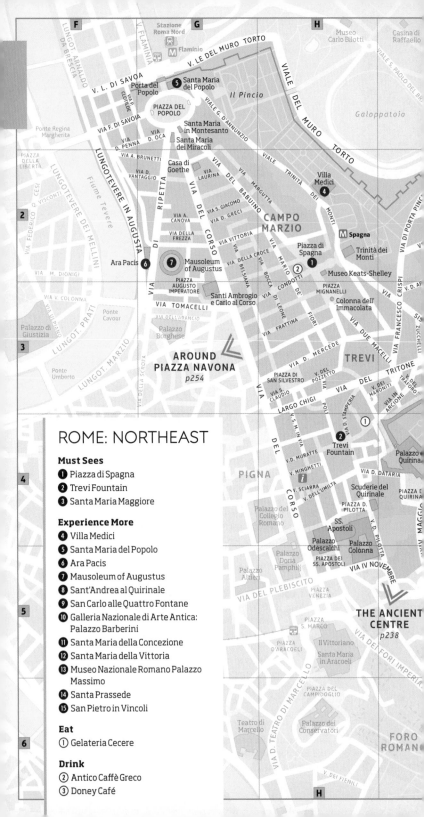

ROME: NORTHEAST

Must Sees

1. Piazza di Spagna
2. Trevi Fountain
3. Santa Maria Maggiore

Experience More

4. Villa Medici
5. Santa Maria del Popolo
6. Ara Pacis
7. Mausoleum of Augustus
8. Sant'Andrea al Quirinale
9. San Carlo alle Quattro Fontane
10. Galleria Nazionale di Arte Antica: Palazzo Barberini
11. Santa Maria della Concezione
12. Santa Maria della Vittoria
13. Museo Nazionale Romano Palazzo Massimo
14. Santa Prassede
15. San Pietro in Vincoli

Eat

1. Gelateria Cecere

Drink

2. Antico Caffè Greco
3. Doney Café

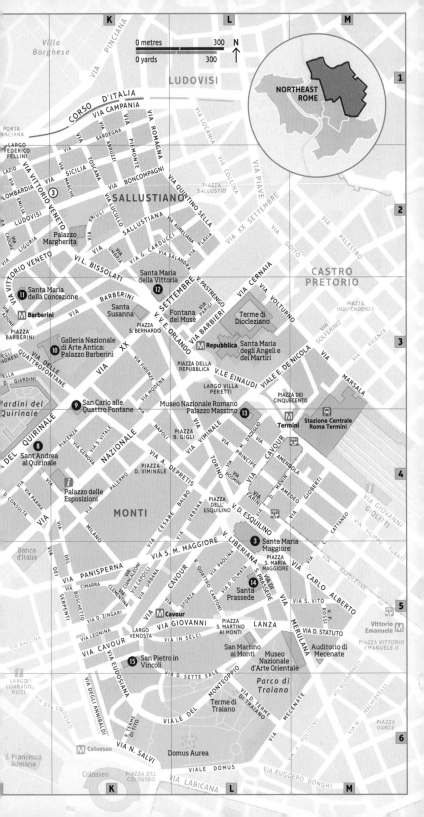

❶
PIAZZA DI SPAGNA

📍 H2 🚌 116, 117, 119 Ⓜ Spagna

Shaped like a crooked bow tie and surrounded by tall, shuttered houses painted in muted shades of ochre, pink and cream, Piazza di Spagna is crowded all day and (in summer) most of the night. It is the most famous square in Rome, long the haunt of expatriates and foreign visitors.

↑ View from outside the Trinità dei Monti, at the top of the Spanish Steps

History of Piazza di Spagna

In the 17th century the Spanish embassy was on the square, and the area around it was deemed to be Spanish territory – anyone who unwittingly trespassed was in danger of being dragooned into the Spanish army. In the 18th and 19th centuries the square stood at the heart of the main hotel district, attracting aristocrats doing the Grand Tour, as well as artists, writers and composers.

Spanish Steps

In 1700, the Bourbon royal family became the rulers of Spain as well as France. It was decided to symbolize their power by linking the French church of Trinità dei Monti with the Spanish Embassy by building the steps.

←

Frescoes by Daniele di Volterra inside the Trinità dei Monti

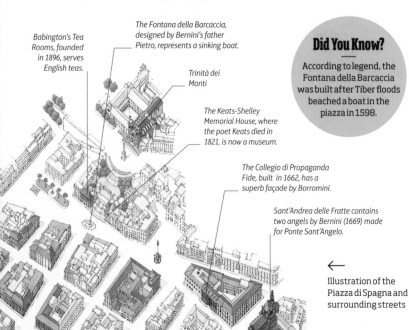

Babington's Tea Rooms, founded in 1896, serves English teas.

The Fontana della Barcaccia, designed by Bernini's father Pietro, represents a sinking boat.

Trinità dei Monti

The Keats-Shelley Memorial House, where the poet Keats died in 1821, is now a museum.

The Collegio di Propaganda Fide, built in 1662, has a superb façade by Borromini.

Sant'Andrea delle Fratte contains two angels by Bernini (1669) made for Ponte Sant'Angelo.

Did You Know?
—
According to legend, the Fontana della Barcaccia was built after Tiber floods beached a boat in the piazza in 1598.

←

Illustration of the Piazza di Spagna and surrounding streets

The Fontana della Barcaccia at
the foot of the Spanish Steps ↑

②

TREVI FOUNTAIN

◉ H4 🚌 52, 53, 61, 62, 63, 71, 80, 116, 119 and other routes along Via del Corso and Via del Tritone

Tucked away on a tiny piazza, this is the most famous – and the largest – fountain in Rome. Built in 1762 by Italian architect Nicola Salvi, in the flamboyant Rococo style, the Trevi Fountain is a creamy travertine extravaganza of rearing sea-horses, conch-blowing Tritons, craggy rocks and flimsy palm trees built into the side of the Palazzo Poli.

Trevi Water

Legend has it that the fountain is named after a young virgin named Trivia who showed Roman engineers the location of a freshwater spring. The water now comes from the Acqua Vergine, a Roman aqueduct built in 19 BC and fed by springs some 22 km (14 miles) from the city.

In the 19th century, Trevi water was considered the sweetest in Rome, and English residents are said to have kept supplies at home for making tea. These days chemicals are added to the water to keep algae at bay. A long-standing tradition states that anyone who wants to guarantee their return to the city should throw a coin in the water – around €3,000 is thrown into the fountain daily.

→

Relief depicting Trivia revealing the location of the freshwater spring

EAT

Gelateria Cecere
The simple, long-established Cecere has a loyal following among Romans for its ice cream, made to an old (and secret) family recipe. It is famous for its rich marsala-spiked *zabaglione* flavour, but the pistachio and chocolate are fabulous too.

◉ H4 🏠 Via del Lavatore 85 **☎** 06 679 2060

Ⓢ Ⓢ Ⓢ

LA DOLCE VITA

Federico Fellini's 1960 film is about a *paparazzo* (played by Marcello Mastroianni) drifting through the decadent nightlife of Rome, and meeting a beautiful Swedish actress played by Anita Ekberg. The well-known scene – Ekberg taking a shower in the Trevi Fountain – may be largely responsible for making the Trevi the most famous and photographed fountain in the city.

Sculptures

The central statue of Neptune, Roman God of the Sea, was executed by Pietro Bracci, who took over work on the fountain after the death of Nicola Salvi, his long-time friend, in 1751. The theme of the work, ingeniously grafted onto the back of a palazzo, is the taming of the waters.

Neptune's conch-shell chariot is powered by two sea-horses steered by Tritons. One Triton struggles to master an unruly beast, while the other leads a far more docile animal. The horses symbolize the different moods of the sea. In the niches next to Nepture are figures representing Abundance (to his left), with her cornocopia of fruit, and Salubrity (on his right), who holds a cup from which a snake drinks.

→

Detail of a conch-blowing Triton leading a *hippocampo* (sea-horse)

↓ The Trevi Fountain, set against the façade of the Palazzo Poli

↑ Façade of the basilica, seen from Piazza di Santa Maria Maggiore

3 🛍

SANTA MARIA MAGGIORE

📍L4 🏛Piazza di Santa Maria Maggiore 📞06 69 88 68 00 🚌16, 70, 71, 714
🚊14 Ⓜ Termini, Cavour 🕐7am-6:45pm daily

The biggest among the 26 churches in Rome dedicated to the Virgin Mary, Santa Maria Maggiore was originally built in the 5th century. It was adapted by many popes over the centuries, giving it an unusual mix of different architectural styles.

Legend has it that Pope Liberius had Santa Maria Maggiore built after he dreamt the Virgin told him to construct a church on the spot where he found snow. When it fell on the Esquiline in the middle of a baking hot August day, he set to work. Santa Maria Maggiore's colonnaded nave is part of the original 5th-century building. The Cosmatesque marble floor and Romanesque bell tower are medieval. The Renaissance saw a new coffered ceiling, and the Baroque gave the church twin domes and its imposing front and rear façades. The mosaics are Santa Maria's most famous feature.

The biblical scenes in the aisle and the mosaics on the triumphal arch date from the 5th century. Medieval highlights include a 13th-century enthroned Christ in the loggia.

↑ Mosaics and baldacchino inside Santa Maria Maggiore

←

Virgin and Child sculpture in Piazza di Santa Maria Maggiore

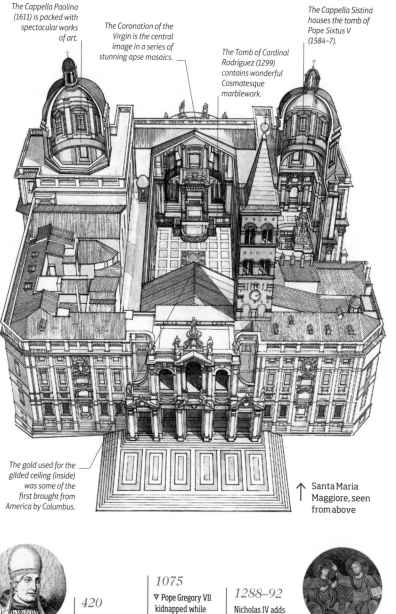

The Cappella Paolina (1611) is packed with spectacular works of art.

The Coronation of the Virgin is the central image in a series of stunning apse mosaics.

The Tomb of Cardinal Rodriguez (1299) contains wonderful Cosmatesque marblework.

The Cappella Sistina houses the tomb of Pope Sixtus V (1584–7).

The gold used for the gilded ceiling (inside) was some of the first brought from America by Columbus.

↑ Santa Maria Maggiore, seen from above

Timeline

356
△ Virgin appears to Pope Liberius

420
Probable founding date

432–40
Sixtus III completes church

1075
▽ Pope Gregory VII kidnapped while saying Christmas Mass here

1288–92
Nicholas IV adds apse and transepts

1347
Cola di Rienzo crowned Tribune of Rome in Santa Maria Maggiore

1673
△ Carlo Rainaldi rebuilds apse

The elegant location of the 16th-century Villa Medici

EXPERIENCE MORE

4 🏛🅜🖼

Villa Medici

◉ H2 **⌂** Accademia di Francia a Roma, Viale Trinità dei Monti 1 ▦117 **Ⓜ** Spagna **◷** For tours 11am & 3:30pm Tue-Sun **Ⓦ** villamedici.it

Superbly positioned on the Pincio Hill, above Piazza di Spagna, this 16th-century villa has retained the name that it assumed when Cardinal Ferdinando de' Medici bought it in 1576. From the terrace you can look across the city to Castel Sant'Angelo. It is now home to the French Academy, founded by Louis XIV in 1666 to give artists the chance to study in Rome. From 1803 musicians were also allowed to study here: both Berlioz and Debussy were students.

The villa is only open for exhibitions and guided tours. Tours include the formal gardens, which feature a gorgeously frescoed pavilion and copies of ancient statues.

5

Santa Maria del Popolo

◉ G1 **⌂** Piazza del Popolo 12 **☎** 06 361 08 36 ▦117, 119, 490, 495, 926 **Ⓜ** Flaminio **◷** 7:30am-12:30pm & 4-7pm Sun-Thu, 7:30am-7pm Fri & Sat

Santa Maria del Popolo, one of the first Renaissance churches in Rome, was commissioned by Pope Sixtus IV in 1472.

↑ Trompe l'oeil cupola in the church of Santa Maria del Popolo

Lavish endowments have made it one of Rome's greatest artistic treasures.

Shortly after Sixtus died in 1484, Pinturicchio and his pupils frescoed two chapels (first and third right) for the della Rovere family. On the altar of the first chapel there is a lovely *Nativity* from 1490 that depicts a stable at the foot of a Classical column.

In 1503 Sixtus IV's nephew Giuliano became Pope Julius II and had Bramante build a new apse. Pinturicchio was called in again to paint its vaults with Sibyls and Apostles framed in an intricate tracery of freakish beasts.

In 1513 Raphael created the Chigi chapel (second left) for the wealthy banker Agostino Chigi. The design is a bold Renaissance fusion of the sacred and profane; there are pyramid-like tombs and a ceiling mosaic of God holding the signs of the zodiac describing Chigi's horoscope. Raphael died before the chapel was finished and it was completed by Bernini, who added the dynamic statues of Daniel and Habakkuk. In the Cerasi chapel, left of the altar, there are two realistic works painted by Caravaggio in 1601: the *Conversion of St Paul* and the *Crucifixion of St Peter*. The artist uses daringly exaggerated lighting and foreshortening techniques to intensify the dramatic effect.

Ara Pacis

♀ G2 ⌂ Lungotevere in Augusta 🚌 70, 81, 117, 119, 186, 628 🕐 9am-7:30pm daily (last adm: 6:30pm) 🚫 1 Jan, 25 Dec 🌐 arapacis.it

Painstakingly reconstructed over many years from its scattered fragments, the exquisitely carved Ara Pacis (Altar of Peace) celebrates the peace created by Emperor Augustus throughout the Mediterranean. Commissioned in 13 BC and completed four years later, the altar stands in a square enclosure of Carrara marble, carved with realistic reliefs of such quality that experts think the craftsmen may have been Greek.

The reliefs on the north and south walls depict a procession that took place on 4 July 13 BC, in which the members of the emperor's family can be identified, including Augustus's grandson, Lucius, clutching at the skirt of his mother, Antonia. The site is housed in a building by architect Richard Meier.

DRINK

Antico Caffè Greco

Founded in 1760, this café was once a meeting place for artists and intellectuals, including Keats and Byron, and it still retains the feel of a refined salon. Coffee and cake here is a (pricey) treat.

♀ H2 ⌂ Via dei Condotti 862 🌐 anticocaffegreco.eu

Mausoleum of Augustus

♀ G2 ⌂ Piazza Augusto Imperatore 📞 06 06 08 🚌 81, 117, 492, 628, 926 🕐 For events; call for info

Now just a weedy mound ringed with cypresses, this was once the most prestigious burial place in Rome. Augustus had the mausoleum built in 28 BC as a tomb for himself and his descendants. The circular building was 87 m (270 ft) in diameter with two obelisks. Inside were four concentric passageways linked by corridors where urns holding the ashes of the Imperial family were placed, including those of Augustus who died in AD 14.

Sant'Andrea al Quirinale

♀ J4 ⌂ Via del Quirinale 29 📞 06 487 45 65 🚌 116, 117 🕐 9am-noon, 3-6pm Tue-Sun

Sant'Andrea was designed for the Jesuits by Bernini and executed between 1658 and 1670. The site was wide but shallow, so Bernini took the radical step of pointing the long axis of his oval plan towards the sides. At the altar he combined sculpture and painting to create a theatrical crucifixion of Sant'Andrea (St Andrew); the diagonally crucified saint on the altar-piece looks up at a stucco effigy of himself ascending to the lantern, where the Holy Spirit and cherubs await him in heaven.

---

⑨ San Carlo alle Quattro Fontane

♀ K3 ⌂ Via del Quirinale 23 📞 06 488 32 61 🚌 116 & routes to Piazza Barberini Ⓜ Barberini 🕐 10am-1pm & 3-6pm Mon-Fri, 10am-1pm Sat & Sun

In 1638, Borromini was commissioned by the Trinitarians to design a church and convent on a tiny cramped site at the Quattro Fontane crossroads. The church, so small that it is said it would fit inside one of the piers of St Peter's, is designed with bold, fluid curves on both the façade and interior.

In a small room off the sacristy hangs a portrait of Borromini. He committed suicide in 1667, and a chapel that was reserved for him in the crypt remains empty.

←

Detail of the reliefs on the Ara Pacis, a marble altar created in 9 BC

10

Galleria Nazionale di Arte Antica: Palazzo Barberini

📍 K3 ⧉ Via delle Quattro Fontane 13 🚌 52, 53, 61, 62, 63, 80, 116, 175, 492, 590 Ⓜ Barberini 🕐 8:30am-7pm Tue-Sun (last adm: 6:30pm) 🔒 1 Jan, 25 Dec 🌐 barberini corsini.org

When Maffeo Barberini became Pope Urban VIII in 1623, he decided to build a grand family palazzo. Designed by Carlo Maderno as a typical country villa on the fringes of the city, it now overlooks Piazza Barberini, where traffic hurtles around Bernini's Triton fountain. Maderno died shortly after the foundations had been laid, and Bernini and Borromini took over.

Of the many sumptuously decorated rooms, the most striking is the Gran Salone, with an illusionistic ceiling frescoed by Pietro da Cortona in 1633–9.

The palazzo also houses part of the Galleria Nazionale d'Arte Antica, with works by Titian, Filippo Lippi, Caravaggio and Artemisia Gentileschi. The most famous is a portrait of a courtesan, reputedly Raphael's lover, *La Fornarina*, although not painted by the artist himself.

11

Santa Maria della Concezione

📍 J3 ⧉ Via Veneto 27 ☎ 06 88 80 36 95 🚌 52, 53, 61, 62, 63, 80, 116, 175 Ⓜ Barberini 🕐 7am-1pm & 3-6pm daily (church); 9am-7pm daily (crypt)

Below this unassuming church is a crypt decked with the dearticulated skeletons of 4,000 Capuchin monks. They form a macabre reminder of the transience of life, with vertebrae wired together to make sacred hearts and

crowns of thorns, and, in one chapel, the skeleton of a tiny Barberini princess.

12

Santa Maria della Vittoria

📍 K3 ⧉ Via XX Settembre 17 ☎ 06 42 74 05 71 🚌 61, 62, 175, 910 Ⓜ Repubblica 🕐 8:30am-noon & 3:30-6pm daily

Santa Maria della Vittoria is an intimate Baroque church with a lavish, candlelit interior. Inside the Cornaro chapel you will find one of Bernini's most ambitious sculptures, the *Ecstasy of St Teresa* (1646). The physical nature of St Teresa's ecstasy is apparent as she appears collapsed on a cloud with her mouth half open and eyes closed, struck by the arrow of a smiling angel. On either side, past and present ecclesiastical members of the Venetian Cornaro family, who

↑ The crypt of Santa Maria della Concezione, decorated with thousands of human bones

commissioned the chapel, sit in boxes as if watching and discussing the scene being played out in front of them.

Museo Nazionale Romano: Palazzo Massimo

📍 L4 🏛 Palazzo Massimo, Largo di Villa Peretti 1 (1 of 5 sites) 📞 06 39 96 77 00 🚌 All routes to Termini Ⓜ Repubblica 🕐 9am–7:45pm Tue–Sun

Founded in 1899, the Museo Nazionale Romano – one of the world's leading museums of Classical art – houses most of the antiquities found in Rome since 1870, as well as important older collections. During the 1990s it underwent a major reorganization and now has five branches: the Palazzo Altemps *(p262)*; the Baths of Diocletian; the Aula Ottagona; the Crypta Balbi; and the Palazzo Massimo. One ticket is valid for all sites. In the Palazzo Massimo, exhibits dating from the 2nd century BC to the late 4th century AD

are displayed in a series of rooms over three floors. Highlights include the *Quattro Aurighe* mosaics from a villa in northern Rome, the breathtaking series of frescoes from Livia's summer villa, and the famous statue of her husband, the Emperor Augustus.

↑ Classical statuary on display in the Museo Nazionale Romano: Palazzo Massimo

---

DRINK

Doney Café
Located right in the heart of Via Veneto, the Doney recreates *Dolce Vita*-era glamour with enormous chandeliers and retro furnishings. There's a rather pricey restaurant here, or you can come at *aperitivo* time for a cocktail and a spot of people-watching.

📍 K2 🏛 Via Veneto 125 🌐 restaurant doney.com

Santa Prassede

📍 L5 🏛 Via Santa Prassede 9a 📞 06 488 24 56 🚌 16, 70, 71, 75, 714 Ⓜ Vittorio Emanuele 🕐 7:30am–noon & 4–6:30pm daily

The church was founded by Pope Paschal II in the 9th century and decorated by Byzantine artists with the most important glittering mosaics in Rome. In the apse Christ stands between Santa Prassede and her sister, dressed as Byzantine empresses, among white-robed elders, lambs, feather-mop palms and bright red poppies. The Cappella di San Zeno is even lovelier, a jewel-box of a mausoleum, built by Pope Paschal II for his mother, Theodora. Her square halo shows that she was still alive when the mosaic was created.

San Pietro in Vincoli

📍 K5 🏛 Piazza di San Pietro in Vincoli 📞 06 97 84 49 50 🚌 75, 85, 117 Ⓜ Colosseo 🕐 8am–12:30pm & 3–7pm daily (Oct–Mar: to 6pm)

This church's name means "St Peter in Chains", so called because it houses what are said to be the chains with which St Peter was shackled in the Mamertine Prison *(p252)*.

San Pietro is now best known for the Tomb of Julius II, commissioned by the pope from Michelangelo in 1505. Much to the artist's chagrin, Julius soon became more interested in the building of a new St Peter's and the tomb project was laid to one side. After the pope died in 1513, Michelangelo resumed work on the tomb, but had only completed the statues of the *Dying Slaves* (now found in Paris and Florence) and *Moses* when he was called away to paint the *The Last Judgment* in the Sistine Chapel.

ROME: THE VATICAN AND TRASTEVERE

Vatican City, the world capital of Catholicism, is the world's smallest state. It occupies 43 ha (106 acres) within high walls watched over by the Vatican guard. It was the site where St Peter was martyred (c.AD 64) and buried, and it became the residence of the popes who succeeded him. The papal palaces, next to the great basilica of St Peter's, are home to the Sistine Chapel and the eclectic collections of the Vatican Museums, as well as being the residence of the pope. Neighbouring Trastevere is quite different: a picturesque old quarter, whose inhabitants consider themselves to be the only true Romans. Sadly, the proletarian identity of the place is in danger of being destroyed by the proliferation of trendy restaurants, clubs and shops.

Today, crowds flock to the Vatican, where kitsch religious souvenir shops and tourist-orientated cafés now line the hallowed streets. The green spaces on the fringes of Trastevere are ideal for winding down after a tiring day of sightseeing, while its maze of narrow streets are full of great places to eat.

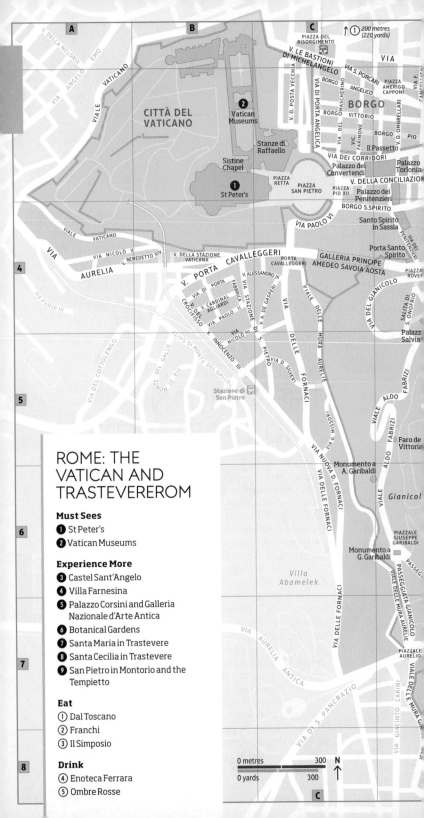

A   **B**   **C**

↑ ① 200 metres (220 yards)

PIAZZA DEL RISORGIMENTO

V. LE BASTIONI DI MICHELANGELO

VIA

VIA S. PORCARI

PIAZZA AMERIGO CAPPONI

BORGO

CITTÀ DEL VATICANO

❷ Vatican Museums

BORGO ANGELICO

V. DI PORTA ANGELICA

V. D. POSTA VECCHIA

BORGO VITTORIO

VIC. DEL MASCHERINO

VIA FARINONE

BORGO

Il Passetto

V. D. OMBRELLARI

BORGO PIO

Stanze di Raffaello

VIA DEI CORRIDORI

Palazzo Torlonia

Sistine Chapel

Palazzo dei Convertendi

Palazzo Penitenzieri

PIAZZA RETTA

PIAZZA SAN PIETRO

V. DELLA CONCILIAZIO

❶ St Peter's

PIAZZA PIO XII

Palazzo dei Penitenzieri

BORGO S.SPIRITO

VIA PAOLO VI

Santo Spirito in Sassia

Porta Santo Spirito

4

VIALE VATICANO

VIA NICOLÒ V

V. BENEDETTO XIV

V. DELLA STAZIONE VATICANA

CAVALLEGGERI

GALLERIA PRINCIPE AMEDEO SAVOIA AOSTA

PIAZZA ROVE

VIA

AURELIA

V. PORTA

PORTA CAVALLEGGERI

V. ALESSANDRO III

VIA DELLE MURA AURELIE

VIA DEL GIANICOLO

SALITA DI S. ONOFRIO

VIA PAOLO III

FABBRICA

V. DI PORTA

V. CARDINAL AGLIARDI

VIA STAZIONE DI S. PIETRO

V. A. DE GASPERI

Palazz Salvia

V. DEL CROCIFISSO

VIA PAOLO II

VIA NICOLÒ III

VIA D. SILVERI

FABRIZI

CLIVO DI MONTE DEL GALLO

VIA DI MONTE DEL GALLO

VIA INNOCENZO III

5

VIA DEL COTTOLENGO

VIA DEL GALLO

Stazione di San Pietro

VIALE ALDO FABRIZI

Faro de Vittoria

VIA DELLE FORNACI

VIA G. MISSORI

VIA NUOVA D. FORNACI

Monumento a A. Garibaldi

VIALE ALDO FABRIZI

Gianicol

PIAZZALE GIUSEPPE GARIBALDI

Monumento a G. Garibaldi

PASSEGGIATA

VIALE DELLE MURA AURELIE

ROME: THE VATICAN AND TRASTEVEREROM

Must Sees
❶ St Peter's
❷ Vatican Museums

Experience More
❸ Castel Sant'Angelo
❹ Villa Farnesina
❺ Palazzo Corsini and Galleria Nazionale d'Arte Antica
❻ Botanical Gardens
❼ Santa Maria in Trastevere
❽ Santa Cecilia in Trastevere
❾ San Pietro in Montorio and the Tempietto

Eat
① Dal Toscano
② Franchi
③ Il Simposio

Drink
④ Enoteca Ferrara
⑤ Ombre Rosse

Villa Abamelek

VIA DELLE FORNACI

VIA AURELIA ANTICA

PIAZZALE AURELIO

VIALE DELLE MURA G

VIA GIACINTO CARINI

VIA DI S. PANCRAZIO

0 metres   300
0 yards   300

N ↑

C

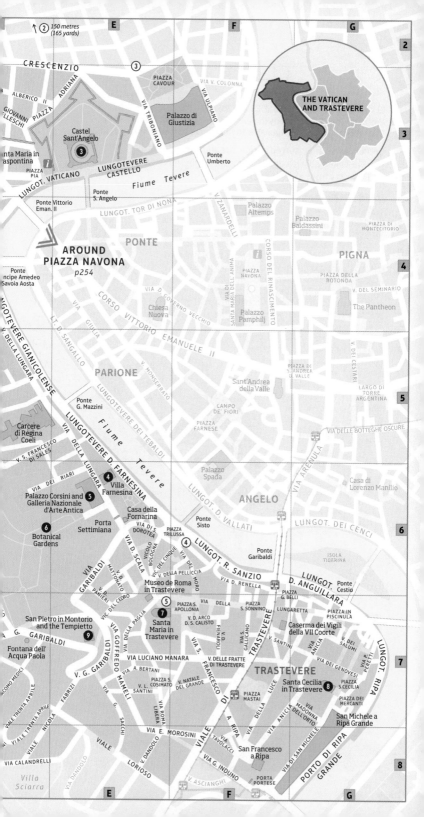

↑ ② 150 metres
(165 yards)

E F G

2

CRESCENZIO

ALBERICO II
ADRIANA

GIOVANNI
PIAZZA
LLESCHI

③

PIAZZA
CAVOUR

VIA V. COLONNA

VIA ULPIANO

VIA TRIBONIANO

Palazzo di
Giustizia

THE VATICAN
AND TRASTEVERE

3

Castel
Sant'Angelo
③

nta Maria in
aspontina

PIAZZA
PIA

LUNGOT. VATICANO

Ponte
Umberto

LUNGOTEVERE
CASTELLO

Fiume Tevere

Ponte
S. Angelo

Ponte Vittorio
Eman. II

LUNGOT. TOR DI NONA

V. ZANARDELLI

Palazzo
Altemps

Palazzo
Baldassini

PIAZZA DI
MONTECITORIO

Ponte
ncipe Amedeo
Savoia Aosta

PONTE

AROUND
PIAZZA NAVONA
p254

PIGNA

4

LT. D. SANGALLO

LUNGOTEVERE GIANICOLENSE

V. DELLA LUNGARA

VIA D. GOVERNO VECCHIO

VIA
GIULIA

Chiesa
Nuova

VIA DI SANTA MARIA DELL'ANIMA

CORSO DEL RINASCIMENTO

PIAZZA
NAVONA

Palazzo
Pamphilj

PIAZZA DELLA
ROTONDA

V. DEL SEMINARIO

The Pantheon

CORSO VITTORIO EMANUELE II

PARIONE

V. MONSERRATO

Sant'Andrea
della Valle

PIAZZA DI
S. ANDREA
D. VALLE

V. DEI CESTARI

LARGO DI
TORRE
ARGENTINA

5

Ponte
G. Mazzini

LUNGOTEVERE DEI TEBALDI

Fiume

CAMPO
DE' FIORI

PIAZZA
FARNESE

VIA DELLE BOTTEGHE OSCURE

Carcere
di Regina
Coeli

V. S. FRANCESCO
DI SALES

VIA DEI RIARI

Tevere

Palazzo
Spada

VIA ARENULA

Casa di
Lorenzo Manilio

LUNGOTEVERE D. FARNESINA

④ Villa
Farnesina

Palazzo Corsini and ⑤
Galleria Nazionale
d'Arte Antica

⑥
Botanical
Gardens

Porta
Settimiana

Casa della
Fornarina

VIA DI S.
DOROTEA

LUNGOT. D. VALLATI

ANGELO

Ponte
Sisto

LUNGOTEVERE DEI CENCI

ISOLA
TIBERINA

6

PIAZZA
TRILUSSA

④ LUNGOT. R. SANZIO

Ponte
Garibaldi

LUNGOT.
D. ANGUILLARA

Ponte
Cestio

VIA D. SCALA

VICOLO
BOLOGNA

WC. DEL CINQUE

VIA DEL MORO

V. DELLA PELLICCIA

VIA D. RENELLA

Museo de Roma
in Trastevere

WC. DEL CEDRO

VIA DELLA PAGLIA

⑤ PIAZZA S.
APOLLONIA

VIA DELLA

PIAZZA
S. SONNINO

PIAZZA
G. BELLI

LUNGARETTA

PIAZZA IN
PISCINULA

San Pietro in Montorio
and the Tempietto ⑨

VIA
GARIBALDI

V. D.
PAMIERI

⑦
Santa
Maria in
Trastevere

V. D. ARCO
D. S. CALISTO

V.D.
FIENAROLI

VIA S.
GALLICANO

TRASTEVERE

V. SANTINI

Caserma dei Vigili
della VII Coorte

V. DEI
SALUMI

LUNGOT. RIPA

7

Fontana dell'
Acqua Paola

ACOMO MEDICI

G. GARIBALDI

VIA GOFFREDO MAMELI

VIA LUCIANO MANARA

A. BERTANI

PIAZZA S.
V. L. COSIMATO
SANTINI

VIA DELLE FRATTE
DI TRASTEVERE

VIA S. FRANCESCO

VIA NATALE
DEL GRANDE

PIAZZA
MASTAI

VIA DELLA
LUCE

VIA DELLA

VIA S.
FRANCESCO A RIPA

Santa Cecilia ⑧
in Trastevere

VIA
MADONNA
DELL'ORTO

VIA ANICIA

PIAZZA
S.CECILIA

VIA DEI GENOVESI

TRASTEVERE

PIAZZA DEI
MERCANTI

San Michele a
Ripa Grande

VIA P.
PERETTI

VIALE TRENTA APRILE

VIALE NICOLA
FABRIZI

V. G. GARIBALDI

VIA DANDOLO

VIA E. MOROSINI

VIA G. SACCHI

PIAZZA
ROMA
LIBERA

VIA ROMA
LIBERA

San Francesco
a Ripa

VIA DI SAN MICHELE

PORTO DI RIPA

8

Villa
Sciarra

VIALE
TRENTA APRILE

VIA CALANDRELLI

VIALE

LORIOSO

VIA G. INDUNO

PORTA
PORTESE

V. ASCIANGHI

GRANDE

E F G

ST PETER'S

📍1 B3 🏛Piazza San Pietro 🚌23, 49, 70, 180, 492 Ⓜ Ottaviano San Pietro 🕐7am–6:30pm daily (basilica); 8am–6:15pm daily (treasury); 8am–5:30pm (grottoes); 8am–5pm daily (dome) 🌐stpetersbasilica.info

Catholicism's most sacred shrine, the sumptuous, marble-caked basilica of St Peter's draws pilgrims and tourists from all over the world.

Inside St Peter's

Marking the site where St Peter was martyred and buried, the basilica holds hundreds of precious works of art, some salvaged from the original 4th-century basilica built by Constantine, others commissioned from Renaissance and Baroque artists. The dominant tone is set by Bernini, who created the baldacchino twisting up below Michelangelo's huge dome. He also created the *cathedra* in the apse, with four saints supporting a throne that contains fragments once thought to be relics of the chair from which St Peter delivered his first sermon. From the basilica you can visit the Grottoes, where the late Pope John Paul II is buried, the Treasury and St Peter's Sacristy, or the terrace for panoramic views. You can can also book in advance online (*www. papalaudience.org*) for an audience with the pope, which takes place at 10am every Wednesday in Piazza San Pietro or in the Papal Audience Chamber.

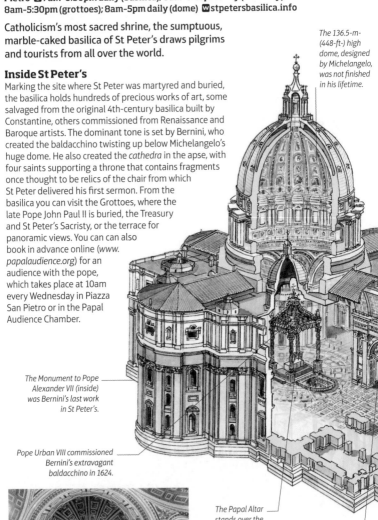

The 136.5-m-(448-ft-) high dome, designed by Michelangelo, was not finished in his lifetime.

The Monument to Pope Alexander VII (inside) was Bernini's last work in St Peter's.

Pope Urban VIII commissioned Bernini's extravagant baldacchino in 1624.

The Papal Altar stands over the crypt where St Peter is buried.

The foot of St Peter, sculpted in the 13th century, has worn thin from pilgrims touching it over the centuries.

←

Michelangelo's dome and the top of the baldacchino

AD 61
▼ Burial of St Peter.

200
Altar built marking grave of St Peter.

1452
Nicholas V plans restoration.

1547
Michelangelo named as chief architect of St Peter's.

324
Constantine builds basilica.

800
△ Charlemagne crowned Emperor of the Romans in St Peter's.

1514
Raphael named director of works.

1626
New basilica of St Peter's consecrated.

→ Piazza San Pietro, the grand oval plaza surrounding the basilica

Protected by glass since an attack in 1972, Michelangelo's Pietà (1499), located in the first chapel on the right, was created when the sculptor was only 25.

POPE'S BLESSING

On Sundays (at noon), religious festivals and special occasions such as canonizations, the pope stands on the balcony at the Library window and blesses the faithful crowds gathered in Piazza San Pietro below.

These bronze doors from the old basilica were decorated with biblical reliefs by Filarete between 1439 and 1445.

From this Library window, the pope blesses the faithful.

← St Peter's, centre of the Catholic faith

287

→ The monumental spiral staircase designed by Giuseppe Momo in 1932

2 ⊘ ⊛ ⊕ ⊡ ⊕

VATICAN MUSEUMS

📍C3 🏛Città del Vaticano (entrance in Viale Vaticano) 🚌49 to entrance, 23, 81, 492, 990 Ⓜ Ottaviano San Pietro, Cipro 🕐9am–6pm Mon-Sat (last admission 4pm), 9am–2pm last Sun of month - free entry (last admission 12:30pm); low-cut or sleeveless clothing, shorts, mini-skirts and hats are not allowed 🚫Religious and public hols 🌐museivaticani.va

Home to the Sistine Chapel and Raphael Rooms as well as to one of the world's most important art collections, the Vatican Museums are housed in palaces originally built for Renaissance popes Julius II, Innocent VIII and Sixtus IV. Most of the later additions were made in the 18th century, when priceless works of art accumulated by earlier popes were first put on show. Strung along 7 km (over 4 miles) of corridors, these incredible collections form one of the world's largest museums.

Among the Vatican's greatest treasures are its superlative Greek and Roman antiquities, together with the magnificent artifacts excavated from Egyptian and Etruscan tombs during the 19th century. Some of Italy's leading artists, such as Raphael, Michelangelo and Leonardo da Vinci, are represented in the Pinacoteca (art gallery) and parts of the former palaces, where they were employed by popes to decorate sumptuous apartments and galleries. The absolute highlights of this complex of museums are the Sistine Chapel and the Raphael Rooms, which should not be missed.

↑ The Cortile della Pigna, with a spherical bronze sculpture by Arnaldo Pomodoro

INSIDER TIP
Skipping the Queue

Book a ticket for the first slot of the day online. You can head straight to the Sistine Chapel, then make your way slowly backwards. For an extra fee, book a Breakfast Visit, which gives entry from 7:15am and includes breakfast and an audio guide.

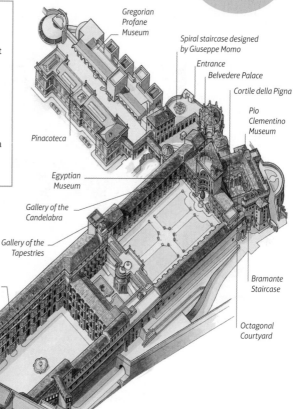

Gregorian Profane Museum

Spiral staircase designed by Giuseppe Momo

Entrance

Belvedere Palace

Cortile della Pigna

Pio Clementino Museum

Pinacoteca

Egyptian Museum

Gallery of the Candelabra

Gallery of the Tapestries

Gallery of the Maps

Bramante Staircase

Sistine Chapel

Octagonal Courtyard

↑ Hightlights of the Vatican Museums complex

Borgia Apartment

Raphael Rooms

Timeline

1473 △ Pope Sixtus IV builds Sistine Chapel

1503-13 Pope Julius II starts Classical sculpture collection

1508 ▽ Raphael begins work on Rooms; Michelangelo begins painting the Sistine Chapel ceiling

1541 Michelangelo's Last Judgment is unveiled

1655 △ Bernini designs Royal Staircase

1758 Founding of Gregorian Profane Museum

1771 △ Founding of Pio Clementino Museum

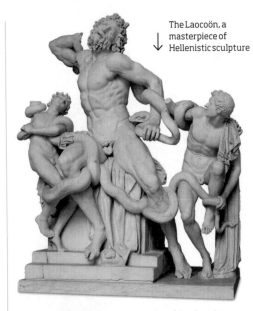

The Laocoön, a masterpiece of Hellenistic sculpture

HIGHLIGHTS OF THE VATICAN COLLECTION

EXPERIENCE Rome: The Vatican and Trastevere

Pio Clementino Museum

The Vatican's prize pieces of Greek and Roman sculpture form the nucleus of this museum. Most of the works are Roman copies of lost ancient Greek originals, notably *The Laocoön*, a violenty contorted Hellenistic work showing the Trojan priest Laocoön and his two sons struggling to escape from the writhing coils of a sea serpent. Also here is the *Apollo Belvedere*, considered a paragon of physical perfection by Renaissance artists, and the muscular, contorted Belvedere Torso, whose influence can be seen on Michelangelo's *ignudi* (male nudes) in the Sistine Chapel. A menagerie of animal- themed sculptures and mosaics are gathered together in the Room of the Animals.

On either side of the museum are two staircases. The original spiral stairway designed by Bramante in 1505 is open only to special tours. The modern double helix stairway, commonly called the Snail or Momo Staircase, was designed by Giuseppe Momo in 1932. It was inspired by Bramante's original.

Did You Know?

Bramante designed the spiral staircase so that it could be ridden up on horseback.

Gregorian Profane Museum

In a space infused with natural light, the Gregorian Profane museum spans Classical antiquity and includes large marble fragments from the Athens Parthenon, Roman copies of Greek sculptures and a striking mosaic from the Baths of Caracalla portraying full-length figures of athletes.

Egyptian Museum

Egyptian culture and mythology became extremely fashionable in Imperial Rome, and the collection here consists chiefly of Egyptian antiquities brought to the city to adorn buildings such as the Temple of Isis (which once stood near the Pantheon), Villa Adriana at Tivoli, and the Gardens of Sallust to the southeast of the Villa Borghese park. Also on display are painted mummy cases and tomb finds.

Galleries of Maps, Tapestries and Candelabra

A long corridor is divided into three contiguous galleries. The Gallery of the Maps displays 16th-century maps of Italy's regions and papal territories painted as if Rome were literally at the centre of the world, with areas south

←

Classical sculptures gallery in the Pio Clementino Museum

→

The Gallery of the Maps; detail of a map by Egnazio Danti (1580)

The modern double helix stairway, commonly called the Snail or Momo Staircase, was designed by Giuseppe Momo in 1932.

of Rome, such as Sicily and Calabria, appearing "upside down". The Gallery of the Tapestries has early 16th-century silk, gold and wool tapestries woven in Brussels to designs inspired by Raphael, while the Gallery of the Candelabra has immense marble candle holders.

Pinacoteca

There are some splendid Renaissance works from all over Italy in the 18 rooms of the art gallery. Don't miss the fragments of frescoes of apostles and angel musicians in Room IV by Melozzo da Forlì or the exquisitely romantic Madonna paintings by Filippo

Lippi and Fra Angelico in Room III. Room VI is devoted to the fabulous world of the Crivelli brothers, 16th-century Venetian artists who depicted fragile doll-like Madonnas enclosed within elaborate painted frames of fruit and flowers. Raphael has an entire room (VIII) devoted to his work, notably *The Transfiguration*, which includes a woman with red-gold hair, who is thought to have been his lover, La Fornarina. Next door in Room IX is a single, rare work by Leonardo da Vinci depicting St Jerome in the desert. There are also notable paintings by Titian, Crespi, Veronese and Caravaggio.

GALLERY GUIDE

The museum complex is vast: the Sistine Chapel is 20 to 30 minutes' walk from the entrance, so allow plenty of time. There is a strict one-way system. It is best to be selective or choose one of four colour-coded itineraries, which vary from 90 minutes to a five-hour marathon.

Michelangelo's
breathtaking
ceiling frescoes ↑

SISTINE CHAPEL: THE CEILING

Although Michelangelo had studied fresco-painting under Ghirlandaio, until 1508 he had mainly gained fame through his work as a sculptor. Nonetheless, Pope Julius II commissioned him to paint the ceiling of the Sistine Chapel, which would result in one of the greatest masterpieces of Western art.

At the time, the ceiling was painted simply blue, with golden stars. Michelangelo frescoed over the old ceiling painting between 1508 and 1512, working on specially designed scaffolding. He persuaded the pope to give him a free hand, and spent four years painting 366 figures from the Old and New Testaments, illustrating the bibilical stories of the Creation of the World, the Fall of Man and the Coming of Christ. *Ignudi* (male nudes) are depicted around these frescoes. In the spandrels surrounding the vault are sibyls, prophetesses from pagan mythology, which, in the Renaissance, were adopted by Christian artists as figures who could foresee the Coming of Christ. The central painting, *The Creation of Adam*, portraying God reaching down from a cloudy heaven to create Adam, is one of the most reproduced religious paintings of all time.

RESTORATION OF THE CEILING

From 1979 until 1994 a huge restoration programme was carried out. Five hundred years of soot, candle smoke and glue - along with breadcrumbs and retsina used by earlier restorers, and brush hairs and fingerprints left behind by Michelangelo - were removed. The faded, eggshell-cracked figures were discovered to have rose-petal skin, lustrous hair and to be wearing luscious strawberry-pink, lime-green, lemon and orange shot-silk robes. Critics were surprised that Michelangelo's palette was so bright.

The Last Judgment by Michelangelo, showing souls meeting the wrath of Christ

Hall of Constantine

The frescoes here, started in 1517, were executed mainly by Raphael's pupils and show the triumph of Christianity over paganism, focusing on key moments in the life of Emperor Constantine.

Room of Heliodorus

The theme here is divine intervention and includes *The Expulsion of Heliodorus from the Temple* and the dazzling *Liberation of St Peter*, in which an angel frees St Peter (a portrait of Julius II) from prison.

Room of the Segnatura

The frescoes here celebrate the Renaissance ideal – the ability of the intellect to discover the truth. The key work is *The School of Athens* in which Raphael painted leading Greek philosophers in a vaulted hall.

Room of the Fire in the Borgo

This celebrates a miracle in 847, when Pope Leo IV is said to have extinguished a fire in the quarter around the Vatican by making the sign of the cross.

SISTINE CHAPEL: THE WALLS

Wall Frescoes

The massive walls of the Sistine Chapel were frescoed by some of the finest artists of the 15th and 16th centuries. The twelve paintings by artists, including Perugino, Ghirlandaio, Botticelli and Signorelli, show parallel episodes from the lives of Moses and Christ. The decoration of the walls was completed between 1534 and 1541 by Michelangelo.

The Last Judgment

Twenty-four years after he had finished the Sistine ceiling, Michelangelo was commissioned by Pope Paul III Farnese to cover the altar wall of the chapel with a fresco of *The Last Judgment*. Michelangelo drew on Dante's *Inferno*. The painting is a bleak, harrowing work, showing the damned hurtling towards a putrid hell, the blessed being dragged up to heaven, and saints demanding vengeance for their martyrdoms, a theme chosen by the Pope

Did You Know?

Michelangelo's self-portrait is seen on the flayed skin held by St Bartholomew in *The Last Judgment*.

to warn Catholics to adhere to their faith in the turmoil of the Reformation.

RAPHAEL ROOMS

In 1508, Pope Julius II asked Bramante to recommend an artist to redecorate his private suite of four rooms. Bramante suggested a young artist named Raphael. The resulting frescoes swiftly established Raphael as one of the leading artists in Rome, putting him on a par with Michelangelo. Raphael and his pupils took over 16 years to fresco the rooms.

→ Detail of *The School of Athens*, with Plato and Aristotle in the centre

←
Hall of Constantine, a
celebration of the triumph of
Christianity over paganism

EXPERIENCE MORE

3

Castel Sant'Angelo

Q E3 **A** Lungotevere Castello **⊞** 34, 280 **Q** 9am-7:30pm daily (last entry 6:30pm) **Q** 1 Jan, 25 Dec **W** castelsantangelo. beniculturali.it

This massive fortress takes its name from the vision of the Archangel Michael by Pope Gregory the Great in the 6th century as he led a procession across the bridge, praying for the end of the plague.

The castle began life in AD 139 as the Emperor Hadrian's mausoleum. Since then it has been a bridgehead in the Emperor Aurelian's city wall, a medieval citadel and prison, and a place of safety for popes during times of political unrest. A corridor links it with the Vatican Palace, providing an escape route for the pope.

From dank cells to fine apartments of Renaissance popes, the museums cover all aspects of the castle's history, including the Sala Paolina, with illusionistic frescoes (1546–8) by Pellegrino Tibaldi and Perin del Vaga, and the Courtyard of Honour.

4

Villa Farnesina

Q E6 **A** Via della Lungara 230 **C** 06 68 02 72 68 **⊞** 23, 280 **Q** 9am-2pm Mon-Sat & every 2nd Sun of the month

The fabulously wealthy Sienese banker Agostino Chigi commissioned this villa in 1508 from his fellow Sienese Baldassare Peruzzi. Chigi's main home was across the Tiber, and the villa was designed purely for lavish banquets. Artists, poets, cardinals, princes and the pope himself were entertained here in magnificent style. Chigi also used the villa for sojourns with the courtesan Imperia, who allegedly inspired one of the *Three Graces* painted by Raphael in the Loggia of Cupid and Psyche.

The simple, harmonious design of the Farnesina, with a central block and projecting wings, made it one of the first true villas of the Renaissance. Peruzzi decorated some of the interiors himself, such as the Sala della Prospettiva upstairs, in which the illusionistic frescoes create the impression of looking out over 16th-century Rome through a marble colonnade.

Other frescoes, by Sebastiano del Piombo and Raphael and his pupils, depict Classical myths, while the vault of the main hall, the Sala di Galatea, is adorned with astrological scenes showing the position of the stars at the time of Chigi's birth. After his death in 1920 the banking business collapsed, and in 1577 the villa was sold off to the Farnese family.

The formidable fortress of Castel Sant'Angelo, rising above the Tiber ↓

5 ⟨⟩ ⟨⟩ ⟨⟩

Palazzo Corsini and Galleria Nazionale d'Arte Antica

⦿E6 **⌂**Via della Lungara 10 **🚌**23, 280 **⌚**8:30am-7pm Wed-Mon **🗓**1 Jan, 25 Dec, 31 Dec **🌐**barberini corsini.org

The history of Palazzo Corsini is intimately entwined with that of Rome. Built for Cardinal Domenico Riario in 1510–12, it has boasted among its many distinguished guests Bramante, the young Michelangelo, Erasmus, the mother of Napoleon and Queen Christina of Sweden, who died here in 1689. The palazzo was rebuilt by Ferdinando Fuga, who planned the façade to be viewed from an angle, as Via della Lungara is too narrow for a full-frontal view.

When the palazzo was bought by the state in 1893, the Corsini family donated their collection of paintings, which formed the core of the national art collection,

↑ Raphael's *Triumph of Galatea* fresco in Villa Farnesina

and was soon augmented. The collection is now split between Palazzo Barberini and Palazzo Corsini. Although the best works are in the Barberini, there are paintings by Van Dyck, Rubens, Murillo and, notably, an androgynous *St John the Baptist* (c.1604) by Caravaggio and a *Salome* (1638) by Reni. The strangest work is a portrait of the rotund Queen Christina as the goddess Diana by J Van Egmont.

6 ⟨⟩ ⟨⟩

Botanical Gardens

⦿D6 **⌂**Largo Cristina di Svezia 24 **📞**06 49 91 71 07 **🚌**23, 280 **⌚**9:30am-6:30pm (Oct-Mar: 5:30pm) Mon-Sat **🗓**Public hols

Sequoias, palm trees and splendid collections of orchids are among the 7,000 plants represented in the Botanical Gardens. Species are grouped to illustrate their botanical families and their adaptation to different climates. There are also some curious plants like the ginkgo that have survived virtually unchanged from prehistoric eras. Now owned by the University of Rome, the gardens were originally part of the Palazzo Corsini.

DRINK

Enoteca Ferrara

This cosy *enoteca* has a vast wine list with a good selection of wines by the glass and helpful staff. There's a smart restaurant attached, although the aperitivo buffet might leave you with little room for dinner.

⦿F6 **⌂**Piazza Trilussa, 41 **🌐**enotecaferrara.it

Ombre Rosse

This friendly bar's pleasant terrace on little Piazza di Sant' Egidio is a great spot for a prosecco as you take in the predinner Trastevere whirl. There's live music - from rock'n'roll to blues - several nights a week.

⦿E7 **⌂**Piazza di Sant'Egidio 12 **🌐**ombre rosseintrastevere.it

EAT

Dal Toscano

This classic trattoria specializes in steak, but it also offers a superb thick Tuscan soup and a great range of pasta dishes.

♀C2 ♠Via Germanico 58 ⓦristorante daltoscano.it

€€€

Franchi

A first-class delicatessen with a tantalizing array of lunchtime snacks.

♀D2 ♠Via Cola di Rienzo 200 ☎06 686 55 64

€€€

Il Simposio

A fine-dining restaurant specializing in fish.

♀E3 ♠Piazza Cavour 16 ⓦilsimposioroma.it

€€€

7

Santa Maria in Trastevere

♀E7 ♠Piazza Santa Maria in Trastevere ☎06 581 48 02 🚌H, 23, 280 🕐7:30am–9pm daily

Santa Maria in Trastevere was probably the first Christian place of worship in Rome, founded by Pope Callixtus I in the 3rd century, when emperors were still pagan and Christianity a minority cult. According to legend,

it was built on the site where a fountain of oil had miraculously sprung up on the day that Christ was born. The basilica became the focus of devotion to the Madonna and, although today's church and its mosaics date largely from the 12th and 13th centuries, images of the Virgin continue to dominate. The façade mosaics probably date from the 12th century, and show Mary, Christ and ten lamp-bearing women. Inside in the apse is a stylized 12th-century *Coronation of the Virgin* and, below, a 13th-century series of realistic scenes from the life of the Virgin by Pietro Cavallini. The oldest image of the Virgin is a 7th-century icon, the *Madonna di Clemenza*, which

depicts her as a Byzantine empress flanked by a guard of angels. It sits above the altar in the Cappella Altemps.

8

Santa Cecilia in Trastevere

♀G7 ♠Piazza di Santa Cecilia ☎06 589 92 89 🚌H, 23, 44, 280 🕐10am–1pm & 4-7pm daily (main church); 10am–12:30pm Mon–Sat (Cavallini fresco)

St Cecilia, aristocrat and patron saint of music, was martyred here in AD 230. After an unsuccessful attempt to suffocate her by locking her in the hot steam bath of her

→ Remarkably brilliant mosaics in the church of Santa Maria in Trastevere

Bramante's elegant Tempietto, a small Renaissance gem ↓

house for three days, she was beheaded. A church was built, possibly in the 4th century, on the site of her house (still to be seen beneath the church). Her body was lost, but it turned up again in the Catacombs of San Callisto (*p317*). In the 9th century it was reburied here by Pope Paschal I, who rebuilt the church. A fine apse mosaic survives from this period. The altar canopy by Arnolfo di Cambio and the fresco of *The Last Judgment* by Pietro Cavallini can be reached through the adjoining convent; they date from the 13th century, one of the few periods when Rome had a distinctive artistic style.

In front of the altar is a delicate statue of St Cecilia by Stefano Maderno, which is based on sketches made of her perfectly preserved relics when they were briefly disinterred in 1599.

---

⑨

San Pietro in Montorio and the Tempietto

📍 E7 🏛 Piazza di San Pietro in Montorio 2 📞 06 581 39 40 🚌 44, 75, 115 🕐 8am-noon & 3-4pm daily (main church); 10am-6pm Tue-Sun (Tempietto)

The Tempietto, a diminutive masterpiece of Renaissance architecture completed by Bramante in 1502, stands in the courtyard of San Pietro in Montorio. Its circular shape is an echo of early Christian *martyria*, chapels built on the site of a saint's martyrdom. This was erroneously thought to be the spot in Nero's Circus where St Peter was crucified. Bramante ringed the chapel with Doric columns, a Classical frieze and a fine balustrade.

SAN COSIMATO MARKET

In the heart of Trastevere, this lively market in Piazza San Cosimato has abundant fruit and vegetables along with some excellent cheeses and cured meats. There's also a fantastic playground to keep the kids entertained while you browse for bargains.

ROME: AVENTINE AND LATERAN

The southernmost of the seven hills in Rome and, according to legend, Remus's preferred spot for the foundation of the city, the Aventine stood outside the city walls for centuries after Romulus set up camp at the Palatine Hill. During the Imperial period, this former working-class suburb gained in prestige and became one of the more affluent parts of the city. The nearby Lateran was the residence of the popes in the Middle Ages, and the Basilica of San Giovanni beside it rivalled St Peter's in splendour. After the return of the popes from Avignon at the end of the 14th century, the area declined in importance.

This is one of the greenest parts of the city, taking in the Celian and Aventine Hills, as well as the very congested area around San Giovanni in Laterano. The Celian, now scattered with churches, was a fashionable place to live in Imperial Rome. Some of the era's splendour is still apparent in the ruins of the Baths of Caracalla. Behind the Baths rises the Aventine Hill, a peaceful, leafy area, with the superb basilica of Santa Sabina, and lovely views across the river to Trastevere and St Peter's. By contrast, in the valley below, cars and Vespas skim around the Circus Maximus, following the ancient charioteering track, while to the south lies Testaccio, a lively working-class district.

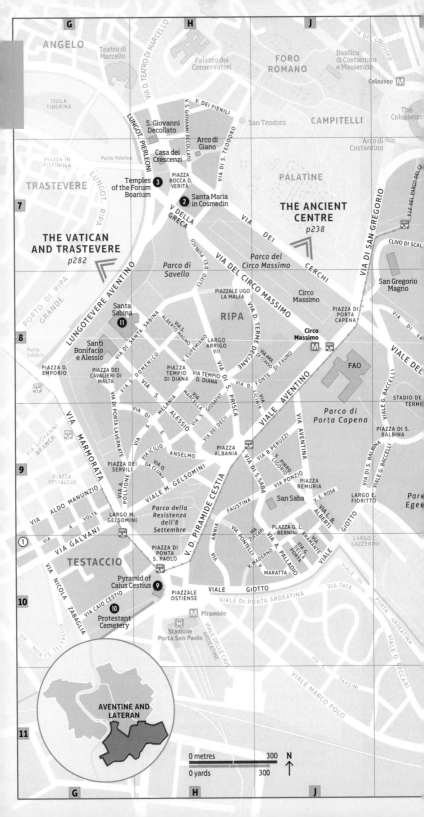

ROME: AVENTINE AND LATERAN

Must See
1 San Giovanni in Laterano

Experience More
2 Santa Maria in Cosmedin
3 Temples of the Forum Boarium
4 Santa Maria in Domnica
5 Santi Quattro Coronati
6 Santo Stefano Rotondo
7 San Clemente
8 Baths of Caracalla
9 Pyramid of Caius Cestius
10 Protestant Cemetery
11 Santa Sabina

Shop
① Mercato di Testaccio

SAN GIOVANNI IN LATERANO

**◉ M7 ⬛ Piazza di San Giovanni in Laterano 🚌 16, 81, 85, 87, 650 🚊 3 Ⓜ San Giovanni
📞 06 69 88 64 93 ⏰ 7am–6:30pm daily (cathedral); 9am–6pm daily (cloisters); 10am–5:30pm daily (museum); 7am–12:30pm & 4–6:30pm daily (baptistry)**

Until the Middle Ages, this basilica was the most important religious building in Rome. Popes resided in the adjacent Lateran Palace and were crowned here. After the papacy moved to Avignon in 1309, the basilica declined in importance, but it continues to house the *cathedra* of the Bishop of Rome, the pope.

Early in the 4th century, the Laterani family were disgraced and their land taken by Emperor Constantine to build Rome's first Christian basilica. Today's church retains the original shape, but has been rebuilt several times, most notably in 1646 when Borromini restyled the interior. Until 1870 all popes were crowned in the basilica. It still remains the city's main cathedral, and the seat of the Bishop of Rome, the pope, who celebrates Maundy Thursday Mass here and attends the annual blessing of the people.

TRIAL OF A CORPSE

Fear of rival factions led the early popes to extraordinary lengths. An absurd case took place at the Lateran Palace in 897 when Pope Stephen VI tried the corpse of his predecessor, Formosus, for disloyalty to the Church. The corpse was found guilty; its right hand was mutilated and it was thrown into the Tiber.

Grand façade of the basilica seen from Piazza di San Giovanni in Laterano; ↓ Borromini's restyled interior (inset)

Timeline

314–18
Five-aisled basilical church is built

1144
Church dedicated to San Giovanni in Laterano

1646
Borromini rebuilds interior

1730–40
▽ Alessandro Galilei constructs main façade

AD 313
△ Constantine gives Laterani site to Pope Melchiades for a church

324
Basilica consecrated by Pope Sylvester I and dedicated to the Redeemer

1308–9
Church destroyed by fire; papacy moves to Avignon

The domed baptistry dates back to Constantine's time. Its octagonal shape has served as the model for baptistries throughout the Christian world.

The Chapel of San Venanzio is decorated with 7th-century mosaics.

Apse

The pope gives his annual blessing from the upper loggia of the North Façade.

Only the pope can celebrate mass at this altar.

Possibly by Giotto, the Boniface VIII Fresco shows the pope announcing the Holy Year of 1300.

Museum entrance

Built by the Vassalletto family in about 1220, the cloisters are remarkable for their inlaid marble mosaics.

The altarpiece in the Corsini Chapel is a mosaic copy of Guido Reni's painting of Sant'Andrea Corsini.

The main entrance, on the East Façade (1735), is adorned with statues of Christ and the Apostles.

Basilica of San Giovanni in Laterano ↑

305

EXPERIENCE MORE

2

Santa Maria in Cosmedin

📍H7 🏛Piazza della Bocca della Verità 📞06 678 77 59 🚌23, 44, 81, 160, 170, 280, 628, 715, 716 🕐9:30am–6pm daily (5pm in winter)

This church was built in the 6th century on the site of the ancient city's food market. The Romanesque bell tower and portico were added in the 12th century. In the 1800s a Baroque façade was removed,

---

🔍 **HIDDEN GEM**
Aventine Orange Garden

Take a break from sightseeing in a pretty orange garden just off Via di Santa Sabina, on the Aventine Hill. It has some truly spectacular views of the Tiber.

---

and the church restored to its original simplicity. It contains many fine examples of Cosmati work, in particular the mosaic pavement, the raised choir, the bishop's throne, and the canopy over the main altar.

Set into the wall of the portico is the Bocca della Verità (Mouth of Truth), a grotesque marble face, thought to have been an ancient drain cover. Medieval tradition had it that the jaws would snap shut on liars – a way of testing the faithfulness of spouses.

3

Temples of the Forum Boarium

📍H7 🏛Piazza della Bocca della Verità 📞06 39 96 77 00 🚌23, 44, 81, 160, 170, 280, 628, 715, 716 🕐1st & 3rd Sun of month for guided tours only

These wonderfully well-preserved Republican-era

temples are at their best in moonlight, standing in their grassy enclave beside the Tiber sheltered by umbrella pines. During the day, they look less romantic, stranded in a sea of traffic. They date from the 2nd century BC, and were saved from ruin by being consecrated as Christian churches in the Middle Ages by the Greek community then living in the area. The rectangular temple, formerly known as the Temple of Fortuna Virilis, was probably dedicated to Portunus, the god of rivers and ports. Set on a podium, it has four Ionic travertine columns fluted at the front and 12 half-columns embedded in the tufa wall of the *cella* – the room that housed the image of the god. In the 9th century the temple was converted into the church of Santa Maria Egiziaca, after a 5th-century prostitute who reformed and became a hermit.

The smaller circular temple, made of solid marble and

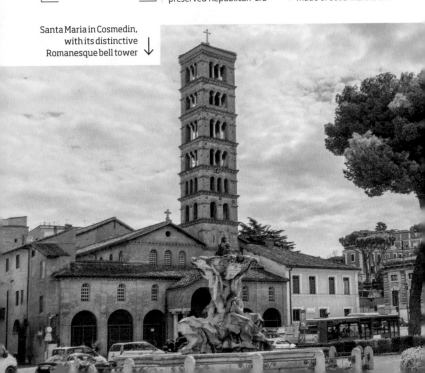

Santa Maria in Cosmedin, with its distinctive Romanesque bell tower ↓

The circular Temple of Hercules Victor, one of the Temples of the Forum Boarium ↑

surrounded by 20 fluted columns, was dedicated to Hercules but was long thought to be a Temple of Vesta because of its similarity to the one in the Forum.

 4

Santa Maria in Domnica

L8 **Piazza della Navicella 12** **06 77 20 26 85** **81, 117, 673** **Colosseo** **For church services only**

Santa Maria in Domnica was probably founded in the 7th century, and renovated in the 9th century. By this time the Romans had lost the art of making mosaics, so Pope Paschal I imported mosaicists from Byzantium. They created an exquisite apse mosaic showing the Virgin, Child and angels in a garden of paradise. Paschal I is kneeling at the Virgin's feet wearing a square halo, indicating that he was alive when it was made.

In 1513 Andrea Sansovino added a portico decorated with lions' heads, a punning homage to Pope Leo X.

 5

Santi Quattro Coronati

L7 **Via dei Santi Quattro Coronati 20** **06 70 47 54 27** **85, 117, 810** **3** **10–11:45am Mon-Sat, 4–5:45pm daily**

The name of this fortified convent (Four Crowned Saints) refers to four Christian soldiers martyred after refusing to worship a pagan god. For centuries it was the bastion of the pope's residence, the

↑ The Bocca della Verità, in the portico of Santa Maria in Cosmedin

Lateran Palace. Erected in the 4th century AD, it was rebuilt after invading Normans set fire to it in 1084.

Highlights are a delightful garden cloister and the Chapel of St Sylvester, where 12th-century frescoes tell the story of Emperor Constantine's conversion to Christianity.

 6

Santo Stefano Rotondo

L8 **Via di Santo Stefano Rotondo 7** **06 42 11 99** **81, 117, 673** **9:30am–12:30pm & 3–6pm (2–5pm in winter) Tue–Sat, 9:30am–noon Sun**

Santo Stefano Rotondo was built between 468 and 483 on a circular plan with four chapels in a cruciform shape. Its circular inner area is enclosed by two concentric corridors. A third, outer corridor was demolished on the orders of Leon Battista Alberti. In the 1500s Niccolò Pomarancio, Antonio Tempesta and others covered the walls with 34 frescoes detailing the martyrdoms of saints.

San Clemente

📍 L7 🏛 Via di Labicana 95
🚌 85, 87, 117, 186, 810
Ⓜ Colosseo 🚋 3 📞 06 774
00 21 🕐 9am-12.30pm,
3-6pm Mon-Sat, noon-6pm
Sun & bank hols); last adm:
20 mins before closing

In 1857 Father Mullooly, the Irish Dominican prior of San Clemente, began excavations beneath the existing 12th-century basilica. He and his successors discovered a 4th-century church and, below that, a number of ancient Roman buildings. On the lowest level is a temple devoted to the cult of Mithras, a mystical all-male religion that was imported from Persia and rivalled Christianity for popularity in the 2nd and 3rd centuries AD.

The centrepiece of the upper church is the 12th-century apse mosaic *Triumph of the Cross*, in which the crucified Christ is represented as the tree of life, nourished by the rivers of Paradise and

surrounded by foliage and animals. Also worth seeing is the splendid 12th-century spiral paschal candlestick, striped with glittering Cosmati mosaics, and the 8th-century *scola cantorum* (choir enclosure), salvaged from the church below.

It took 40 years to shovel out the rubble from the lower church, revealing a three-aisled basilica with traces of frescoes, including one of Byzantine Empress Theodora converted into a *Madonna and Child* by the later addition of a haloed baby. From this level, steps lead down to the foundations of a Roman apartment block with the temple to Mithras – complete with sacrificial altar – in what was once its courtyard.

↑ Sumptuous interior of the church of San Clemente

Baths of Caracalla

📍 K9 🏛 Viale delle Terme di
Caracalla 52 📞 06 39 96 77
00 🚌 160, 628 🚋 3 🕐 9am-
2pm Mon, 9am to 1 hour
before sunset Tue-Sun
🚫 1 Jan, 25 Dec

Rearing up at the foot of the Aventine Hill are the red-brick ruins of the Baths of Caracalla. Begun by Emperor Septimius Severus in AD 206, and completed by his son Caracalla in AD 217, they remained in use until the 6th century, when the Goths sabotaged the city's aqueducts.

→ The monolithic remains of the vast Baths of Caracalla complex

Going for a bath was a social event in ancient Rome, and complexes such as Caracalla offered an impressive array of facilities: art galleries, gymnasia, gardens, libraries, lecture rooms and shops selling food and drink.

A Roman bath was a long and complicated business, beginning with a form of Turkish bath, followed by a spell in the *caldarium*, a large hot room with pools of water to moisten the atmosphere. Then came the lukewarm *tepidarium*, followed by a visit to the large central meeting place known as the *frigidarium*, and finally a plunge into the *natatio*, an open-air swimming pool. For the wealthy, this was followed by a rub-down with scented woollen cloth.

Most of the rich marble decorations of the baths were scavenged by the Farnese family in the 16th century to adorn the rooms of Palazzo Farnese (*p264*). There are, however, statues and mosaics from the Baths in the Museo Archeologico Nazionale in Naples (*p452*) and in the Vatican's Gregorian Profane Museum (*p290*).

So dramatic is the setting that it is the regular venue for the open-air opera season.

Pyramid of Caius Cestius

Q H10 **A** Piazzale Ostiense
C 06 39 96 77 00 (for tours)
🚌 23, 280 **🚋** 3 **Ⓜ** Piramide

Caius Cestius was a wealthy but unimportant 1st-century BC *praetor*, or senior magistrate. At the time, inspired by the Cleopatra scandals, there was a craze for all things Egyptian, and Caius decided to commission himself a pyramid as a tomb. Set into the Aurelian Wall near Porta San Paolo, it is built of brick and faced with white marble; according to an inscription, it took just 330 days to build in 12 BC.

10 Protestant Cemetery

Q G10 **A** Cimitero Acattolico, Via di Caio Cestio **C** 06 574 19 00
🚌 23, 280 **🚋** 3 **🕐** 9am–5pm Mon–Sat, 9am–1pm Sun; last adm: 30 mins before closing

Non-Catholics have been buried in this cemetery behind the Aurelian Wall since 1738. In the oldest part

(on the left as you enter) is the grave of the poet John Keats, who died in 1821 in a house on Piazza di Spagna (*p272*). He wrote his own epitaph: "Here lies one whose name was writ in water". Close by rest the ashes of Percy Bysshe Shelley, who drowned in 1822.

11 Santa Sabina

Q G8 **A** Piazza Pietro d'Illiria 1 **C** 06 57 94 01
🚌 23, 44, 170, 781
🕐 8:15am–12:30pm & 3:30–6pm daily

High on the Aventine stands an early Christian basilica, founded by Peter of Illyria in AD 425 and later given to the Dominican order. It was restored to its original simplicity in the early 20th century. Light filters through 9th-century windows onto a nave framed by pale Corinthian columns. Above the main door is a blue and gold 5th-century mosaic inscription to Peter. In the side portico outside is a 5th-century panelled door carved with biblical scenes, notably one of the oldest images of the Crucifixion (top left-hand corner).

SHOP

Mercato di Testaccio
This is a must for anyone who takes food seriously - as well as the market stalls, there are takeaway food stands offering everything from assorted tasty morsels to freshly squeezed juices.

Q G10 **A** Via Lorenzo Ghiberti
W mercatoditestaccio.it

↑ Weeping angel statue at the Protestant Cemetery

A SHORT WALK

PIAZZA DELLA BOCCA DELLA VERITÀ

Distance 0.8 km (0.5 miles) **Nearest bus stops** 23, 44, 81, 160, 170, 280, 628, 715, 716, 780 **Time** 20 minutes

A quiet corner of the city, this area beside the Tiber is great for escaping the crowds. It was ancient Rome's first port and its busy cattle market. Substantial Classical remains include two small temples from the Republican age and the Arch of Janus from the later Empire. In the 6th century the area became home to a Greek community from Byzantium, who founded the churches of San Giorgio in Velabro and Santa Maria in Cosmedin. Follow tradition and place your hand inside the Bocca della Verità (the Mouth of Truth), a mythological stone sculpture in the portico of Santa Maria in Cosmedin.

Sant'Omobono, dating to the 16th-century, stands in isolation in the middle of an important archaeological site where the remains of sacrificial altars and two temples from the 6th century BC have been discovered.

START

The 11th-century Casa dei Crescenzi features columns and capitals from ancient Roman temples.

The Temples of the Forum Boarium are the best preserved of Rome's Republican temples (p306).

Ponte Rotto, as this forlorn ruined arch in the Tiber is called, means simply "broken bridge". Built in the 2nd century BC, its original name was Pons Aemilius.

LUNGOTEVERE DEI PIERLEONI

Tevere

PONTE PALATINO

The Fontana dei Tritoni, by Carlo Bizzaccheri, was built here in 1715. The style shows the powerful influence of Bernini.

↑ The well-preserved Temple of Hercules in the Forum Boarium

Medieval interior ↑
of Santa Maria
in Cosmedin

Locator Map
For more detail see p302

Santa Maria della Consolazione is named after an icon that consoled criminals at Tarpeian Rock (p245).

FINISH

VIA DEI FIENILI

V
I
A

D
I

S
A
N

T
E
O
D
O
R
O

VIA DI SAN TEODORO

GIOVANNI DECOLLATO

PIAZZA DELLA
BOCCA DELLA
VERITA

VIA DEI CERCHI

VIA DELLA GRECA

The 15th-century portal of the ancient round San Teodoro church is decorated with the insignia of Pope Nicholas V.

The plain Renaissance façade of San Giovanni Decollato was completed in about 1504.

San Giorgio in Velabro's simple 12th-century portico of Ionic columns was destroyed by a bomb in 1993 but has been restored.

The Arco degli Argentari, dedicated to Emperor Septimius Severus in AD 204, is decorated with scenes of religion and war.

The square Arch of Janus with arches on each side dates from the 4th century AD.

The medieval church of Santa Maria in Cosmedin has a fine marble mosaic floor and a Gothic baldacchino (p306).

0 metres		100
0 yards		100

N
↑

ROME: BEYOND THE CENTRE

Must See

❶ Museo e Galleria Borghese

Experience More

❷ MAXXI (National Museum of 21st Century Arts)

❸ Villa Giulia

❹ Catacombs

❺ Centrale Montemartini

❻ MACRO Testaccio

❼ EUR

❽ Cinecittà Si Mostra

It is well worth making the effort to see some of Rome's outlying sights. Just outside the centre are the Villa Giulia, home to a magnificent Etruscan museum, and the Museo Borghese on the splendid Villa Borghese estate, with its extraordinary collection of virtuoso statues by Bernini. South of the city, follow the atmospheric Via Appia Antica to the outskirts of the modern city and discover the evocative ruins of ancient churches and early Christian catacombs. Further north, MAXXI gives a tantalising taste of the Rome of the future.

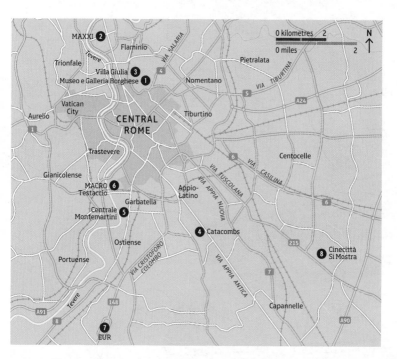

1 🔨 ⟨M⟩ 🖥 📱

MUSEO E GALLERIA BORGHESE

📍 D4   🏠 Villa Borghese, Piazzale Scipione Borghese   🚌 52, 53, 116, 910   🚊 3, 19
🕐 9am–7pm Tue–Sun   🚫 1 Jan, 25 Dec   🌐 galleriaborghese.beniculturali.it

There are few places in the world where it is possible to weave together a day in a park with high culture as easily as at the Villa Borghese. Some of Bernini's best sculptures and paintings by Caravaggio, Titian and Raphael sit alongside Classical works in this beautiful frescoed 17th-century villa set in extensive grounds.

The villa and park were laid out by Cardinal Scipione Borghese, favourite nephew of Pope Paul V, who had the estate designed for pleasure and entertainment. The hedonistic cardinal was an extravagant patron of the arts and commissioned sculptures from Bernini which now rank among the artist's most famous works. Today the villa houses the superb private Borghese collection of sculptures and paintings.

Sculpture

The sculpture collection is on the ground floor of the villa. Among the highlights is one of Bernini's finest works, *Apollo and Daphne* (1624) in room 3, which shows the nymph Daphne metamorphosing into a laurel tree in order to escape abduction by Apollo. Abduction is also the theme of *The Rape of Proserpina*, again by Bernini, in room 4.

Bernini's masterful representation of flesh in *The Rape of Proserpina* ↓

THE BORGHESE COLLECTORS

Scipione used this villa to display the antiquities collection given to him by his uncle, Pope Paul V, to which he added sculptures by Bernini. When later heir Camillo Borghese married Pauline Bonaparte, he gave the bulk of the Classical sculpture collection to his brother-in-law, Napoleon. They now form the core of the Louvre's antiquities wing.

← Bust of Cardinal Scipione Borghese

Here, muscular Hades throws his head back with laughter, his strong fingers pressing into the maiden's soft flesh as she struggles to break free of his grasp.

Paintings

The upper floor of the villa is devoted to Baroque and Renaissance paintings. Works on display include Raphael's masterpiece *Deposition*, Titian's *Sacred and Profane Love*, and various works by Caravaggio, including the sensuous *Boy with a Basket of Fruit*.

The Park

The estates of the Villa Borghese, Villa Giulia and the Pincio gardens form one vast park, with the Giardino del Lago, at its centre, named after an artificial boating lake. Dotted around it are an array of attractions, including artificial ponds, mock temples, a children's play centre, a zoo, an outdoor theatre, the world's smallest purpose-built cinema and a horse-riding track.

↑ Exterior of the villa, now the Museo e Galleria Borghese

↑ Raphael's bold and moving masterpiece *Deposition*

EXPERIENCE MORE

②

MAXXI (National Museum of 21st Century Arts)

📍D4 🏛Villa Guido Reni 4A 🚌53, 217, 910 🚊2 🕐11am–7pm Tue–Sun (to 10pm Sat) 🚫1 May, 25 Dec 🌐maxxi.art

Along with the nearby Parco della Musica, MAXXI has put Rome on the contemporary arts map. Completed in 2009, it is located in a stunning building designed by the late architect Zaha Hadid. The museum showcases emerging Italian and international artists. An impressive amount of space is also given over to architecture.

③

Villa Giulia

📍D4 🏛Piazzale di Villa Giulia 9 📞06 322 65 71 🚌52 🚊3, 19 🕐9am–8pm Tue–Sun 🚫1 Jan, 25 Dec

Villa Giulia was built in the mid-16th century as a country retreat and pleasure palace for Pope Julius III, who would regularly float up the River Tiber from the Vatican on a flower-decked barge to check on its progress. The gardens were planted with 36,000 trees and studded with statues, grottoes, pavilions and fountains. The house was filled

SHOP

Eataly

As well as a bewildering range of niche producers of everything from artisanal cheese to craft beer, this cathedral to gastronomy houses bars, restaurants and cookery schools. There's a packed calendar of tastings and other food-related events.

📍D4 🏛Piazzale 12 Ottobre 1492 🌐eataly.net

with an outstanding collection of sculptures: 160 boats packed with statues and ornaments were sent to the Vatican after the Pope died in 1555.

Since 1889 the villa has been home to the Museo Nazionale Etrusco, devoted to the Etruscan civilization that lived in central Italy before the Romans and traded metals for ceramics and luxury objects made by the Greeks and Phoenicians. The museum's collection includes several important pieces that were repatriated to Italy after being illegally excavated and sold to collectors and museums. Included among these is the 6th-century-BC *Euphronius Vase*, painted with spectacular images of Hypnos, god of sleep, and Thanatos, god of death; it was returned to Italy from the Metropolitan Museum in New York in 2008. Other highlights include the *Ficoroni Cist*, an exquisitely engraved 4th-century-BC bronze marriage coffer designed to hold mirrors and cosmetics; the spiral-handled *Faliscan Crater*, a beautifully

Futuristic MAXXI museum, designed by Zaha Hadid

painted vase used to hold wine or oil, dating back to the 4th century BC; and the famous *Husband and Wife Sarcophagus*, a 6th-century-BC tomb on which the deceased couple are shown banqueting in the afterlife.

Admission to Villa Giulia is free on the first Sunday of the month.

 4

Catacombs

D4 **Via Appia Antica 126** **118, 218**

The first part of the Via Appia was built in 312 BC by Appius Claudius Caecus. In 190 BC, when it was extended to the southern ports of Taranto and Brindisi, the road became Rome's link with its empire in the East. It was also the route taken by the funeral processions of the dictator Sulla (78 BC) and Emperor Augustus (AD 14), and it was along this road that St Paul

was led as a prisoner to Rome in AD 56. The church of Domine Quo Vadis marks the spot where St Peter is said to have met Christ when fleeing Rome. The road is lined with ruined family tombs, decaying monuments and collective burial places (*columbaria*). Beneath the fields on either side lies a maze of catacombs.

In burying their dead in underground cemeteries outside the city walls, the early Christians were simply obeying the laws of the time. They were not forced to use them because of persecution, as later popular myth has suggested. Many saints were buried here, and the catacombs later became shrines and places of pilgrimage.

Today several catacombs are open to the public. The vast **Catacombs of San Callisto**, hewn from volcanic tufa, contain niches, or *loculi*, which held two or three bodies, as well as the burial places of several early popes. Close by, walls in the Catacombs of San Sebastiano are covered in graffiti invoking St Peter and St Paul, whose remains may once have been moved here.

Catacombs of San Callisto

06 513 01 580 **9am-noon, 2-5pm Thu-Tue** **1 Jan, late Jan-late Feb, Easter Sun, 25 Dec**

 5

Centrale Montemartini

D4 **Via Ostiense 106** **06 06 08** **23, 769** **9am-7pm Tue-Sun (last adm: 6:30pm)** **1 Jan, 1 May, 25 Dec**

An enormous former industrial site, originally housing Rome's first power station, has been restored and turned into a fascinating art centre. Two enormous generators still occupy the central machine room, creating quite an intriguing contrast to the exhibitions.

On display at Centrale Montemartini are Roman statues and artifacts belonging to the Capitoline Museums (*p250*). Many of the statues were discovered during excavations in the late 19th and early 20th centuries, including some from the Area Sacra di Largo Argentina (*p265*).

Ruins of a Roman-era aqueduct along the Via Appia Antica ↓

Monumental Fascist-era
architecture at the
↓ EUR quarter

MACRO Testaccio

D4 Piazza Orazio Giustiniani 4 4-10pm Tue-Sun (only during exhibitions) museo macro.org

For much of the 20th century, the Testaccio neighbourhood was a working-class quarter, dominated by its vast 19th-century slaughterhouse, the Mattatoio. It has now become one of the city's trendiest areas, and the Mattatoio, considered an important industrial architectural landmark, has been transformed into the second seat of the Museo d'Arte Contemporanea Roma (MACRO). It hosts temporary modern and contemporary art exhibitions and art-related events.

EUR

D4 170, 671, 714 EUR Fermi, EUR Palasport

The Esposizione Universale di Roma (EUR), a suburb to the south of the city, was originally built for an international exhibition, a kind of "Work Olympics", that was planned for 1942, but never took place because of the outbreak of war. The architecture was intended to glorify Fascism, and as a result the bombastic style of the buildings can look overblown and rhetorical to modern eyes. Of all the buildings the best known is probably the Palazzo della Civiltà del Lavoro (the Palace of the Civilization of Work), an unmistakable landmark for people arriving from Fiumicino airport.

→

Entrance to the film studios at Cinecittà, now open to the public

EAT

Sibilla

The location - a wisteria-clad terrace with a view of a Greek temple - can hardly be beaten, and the food at Sibilla is pretty special too: expect refined versions of traditional Italian cuisine.

D4 Via della Sibilla 50, Tivoli ristorantesibilla.com

€€€

Despite the area's dubious architecture, EUR has been a planning success, and people are keen to live here. As well as residential housing, the vast marble halls along the wide boulevards are also home to a number of government offices and museums. Best among the latter is the **Museo della Civiltà Romana**, famous for its casts of the reliefs from the Column of Trajan, and for a large-scale model depicting 4th-century Rome. The south of the suburb features a lake and shady park, and the huge Palazzo dello Sport, built for the 1960 Olympics.

Museo della Civiltà Romana

Piazza G Agnelli 10 06 06 08 For restoration; call ahead for details

Cinecittà Si Mostra

D4 Via Tuscolana 1055 9:30am-5:30pm Wed-Mon cinecitta simostra.it

Cinecittà Si Mostra (literally Cinecittà Shows Off) offers the chance to step behind the scenes of Italy's most famous film studio. Costumes and props are exhibited, including the dress worn by Elizabeth Taylor in *Cleopatra* (1963). Visits include tours of film sets, such as a replica Broadway created for the Martin Scorsese film *Gangs of New York* (2002) and a mock ancient Rome (which stood in for ancient Pompeii in a 2008 episode of *Doctor Who*), along with a visit to the working film studio.

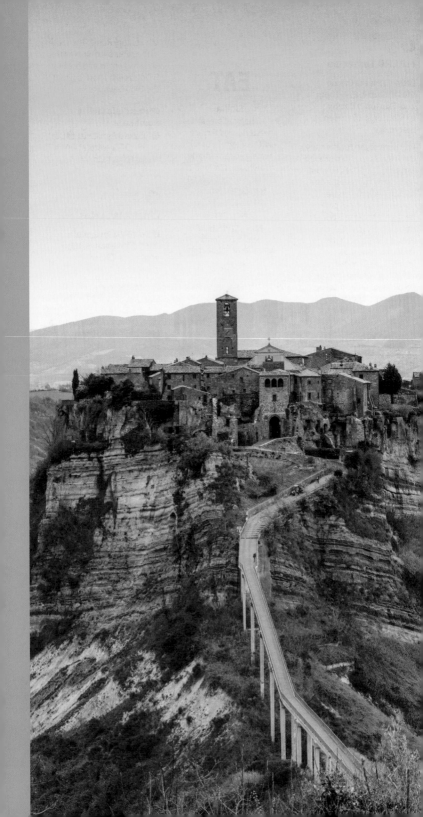

LAZIO

With its ancient forests, volcanic lakes, wetlands, mountains and beaches, Lazio is a region of fascinating contrasts. In addition to its many archaeological sites, Lazio today offers skiing, swimming and watersports.

Lazio was inhabited at least 60,000 years ago, although the first signs of a civilization date back to the 10th century BC. By the 7th century BC a flourishing Etruscan and Sabine civilization based on trade and agriculture existed in the north, while the region's southern margins were colonized by the Latins, Volsci and Hernici. History mingles with myth in the writings of Virgil, who describes how Aeneas landed in Lazio, where he married the daughter of the king of the Latins. Romulus and Remus (legendary founders of Rome) were descendants of this alliance.

With the rise of Rome as a power, the Etruscan and Latin peoples were, in time, overwhelmed and the focus of the region turned to the city of Rome. Great roads and aqueducts extended out of the city like spokes of a wheel, and wealthy patricians built lavish villas in the surrounding countryside.

The early Middle Ages saw the rise of the Church's temporal power and, with the foundation of monasteries at Subiaco and Montecassino, Lazio became the cradle of western monasticism, and eventually part of the Papal States. In the 16th and 17th centuries, wealthy papal families competed with one another to build luxurious villas and gardens.

Throughout its history, however, Lazio has been eclipsed and neglected by Rome. The Pontine marshes were a malaria-ridden swamp until the 1920s, when Mussolini had them drained and brought new roads and agricultural improvements.

LAZIO

Experience

EXPERIENCE MORE

Viterbo

D4 🚆 *i* **Via Ascenzi 1;**
www.visit.viterbo.it

Viterbo was an important Etruscan centre before falling to the Romans in the 4th century BC. Its heyday came when it briefly became the papal seat (1257–81). It was devastated in World War II, but the medieval core has been carefully restored.

In San Pellegrino, Viterbo's oldest and best-preserved quarter, medieval houses with towers, arches and external staircases line narrow streets.

On Piazza San Lorenzo the 12th-century Duomo boasts a striped bell tower, a solemn 16th-century façade and a stark Romanesque interior. The adjacent 13th-century Palazzo Papale, with a finely carved loggia, was built for popes on their visits to the city.

The town's civic buildings border Piazza del Plebiscito. The most interesting is the 15th-century **Palazzo dei Priori**, frescoed inside by Baldassare Croce with scenes from the town's history and mythological past.

The **Villa Lante**, northeast of Viterbo, was begun in 1562 by Vignola for Cardinal Gambara. The main attractions are the Renaissance gardens and fountains. Be aware that many of the fountains will spray people without warning.

Palazzo dei Priori

🏛 ⌂ Piazza Plebiscito
📞 0761 30 47 95 ⊙ Daily

Villa Lante

🏛 ⌂ Bagnaia 📞 0761 28 80 08 ⊙ 8:30am to 1 hour before sunset Tue–Sun
🗓 1 Jan, 1 May, 25 Dec

Montefiascone

D4 ⌂ Viterbo 🚆🚌
i **Piazza V. Emanuele;**
0761 64 79 41

This pretty town sits on the edge of a defunct volcanic crater between the shores of Lake Bolsena and the Via Cassia. It is dominated by the bulk of its cathedral, Santa Margherita, whose 1670s dome is second in size only to St Peter's.

On the town's outskirts, towards Orvieto, lies San Flaviano, a lovely building with a 12th-century church oriented east over an 11th-century church pointing west. Inside are some fine 14th-century frescoes and freely carved capitals.

The popular lakeside resort of Bolsena, 15 km (9 miles) north on Lake Bolsena, has a medieval castle, as well as boats to the islands of Bisentina and Martana.

Tuscania

C4 ⌂ Viterbo
🚌 *i* **Piazzale Trieste;**
0761 445 42 59

Tuscania's trim walls and towers are visible from afar

↑ Geometric garden at Villa Lante, just outside Viterbo

→

View across the city of Tuscania, with its towers visible

on the empty low-lying plains between Viterbo and Tarquinia. Although shaken by an earthquake in 1971, its medieval and Renaissance buildings have been carefully reconstructed. Just outside the city walls, on the rocky Colle San Pietro, two remarkable churches of the Lombard-Romanesque period occupy the site of Tuscana, a major Etruscan centre conquered by Rome in 300 BC.

Santa Maria Maggiore, at the foot of the hill, has a Lombard-Romanesque asymmetric façade with blind arcades and a bold rose window. Over the central door lies a simple marble Madonna and Child, framed by abstract motifs and biblical scenes.

The Lombard-Romanesque church of San Pietro, on top of the hill, is a striking building of ochre-hued tufa and white marble details. It stands on a grassy piazza, along with two medieval towers and a bishop's palace. The façade features an intricately inlaid rose window flanked by strange reliefs, including three-headed bearded demons.

4

Bomarzo

◬D4 🏛Parco dei Mostri, Bomarzo 🚌To Viterbo 🚌From Viterbo (not Sun or public hols) 🕐8:30am-7pm (winter: to sunset)
🌐sacrobosco.it

The Monster Park beneath the town of Bomarzo was created between 1522 and 1580 by Duke Vicino Orsini as a bizarre memorial to his late wife, and is essentially the world's first theme park. Orsini embraced the artificiality and distortion of the Mannerist period by creating lopsided buildings and sculpting huge boulders

of stone into fantastic creatures and vast allegorical monsters. Most famous of all is a huge screaming face, but there is also a giant ripping a man in two, a life-size elephant crushing a Roman soldier, and a series of dragons, nymphs, mermaids and sphinxes.

5

Caprarola

◬D4 🏛Viterbo 🚌
🛈Via Filippo Nicolai 2; www.caprarola.com

Perhaps the grandest of the country villas created during the 17th century by the wealthy families of Rome, **Palazzo Farnese** is the focal point of the medieval village of Caprarola. Designed by Vignola, it was built between 1559 and 1575 and takes its star shape from the foundations of a large pentagonal fortress designed by Antonio da Sangallo the Younger half a century earlier.

Created, according to legend, by Hercules ramming his club into the ground, Lago di Vico, 5 km (3 miles) west of Caprarola, occupies the remnants of a volcanic crater. An idyllic enclave, the lake is encircled by the wooded slopes of the Cimini Hills.

Palazzo Farnese
 🏛Caprarola 📞0761 64 60 52 🕐Tue-Sun 🔒1 Jan, 25 Dec

EAT

Hostaria del Ponte da Lorena
Set inside an 18th-century palace, this restaurant has a lovely courtyard and a terraced garden.

◬D4 🏛Piazza G Battista 1 Lubriano 🔒Tue 🌐hostaria delponte.it

€€€

La Piazzetta del Sole
This little spot is tucked into a tiny hamlet and run by two visionary women - one in the kitchen and one front of house.

◬C4 🏛Via XX Settembre 129, Farnese 🔒Mon; D Sat & Sun 🌐piazzettadelsole.com

€€€

Trattoria Zi Maria
First-rate traditional regional food is served in this trattoria. The venison with wild berries is exceptional.

◬C4 🏛Via Sasso Manziana 2, Sasso-Cerveteri 🔒Tue 🌐trattoria zimaria.com

€€€

Dusk at the idyllic Lake Bracciano, popular with watersports enthusiasts

SLEEP

Villa Clementina

This enchanting hotel has beautifully frescoed rooms and lush grounds with a botanical garden, a saline-mineral water swimming pool and a wellness centre. A gorgeous restaurant serves traditional Italian cuisine.

D4 Traversa Quarto del Lago, Bracciano hotelvilla clementina.it

€€€

6 Lake Bracciano

D4 Roma Bracciano Piazza IV Novembre, Bracciano; 06 99 81 62 62

Bracciano is a large lake famous for its fish, and popular for watersports and lakeside lunches.

Medieval Anguillara, to the south, is the prettiest of the lakeside towns with romantic views over the water. The main town, Bracciano, on the east shore, is dominated by **Castello Orsini-Odescalchi**, a pentagonal 15th-century structure with frescoes by Antoniazzo Romano and other Tuscan and Umbrian artists.

Castello Orsini-Odescalchi

Piazza Mazzini 14 06 99 80 23 79 Tue-Sun 1 Jan, 25 Dec

HIDDEN GEM
Calcata

For some 30 years, the town of Calcata was left to ruin. But in the late 1960s, a group of artists, musicians and bohemian intellectuals began to breathe life back into it, establishing a creative colony that continues to thrive to this day.

---

7 Cerveteri

D4 Roma Piazza Risorgimento 19; 06 99 55 26 37

In the 6th century BC Cerveteri (ancient Kysry) was one of the largest and most culturally rich towns of the Mediterranean. The Etruscan **necropolis**, a city of the dead 2 km (1 mile) outside town, is a network of streets lined with tombs dating from the 7th to the 1st century BC. The Tomba dei Rilievi is decorated with plaster reliefs of tools, pets and mythological figures. While the best finds from the necropolis are in museums such as the Vatican Museums, Villa Giulia and the British Museum in London, some can be seen in the small **Museo Nazionale Cerite**.

There are more traces of the Etruscans to be seen at Norchia, where the tombs are carved out of a rock face, and Sutri, whose amphitheatre is one of the few relics of the living Etruscans.

Necropolis

Via Necropoli 06 994 06 51 Tue-Sun Some pub hols

Museo Nazionale Cerite

Piazza Santa Maria 06 994 06 51 Tue-Sun Pub hols

8 Ostia Antica

D5 Viale dei Romagnoli 717, Ostia 06 56 35 80 99 Piramide, then train from Porta San Paolo 8:30am to 1 hour before sunset Tue-Sun 1 Jan, 1 May, 25 Dec

For more than 600 years Ostia was Rome's main port and a busy trading centre, until the 5th century AD when a disastrous combination of malaria and commercial competition sent the town into decline. Silt preserved its buildings and it now lies 5 km (3 miles) inland.

The ruins of Ostia give a vivid idea of life in Classical times. The main thoroughfare, the Decumanus Maximus, runs through the Forum, which houses Ostia's largest temple, the Capitol, and past the restored theatre, still used for open-air concerts in the summer. The road is lined with baths, shops and multistorey buildings. There is even a Thermopolium, or bar, with a marble counter and paintings advertising food and drink.

9

Frascati and the Castelli Romani

D4 **Roma** **FS** **Frascati**

The Alban hills have long been a country retreat for Romans. In Classical times they were scattered with villas; during the Middle Ages with fortified castles (hence the name); and in the 16th and 17th centuries with luxurious residences surrounded by spectacular parks. During World War II German defences were based in the Alban hills and many Castelli towns were damaged by Allied bombs. Partly protected by a nature reserve, the hilltop towns are popular day-trip destinations and famous for their white wine. Frascati's central piazza is a belvedere overlooked by the **Villa Aldobrandini**, a majestic 17th-century building in a splendid park of grottoes and fountains.

The fortified Abbazia di San Nilo in Grottaferrata, 3 km (2 miles) south, was founded in 1004 and contains some lovely 17th-century frescoes by Domenichino in the chapel. Overlooking Lake Albano, 6 km (4 miles) south, Castel Gandolfo is the site of the pope's summer palace.

Villa Aldobrandini
06 94 18 41 Mon-Fri

10

Tarquinia

C4 **Viterbo** **FS**
Barriera di San Giusto; 0766 84 92 82

Ancient Tarquinia (Tarxuna) was one of Etruria's most important centres. It occupied a strategic position on a ridge to the northeast of the present town until the 4th century BC, when it fell to Rome.

Tarquinia is worth a wander for its crumbling medieval churches and spacious main square, though the main reason to visit is the **Museo Archeologico e Necropoli**, which has one of Italy's better collections of Etruscan finds. The star attraction is a group of terracotta winged horses from the 4th century BC.

↑ A decorative jug in the Museo Archeologico in Tarquinia

On a hilltop 2 km (1 mile) southeast of town are the frescoed tombs of the necropolis dug into the soft volcanic tufa. There are almost 6,000 tombs but only about 15 can be visited at a time. The frescoes that decorate them, designed to remind the dead of life, range from frenetic dancing figures in the Tomb of the Triclinium to diners reclining in the Tomb of the Leopards.

Museo Archeologico e Necropoli
Piazza Cavour 0766 85 00 80 Tue-Sun 1 Jan, 1 May, 25 Dec

↓ Roman remains at Ostia Antica, a former port

⓫ Tivoli

△D4 △Roma 🚊🚌
🛈 Piazzale Nazioni Unite;
0774 31 35 36

Hill-town Tivoli, a popular excursion from Rome, was a favoured resort of the ancient Romans, attracted by its fresh water and sulphur springs, and beautiful countryside. The temples that once covered Tivoli's hilltop are still visible in places. Some are half buried in medieval buildings, others, such as the temples of Sibyl and Vesta, are relatively intact.

The town's most famous sight is the **Villa d'Este**, a sumptuous country residence created in the 16th century by Pirro Ligorio for Cardinal Ippolito d'Este from the shell of a Benedictine monastery. It is known primarily for its gardens, steeply raked on terraces, and studded with spectacular, if somewhat faded and moss-hung, fountains. Although suffering from reduced water pressure and polluted water due to centuries of neglect, the gardens give a vivid impression of the frivolous luxury enjoyed by the papal families. Highlights include the Viale delle Cento Fontane and the Fontana dell'Organo Idraulico, which, thanks to a hydraulic

↑ A waterfall within the gardens of the famed Villa d'Este, Tivoli

system, can play music. At the other end of town, the **Villa Gregoriana**, now a hotel, is set in a lush wooded valley where paths wind down into a deep ravine.

About 5 km (3 miles) west of Tivoli are the ruins of **Hadrian's Villa**. Easily seen in conjunction with a visit to the town, this is one of the largest and most spectacular villas ever built in the Roman Empire (it once covered an area greater than the centre of Imperial Rome).

Hadrian was an inveterate traveller and his aim in creating the villa was to reproduce some of the wonders he had seen around the world. The Stoa Poikile, for example, a walkway around a rectangular pool and garden, recalls the painted colonnade of the Stoic

philosophers in Athens, while the Canopus evokes the grand sanctuary of Serapis in Alexandria. There are also ruins of two bath complexes, a Latin and a Greek library, a Greek theatre, and a private study on a little island known as the Teatro Marittimo.

Today the rambling ruins make a lovely place to relax, picnic or explore.

Villa d'Este

🏛 △Piazza Trento 1 📞0774 33 29 20 🕐Tue-Sun 🚫1 Jan, 25 Dec

Villa Gregoriana

△Largo Sant'Angelo
📞0774 33 26 50 🕐Apr-Oct: daily; Nov-Mar: Tue-Sun

Hadrian's Villa

🏛 △ Largo Marguerite Yourcenar 📞0774 53 02 03 🚫Public hols

⓬ Palestrina

△D4 △Roma 🚌

Medieval Palestrina grew up over the terraces of a huge temple dedicated to the goddess Fortuna Primigenia, the mother of all gods. The temple, founded in the 8th century BC and rebuilt in the 2nd century BC by Sulla, housed one of the most important oracles of ancient times. The terraces of the sanctuary, littered with fragments of columns and porticoes, lead up to the curved Palazzo Barberini. Built over the site of a circular temple, the Palazzo now houses the **Museo Nazionale Prenestino**, best known for a 1st-century-BC mosaic of the Nile in flood. This museum also boasts a famous sculpture of the Capitoline Triad.

Museo Nazionale Prenestino

🏛 △Via Barberini 📞06 953 81 00 🕐Daily 🚫1 Jan, 1 May, 25 Dec

LAZIO MONASTERIES

St Benedict founded the Abbey of Montecassino around 529 and there wrote his famous *Rule*, which became the fundamental monastic code of western Europe. The Cistercians, an offshoot of the Benedictines, were followers of St Bernard, whose creed was based on austerity and self-sufficiency. Cistercian abbeys in Lazio include Valvisciolo and San Martino in Cimino.

The stunning cliff-side location of the Benedictine monastery at Subiaco ↑

13
Subiaco

🅰D4 🚉Roma 🚌 ℹ️Town Library, Viale della Repubblica 26; 0774 85050

In the 6th century, weary of the decadence of Rome, St Benedict left the city to become a hermit in a cave above Subiaco. Others joined him, and eventually there were 12 monasteries in the area.

Only two of these now survive: **Santa Scolastica**, dedicated to Benedict's sister, is organized around three cloisters, one Renaissance, one early Gothic and the third Cosmatesque. Higher up, the 12th-century **San Benedetto** is a more rewarding desti-nation. Overhanging a deep gorge, it comprises two churches built on top of each other. The upper is decorated with 14th-century Sienese frescoes; the lower, built over several levels, incorporates the original cave where Benedict spent three years after fleeing Rome.

Santa Scolastica
🏠3 km (2 miles) E of Subiaco ☎0774 824 21 🕐Daily

San Benedetto
🏠3 km (2 miles) E of Subiaco ☎0774 85 039 🕐Daily

14
Montecassino

🅰E5 🚉Cassino ☎0776 31 1529 🚆Cassino, then bus 🕐Apr-Oct: 8:45am-7pm daily; Nov-Mar: 9am-4:45pm Mon-Sat, 8:45am-5:15pm Sun

The Abbey of Montecassino, the mother church of the Benedictine Order and an important centre of medieval art, was founded in 529 by St Benedict. By the 8th century it was an important centre of learning, and by the 11th century it had become one of the richest monasteries in Europe.

In 1944 Montecassino was a German stronghold and therefore a target for Allied bombing campaigns. Most of the complex was devasta-ted, including the lavish Baroque church, but the walls remained intact and the abbey withstood for three months before falling to the Allies. The adjoining war cemeteries commemorate the 30,000 soldiers killed.

STAY

Here are some of the best monastery stays in Lazio.

Monasteri Benedettini
Built into a cliff, this monastery offers incredible valley views.

🅰D4 🏠Largo San Benedetto 1, Subiaco 🌐benedettini-subiaco.org

———————

Benedictine Abbey of Santa Maria di Farfa
A national monument with a strong artistic and architectural past.

🅰D4 🏠Via del Monastero 1, Fara in Sabina 🌐abbaziadi farfa.com

———————

Abbazia di Casamari
Pristine 13th-century abbey – a fine example of Burgundian and early Gothic architecture.

🅰D5 🏠Via Maria, Veroli 🌐abbaziadicasamari.it

↑ Interior of the nave of Anagni's imposing Romanesque Duomo

15 Anagni

 D5 🚗 Frosinone 🚆🚌
🛈 Largo Gismondi; 0775 72 78 52

According to legend, Saturn founded five towns in south-east Lazio, including Anagni, Alatri and Arpino. This area is now known as La Ciociaria, from *ciocie*, the bark clogs worn in the area until about 30 years ago.

Before the Romans conquered this part of Lazio it was inhabited by several different tribes: the Volsci, the Sanniti, and the Hernici. Little is known of them, apart from the extraordinary walls with which they protected their settlements. In later years these were believed to have been built by the Cyclops, a mythical giant, which gave them their present name of Cyclopean walls.

Anagni was the most sacred Hernician centre until its destruction by the Romans in 306 BC. In the Middle Ages it was the birthplace and family seat of several popes, an era from which many buildings survive, most notably Boniface VIII's 13th-century mullion-windowed palace.

The beautiful Romanesque Duomo, Santa Maria, built over the ancient Hernician acropolis, boasts a fine Cosmati mosaic floor from the 13th century as well as 14th-century Sienese frescoes.

The crypt of San Magno is frescoed with one of the most complete surviving cycles of the 12th and 13th centuries.

Alatri, perched on an olive-covered slope 28 km (17 miles) east of Anagni, was an important Hernician town. It has an impressive double set of Cyclopean walls, 2 km (1 mile) long and 3 m (10 ft) high, from its 7th-century-BC acropolis.

The bustling town of Arpino, 40 km (25 miles) east of Alatri, was the birthplace of the Roman orator Cicero. About 3 km (2 miles) above Arpino, at the site of the ancient town of Civitavecchia, is a tremendous stretch of Cyclopean walls with a rare gateway with a pointed arch.

16 Terracina

 D5 🚗 Latina 🚆🚌
🛈 Viale Europa 204; 0773 70 77 02

Roman Terracina was an important commercial centre on the Via Appia (p317). Today it is a popular seaside resort, with fascinating medieval buildings and Roman ruins in its historic centre. The more modern part of town by the sea is full of restaurants, bars and hotels.

Bombing in World War II uncovered many of the town's ancient structures, notably a stretch of the Appian Way and the original paving of the Roman Forum in Piazza del Municipio. The 11th-century Duomo was built in the shell of a Roman temple, and is still entered by the temple's steps. The medieval portico is adorned with a lovely 12th-century mosaic. Next door, the modern town hall is home to the **Museo Archeologico**, devoted to local Greek and Roman finds.

About 3 km (2 miles) above the town are the podium and foundations that once supported the Temple of Jove Anxur, dating back to the 1st century BC. This huge arcaded platform offers vertiginous views of Terracina and its bay.

Museo Archeologico
 🚗 Piazza Municipio
📞 0773 707313 🕐 Daily
🚫 Mon pm, some pub hols

17 Sermoneta and Ninfa

 D5 🚗 Latina 🚆 Latina Scalo 🚌 From Latina
🛈 Via Varsavia, Latina (0773 48 06 72)

Sermoneta is a lovely hilltop town overlooking the Pontine Plains, with narrow cobbled streets winding around medieval houses, palaces and churches. The Duomo has a fine 15th-century panel by

→

Wisteria in bloom in the picturesque gardens of Ninfa

EAT

Il Granchio

Teeming with elegance and exuberance, this outstanding seafood restaurant uses only the highest-quality ingredients sourced from Terracina's fish auctions – the fishermen's catch determines the daily menu. A top-notch gastronomic experience, Il Granchio also offers a cosy bistro for less formal dining occasions.

 D5 🚗 Via S Francesco Nuovo 80, Terracina
🚫 Mon, L Tue-Sat
🌐 ilgranchio.it

€€€

Benozzo Gozzoli showing the Virgin cradling Sermoneta in her hands. At the top of the town is the fairy-tale Castello Caetani, frescoed by a pupil of Pinturicchio.

In the valley below lies the abandoned medieval village of **Ninfa**, converted into lush gardens by the Caetani family in 1921.

Ninfa

 Via Provinciale Ninfina 68 📞 0773 35 42 41 🕐 Apr–Nov: 1st Sat & Sun of the month

---

18
Sperlonga

🅰D5 🅰 Latina
📧 ℹ Corso San Leone 22; 0771 55 70 00

Sperlonga is a seaside resort surrounded by sandy beaches. The old town sits on a rocky promontory, a picturesque labyrinth of narrow alleyways and piazzettas offering an occasional glimpse of the sea below. It is full of bars, restaurants and boutiques.

The area around Sperlonga was a summer retreat for the ancient Romans. They built villas along the coast, and converted natural caves into places to dine and relax.

In 1957, archaeologists excavating the complex of Tiberius's luxury villa, just outside the town, found some 2nd-century-BC Hellenistic sculptures in a cave open to the sea. These sculptures, depicting Homer's *Odyssey*, are thought to be by the same artists from Rhodes responsible for *The Laocoön (p290)*. They are displayed in the **Zona Archeologica**'s Museo Archeologico Nazionale.

Zona Archeologica

 Via Flacca 📞 0771 54 80 28 🕐 Daily 🔒 1 Jan, 25 Dec

19
Gaeta

🅰D5 🅰 Latina
📧 ℹ Piazza XIX Maggio; 0771 46 91

According to Virgil, Gaeta was named after Aeneas's wet nurse Caieta, who was allegedly buried here. The town sits on the southern headland of the gulf of Gaeta, under Monte Orlando. The historic centre is dominated by a mighty Aragonese castle and the pinnacles of mock-Gothic San Francesco. To the north, the modern quarter links Gaeta to the picturesque bay of Serapo.

↑ A bright, sunny day on the beautiful sandy beach at Sperlonga

---

TOP 5 BEACHES IN LAZIO

Sperlonga
🅰D5
Beach resort village with charming alleyways, ancient stone houses and the famed Cave of Tiberius.

Gaeta
🅰D5
With seven sandy beaches to choose from, Gaeta is a popular summertime getaway.

Tor Caldara (Anzio)
🅰D5
Opposite a nature reserve, this beach has golden sands and blue, crystal-clear waters.

San Felice Al Circeo
🅰D5
With underwater coves and grottoes ideal for diving, this seaside town is also a surfer's paradise.

Cala Feola
🅰D5
In a beautiful cove on Ponza, this is the only sandy beach to be found on the island.

Diners on a narrow street near Palazzo Vecchio

FLORENCE

The cradle of the Renaissance, Florence was at the centre of a cultural and artistic revolution during the 15th century. Inspired by the rediscovery of Classical culture, and under the lavish patronage of the Medici – then the richest family in Europe – artists like Michelangelo, Botticelli and Donatello, and architects such as Brunelleschi and Leon Battista Alberti, created a city that remains one of the world's greatest artistic capitals.

While the Etruscans had long settled in the hills around Fiesole, Florence first sprang to life as a Roman colony in 59 BC. Captured by the Lombards in the 6th century, the city later emerged from the Dark Ages as an independent city state. By the 13th century a burgeoning trade in wool and textiles, backed by a powerful banking sector, had turned the city into one of Italy's leading powers. Political control was wielded first by the guilds, and later by the Florentine Republic. In time, power passed to leading noble families, of which the most influential were the Medici, a hugely wealthy banking dynasty. Florence, and later Tuscany, remained under the family's almost unbroken sway for three centuries. During this time the city was at the cultural and intellectual heart of Europe, its cosmopolitan atmosphere and wealthy patrons providing the impetus for a period of unparalleled artistic growth. By 1737 the Medici had died out, leaving the city under Austrian (and briefly Napoleonic) control until Italian Unification in 1860.

FLORENCE

Must Sees
1. Duomo and Baptistry
2. Uffizi
3. Piazza della Signoria
4. Galleria dell'Accademia
5. Palazzo Pitti

Experience More
6. Convento di San Marco
7. Santissima Annunziata
8. Museo Archeologico
9. Spedale degli Innocenti
10. Museo dell'Opera del Duomo
11. Bargello
12. Santa Croce
13. Museo Galileo
14. Ponte Vecchio
15. Palazzo Vecchio
16. Orsanmichele
17. Palazzo Davanzati
18. Palazzo Strozzi
19. San Lorenzo
20. Cappelle Medicee
21. Mercato Centrale
22. Palazzo Antinori
23. Palazzo Rucellai
24. Santa Maria Novella
25. Museo Nazionale Alinari della Fotografia
26. Ognissanti
27. Santo Spirito
28. Santa Felicita
29. Piazzale Michelangelo
30. San Miniato al Monte
31. Cappella Brancacci

Eat
1. Osteria Antica Mescita San Niccolò
2. Il Rifrullo
3. Enoteca Fuori Porta
4. I Bastioni di San Niccolò

Drink
5. Cantinetta Antinori
6. Casa del Vino
7. Fratelli Zanobini

Stay
8. Hotel Brunelleschi

Shop
9. Scuola del Cuoio
10. Officina Profumo Farmaceutica di Santa Maria Novella

$\rightarrow$

1 The Duomo dominating Florence's skyline.

2 Designer shop on Via Tornabuoni.

3 Piazza Santo Spirito.

4 Interior of Palazzo Pitti.

2 DAYS

A Tour of Florence

Day 1

Morning Start the day at the magnificent Piazza Duomo *(p342)*; climb Brunelleschi's enormous dome and admire the famous bronze Baptistery doors before strolling to Piazza della Signoria *(p346)*, where a replica of Michelangelo's *David* and an array other statues can be seen. Just around the corner, Mercato Nuovo sells exquisite Florentine souvenirs, including leather goods and speciality paper. After crossing Ponte Vecchio *(p356)*, turn left and walk along the river for lunch at Osteria Antica Mescita San Niccolò *(p362)*.

Afternoon Refuelled and refreshed, you will be ready for the walk up to Piazzale Michelangelo *(p362)* for awe-inspiring views. Carry on to San Miniato al Monte before taking the shorter – but steeper – Salita al Monte back down the hill, stopping at the rose garden. Cross the Ponte alle Grazie bridge to reach Santa Croce *(p355)*. Explore the interior of this awe-inspiring church – paying your respects to the tombs of Michelangelo, Machiavelli and Galileo – and visit the leather school at the rear.

Evening Have dinner at the excellent Gucci Garden *(Piazza della Signoria 10)*.

Day 2

Morning Make the San Lorenzo complex, including the startling Cappelle Medicee *(p358)*, today's first stop, followed by a look around the adjacent Mercato Centrale. See the frescoes at Santa Maria Novella *(p360)* nearby before making a tiny detour to the extraordinary Officina Profumo Farmaceutica historic perfumery *(p61)*. For a tasty lunch and a glass of wine, try Cantinetta Antinori *(p358)*, just beyond Santa Maria Novella.

Afternoon After lunch, stroll past the designer stores of Via Tornabuoni, stopping just before the river at the Museo Ferragamo *(p358)* to see shoes worn by some of Hollywood's classic stars. Cross the bridge to the Oltrarno district where the shopping theme changes to antiques on the way to Palazzo Pitti *(p350)*. After visiting the rich interiors and galleries of this incredible 15th-century palace, end the afternoon with a relaxing stroll around the Boboli Gardens *(p351)*.

Evening Reward yourself with an aperitivo in Piazza Santo Spirito *(p361)* before dining at one of the Oltrarno's authentic eateries, such as L'Brindellone *(Piazza Piattellina 10)*.

Primavera, Botticelli, Uffizi

This Renaissance masterpiece *(p344)* is rich in allegory (though interpretations vary). Set in an orange grove, it shows Venus with Cupid above her at the centre, flanked by the Three Graces on the left and Flora on the right. Blue-tinged Zephyrus blows in the west wind on the far right, while Mercury stirs the clouds with a caduceus on the left.

←

Botticelli's masterpiece *Primavera* (late 1470s or early 1480s) in the Uffizi

FLORENCE FOR
ART LOVERS

Known as the cradle of the Renaissance, Florence is home to an incredible concentration of world-famous art. This is largely thanks to the patronage of the powerful Medici family, the dynasty of bankers that backed such artists as Botticelli, Leonardo da Vinci, Raphael and Michelangelo.

BRUNELLESCHI'S DOME

Dominating Florence's skyline, Brunelleschi's octagonal dome is a striking symbol of the city. Building the vast structure posed a monumental challenge and the architect drew inspiration from the ancient Romans to find a solution, most notably from the Pantheon in Rome. He used wooden supports, a fishbone layout of bricks, and created an inner and outer shell. The gallery on one side of the base, a later addition, was left unfinished due to the disapproval of Michelangelo, among others.

Annunciation, Fra Angelico, San Marco

Located at the top of the stairs to the dormitory of the monastry *(p353)*, this simple yet striking fresco is the most remarkable among the many decorations carried out by Fra Angelico at San Marco in the decade he lived here as a friar.

Pietà, Michelangelo, Museo dell'Opera del Duomo

Michelangelo originally intended this sculpture (p354) of the aftermath of the Crucifixion for his own tomb but abandoned the work after damaging it in several places, probably frustrated by a flaw in the marble. It depicts Nicodemus cradling Christ, supported by the Virgin Mary and Mary Magdalene. The hooded figure of Nicodemus is thought to represent the artist himself.

→

Michelangelo's *Pietà* (c.1547–55) in the Museo dell'Opera del Duomo

Madonna della Seggiola, Raphael, Palazzo Pitti

The Galleria Palatina (p352) has a rich collection of works by Raphael and this painting, probably commissioned by Pope Leo X, is the highlight: a strikingly natural and immediate rendering of the Madonna and Child with the young John the Baptist.

←

Raphael's *Madonna della Seggiola* (1514) in the Palazzo Pitti

Holy Trinity, Masaccio, Santa Maria Novella

This fresco, considered to be Masaccio's great masterpiece, adopts an extraordinary use of perspective, from the depth of the barrel vaulted ceiling to the kneeling patrons, who appear to be outside the painting in the foreground (p360).

→

Masaccio's *Holy Trinity* (1427–8) fresco in Santa Maria Novella

↑ Fra Angelico's serene *Annunciation* (1437–46) at San Marco

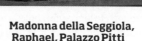

Panini

Tuscan bread is traditionally salt-free and ideal with local Pecorino (sheep's cheese), cured Tuscan ham and other cold cuts such as *finocchiona* (a kind of salami with fennel seeds). Prestigious Procacci is famed for its truffle panini.

Florence's best panini:
I Fratellini (Via dè Cimatori 38R), *All'Antico Vinaio* (Via de' Neri 65R) *and Procacci* (Via Tornabuoni 64R).

←

Paninis stuffed with *prosciutto crudo* on sale at a bakery in Florence

FLORENCE FOR
FOODIES

One of the great joys of any visit to Tuscany is the magnificent food and wine. Strolling around Florence you come across so many tempting aromas wafting from restaurants and colourful displays of fresh produce at market stalls that it can be hard to choose where and what to eat or buy.

FLORENTINE STREET FOOD

Central Florence is peppered with kiosks and stalls laden with steaming pans of tripe or *lampredotto* (a typical Florentine dish made from the fourth stomach of a cow), the city's most traditional and popular street food. Join the locals queuing for a panino softened with *salsa verde* (a green herby sauce) before being filled. The most popular stalls in the city include Nencioni (Piazza Mercato Nuovo), Nerbone (Mercato Centrale) and L'Antico Trippaio (Piazza de' Cimatori).

Markets

Colourful and full of life, Florence's two main markets are the place to go for fresh produce, fragrant bread, local cheeses and street food.

Florence's top markets:
Mercato Centrale (Via dell' Ariento) *and Mercato di Sant' Ambrogio* (Piazza Ghiberti).

Wine Bars

Florence's many atmospheric wine bars - much-frequented by the locals - are ideal for enjoying a glass of Chianti Classico or white Vernaccia at lunch or at the end of a long day of sightseeing. Some just serve wine, but most can provide an array of delicious snacks and even full meals. **Florence's finest wine bars:** *Cantinetta Antinori* (Piazza Antinori 3), *Casa del Vino* (Via dell'Ariento 16R) *and Fratelli Zanobini* (Via Sant'Antonino 47R).

$\rightarrow$

Bartender serving wine and snacks at one of Florence's wine bars

Traditional Florentine Food

Florence's typical dishes are famously hearty and tasty *(p27)*. Specialities include Fiorentina (t-bone) steaks, *panzanella* (tomato, onion and dry bread salad) and crostini. **First-rate Florentine food:** *Il Latini* (p371), *All'Antico Ristoro de' Cambi* (Via Sant'Onofrio 1R) and *Osteria Antica Mescita San Niccolò* (p362).

$\leftarrow$

Bistecca Fiorentina steaks on the grill

Fine-Dining

Central Florence has a high concentration of restaurants run by some of Italy's top chefs. Book a table for some spectacular contemporary cuisine. **Florence's fine dining:** *Enoteca Pinchiorri* (Via Ghibellina 87) *and La Bottega del Buon Caffè* (Lungarno Benvenuto Cellini 69/R).

$\rightarrow$

Dish at Enoteca Pinchiorri, a fine-dining restaurant in Florence

$\uparrow$ Market stall selling fresh produce and street food

DUOMO AND BAPTISTRY

📍 C2 🏠 Piazza del Duomo 🚌 1, 6, 14, 17, 23 🕐 Opening times vary, check website 🚫 1 Jan, Easter, 15 Aug, 8 Sep & 25 Dec 🌐 ilgrandemuseodelduomo.it

Rising above the heart of the city, the richly decorated Duomo – Santa Maria del Fiore – and its orange-tiled dome have become Florence's most famous symbols.

Typical of the Florentine determination to lead in all things, the cathedral is Europe's fourth-largest church. It can hold 20,000 people and to this day remains the city's tallest building. One of the great Renaissance structures, its foundation stone was laid in 1296, but the Neo-Gothic patterned marble façade, inspired by the decoration of the Campanile alongside, was not completed until 1887. Clad in white, green and pink Tuscan marble, the Campanile was designed by Giotto in 1334 and completed after the artist's death. Opposite the Duomo stands the Baptistry of San Giovanni; with its celebrated bronze doors and precious mosaics, it holds the octagonal font where many famous Florentines, including Dante, were baptized. The Baptistry may date back to the 4th century, making it one of Florence's oldest buildings.

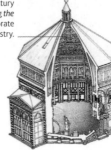

↑ Mosaics in the interior of the Baptistry

Colourful 13th-century mosaics illustrating *the Last Judgment* decorate the ceiling of the Baptistry.

→ Florence's octagonal Baptistry

Frescoed interior of
Brunelleschi's dome

← The Duomo's enormous dome
and Campanile towering
above Florence's skyline

BAPTISTRY DOORS

In 1401, Lorenzo
Ghiberti won a compet-
ition to design the
north Baptistry doors.
In 1425-52 he designed
the east doors, which
Michelangelo dubbed
the "Gate of Paradise".
The original ten relief
panels are in the Museo
dell'Opera del Duomo
(p354); those on the
Baptistry are copies.

The top of the dome
offers spectacular
views over the city.

Bricks in the dome
were set between
marble ribs in a
self-supporting
herringbone
pattern.

The dome, designed by
Brunelleschi (1420–36), was
the largest of its time to be
built without scaffolding.

Domenico di Michelino's
Dante Explaining the
Divine Comedy *(1465)*
fresco shows the poet
outside Florence against a
backdrop of Purgatory,
Hell and Paradise.

The colourful, intricately
inlaid pavement dates
from the 16th century.

Copies of reliefs by Andrea
Pisano on the Campanile's
first storey depict the
Creation of Man, and the
Arts and the Industries.

The Duomo, seen from ↑
the Piazza del Duomo ↑

② ✏️ 🎨 🖥️ 🏛️

UFFIZI

📍 C3 🏛️ Piazzale degli Uffizi 6 🚌 B, 23 🕐 8:15am–6:50pm Tue–Sun (to 10pm Tue) 🗓️ 1 Jan, 1 May, 25 Dec 🌐 uffizi.firenze.it

The Uffizi is one of Italy's greatest art galleries. It covers the whole sweep of Florentine art, from stylized Byzantine icons to the flowing lines of early medieval works, through Renaissance masterpieces to the colourful complexities of Mannerist paintings.

The Uffizi was built in 1560–80 to house offices (*uffici*) for Duke Cosimo I. The architect Vasari used iron as reinforcement, enabling his successor, Buontalenti, to create an almost continuous wall of glass on the upper storey. From 1581, the Medicis used this well-lit space to display the family art treasures, creating what is now the oldest gallery in the world. Today, the paintings are hung chronologically to show the development of Florentine art from Gothic to Renaissance and beyond.

Gothic Art

Rooms 2 to 6 of the gallery are devoted to Tuscan Gothic art from the 12th to the 14th century. Giotto (1266–1337) introduced a degree of naturalism that was new in Tuscan art. The angels and saints in his *Ognissanti Madonna* (1310), in room 2, express a range of emotions, from awe and reverence to puzzlement.

Early Renaissance

The Botticelli paintings in rooms 10–14 are the highlight of the Uffizi's collection. The brilliant colours of *Primavera* (c.1482) are a reminder that Renaissance artists often experimented with

Elegant exterior of the ↑ Uffizi, designed by Vasari and Buontalenti

GALLERY GUIDE

Book your ticket in advance to avoid queues. The earliest works are on the second floor – start here to explore the collection. There are many well-known Early Renaissance paintings in rooms 7-18. Ancient Greek and Roman sculptures are in the second-floor corridor, as well as room 56 on the first floor. Some familiar High Renaissance masterpieces are hung on the first floor, and masters from other European countries are in rooms 44-55.

←

Visitors marvelling at Botticelli's famous masterpiece *Primavera*

Michelangelo's vibrant and expressive *Holy Family* tondo →

new pigments to achieve striking effects. A celebration of spring, the painting is populated with goddesses and over 500 species of plant. Zephyrus, the west wind, blows in from the right, while Mercury dispels clouds on the left.

Room 15 contains works attributed to the young Leonardo. Still under the influence of his tutor Andrea del Verrocchio, he was already developing his own highly naturalistic style in *The Annunciation* (1472–5) and in his first independent commission, the unfinished *Adoration of the Magi* (1481).

High Renaissance

Michelangelo's *The Holy Family* (1506–8), in room 35, is striking for its bright colours and the unusually twisted pose of the Virgin. Room 66 on the first floor is dedicated to Raphael. The tender *Madonna of the Goldfinch* (1506) shows signs of earthquake damage dating from 1547. Works by Titian (1488–1576) are in room 83, including *The Venus of Urbino* (1538), said to be one of the most beautiful nudes ever painted.

Later Paintings

Rooms 90 to 93 are dedicated to Caravaggio (1571–1610) and his legacy in the 17th century. There are works by several of his followers, including Gerard van Honthorst (1592–1656), a Dutch artist renowned for his artificially lit scenes, and Artemisia Gentileschi (1593–1656), a female painter best known for her brutal masterpiece *Judith Slaying Holofernes* (1611–12).

↑ Raphael's serene *Madonna of the Goldfinch*

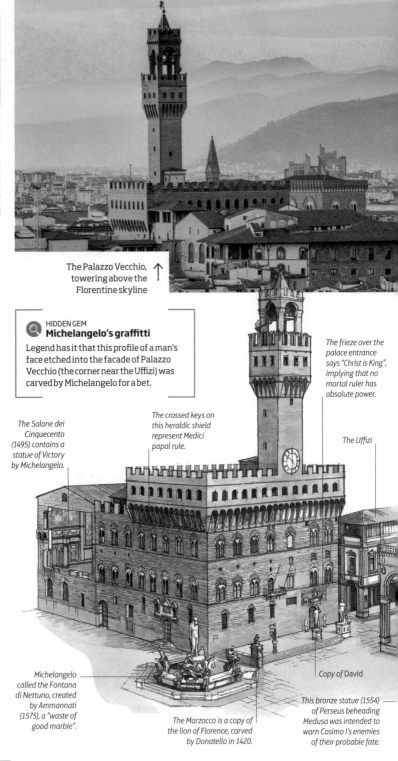

The Palazzo Vecchio, towering above the Florentine skyline ↑

HIDDEN GEM
Michelangelo's graffitti

Legend has it that this profile of a man's face etched into the facade of Palazzo Vecchio (the corner near the Uffizi) was carved by Michelangelo for a bet.

The frieze over the palace entrance says "Christ is King", implying that no mortal ruler has absolute power.

The Salone dei Cinquecento (1495) contains a statue of Victory by Michelangelo.

The crossed keys on this heraldic shield represent Medici papal rule.

The Uffizi

Michelangelo called the Fontana di Nettuno, created by Ammannati (1575), a "waste of good marble".

The Marzocco is a copy of the lion of Florence, carved by Donatello in 1420.

Copy of David

This bronze statue (1554) of Perseus beheading Medusa was intended to warn Cosimo I's enemies of their probable fate.

❸

PIAZZA DELLA SIGNORIA

⊙ C3 ⏰ **9am–7pm Mon–Wed & Fri–Sun, 9am–2pm Thu (Palazzo Vecchio)** 🌐 **museicivicifiorentini.comune.fi.it**

Florence's public living room and outdoor sculpture gallery, the Piazza della Signoria has been at the heart of the city's political and social life for centuries.

The great bell of the Palazzo Vecchio, the city's imposing town hall, once used to summon citizens to *parlamento* (public meetings) here, and the square has long been a popular promenade for both visitors and Florentines. The piazza's statues (some are copies), sheltered by the lovely 14th-century Loggia dei Lanzi, commemorate the city's major historical events, though its most famous episode is celebrated by a simple pavement plaque near the Loggia: the execution of the fanatical religious leader Girolamo Savonarola.

The Palazzo Vecchio, seen from the Piazza della Signoria ↓

← Tourists admiring the many marble statues in the Loggia dei Lanzi

The Loggia dei Lanzi, designed by Orcagna (1382), is named after the Lancers, the body-guards of Cosimo I.

Roman statues, possibly of emperors, line the Loggia.

→ The beautifully decorated first courtyard of the Palazzo Vecchio

Giambologna's famous Rape of the Sabine Women (1583) was carved from a single block of flawed marble.

DAVID

The famous Michelangelo statue symbolizes triumph over tyranny. The original sculpture stood in the piazza until 1873. Damaged during an anti-Medici riot, it was wheeled over to the Accademia for safe-keeping (p348) and replaced with a replica.

Michelangelo's monumental masterpiece *David* (1501–4), in the Galleria dell'Accademia ↑

4

GALLERIA DELL' ACCADEMIA

🔲 D1 🚪 Via Ricasoli 60 🕐 8:15am-6:50pm Tue-Sun 🔒 Pub hols
🌐 accademia.org

Michelangelo's proud *David* (1501–4) towers over visitors in the Accademia, Europe's first art school. A spectacular collection of art was amassed here for students to copy, including paintings by Botticelli, Lorenzo di Credi, Orcagna, Perugino and del Sarto.

Founded in 1563, the Academy of Fine Arts was the first school established in Europe specifically to teach the techniques of drawing, painting and sculpture. The art collection displayed here was formed in 1784 to provide material for students to study and copy.

Michelangelo's Sculptures

The Accademia's most treasured sculpture is Michelangelo's *David*, a colossal (5.2-m-/17-ft- tall) nude of the biblical hero who killed the giant Goliath. The sculpture, which originally stood in Piazza della Signoria, established Michelangelo, at the age of 29, as the foremost sculptor of his time.

The gallery is also home to Michelangelo's *Quattro Prigionieri (Four Prisoners)*, sculpted between 1521 and 1523 and intended to adorn the tomb of Pope Julius II. The muscular figures struggling to free themselves from the stone are among the artist's most dramatic works.

Florentine Paintings

Among the Accademia's collection of 15th- and 16th-century Florentine paintings are important works by Filippino Lippi, Fra Bartolomeo, Bronzino and Ridolfo Ghirlandaio. Star pieces include the *Madonna del Mare (Madonna of the Sea)*, attributed to Botticelli (1445–1510), and *Venus and Cupid* by Jacopo Pontormo (1494–1556), based on a preparatory drawing by Michelangelo.

↑ Crowds gathering on the street outside the Galleria dell'Accademia

Did You Know?

The scale of *David*'s hands and head are exaggerated because he was originally meant to be placed high up on Florence Cathedral.

CASSONE ADIMARI

One of the highlights of the Accademia's collection is an elaborately painted wooden chest, the *Cassone Adimari* (1440-45), by Lo Scheggia, the stepbrother of Masaccio. Originally part of a wealthy bride's trousseau, it is decorated with details of Florentine life, clothing and architecture. A scene of the bridal party appears on the chest in front of the Baptistry.

PALAZZO PITTI

◉ B4 **⌂ Piazza de' Pitti** **🚌 11, C3, D** **🕐 Opening times vary, check website**
🌐 uffizi.it/palazzo-pitti

This one-time residence of the Medici family is a treasure trove, with its lavish royal apartments and galleries of modern art, costume, silverware and porcelain. The palace's true jewel is the Galleria Palatina: frescoed by Pietro da Cortona, it holds one of the best collections of Raphaels and Titians in the world, second only to the Uffizi.

Galleria Palatina

The Palatine Gallery, which forms the heart of the Pitti museum complex, contains countless masterpieces by artists such as Botticelli, Titian, Perugino, Andrea del Sarto, Tintoretto, Veronese, Giorgione and Gentileschi. The works of art, accumulated by the Medici family and the house of Habsburg-Lorraine, are still hung much as the grand dukes wished, regardless of subject or chronology. Highlights of the collection include Antonio Canova's statue of the *Venus Italica* (1810), Titian's *Portrait of a Gentleman* (1540), Raphael's *Madonna della Seggiola* or *"Madonna of the Chair"* (c.1513–14) and Caravaggio's *The Sleeping Cupid* (1608). The gallery consists of eleven main salons, the first five of which are painted with allegorical ceiling frescoes glorifying the Medici.

Appartamenti Reali

The Royal Apartments on the first floor of the south wing of the Palazzo were built in the 17th century. They are decorated with frescoes by various Florentine artists, a series of portraits of the Medici by the Flemish painter Justus Sustermans, and a group of 18th-century Gobelins tapestries. In the late 18th

Palazzo Pitti's façade, thought to be the work of Brunelleschi ↓

and early 19th centuries, the apartments were revamped in Neo-Classical style by the Dukes of Lorraine when they succeeded the Medici dynasty as the rulers of Florence.

The apartments are lavishly appointed with ornate gold-and-white stuccoed ceilings and rich decoration, notably the walls of the Parrot Room, which are covered with an opulent crimson fabric detailed with a bird design. The Tapestry Rooms are hung with 17th- and 18th-century tapestries made by French, Belgian and Italian workshops.

Other Collections

The Museo degli Argenti (Silverware Museum) is housed in rooms formerly used by the Medici as summer apartments. The family's lavish taste is reflected in the vast array of precious objects on display: Roman glassware, ivory, carpets, crystal, amber and fine works by Florentine and German goldsmiths. The Galleria del Costume, which opened in 1983, reflects changing tastes in courtly fashion from the late 18th century up to the 1920s. Highlights of the Galleria d'Arte Moderna (Modern Art Gallery) are the wonderful paintings of the Macchiaioli (spot-makers), a group of Tuscan artists with a style similar to that of the French Impressionists.

↑ Masterpieces and frescoes adorning the Galleria Palatina

THE BOBOLI GARDENS

The Boboli Gardens are a lovely place to escape the rigours of sightseeing. Laid out for the Medici in 1549, they were opened to the public in 1766 and present an excellent example of stylized Renaissance gardening. The neatly clipped box hedges of the formal gardens lead to wilder groves of ilex and cypress trees, planted to create a contrast between artifice and nature. Baroque and Rococo influences are evident in the gardens' burbling fountains, cypress avenues and countless hidden statues.

EXPERIENCE MORE

⑥
Convento di San Marco

🅿 D1 📍 Piazza di San Marco
📞 055 28 76 28 🕐 7am–noon & 4–8pm daily

The Convent of San Marco was founded in the 13th century and enlarged in 1437, when Dominican monks from nearby Fiesole moved to Florence at the invitation of Cosimo il Vecchio. He had the convent rebuilt by his favourite architect, Michelozzo, whose simple cloisters and cells provide the setting for a remarkable series of devotional frescoes (c.1438–45) by Florentine painter and Dominican friar Fra Angelico. The convent and art collections form the **Museo di San Marco**.

Michelozzo's magnificent Chiostro di Sant'Antonino was named after the convent's first prior, Antonino Pierozzi (1389–1459). Most of the faded frescoes in this cloister describe scenes from the saint's life by Bernardino Poccetti. The panels in the corner are by Fra Angelico. A door in the right side of the cloister leads to the Ospizio dei Pellegrini (Pilgrims' Hospice). Today it houses the museum's freestanding paintings, including three famous masterpieces: Fra Angelico's *Deposition* (c.1432–4), an altarpiece painted for the church of Santa Trinità; the *Madonna dei Linaiuoli*, commissioned by the Linaiuoli (flaxworkers' guild) in 1433; and the moving *Lamentation over Christ* (c.1436–41).

In the courtyard, right of the convent's former bell, is the vaulted Sala Capitolare (Chapterhouse), decorated with an over-restored *Crucifixion and Saints* (1440) painted by Fra Angelico.

Covering one wall of the small Refettorio (refectory) is a fresco of the *Last Supper* (c.1480) by Domenico Ghirlandaio. Stairs from the courtyard lead to the first floor, where you suddenly see Fra Angelico's *Annunciation* (c.1440). Beyond, ranged around three sides of the cloister, are the Dormitory Cells. These 44 tiny monastic cells are frescoed with scenes from *The Life of Christ* (1439–45) by Fra Angelico and his assistants. The cells numbered 1 to 11 are generally attributed to Fra Angelico personally, as is the lovely fresco of the *Madonna and Saints* on the right of the corridor.

Cells 12–14 were once occupied by Savonarola, the zealous Dominican monk who became Prior of San Marco in 1491 *(see box)*.

On the opposite side of the courtyard, cells 38 and 39 were reserved for Cosimo il Vecchio when he retreated to the convent to find spiritual sustenance and peace.

Along the third corridor lies a colonnaded hall displaying a series of priceless illuminated manuscripts. This was Europe's first public library, designed by Michelozzo in 1441 for Cosimo il Vecchio.

Museo di San Marco

📞 055 238 86 08 (reservations) 🕐 8:15am–1:50pm daily (to 4:50pm Sat & Sun)
🚫 1 Jan, 1 May, 25 Dec; 2nd & 4th Mon of month; 1st, 3rd & 5th Sun of month

---

⑦
Santissima Annunziata

🅿 D1 📍 Piazza della Santissima Annunziata
📞 055 239 80 34 🕐 7:30am–12:30pm & 4–6:30pm daily

Founded in 1250, the church of the Holy Annunciation was

> **Did You Know?**
>
> San Marco is home to Europe's first public library, which opened in 1441 and contained 400 books.

THE "MAD MONK"

Girolamo Savonarola (1452–98), Prior of San Marco, became popular for his calls for Christian renewal. When France threatened invasion in 1494, Florence expelled the ruling Medici family, installing a republic with the friar at the helm. He led campaigns against the excesses of the Renaissance, burning priceless works of art, but his radical approach enflamed Pope Alexander VI, and he was executed in 1498. At San Marco you can see several relics of the "Mad Monk", including his cloak and a part of the wooden beam he was hanged from.

The first floor contains a splendid series of Etruscan bronzes as well as the famous *Chimera* (4th century BC), a mythical lion with a goat's head imposed on its body and a serpent for a tail. Equally impressive is the 1st-century *Arringatore* bronze found near Lake Trasimeno in Umbria.

A large section on the second floor is dedicated to Greek vases, notably the famed François Vase, found in an Etruscan tomb near Chiusi.

9
Spedale degli Innocenti

📍D1 🏛Piazza della Santissima Annunziata 12
📞055 203 71 🕐1 Jan, Easter, 25 Dec

Named after Herod's biblical Massacre of the Innocents, the "Hospital" opened in 1444 as Europe's first orphanage. Part of the building is still used for this purpose. Brunelleschi's arcaded loggia is decorated with glazed terracotta roundels, added by Andrea della Robbia in around 1498, showing babies wrapped in swaddling bands. At the left end of the portico you can see the *rota*, a rotating stone cylinder on which mothers could anonymously place their unwanted children and ring the bell for them to be admitted to the orphanage.

Within the building lie two elegant cloisters: the Chiostro degli Uomini (Men's Cloister), built between 1422 and 1445 and decorated with *sgraffito* roosters and cherubs; and the smaller Women's Cloister (1438). The upstairs gallery contains a handful of fine works, including terracottas by della Robbia and pictures by Botticelli, Piero di Cosimo and Domenico Ghirlandaio.

rebuilt by Michelozzo between 1444 and 1481. Its atrium contains frescoes by the Mannerist artists Rosso Fiorentino, Andrea del Sarto and Jacopo Pontormo. Perhaps the finest of its panels are *The Journey of the Magi* (1511) and *The Birth of the Virgin* (1514) by del Sarto.

The heavily decorated, dark interior has a frescoed ceiling completed by Pietro Giambelli in 1669. Here is one of the city's most revered shrines: a painting of the Virgin Mary that, according to devout Florentines, was begun by a monk in 1252 but completed by an angel. Newlywed couples traditionally visit the shrine (on the left as you enter the church) to present a bouquet of flowers to the Virgin and to pray for a happy marriage.

A door from the north transept leads to the Chiostrino dei Morti (Cloister of the Dead), so called because it was originally used as a burial ground. Today it is best known for del Sarto's beautiful fresco *The Madonna del Sacco* (1525).

The church is situated on the northern flank of Piazza della Santissima Annunziata, one of the finest Renaissance squares in Florence. Designed by Brunelleschi, the delicate nine-bay arcade fronts the Spedale degli Innocenti to its right, while at the centre of the square stands a bronze equestrian statue of Duke Ferdinando I. Started by Giambologna, it was finished in 1608 by his assistant Pietro Tacca (who designed the square's bronze fountains).

8 🏛
Museo Archeologico

📍D1 🏛Via della Colonna 36 📞055 235 75 🕐8:30am–1:30pm Tue-Fri, 8:30am–2pm Sat-Mon & 1st & 3rd Sun of month 🕐1 Jan, 1 May, 25 Dec

The Archaeological Museum is in a palazzo built by Giulio Parigi for the Princess Maria Maddalena de' Medici in 1620.

Museo dell'Opera del Duomo

📍 D2 🏛 Piazza del Duomo
📞 055 230 28 85 🕐 9am-
7pm Tue-Thu & Sun, 9am-
9pm Mon, Fri & Sat 🔒 1st
Tue of month

The Cathedral Works Museum is dedicated to the history of the Duomo. The main ground-floor room holds statues from Arnolfo di Cambio's workshop which were once placed in the cathedral's niches. Nearby is Donatello's *St John*. Another room contains 14th- and 15th-century religious paintings and reliquaries.

Michelangelo's *Pietà* has pride of place on the staircase. The hooded figure of Nico-demus is widely believed to be a self-portrait.

The first room on the upper floor contains two choir lofts, dating to the 1430s, by Luca della Robbia and Donatello. Carved in crisp white marble and decorated with coloured glass and mosaic, both depict children playing musical instruments and dancing. Among a number of other works by Donatello in this room are his statue of *La Maddalena* (1455) and several Old Testament figures, including the prophet Abakuk (1423–5).

Bargello

📍 D3 🏛 Via del Proconsolo
4 📞 055 238 86 06 🚌 14, A
🕐 8:15am-1:50pm daily (to
4:50pm Sat & Sun) 🔒 1st,
3rd & 5th Sun and 2nd & 4th
Mon of the month; 1 Jan, 1
May, 25 Dec

Florence's second-ranking museum after the Uffizi, the Bargello contains a wonderful medley of applied arts and Italy's finest collection of Renaissance sculpture. Begun in 1255, the fortress-like building was initially the town hall, but it later became a prison and home to the chief of police (the *Bargello*). It also became known for its executions, which took place in the main courtyard until 1786, when the death sentence was abolished by Grand Duke Pietro Leopoldo. The building opened as one of Italy's first

↑ Pietro Francavilla's statue *Jason with the Golden Fleece,* in the Bargello

national museums in 1865. The key exhibits range over three floors, beginning with the Michelangelo Room, with three contrasting works by this artist, the most famous a tipsy-looking *Bacchus* (1497). Close by are a powerful bust of *Brutus* (1539–40) and a circular relief depicting the *Madonna and Child* (1503–5). Countless works by other sculptors occupy the same room. Among them is an exquisite *Mercury* (1564) by the Mannerist genius, Giam-bologna, as well as several virtuoso bronzes by the sculptor and goldsmith Benvenuto Cellini (1500–71).

The courtyard's external staircase leads to the first floor, which opens with a wonderfully eccentric bronze menagerie by Giambologna, and Pietro Francavilla's marble sculpture *Jason with the Golden Fleece* (late 1580s). To the right is the Salone del Consiglio Generale, a cavernous former courtroom that contains the cream of the museum's Early Renaissance sculpture. Foremost among its highlights is Donatello's heroic *St George* (1416) – the epitome of "youth, courage and valour of arms" in the words of

> Michelangelo's *Pietà* has pride of place on the staircase. The hooded figure of Nicodemus is widely believed to be a self-portrait.

Vasari. Commissioned by the Armourers' Guild, the statue was brought here from Orsanmichele in 1892. At the centre of the room, in direct contrast, is Donatello's androgynous *David* (c.1430), famous as the first free-standing nude by a Western artist since antiquity. Among the room's more easily missed works, tucked away on the right wall, are two reliefs depicting *The Sacrifice of Isaac* (1402). Created by Brunelleschi and Lorenzo Ghiberti respectively, both were entries in the competition to design the Baptistry doors.

Beyond the Salone, the Bargello's emphasis shifts to the applied arts, with room after room devoted to rugs, ceramics, silverware and a host of other beautiful objets d'art. The most celebrated of these rooms is the Salone del Camino on the second floor, which features the finest collection of small bronzes in Italy. Some are reproductions of antique models, others are copies of Renaissance statues. Giambologna, Cellini and Antonio del Pollaiuolo are represented here.

Santa Croce

📍 D3 🏛 Piazza di Santa Croce ☎ 055 246 61 05 🚌 C2, C3 🕐 9:30am–5:30pm Mon–Sat, 2–5:30pm Sun) 🚫 During Mass (also 1 Jan, Easter, 13 Jun, 4 Oct, 25 & 26 Dec)

Dating from 1295, the Gothic church of Santa Croce features a magnificent Neo-Gothic

---

SHOP

Scuola del Cuoio

Buy handmade leather goods or simply watch leather crafters at work in frescoed rooms to the rear of the Santa Croce church. This school was founded in 1949 by a local firm to teach war orphans a profession.

📍 E3 🏛 Via San Giuseppe 5R 🌐 leatherschool.biz

---

façade by Niccolò Mattas, added in 1863. The campanile was built in 1842 to replace the original, destroyed by lightning in 1512.

Inside the church are tombs of famous Tuscans, including Galileo and Machiavelli, plus a grand tomb for Michelangelo sculpted by Vasari and a monument to Dante, who was buried in Ravenna, where he died in exile *(p432)*. Among rich collection of the artworks, Cimabue's 13th-century *Crucifixion* is a highlight, as are the magnificent *Last Supper* and *Tree of Life* frescoes by Taddeo Gaddi (c.1355–60) in the refectory. Fresco cycles by Giotto feature the life of St Francis in the Bardi Chapel and, in the Peruzzi Chapel, the life of St John the Baptist (on the left) and St John the Evangelist (right). The Baroncelli Chapel is frescoed by Taddeo Gaddi (1332–8) with scenes from the life of the Virgin. The Cappella de' Pazzi, a spectacular domed chapel with classical proportions begun in 1441 by Brunelleschi, has terracotta roundels created by Luca della Robbia (c.1442–52).

↑ The distinctive Neo-Gothic façade of the church of Santa Croce

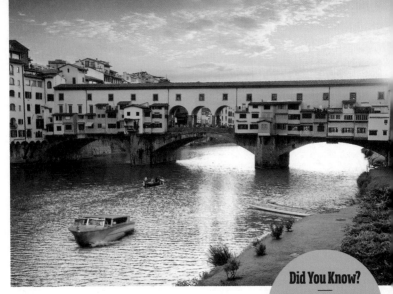

Did You Know?

Ponte Vecchio was the only bridge in Florence to escape Nazi bombing, allegedly because Hitler ordered its survival.

13

Museo Galileo

📍 C3 🏛 Piazza de' Giudici 1 📞 055 26 53 11 🕐 9:30am-6pm daily (to 1pm Tue) 🚫 1 & 6 Jan, 1 May, Easter, 24 Jun, 13 Aug, 1 Nov, 8, 25 & 26 Dec

This lively and superbly presented museum devotes two floors to various scientific themes, illustrating each with countless fine displays and a panoply of old and beautifully made scientific instruments. It is also something of a shrine to the Pisa-born scientist Galileo Galilei (1564–1642), and houses the only surviving instruments he designed and built, including two telescopes and the objective lens from the telescope with which he discovered Jupiter's moons.

Some of the best exhibits on display here are the early maps, globes and astrolabes, antique microscopes, thermometers and barometers. There are also some fine old clocks, mathematical instruments, calculators, a horrifying collection of 19th-century surgical instruments, and some graphic anatomical models. The museum has

installed a large bronze sundial outside the entrance that can be used to read the hour and the date.

14

Ponte Vecchio

📍 C3

Ponte Vecchio, the oldest surviving bridge in the city, was built in 1345, the last in a succession of bridges and fords on the site that dated back to Roman times. Designed by Giotto's pupil Taddeo Gaddi, it was originally the domain of blacksmiths, butchers and tanners (who used the river for disposing of waste). They were reviled for their noise and stench and were evicted in 1593 by Duke Ferdinando I – replaced by jewellers and goldsmiths. The elevated Corridoio Vasariano runs along the eastern side of the bridge, above the shops. Giorgio Vasari designed the corridor in 1565 to allow the Medici family to move about their residences without having to mix with the public. This was the city's only bridge to escape destruction during World War II, and visitors

today come as much to admire the views as to browse among the antique shops and specialized jewellery shops. A bust of the famous goldsmith Benvenuto Cellini stands in the middle of the bridge.

15

Palazzo Vecchio

📍 C3 🏛 Piazza della Signoria (entrance on via della Ninna) 📞 055 276 83 25 🚌 A, B 🕐 Apr-Sep: 9am-11pm daily (to 2pm Thu); Oct-Mar: 9am-7pm daily (to 2pm Thu) 🚫 1 Jan, Easter, 1 May, 15 Aug, 25 Dec

The "Old Palace" still fulfils its original role as town hall. It was completed in 1322 when a huge bell, used to call citizens to meetings or warn of fire, flood or enemy attack, was hauled to the top of the imposing bell tower. While retaining much of its medieval appearance, the interior was remodelled for Duke Cosimo I in 1540. The redecoration

← The Ponte Vecchio, a popular spot for jewellery hunters

was undertaken by Vasari, who incorporated bombastic frescoes (1563–5) depicting Florentine achievements. Michelangelo's *Victory* statue (1525) graces the Salone dei Cinquecento, which also has a tiny study decorated by Florence's leading Mannerist painters in 1569–73. Other highlights include the Cappella di Eleonora, painted by Bronzino (1540–45); the loggia, with its views over the city; the Sala dei Gigli (Room of Lilies) with Donatello's *Judith and Holofernes* (c.1455) and frescoes of Roman heroes by Ghirlandaio (1485). The excellent museum for children and the Secret Itineraries (a series of private rooms and hidden passageways) can be toured by reservation.

Orsanmichele

C3 **Via dell'Arte della Lana** **055 28 49 44** **10am–5pm daily** **1 Jan, 1 May, Mon in Aug, 25 Dec**

Built in 1337 as a grain market, Orsanmichele was later converted into a church which took its name from Orto di San Michele, a monastic garden long since

>
> INSIDER TIP
> **Fontana del Porcellino**
>
> Head to Mercato Nuovo to perform a popular good luck ritual: stroke the shiny snout of the bronze wild boar statue while dropping a coin into the fountain. If it passes through the grating, your wish will come true!

vanished. The arcades of the market became windows, which are today bricked in, but the original Gothic tracery can still be seen. The decoration was entrusted to Florence's major *Arti* (guilds). Over 60 years they commissioned sculptures of their patron saints to adorn the 14 exterior niches; however, today many of the figures on display are copies. Among the sculptors were Lorenzo Ghiberti, Donatello and Verrocchio.

The beautifully tranquil interior contains an opulent 14th-century altar by Andrea Orcagna, a *Virgin and Child* by Bernardo Daddi (1348) and a statue of the *Madonna and Child with St Anne* by Francesco da Sangallo (1522). Upstairs is a small museum dedicated to statuary.

Palazzo Davanzati

C3 **Via Porta Rossa 13** **055 238 86 10** **8:15am–1:50pm daily** **1st, 3rd & 5th Mon of the month; 2nd & 4th Sun of the month; 1 Jan, 1 May, 25 Dec**

This wonderful museum uses original fittings and furniture to recreate a typical well-to-do 14th-century townhouse. Among the highlights is the *Sala dei Pappagalli* (Parrots Room), with its frescoes and rich tapestries.

In one corner of the inner courtyard is a well and a pulley system to raise pails of water to each floor – a real luxury, since most medieval households had to fetch water from a public fountain.

↑ The elegant inner courtyard of Palazzo Vecchio

Palazzo Strozzi

◎ B3 ◿ Piazza degli Strozzi ◷ 10am–8pm daily (to 11pm Thu) ⬡ palazzo strozzi.org

Sheer size accounts for the impact of the Palazzo Strozzi and, although it is only three storeys high, each floor exceeds the height of a normal palazzo. It was commissioned by the wealthy banker Filippo Strozzi, who had 15 buildings demolished to make way for the palazzo. He hoped it would rival the Medici palaces elsewhere in the city.

Work on the building continued until 1536, with three major architects contributing to its design – Giuliano da Sangallo, Benedetto da Maiano and Simone del Pollaiuolo. Look out for the original Renaissance torch-holders, lamps and rings for tethering horses that still adorn the corners and façades. The palace is now primarily used as an exhibition venue.

San Lorenzo

◎ C2 ◿ Piazza San Lorenzo 9 ◖ 055 21 66 34 ◷ 10am–5:30pm Mon–Sat

Built on the site of the city's former cathedral, consecrated in 393, San Lorenzo was the parish church of the Medici

HIDDEN GEM
Museo Ferragamo

On chic Via Tornabuoni, the Museo Ferragamo is a homage to shoe designer Salvatore Ferragamo, and includes an exquisite collection of shoes made for such stars as Marilyn Monroe and Sophia Loren.

family. In 1419 Brunelleschi was commissioned to rebuild it in Classical style, with three naves separated by rows of Corinthian columns. Almost a century later, Michelangelo submitted plans for the façade but the work was never carried out. Michelangelo did, however, work on the Medici tombs and the Biblioteca Laurenziana (library), which features an unusual triple staircase and a carved wooden ceiling. The Old Sacristy presents a harmonious combination of Brunelleschi's classical architecture and a series of reliefs by Donatello, whose last works were the church's two bronze pulpits. Situated in the nave, these were completed by his pupils in 1460 and feature reliefs capturing the flinching pain of Christ's Passion and the glory of the Resurrection. Although accessed by a separate entrance, the Cappelle Medicee are a continuation of the San Lorenzo complex.

Cappelle Medicee

◎ C2 ◿ Piazza di Madonna degli Aldobrandini ◖ 055 238 86 02 (reservations) ▣ Many routes ◷ Jan–Oct: 8:15am–6pm daily; Nov & Dec: to 1:50pm daily; last adm: 30 mins before closing ◖ 1st, 3rd & 5th Mon of each month, 2nd & 4th Sun, 1 Jan, 1 May, 25 Dec

The Medici Chapels divide into three distinct areas. Beyond the entrance hall lies a low-vaulted crypt, a suitably subdued space for the brass-railed tombs of many lesser members of the Medici family. From here steps lead to the octagonal Cappella dei Principi (Chapel of Princes), a vast family mausoleum begun by Cosimo I in 1604. The ceiling is garishly frescoed and the walls are smothered in huge swathes of semi-precious

pietre dure (inlaid stone). Spaced around the walls are the tombs of six Medici Grand Dukes. A corridor leads to Michelangelo's New Sacristy, designed as a counterpoint to Brunelleschi's Old Sacristy in San Lorenzo. Three groups of statues, all carved by Michelangelo between 1520 and 1534, stand around the walls: that on the near left-hand wall is *The Tomb of the Duke of Urbino* (grandson of Lorenzo the Magnificent). Opposite is *The Tomb of the Duke of Nemours* (Lorenzo's third son). Close to the unfinished *Madonna and Child* (1521) is the simple tomb containing Lorenzo the Magnificent and his murdered brother, Giuliano (died 1478).

Mercato Centrale

◎ C1 ◿ Piazza del Mercato Centrale ◷ 7am–2pm Mon–Sat

At the heart of the San Lorenzo street market is the bustling Mercato Centrale, Florence's busiest food

→ Corinthian columns lining San Lorenzo's elegant interior

market. It is housed in a vast two-storey building of cast-iron and glass, built in 1874 by Giuseppe Mengoni.

The ground-floor stalls sell meat, poultry, fish, hams, oils and cheeses. There are also Tuscan takeaway foods such as *porchetta* (roast suckling pig), *lampredotto* (pig's intestines) and *trippa* (tripe). The first floor functions as a large bar/restaurant, with seating. There are food stalls, a bank, a bookshop and a cooking school. On the mezzanine you will find a pizzeria and a restaurant.

22
Palazzo Antinori

📍 B2 🏠 Piazza Antinori 3 🚫 To the public

Palazzo Antinori, originally named the Palazzo Boni e Martelli, was constructed in 1461–6 and, with its elegant courtyard, is one of the finest small Renaissance *palazzi* in Florence. It was acquired by the Antinoris in 1506 and has remained with the same family ever since.

The dynasty owns large estates all over Tuscany and in the neighbouring region of Umbria, producing a range of well-regarded wines, olive oils and liqueurs. You can sample these in the frescoed wine bar to the right of the courtyard, Cantinetta Antinori *(see box)*.

23
Palazzo Rucellai

📍 B2 🏠 Via della Vigna Nuova 16 🚫 To the public

Built in 1446–51, this is one of the most ornate Renaissance palaces in the city. It was commissioned by Giovanni Rucellai, whose enormous wealth derived from the import of a rare and costly red dye made from lichen, found only on the Spanish island of Mallorca. The precious dye was called *oricello,* from which the name Rucellai is derived.

Giovanni commissioned several buildings from the architect Leon Battista Alberti, who designed this palace as a virtual textbook illustration of the major Classical orders.

DRINK

Cantinetta Antinori
Enjoy prestigious Antinori wines by the glass, a meal of Tuscan fare or just see the Chianti cart in the courtyard.

📍 B2 🏠 Piazza Antinori 3
🚫 Sun 🌐 cantinetta-antinori.com

Casa del Vino
Lined with wooden shelves full of bottles, this place is ideal for a glass of Chianti and a *panino*.

📍 C1 🏠 Via dell' Ariento 16R
🚫 Sun
🌐 casadelvino.it

Fratelli Zanobini
An atmospheric wine-bar with standing room only.

📍 B1 🏠 Via Sant'Antonino 47R
📞 055 239 68 50
🚫 Sun

24

Santa Maria Novella

⊠ B2 ⊞ Piazza di Santa Maria Novella ☎ 055 21 92 57 ⊞ C2, D ⊙ Opening times vary, check website ⊡ 1 Jan, Easter, 1 May, 15 Aug, 8 & 25 Dec ⊡ smn.it

The church of Santa Maria Novella was built by the Dominicans between 1279 and 1357. The Romanesque lower façade was completed splendidly by pioneering Renaissance architect Leon Battista Alberti (1456–70). The Gothic interior features a crucifix by Giotto at the centre of the nave, which appears exceptionally long due to a trick of perspective created by the piers being closer together at the altar end. On the left, the superb *Trinity* fresco by Masaccio (painted around 1427) is renowned as one of the Renaissance's first masterpieces of perspective; the kneeling figures flanking the arch are the painting's sponsors, Judge Lorenzo Lenzi and his wife.

There are more extraordinary frescoes to be found elsewhere in the chapels:

💬 INSIDER TIP
Bus 7 to Fiesole

Just 7km (4 miles) from Florence, Fiesole *(p391)* makes an easy day trip. Bus 7 leaves from Piazza San Marco three times an hour and takes around 20 minutes to reach the attractive hilltop town.

works by Nardo di Cione and his brother Andrea Orcagni depict scenes from Dante's *Divine Comedy* in the Cappella Strozzi, and there are images by Filippino Lippi in the Cappella di Filippo Strozzi. Painted by Ghirlandaio, who was probably assisted by the young Michelangelo (1485), the scenes in *The Life of John the Baptist* in the Cappella Tornabuoni show Florentine aristocrats in contemporary dress. Perspective scenes of the *Genesis* by Paolo Uccello adorn the walls of the Green Cloister, while the Cappellone degli Spagnoli, which was used by the Spanish courtiers of Eleonora of Toledo, features frescoes of salvation and damnation by Andrea di Bonaiuto.

25

Museo Nazionale Alinari della Fotografia

⊠ B2 ⊞ Piazza Santa Maria Novella 14 ⊡ For renovation ⊡ mnaf.it

The Alinari brothers began taking pictures of Florence in the 1840s, supplying quality postcards and prints to the city's visitors. The exhibits here offer a vivid insight into the social history of Florence at that time. The museum also houses a collection of cameras, documents and objects that illustrate the history of photography.

26

Ognissanti

⊠ A2 ⊞ Borgo Ognissanti 42 ☎ 055 239 87 00 ⊙ 9:30am–12:30pm & 4–7:30pm Thu–Tue; Ghirlandaio's *Last Supper* fresco: 9am–1pm Mon & Sat

Ognissanti, or All Saints, used to be the parish church of the Vespucci, one of whose members, the 15th-century navigator Amerigo, gave his

↑ Display in the Museo Nazionale Alinari della Fotografia

↑ Splendid façade of the church of Santa Maria Novella

name to the New World. The young Amerigo is depicted in Ghirlandaio's fresco of the *Madonna della Misericordia* (1472) in the second chapel on the right; Ghirlandaio's *The Last Supper* (1480) can be seen in the convent next door.

In a chapel to the left of the transept hangs the 14th-century, 5-m- (16-ft-) high Ognissanti Crucifix by Giotto.

Santo Spirito

📍 B3 🏛 Piazza di Santo Spirito 30 📞 055 210030 🚌 D 🕐 10am-12:30pm & 5-6pm Thu-Tue

The Augustinian foundation of this church dates from 1250. The present building was designed by the architect Brunelleschi in 1435, but not completed until the late 15th century. The unfinished, modest façade was added in the 18th century.

Inside, the harmony of the proportions has been some-what spoiled by the elaborate Baroque baldacchino and the High Altar, which was finished in 1607 by Giovanni Caccini. The church has 38 side altars,

decorated with 15th- and 16th-century Renaissance paintings and sculpture, among them works by Cosimo Rosselli, Domenico Ghirlandaio and Filippino Lippi. The latter painted a magnificent *Madonna and Child* (1466) for the Nerli Chapel in the south transept.

In the north aisle, a door beneath the organ leads to a vestibule with an ornate coffered ceiling. It was designed by Simone del Pollaiuolo in 1491. The sacristy adjoining the vestibule, in which 12 huge columns are crammed into a tiny space, was designed by Giuliano da Sangallo in 1489.

Santa Felìcita

📍 B4 🏛 Piazza di Santa Felìcita 📞 055 213018 🚌 D 🕐 9:30am-12:30pm & 3:30-5pm Mon-Sat

There has been a church on this site since the 4th century. The present structure, begun in the 11th century, was remodelled in 1736-9 by Ferdinando Ruggieri, who retained Vasari's earlier

porch (added in 1564) as well as many of the church's original Gothic features.

The Capponi family chapel to the right of the entrance contains two works by Jacopo da Pontormo: *The Deposition* and *The Annunciation* (1525-8). Their strange composition and remarkable colouring make them two of Mannerism's greatest masterpieces.

SHOP

Officina Profumo Farmaceutica di Santa Maria Novella
First opened in 1612 by Dominican friars, this unique perfumery has been selling popular remedies and fragrances for over 400 years. Explore the frescoed premises, which include a shop, museum and tea room.

📍 B2 🏛 Via della Scala 16 🌐 smnovella.it

29 Piazzale Michelangelo

E5 **Piazzale Michelangelo** 12, 13

Of all the great Florentine viewpoints – such as the Duomo and Campanile – none offers such a magnificent panorama of the city as Piazzale Michelangelo. Laid out in the 1860s by Giuseppe Poggi, and dotted with copies of Michelangelo's statues, its balconies attract many visitors and the inevitable massed ranks of souvenir sellers. However, this square remains an evocative spot, especially when the sun sets over the Arno and distant Tuscan hills.

30 San Miniato al Monte

E5 **Via del Monte alle Croci** 055 234 27 31 12, 13 9:30am–1pm & 3–7pm daily (summer: to 7:30pm) **Public hols**

San Miniato is one of the most beautiful Romanesque churches in Italy. Begun in 1018, it was built over the shrine of San Miniato (St Minias), a rich Armenian merchant beheaded for his beliefs in the 3rd century. The façade, begun around 1090, has the geometric marble patterning typical of Pisan-Romanesque architecture. The statue on the gable shows an eagle carrying a bale of cloth, the symbol of the Arte di Calimala (guild of wool importers), who financed the church in the Middle Ages. The 13th-century mosaic shows Christ, the Virgin and St Minias. The same protagonists appear in the apse mosaic inside the church, which sits above a crypt supported by columns salvaged from ancient Roman buildings. The floor of the nave is covered with seven mosaic panels of animals and signs of the zodiac.

Other highlights include Michelozzo's free-standing Cappella del Crocifisso (1448) and the Renaissance Cappella del Cardinale del Portogallo (1480) with terracotta ceiling roundels (1461) by Luca della Robbia. There is a fresco cycle of *Scenes from the Life of St Benedict* by Spinello Aretino in the sacristy, which was completed in 1387.

31 Cappella Brancacci

A3 **Piazza del Carmine** 055 276 82 24 D 10am–5pm Mon & Wed–Sat, 1–5pm Sun **Public hols**

The Cappella Brancacci, a chapel within the Church of Santa Maria del Carmine, contains the famous frescoes on *The Life of St Peter*, which were commissioned by the Florentine merchant Felice Brancacci around 1424. Although the paintings were begun by Masolino in 1425, many of the scenes are by his more famous pupil Masaccio (who died before completing the cycle) and by Filippino Lippi, who finished the work from 1480.

Masaccio's powerful works were pioneering for the Renaissance, and they were later studied by great artists including Michelangelo. Noteworthy features include the tragic realism he portrayed in scenes such as *The Expulsion of Adam and Eve* and his life-like depiction of beggars in the scene of *St Peter Healing the Sick*, something considered revolutionary at the time.

While Masolino's scenes may appear less immediate and animated in contrast, they do demonstrate a remarkably delicate use of colour. Filippino Lippi contributed such emotional episodes as the *Proconsul Sentencing St Peter to Death*, a scene that includes a self-portrait (on the far right) and a portrayal of Botticelli

→

View across Florence at dusk, as seen from Piazzale Michelangelo

(to the right of the crucifixion, looking out of the painting). St Peter is distinguished from the crowds in every scene by his orange cloak.

EAT

Osteria Antica Mescita San Niccolò

Historic trattoria serving a range of Florentine dishes.

D4 **Via San Niccolò 60R** osteriasanniccolo.it

€€€

Il Rifrullo

Contemporary place with bar service, a lunchtime buffet, Sunday brunch and a garden.

D4 **Via San Niccolò 55R** ilrifrullo.com

€€€

Enoteca Fuori Porta

Popular restaurant dishing up good contemporary and traditional cuisine.

D4 **Via Monte alle Croci 10R** fuoriporta.it

€€€

I Bastioni di San Niccolò

This place serves really exceptional pizzas.

D4 **Via dei Bastioni 9R** 055 247 67 60

€€€

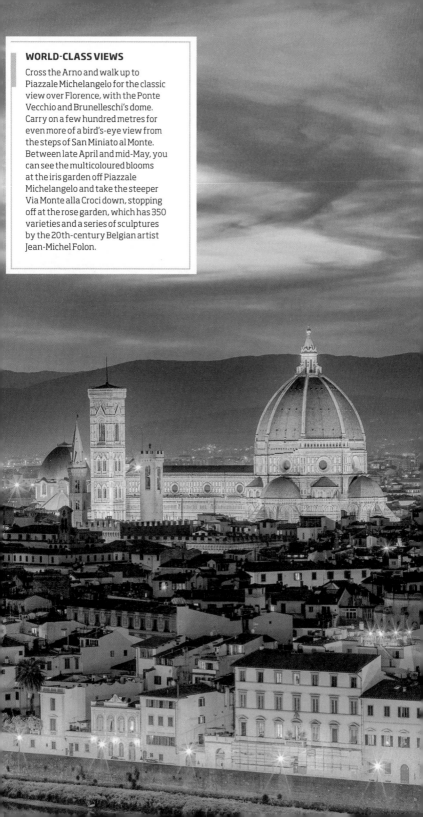

WORLD-CLASS VIEWS

Cross the Arno and walk up to Piazzale Michelangelo for the classic view over Florence, with the Ponte Vecchio and Brunelleschi's dome. Carry on a few hundred metres for even more of a bird's-eye view from the steps of San Miniato al Monte. Between late April and mid-May, you can see the multicoloured blooms at the iris garden off Piazzale Michelangelo and take the steeper Via Monte alla Croci down, stopping off at the rose garden, which has 350 varieties and a series of sculptures by the 20th-century Belgian artist Jean-Michel Folon.

A SHORT WALK
OLTRARNO

Distance 1.2 km (0.75 miles) **Buses** 11, C3 & D
Time 15 minutes

For the most part, the Oltrarno is a homely area of small houses, quiet squares and shops selling antiques, bric-a-brac and foodstuffs. The Via Maggio, a busy thoroughfare, breaks this pattern, but step into the side streets and you can escape the bustle. The restaurants serve authentic, reasonably priced food, and the area is full of studios and workshops restoring antique furniture. Among the things to see are Santo Spirito and Palazzo Pitti, one of the city's largest palaces, which contains an art collection second only to that of the Uffizi.

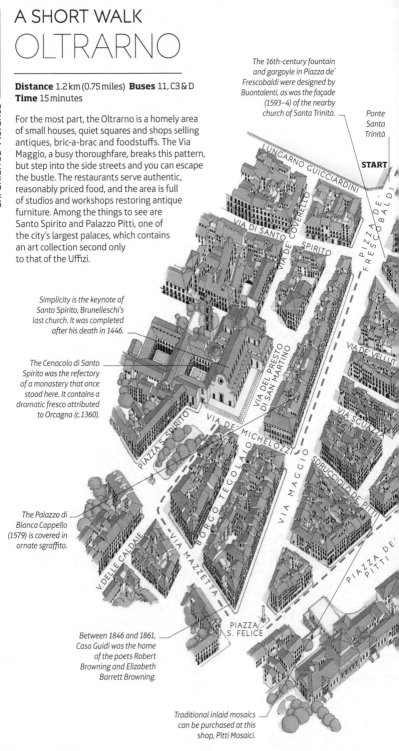

The 16th-century fountain and gargoyle in Piazza de' Frescobaldi were designed by Buontalenti, as was the façade (1593–4) of the nearby church of Santa Trinità.

Ponte Santa Trinità

START

Simplicity is the keynote of Santo Spirito, Brunelleschi's last church. It was completed after his death in 1446.

The Cenacolo di Santo Spirito was the refectory of a monastery that once stood here. It contains a dramatic fresco attributed to Orcagna (c.1360).

The Palazzo di Bianca Cappello (1579) is covered in ornate sgraffito.

Between 1846 and 1861, Casa Guidi was the home of the poets Robert Browning and Elizabeth Barrett Browning.

Traditional inlaid mosaics can be purchased at this shop, Pitti Mosaici.

↑ Elaborate fountain on the corner of Piazza de' Frescobaldi

Locator Map
For more detail see p334

Ponte Vecchio (p289)

FINISH

BORGO SAN JACOPO

VIA TOSCANELLA

V. DI RAMAGLIANTI

VIA DE' GUICCIARDINI

Palazzo Guicciardini was the birthplace of historian Francesco Guicciardini, a friend and contemporary of Niccolò Machiavelli.

Several museums are contained within the Palazzo Pitti (p350), including an outstanding collection of paintings.

Did You Know?

The nearby San Niccolò district is home to lots of great-value bars and restaurants.

0 metres 100
0 yards 100
N ↑

→
Exterior of Palazzo Pitti, seen from the Boboli Gardens

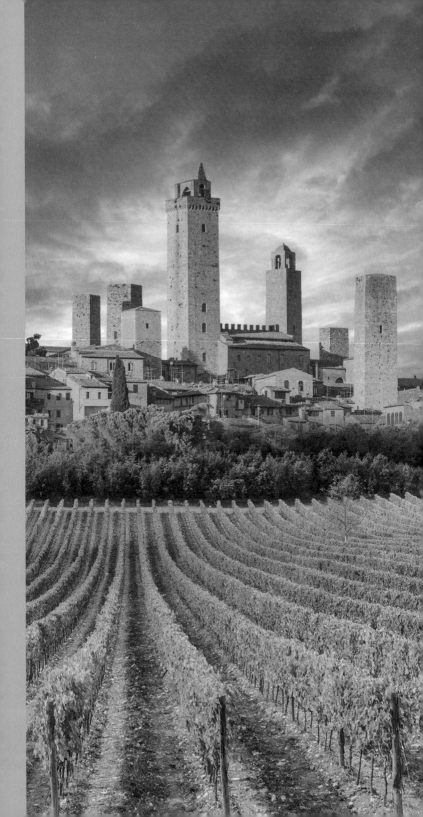

TUSCANY

Tuscany has long held a special place in the hearts of visitors. Its picturesque hill-towns gaze across the countryside, many encircled by Etruscan walls and slender cypress trees. Handsome palaces testify to the region's wealth, while medieval town halls indicate a long-standing tradition of democracy and self-government. In the countryside, among the vineyards and olive groves, there are hamlets and farmhouses, as well as fortified villas and castles – reminders of the violence and strife that tore Tuscany apart during the Middle Ages. Several imposing castles and villas were built for the Medici family, the great patrons of the Renaissance who supported eminent scientists, such as Galileo.

Northern Tuscany, and the heavily populated plain between Florence and Lucca, is dominated by industry, with intensively cultivated land between the cities and the wild mountainous areas. The area centred around Livorno and Pisa is now the region's economic hub. Pisa, at the height of its powers, dominated the western Mediterranean from the 11th to the 13th centuries. Its navy opened up extensive trading routes with North Africa, and brought to Italy the benefits of Arabic scientific and artistic achievement. During the 16th century the Arno estuary began to silt up, ending Pisan power.

At the heart of central Tuscany lies Siena, which was involved in a long feud with Florence. Its finest hour came with its victory in the Battle of Montaperti in 1260, but it was devastated by the Black Death in the 14th century and finally suffered a crushing defeat by Florence in the siege of 1554–5. Northeastern Tuscany, with its mountain peaks and woodland, provided refuge for hermits and saints, while the east was home to Piero della Francesca, the early Renaissance painter whose timeless and serene works are imbued with an almost spiritual perfection.

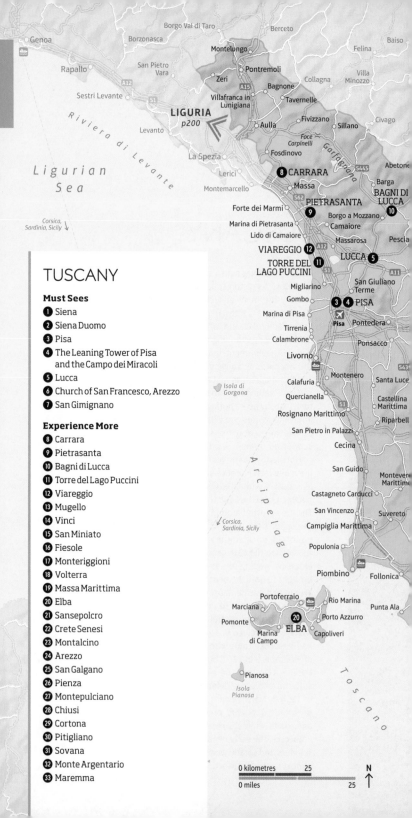

TUSCANY

Must Sees

1. Siena
2. Siena Duomo
3. Pisa
4. The Leaning Tower of Pisa and the Campo dei Miracoli
5. Lucca
6. Church of San Francesco, Arezzo
7. San Gimignano

Experience More

8. Carrara
9. Pietrasanta
10. Bagni di Lucca
11. Torre del Lago Puccini
12. Viareggio
13. Mugello
14. Vinci
15. San Miniato
16. Fiesole
17. Monteriggioni
18. Volterra
19. Massa Marittima
20. Elba
21. Sansepolcro
22. Crete Senesi
23. Montalcino
24. Arezzo
25. San Galgano
26. Pienza
27. Montepulciano
28. Chiusi
29. Cortona
30. Pitigliano
31. Sovana
32. Monte Argentario
33. Maremma

7 DAYS

A Week in Tuscany

Day 1

Morning Begin your week in Pisa at the celebrated Leaning Tower and the Campo dei Miracoli *(p380)*. Climb the tower and explore the impressive Duomo and Baptistry before tucking into a traditional *cecina* (chickpea fritter) for lunch at Il Montino *(Via del Monte 1)*.

Afternoon Wander around the historic streets of central Pisa *(p378)* and then take the train to Florence.

Evening End the day with stroll by the Arno river and a hearty Tuscan dinner at Il Latini *(Via dei Palchetti 6R)*.

Day 2

Morning Dedicate the morning to the Uffizi *(p344)* followed by a *panino* and a glass of wine at I Fratellini *(p340)*, just off Piazza della Signoria.

Afternoon Wander from Piazza Duomo *(p342)* to Ponte Vecchio *(p356)* and explore the antiques shops and quiet backstreets

of the Oltrarno *(p364)*. Afterwards, visit the Cappella Brancacci to see the famous *Life of St Peter* frescoes *(p362)*.

Evening Walk to Piazzale Michelangelo *(p362)* for panoramic views of the city at sunset before dining at Enoteca Fuori Porta *(p362)* at the bottom of the hill.

Day 3

Morning Drive from Florence along the Strada Chiantigiana, through the picturesque vine-covered hills of Chianti *(p391)*. Stop at Casa del Chianti Classico in Radda, and have lunch at the bistrot.

Afternoon Drive to San Gimignano *(p386)* to see its towers, then head for Siena.

Evening En route to Siena, stop in at the walled village of Monteriggioni *(p392)* for dinner at Il Pozzo *(Piazza Roma 2)*.

Day 4

Morning Start your day at Siena's striking tiger-striped Duomo *(p376)* and, after

① Pisa's Leaning Tower.
② Cyclists crossing the Arno.
③ San Gimignano.
④ Pecorino cheese.
⑤ Pitigliano centre.

coffee on Piazza del Campo, climb Torre del Mangia (p372). Nearby Osteria Il Grattacielo (p375) is ideal for lunch.

Afternoon Explore the narrow medieval streets of central Siena, visit the serene Santuario e Casa di Santa Caterina (p374) and stroll in the nearby Orto de' Pecci, a green oasis in the heart of Siena.

Evening For a tasty fresh pasta dinner, head to Osteria da Cice (Via S. Pietro 32).

Day 5

Morning Dedicate today to the region's best food and wine, starting at the hill town of Montalcino (p394), some 40 km (25 miles) from Siena. Enjoy a tasting of Brunello at the Fattoria dei Barbi winery (p394) and settle down for a leisurely lunch at their bistrot.

Afternoon Nearby Pienza (p396) is famous for its Pecorino (sheep's cheese). To buy some of the best, stop into local delicatessen Monaci Remo (Via Tenente Niccolo' Piccolomini 2).

Evening End the day by visiting the ancient wine cellars and trying the Vino Nobile in Montepulciano (p396).

Day 6

Morning Continue south to reach Pitigliano (p398), a picturesque medieval town clamped to a tufa ridge. Explore the narrow streets and take in the dizzying views before grabbing lunch at Trattoria Il Grillo (Via Cavour 18).

Afternoon From here it is a 5-km (3-mile) walk along Vie Cave to pretty Sovana (p398). Walk or take the bus back to Pitigliano and drive to Saturnia (p399).

Evening Spend the evening dining and using the spa at Terme di Saturnia (p399).

Day 7

Spend a leisurely final day at the fishing village of Porto Ercole (p399). Enjoy a meal at one of the many seafood restaurants before making the journey home.

❶

SIENA

🅰 C3 🚉 Piazzale Rosselli 🚌 Piazza S Domenico 🅸 Palazzo Squarcialupi, Piazza Duomo 1; www.terresiena.it

Siena's principal sights cluster in the maze of narrow streets and alleys around the fan-shaped Piazza del Campo. One of Europe's greatest medieval squares, the piazza sits at the heart of the city's 17 *contrade*, a series of parishes whose ancient rivalries are still acted out in the twice-yearly Palio (*p375*). Loyalty to the *contrada* of one's birth is fierce, and as you wander the streets you will see each parish's animal symbols repeated on flags, plaques and carvings. Siena's hilly position also means that city walks offer delightful hidden corners and countless stunning views.

①

Piazza del Campo

Italy's loveliest piazza occupies the site of the old Roman forum, and for much of Siena's early history it was the city's principal marketplace. It began to assume its present shape in 1293, when the Council of Nine, Siena's ruling body at the time, began to acquire land with a view to creating a grand civic piazza. The red-brick paving was begun in 1327 and completed in 1349, its distinctive nine segments designed to reflect the authority of the Council of Nine and to symbolize the protective folds of the Madonna's cloak. The piazza has been the focus of city life ever since, a setting for executions, bullfights and the drama of the Palio (*p375*), a festival centred around a bareback horse race. Cafés, restaurants and fine medieval *palazzi* now line the Campo's fringes, dominated by the Palazzo Pubblico (1297–1342) and Torre del Mangia, built in 1348 (*p374*). This imposing ensemble tends to over-shadow the Fonte Gaia on the piazza's northern edge. The fountain is a 19th-century copy of an original carved by Jacopo della Quercia in 1409–19. Its reliefs depict the *Virtues*, *Adam and Eve* and the *Madonna and Child*. The fountain's water is still supplied by a 500-year-old aqueduct.

← ③ Santuario e Casa di Santa Caterina (50m)

← ⑥ San Domenico (400m)

Striped black-and-white marble pillars support the Duomo's vaulted ceiling.

VIA DI FONTEBRANDA

VIA FRANCIOSA

PIAZ GIO

VIA DEL FUSARI

PIAZZA DEL DUOMO

VIA DE

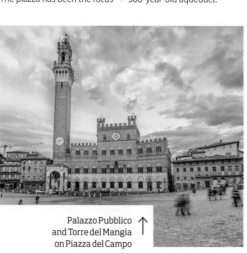

Palazzo Pubblico and Torre del Mangia on Piazza del Campo ↑

Siena's skyline, dominated by the Duomo's bell tower and the Torre del Mangia ↑

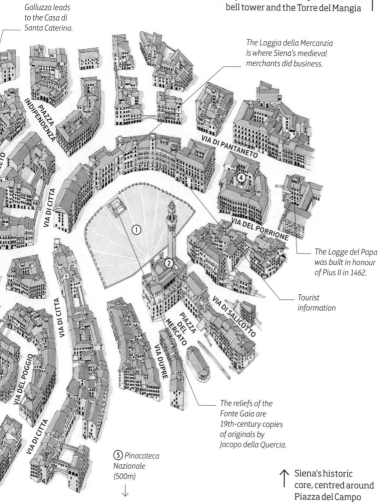

Via della Galluzza leads to the Casa di Santa Caterina.

The Loggia della Mercanzia is where Siena's medieval merchants did business.

PIAZZA INDIPENDENZA

VIA DI PANTANETO

VIA DI CITTA

VIA DEL PORRIONE

The Logge del Papa was built in honour of Pius II in 1462.

Tourist information

VIA DI SALICOTTO

PIAZZA DEL MERCATO

VIA DUPRE

VIA DI CITTA

VIA DEL POGGIO

VIA DI CITTA

The reliefs of the Fonte Gaia are 19th-century copies of originals by Jacopo della Quercia.

⑤ *Pinacoteca Nazionale (500m)* ↓

↑ Siena's historic core, centred around Piazza del Campo

↑ Siena's vast San Domenico church illuminated at night

Palazzo Pubblico

🏛 Piazza del Campo 1
📞 0577 29 22 32 🕐 10am–6pm daily (palazzo); 10am–4pm (tower)

Although it continues in its ancient role as Siena's town hall, the Palazzo Pubblico's medieval rooms, some decorated with paintings of the Sienese school, are open to the public as the Museo Civico.

The main council chamber, or Sala del Mappamondo, is named after a map of the world painted by Ambrogio Lorenzetti in the early 14th century. One wall is covered by Simone Martini's fresco of the *Maestà* (1315), which depicts the Virgin in Majesty as the Queen of Heaven, attended by the Apostles, saints and angels. Opposite is a fresco (attributed to Simone Martini, but possibly later) of the mercenary *Guidoriccio da Fogliano* (1330). The walls of the chapel are covered with frescoes of the *Life of the Virgin* (1407) by Taddeo di Bartolo, and the choir stalls are decorated with wooden panels inlaid with biblical scenes. The Sala della Pace contains the famous *Allegory of Good and Bad Government* (c.1338–40),

a pair of frescoes by Ambrogio Lorenzetti. They form one of the most important series of secular paintings from the Middle Ages. In the *Good Government* fresco civic life flourishes, while the *Bad Government* reveals rubbish-strewn streets and ruins.

The Sala del Risorgimento is covered with late 19th-century frescoes illustrating the events leading up to the unification of Italy under King Vittorio Emanuele II.

In the palace courtyard is the entrance to the Torre del Mangia, the palace's huge 102-m (330-ft) bell tower. Built by the brothers Muccio and Francesco di Rinaldo between 1338 and 1348, it was named after the first bell-ringer, whose idleness led to the nickname Mangiaguadagni (literally "eat the profits").

🔍 HIDDEN GEM
Bird's-Eye View

The small balcony of the San Paolo pub *(Vicolo San Paolo 2)*, directly opposite the Torre del Mangia, is the very best place to go for views over the Campo. Come for a drink or panino.

Santuario e Casa di Santa Caterina

🏛 Costa di Sant'Antonio
📞 0577 28 81 75 🕐 10am–6pm daily

Siena's patron saint, Catherine Benincasa (1347–80), was the daughter of a tradesman. At the age of eight she devoted herself to God and had many visions, as well as later receiving the stigmata (wounds of Christ). Like her namesake, St Catherine of Alexandria, she was believed to have been betrothed to the Christ child in a vision – a scene that inspired many artists. Her eloquence persuaded Pope Gregory XI to return the seat of the papacy to Rome in 1376, after 67 years of exile in Avignon. She died in Rome and was canonized in 1461.

Today Catherine's house is surrounded by chapels and cloisters. Among them is the Church of the Crucifixion, built in 1623 to house the 12th-century crucifix, in front of which she received the stigmata in 1375. The house is decorated with paintings of events from Catherine's life by artists including her contemporaries Francesco Vanni and Pietro Sorri.

④
Palazzo Piccolomini

 Piazza Pio II ☎ 0577 24 71 45 ⏰ 10am-4:30pm Tue-Sun (Apr-Sep: to 6pm) 🔒 7 Jan-14 Feb, 16-30 Nov

Siena's most imposing private palazzo was built for the wealthy Piccolomini family in the 1460s by Florentine architect and sculptor Bernardo Rossellino. It now contains the Sienese state archives, account books and taxation documents dating back to the 13th century. Some of the leading artists of their day were employed to paint the wooden bindings used to enclose the tax and account records. The paintings, now on display in the Sala di Congresso, often show scenes of Siena itself or episodes from the city's past.

Other records include a will attributed to Boccaccio and the council's contract with Jacopo della Quercia for the Fonte Gaia (p372).

⑤
Pinacoteca Nazionale

 Via San Pietro 29 ☎ 0577 28 61 43 ⏰ 8:15am-7:15pm Tue-Sat, 9am-1pm Sun & Mon 🔒 1 May

This fine gallery, which is housed in the 14th-century Palazzo Buonsignori, contains an unsurpassed collection of paintings by artists of the Sienese school. Arranged in chronological order, from the 13th century through to the Mannerist period (1520–1600), highlights include Duccio's *Madonna dei Francescani* (1285), Simone Martini's masterpiece *The Blessed Agostino Novello and Four of His Miracles* (c.1330) and Domenico di Pace Beccafumi's Mannerist *Christ Descending into Limbo* (1536). Pietro Lorenzetti's *Two Views*, from the 14th century, are early examples of landscape painting, and Pietro da Domenico's *Adoration of the Shepherds* (1510) shows how the art of Siena remained visibly influenced by its Byzantine roots long after the naturalism of the Renaissance had reached across the rest of Europe.

⑥
San Domenico

 Piazza San Domenico ⏰ 9am-6:30pm daily

The preserved head of the city's patroness, St Catherine of Siena, can be seen in a gilded tabernacle on the altar of a chapel dedicated to her in the huge, barn-like Gothic church of San Domenico (begun 1226). The chapel itself was built in 1460 for this purpose and is dominated by Sodoma's frescoes (1526), to the right and left of the altar, which show Catherine in states of religious fervour and her early life. The church has the only portrait of St Catherine considered authentic, painted by her friend Andrea Vanni. The fresco by Vanni can be found in the Chapel of the Vaults.

EAT

Osteria Il Grattacielo
This tiny restaurant specializes in local cheeses, cold cuts and vegetable dishes.

 Via Pontani 8 Ⓦ osteriailgrattacielo.it

⑤⑤⑤

Grotta Santa Caterina da Bagoga
A charming trattoria run by a one-time Palio jockey.

 Via della Galluzza 26 🔒 Mon Ⓦ ristorante bagoga.it

⑤⑤⑤

THE PALIO OF SIENA

The Palio is Tuscany's most celebrated festival and it occurs in the Campo each year on 2 July and 16 August at 7pm. This special event is a bareback horse race first recorded in 1283. The jockeys represent 10 of Siena's 17 *contrade* (districts); the horses are chosen by the drawing of lots. Preceded by days of colourful pageantry, processions and heavy betting, the races themselves last only 90 seconds. Thousands crowd into the piazza to watch the race, and rivalry is intense. The winner is rewarded with a silk *palio* (banner). Festivities for the winners can last for weeks.

SIENA DUOMO

C3 **Piazza del Duomo** **Pollicino** **10:30am-5:30pm Mon-Sat, 1:30-5:30pm Sun (duomo); 10:30am-5:30pm daily (library)** **operaduomo.siena.it**

Siena's hulking Duomo (1136–1382) is a treasure house of late Gothic sculpture, early Renaissance painting and Baroque design. The early architects dressed the cathedral in striking Romanesque stripes, but the form is firmly Gothic and one of the best examples of the style in Italy.

Had 14th-century plans to create a new nave come to fruition, this spectacular building would have become the largest church in Christendom. In the event the plan came to nothing, abandoned when the plague of 1348 virtually halved the city's population. Among the Duomo's treasures are sculptural masterpieces by Nicola Pisano, Donatello and Michelangelo, a fine inlaid pavement and a magnificent fresco cycle by Pinturicchio. Equally fascinating are the cathedral outbuildings: the Baptistry, the Museo dell'Opera Metropolitana (housed in the side aisle of the uncompleted nave) and the Santa Maria della Scala hospital across the square, where 1440s frescoes in the wards depict a series of fascinating medieval hospital scenes.

↑ Coffered vaulting inside the dome of Siena Duomo

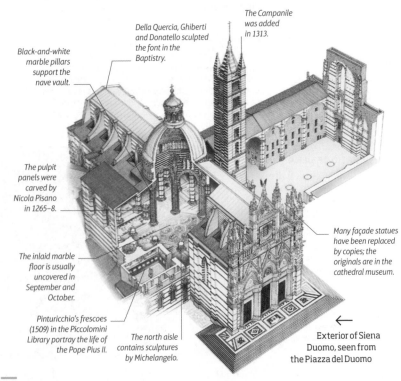

Della Quercia, Ghiberti and Donatello sculpted the font in the Baptistry.

The Campanile was added in 1313.

Black-and-white marble pillars support the nave vault.

The pulpit panels were carved by Nicola Pisano in 1265–8.

The inlaid marble floor is usually uncovered in September and October.

Many façade statues have been replaced by copies; the originals are in the cathedral museum.

Pinturicchio's frescoes (1509) in the Piccolomini Library portray the life of the Pope Pius II.

The north aisle contains sculptures by Michelangelo.

← Exterior of Siena Duomo, seen from the Piazza del Duomo

Did You Know?

The Duomo stripes recall the legend of Siena's founders Senius and Aschius, who arrived on one black horse and one white one.

Campanile and dome of Siena Duomo at sunrise, with the rooftops of Siena in the background

↑ Elegant palazzos lining the banks of the River Arno in central Pisa

❸

PISA

🅐C3 ✈Galileo Galilei 5 km (3 miles) S 🚆Pisa Centrale, Pza della Stazione 🚌Viale Gramsci ℹ Piazza Duomo 7; www.turismo.pisa.it

There is more to Pisa than the Leaning Tower. Instead of heading straight to the Campo dei Miracoli, first take in the lively ambience of the historic centre. Stroll its piazzas, explore its museums and take in its many churches and palazzos. The city's medieval buildings hark back to the Golden Age in the 12th and 13th centuries, when the powerful navy ensured dominance of the seas and brought back vast mercantile riches.

①

Museo Nazionale di San Matteo

🏛Lungarno Mediceo, Piazza San Matteo 1 ☎050 541865 ⏰3-6pm Tue-Sun

This museum is housed in an elegantly fronted medieval convent. Though a little disorganized, it has a good selection of Pisan and Florentine art from the 12th to the 17th centuries. Highlights include Gentile da Fabriano's radiant 15th-century *Madonna of Humility*, Masaccio's *St Paul* (1426) and Donatello's bust of San Rossore (1424–7).

②

Santa Maria della Spina

🏛Lungarno Gambacorti ☎055121919 ⏰3-6pm Tue-Sun

The roofline of this tiny church, located just beyond the Ponte Solferino, bristles with spiky Gothic pinnacles, spires and niches sheltering statues of saints and apostles. The decoration reflects the history of the church, which was built between 1230 and 1323 to house a thorn *(spinas)* from Christ's Crown of Thorns, the gift of a Pisan merchant.

③

Palazzo Blu

🏛Lungarno Gambacorti 9 ⏰10am-7pm Tue-Sun 🌐palazzoblu.it

The striking sky-blue colour of this palazzo, which overlooks the River Arno, dates from the late 18th century, a time when numerous visitors from St Petersburg stayed here. The palazzo regularly hosts world-class temporary exhibitions, while the collection focuses on Pisan art from the 14th to 20th centuries and the beautifully decorated rooms include period furnishings.

④

Tenuta San Rossore

🏛Località Cascine Vecchie 🚌Bus 6 from Pisa 🌐parcosanrossore.org

The San Rossore estate, just outside Pisa, is at the heart of a vast area of parkland that stretches along the coast from Viareggio to Livorno. Hire a bicycle at the Cascine Vecchie visitor centre, join a horse trek or take a tour by a horse-drawn carriage or road-train. There are picnic spots as well as bars and restaurants on the estate.

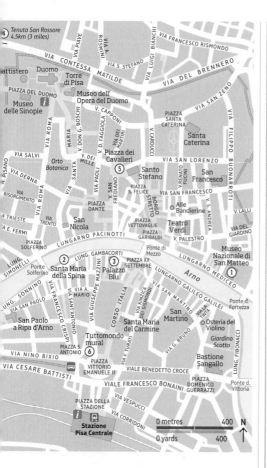

EAT

Ristorante Poldino
At the heart of the San Rossore park, this restaurant serves tasty Tuscan dishes made largely with produce from the estate.

📍 Località Cascine Vecchie 13, Parco San Rossore
🌐 poldino.com

$$ $ $

Osteria del Violino
Watch chunky Fiorentina T-bone steaks being grilled on the open fire at this fantastic Pisan *osteria*.

📍 Via la Tinta 33
📞 050 620 00 56

$ $ $

Alle Bandierine
This popular family-run eatery is the perfect place for delicious spaghetti and plenty of fresh seafood. The house wine is excellent.

📍 Via Mercanti 4
🌐 ristorante allebandierine.it

$ $ $

---

⑤

Piazza dei Cavalieri

The building on the north side of this square is home to Italy's prestigious university the Scuola Normale Superiore. Designed by Giorgio Vasari in 1562, the building was headquarters of the Cavalieri di Santo Stefano, an order of knights created by Cosimo I.

VESPA MUSEUM

Visitors staying in Pisa should not miss the opportunity to visit this great museum in Piaggio, just a 15-minute train ride away. Vespa scooters have been made in Piaggio since the 1940s. The collection includes custom and race versions of the iconic motorbikes *(Viale Rinaldo Piaggio 7, closed Mon & Sun)*.

---

⑥

Tuttomondo mural

📍 Via Zandonai

The last of Keith Haring's characteristically colourful murals decorates the back wall of the 14th-century church of Sant'Antonio Abate. The American artist took four days to complete the mural, which features 30 figures in various positions representing peace in the world. The Keith Art Shop Café opposite is an ideal spot to admire the work.

④ ⊗

THE LEANING TOWER OF PISA AND THE CAMPO DEI MIRACOLI

🅰 C3 🏠 Piazza dei Miracoli 🚌 3, 11 ⏰ Opening times vary, check website 🌐 opapisa.it

Pisa's world-famous Leaning Tower (Torre Pedente) is just one of the splendid religious buildings that rise from the emerald-green lawns of the Campo dei Miracoli, or "Field of Miracles". Located to the northwest of the city centre, the complex also features Pisa's Duomo, the cathedral Baptistry and the Campo Santo cemetery.

Campo dei Miracoli

The famous Leaning Tower started life as a campanile for Pisa's Duomo, begun in 1063, with its four-tiered façade of creamy colonnades. The Baptistry was begun on Romanesque lines in 1152, and completed in a more ornate Gothic style in 1278. The fourth building on the square, the arcaded cemetery, is said to enclose soil brought by the Crusaders from the Holy Land.

The Leaning Tower

All the buildings of the Campo dei Miracoli lean because of their shallow foundations and the sandy silt subsoil, but none tilts so famously as the Leaning Tower. Begun in 1173, the tower began to tip sideways before the third storey was completed, but construction continued until its completion in 1350. More than ten years of engineering work stabilized the tower in 2008, and visitors can now safely climb to the top.

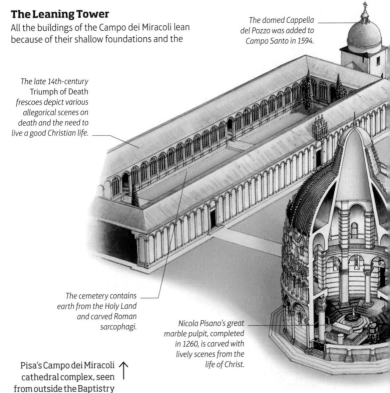

The domed Cappella del Pozzo was added to Campo Santo in 1594.

The late 14th-century Triumph of Death frescoes depict various allegorical scenes on death and the need to live a good Christian life.

The cemetery contains earth from the Holy Land and carved Roman sarcophagi.

Nicola Pisano's great marble pulpit, completed in 1260, is carved with lively scenes from the life of Christ.

Pisa's Campo dei Miracoli cathedral complex, seen from outside the Baptistry ↑

↑ The Campo dei Miracoli, featuring the Leaning Tower and Duomo

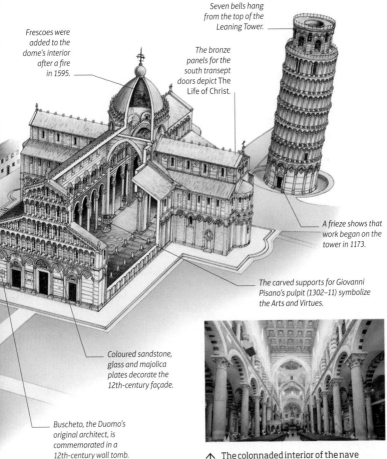

Frescoes were added to the dome's interior after a fire in 1595.

Seven bells hang from the top of the Leaning Tower.

The bronze panels for the south transept doors depict The Life of Christ.

A frieze shows that work began on the tower in 1173.

The carved supports for Giovanni Pisano's pulpit (1302–11) symbolize the Arts and Virtues.

Coloured sandstone, glass and majolica plates decorate the 12th-century façade.

Buscheto, the Duomo's original architect, is commemorated in a 12th-century wall tomb.

↑ The colonnaded interior of the nave in Pisa's Duomo

↑ Market stalls line Piazza Anfiteatreo in central Lucca

5

LUCCA

🅐 C3 🚋 Piazza Ricasoli 🚌 Piazzale Verdi 🛈 Via Carducci 10; www.luccaturismo.it

Lucca's picturesque cobbled streets still follow the grid pattern of the Roman colony founded in 180 BC. The centre is surrounded by imposing 16th- and 17th-century city walls, topped by a wide, tree-lined promenade – a pleasant and popular place to walk. The town has a number of splendid Pisan-Romanesque churches and attractive squares, including the Piazza Anfiteatro, an unusual oval-shaped piazza edged by buildings that retain the shape of the ancient Roman amphitheatre that once stood here.

② Museo Nazionale di Villa Guinigi

🏠 Via della Quarquonia 📞 0583 555 70 🕒 8:30am-7:30pm Tue-Sat 🚫 1 Jan, 1 May, 25 Dec

Built in 1418 for Paolo Guinigi, ruler of Lucca, this sprawling Renaissance villa is home to a collection of artifacts dating from the 8th century BC to the 18th century AD. Exhibits include ancient Etruscan and Roman objects, paintings and sculptures by Fra Bartolomeo, and some fine Romanesque reliefs from Lucca's churches.

① Duomo di San Martino

🏠 Piazza San Martino 📞 0583 95 70 68 🕒 Daily

Dedicated to San Martino, Lucca's cathedral dates from the 11th century. Decorated with Romanesque sculptures and colonnades, the façade (1204) was built after the campanile (begun in 1060), which was originally intended as a defence tower and explains the asymmetric appearance. The main portals contain remarkable carvings by Guidetto da Como and Nicola Pisano. Notable works in the interior include Ghirlandaio's painting *The Madonna and Saints* (c.1479) in the sacristy, a *Last Supper* by Tintoretto and the tomb of Ilaria del Carretto (1405–6), a beautiful marble sarcophagus by Jacopo della Quercia. The Volto Santo is a venerated crucifix said to be a medieval copy of one carved at the time of the Crucifixion. Ornaments used to adorn the crucifix during religious festivals are on display in the Museo Dell'Opera del Duomo, along with other cathedral treasures.

③ Casa Natale di Puccini

🏠 Corte San Lorenzo 9 📞 0583 58 40 28 🕒 Daily: Mar-Apr: 10am-6pm; May-Sep: 10am-7pm; Nov-Jan: 10am-5pm 🚫 25 Dec

The 15th-century house where the great composer Giacomo Puccini (1858–1924) was born contains some of his furniture and clothes as well as costumes used for his operas. Also on display is the piano he used to compose many works, including his last opera, *Turandot*.

→ Marble statues in the formal gardens of Palazzo Pfanner

④ Torre Guinigi

🏠 Via Sant'Andrea 45
🕐 9:30am–4:30pm daily

Dating from the 1300s, this 44-m- (144-ft-) high tower is one of the many structures built by the Guinigi family. The holm oaks growing at the top of the tower make this a popular attraction.

⑤ Via Fillungo

Lucca's principal shopping street winds its way through the heart of the city towards the Anfiteatro Romano. The deconsecrated church of San Cristoforo, built in the 13th century, lies halfway down.

🔍 HIDDEN GEM:
Santa Maria Forisportam

Located beyond the Roman walls of Lucca (Forisportam meaning "outside the gate"), this 12th-century church (*Vicolo Tommasi 1*) contains two great paintings by Guercino.

⑥ Palazzo Pfanner

🏠 Via degli Asili 33
🌐 palazzopfanner.it

This elegant villa (1667) is best known for its formal 18th-century gardens, which feature statues of classical gods.

⑦ San Michele in Foro

🏠 Piazza San Michele 🕐 8am–10:30am 3–5pm daily

The towering façade of San Michele – topped by the huge winged figure of the Archangel Michael slaying a dragon – is one of Tuscany's most lavish Romanesque churches.

Did You Know?

Parts of *Portrait of a Lady*, starring John Malkovich and Nicole Kidman, were filmed at Palazzo Pfanner.

⑧ San Frediano

🏠 Piazza San Frediano 📞 05 83 535 76 🕐 Call for times

San Frediano's striking façade features a colourful 13th-century mosaic, *The Ascension*, a fine prelude to the church's interior. Pride of place goes to a Romanesque font carved with scenes from the life of Christ and the story of Moses.

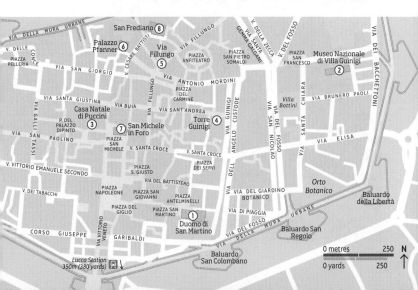

EXPERIENCE Tuscany

CHURCH OF SAN FRANCESCO, AREZZO

🅰C3 🏛Piazza San Francesco 🕐9am-7pm Mon-Fri, 9am-6pm Sat, 1-6pm Sun 🚫1 Jan, 25 Dec 🌐pierodellafrancesca.it

The 13th-century Church of San Francesco houses one of Italy's greatest fresco cycles, the *Legend of the True Cross* (1452–66), Piero della Francesca's masterpiece. The cycle tells the tale of the cross that Christ was crucified on, the True Cross, in 12 episodes. The paintings combine robust realism, vivid figures and lively battle scenes.

Narrative of the Fresco Cycle

Della Francesca presents the story of the True Cross in dramatic detail. The narrative begins on the right-hand wall with a scene showing a sprig from the Tree of Knowledge being planted over Adam's grave. The Queen of Sheba then visits Solomon and foresees that a bridge made from the Tree will be used to crucify the world's greatest king. Solomon, assuming he is that king, orders the bridge to be buried. We then see the Annunciation and Christ on the Cross at the centre of the fresco cycle. Centuries later, Constantine has a vision of the Cross and hears a voice saying "in this sign you shall conquer". Constantine goes on to defeat his rival Maxentius, while Judas Kyriakos is tortured into revealing the location of the True Cross. Three crosses are then dug up and Constantine's mother Helena recognizes the True Cross. The Persian kind Chosroes is defeated after stealing the Cross and the True Cross is finally returned to Jerusalem.

↑ Exterior of the Church of San Francesco in Arezzo

1️⃣ A sprig from the Tree of Knowledge is planted over Adam's grave; The Queen of Sheba visits Solomon; Constantine defeats Maxentius.

2️⃣ The true Cross is returned to Jerusalem; Helena recognizes the True Cross; The Persian king Chosroes is defeated after stealing the Cross.

3️⃣ Judas Kyriakos reveals the location of the True Cross; the Annunciation; Solomon buries the bridge; Constantine has a vision about the Cross.

San Gimignano's skyline, bristling with medieval towers ↑

7

SAN GIMIGNANO

🅰C3 🚌Porta San Giovanni 🚺Piazza del Duomo 1; www.san gimignano.com

The 13 towers that dominate San Gimignano's skyline were built by noble families in the 12th and 13th centuries, when the town's position – on the main pilgrim route from northern Europe to Rome – brought it great prosperity. The plague of 1348, and the diversion of the pilgrim route, led to its decline, as well as its preservation. San Gimignano is rich in works of art, and has lots of good shops and restaurants, although many close from November to March.

① Museo Civico

🏠Palazzo del Popolo, Piazza del Duomo 📞0577 28 63 00 🕐1 Apr-30 Sep: 10am-6:30pm daily; 1 Oct-31 Mar: 11am-5pm daily 🚫25 Dec

Frescoes in the courtyard of this museum feature the coats of arms of city mayors, as well as a 14th-century *Virgin and Child* by Taddeo di Bartolo. The first room is the Sala di Dante, where an inscription recalls a visit by the poet in 1300. The floor above has an art collection, which includes excellent works by Bartolo di Fredi, Pinturicchio, Benozzo Gozzoli and Filippino Lippi.

② Sant'Agostino

🏠Piazza Sant'Agostino 🕐Daily

Consecrated in 1298, this church has a simple façade, contrasting markedly with the heavily decorated Rococo interior (c.1740) by Vanvitelli. Above the main altar is the *Coronation of the Virgin* (1483) by Piero del Pollaiuolo.

③ Collegiata

🏠Piazza del Duomo 🕐Daily

This 12th-century Romanesque church contains a feast of frescoes. In the north aisle the frescoes comprise 26 episodes from the Old Testament (1367) by Bartolo di Fredi.

④ Museo San Gimignano 1300

🏠Via San Giovanni 50 📞327 439 51 65 🕐10am-5pm daily (May-Nov: to 6pm)

A reconstruction of San Gimignano as it was in the 13th and 14th centuries is the main highlight of this museum. The exhibits – all handmade – include 72 "tower houses", a symbol of the city's power in the Middle Ages.

Must See

DRINK

Vernaccia di San Gimignano Wine Museum

Try San Gimignano's famous white wine and its lesser known reds, rosé and Vin Santo, at this regional wine museum. A fascinating multimedia experience also recounts the history and culture surrounding the wines.

🏠 Via della Rocca 1
🌐 san gimignanomuseo vernaccia.com

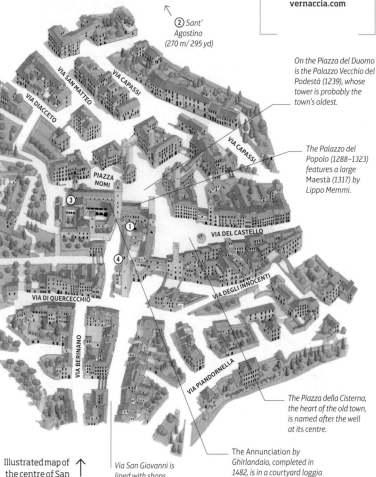

② *Sant'
Agostino
(270 m/ 295 yd)*

VIA SAN MATTEO

VIA CAPASSI

VIA DIACCETO

VIA CAPASSI

PIAZZA NOMI

③

①

VIA DEL CASTELLO

④

VIA DEGLI INNOCENTI

VIA DI QUERCECCHIO

VIA BERINANO

VIA PIANDORNELLA

On the Piazza del Duomo is the Palazzo Vecchio del Podestà (1239), whose tower is probably the town's oldest.

The Palazzo del Popolo (1288–1323) features a large Maestà (1317) by Lippo Memmi.

The Piazza della Cisterna, the heart of the old town, is named after the well at its centre.

The Annunciation by Ghirlandaio, completed in 1482, is in a courtyard loggia alongside the Collegiata.

Illustrated map of the centre of San Gimignano

Via San Giovanni is lined with shops selling local goods.

EXPERIENCE MORE

⑧
Carrara

C3 🏛Massa Carrara 🚇
ℹ️Lungomare Vespucci 24;
0585 24 00 63

Carrara's white stone has been prized for centuries by famous sculptors from Michelangelo to Henry Moore. The region's 300 or more quarries date back to Roman times, making this one of the world's oldest industrial sites in continuous use. Many of the town's marble-sawing mills and workshops offer visitors the chance to see the ways in which marble and quartz are worked. These techniques – along with marble artifacts old and new – can be seen at the **Museo Civico del Marmo**.

Local marble is put to good use in the town's Duomo on Piazza del Duomo, particularly in the fine Pisan-Romanesque façade with its delicate rose window. The cathedral square also contains Michelangelo's house, used by the sculptor during his visits to select blocks of marble. The town has some lovely corners to explore, in particular the elegant Piazza Alberica. Most visitors head for the stone quarries at nearby Colonnata and at Fantiscritti (take a bus or follow the signs to the "Cave di Marmo").

Museo Civico del Marmo
🏛 Viale XX Settembre
📞0585 84 57 46 🕐Mon–Sat

---

⑨
Pietrasanta

C3 🚆 ℹ️Piazza Statuto

This medieval town has long been a draw for sculptors from all over the world, thanks to the white marble quarried from the Alpi Apuane mountains that form the town's backdrop. More recently, artistic metal-casting foundries have been established here alongside the many marble workshops. The **Museo dei Bozzetti**, in a former monastery, contains a fascinating collection of maquettes and scale models that have been used in preparation for artworks, including César's famous thumb sculpture. The town's Piazza Duomo is dominated by the 13th-century Duomo di San Martino, with its splendid 14th-century façade. Inside the adjacent brick campanile is a spectacular helical staircase by Donato Benti, a Florentine sculptor and architect.

Dotted around the town are over 70 sculptures by contemporary artists. Among them are works by Fernando Botero (born 1932) and Igor Mitoraj (1944–2014), both of whom had studios here.

Museo dei Bozzetti
🏛 Via Sant'Agostino 1
🕐Opening times vary, check website 🌐museo
deibozzetti.it

MICHELANGELO'S QUARRY

Michelangelo discovered exceptional marble on Monte Altissimo, and he even began his own access road to the precious stone following his commission to decorate the façade of Florence's San Lorenzo (p358). Although the project was abandoned (and San Lorenzo remains unadorned), the quarry is still in use today.

A white-marble quarry in the vicinity of Carrara

→
Sandy beach at
Viareggio, on the
Versilia coast

Bagni di Lucca

C3 **Lucca** **Via Umberto I, inside the town hall; 0583 80 57 45**

All over Tuscany there are hot springs of volcanic origin, like Bagni di Lucca. The Romans first exploited the springs and built bath complexes where army veterans who settled in the area could relax. More spas came into prominence in the Middle Ages and the Renaissance, and they continue to be recommended for relieving a variety of ailments, such as arthritis.

Tuscan spas really came into their own in the early 19th century, when Bagni di Lucca reached its heyday as one of Europe's most fashionable spas, frequented by emperors, kings and aristocrats. Visitors came not only for thermal cures, but also for the Casino (1837), one of Europe's first licensed gambling houses. These days the town is rather sleepy, and its main sights are the 19th-century monuments, including the Neo-Gothic English Church (1839) on Via Crawford and the Cimitero Anglicano (Protestant Cemetery) on Via Letizia.

Southeast of Bagni di Lucca lies another popular spa town, Montecatini Terme. Developed in the 18th century, this town features a wide range of spa architecture, from Neo-Classical to Art Nouveau establishments.

Torre del Lago Puccini

C3 **Lucca** **Viale Kennedy 2; 0584 96 22 23**

A glorious avenue of lime trees, the Via dei Tigli, links Viareggio with Torre del Lago Puccini, once the home of the opera composer Giacomo Puccini (1858–1924). He and his wife are buried in their former home, now the **Museo Villa Puccini**, which houses the piano on which the maestro composed many of his most famous works. Lago Massaciuccoli, a nature reserve for rare and migrant birds, provides a pretty backdrop for open-air performances of Puccini's works.

Museo Villa Puccini

 Piazzale Belvedere Puccini 226 **0584 34 14 45** **Mon pm–Sun** **Nov, 25 Dec**

HIDDEN GEM:
Scottish Barga

A depression in the 1800s resulted in many residents of the medieval town of Barga ending up in Glasgow. The links with Scotland remain strong today, with tartan a regular sight, and an annual fish and chips festival.

Viareggio

C3 **Lucca** **Viale Carducci 10; 0584 96 22 33**

Known for its carnival, held in January and early February, this is the most popular of the resorts on the Versilia coast. Its famous "Liberty" (Art Nouveau) style of architecture can be seen in the grand hotels, villas and cafés built in the 1920s after the original boardwalk and timber chalets went up in flames in 1917. The finest example of Liberty architecture is the Gran Caffè Margherita at the end of Passeggiata Margherita, designed by the prolific father of Italian Art Nouveau, Galileo Chini.

←

A pretty square in the hilltop town of San Miniato

semi-derelict Rocca (castle), built for Frederick II, German Holy Roman Emperor, in the 13th century. Close by stands the **Museo Diocesano**, which is home to a *Crucifixion* (c.1430) attributed to Filippo Lippi, a terracotta bust of Christ attributed to Verrocchio (1435–88), and the *Virgin of the Holy Girdle* by Andrea del Castagno (c.1417–57). Next door, the red-brick Romanesque façade of the Duomo dates from the 12th century. Its inset majolica plates, evidence of trade with Spain or North Africa, probably represent the North Star and the constellations of Ursa Major and Minor (all three were key points of reference for early navigators).

Museo Diocesano

⊛ ⬛ Piazza Duomo ⬛ Opening times vary, check website ⬛ museodiocesano.it

⑬ Mugello

⬛ C3 ⬛ Florence ⬛
🚩 Via Palmiro Togliatti 45 & Borgo San Lorenzo;
www.mugellotoscana.it

Mugello is an area of wooded hillsides, Renaissance villas and villages. The **Parco di Pratolino** has fountains, grottoes and statues, including Giambologna's imposing *Apennine Colossus*.

In Scarperia, the 14th-century **Palazzo dei Vicari** has a curious façade decorated with the heraldic shields of successive governors, and a Brunelleschi clock that was used for the panoramic bell-tower timepiece.

Parco di Pratolino

⊛ ⊜ ⬛ Via Fiorentina 276, Loc Pratolino, Vaglia ⬛ Apr-Oct: 10am-8pm Fri-Sun

Palazzo dei Vicari

⊛ ⊛ ⊜ ⬛ Piazza dei Vicari, Scarperia ⬛ 055 846 81 65 ⬛ 10am-1pm Wed-Sun (Jun-Aug: also 3-7pm)

⑭ Vinci

⬛ C3 ⬛ Florence ⬛
🚩 Via Montalbano 1;
0571 93 32 85

The birthplace of Leonardo da Vinci (1452–1519), this hilltop town celebrates its most famous resident in the **Museo Leonardiano**. On display are wooden models of Leonardo's machines and inventions, including a bicycle, a car, an armoured tank and even a machine-gun.

Museo Leonardiano

⊛ ⬛ Castello dei Conti Guidi ⬛ 0571 93 32 51 ⬛ 9:30am-6pm daily (Mar-Oct: to 7pm)

⑮ San Miniato

⬛ C3 ⬛ Pisa ⬛ 🚩 Piazza del Popolo; 0571 41 87 39

This hilltop town manages to remain aloof from the vast industrial sprawl of the Arno Valley. Its key building is the

---

STAY

Il Borro

Il Borro offers country-chic accommodation in charming stone houses around a stunning medieval village, plus self-catering villas elsewhere on the estate. Non-residents are welcome to shop at the craft workshops or join a wine-tasting tour. There's a choice of dining, a spa, two pools, horse riding and golf.

⬛ C3 ⬛ Località Borro 1, San Giustino Valdarno ⬛ ilborro.it

€€€

Fiesole

C3 **Florence**
**Via Portigiani 3; 055
596 13 11**

Fiesole stands in rolling hilly countryside 8 km (5 miles) north of Florence. It is a popular retreat from the city thanks to its hilltop position which attracts cool breezes. Founded in the 7th century BC, the original Etruscan colony was a powerful force in central Italy, only surrendering its supremacy following the foundation of Florence (1st century BC).

The restored Duomo of San Romolo in Piazza Mino da Fiesole was begun in 1028. It has a massive bell tower and a bare Romanesque interior. Behind the Duomo, an archaeological area contains the remains of a 1st-century-BC Roman theatre, traces of Etruscan walls from the 4th century BC and the **Museo Civico Archeologico**, with a collection of bronzes, ceramics and jewellery.

CHIANTI

With its vine-covered hillsides, pretty villages and grand villas and castles, Chianti is a lovely place to explore. The panoramic SS222 Strada Chiantigiana runs the length of the Chianti winemaking zone, a large area between Florence and Siena; the best wines, however, are from the much more restricted Chianti Classico territory – look for the Chianti Classico black cockerel (Gallo Nero) symbol. For the very best, opt for a Chianti Classico Riserva or Chianti Classico Gran Selezione.

Via di San Francesco, a steep lane offering lovely views, leads to the Franciscan friary of San Francesco (14th century) and the interesting 9th-century church of Sant'Alessandro, with a Neo-Classical façade.

Via Vecchia Fiesolana leads to the hamlet of San Domenico, where the 15th-century church of the same name contains a painting of the *Madonna with Angels and Saints* (c.1430) by Fra Angelico and the Chapter House

contains a fresco of *The Crucifixion* (c.1430), by the same artist. Close by, on the Via della Badia dei Roccettini, is the Badia Fiesolana, a pretty Romanesque church with a striped marble façade and interior of local grey sandstone, *pietra serena*.

**Museo Civico
Archeologico**
 Via Portigiani 1
 Opening times vary, check website **museidifiesole.it**

↑ A panorama of Florence from the hill of Fiesole

⓱ Monteriggioni

🅰C3 🅾Siena 🚌
ℹ Piazza Roma 23; www. monteriggioniturismo.it

Monteriggioni is a gem of a medieval hilltop town. It was built in 1203 and ten years later became a garrison town. It is completely encircled by high walls with 14 heavily fortified towers, built to guard the northern borders of Siena's territory against invasion by Florentine armies.

Dante used Monteriggioni as a simile for the deepest abyss at the heart of his *Inferno*, which compares the town's "ring-shaped citadel... crowned with towers" with giants standing in a moat. The perfectly preserved walls are best viewed from the Colle di Val d'Elsa road. Within the walls, the sleepy town consists of a large piazza, a pretty Romanesque church (on the piazza), a few houses, a couple of craft shops, restaurants, and shops selling many of the locally produced Castello di Monteriggioni wines.

West of Monteriggioni by 3 km (2 miles) lies the former Cistercian Abbey of Abbadia dell'Isola (12th century). This Romanesque church was largely rebuilt in the 18th century. It contains frescoes by Taddeo di Bartolo and Vincenzo Tamagni.

⓲ Volterra

🅰C3 🅾Pisa 🚌 **ℹPiazza dei Priori 20; www. volterratur.it**

Like many Etruscan cities, Volterra is situated on a high plateau, offering fine views over the surrounding hills. In many places the ancient Etruscan walls still survive. The **Museo Etrusco Guarnacci** contains one of the best collections of Etruscan artifacts in Italy. Of special interest is the group of over 600 cinerary urns, made from alabaster or terracotta, many of which were gathered from local tombs.

The Palazzo dei Priori, the medieval seat of government on Piazza dei Priori, is the oldest of its kind in Tuscany. It was begun in 1208 and there are 14th-century frescoes inside. The Pisan-Romanesque Duomo, located on Piazza San Giovanni, has a fine 13th-century pulpit with sculptured panels.

Volterra's excellent art gallery and museum, the **Pinacoteca e Museo Civico**, features works by Florentine artists. *Christ in Majesty* (1492) by Ghirlandaio shows Christ hovering above an idealized Tuscan landscape. Luca Signorelli's *Virgin and Child with Saints* (1491) states his debt to Roman art through the reliefs on the base of the Virgin's throne. Painted in the same year, his *Annunciation* is a beautifully balanced composition. Another

View over the hills and rooftops of Massa Marittima

→ Charming marina on Elba's east coast

highlight is Rosso Fiorentino's Mannerist painting, *The Deposition* (1521).

Volterra is famous for its craftsmen, who have been carving elaborate statues and objets d'art from locally mined alabaster for 2,500 years.

Museo Etrusco Guarnacci
 🏛 Via Don Minzoni 15
📞 0588 863 47 🕐 Daily
🚫 1 Jan, 25 Dec

Pinacoteca e Museo Civico
🏛 Via dei Sarti 1
📞 0588 875 80 🕐 Daily
🚫 1 Jan, 25 Dec

---

⑲
Massa Marittima

🗺 C4 🚉 Grosseto 🚌
ℹ Amatur, Via Todini 3-5;
0566 90 65 54

Set in the Colline Metallifere (metal-bearing hills) where lead, copper and silver ores have been mined for centuries, Massa Marittima is far from being a grimy industrial town. Many Romanesque buildings still survive from the time when the town became an independent republic (1225–1335). The Romanesque-Gothic Duomo in Piazza Garibaldi is dedicated to St Cerbone, a 6th-century saint whose story is sculpted in stone above the main portal. Inside the building, the *Maestà* is attributed to Duccio (c.1316).

The **Museo della Miniera** (Museum of Mining) is located partially inside a former mine shaft and has exhibits that explain mining techniques, tools and minerals.

The **Museo Archeologico e Museo d'Arte Sacra** has material from Paleolithic to Roman times. Other attractions include the Fortezza Senese and the Torre della Candeliera.

Museo della Miniera
🏛 Via Corridoni 📞 0566 90 22 89 🕐 Tue-Sun

Museo Archeologico e Museo d'Arte Sacra
🏛 Palazzo del Podestà, Piazza Garibaldi 📞 0566 90 22 89 🕐 Tue-Sun

---

⑳
Elba

🗺 C4 🚉 Livorno 🚌 Portoferraio 🚌 ℹ Viale Elba 4; www.visitelba.info

Elba's most famous resident was Napoleon, who was exiled for nine months here after the fall of Paris in 1814. Today

Did You Know?

During his exile, Napoleon oversaw a series of major infrastructure reforms on Elba.

Italy's third-largest island is mainly populated by holiday-makers, who come by ferry from Piombino, 10 km (6 miles) away on the mainland. The main town is Portoferraio, with an old port, and a modern seafront of hotels and fish restaurants.

The landscape of the island is varied. On the west coast, which tends to be a little quieter and less touristy, there are sandy beaches suitable for all watersports. The east coast, centred on the town of Porto Azzurro, the island's second port, is more rugged, with high cliffs and stony beaches. Inland, olive groves and vineyards line hillsides, and vegetation covers the mountains. A good way to see the interior is to take the road from Marciana Marina to the medieval village of Marciana Alta. Close by, a minor road leads to a cable car that runs to Monte Capanne (1,018 m/3,300 ft), a magnificent viewpoint.

> **Volterra is famous for its craftsmen, who have been carving elaborate statues and objets d'art from locally mined alabaster for 2,500 years.**

㉑ Sansepolcro

 D3 **Arezzo** 🚌
ℹ Via Matteotti 8; www.
prolocosansepolcro.it

Sansepolcro is the birthplace
of Piero della Francesca
(1410–92). The town's **Museo
Civico** contains two of his
masterpieces: *The Resurrection*
(1463) and the *Madonna della
Misericordia* (1462). It also has
a 15th-century *Crucifixion* by
Luca Signorelli. In the church
of San Lorenzo on Via Santa
Croce there is a *Deposition* in
the Mannerist style by Rosso
Fiorentino (1494–1541).

Museo Civico
⊛ ⊛ **⌂** Via Aggiunti 65
☎ 0575 73 22 18 **⊙** Daily
⊗ Public hols

㉒ Crete Senesi

 C3 **Asciano** 🚌🚗 **ℹ** Via
delle Fonti; 0577 71 88 11

To the south of Siena and
central Tuscany is the area
known as the Crete Senesi,
which is characterized by
round clay hillocks eroded by
heavy rain over the centuries.
Dubbed the "Tuscan desert",
it is almost completely barren.
Cypress and pine trees, planted
to provide windbreaks along
roads and around isolated
farmhouses, are an important
feature in this empty, primeval
landscape. Shepherds tend
to flocks of sheep here; the
milk is used to produce the
strongly flavoured pecorino
cheese that is popular
throughout Tuscany.

㉓ Montalcino

 C4 **Siena** 🚌 **ℹ** Costa
del Municipio 1; www.
prolocomontalcino.it

Hilltop Montalcino sits at the
heart of the vineyards that
produce Brunello, one of Italy's
finest red wines. It can be
sampled in the **Enoteca La
Fortezza di Montalcino** (a
wine shop) situated in the
14th-century Fortezza with its
impressive ramparts. On the
way from the fortress into
town is the monastery of Sant'
Agostino and its 14th-century
church and, just beyond, the
Palazzo Vescovile. On Piazza
del Popolo the slim tower of
the Palazzo Comunale,
constructed in the 13th and
14th centuries, stands tall
above the town.

**Enoteca La Fortezza di
Montalcino**
⌂ Piazzale della Fortezza
⊙ Daily **🌐** enotecala
fortezza.com

TOP 3 MONTALCINO WINERIES

Castello di Banfi
C4 **⌂** Poggio alle
Mura, Sant'Angelo Scalo
🌐 castellobanfi.com
Based around a hilltop
castle, this winery runs
tours and tastings.

Fattoria dei Barbi
C4 **⌂** Località Pordernovi,
Montalcino **🌐** fattoria
deibarbi.it
Cellar tours, a wine
museum and a tavern
draw the crowds here.

Podere Le Ripi
C4 **⌂** Castelnuovo Abate,
Montalcino **🌐** podere
leripi.it
Biodynamic winery
with tastings and tours.

↑ The typically
desert-like
landscape of the
Crete Senesi

→ Market stalls on a picturesque square in Arezzo

Arezzo

C3 ⊞ *i* Piazza della Repubblica 22–23; 0575 268 50

Arezzo is one of Tuscany's wealthiest cities, its prosperity based on a thriving jewellery industry. Although much of its medieval centre was destroyed during World War II, the city preserves some outstanding sights: foremost are Piero della Francesca's famous frescoes in the church of San Francesco (p384). Nearby, the Pieve di Santa Maria boasts an ornate Romanesque façade. To its rear stretches the steeply sloping Piazza Grande, flanked by an arcade (1573) by Vasari, and by the Palazzo della Fraternità dei Laici (1377–1552).

The huge **Duomo** to the north is best known for its 16th-century stained glass and a small fresco of *Mary Magdalene* by Piero della Francesca (1416–92).

The **Museo Diocesano (Mudas)** features three wooden crucifixes, dating from the 12th and 13th centuries, a bas-relief of *The Annunciation* (1434) by Rossellino and paintings by Vasari. More works by Vasari can be seen in the **Casa di Vasari**, a house built by the artist in 1540.

Still more of Vasari's frescoes are displayed in the **Museo d'Arte Medioevale e Moderna**, a museum famed for its excellent collection of majolica pottery.

The **Fortezza Medicea**, a ruined Medici castle built by Antonio da Sangallo in the 16th century, has fine views.

Duomo

⌂ Piazza Duomo 1 ☎ 0575 239 91 ⊙ Daily

Museo Diocesano (Mudas)

⊛ ⌂ Piazzetta Dietro il Duomo 12 ☎ 0575 402 72 68 ⊙ Daily

Casa di Vasari

⊛ ⌂ Via XX Settembre 55 ☎ 0575 35 44 49 ⊙ Wed–Mon

Museo d'Arte Medioevale e Moderna

⊛ ⌂ Via di San Lorentino 8 ☎ 0575 40 90 50 ⊙ Tue, Thu, Sat & Sun

Fortezza Medicea

⌂ Parco il Prato ☎ 0575 37 76 78 ⊙ Tue–Sun

San Galgano

C3 ⌂ Siena ⊞ ⊙ 9am–6pm daily ⊡ comune.chiusdino.siena.it

This remote Cistercian abbey lies in a superb setting. San Galgano (1148–81) was a brave but dissolute knight who turned to God, renouncing the material world. When he tried to break his sword against a rock as a symbol of his rejection of war, it was swallowed by the stone. This he interpreted as a sign of God's approval. He built a hut on a hill above the abbey (the site of today's beehive-shaped chapel at Montesiepi, built c.1185).

The abbey, begun in 1218, is Gothic in style, reflecting the French origins of the Cistercian monks who designed it. They divided their lives between prayer and labour, but despite an emphasis on poverty, the monks became wealthy from the sale of wood. By the middle of the 14th century, the abbey was corruptly administered and gradually fell into decline. It was eventually dissolved in 1652.

St Galgano's sword stands embedded in a stone just inside the door of the circular oratory. The 14th-century stone walls of the side chapel are frescoed with scenes from Galgano's life by Ambrogio Lorenzetti (1344).

26
Pienza

 C4 Siena Via delle Case Nuove 4; www.prolocopienza.it

Pienza is a delightful village whose intimate centre was almost completely redesigned in the 15th century by Pope Pius II. Born as Aeneas Sylvius Piccolomini in 1405, when the village was known as Corsignano, he became a leading Humanist scholar and philosopher. Elected pope in 1458, he rebuilt his birthplace, renaming it Pienza in his own honour. Florentine architect and sculptor Bernardo Rossellino was commissioned to build a cathedral, papal palace and town hall (all completed 1459–62), but a planned model Renaissance town was never realized. Some idea of what might have been, however, can still be gained from the **Palazzo Piccolomini**, the former papal palace, home to Pius's descendants until 1968.

The airy Duomo next door contains six altarpieces of the *Madonna and Child*, each commissioned from leading Sienese painters of the day. Rossellino was forced to build the Duomo on a cramped site with poor foundations, and cracks started to appear in the building before it was even completed. Today, the church's eastern end suffers from severe subsidence.

Palazzo Piccolomini

 Piazza Pio II 0577 286300 10am-6:30pm Tue-Sun (mid-Oct-mid-Mar: to 4:30pm) Jan-mid-Feb, mid-end Nov

27
Montepulciano

C4 Siena Piazza Don Minzoni 1; www.prolocomontepulciano.it

This is one of Tuscany's highest hill-towns, its walls and fortifications offering broad views over Umbria and southern Tuscany, and over the vineyards providing the Vino Nobile wine that has made its name famous. The streets are

---

HIDDEN GEM
Ancient Cellars

Below Montepulciano's town centre is a network of ancient cellars, many of which are open to the public, accessed from several restaurants, shops and wine stores, including the historic winemaker Contucci (*Via del Teatro 1*).

Verdant rolling hills in the countryside around Pienza

brimming with Renaissance palazzi. The main street, the Corso, climbs to the Duomo (1592–1630), the setting for one of the masterpieces of the Sienese School, the *Assumption* (1401), created by Taddeo di Bartolo. The High Renaissance church, Tempio di San Biagio (1518–34), lies off the road to Pienza.

28
Chiusi

 D4 Siena Via Porsenna 79; www.prolocochiusi.it

Chiusi used to be one of the most powerful cities in the Etruscan league, reaching the height of its influence in the 7th and 6th centuries BC. Many Etruscan tombs dot the surrounding countryside, the source of exhibits like vases and urns in the town's **Museo Archeologico Nazionale**.

The Romanesque **Duomo** includes recycled Roman pillars and capitals. The wall decorations in the nave were painted by Arturo Viligiardi in 1887. There is a Roman mosaic underneath the high altar. Visits can be made to several

Etruscan tombs under the town from the **Museo della Cattedrale**, a museum in the cloister of the Duomo.

Museo Archeologico Nazionale

 ▢ Via Porsenna 93 ☎ 0578 201 77 ◷ 9am–8pm Mon–Sat (to 2pm Sun & public hols)

Duomo & Museo della Cattedrale

◈ ▢ Piazza del Duomo ◷ Opening times vary, check website ⓦ museum florence.com

---

㉙

Cortona

▲ D3 ▢ Arezzo 🚉🚌 ℹ Piazza Signorelli 9; 0575 63 72 23

One of the oldest hill-towns in Tuscany, Cortona, founded by the Etruscans, is also one of the most scenic. A major power in the Middle Ages, it was able to hold its own against Siena and Arezzo. Today it is a charming maze of old streets and medieval buildings. The town's early history is traced in the **Museo dell'Accademia Etrusca**, which contains Etruscan artifacts as well as Egyptian and Roman remains. The small **Museo Diocesano** features several fine paintings, in particular a *Deposition* (1502) by Luca Signorelli and a sublime *Annunciation* (c.1434) by Fra Angelico. Signorelli, born in Cortona, is buried in the church of San Francesco (built in 1245), which contains an *Annunciation* painted in Baroque style by Pietro da Cortona, another native artist.

Museo dell'Accademia Etrusca

◈ ▢ Palazzo Casali, Piazza Signorelli 9 ☎ 0575 63 72 35 ◷ Daily (except Mon in winter)

Museo Diocesano

◈ ▢ Piazza del Duomo 1 ☎ 0575 628 30 ◷ Daily (Tue–Sun in winter)

PECORINO DI PIENZA

Pienza is famous for its delicious sheep's cheese, which is aged for at least 90 days in oak barrels. Try some of the variously aged cheeses and other produce at the Taverna del Pecorino *(Via Condotti 1)*.

→

Wheel of pecorino di Pienza cheese

↑ Beautiful Piazza Grande in Montepulciano

30 Pitigliano

C4 Grosseto
🚌 Piazza Garibaldi 51; 0564
61 71 11

Perched on a plateau, high above cliffs carved out by the river Lente, Pitigliano looks spectacular. The houses seem to grow out of the cliffs, which are riddled with caves cut out of the soft limestone. Its maze of tiny medieval streets includes a small Jewish ghetto, formed in the 1600s by Jews fleeing persecution in the papal states.

The **Museo di Palazzo Orsini** displays a small exhibition of work by local artist Francesco Zuccarelli (1702–88). He also painted two of the altarpieces in the medieval Duomo in Piazza San Gregorio.

The **Museo Etrusco** contains finds from ancient local settlements.

Museo di Palazzo Orsini
⊚ 🏛 Piazza della Fortezza Orsini 4 📞 0564 61 60 74
🕐 10am–1pm & 3–5pm Tue–Fri

Museo Etrusco
⊚ 🏛 Piazza della Fortezza Orsini 59c 📞 0564 61 40 67
🕐 Times vary, call ahead

31 Sovana

C4 Grosseto 🚌 Piazza Busatti 8; 0564 61 40 74

Sovana's single little street ends in Piazza del Pretorio, home to the ancient church of Santa Maria, which contains frescoes and a 9th-century altar canopy. A lane beyond leads through olive groves to the Romanesque Duomo, filled with reliefs and carvings from an earlier church on the site. Some fine Etruscan tombs lie in the surrounding countryside, many clearly signposted.

 INSIDER TIP
Tuscia's Etruscan Footpaths

Bordering Tuscany, Lazio and Umbria, the area known as Tuscia is rich in Etruscan remains such as the Vie Cave, walled footpaths carved into the rock. There are several examples of these near Pitigliano.

32 Monte Argentario

C4 Grosseto 🚌 Piazzale del Valle, Porto Santo Stefano; 0564 81 42 08

Monte Argentario was an island until the early 1700s, when the shallow waters separating it from the mainland began to silt up, creating two sandy spits of land, known as

Lion statue at Palazzo Orsini, in the centre of Pitigliano ↑

Sunset at the Cala
Violina beach
in Maremma

tomboli, which enclose the
Orbetello lagoon. Today the
lagoon is host to a beautiful
nature reserve that is well
worth visiting. Orbetello itself,
a lively and relatively unspoilt
little town, was linked to
the island in 1842, when a
dyke was constructed from
the mainland.

Porto Ercole and Porto
Santo Stefano, the main
harbour towns on the
peninsula, are upmarket
resorts that are favoured by
wealthy yacht owners and
become busy in peak season.
In the summer, ferries from
Porto Santo Stefano call at
Giannutri, a privately owned
island. Interior roads – notably
the Strada Panoramica – offer
peaceful drives past rocky
coves and bays.

33 ⊘ ⊗

Maremma

C4 ⚑ Grosseto ⏱ Daily
🚌 From Alberese to
entrances & to tour
departure point for Inner
Park Areas 🛈 Piazza del
Popolo 3 Grosseto; www.
quimaremmatoscana.it

The Etruscans, followed by
the Romans, were the first
to cultivate the marshes and
low hills of the Maremma.
Following the collapse of the
Roman Empire, however, the
area fell prey to flooding and
malaria and was left virtually
uninhabited until the 1700s.
Since then the land has
been reclaimed, the irrigation
canals unblocked and farming
developed on the fertile soil.

> **Did You Know?**
>
> Traditional *butteri*,
> Tuscan cowboys, are
> still employed in
> the Maremma.

The Parco Naturale della
Maremma was set up in 1975
to preserve the native flora
and fauna, and to prevent
development on the coastline.
Entrance to much of the park
is restricted to access on foot
or by a park bus from Alberese.
Other more marginal areas,
however, such as the excellent
beach at Marina di Alberese,
are easier to see.

SATURNIA'S SPA WATER

Holiday-makers come to Saturnia for
the water. The Cascate del Mulino
consists of a series of natural pools,
with rocks stained coppery green, on
the Gorello river just outside Saturnia.
It is possible to bathe in the warm
(37°C/98°F) sulphur water here at any
time, all year round, free of charge.

The Terme di Saturnia, on the other
hand, is a resort hotel that provides
excellent spa facilities, health
treatments and even an 18-hole
golf course (*Località Follonata*).

UMBRIA

Long dismissed as Tuscany's "gentler sister", Umbria has finally emerged from the shadow of its more famous western neighbour. Forming an expanse of gentle pastoral countryside and high mountain wilderness, this picturesque region is full of historic hill-towns. With its dramatic landscapes, it is a popular destination for walkers, while the beach-fringed shores of Lake Trasimeno offer great swimming and sailing opportunities.

The region was inhabited in the 8th century BC by the Umbrians, a peaceable farming tribe, and later colonized by the Etruscans and Romans. In the Middle Ages, the Lombards established a dukedom centred around Spoleto. By the 13th century much of the region was scattered with independent city-states, most of them eventually absorbed by the Papal States, where they remained until Italian unification in 1860.

Today the old towns are Umbria's chief glory. In Perugia, the region's capital, and the smaller centres of Gubbio, Montefalco and Todi, there are numerous Romanesque churches, civic palaces, vivid fresco cycles and endless medieval nooks and crannies. Spoleto, renowned for its summer arts festival, blends grandiose medieval monuments with Roman remains and some of Italy's oldest churches. Assisi, the birthplace of St Francis, contains the Basilica di San Francesco, frescoed in part by Giotto. At Orvieto, magnificently situated on its volcanic crag, there are Etruscan remains and one of Italy's finest Romanesque-Gothic cathedrals.

Umbria's oak woods, ice-clear streams and rich soils yield many delicacies. Chief among these are trout and truffles, olive oils to rival those of Tuscany, prized lentils from Castelluccio, cured meats from Norcia and tangy mountain cheeses. Sadly, this beautiful area is also frequently hit by earthquakes, which cause considerable damage to its many artistic monuments.

UMBRIA

Must See

1 Basilica di San Francesco, Assisi

Experience More

2 Gubbio
3 Perugia
4 Lake Trasimeno
5 Assisi
6 Spello
7 Montefalco
8 Cascata delle Marmore
9 Orvieto
10 Todi
11 Spoleto
12 Monti Sibillini
13 Valnerina

LE MARCHE
p414

BASILICA DI SAN FRANCESCO, ASSISI

🅰D4 **🏛Piazza San Francesco** **🕐6am– 6pm daily (lower church); 8:30am–6pm daily (upper church)** **🚌 FS** **🌐sanfrancescoassisi.org**

The burial place of St Francis, this basilica was begun in 1228, two years after the saint's death. With its stunning frescoes by the great painters Giotto and Cimabue, the Basilica remains among the most influential monuments of Western art today.

Over the 13th and 14th centuries, the Basilica's Upper and Lower Churches were decorated by the foremost artists of their day, among them Cimabue, Simone Martini, Pietro Lorenzetti and Giotto, whose frescoes on the *Life of St Francis* are some of the most renowned in Italy. The pictorial style created in Assisi was reproduced in many new Franciscan churches across the country. The Basilica, which dominates Assisi, is one of the world's great Christian shrines and receives vast numbers of pilgrims.

↑ Lower Church entrance, seen from the Lower Plaza

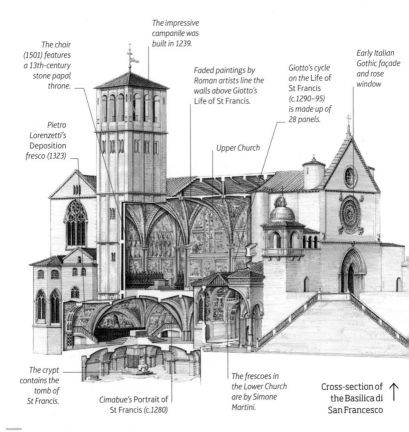

The choir (1501) features a 13th-century stone papal throne.

The impressive campanile was built in 1239.

Faded paintings by Roman artists line the walls above Giotto's Life of St Francis.

Giotto's cycle on the Life of St Francis (c.1290–95) is made up of 28 panels.

Early Italian Gothic façade and rose window

Pietro Lorenzetti's Deposition fresco (1323)

Upper Church

The crypt contains the tomb of St Francis.

Cimabue's Portrait of St Francis (c.1280)

The frescoes in the Lower Church are by Simone Martini.

Cross-section of the Basilica di San Francesco ↑

Gothic arches soaring above the
13th-century Upper Church ↑

EXPERIENCE MORE

② Gubbio

▲D3 ⚫Perugia 🚆**Fossato di Vico-Gubbio** 🚌 *i* **Via della Repubblica 15; 075 922 06 93**

Founded by the Umbrians in the 3rd century BC as Tota Ikuvina, Gubbio assumed greater prominence in the 1st century AD as a Roman colony (Eugubium). It emerged as an independent commune in the 11th century, having spread up the slopes of Monte Ingino. From 1387 to 1508 Gubbio was ruled from Urbino by the Dukes of Montefeltro.

The 13th-century Duomo is distinguished by a wagon-vaulted ceiling whose curved arches symbolize hands in prayer. Medieval Via dei Consoli leads to the 13th-century Palazzo del Bargello – a stone-faced building formerly the headquarters of the chief of police. Also here is the Fontana dei Matti (Fountain of the Mad), named after the tradition that anyone who walks around it three times will go insane.

In the lower town, the church of San Francesco (1259–82) is known for 17 faded frescoes showing scenes from the *Life of the Virgin* (1408–13) by Ottaviano Nelli.

Palazzo dei Consoli

⊗ ⚫**Piazza Grande** 📞**075 927 42 98** 🕙**10am–1pm & 3–6pm daily (Nov–Mar: 10am–1pm & 2:30–5:30pm)** 🚫**1 Jan, 13–15 May, 25 Dec**

Dominating Gubbio's skyline is this mighty civic palace, begun in 1332 by Gattapone. It houses the Museo Civico, best known for the Eugubine Tablets (250–150 BC). These seven bronze slabs are inscribed with Etruscan and Roman characters, probably a phonetic translation of prayers and rituals from the ancient Umbrian and Etruscan languages.

Palazzo Ducale

⊗ ⚫**Via Federico da Montefeltro** 📞**075 927 58 72** 🕙**8:30am–7:30pm Tue–Sun** 🚫**1 Jan, 25 Dec**

Attributed to Francesco di Giorgio Martini, this palace was built in 1470 for the Montefeltro as a copy of the family home in Urbino *(p418)*. It also has a pretty Renaissance courtyard.

---

③ Perugia

▲D4 🚆🚌**Piazza Vittorio Veneto** *i* **Piazza Matteotti 18; www.turismo.comune. perugia.it**

Perugia's old centre hinges around the pedestrianized Corso Vannucci, named after the local painter Pietro Vannucci (Perugino). At its northern end is Piazza IV Novembre, dominated by the Fontana Maggiore, a 13th-century fountain by Nicola and Giovanni Pisano. To the rear rises the 15th-century Duomo. Its Cappella del Santo Anello contains the Virgin's "wedding ring", a weighty piece of agate said to change colour according to the character of the person wearing it. The third pillar in the south nave holds a Renaissance painting of the *Madonna delle Grazie* by Gian Nicola di Paolo.

↑ The sun rising over the medieval town of Gubbio

Perugia's old centre, home to the medieval Palazzo dei Priori (inset)

The figure is credited with miraculous powers, and mothers bring newly baptized children and kneel before it.

Away from the Corso is the Oratorio di San Bernardino (1457–61) on Piazza San Francesco, with a colourful façade by Agostino di Duccio.

On Piazza Giordano Bruno is San Domenico (1304–1632), with decoration by Agostino di Duccio and the Gothic tomb of Benedict XI (c.1304).

Museo Archeologico Nazionale dell'Umbria

 San Domenico, Piazza Giordano Bruno 10 ☎ 075 572 71 41 ⏰ Daily ⌚ 1 Jan, 1 May, 25 Dec

Housed in the cloisters of San Domenico, this museum exhibits prehistoric, Etruscan and Roman artifacts.

HIDDEN GEM:
Perugina Chocolate Factory

Visit the Perugina Chocolate Museum and Factory (Viale San Sisto 207/C) and enjoy tastings or a chocolate-making course. Every October, chocoholics gather here for the Eurochocolate festival.

Palazzo dei Priori

Corso Vannucci 19 ☎ 075 573 64 58 ⏰ Daily (Sun: am only) ⌚ 1 Jan, 1 May, 25 Dec & 1st Mon of month

The monumental walls and bristling crenellations of this palace mark it as Umbria's finest public building. Among its fine rooms is the Sala dei Notari (c.1295), the former lawyers' hall, vividly frescoed with scenes from the Old Testament – the work of a follower of Pietro Cavallini. The doorway is guarded by a pair of large bronzes made in 1274: a Guelph lion and a griffin, the medieval emblem of Perugia. The Sala di Udienza del Collegio della Mercanzia, built around 1390, was formerly used by the Merchants' Guild. This room is late Gothic in style, with exquisite panelling and 15th-century inlaid wood.

Also in the palace is the Collegio del Cambio, Perugia's former money exchange, which was begun in 1452. Its walls are covered with superlative frescoes (1498–1500) by Perugino, works devoted to Classical and religious scenes. A glum self-portrait scowls down from the centre of the left wall, while the hand of Perugino's pupil Raphael may be evident in some panels on the right wall.

Galleria Nazionale dell'Umbria

Palazzo dei Priori, Corso Vannucci 19 ☎ 075 58 66 84 10 ⏰ Tue-Sun ⌚ 1 Jan, 1 May, 25 Dec

Most of the works in this fine collection are 13th- to 18th-century paintings by local artists, but the highlights are altarpieces by Piero della Francesca and Fra Angelico.

---

❹

Lake Trasimeno

D3 Perugia FS Castiglione del Lago Piazza Mazzini 10, Castiglione del Lago; www.umbriatourism.it

Edged with low hills, this is Italy's fourth-largest lake. The town of Castiglione del Lago has small sandy beaches and a 16th-century castle used for summer concerts. The church of Santa Maria Maddalena has a Madonna and Child (c.1500) by Eusebio di San Giorgio.

The town of Passignano sul Trasimeno offers boat trips to Isola Maggiore. The island's charming village is known for lace-making.

→

The Fontana dei Tre Leoni, in Assisi's main square

⑤

Assisi

🅐D4 🅰Perugia 🚉🚌
ℹ️Piazza del Comune 22;
www.visit-assisi.it

This medieval town, with its geranium-hung streets and fountain-splashed piazzas, is heir to the legacy of St Francis (c.1181–1226), who is buried in the Basilica di San Francesco (p404).

Piazza del Comune, Assisi's main square, is dominated by the columns of the Tempio di Minerva, a Roman temple front from the Augustan age. The Palazzo Comunale, opposite, is home to the Pinacoteca Comunale, an art gallery with works by local medieval artists. Also on the square, the Fontana dei Tre Leoni incorporates three lion statues representing the three city districts.

Down Corso Mazzini lies the Basilica di Santa Chiara, the burial place of St Clare – Francis's companion and the founder of the Poor Clares (an order of nuns). One of its chapels contains the crucifix that is said to have bowed its head and ordered Francis to "repair God's church". The crucifix originally came from San Damiano, a sublime church set amid olive groves south of Porta Nuova.

The Abbazia di San Pietro, on Piazza San Pietro, has a Romanesque façade and 13th-century frescoes in the chapel on the left. The nearby Oratorio dei Pellegrini, a 15th-century pilgrims' hospice, contains well-preserved frescoes by Matteo da Gualdo.

Assisi's Duomo (San Rufino) dates from the 12th and 13th centuries and has a superb Romanesque façade. Inside, archaeological items are displayed in the attractive crypt, and there is a small museum of paintings. You can also see the font where St Clare and St Francis were baptized. From the Duomo, head up to Rocca Maggiore, an imposing castle with wide-reaching views across the Umbrian countryside.

At the foot of the town, near the station, the 16th-century church of Santa Maria degli Angeli was built around the Porziuncola, a tiny frescoed chapel where both St Francis and St Clare founded their religious orders. The church grounds also include a rose garden and the Cappella del Transito, the infirmary where St Francis died.

About 4 km (2 miles) out of Assisi, towards Monte Subasio, is the Eremo delle Carceri, a stone-built monastery surrounded by peaceful woodland. Here you can see the grottoes where St Francis and his companions used to withdraw to contemplate.

⑥

Spello

🅐D4 🅰Perugia 🚉🚌
ℹ️Piazza Matteotti 3;
0742 30 10 09

Spello is one of the better-known villages in the Vale of Spoleto. Although not badly damaged in the 2016 earth-quake, some sites may remain closed in 2019 to rule out structural damage. Spello is renowned for a fresco cycle by Pinturicchio in the Cappella Baglioni of the church of Santa Maria Maggiore (12th–13th century), on Via Consolare. Painted around 1500, the frescoes depict scenes from the New Testament. Towards the centre of the village is the Gothic church of Sant'Andrea (13th century), on Via Cavour. This road becomes Via Garibaldi, which leads to San Lorenzo, a Baroque gem of a church dating from the 12th century.

Spello also boasts Roman ruins from the age of Augustus, including the Porta Consolare at the end of Via Consolare, and the twin-towered Porta Venere by Via Torri di Properzio.

The road to Assisi over Monte Subasio offers stunning views from the top of the mountain above Spello.

> The 16th-century church of Santa Maria degli Angeli was built around the Porziuncola, a tiny frescoed chapel where both St Francis and St Clare founded their religious orders.

Like Spello, the nearby village of Bevagna sprang to life as a way station on the Via Flaminia (the Roman road that ran through this part of Umbria). The medieval Piazza Silvestri is the setting for two Romanesque churches. San Silvestro (1195) is the more atmospheric of the pair, thanks to its ancient crypt, but San Michele (late 12th century) has an elegant portal, famed for the little gargoyles on either side. Both churches are the work of Maestro Binello.

Montefalco

A D4 **↑ Perugia** **🚌** **🛈 Via Ringhiera Umbra 25; 0742 37 92 43**

Montefalco, whose name (Falcon's Mount) draws inspiration from its lofty position and sweeping views, is the best of the villages in the Vale of Spoleto. You might happily spend a morning here, most of it in the polished **Museo Civico di San Francesco** housed in the former church of San Francesco. Its highlight is Benozzo Gozzoli's *Life of St Francis* (1452), a radiant fresco cycle that borrows heavily from Giotto's cycle in Assisi (*p404*). Other painters represented here are Perugino, Tiberio d'Assisi and Niccolò Alunno, all leading medieval Umbrian artists.

Just outside the town walls, the church of Sant'Illuminata is covered with frescoes by the local 16th-century artist Francesco Melanzio. About 2 km (1 mile) beyond, the prettily situated church of San Fortunato is decorated with frescoes by Gozzoli and Tiberio d'Assisi.

The village with the most spectacular setting in the Vale of Spoleto is Trevi. The churches of San Martino (16th century), on Passeggiata di San Martino, and Madonna delle Lacrime (1487–1522), south of Trevi on the road into the village, contain paintings by Perugino and Tiberio d'Assisi, among others.

Museo Civico di San Francesco

 ↑ Via Ringhiera Umbra 6 **☎ 0742 37 95 98** **⏰ Mar–Oct: daily; Nov–Feb: Tue–Sun** **📅 1 Jan, 25 Dec**

Cascata delle Marmore

A D4 **↑ Terni; Voc Cascata 30 (Belvedere Superiore) & Piazzale F Fatati 6 (Belvedere Inferiore)** **🌐 marmorefalls.it**

Created by the Romans during works to link the Nera and Velino rivers in 271 BC, this spectacular 165-m- (540-ft-) high waterfall

STAY

Etruscan Chochotel
A contemporary, chocolate-themed hotel with a rooftop pool.

A D4 **↑ Via Campo di Marte 134, Perugia** **🌐 chocohotel.it**

€€€

Nun Assisi Relais
Set in a former convent, this spa-hotel has a mixture of ancient and contemporary features.

A D4 **↑ Via Eremo delle Carceri 1a, Assisi** **🌐 nunassisi.com**

€€€

Hotel La Badia
In a 12th-century abbey, this hotel offers a pool and tennis courts.

A D4 **↑ Località La Badia 8, Orvieto** **🌐 hotellabadia.it**

€€€

is located near the town of Terni. Its powerful flow is diverted for hydroelectric power for much of the time, so you can only view it during certain periods (check online). The park has two main viewpoints, with a shuttle bus running between them. At the Belvedere Superiore, the Specola viewing tower, built in 1781 by Pope Pius VI, is the ideal spot to witness the falls' rainbow phenomenon. There's also a series of footpaths between the viewpoints and through woodland.

←

The Romanesque façade of Spello's San Michele church, designed by Maestro Binello

9

Orvieto

A D4 **B** Terni **C D**
i Piazza Duomo 24;
www.inorvieto.it

Set on a huge slab of tufa, Orvieto was colonized nine centuries before Christ and flourished in the Etruscan period as Velzna. After the Romans destroyed it in 264 BC, the town didn't revive until the medieval period, when it became the residence of the popes. Etruscan finds and medieval art make Orvieto a compelling place to visit.

Duomo

A Piazza Duomo **C** 0763
34 11 67 **D** Daily

Some 300 years in the building, Orvieto's Duomo (begun 1290), with its breathtaking façade, is one of Italy's greatest cathedrals. It was inspired by the Miracle of Bolsena in which real blood from a consecrated host supposedly fell on the altar cloth of a church in nearby Bolsena.

Museo dell'Opera del Duomo & Museo d'Arte Moderna "Emilio Greco"

A Piazza Duomo
C 0763 34 35 92 **D** Apr-Sep:
9:30am-7pm daily; Nov-
Feb: 10am-1pm & 2-5pm
Wed-Mon; Mar & Oct: 10am-
5pm Wed-Mon **W** opsm.it

The Museo dell'Opera del Duomo is an interesting little museum containing an

INSIDER TIP
Orvieto Underground

Book yourself onto a fascinating tour through the numerous caves and chambers carved into the rock below Orvieto since Etruscan times. Tours leave from Piazza Duomo 23 *(www. orvietounderground.it).*

↑ Strikingly ornate decoration inside the Duomo of Orvieto

eclectic collection of treasures given to the Duomo. Among the highlights are paintings by Lorenzo Maitani (died 1330) and sculptures by Andrea Pisano (c.1270–1348).

The "Emilio Greco" museum is devoted to the modern Sicilian sculptor Emilio Greco, who is responsible for the bronze doors (1964–70) of the Duomo in Orvieto.

Museo Archeologico Faina & Museo Civico

A Piazza Duomo 29
C 0763 34 10 39 **D** 8:30am-
7:30pm daily **D** 1 Jan, 1 May,
25 Dec

The first of these two museums has a well-known, low-key collection of Etruscan remains, including a large number of Greek vases that were found in Etruscan tombs in the surrounding area. The Museo Civico contains ancient Greek artifacts and Etruscan copies of Greek works.

Pozzo di San Patrizio

A Viale San Gallo
C 0763 34 37 68 **D** Daily

This well was commissioned in 1527 by Pope Clement VII and designed by the Florentine architect Antonio da Sangallo to provide the town with a water supply in case of attack. Two 248-step staircases drop into its dank interior, cleverly arranged as a double helix

(spiral) so as not to intersect. The 62 m (203 ft) shaft took ten years to complete.

Necropoli Etrusca - Crocifisso del Tufo

A Strada Statale 71 to
Orvieto Scalo, km 1,600
C 0763 34 36 11 **D** 10am-
5pm (Apr-Sep: to 7pm) daily
D 1 Jan, 1 May, 25 Dec

This Etruscan necropolis has burial chambers built of blocks of tufa. Etruscan letters, thought to be the names of the deceased, are inscribed on the tombs.

San Lorenzo de' Arari

A Via Scalza **C** 0763 34 17 72

The walls of this tiny 14th-century church feature frescoes describing the martyrdom of St Lawrence. The altar is made from an Etruscan sacrificial slab.

Sant'Andrea

A Piazza della Repubblica
C 0347 809 43 97

This church is distinguished by a curious 12-sided campanile, part of the original 12th-century building.

10

Todi

A D4 **O** Perugia **FS** 🚌
i Via del Monte 23; 075
895 65 29

An ancient Etruscan, and then Roman, settlement, the hill-town of Todi still preserves a picturesque medieval centre.

The main square, Piazza del Popolo, is flanked by the lovely plain-faced Duomo. Built in the 13th century on the site of a Roman temple to Apollo, it has a dusky interior and one of Umbria's finest choirs (1521–30). Note the altarpiece at the end of the right aisle by Giannicola di Paolo (a follower of Perugino).

Also flanking the piazza are the Palazzo dei Priori (1293–1337) and the linked Palazzo del Capitano (1290) and Palazzo del Popolo (1213). Inside the Palazzo del Capitano, distinguished by its redoubtable medieval interior, lies the **Museo Etrusco-Romano**, with a collection of local Etruscan and Roman artifacts. There are altarpieces

and sacred objects in the **Pinacoteca Comunale**, also housed in the palace.

A few steps from the piazza rises San Fortunato (1292–1462), named after Todi's first bishop, with a florid Gothic doorway (1415–58). The choir (1590) is superb, but the church's most famous work is *Madonna and Child* (1432) by Masolino da Panicale (fourth chapel on the right). The crypt contains the tomb of Jacopone da Todi (c.1228–1306), a noted medieval poet and mystic.

To the right of the church are some shady gardens, from which a path (past the tiny castle) drops through the trees to emerge just in front of Santa Maria della Consolazione (1508–1607), near the N79. One of central Italy's finest Renaissance churches, and based on a Greek cross, it may have been built to a plan by Bramante.

**Museo Etrusco-Romano
and Pinacoteca Comunale**
♿ **O** Piazza del Popolo 29/30
☎ 075 894 41 48 ◷ 10:30am-
1pm & 2:30-5pm Tue-Sun

TOP 3 MONTEFALCO SAGRANTINO WINERIES

Scacciadiavoli
A D4 **O** Località Cantinone 31, Montefalco **W** cantina scacciadiavoli.it
Visit to see how Sagrantino and other local wines are made. Founded in 1884, this is one of Montefalco's oldest wineries.

Tenuta Bellafonte
A D4 **O** Via Colle Nottolo 2, Bevagna **W** tenuta bellafonte.it
As well as tours of the winery, accommodation is on offer here.

Lungarotti
A D4 **O** Viale Lungarotti 2, Torgiano **W** lungarotti.it
The main cellar of this winery is at Torgiano, along with fascinating wine and olive oil museums.

↑ The town of Todi, dominated by the church of San Fortunato

→ Approach to Spoleto's Duomo

⑪ Spoleto

🅐D4 🅐Perugia 🅵🅂 🚌
🛈 Piazza della Libertà 7; www.spoletocard.it

Within its wooded setting, Spoleto is the loveliest of the Umbrian hill-towns. Founded by the Umbrians, it was one of central Italy's main Roman colonies, a prominence maintained by the Lombards, who in the 7th century made it the capital of one of their three Italian dukedoms. After a spell as an independent city state, in 1354 Spoleto fell to the papacy.

The church of San Pietro was founded in 419 AD and built on an ancient necropolis. Its façade is covered in Romanesque relief sculptures, considered some of the finest examples in Umbria. From here, head north towards the town centre on Viale Giacomo Matteotti and Via San Carlo.

At the southern end of Piazza del Mercato is the Arco di Druso, a 1st-century-AD Roman arch. Via Aurelio Saffi, at the piazza's northern end, leads to Romanesque church Sant'Eufemia.

A short way beyond, the fan-shaped Piazza del Duomo opens out to reveal Spoleto's 12th-century Duomo, graced with an elegant Romanesque façade. Filling the apse of the Baroque interior is a great fresco cycle. The final work of Fra Lippo Lippi, from 1467–9, it describes episodes from the *Life of the Virgin*. The Cappella Erioli is adorned with Pinturicchio's unfinished *Madonna and Child* (1497).

The best of the exceptional churches in the lower town is 4th-century San Salvatore, located in the main cemetery. Nearby stands San Ponziano, fronted by a captivating three-tiered Romanesque façade. Its crypt is decorated with Byzantine frescoes.

ROMANESQUE CHURCHES IN UMBRIA

Umbria's church-building tradition had its roots in ancient Roman basilicas. The region's Romanesque façades are usually divided into three tiers, often with three rose windows arranged above a trio of arched portals. The three doors usually correspond to the interior's nave and two aisles, which derive from the simple barn-like plan of Roman basilicas. Inside, the presbytery is often raised in order to allow for the building of a crypt, which usually contained the relics of a saint or martyr. Many of the churches took centuries to build, or were repeatedly modified over time, often acquiring elements of Gothic, Baroque or Renaissance styles.

1 Spoleto's Duomo (1198) has eight rose windows, a mosaic (1207) and a Renaissance portico (1491).

2 The Duomo (1253) in Assisi is a fine example of a three-tiered façade (p408). It also has a pointed arch.

3 Todi's Duomo was begun in the 13th century, but construction work continued until the 17th century (p411).

San Gregorio
🏠 Piazza Giuseppe Garibaldi, 34 **📞 0743 441 40**

This church dates from 1069, but its façade and campanile incorporate fragments of Roman buildings. Inside is a raised presbytery and a lovely multi-columned crypt. Some 10,000 Christian martyrs are supposedly buried near the church. They were reputedly slaughtered in the town's Roman amphitheatre, traces of which can be seen in the barracks on Via del Anfiteatro.

Ponte delle Torri
🏠 Via Giro del Ponte

This magnificent 14th-century aqueduct, the "bridge of towers", is 80 m (262 ft) high. Designed by Gattapone (from Gubbio), it is the town's most famous monument. From the bridge, there are views of the bastions of the Rocca Albornoz, a huge papal fortress built in 1359–64, also by Gattapone.

Museo del Tessile e del Costume
🚾 🏠 Via delle Terme
📞 0743 459 40 **🕐 3:30-7pm Sat & Sun** **🚫 1 Jan, 25 Dec**

Among the exhibits in this exquisite collection are sacred vestments and a series of 17th-century tapestries that once belonged to Queen Christina of Sweden.

🔟2️⃣ Monti Sibillini

🗺️ D4 **🏠 Macerata** **🚉 Spoleto**
🚌 Visso **ℹ️ Piscina Comunale, Visso; www.sibillini.net**

The national park of the Monti Sibillini in eastern Umbria provides the region's wildest and most spectacular scenery. A range 40 km (25 miles) long, the mountains form part of the Apennines, a chain that runs the length of the Italian peninsula. Monte Vettore is the loftiest point, and the peninsula's third highest; it stands at 2,476 m (8,123 ft), a great whale-backed peak close to the cave of the mythical sibyl that gave the region its name.

Good maps and trails make this a superb walking area, while drivers can follow hairpin roads to some of Italy's most spectacular landscapes. Chief of these is the Piano Grande, a huge upland plain surrounded by a vast amphitheatre of mountains. Bare but for flocks of sheep and bedraggled haystacks, the plain blazes with wild flowers in spring and lentils grow later in the year. The only habitation was Castelluccio, a beautiful, neglected mountain village that was sadly nearly destroyed by the November 2016 earthquake.

SPOLETO FESTIVAL

Each year, Spoleto becomes one big stage for 17 days between late June and mid-July during the Spoleto Festival, held since 1958. Operas, concerts, plays, dance shows, talks and visual art displays are held at venues throughout this medieval town.

🔟3️⃣ Valnerina

🗺️ D4 **🏠 Perugia**
🚉 Spoleto, then bus
ℹ️ Piazza Aldo Moro 3, Cascia; 0743 711 47

The Valnerina (Valley of the River Nera) curves through a broad swathe of eastern Umbria before emptying into the Tiber. It is edged with craggy, tree-covered slopes and dotted with upland villages and fortified hamlets.

The star attraction is **San Pietro in Valle**, an 8th-century monastery. Its nave walls are covered in 12th-century frescoes. Some of the best Romanesque carvings in Umbria can be found here.

San Pietro in Valle
🏠 Località Ferentillo, Terni
📞 0744 78 01 29 **🕐 Daily (Sat & Sun in winter)**

1   2   3

LE MARCHE

Tucked away in a remote corner between the Adriatic Sea and the Apennine mountains, Le Marche (the Marches) is an enchanting rural patchwork of old towns, hill country and long, sandy beaches. In pre-Christian times the area was settled by the Piceni, a tribe eventually assimilated by the Romans. In the 4th century BC, exiles from Magna Graecia colonized much of the region. The most notable town was Ancona, also the northernmost point of Greek influence on the Italian peninsula. During the early Middle Ages the region marked the edge of the Holy Roman Empire, giving rise to its present name (march meant "border area").

The region's historical peak was reached in the 15th century under Federico da Montefeltro, whose court at Urbino became one of Europe's leading cultural centres. Much of Urbino's former grandeur survives, particularly in Federico's magnificent Renaissance Palazzo Ducale, now home to a regional art collection. Ascoli Piceno is almost as enchanting as Urbino, its central Piazza del Popolo among the most evocative old squares in Italy. Smaller towns like San Leo and Urbania and the republic of San Marino also boast fine medieval monuments.

Today, probably as many people come to Le Marche for its beaches and towns as for its hilly, unspoiled interior. Especially beautiful are the snow-capped peaks of the Monti Sibillini, situated in magnificent walking and skiing country.

Regional cuisine encompasses the truffles and robust cheeses of the mountains, tender hams and salamis, olive *ascolane* (olives stuffed with meat and herbs) and *brodetto*, fish soup made in several versions up and down the coast. Dry, white Verdicchio is the best-known wine, although more unusual names, such as Bianchello del Metauro, are gaining in popularity.

LE MARCHE

Must See

1 Urbino

Experience More

2 San Marino
3 Pèsaro
4 Fano
5 Macerata
6 Urbania
7 Grotte di Frasassi
8 Senigallia
9 Ancona
10 Conero Peninsula
11 Loreto
12 Ascoli Piceno

The 15th-century Palazzo Ducale above the town of Urbino

❶ URBINO

🅐 D3 🚌 ℹ️ Via Puccinotti; www.turismo.marche.it

Central Urbino is a wonderful tangle of steeply sloping medieval and Renaissance streets, dominated by the stunning Palazzo Ducale with its fairytale twin-towered façade. Italy's most beautiful Renaissance palace, it was built for Duke Federico da Montefeltro, ruler of Urbino (1444–82) and became a major centre for Renaissance development. The city was also home to one of history's most remarkable artists, Raphael.

①

Palazzo Ducale and Galleria Nazionale

🅐 Piazza Duca Federico 13
🕐 8:30am-2pm Mon,
8:30am-7:15pm Tue-Sun;
last adm: 75 mins before
closing 🚫 1 Jan, 25 Dec
🌐 palazzoducale urbino.it

Duke Federico da Montefeltro was a soldier but also a patron of the arts, and his palace – with its library, paintings and refined architecture – is a tribute to courtly life and to the artistic and intellectual ideals of the Renaissance. Architect Luciano Laurana was responsible for much of the design – including the courtyard – but it was Francesco di Giorgio Martini who completed the work with some additions, including a remarkably complex plumbing system.

Did You Know?

After losing an eye while jousting, Federico da Montefeltro had the bridge of his nose removed to increase his vision.

The palazzo houses the Galleria Nazionale delle Marche, which has numerous masterpieces. The gallery's most famous works are Piero della Francesca's enigmatic *The Flagellation* (c.1460), often cited as the world's greatest small painting; *The Ideal City*, a perspective study attributed to Piero or his students; and the gorgeous portrait *La Muta* (1507) by Raphael.

②
Casa Natale di Raffaello

🅐 Via di Raffaello 57
📞 0722 32 01 05 🕐 Mar-Oct:
9am-1pm & 3-7pm Mon-Sat; Nov-Feb: 9am-2pm Mon-Sat, 10am-1pm Sun
🚫 1 Jan, 25 Dec

Urbino's famous son, the painter Raphael (1483–1520), was born in the Casa Natale di Raffaello and received his early training here under his father, the artist Giovanni Santi. The house retains an evocative historic atmosphere. The stone on which father and son mixed their pigments is on display, alongside a sweet *Madonna and Child* by Raphael.

PIADINA

Central Italy's most loved speciality is this simple and delicious flatbread. Cold cuts of cured ham, rocket and soft cheese, particularly the tangy local kind called Squacquerone, make an ideal accompaniment to the bread. Try *piadina* and other local specialities at Piadineria L'Aquilone (*Via Cesare Battisti 23*).

③
Duomo and Museo Diocesano

🅰 Piazza Pascoli 1 🄲 0722 48 18 🕒 9:30am-1.30pm & 2-6pm daily

The Neo-Classical Duomo, on Piazza Federico, was founded in 1062, but mostly built in 1789. Of interest here is the painting of *The Last Supper* by Federico Barocci (c.1535–1612). The Museo Diocesano contains a fine collection of ceramics, glass and religious artifacts ranging from the 13th century to the present.

④
Oratorio di San Giovanni Battista

🅰 Via Federico Barocci 31 🄲 0722 91 02 59 🕒 10am-1pm & 3-6pm Mon-Sat, 10am-12:30pm Sun

The 14th-century Oratorio di San Giovanni Battista has some minutely detailed frescoes from 1416 of the *Crucifixion* and the *Life of St John the Baptist* by Giacomo and Lorenzo Salimbeni.

⑤
Fortezza dell'Albornoz

🅰 Parco della Resistenza

There are magnificent views over the rooftops of Urbino and beyond from this 15th-century fortress, which is the defensive focus of the town's surviving 16th-century walls and bastions. The views are also excellent from the surrounding public park, located just a short walk above the town on Viale Bruon Buozzi.

EAT

Il Cortegiano
Located close to the Palazzo Ducale, this restaurant provides quick snacks or proper dining in a courtyard.

🅰 Via Pucinotti 13 🄲 0722 373 07 🚫 Sun

⑤⑤⑤

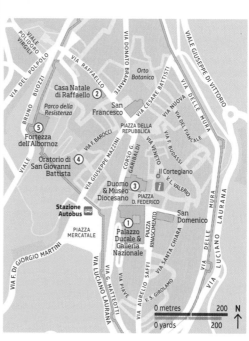

EXPERIENCE MORE

❷
San Marino

 D3 🚌 San Marino Città (from Rimini) 🛈 Contrada Omagnano; www.visit sanmarino.com

Europe's oldest republic, San Marino was reputedly founded by St Marinus, a 4th-century monk. On the slopes of Monte Titano, this tiny country has its own Mint, stamps, football team – even its own army.

There are no customs formalities in San Marino, whose borders are just 12 km (7 miles) apart at the widest point. The town of Borgomaggiore, at the foot of Monte Titano, has a cable car to the medieval citadel of San Marino, which is now sadly overrun with visitors and souvenir stalls.

❸
Pèsaro

 D3 FS 🚌 🛈 Viale Trieste 164; 0721 693 41

One of the Adriatic's larger seaside resorts, Pèsaro has

managed to retain a stylish air. Behind the promenade and the wall of white stucco hotels is a lively, attractive medieval area.

The **Musei Civici** contains Giovanni Bellini's sumptuous *Coronation of the Virgin* (c.1470) polyptych and a collection of Renaissance ceramics.

The **Museo Archeologico Oliveriano** presents a range of historical artifacts, including Roman remains and Iron Age finds from the necropolis of nearby Novilara.

The church of Sant'Agostino, on Corso XI Settembre, is known for its choir stalls, each a patchwork of inlaid landscapes and narrative scenes.

The composer Gioacchino Rossini was born in Pèsaro in 1792. His home, **Casa Rossini**, contains memorabilia, while his piano and some original manuscripts lie in the **Conservatorio Rossini**. His operas are performed in Teatro Rossini during the annual August music festival.

Gradara, about 13 km (8 miles) from Pesaro, is a well-preserved hilltop village dominated by a majestic 14th-century castle, the

Rocca, which was the scene of the tragic love story of Paolo and Francesca, mentioned by Dante in his *Divine Comedy*.

Musei Civici
⌀ 🏠 Piazza Mosca 29 📞 0721 38 75 41 & 199 152 123 🕐 Tue-Sun 🚫 1 Jan, 25 Dec

Museo Archeologico Oliveriano
🏠 Via Mazza 97 📞 0721 333 44 🕐 Mon-Sat

Casa Rossini
⌀ 🏠 Via Rossini 34 📞 0721 38 75 41 🕐 Tue-Sun

Conservatorio Rossini
🏠 Piazza Olivieri 5 📞 0721 336 71 🕐 Mon-Fri, but phone first to arrange 🚫 Public hols

---

Did You Know?

At 60 sq km (23 sq miles), San Marino is the world's smallest republic.

← Dusk falling over San Marino citadel

4
Fano

D3 **Pèsaro** 🚆🚌🚍
Via Cesare Battisti 10; 0721 88 73 14

Named after Fanum Fortunae, a pagan temple to the goddess Fortuna, Fano became the terminus of the Via Flaminia (an important consular road from Rome) and the largest Roman colony on the Adriatic coast. The Arco d'Augusto (AD 2), on Via Arco d'Augusto, is Fano's most significant ancient monument. In 1463 Federico da Montefeltro destroyed its upper section while besieging the town as a papal *condottiere*.

The 16th-century Fontana della Fortuna, in Piazza XX Settembre, is dedicated to the goddess Fortuna. Also on the square, the imposing Palazzo Malatesta was built around 1420 and enlarged in 1544 for Fano's rulers, the Rimini-based Malatesta family. Inside is the small **Museo Civico** and the **Pinacoteca Malatestiana**, with works by Guercino and Guido Reni.

Museo Civico and Pinacoteca Malatestiana
 Piazza XX Settembre
📞0721 88 78 44 🕒Tue-Sun
🗓1 Jan, 25 & 26 Dec

5
Macerata

D3 **Corso della Repubblica 32; 9am-1pm & 3-6pm Mon-Fri (am only Sat); www.turismo.provinciamc.it**

The elegant walled town of Macerata is best known for its Sferisterio, an open-air arena that hosts concerts and an annual opera festival.

Palazzo Buonaccorsi houses a museum of carriages and collections of modern and ancient art, including a *Madonna and Child* by Carlo Crivelli (1470). The **Basilica della Misericordia**, built by Luigi Vanvitelli (1736–41), is set over a votive chapel erected in 1447 to celebrate the end of the plague. It has a richly decorated interior.

Palazzo Buonaccorsi
🖼 Via Don Minzoni 24
🕒10am-6pm daily (Jul-Aug: to 7pm) 🌐maceratamusei.it

Basilica della Misericordia
🖼 Piazza San Vincenzo Strambi 🕒7:30am-12:30pm & 3-6pm daily 🌐basilica misericordia.it

6
Urbania

D3 **Pèsaro** 🚌 **Corso Vittorio Emanuele 21; 0722 31 31 40**

Urbania, with its elegant arcaded centre, takes its name from Pope Urban VIII (1623–44), who entertained the notion of converting an old medieval village into a model Renaissance town.

Its chief attraction is the huge **Palazzo Ducale**, built by the dukes of Montefeltro as a residential alternative to the Palazzo Ducale in nearby Urbino. It was begun in the 13th century, and then rebuilt in the 15th and 16th centuries. Situated alongside the River Metauro, it houses a small

STAY

La Grotta
Cosy, contemporary rooms and a great position in San Marino's historic centre.

D3 **Contrada Santa Croce, San Marino** 🌐lagrottahotel sanmarino.com

€€€

Palazzo Guiderocchi
Stay in a prestigious 16th-century palazzo with original frescoes.

E4 **Via Cesare Battisti 3, Ascoli Piceno** 🌐hotelguiderocchi.it

€€€

art gallery, a modest museum, old maps and globes, and the remnants of Duke Federico's famous library.

Palazzo Ducale
 📞0722 31 31 51
🕒Tue-Sun 🗓Public hols

7
Grotte di Frasassi

D3 **Ancona** 🚆**Genga San Vittore Terme** 🕒**Daily** 🗓**1 Jan & 10-30 Jan, 4 & 25 Dec** 🌐**frasassi.com**

Some of Europe's largest publicly accessible caverns lie in the cave network gouged out by the River Sentino southwest of Jesi. The colossal Grotta del Vento is large enough to contain Milan cathedral – its ceiling extends to a height of 240 m (787 ft). This cavern has been used for a range of experiments, from sensory deprivation to an exploration of the social consequences of leaving a group of people alone in its depths for long periods.

HILL-TOWNS IN LE MARCHE

Charming medieval towns and villages - many of them walled and incorporating castles - dot the hillsides of Le Marche. Sarnano, for one, is a medley of narrow lanes, steps and archways arranged in concentric circles; from the nearby ski area in the Monti Sibillini, you can see the coast on a clear day. A 14th-century castle with stunning views dominates Acquaviva Picena. Offida, famous both for lace and winemaking, is surrounded by vine-covered hills. Just inland from Senigallia, Corinaldo is centred on the striking Piaggia, a flight of 109 steps with a well halfway up, and has particularly well-preserved walls.

← The fortress at Acquaviva Picena

8
Senigallia

🅰D3 🅰Ancona 🚉
𝑖 Via Manni 7; 9am-1pm Mon-Sat (summer: also pm); www.feelsenigallia.it

Famous for its sandy beach, Senigallia also has some fascinating sights. On pedestrianized Piazza del Duca are the imposing **Rocca Roveresca**, a 14th- and 15th-century castle, and **Palazzetto Baviera**, featuring some remarkable stucco decoration by Federico Brandani (16th century). Nearby, the Baroque **Chiesa della Croce** (1608) has a richly decorated interior, including an altarpiece with the *Entombment of Christ* by Federico Barocci (1592). The elegant Foro Annonario is a circular colonnaded piazza and marketplace.

Rocca Roveresca
⊛ ⊛ 🅰Piazza del Duca 2 📞 071 63 258 🕐8:30am-7:30pm

Palazzetto Baviera
⊛ 🅰Via Manni 1 📞071 63 258 🕐10am-1pm & 3-7pm

Chiesa della Croce
🅰Via Fagnani 1 🕐11am-noon Mon-Sat, 4-5pm Sun

9
Ancona

🅰D3 🚇🚉🚌🚢𝑖 Banchina Nazario Sauro 50; www. turismo.marche.it

The capital of Le Marche and its largest port, Ancona dates back to at least the 5th century BC, when it was settled by the Greeks. Its name derives from *ankon* (Greek for "elbow"), a reference to the rocky spur that juts into the sea to form the town's fine natural harbour.

Heavy bombing during World War II destroyed much of the medieval town, but the 15th-century Loggia dei Mercanti (Merchants' Exchange) on Via della Loggia survives.

Just north of the loggia is the **Pinacoteca Comunale F Podesti e Galleria d'Arte Moderna**, with canvases by Titian and Lorenzo Lotto. In the **Museo Archeologico Nazionale delle Marche** there are displays of Greek, Gallic and Roman art. The Arco di Traiano, by the harbour, was erected in AD 115 and is one of Italy's better-preserved Roman arches.

Pinacoteca Comunale F Podesti e Galleria d'Arte Moderna
⊛ 🅰Via Pizzecolli 17 📞071 222 50 41 🕐Tue-Sun 🔒Public hols

Museo Archeologico Nazionale delle Marche
⊛ 🅰Via Ferretti 1 📞071 20 26 02 🕐Tue-Sun 🔒1 Jan, 1 May, 15 Aug, 25 Dec

10
Conero Peninsula

🅰D3 🅰Ancona 🚉 🚌Ancona 🚌From Ancona to Sirolo or Numana 𝑖 Via Peschiera 30a, Sirolo; www.parcodelconero.org

Easily accessible from Ancona to the north, the beautiful cliff-edged Conero Peninsula is a semi-wild area known for

its scenery, its wines (notably Rosso del Conero) and for a collection of coves, beaches and little resorts.

The best of these resorts is Portonovo, above whose beach stands Santa Maria di Portonovo, a pretty 11th-century Romanesque church mentioned by Dante in Canto XXI of *Paradiso*. Sirolo and Numana are busier, but you can escape the crowds by hiking the flower-swathed slopes of Monte Conero, or by taking a boat trip to the smaller beaches.

Loreto

🅐D3 🏠Ancona 🚇🚌
🛈 Corso Boccalini 2; 071 97 77 48

Legend has it that in 1294 the house of the Virgin Mary (Santa Casa) miraculously uprooted itself from the Holy Land and was brought by angels to a laurel grove (*loreto*) south of Ancona.

Each year millions of pilgrims visit the **Santa Casa** in Loreto and its **Basilica**. Begun in 1468, the latter was designed by architects Bramante, Sansovino and Giuliano da Sangallo. Its paintings include works by Luca Signorelli. The **Museo-Pinacoteca** has 16th-century art by Lorenzo Lotto.

Basilica and Santa Casa
🏠Piazza Santuario 📞071 97 01 04 🕐Daily

Museo-Pinacoteca
🅰 🏠Palazzo Apostolico
📞071 974 71 98 🕐Apr-Oct: Tue-Sun; Nov-Mar: Fri-Sun

Ascoli Piceno

🅐D4 🚌 🛈Palazzo Comunale, Piazza Arringo; 0736 25 30 45

This alluring town takes its name from the Piceni, a tribe eventually conquered by the Romans in 89 BC. The gridiron plan of Roman Asculum Picenum is visible in the streets today, but it is the town's medieval heritage that attracts most visitors.

The enchanting Piazza del Popolo is dominated by the 13th-century Palazzo dei Capitani del Popolo and the church of San Francesco, a large and faintly austere Gothic ensemble built between 1262 and 1549.

Around Piazza dell'Arringo is the 12th-century Duomo. Its Cappella del Sacramento contains a polyptych by the 15th-century artist Carlo Crivelli. The **Pinacoteca Civica** has more works by Crivelli and by Guido Reni, Titian and Alemanno. The **Museo Archeologico** contains Roman, Piceni and Lombard artifacts.

Pinacoteca Civica
🅰 🏠Palazzo Comunale, Piazza Arringo 📞0736 29 82 13 🕐Tue-Sun

Museo Archeologico
🅰 🏠Piazza Arringo 28
📞0736 25 35 62 🕐Tue-Sun
🚫1 Jan, 1 May, 25 Dec

↑ Dramatic coastline around the Conero Peninsula

EMILIA-ROMAGNA

The heartland of central Italy, Emilia-Romagna has many attractive towns: the lively regional capital, Bologna, with its arcaded streets and delicious pasta; Ferrara, with its fantastic fortress; Palma, famed for its tasty cheese and ham; Ravenna, gleaming with Byzantine mosaics; and Rimini with its long sandy beaches.

Most of the major towns in Emilia-Romagna lie near the Via Aemilia, a Roman road built in 187 BC, which linked Rimini on the Adriatic coast with the garrison town of Piacenza. Prior to the Romans, the Etruscans ruled from their capital, Felsina, located on the site of present-day Bologna. After the fall of Rome, the region's focus moved to Ravenna, which became a principal part of the Byzantine Empire.

During the Middle Ages pilgrims heading for Rome continued to use the Via Aemilia. Political power, however, passed to influential noble families. Great courts grew up around them, attracting poets such as Dante and Ariosto, as well as painters, sculptors and architects.

Cobbled together from separate Papal States in 1860, modern Emilia-Romagna was given its present borders in 1947. Emilia, the western part of the region, is traditionally associated with a more northern outlook and a tendency towards the left in politics. Romagna, on the other hand, has witnessed an increase in the support for right-wing parties calling for political independence from Rome.

With its rich agricultural land, historic cities and thriving industry, Emilia-Romagna is now one of the most prosperous areas in Italy. The entire region has a reputation as a great gastronomic centre.

EMILIA-ROMAGNA

Must Sees
1. Bologna
2. Ravenna

Experience More
3. Castell'Arquato
4. Modena
5. Parma
6. Ferrara
7. Po Delta
8. Rimini
9. Cesenatico
10. San Leo

LOMBARDY AND
THE LAKES
p162

LIGURIA
p200

TUSCANY
p366

0 kilometres 25

0 miles 25

N

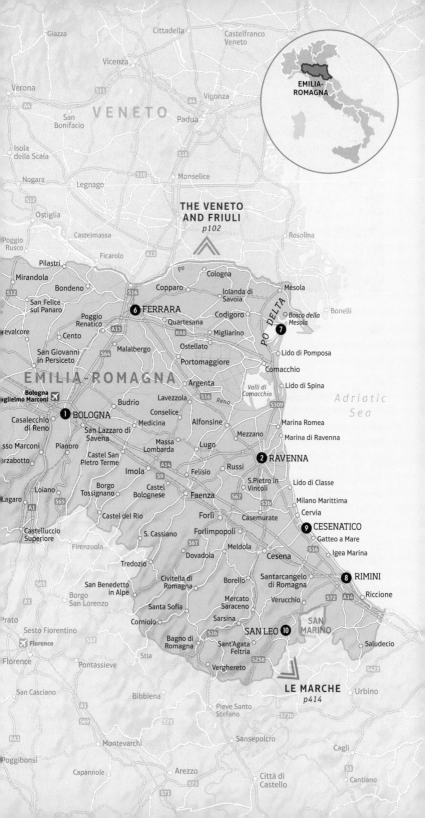

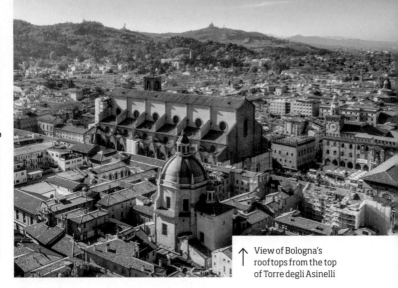

↑ View of Bologna's rooftops from the top of Torre degli Asinelli

①

BOLOGNA

🅰C2 ✈Marconi 9 km (5 miles) NW 🚆Piazza Medaglia d'Oro 🚌Piazza XX Settembre 🛈 Piazza Maggiore 1/e; www. bolognawelcome.com

Widely recognized as Italy's gastronomic capital, Bologna is home to an almost overwhelming number of eateries and food markets. The city's historic core is a handsome ensemble of brick buildings and charming porticoed streets. Medieval palaces are clustered around the central Piazza Maggiore, which is dominated by the Basilica di San Petronio. The University of Bologna is the oldest in Europe and the venerable Archiginnasio was its first official building. The city's main landmark is its pair of medieval towers – the 97-m- (318-ft-) high Asinelli and the leaning Garisenda tower.

①

Due Torri

🏛Piazza di Porta Ravegnana

Only 20 of the original 100 towers that shaped Bologna's skyline in medieval times are still standing today and this eye-catching pair is in prime position in the centre of town. At 97 m (319 ft), **Torre degli Asinelli** is Italy's fourth-tallest tower. The reward for climbing the 498 steps to the top is a

fine view that stretches over the rooftops and hills. Torre della Garisenda, which was mentioned by Dante in his *Inferno*, was reduced in height from 60 m (197 ft) to 48 m (157 ft) in the mid-14th century, when it was feared it would collapse due to its lean from the vertical of 3 m (10 ft). Torre degli Asinelli also has a lean of around 2 m (7 ft).

Torre degli Asinelli

 ⏰9:30am–5pm daily 🌐duetorribologna.com

②

San Giacomo Maggiore

🏛Piazza Rossini ⏰Daily

This Romanesque-Gothic church, begun in 1267 but altered substantially since, is visited mainly for the Cappella Bentivoglio, a superb family chapel founded by Annibale Bentivoglio in 1445 and consecrated in 1486. Pride of place naturally goes to a portrait with subtle characterization of the patrons by Lorenzo Costa (1460–1535), who was also responsible for the frescoes of the *Apocalypse*, the *Madonna Enthroned* and the *Triumph of Death*. The chapel's altarpiece, depicting the *Virgin and Saints with Two Angel Musicians* (1488), is the work of painter Francesco Francia. The Bentivoglio

 INSIDER TIP
Dozza

Take a trip to the hilltop village of Dozza, 25 km (15 miles) from Bologna. The medieval buildings here are decorated with bright murals, thanks to a biennial art festival.

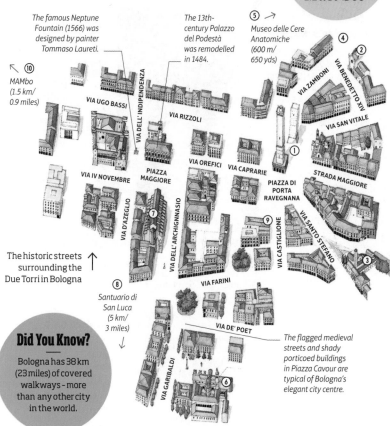

The famous Neptune Fountain (1566) was designed by painter Tommaso Laureti.

The 13th-century Palazzo del Podestà was remodelled in 1484.

⑤ ↗
Museo delle Cere Anatomiche (600 m/ 650 yds)

④

② VIA BENEDETTO XIV

↖ ⑩
MAMbo (1.5 km/ 0.9 miles)

VIA UGO BASSI

VIA DELL'INDIPENDENZA

VIA RIZZOLI

VIA ZAMBONI

VIA SAN VITALE

VIA IV NOVEMBRE

PIAZZA MAGGIORE

VIA OREFICI VIA CAPRARIE

①

STRADA MAGGIORE

PIAZZA DI PORTA RAVEGNANA

VIA D'AZEGLIO

VIA DELL'ARCHIGNNASIO

⑦

⑨

VIA CASTIGLIONE

VIA SANTO STEFANO

③

The historic streets surrounding the Due Torri in Bologna ↑

⑧
Santuario di San Luca (5 km/ 3 miles) ↓

VIA FARINI

VIA DE' POET

The flagged medieval streets and shady porticoed buildings in Piazza Cavour are typical of Bologna's elegant city centre.

VIA GARIBALDI

⑥

Did You Know?

Bologna has 38 km (23 miles) of covered walkways - more than any other city in the world.

family is further glorified in the tomb of Anton Galeazzo Bentivoglio (1435) opposite the chapel. It was among the last works of the noted Sienese sculptor Jacopo della Quercia. The Oratory of Santa Cecilia features frescoes on the lives of Santa Cecilia and San Valeriano by Costa and Francesco Francia (1504–6).

---

③

Basilica di Santo Stefano

◪ Via Santo Stefano 24
☎ 051 648 06 11
◷ 9:15am-6pm daily (summer: to 7:15pm)

Standing on central Bologna's prettiest piazza, this is a complex of ecclesiastical

buildings also known as the Sette Chiese, or the Seven Churches. It is a curious collection of four medieval churches (originally seven) jumbled together under one

↑ Light streaming into the Church of the Crucifix, Basilica di Santo Stefano

roof. The 11th-century church of the Crocifisso provides little more than a corridor leading to the polygonal San Sepolcro, the most appealing of the quartet. Also dating from the 11th century, its centrepiece is the tomb of St Petronius, a marvellously overstated affair that is modelled on the Holy Sepulchre of Jerusalem.

Parts of the church – those dedicated to saints Vitale and Agricola – date back to ancient times. To the rear of the complex is a courtyard with the Fontana di Pilata (a fountain incorporating an 8th-century marble basin), the Chiesa della Trinità, a 12th-century cloister with a Romanesque double-loggia, and a small museum featuring minor paintings and religious artifacts.

④
Pinacoteca Nazionale

📍 Via delle Belle Arti 56
🕐 8.30am-7.30pm Tue-Sun & pub hols (last adm: 30 mins before closing)
🚫 1 Jan, 1 May, 15 Aug, 25 Dec 🌐 pinacotecabologna.beniculturali.it

Bologna's principal art gallery, and one of the region's most important collections, stands on the edge of the city's university district, a bustling area of bars, bookshops and cheap restaurants. The gallery is mainly dedicated to work by Bolognese painters, notably Vitale da Bologna, Guido Reni, Guercino and the Carracci family. Members of the Ferrarese school are also represented, in particular Francesco del Cossa and Ercole de' Roberti. The two highlights are *Madonna in Glory* (c.1491) and *Ecstasy of St Cecilia* (c.1515) by Perugino and Raphael respectively, both artists who worked in Bologna.

⑤
Museo delle Cere Anatomiche

📍 Via Irnerio 48 ☎ 051 209 15 33 or 051 209 15 56 🕐 9am-1pm Mon-Fri, 10am-6pm Sat & Sun
🚫 1 Jan, Easter, 1 May, 25 Dec, pub hols

The Museum of Anatomical Waxworks is one of the more interesting and memorable of Bologna's smaller museums, featuring occasionally gruesome, visceral waxworks and numerous models of organs, limbs and flayed bodies. Sculpted rather than made from casts, the exhibits have an artistic as well as scientific appeal. The models were used as medical teaching aids until the 19th century. Exhibits from the 18th century are in Palazzo Poggi, which also contains the Geografia e Nautica collection.

FOOD MARKETS

Just off Piazza Maggiore, Mercato di Mezzo is great for a snack while Mercato delle Erbe has good restaurants. The weekly Mercato Ritrovato *(Via Azzo Gardino)* includes high-quality Slow Food produce. FICO *(Via Paolo Canali)* is a veritable agri-food theme park with a wide range of eateries, factories and activities.

⑥
San Domenico

📍 Piazza di San Domenico 13
☎ 051 640 04 11 🕐 9am-noon & 3-5pm Mon-Sat, 3-5pm Sun

Bologna's San Domenico can lay claim to being the most important of Italy's many Dominican churches. Begun in 1221, after St Dominic's death, it was built to house the body of the saint, who died here and lies buried in a tomb known as the Arca di San Domenico, a magnificent composite work. The tomb's statues were executed by Pisan sculptor Nicola Pisano; the reliefs of scenes from the *Life of St Dominic* were the work of Pisano and his assistants; the canopy (1473) is attributed to Nicola di Bari; while the figures of the angels and saints Proculus and Petronius are early works by Michelangelo. The reliquary (1383) behind the simple marble sarcophagus contains St Dominic's head.

⑦
San Petronio

📍 Piazza Maggiore
☎ 051 23 14 15 🕐 7:45am-6pm daily

Dedicated to the city's 5th-century bishop, this church ranks among the greatest of Italy's brick-built medieval buildings. Founded in 1390, it was originally intended to be larger than St Peter's in Rome, but its size was scaled down when the church authorities diverted funds to the nearby Palazzo Archiginnasio. The resulting financial shortfall left the church decidedly lopsided, with a row of columns on its eastern flank that were intended to support an additional internal aisle. The project's financial recklessness, nonetheless, was said to have been instrumental in turning Martin Luther against Catholicism.

The airy Gothic interior features graceful pillars supporting the roof and a 67-m- (219-ft-) long meridian line on the floor which was traced in 1655 by the astronomer Gian Domenico Cassini. Twenty-two chapels, shielded by screens, open off the nave.

↑ The arcaded cloisters of San Domenico

In 1547 the Council of Trent was temporarily moved here due to the plague.

Santuario di San Luca

A Via San Luca 36 **O** 7am–6pm daily **W** santuario beataverginesanluca.com

The longest uninterrupted section of the city's porticoes leads the 4 km (2.5 miles) from the Porta Saragozza city gate to this hilltop church, a familiar beacon to travellers.

The current church, built between 1723 and 1757, presents an elegant exterior, while the interior contains a Byzantine Madonna and Child, which is carried in procession to the city's San Pietro cathedral for a week each May. There are marvellous views out over the surrounding hills from the terraces.

Palazzo Pepoli

A Via Castiglione 8 **W** genusbononiae.it/palazzi/palazzo-pepoli

The medieval Palazzo Pepoli, built between 1276 and 1344, houses a multimedia museum that takes visitors on a sensory journey through 2,500 years of Bolognese history, from the Etruscan period to the present day. The chronological displays are interspersed with thematic rooms, such as the City of Water room.

MAMbo

A Via Don Minzoni 14 **W** mambo-bologna.org

The nine thematic sections of the permanent collection at Bologna's modern art museum cover contemporary Italian art from the second half of the 20th century to today. Regular temporary exhibitions are also hosted in this former bakery.

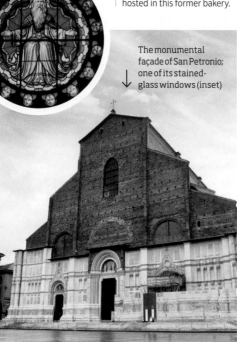

The monumental façade of San Petronio; one of its stained-glass windows (inset)

EAT

Serghei
A traditional trattoria, Serghei serves tasty dishes like stuffed zucchini with meatballs.

A Via Piella 12
C 051 23 35 33
O Sat D, Sun

$$$

E' Cucina
An unassuming looking place with a bright and modern interior, E' Cucina dishes up a selection of inspired dishes at low prices.

A Via Leopardi 4 **C** 051 275 00 69 **O** Aug

$$$

Caminetto d'Oro
This restaurant serves quality regional specialities in a refined environment.

A Via de' Falegnami 4 **O** Sun **W** caminetto doro.it

$$$

Cesarina
Authentic Bolognese dishes are served here in attractive Piazza Santo Stefano.

A Via Santo Stefano 19B **O** Mon, Tue L **W** ristorantecesarina.it

$$$

Osteria Bartolini
Enjoy seafood, including mixed fried fish, in the courtyard garden here.

A Piazza Malpighi 16 **W** osteriabartolini bologna.com

$$$

↑ Saints Apollinare and Vitale atop their columns in Piazza del Popolo

The apse mosaics show Christ, San Vitale and Bishop Ecclesius, who began the church.

②

RAVENNA

⚑ D3 **FS🚌** **ℹ** Piazza San Francesco; www.turismo.ra.it **ⓦ** ravennamosaici.it (for combined tickets for all the mosaic sites)

Famed for its glittering Byzantine mosaics, Ravenna's centre is a pleasant medley of historic cobbled streets, fine shops and piazzas, and is close to some excellent beaches. The city rose to power in the 1st century BC under Emperor Augustus. As Rome's power declined, Ravenna was made capital of the Western Empire in AD 402, a role it had during the Ostrogoth and Byzantine rule in the 5th and 6th centuries, when many of the city's spectacular churches and basilicas were built.

①
Piazza del Popolo

This elegant square is famed for its two Venetian-style columns with saints Vitale and Apollinare perched on top. Behind is Palazzo Communale and Palazzo Veneziano, built when Ravenna was part of the Venetian Republic in the 15th century. The archway in Palazzo Veneziano leads to Via Cairoli, a narrow shopping street. Nearby is Piazza Andrea Costa, home to a covered market that sells all manner of fresh local produce every morning.

②
Basilica di San Vitale

⚑ Via Argentario 22
🕐 Daily; Mar–Oct: 9am–7pm; Nov–Feb: 10am–5pm
🔒 1 Jan, 25 Dec

Finished in 548, this octagonal basilica is the only major church from the period of Emperor Justinian I to survive virtually intact. Its colourful mosaics are the height of Byzantine splendour. Look out for the emperor portrayed with court officials and, on the opposite wall, the Empress Theodora.

③
Tomba di Dante

⚑ Via Dante Alighieri
📞 0544 21 56 76 **🕐** 10am–4pm daily **🔒** 1 Jan, 25 Dec

The interior of Dante's tomb, which was built in the late 18th century, contains a bas-relief by Pietro Lombardo (1483) and a votive lamp that continually burns olive oil donated by Florence each year on the anniversary of Dante's death. The adjacent Dante museum includes paintings of the poet as well as research findings.

🔍 HIDDEN GEM
Ravenna's Beaches

Relaxed, surfer-style beach bars and restaurants abound at Marina di Ravenna and its nearby resorts. For ultimate seaside refinement, head for Milano Marittima.

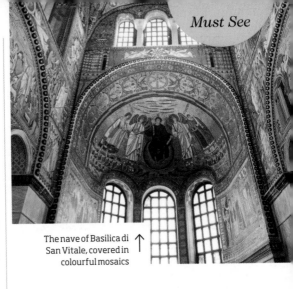

④
Basilica di San Francesco

🏠 Piazza San Francesco 1
🕐 7am–noon & 3–7pm daily
📞 0544 333 56

The main feature of interest in this church is the flooded crypt, which contains 10th-century mosaics and columns.

⑤
Battistero degli Ariani

🏠 Via degli Ariani 📞 0544 54 37 24 🕐 8:30am–4:30pm daily (summer: to 7:30pm) 🚫 1 Jan, 1 May

The cupola of this tiny late 5th-century baptistry has an impressive mosaic showing the 12 Apostles ringed around a scene depicting the baptism of Christ.

⑥
Basilica di Sant' Apollinare Nuovo

🏠 Via di Roma 53 🕐 Same as San Vitale

This glorious 6th-century church has a cylindrical bell tower and some of the largest Byzantine mosaics in the city.

The nave of Basilica di San Vitale, covered in colourful mosaics ↑

Look out for the two rows of mosaics showing processions of martyrs and virgins bearing gifts for Christ and the Virgin.

⑦
Domus dei Tappeti di Pietra

🏠 Via Gian Battista Barbiani 16 🕐 10am–5pm daily 🚫 Jan & Feb 🌐 domus deitappetidipietra.it

A Byzantine house dating from the 5th and 6th centuries, Tappeti di Pietra was only discovered in the 1990s and

has beautiful mosaics on the floors of the 14 rooms.

⑧
Battistero Neoniano

🏠 Piazza Battistero
🕐 Same as San Vitale

The Neonian Baptistry dates from the 5th century and is named after the bishop who may have commissioned its decoration, which includes a mosaic of the baptism of Christ. Built near the ruins of a Roman bathhouse, it is Ravenna's oldest monument.

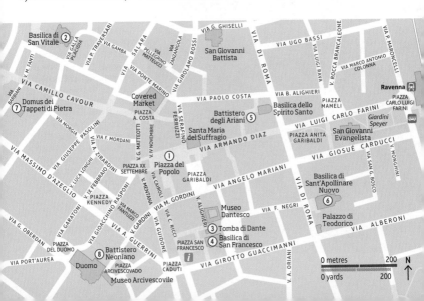

EXPERIENCE MORE

 3

Castell'Arquato

A C2 **Q** Piacenza **⬛**
ℹ Piazza Municipio 1;
0523 80 32 15

Castell'Arquato is one of
the prettiest villages in the
countryside south of the Po.
Day visitors come at the
weekends, thronging the
restaurants and bars around
the beautiful Piazza Matteotti.
The best building on the piazza
is the 13th-century Palazzo
Pretorio, a Romanesque
basilica. The impressive Rocca
Viscontea (14th century), a
former fortress, is on Piazza
del Municipio. The village's
hilltop site offers good views,
particularly over the verdant
Arda Valley to the east.

 4

Modena

A C2 **FS** **⬛** **ℹ** Piazza
Grande 14; www.visit
modena.it

To most Italians Modena
means fast cars (both Ferrari
and Maserati have factories
in its industrial outskirts)
and opera (this is the birthplace of Luciano Pavarotti).
Monuments to an earlier age,
however, make this one of
Emilia's most enticing historic
destinations. A thriving colony
since Roman times, the city
rose to medieval prominence
with the arrival in 1598 of the
d'Este nobles from Ferrara.
This family continued to
rule the city until the end
of the 18th century.

Duomo
⊛ **Q** Corso Duomo
☎ 059 21 60 78 **Ⓞ** 7am–
12:30pm & 3:30–7pm Mon,
7am–7pm Tue–Sun
Ⓠ Lunchtime Tue–Fri
Modena's Romanesque
Duomo was founded by
Countess Matilda of Tuscany,
ruler of Modena in the 11th
century. It was dedicated to
San Geminiano, the city's
patron saint, whose stone
coffin lies under the choir. Its
most noticeable feature is the
Torre Ghirlandina, a leaning
tower begun at the same time
as the Duomo and completed
two centuries later. It once
housed the *Secchia*, a wooden
bucket whose 1325 theft from
Bologna allegedly sparked a
war between the two cities.
It also inspired Tassoni's
17th-century mock epic
poem *La Secchia Rapita*
(The Stolen Bucket).
    The large reliefs on the
Duomo's main (west) façade
are the work of the 12th-
century sculptor Wiligelmus.
The highlight of the rather
severe interior is a large
carved *tribuna* (rood screen)
decorated with 12th-century
scenes from the Passion.

Palazzo dei Musei
⊛ ⊛ ⊛ **Q** Largo di Porta
Sant'Agostino 337 **☎** 059
203 31 25 (Galleria Estense);
059 22 22 48 (Biblioteca
Estense) **Ⓞ** Daily (summer:
Sun pm only) **Ⓠ** Pub hols
Formerly an arsenal and
workhouse, the Palazzo dei
Musei is now home to the
city's best museums and
galleries. Its finest section is
the Galleria Estense, given
over to the d'Este private
art collection. Most of the
paintings are by Emilian

 ←

Castell'Arquato's Rocca
Viscontea, dominating the
surrounding landscape

artists, but there are also works by Velázquez, Tintoretto, Bernini and Veronese.

Among the permanent displays in the Biblioteca Estense, the d'Este Library, are a 1481 edition of Dante's *Divine Comedy* and dozens of fascinating maps and diplomatic letters, many dating back centuries. The jewel of the collection is the illuminated Borso d'Este Bible, whose pages contain over 1,200 miniatures by 15th-century artists of the Ferrara school.

Museo Ferrari
⊕ 🚗 Via Dino Ferrari 43, Maranello 📞 0536 94 97 13 🕐 9:30am-6pm daily (to 7pm summer) 🚫 1 Jan, 25 Dec

The Ferrari factory, 20 km (12 miles) south of Modena, was founded by Enzo Ferrari in 1945. The Fiat-owned manufacturer now produces around 2,500 cars annually. The Galleria Ferrari has an excellent exhibition featuring memorabilia, classic engines and many vintage cars.

TOP 3 CASTLES OF PIACENZA & PARMA

Castello di Bardi
🅰 B2 🏰 Bardi 🌐 castello dibardi.info
This castle dominates the surrounding area from a rocky spur.

Rocca Sanvitale
🅰 C2 🏰 Fontanellato 📞 0521 82 90 55
Surrounded by a moat, this fortress contains Parmigianino frescoes.

Grazzano Visconti
🅰 B2 🏰 Grazzano 📞 0523 87 01 51
Rebuilt in the early 20th century around a 14th-century castle, this village is filled with workshops and taverns.

PARMESAN CHEESE AND PARMA HAM

A visit to a Parmigiano Reggiano dairy, such as Giansanti Di Muzio *(Strada Traversetolo 228, Parma)* shows how this unique product is made, a method that has barely changed since the 12th century.

Prosciutto di Parma also involves a strictly regulated process - only salt may be added. Parma Gustibus *(Strada della Repubblica 54A, Parma)* is a traditional deli.

5
Parma

🅰 C2 🚆🚌 🛈 Piazza Garibaldi 1; www.turismo.comune.parma.it

A byword for fine food and good living, Parma is also a treasure trove of superlative art and fine medieval buildings.

The Lombard-Romanesque Duomo on Piazza Duomo is renowned for the painting that fills its main cupola, the *Assumption* (1526–30) by Antonio da Correggio. The south transept features a carved frieze of *The Deposition* (1178) by Benedetto Antelami, who was also responsible for much of the Baptistry (1196) just south of the cathedral. The reliefs inside and outside the latter – particularly those describing the months of the year – are among the most important of their age in Italy.

East of the Duomo is the church of San Giovanni Evangelista (rebuilt 1498–1510), whose dome features a fresco (c.1520) of the *Vision of St John at Patmos* by Correggio. Frescoes by Parmigianino can also be seen here.

Palazzo della Pilotta
⊕ 🏛 Piazzale della Pilotta 15 📞 0521 23 36 17 (Galleria Nazionale); 0521 23 37 18 (Museo Archeologico Nazionale) 🕐 Tue-Sun am

This vast palace was built for the Farnese family during the 1500s. It comprises several parts, including the Teatro Farnese (1628), a copy of Palladio's ravishing theatre in Vicenza, built entirely of wood.

Both Parmigianino and Correggio are represented in the palace's Galleria Nazionale, which also houses works by Fra Angelico, Bronzino and El Greco, and two by Ludovico Carracci: the *Apostles at the Sepulchre* and the *Funeral of the Virgin* (late 1500s).

The Museo Archeologico Nazionale, on the lower floor, has exhibits from Velleia, an Etruscan necropolis, and from prehistoric sites around Parma.

Camera di Correggio
⊕ 🏛 Via Melloni 📞 0521 23 33 09 🕐 8:30am-2pm Tue-Fri & Sun, 8:30am-6pm Sat
Originally the refectory of the Benedictine convent of San Paolo, this room was frescoed by Correggio in 1518 with mythological scenes.

> A byword for fine food and good living, Parma is also a treasure trove of superlative art and fine medieval buildings.

Cycling past majestic
Renaissance buildings
in Ferrara

Museo Schifanoia
◈ ⌂ Via Scandiana 23
☎ 0532 641 78 ⏱ Tue-Sun
✖ Public hols

The d'Este summer retreat
is famous for its Salone dei
Mesi (Room of the Months),
decorated with detailed
15th-century murals depicting
the 12 different months of
the year.

Museo Archeologico Nazionale
◈ ⌂ Palazzo di Ludovico
il Moro, Via XX Settembre
122 ☎ 0532 662 99 ⏱ Tue-
Sun ✖ 1 May, 25 Dec

The most interesting exhibits
in this museum are artifacts
that were excavated from
Spina, a Greco-Etruscan
trading post near Comacchio
on the Po Delta.

Palazzo dei Diamanti
◈ ◈ ⌂ Corso Ercole d'Este
21 ☎ 0532 24 49 49 ⏱ Daily

Named after the diamond
motifs on its façade, this
palace houses a modern art
gallery, a museum devoted to
the Risorgimento, and the
Pinacoteca Nazionale, which
contains works from leading
exponents of the local
Renaissance school.

6

Ferrara

⌂ C2 🚆🚌 🛈 Castello
Estense, Largo Castello;
www.ferrarainfo.com

The d'Este dynasty has left an
indelible mark on the walled
town of Ferrara. The noble
family took control of the
town in the late 13th century,
holding power until 1598,
when they were forced by the
papacy to move to Modena.

Castello Estense
◈ ⌂ Largo Castello ☎ 0532
29 92 33 ⏱ Tue-Sun (Sep-
Mar: daily) ✖ Public hols

With its battlements and
towers, the d'Este family's
dynastic seat (begun 1385)
looms over the town centre.
Ferrante and Giulio d'Este were
incarcerated in its dungeons
for plotting to overthrow
Alfonso I d'Este. Parisina d'Este,
wife of Nicolò III, was executed
here for having an affair with
Ugo, her illegitimate stepson.

Palazzo del Comune
⌂ Piazza Municipale

Bronze statues of Nicolò III
and Borso d'Este, one of
Nicolò's reputed 27 children,
adorn this medieval palace
(begun 1243). Both are copies
of the 15th-century originals
by Leon Battista Alberti.

Museo della Cattedrale
◈ ⌂ Via San Romano
☎ 0532 76 12 99 ⏱ Tue-
Sun ✖ 1 & 6 Jan, Easter,
25 & 26 Dec

Ferrara's 12th-century Duomo
was designed by Wiligelmus,
widely regarded as the first
great Italian sculptor. Fine
reliefs on the façade depict
scenes from the Last
Judgment. The excellent
museum contains a fine set of
marble reliefs of the *Labours
of the Months* (late 1100s),
two painted organ shutters
(1469) of *St George* and the
Annunciation by Cosmè Tura,
and the *Madonna of the
Pomegranate* (1408) by
Jacopo della Quercia.

CERVIA SALT FLATS & FLAMINGOES

A particularly pure
type of salt has been
produced at the salt
flats just outside
the coastal town of
Cervia since ancient
times. The area, now
a nature reserve, is
year-round home
to a community of
flamingoes. Tours on
foot, by bicycle or by
boat are available
March-November.

Museo Nazionale dell'Ebraismo Italiano e della Shoah

🏛 📍 Via Piangipane 81
🕐 Tue–Sun 🗓 31 Mar, 10 Sep
🌐 meisweb.it

Ferrara has been a major centre for Jewish communities since the 15th century, when the d'Este family guaranteed a safe welcome for Jews persecuted elsewhere. This museum (an ongoing project; completion due 2020) features multimedia displays and exhibits related to the history of Judaism in Italy.

Abbazia di Pomposa

📍 Via Pomposa Centro 1, Codigoro 🕐 9am–7pm Mon (church open daily)
🌐 abbaziadipomposa. altervista.org

Dating in parts from the 7th and 8th centuries, this abbey sits 42 km (26 miles) east of Ferrara. It incorporates a fine Romanesque bell tower (1063) and the Basilica di Santa Maria, which has a mosaic floor with geometric designs and animal motifs, plus richly frescoed walls, including *The Last Judgment*.

❼ Po Delta

📍 D2 🚉 Ferrara 🚌 Ferrara Ostellata 🚌 To Goro or Gorino 🚌 From Porto Garibaldi, Goro & Gorino ℹ Corso Mazzini 200, Comacchio; www. parcodeltapo.it

The Po is Italy's longest river, and its vast basin covers some 15 per cent of the country. Although ravaged in many places by industrial pollution, at its finest it offers beautiful landscapes – rows of poplar trees across misty fields and vistas over the shifting sands of its vast delta, an estuary of marshes, dunes and islands.

The immense Parco Delta del Po is a national park stretching all the way to the Veneto. Wetland areas such as the Valli di Comacchio (north of Ravenna) have long been nature reserves, a winter home to thousands of breeding and migrating birds. Ornithologists gather here to see gulls, coots, bean geese and black terns, and far rarer species such as the white egret, hen harrier and pygmy cormorant. Comacchio, the nearest settlement, comprises 13 tiny islands connected by bridges.

The Bosco della Mesola, a tract of ancient woodland planted by the Etruscans, is home to large herds of deer.

It is possible to take a boat trip to some of the delta's more remote corners: key departure points include the villages of Ca' Tiepolo, Ca' Vernier and Taglio di Po. Most areas also offer the possibility of hiring bicycles. The 125-km (78-mile) ride along the right bank of the Po is very popular with cyclists.

EAT

La Sangiovesa
The wine and much of the produce used in the kitchen come from the restaurant's estate nearby.

📍 D3 📍 Piazza Beato Simone Balacchi 14, Santarcangelo di Romagna 🕐 L Mon–Sat
🌐 sangiovesa.it

€€€

Fishermen's boats on a canal in the Po Delta

8

Rimini

D3 FS🚌 🛈Piazzale Fellini 3; www.rimini turismo.it

Rimini was once a quaint seaside resort, whose relaxed charms were celebrated in the early films of Federico Fellini (1920–93), the director born and raised here. Today it is the largest beach resort in Europe. The seafront, which stretches unbroken for almost 15 km (9 miles), is lined with clubs, bars, cafés and restaurants. The crowded beaches are clean and well maintained, though entrance fees are charged at private beaches.

The town's old quarter, by contrast, is pleasantly quiet. Its charming cobbled streets gather around Piazza Cavour, dominated by the 14th-century Palazzo del Podestà. Rimini's finest building is its main cathedral, the **Tempio Malatestiano**. Built as a Franciscan church, it was converted in 1450 by Leon Battista Alberti, the great Florentine architect, into one of Italy's great Renaissance monuments. The work was commissioned by Sigismondo Malatesta (1417–68), a descendant of Rimini's ruling medieval family, and reputedly one of the most evil and debauched men of his time. Ostensibly designed as a chapel, the Tempio became little more than a monument to Malatesta. Inside are sculptures by Agostino di Duccio and a fresco (1451)

Did You Know?

San Leo has only been part of Emilia-Romagna since 2006, when the town voted to leave Le Marche in a referendum.

STAY

Grand Hotel Rimini

This statuesque building, which dates from 1908 and appears in films by local director Federico Fellini, is more than just a hotel - it's a landmark in itself. It has classic interiors, ample gardens, a pool, a spa and its own private beach opposite.

D3 🏛Parco Federico Fellini, Rimini 🌐grand hotelrimini.com

€€€

---

by Piero della Francesca of Malatesta kneeling before St Sigismund (1451).

The entwined initials of Sigismondo Malatesta and his fourth wife, Isotta degli Atti, provide a recurring decorative motif, and there are reliefs depicting scenes of bacchanalian excess and oddities such as strangely posed elephants (a Malatesta family emblem). All this led Pope Pius II to condemn the building as "a temple of devil-worshippers", and to burn Malatesta's effigy for acts of "murder, violation, adultery, incest, sacrilege and perjury".

Tempio Malatestiano

🏛Via IV Novembre ☎0541 511 30 🕐8:30am-12:30pm & 3:30-6:30pm Mon-Sat (from 9am Sun)

9

Cesenatico

D3 🏛Forlì-Cesena 🚉 🛈Via Roma 112; www.cesenatico.it

The heart of Cesenatico, a city 18 km (11 miles) north of Rimini, lies around its attractive canal-port,

---

which was designed by Leonardo da Vinci in 1502. Today it hosts an open-air museum of historic boats with mustard-yellow sails decorated with deep-red designs. At Christmas, nativity figures positioned on the boats add to the atmosphere.

The town, one of the area's top fishing centres, has an important fish market and the canal-port is lined on both sides with an impressive selection of seafood eateries, including the Michelin-starred La Buca and the more low-key Osteria del Gran Fritto next door, both run by the same family. The sandy beach, popular with families, is well equipped for young children.

10

San Leo

D3 🏛Rimini 🚌From Rimini, change at Villanova 🛈Piazza Dante Alighieri 14; www.san-leo.it

The captivating village of San Leo has a quaint cobbled

← Colourful historic sail-boats in the canal-port of Cesenatico

square with a superb 9th-century Pieve (parish church). Built partly with stone collected from the ruined Mons Feretrius, the church was raised over the site of a 6th-century chapel.

Just behind the Pieve is the 12th-century Duomo, a fine Romanesque building with Corinthian capitals and Roman columns from the Mons Feretrius. The lid of St Leo's sarcophagus is in the crypt. Ancient pagan carvings can be seen on the wall behind the altar.

Few castles are as impressive as the great **Fortress** that towers over San Leo. Dante used this crag-top site as a model for the landscapes of *Purgatorio*, while Machiavelli considered the citadel to be the finest piece of military architecture in Italy. Its rocky ramparts once contained the Mons Feretrius, a Roman temple dedicated to Jupiter.

An earlier Roman fortress on the site became a papal prison in the 18th century. Its most famous inmate was the larger-than-life Conte di Cagliostro. A swindler, womanizer, necromancer, quack and alchemist, Cagliostro was imprisoned for heresy in the 1790s. His tiny cell – known as *pozzetto* (little well), because he had to be lowered into it from the ceiling – was specially built so that its window faced the village's two churches. It is still visible, together with a small picture gallery, state rooms and the majestic Renaissance ramparts, built by Francesco di Giorgio Martini for the dukes of Montefeltro in the 15th century.

Fortress

⊗ 🏠 Via Leopardi
📞 0541 91 63 06 ⏰ Daily

FAENZA CERAMICS

Faenza has been a major player in the world of ceramics since 16th-century craftsmen introduced a new white majolica and light painted blue designs. The town has an important museum *(Museo Internazionale delle Ceramiche, Viale Baccarini 19, closed Mon)* displaying a collection of ancient and modern pieces, including works by Picasso and Matisse.

↑ Typical example of Faenza ceramics

SOUTHERN ITALY

La Corricella Harbour in Procida, an island in the Bay of Naples

EXPLORE SOUTHERN ITALY

This section divides southern Italy into six colour-coded sightseeing areas, as shown on the map below. Find out more about each area on the following pages.

TUSCANY
Arezzo

Perugia　Assisi

UMBRIA

Orvieto

Viterbo
Tarquinia

LAZIO

Cerveteri　Tivoli
Rome

Aprilla
Latina

Santa Teresa Gallura

Porto Torres

Olbia

Alghero

Siniscola

Bosa　Nuoro

Tyrrhenian
Sea

Oristano　Tortoli

SARDINIA
p526

Carbonia

Cagliari
Pula

ITALY

Palermo
Trapani

GETTING TO KNOW
SOUTHERN ITALY

Rich in archaeological sites, as well as some extraordinarily varied landscapes and coasts, southern Italy is a fascinating region. Although the Roman site of Pompeii is high on everyone's list, there are also Greek ruins in Sicily and mysterious *nuraghi* (ancient structures) in Sardinia. The cuisine alone, with its eclectic heritage and diverse flavours, provides an excuse to dawdle on the coast or in pretty mountain villages.

NAPLES

PAGE 448

A chaotic yet spectacular metropolis, Naples sprawls noisily and dirtily around the edge of the magnificent Bay of Naples. To one side is Mount Vesuvius, to the other the smouldering sulphurous fields of the Campi Flegrei, while out at sea, across from the city, are the enticing islands of Capri, Ischia and Procida. Everything about Naples is exuberant, from its streetlife and traditional music to the lavish interiors of its many churches and two royal palaces. Naples is also home to what is reckoned to be the best pizza in Italy.

Best for
Full-on streetlife and lavish religious festivals

Home to
Museo Archeologico Nazionale

Experience
The original pizza Margherita

CAMPANIA

PAGE 462

To the north of Naples, fertile plains sweep down to the town of Santa Maria Capua Vetere, home to one of the largest remaining amphitheatres in Italy. The remote, mountainous and little-visited interior of Campania is overshadowed by the glories of the Amalfi Coast with its famous cornice road, and the astonishing Roman towns of Pompeii and Herculaneum, preserved under ash from the volcano that destroyed them in AD79. Before the Romans, the area was colonized by the Greeks, who left behind the ruins of a beautiful temple at Paestum.

Best for
Celebrity spotting in Capri

Home to
Pompeii, Herculaneum and the winding roads of the Amalfi Coast

Experience
Diving above the ruins of the sunken Roman city of Baie

ABRUZZO, MOLISE AND PUGLIA

PAGE 476

Puglia is the "heel" of the Italian boot, the picturesque, serrated coastline of the Gargano Peninsula is its "spur" and Abruzzo and Molise together form the "ankle". The mountainous regions of Abruzzo and Molise are wonderful for hiking and exploring rarely visited villages. Puglia is a wealthy, agricultural region with a beautiful coastline. Its jewel is Baroque Lecce, but the curious trulli houses around Alberobello, the labyrinthine centre of old Bari, and the Castel del Monte, are all worth visiting.

Best for
Eating sundried tomatoes and freshly picked produce

Home to
The florid Baroque buildings of Lecce and the Parco Nazionale d'Abruzzo, Lazio e Molise

Experience
Burrata from the region's cheese makers

→

BASILICATA AND CALABRIA

Basilicata and Calabria receive relatively few tourists, except for the incredible cave-city of Matera and the fabulous coastline between Tropea and Maratea. Mostly upland country, Basilicata is peppered with Greek ruins, medieval abbeys and Norman castles. Calabria, bounded by the Ionian and Tyrrhenian seas, has many lovely beaches. Greek ruins can be found at Locri Epizephiri, while the slopes of the Aspromonte and Sila mountains are popular with walkers and skiers.

Best for
Getting off the beaten track

Home to
Matera, wild mountains and beautiful beaches

Experience
Sleeping in a cave hotel

PAGE 500

SICILY

Lying at the heart of the Mediterranean, the island of Sicily has been fought over and colonized by Greeks, Phoenicians, Romans, Arabs, Normans, Spanish, English and French, all of whom influenced the food and the language, as well as its art and architecture. Palermo, the busy capital, and Siracusa, with its island centre Ortigia, are the most interesting cities. The island's coastline has hundreds of sandy beaches, while the varied interior is characterized by remote hill-towns and plains punctuated by mountains. Among the most famous sights are the Mount Etna and Stromboli volcanoes.

Best for
Visiting ancient Greek temples and lazing on the beach

Home to
Palermo, the Valley of the Temples and Mount Etna

Experience
The aperitivo scene on the Baroque island of Ortigia

PAGE 526

SARDINIA

With an interior of dramatic, soaring uplands and a coastline of beguiling sandy beaches and marine caves, Sardinia is extraordinarily beautiful – and in places still utterly wild. Cagliari, Alghero and Sassari are all worth visiting, but the true highlight of the island is its amazingly varied coastline, ranging from the white quartz beaches of the Sila peninsula to the exclusive resorts of the Costa Smeralda. Sardinia's ancient inhabitants are known as *nuraghic* after the strange truncated drystone structures with which they peppered the island.

Best for
Snorkelling in crystalline waters

Home to
Relics of the nuraghic *civilization, the exclusive resorts of the Costa Smeralda*

Experience
Flamingoes flying above Cagliari on their way to the salt flats on a spring evening

NAPLES

Naples is a vibrant cacophony of world-class museums, ancient ruins, crumbling churches and Baroque palaces blended into the fabric of a bustling modern city. Founded by the Greeks, it is one of only a few Italian cities that have remained continuously occupied from ancient times to the present day. The Romans enlarged and embellished it and in later centuries it was the much sought-after prize of foreign invaders and Imperialists – most notably the Normans, Hohenstaufen, French and Spanish.

Greek colonists founded a settlement overlooking the Bay of Naples as early as the 4th century BC, calling it Parthenope. As the settlement continued to expand, they established Neapolis (new city) next to the Palaeopolis, or old city. Neapolis was a leading commercial centre, and the Greek language and customs survived even during the Roman period, when this was a favourite area of the elite.

After the fall of the Roman Empire and a wave of invasions, the city came under Byzantine influence and went through a period of rebirth. In the 12th century, the invading Normans succeeded in conquering the whole of southern Italy. Naples itself became a capital, and the court began to attract famous artists. The 1400s were a golden era for Naples, but there followed two centuries of oppressive rule by Spain. In 1734 King Charles began the period of Bourbon hegemony. With the exception of the short-lived republican government in 1799 and the subsequent decade of French dominion, the Bourbons ruled Naples until 1860.

Since the unification of Italy, in the mid-19th century, the city's problems have become national issues – most notably the wealth gap between northern and southern Italy.

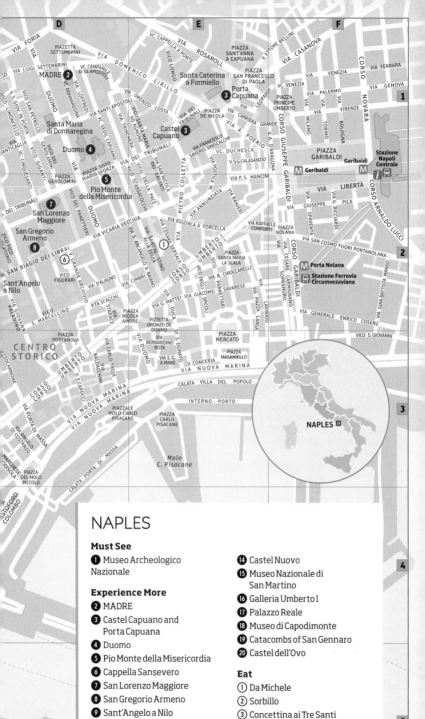

NAPLES

Must See

1 Museo Archeologico Nazionale

Experience More

2 MADRE
3 Castel Capuano and Porta Capuana
4 Duomo
5 Pio Monte della Misericordia
6 Cappella Sansevero
7 San Lorenzo Maggiore
8 San Gregorio Armeno
9 Sant'Angelo a Nilo
10 San Domenico Maggiore
11 Santa Chiara
12 Gesù Nuovo
13 Sant'Anna e San Bartolomeo dei Lombardi
14 Castel Nuovo
15 Museo Nazionale di San Martino
16 Galleria Umberto I
17 Palazzo Reale
18 Museo di Capodimonte
19 Catacombs of San Gennaro
20 Castel dell'Ovo

Eat

① Da Michele
② Sorbillo
③ Concettina ai Tre Santi

Stay

④ Constantinpoli 104
⑤ Hotel Romeo
⑥ Decumani

❶ ⊗ ⊗

MUSEO ARCHEOLOGICO NAZIONALE

⬛ C1 🏛 Piazza Museo Nazionale 19 Ⓜ Piazza Cavour-Museo 🚌 C64, C83, E1, R1, R4, 24, 47, 110, 135 ⏰ 9am–7:30pm Wed–Mon 🚫 1 Jan, 25 May, 25 Dec 🌐 cir.campania. beniculturali.it/museoarcheologiconazionale

Among the world's top museums of ancient art, Naples' Archaeological Museum overwhelms with its wealth of beautiful and priceless objects. Many of the treasures on display were excavated from Pompeii and Herculaneum.

Sculptures

The fine collection of Greco-Roman sculpture consists mostly of works found in excavations around Vesuvius and the Phlegraean Fields, as well as the treasures from the Farnese Collection (King Ferdinando IV's Roman antiquities, inherited from his grandmother Elizabeth Farnese). The sculptures – most of which are the only existing Roman copies of lost Greek originals – are displayed on the ground floor. Among the numerous fine works are the *Farnese Hercules*, an enlarged Roman copy of a sculpture by the Greek master Lysippus, and the *Farnese Bull*, the largest sculptural group to have survived from antiquity (c.200 BC).

Frescoes

Most of the frescoes in the collection were removed from buildings in cities buried by the eruptions of Vesuvius, and assembled here from the mid-1700s onwards. The most important of these came from the Basilica in Herculaneum. Others were taken from the Villa di Fannio Sinistore at Boscoreale and from the extensive landed property of Julia Felix in Pompeii. The frieze from her house, with a still life of apples and grapes and scenes from the forum, gives a fascinating glimpse of everyday life in a 1st-century-AD city.

GALLERY GUIDE

The Farnese Collection and sculpture from Herculaneum, Pompeii and other Vesuvian cities can be seen on the ground floor, the mezzanine level and the first floor. Mosaics, on the mezzanine level, and domestic items, weapons and murals, on the first floor, show daily life in the ancient cities. A lower-ground-floor level houses the Egyptian Collection. The arrangement aims to display the exhibits in context.

←
Mosaic found at Pompeii depicting the Battle of Alexander

Timeline

1616
The building is adapted and becomes the seat of Naples university.

1957
Museo Archeologico Nazionale is renamed after the picture collection moves.

1980
▼ An earthquake causes serious damage to many of the exhibits.

Must See

1500s
The structure that will house the museum is built as the home of the royal cavalry.

1738
▲ Excavations of Vesuvian towns begin. King Charles III collects finds.

1860
The collection becomes public property and known as the Museo Nazionale.

Mosaics

The majority of the mosaics on display in the museum come from Pompeii, Stabiae, Herculaneum and Boscoreale and date from the 2nd century BC to AD 79. The realistic images, such as the female portraits from Pompeii, are particularly fascinating. Among the highlights is a depiction of the Battle of Alexander, found at Pompeii. This large, detailed mosaic was based on a Hellenistic painting and depicts Alexander the Great leading his cavalry against Darius III.

Egyptian Collection

The museum is home to many valuable works of Egyptian art from the Ancient Kingdom (2700–2200 BC) to the Roman age. As well as human and animal mummies, the Egyptian section includes Canopic vases and containers for the internal organs of the deceased. The collection of *shabti* comprises wood, stone and faïence statuettes representing workers for the deceased in the afterlife.

Elegant exterior of the Museo Archeologico Nazionale

↑ Visitors admiring the *Farnese Hercules* and other Classical sculptures in the collection

EXPERIENCE MORE

2
MADRE

📍D1 🏛Via Settembrini 79
🕐10am-7:30pm Mon &
Wed-Sat, 10am-8pm Sun
🌐www.madrenapoli.it

Opened in 2005, the Museo d'Arte Contemporanea Donna Regina Napoli (MADRE) is located in the Palazzo Donnaregina, from which it gets its name. The museum houses a remarkable collection by well-known artists, such as Andy Warhol, Robert Rauschenberg, Mimmo Paladino, Claes Oldenburg, Robert Mapplethorpe and Roy Lichtenstein among others. On the first floor is a library and a children's area, while the third floor is used for temporary exhibitions. The museum often hosts special events such as cinema screenings, concerts and theatrical performances. The church of Santa Maria Donnaregina, at the back of the museum, provides additional exhibition space in a beautiful setting.

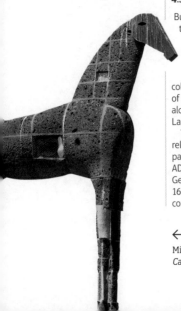

Mimmo Paladino's
Cavallo, at MADRE

3
Castel Capuano and Porta Capuana

📍E1 🏛Piazza Enrico de Nicola

Begun in 1165 by Norman King William I and completed by Frederick II, Castel Capuano was a royal palace until 1540, when Don Pedro de Toledo turned it into law courts, a function it maintains to the present day.

Nearby, between the Aragonese towers of the Capua Gate and facing a market, is a rare sculpture in the Florentine-Renaissance style. Created by Giuliano da Maiano (and finished in 1490 by Luca Fancelli) as a defensive gate, Porta Capuana is perhaps Italy's finest Renaissance gateway.

4
Duomo

📍D1 🏛Via Duomo 147
📞081 44 90 97 🕐8:30am-
1:30pm & 2:30-7:30pm
Mon-Sat; 8am-1:30pm &
4:30-7:30pm Sun & hols

Built between 1294 and 1323, the Cattedrale di Santa Maria Assunta, or Duomo, lies behind a mostly 19th-century façade. The nave is lined with ancient columns, and there is an array of monuments to past rulers, along with paintings by Lanfranco and Domenichino.

The Duomo houses the relics of San Gennaro, Naples' patron saint (martyred AD 305). The Cappella San Gennaro, erected in the 1600s, holds phials of his congealed blood, which miraculously liquefies three times a year (the Saturday before the first Sunday in May, 19 September and 16 December). The Cappella Carafa, a Renaissance master-piece built from 1497 to 1506, contains the saint's tomb.

Accessible from the Duomo's north aisle is the Cappella di Santa Restituta, founded in the 4th century on the site of a former Temple of Apollo, and rebuilt in the 1300s. It has ceiling paintings by Luca Giordano (1632–1705) and a 5th-century baptistry. The nearby Museo del Tesoro di San Gennaro exhibits a range of gold, silverware, jewels, statues and art.

EAT

Here are some of the best pizzerias in Naples.

Da Michele
This pizzeria serves only Margherita and Marinara varieties.

📍E2 🏛Via Cesare Sersale 1
🌐damichele.net
€€€

Sorbillo
The pizza here is well worth queueing up for.

📍C2 🏛Via dei Tribunali 32 🌐sorbillo.it
€€€

Concettina ai Tre Santi
A fourth-generation pizzaiolo.

📍C1 🏛Via Arena alla Sanità 7 Bis
🌐pizzeriaoliva.it
€€€

Via Nilo, just round the corner from Cappella Sansevero

5

Pio Monte della Misericordia

📍 D2 🏛 Via dei Tribunali 253 📞 081 44 69 44/73 🕐 9am-6pm Mon-Sat (to 2:30pm Sun) 🚫 Easter, Christmas

Pio Monte is one of the most important charitable institutions in Naples. It was founded in 1601 to aid the poor and ill, and to free the Christian slaves in the Ottoman Empire. After passing through the five-arch loggia (where pilgrims could shelter), you enter the octagonal church. The eye is immediately drawn to the extraordinary altarpiece, Caravaggio's *Seven Acts of Mercy* (1607). The art gallery has paintings by Luca Giordano and Mattia Preti. Access to the church is free, but there is an entry fee for the art gallery.

6

Cappella Sansevero

📍 C2 🏛 Via F de Santis 19 🕐 9:30am-6:30pm Wed-Mon 🌐 museosansevero.it

This tiny 16th-century chapel is the burial sepulchre of the Princes of Sangro di Sansevero. Featuring both Christian and Masonic symbolism, it has an unusual character.

The chapel is filled with remarkable 18th-century sculpture, including *The Resurrection of the Prince*, by an unknown artist, and Giuseppe Sammartino's *Veiled Christ*, an alabaster figure beneath a marble veil.

Prince Raimondo, an 18th-century alchemist, is associated with the chapel. He performed gruesome experiments on human bodies, for which he was excommunicated. The results of some of his experiments can be seen in the crypt.

THE STORY OF PIZZA

Deeply engrained in Naples' gastronomic identity, pizza first emerged in southern Italy in the late 1700s, quickly becoming a working-class staple. In 1889, when touring the kingdom, Queen Margherita of Savoy developed a taste for this peasant delicacy. After she summoned chef Raffaele Esposito to the royal-palace ovens, pizza Margherita was born. In order to raise awareness of pizza-making's endangered status, in 2017 the culinary art was added to UNESCO's Intangible Cultural Heritage of Humanity list.

7

San Lorenzo Maggiore

D2 Piazza San Gaetano 316 081 211 08 60
9:30am-5:30pm daily

This Franciscan church is mainly 14th-century (with an 18th-century façade) and was built during the reign of Robert the Wise of Anjou. The storyteller Giovanni Boccaccio (1313–75) reputedly based the character Fiammetta on King Robert's daughter Maria, whom he saw here on Easter Eve in 1334. For Naples, San Lorenzo Maggiore is a rare Gothic edifice. Its nave and the apse ambulatory have a magnificent period simplicity. The church houses medieval tombs that include the Gothic tomb of Catherine of Austria, who died in 1323, by a pupil of Giovanni Pisano. Excavations in the monastic cloister, where the lyric poet and scholar Petrarch (p118) once stayed, have revealed the remains of a Roman basilica. There are also important Greek and medieval excavations, for which there is an admission fee.

← Sculpture in the church of San Lorenzo Maggiore

↑ Ceiling of San Lorenzo Maggiore

traditionally from noble families, were accustomed to lavish living. The Baroque interior of the church sports frescoes by Luca Giordano. There is a lovely fountain in the cloister with a statue of *Christ and the Samaritan*.

The church is located in a street known to locals as "Christmas Alley" because it is lined with workshops manufacturing and selling Nativity figures (*presepi*).

8

San Gregorio Armeno

D2 Via San Gregorio Armeno 44 081 552 01 86
9:30am-noon daily (hols: 9am-12:30pm)

Benedictine nuns still preside over this church. The attached convent earned a reputation for luxury since the nuns,

9

Sant'Angelo a Nilo

D2 Piazzetta Nilo 23 081 211 08 60 9am-1pm & 4:30-7pm Mon-Sat (am only Sun & public hols)

This 14th-century church holds a fine Renaissance work: the Tomb of Cardinal Rinaldo Brancaccio. Designed by Michelozzo, it was sculpted in Pisa, then shipped to Naples upon completion in 1428. Donatello reputedly carved the right-hand angel drawing back the curtain, the shallow-relief *Assumption* and the cardinal's head. From the church you can visit the courtyard of Palazzo Brancaccio, home to Naples' first public library (1690).

10

San Domenico Maggiore

📍 C2 🏛 Piazza San Domenico Maggiore 8
📞 081 557 32 04 🕐 7:15am-noon & 5-7pm daily (hols: 9am-1pm & 5-9pm)

In 1283 Charles I of Anjou ordered the construction of a new church and monastery for the Dominican order. The Gothic three-nave building was built onto the pre-existing church of Sant'Arcangelo a Morfisa, which was the original seat of Naples' University of Theology, headed by St Thomas Aquinas. A relic of the saint's arm is said to be kept inside the monastery. In 1850–53 Federico Travaglini rebuilt the interior in Neo-Gothic style. The sacristy houses 42 coffins arranged along the balcony. Some contain the corpses of the Aragonese kings, including Alphonse and Ferdinand I.

STAY

Constantinpoli 104
Impeccably appointed boutique hotel.

📍 E5 🏛 Via S Maria di Costantinopoli 104
🌐 costantinopoli104.it

€€€

Hotel Romeo
Rooms in the old town.

📍 C4 🏛 Via C Colombo 45
🌐 romeohotel.it

€€€

Decumani
Tasteful furnishings in a 20th-century palazzo.

📍 D2 🏛 Via del Grande Archivio 8
🌐 decumani.com

€€€

↑ The cloister of San Gregorio Armeno, in an idyllic garden setting

⓫
Santa Chiara

📍 C3 🏛 Via Santa Chiara 49
📞 081 797 12 31 🕐 9:30am-
5:30pm Mon-Sat, 10am-
2pm Sun

This 14th-century church was
bombed in World War II, but a
reconstruction uncovered the
original Provençal-Gothic
structure. The tombs of the
Angevin monarchs are housed
here. The tomb of Robert the
Wise (died 1343) is by
Giovanni and Pacio Bertini;
that of his son, Charles of
Calabria (died 1328), is by Tino
da Camaino; and the tomb of
Charles's wife, Mary of Valois
(died 1331), is by da Camaino
and his followers. Adjacent is
a convent with a **cloister**
designed by Vaccaro (1742).
There is also a museum with
ornaments and sculptures
from Santa Chiara, as well as
a Roman bathhouse (AD 1).

Cloister

📞 081 797 12 24 or 081 551
66 73 🕐 9:30am-5:30pm
Mon-Sat, 10am-2:30pm Sun
& public hols

⓬
Gesù Nuovo

📍 C2 🏛 Piazza del Gesù
Nuovo 2 📞 081 557 81 11
🕐 7am-1pm & 4-8pm daily

This 16th-century Jesuit church
was constructed by Valeriano
(and later Fanzago and Fuga)
from the Severini palace (15th
century), of which only a
façade survives. The interior
decoration (1600s) is in accordance with the needs of the
Jesuits, who used dramatic
and emotional appeal to draw
the faithful. It is resplendent
with coloured marble and
paintings, including works by
Ribera and Solimena, such as
the latter's *Expulsion of
Heliodorus from the Temple*
fresco. In 1688 an earthquake
destroyed the dome – the
present one is 18th century.

⓭
Sant'Anna e San Bartolomeo dei Lombardi

📍 C3 🏛 Piazza Monteoliveto
44 📞 081 551 33 33
🕐 8:30am-noon Mon-Sat
(Sat: also 5:30-6:30pm)

Also known as Santa Maria di
Monteoliveto, this church –
the favourite of the Aragonese
kings – was built in 1411 and
restored after World War II. It
is a repository of Renaissance
art. Entering, past the tomb
(1627) of Domenico Fontana
(who completed the dome
of St Peter's in Rome after
Michelangelo's death), the
richness of the interior unfolds.

The Cappella Mastrogiudice
contains an *Annunciation*
panel by Florentine sculptor
Benedetto da Maiano (1489).
In the Cappella Piccolomini
is Antonio Rossellino's
monument (c.1475) to Maria
d'Aragona (completed by da
Maiano). The Cappella del
Santo Sepolcro houses a *Pietà*
by Guido Mazzoni (1492). Its
eight terracotta figures are
considered life-size portraits
of the artist's contemporaries.
The old Sacristy, frescoed by
Vasari (1544), has inlaid stalls
by Giovanni da Verona (1510).

⓮
Castel Nuovo

📍 C4 🏛 Piazza Municipio
📞 081 795 77 13 🕐 9am-
7pm Mon-Sat (last adm:
6pm) 🚫 Some public hols

Also known as the Maschio
Angioino, this Angevin
fortress was built for Charles
of Anjou in 1279–82 and
given the *nuovo* ("new") part
of its name to distinguish it
from two earlier castles.
Despite its origins, apart
from the squat towers
and the Cappella Palatina
(which features Francesco
Laurana's *Madonna* of 1474
above the portal), most of
the structure is Aragonese.

TOP 3 NAPLES NIGHTSPOTS

Arenile di Bagnoli
🅰 E5 🏛 Via Coroglio 14b
🌐 areniledibagnoli.it
This lively spot is a local
and international music
mecca. There's a stage
along the sea in summer.

Cammarota Spritz
📍 B4 🏛 Vico Lungo Teatro
Nuovo 31 📞 320 277 5687
With a hip, grungy vibe,
this place serves Aperol
in plastic cups for €1.

Enoteca Belledonne
📍 A5 🏛 Vico Belledonne a
Chiaia 18 🌐 enoteca
belledonne.it
This bottle-lined wine
bar is always hopping.

The castle was the main royal residence. In the Sala dei Baroni, Ferdinand I of Aragon brutally suppressed the ringleaders of the Barons' revolt of 1486. The Aragonese were capable of violence, but they were also patrons of the arts.

The triumphal arch of the castle's entrance (begun 1454) is theirs. Commemorating Alfonso of Aragon's entry to Naples in 1443, this ingenious application of the ancient triumphal arch design was worked on, in part, by Laurana. The original bronze doors by Guillaume le Moine (1468) are in the Palazzo Reale. Part of the castle houses the **Museo Civico**.

Museo Civico

📞 081 795 77 22
🕐 9am–6pm Mon–Sat

The castle was the main royal residence. In the Sala dei Baroni, Ferdinand I of Aragon brutally suppressed the ringleaders of the Barons' revolt of 1486.

15

Museo Nazionale di San Martino

📍 A3 🏛 Largo San Martino 5 📞 081 229 45 02/03 🕐 8:30am–7:30pm Thu-Tue

Standing proudly high above Santa Lucia, the Baroque Certosa di San Martino, founded in the 1300s as a Carthusian monastery, offers great views out across the Bay of Naples. It contains a museum housing a variety of *presepi*, Christmas cribs of Neapolitan tradition, some featuring hundreds of figures. The cloister was completed in 1623–9 by Cosimo Fanzago (the creator of Neapolitan Baroque) to the 16th-century designs of Dosio. The church and choir are other examples of his virtuosity. Next to the Certosa is **Castel Sant'Elmo**, built from 1329–43 and rebuilt in the 1500s, from where there are further stunning views.

Castel Sant'Elmo

🕐 8:30am–5pm daily

↑ Castel Nuovo, the medieval seat of Naples' kings

←
The majestic arcades of
Galleria Umberto I, with
its handsome glass roof

Galleria Umberto I

📍 B4 🏛 Via Toledo
🕐 Daily

Once a focus for fashionable Neapolitans, the handsome arcades of the Galleria Umberto I were built in 1887 and rebuilt after World War II. They face Italy's largest and oldest opera house: the **Teatro San Carlo**, first built for Charles of Bourbon in 1737.

Teatro San Carlo
 🕐 Jan–Jul
🌐 teatrosancarlo.it

Palazzo Reale

📍 C5 🏛 Piazza Plebiscito 1
🕐 9am–8pm Thu–Tue
🔒 1 Jan, 25 Dec 🌐 palazzo realenapoli.it

Begun by Domenico Fontana in 1600, and later expanded, Naples' royal palace is a handsome edifice filled with furniture, tapestries, paintings and porcelain. The small private Teatro di Corte (1768) was built by Ferdinando Fuga. The building houses the **Biblioteca Nazionale** (library). The exterior has been partly restored and Piazza del Plebiscito has been cleaned up. The great colonnades sweep towards 19th-century San Francesco di Paola, modelled on Rome's Pantheon.

Biblioteca Nazionale
📞 081 781 92 31 🕐 8am–6:45pm Mon–Fri, 9am–1:45pm Sat; bring ID

Museo di Capodimonte

📍 A1 🏛 Via Miano 2
🕐 8:30am–7:30pm Thu–Tue
🌐 museocapodimonte. beniculturali.it

Begun in 1738 by the Bourbon king Charles III as a hunting

💬 **INSIDER TIP**
Street Food

For great street food, head to Spaccanapoli – a street crisscrossing the old centre. Try a *pizza a portafoglio* (folded pizza) and deep-fried *palle 'e riso* (balls of rice). Don't miss *baba* (rum-soaked dough) at Naples' oldest patisserie, Scaturchio.

lodge, the Palazzo Reale di Capodimonte houses this museum and its magnificent collections of Italian paintings. Included are works by Titian, Botticelli, Raphael and Perugino, much of it originating in the Farnese family collections. There is also a gallery of 19th-century art, largely from southern Italy.

Catacombs of San Gennaro

📍 A1 🏛 Via di Capodimonte 13 🕐 10am–5pm Mon–Sat (to 2pm Sun) 🌐 catacombe dinapoli.it

These catacombs – the original burial place of San Gennaro – are near the church of San Gennaro in Moenia. The small church was founded in the 8th century, and is adjoined by a 17th-century workhouse. Two tiers of catacombs dating from the 2nd century penetrate the tufa, and there are mosaics and early Christian frescoes. Further along the street, the Catacombs of San Gaudioso honour the 5th-century saint who founded a monastery on the spot. Above is the 17th-century church of Santa Maria della Sanità.

Castel dell'Ovo

📍 A2 🏛 Via Eldorado 3
📞 081 795 45 93 🕐 8:30am–7pm Mon–Sat (to 1:30pm Sun & hols)

Begun in 1154, the Castel dell'Ovo is the oldest castle in Naples. It is set on a small island facing, and joining, the Santa Lucia district – once the site of the city's shellfish market. A royal residence under the Normans and Hohenstaufen, today it belongs to the army. It is now used for cultural events, and there are great views from the ramparts.

Beneath its ramparts, tiny Porta Santa Lucia is filled with seafood restaurants. The Via Partenope, running past it, makes a really lovely promenade.

→ Statue of Frederick II in the Palazzo Reale

CAMPANIA

Set beneath the shadow of Mount Vesuvius,
Campania is a region of dramatic contrasts.
The hinterland, home to rich, well-cultivated plains,
is eclipsed by the Amalfi coastline with its
breathtaking views and the spectacular Cilento
seaboard. The mountainous interior, remote and
unvisited, contains small towns that were settled
by the Greeks, developed by the Romans and often
abandoned in the wake of malaria and Saracen
attacks. Elsewhere, extraordinary Roman towns
and Greek ruins, preserved by a blanket of volcanic
ash, reveal the area's ancient history.

Campania was first settled by the Etruscans and
the Greeks, whose massive ruins can be seen at
Paestum. Next came a time of great prosperity
under the Romans; archaeological evidence of which
still exists at Benevento, Santa Maria Capua Vetere
and, of course, Pompeii and Herculaneum.

Today, a visit to Pompeii is a high priority for
tourists, but this was not always so. Travellers on
the Grand Tour in the 1600s and early 1700s
preferred the volcanic phenomena of the Solfatara
crater and the Phlegraean Fields to the west of
Naples. Only when the first archaeological digs
unearthed the remains of Paestum and the
buried cities around Mount Vesuvius did a tour
of the ancient ruins become popular.

The beautiful colour, light and atmosphere found
on the islands of Capri and Ischia, and on the
Sorrento Peninsula, began to interest landscape
painters in the 19th century. The southern flank of
the peninsula – the Amalfi coast – remained isolated
until the mid-1960s, when it attracted visitors in
search of an alternative, remote lifestyle. Ironically,
the area has since become a popular holiday spot.

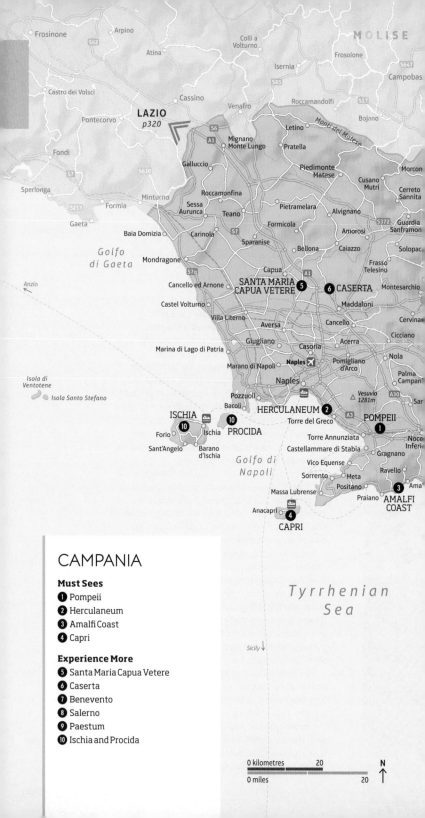

CAMPANIA

Must Sees

1 Pompeii
2 Herculaneum
3 Amalfi Coast
4 Capri

Experience More

5 Santa Maria Capua Vetere
6 Caserta
7 Benevento
8 Salerno
9 Paestum
10 Ischia and Procida

↑ Ruins of Pompeii against the backdrop of Mount Vesuvius

❶ 🛝 🅜 🖥

POMPEII

🅐 E5 🏠 Piazza Esedra 5 🕐 Apr-Oct: 9am-7:30pm daily (last adm: 6pm); Nov-Mar: 9am-5pm daily (last adm: 3:30pm) 🕐 1 Jan, 25 Dec 🌐 pompeiisites.org

When Vesuvius erupted in AD 79 the port of Pompeii and its 20,000 inhabitants were frozen in time, perfectly preserved by the volcano's ashes. The city has transfixed visitors since it was discovered in the 18th century.

↑ Plaster cast of one of Vesuvius's victims at Pompeii

Today, haunting plaster casts of Pompeii's inhabitants lie sprawled where they died, while exquisite mosaics and wall paintings – among the ruins of shops, homes and temples – offer total immersion into the Roman world.

Villas

Pompeii contains the remains of many large houses of great historical and architectural value. Highlights include the House of the Tragic Poet, with its *cave canem* ("beware of the dog") mosaic at the entrance, and the Villa of the Mysteries, with a fresco cycle showing an adolescent girl preparing for an initiation rite.

The Forum

The Forum was the centre of public life. Set around it were important administrative and religious institutions, including the Basilica and the temples of Apollo, Jupiter and Vespasian.

MOUNT VESUVIUS

Nearly 2,000 years after the eruption that destroyed Pompeii and Herculaneum, Vesuvius remains the most dangerous volcano in Europe, with an estimated 700,000 people living in the danger zone. Consequently the volcano, which last erupted in 1944, is constantly monitored. When it explodes again, scientists fear an eruption will put Naples in danger. If signs of activity increase to a potentially dangerous level, a 72-hour evacuation programme will be implemented.

To experience the volcano close-up take a minibus from Ercolano Scavi train station to the Mount Vesuvius car park, from where it's a half-hour climb to the steaming crater. For more volcanic experiences, head to the Solfatara, 30 minutes' drive west of Naples, where you can have the unforgettably bizarre experience of walking on the hot, spongy, stinking fields of sulphur in another volcanic crater.

←

Vibrant frescoes decorating the walls of the Villa of the Mysteries

Perhaps the most impressive ruins in the forum are its public baths. Built after 80 BC, the baths would have been widely used for daily ablutions. They follow a sequence from dressing room to *frigidarium* (cold room), then on to *tepidarium* (warm room) and *calidarium* (hot room). Mythological figures decorate the vaults of the *tepidarium*, and the *calidarium* contains a mammoth marble basin.

Theatres

Performance spaces included the Odeon (a small theatre for 1,500 people), the Great Theatre (which held 5,000 people) and the Amphitheatre (for up to 20,000 spectators of gladiotorial combat). Beautifully preserved, the Great Theatre is still used for modern productions in the summer months.

Brothels

Numerous *lupanare* (brothels) have been discovered during excavation work. The most striking is on a street parallel to Via Stabiana. Here, erotic frescoes and ancient graffiti line the walls, indicating the services offered by prostitutes, including boys, to satisfy their clients and lovers.

↓ Ruins lining a cobbled street in Pompeii

HERCULANEUM

🅐E5 **🏠Ercolano Scavi, Corso Resina** **⏰Apr–Oct: 8:30am–7:30pm daily (last adm: 6pm); Nov–Mar: 8:30am–5pm daily (last adm: 3:30pm)** **🌐pompeiisites.org**

Named after Hercules, this ancient Roman town was destroyed by Vesuvius in AD 79 – the same blast that engulfed Pompeii with rocks and ash. Herculaneum was entombed in superheated mud and ash, and is now the best-preserved ancient Roman city in Italy. Along with the town's buildings and decorations, wood, plants, textiles and other perishable materials have been uncovered in excavations.

Before the eruption of Vesuvius, Herculaneum fell under Greek influence around the 5th century BC and then under Samnite rule. In 89 BC the town became part of the Roman Empire, a residential *municipium* and resort.

Excavations began in the 18th century, and uncovered Roman houses built around a rectangular plan. Ancient Herculaneum is well below the level of the modern town, and the area is still being excavated. Highlights include the frescoes of the Villa dei Papiri (so-called because papyrus scrolls were discovered here), the frescoes in the College of the Augustales, the mosaics in the House of Neptune and Amphitrite, the changing rooms and mosaics of the City Baths, the two-storey Trellis House, and the replica sculptures in the courtyard of the House of the Stags. Look out for the remains of a wooden boat (complete with a coil of rope) in the Boat House, and for

↑ Visitors admiring the frescoes in the College of the Augustales

terracotta amphorae set into marble counters in the Thermopolia (the Roman answer to fast-food outlets). Many of the best-preserved sculptures and frescoes from Herculaneum are now on display in the Museo Archeologico Nazionale (*pp452–3*).

← Mosaic in the summer dining room of the House of Neptune and Amphitrite

→ Stag and dog sculpture discovered in the courtyard of the House of the Stags

Did You Know?

The J Paul Getty Museum
in Malibu is a re-creation
of Herculaneum's
Villa dei Papiri.

Ruined houses and ↑
shops lining a street in
Herculaneum

Colourful villas spilling down the hillside to the sea in Positano

3

AMALFI COAST

 E5 Amalfi *i* Corso delle Repubbliche Marinare 27, Amalfi; www.amalfitouristoffice.it

Suspended between sea, sky and earth, state road 163, which twists and turns along the full length of the Amalfi coast, offers stunning views at every corner. Until the 19th century, this stretch of the "divine coast" was isolated but by the early 1900s it had began to attract travellers, artists and writers. Today, popular pleasures here include beach-hopping and taking trips to coastal summits to admire the breathtaking views.

①
Sorrento

 i Azienda Autonoma di Soggiorno Sorento-Sant'agnello, Via de Maio 35; www.sorrento tourism.com

On the cliffs at the southern end of the Bay of Naples, Sorrento has ancient origins, seen in the original Greek town plan in the centre. In the summer the town fills with tourists taking in the views or relaxing at cafés. Both Marina Grande and Marina Piccola have small beaches.

②
Positano

 i AAST, Via del Saracino 4; www.azienda turismopositano.it

Pastel-coloured houses here clamber down a vertiginous slope into the sea, with the oldest houses in the upper part of Positano decorated with pretty Baroque stuccoes. The traffic-free street going down to the sea, Via Pasitea, penetrates the heart of town with its narrow-stepped alleys, houses with vaulted roofs, terraces and tiny

gardens that defy the rock. Near the beach is the small church of Santa Maria dell' Assunta, whose cupola is covered with yellow, blue and green majolica tiles. The descent ends at Marina Grande, lined with high-end bars and restaurants.

---

③
Amalfi

 i AAST, Corso Repubbliche Marinare 27; www.amalfi.it

Tucked in between mountains and sea, Amalfi is a perennial favourite with visitors for its scenic beauty and original architecture. It also has a glorious history as a powerful maritime republic. Amalfi's

> HIDDEN GEM
> ### Nocelle
>
> Positano can get very busy with day-trippers. To escape the crowds, make the steep ascent to Montepertuso, from where a splendid scenic path leads to the quiet mountain village of Nocelle, a pleasant place to pause for lunch.

cathedral, the **Duomo di Sant'Andrea**, founded in the 9th century, was rebuilt in Romanesque style in the 11th century and altered several times. Heading inland from Amalfi, you can visit the Valle dei Mulini (Valley of the Mills), known for its traditional paper production, and the **Museo della Carta** or Paper Museum.

Duomo di Sant'Andrea

Ⓐ Via Duca Mansone I ⓒ Mar-Oct: 7:30am-7pm daily; Nov-Feb: 9-11:30am, 4:30-7pm daily

Museo della Carta

Ⓐ Via delle Cartiere ⓒ 089 830 45 61 ⓒ Mar-Oct: 10am-6:30pm Tue-Sun; Nov-Feb: 10:30am-3:30pm Tue-Sun

---

④
Ravello

🚇 🚌 ℹ AAST, Via Roma 18; www.ravello-time.it

Somewhat off the beaten track, Ravello is for those who love peace and quiet – though it does liven up for the Ravello Festival in July and August. The town's architectural highlights include the **Duomo**, dedicated to San Pantaleone, the town's patron saint; **Villa Rufolo**, famed for its tropical gardens; and **Villa Cimbrone**, now a small luxury hotel *(see box)* with spellbinding views of the coast to Punta Licosa.

Duomo

Ⓐ Piazza Duomo ⓒ 9am-7pm daily ⓦ chiesaravello.it

Villa Rufolo

Ⓐ Piazza Duomo ⓒ Summer: 9am-9pm ⓦ villarufolo.it

The marble façade of Duomo di Sant'Andrea in Amalfi

STAY

Hotel Villa Cimbrone
Perched high atop the town of Ravello, this graceful hotel has memorable gardens with idyllic views along the coast, a Michelin-starred restaurant, a pool, and delicately frescoed rooms that once hosted Greta Garbo, D H Lawrence and Gore Vidal.

Ⓐ Via Santa Chiara 26 ⓦ hotelvilla cimbrone.com

$ $ $

↑ View of Capri Town and I Faraglioni from Mount Solaro

 4

CAPRI

E5 🚢 Capri 🛈 Piazza Umberto I, Capri; www.capritourism.com

Nestled at the southern end of the Bay of Naples, this small, rugged island has a long history of attracting well-heeled visitors. Roman emperors Augustus and Tiberius enjoyed lengthy stays here, the latter spending his last years ruling from his luxurious Capri villa. In the 19th century, the island ushered in the arrival of foreign artists, politicians and intellectuals. It remains a tourist mecca and, while it can swell with crowds of day-trippers, its charm and beauty make it well worth a visit.

① Capri Town

Straddling the eastern part of the island, the town of Capri is from where most excursions around the island begin. Visitors usually arrive by boat into the main harbour, Marina Grande, a colourful village of seafood restaurants, bars and shops. From here, a ride on the funicular leads straight to the heart of the old town within a few minutes. Stroll along Via Camerelle, Capri's answer to New York's Fifth Avenue, for luxury brand shopping. The picturesque dome of Baroque church Santo Stefano overlooks the bustling scene.

② Piazza Umberto I

The famous "Piazzetta" in Capri Town is an outdoor living room, crowded day and night. A prime people-watching and celebrity-spotting venue, it is packed with café tables buzzing with gossip and animated discussion. The narrow alleys surrounding the piazza are also a delight to explore.

③ Anacapri

🛈 AAST, Via Orlandi 59; 081 837 15 24

On the slopes of Monte Solaro is the second town on the island, Anacapri. A refreshing contrast to the pomp of Capri Town, its relatively quiet lanes and piazzas feature churches, museums and artisanal shops. Here you can visit the church of San Michele, the Villa San Michele (former home of the Swedish physician Axel Munthe) and the excavations at Emperor Tiberius's imperial

EAT

L'Olivo
One of two Michelin-starred restaurants at the luxurious Capri Palace Hotel, L'Olivo is a study in masterful Mediterranean cuisine.

🏠 Via Capodimonte 14, Anacapri ⏱ Oct–mid-Apr 🌐 capripalace.com

💲💲💲

→ Fishing vessels moored in Marina Grande, Capri Town

Villa Damecuta and, of course, appreciate the magnificent view from the top of the hill.

④ Grotto Azzurra

🚤 **Boat tours from the Marina Grande, Capri Town**

One of the island's most popular sights, this large sea cave is illuminated by an incredible, otherworldly blue light, created by the sunlight that streams through the small entrance and is then reflected from the bottom of the sea. Trips are often cancelled during high tide or in rough seas.

⑤ Villa Jovis

🏛 **Via A Maiuri** 🕐 **9am-1 hr before sunset daily**

The retreat built by Emperor Tiberius stands proudly on the mountain named after him, the dramatic setting chosen for its seclusion. Excavations of the site have unearthed baths, apartments and the infamous "Tiberius's drop", from which the emperor's victims were said to be thrown into the sea. The ruins also include the remains of a tower once used to communicate with the mainland.

⑥ Marina Piccola

Occupying a picturesque bay dotted with yachts, the laid-back Marina Piccola has bars and restaurants pressed along the water and a few spits of sand wedged between rocky outcrops. It is a great spot for swimming and sunbathing,

Did You Know?

Emperor Augustus decided to build villas on Capri after he saw a dead tree miraculously sprout leaves on the island.

with views of I Faraglioni, the rock formations soaring up to 109 m (360 ft) out of the sea. Commissioned by the German industrialist Alfred Krupp, the famous Via Krupp (often closed due to renovations) makes a vertiginous descent towards the marina from Capri Town in a series of striking hairpin bends. A quicker and more reliable route is to follow Via Roma and Via Mulo.

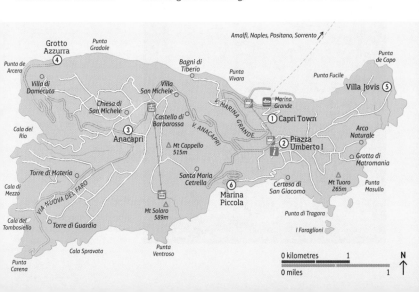

EXPERIENCE MORE

5

Santa Maria Capua Vetere

🅰E5 🏛 Caserta 🚇 ⓘ Palazzo Reale, Caserta; 0823 32 22 33

This town's 1st-century-AD Roman **amphitheatre** used to be Italy's largest after the Colosseum. There are well-preserved tunnels beneath it. The town occupies the site of ancient Capua, the scene of the revolt of the gladiators led by Spartacus in 73 BC. The on-site Gladiator Museum recreates their history. Nearby is a Mithraeum (2nd–3rd century) with well-preserved frescoes. Finds from the sites are shown in the **Museo Archeologico dell'Antica Capua** in Capua.

Amphitheatre
⊛ 🏛 Piazza 1 Ottobre
☎ 0823 79 88 64 ⏰ Tue-Sun

Museo Archeologico dell'Antica Capua
⊛ 🏛 Via Roberto d'Angio 48, Capua ☎ 0823 84 42 06 ⏰ Tue-Sun

6

Caserta

🅰E5 🚇 ⓘ Palazzo Reale; www.reggiadicaserta. beniculturali.it

The magnificently opulent **Palazzo Reale** dominates Caserta. Built for the Bourbon King Charles III, Italy's largest royal palace boasts over 1,000 rooms, grand staircases and richly adorned apartments.

It was designed by Luigi Vanvitelli, and construction started in 1752. The surrounding park is dotted with fountains, ornamental waterworks and statuary.

San Leucio, 3 km (2 miles) northwest of Caserta, is a model town built by Ferdinand IV, who also founded its silk industry.

Palazzo Reale
⊛ 🏛 Viale Douhet 2a
☎ 0823 44 80 84 ⏰ 8:30am-7:30pm Wed-Mon 🚫 Pub hols

7

Benevento

🅰E5 🚇 ⓘ Via Sala 31; www.comune.benevento.it

The Roman city Beneventum was an important centre at the end of the first extension of the Via Appia from Capua. The well-preserved Arch of Trajan on Via Traiano was built of marble in AD 114–166. The relief sculpture adorning it – scenes from the life of Trajan and mythological subjects – is in excellent condition.

Elsewhere, evidence of the Romans is to be found in the ruined **Roman theatre**, built during Hadrian's reign, and in the **Museo del Sannio**, which contains artifacts from the region, from ancient Greek finds to modern art.

During World War II, the city stood directly in the way of the Allied advance from the south. It was heavily bombed, hence its largely modern appearance. Benevento has centuries-old associations with pagan worship, and a liqueur called Strega (witch) is made here.

A marble-covered hall in the Palazzo Reale of Caserta, Italy's largest royal palace

Corricella, a colourful village on the island of Ischia

Roman Theatre
◈ 🏠 Via Teatro Romano 3
📞 082 45 04 06 ⏰ Mon-Sat
🚫 Public hols

Museo del Sannio
◈ 🏠 Piazza Santa Sofia 1
⏰ 9am-7pm Tue-Sun 🚫 1 Jan,
25 Dec 🌐 museodelsannio.it

Museo Diocesano
🏠 Largo Plebiscito 12 📞 089
23 91 26 ⏰ 9am-1pm &
3-7pm Thu-Tue

Museo Provinciale
🏠 Via San Benedetto 28
📞 089 23 11 35 ⏰ 9am-
7:30pm Tue-Sun

the extensive finds from the site, including tomb treasures, some terracotta votive offerings, architectural fragments and sculpture.

Museum
◈ ⏰ Daily 🚫 From 1:40pm on 1st & 3rd Mon of month

---

⑧ Salerno

🅰 E5 FS 🚆 🚌 Salerno
🛈 Via Lungomare Trieste
7-9; 089 23 14 32

The big, busy port of Salerno is visited today for its 11th-century Duomo. Its best feature is the Atrium, whose columns came from Paestum. In the crypt is the Tomb of St Matthew, brought here in 954.

The **Museo Diocesano** is home to most of the cathedral treasures, while local archaeological finds are in the **Museo Provinciale**.

South of Salerno, the Cilento is a mountainous region with a remote interior and a lovely coastline. Outside Castellammare di Velia, 70 km (43 miles) south of Salerno, are the ruins of the Greek town of Elea (founded 6th century BC). Excavations have revealed a magnificent 4th-century Roman gateway, Roman baths and the remains of the acropolis.

⑨ Paestum

🅰 E5 🚌 From Salerno
FS Paestum ⏰ 8:30am-
7:30pm daily 🛈 Via Magna
Grecia 919; 0828 81 10 23

The Greeks founded this city in the 6th century BC and called it Poseidonia, the City of Poseidon. The Romans renamed Paestum in 273 BC. It was abandoned in the 9th century due to malaria and a Saracen assault, and rediscovered in the 1700s.

Paestum has three massive Doric temples in an excellent state of repair: the Basilica or Temple of Hera I (mid-6th century BC); the Temple of Neptune (5th century BC), the largest and most complete at Paestum; and the Temple of Ceres, thought to date between its two neighbours.

Excavations have revealed the remains of the ancient city, its public and religious buildings, roads and protective walls. A **museum** contains

⑩ Ischia and Procida

🅰 E5 🏠 Napoli 🚢 Ischia & Procida 🛈 Via Sogliuzzo 72, Ischia; www.infoischia procida.it

Ischia is the biggest island in the Bay of Naples and, with its beach resorts, thermal springs and therapeutic mudbaths, it is nearly as popular as Capri. The northern and western shores are developed; the southern flank of the island is the quietest. Here, the village of Sant'Angelo is dominated by a long-extinct volcano, Monte Epomeo, whose summit offers views across the bay. Also worth a visit are the gardens of **La Mortella** in Forio.

The tiny, picturesque island of Procida is less visited and very tranquil, with good swimming at Chiaiolella.

La Mortella
◈ 📞 081 98 62 20 ⏰ Apr-Oct: 9am-7pm Tue, Thu, Sat & Sun

ABRUZZO, MOLISE AND PUGLIA

Hugging the southeastern seaboard of Italy and looking towards the Balkans, the mountainous regions of Abruzzo and Molise, separated in 1963, are sparsely populated, quiet places where the wild landscape exerts a strong influence. Settled by various Apennine tribes in the Middle Bronze Age, Abruzzo and Molise were later subdued by the Romans, united under the Normans in the 12th century and, thereafter, ruled by a succession of dynasties based in Naples. Abruzzo, dominated by the Apennines, is a brooding region characterized by tracts of forest, sandy shores and breathtaking mountain scenery. Vertiginous drops preface the ascent to ramshackle hill-towns clinging to the sides of mountains. Molise's landscape is less dramatic, featuring high plains, gentle valleys and lonely peaks.

Bathed in ivory light, Puglia radiates warmth all year round. Pheonicians, Greeks and Romans, medieval Crusaders and pilgrims have all been drawn here by its fertile lands and easy access to the East. Its lively commercial centres – Lecce, Bari and Taranto – continue to draw visitors to the area. Puglia has glorious architecture, particularly in the churches and castles of the north. The curious *trulli* houses in central Puglia, the florid Baroque of Lecce and the Levantine atmosphere of its merchant cities complete the picture of an ancient land subject to more influences from outside the Italian peninsula than from within it.

Adriatic Sea

Isola Pianosa

Rodi Gargánico

Péschici

Vieste

GARGANO PENINSULA

8

Pugnochiuso

Mattinata

Manfredonia

Golfo di Manfredonia

Greece, Albania, Croatia →

Lupara

Margherita di Savoia

Barletta

Cerignola

Andria

11 TRANI

Molfetta

Canosa di Puglia

Bari

CASTEL DEL MONTE 12

Corato

Bítonto

13

15 BARI

Modugno

Mola di Bari

RUVO DI PUGLIA

Polignano a Mare

pinazzola

PUGLIA

Rutigliano

Monopoli

Gravina in Puglia

Altamura

Turi

Putignano

Fasano

ALBEROBELLO 14

Martina Franca

Torre Sabina

Greece →

Mottola

16 OSTUNI

BASILICATA AND CALABRIA *p490*

Matera

S7

Ginosa

Massafra

Ceglie Méssapica

Mesagne

Salento

Brindisi

Torre Mattarelle

BASILICATA

Palagiano

Francavilla Fontana

San Pietro Vernotico

Montemurro

TARANTO 17

Pulsano

Manduria

San Pancrazio Salentino

San Cataldo

Policoro

Librari

Veglie

Lequile

1 LECCE

Melendugno

Latronico

Torre Lapillo

Rocca Imperiale

Golfo di Taranto

GALATINA 18

19 OTRANTO

Maglie

Castrovillari

Amendolara

Gallipoli

Posto Racale

Taurisano

Tricase

Trebisacce

Torre Pali

Santa Maria di Leuca

San Sosti

CALABRIA

Rossano

Cariati

Cetraro

Acri

0 kilometres 40

0 miles 40

N ↑

↑ The 1st-century-BC Roman amphitheatre on Piazza Sant'Oronzo

LECCE

 G6 🚉 **Viale Oronzo Quarta** 🚌 **Via Boito and Via Adua**
ℹ **Via Vittorio Emanuele 23; www.ilecce.it**

With scores of Baroque churches and palazzi, their golden façades a frolic of scrolls, curlicues, flowers, foliage, monsters, dragons, cherubs and angels, Lecce is a lively provincial capital and university town. It has always been beautiful, but in recent years, this part of Puglia has become fashionable. Churches and palaces have been restored, much of its historic centre has been pedestrianized, and its cobbled streets are full of stylish bars, restaurants and hip hotels.

① Piazza del Duomo

This elegant square is home to the Bishop's Palace (rebuilt 1632), the grand Duomo and the Seminary. Originally built around 1100, the present Duomo dates from the middle of the 17th century and was designed by Giuseppe Zimbalo, who also designed the five-storey bell tower. The Seminary once supplied the Vatican with *castrato* singers – eunuchs noted for their high voices.

② Chiesa del Rosario

 Via Giuseppe Libertini 5
🕿 **0832 30 85 40** 🕐 **Opening times vary, call ahead**

Said to be the finest work by Zimbalo (begun 1691), the exterior of this church is ornate and idiosyncratic in its detail. Set on a Greek-cross plan, the church was due to be topped by a dome, but the plans were abandoned in favour of a simple wooden roof after Zimbalo's death in 1710.

③ Basilica di Santa Croce

 Via Umberto I 3 🕿 **0832 24 19 57** 🕐 **Opening times vary, call ahead**

Built 1549–1679, this is perhaps Lecce's most famous Baroque

STAY

La Fiermontina Urban Resort

This luxurious boutique hotel inhabits a former 17th-century residence in the fashionable old quarter known for its Baroque architecture. Expect sleek Italian furniture, vintage star-pinnacle ceilings, Trani stone floors and contemporary art. A dimly lit bar and Pugliese restaurant top things off.

🏠 **Piazzetta Scipione de Summa 4**
ⓦ **lafiermontina.com**

€€€

LECCESE BAROQUE

Lecce's architecture is mostly in the highly decorative Baroque style, which flourished in the 1600s and earned the city the nickname "Florence of the South". This style was possible due to the pietra di Lecce, an easily carved golden sandstone used by the city's architects. Giuseppe Zimbalo (1620–1710) was the greatest exponent of the style.

building. The extravagantly decorated façade is a riot of grotesque beasts, animals and allegorical figures set around a large rose window by Zimbalo. The slightly more subdued interior features 17 altars.

---

⑥ Castello di Lecce

A Norman castle expanded by Charles V, the Castello di Lecce is Puglia's biggest fortress. Part of the building is now home to the **Museo della Cartapesta**, a museum of papier-mâché sculptures.

Museo della Cartapesta
🏛 Viale 25 Luglio 🕐 9:30am–1pm & 4–8pm daily

---

④ Museo Provinciale Sigismondo Castromediano

🏛 Viale Gallipoli 28 ☎ 0832 68 35 03 🕐 8:30am–7:30pm Mon–Sat, 9am–1pm Sun

This fascinating museum contains objects dating from the Bronze Age and an excellent collection of Attic vases. The exhibit labels are mainly in Italian, but the staff speak good English and are generally eager to help.

---

⑤ Piazza Sant'Oronzo

Standing in this square is a large 1739 bronze statue of St Oronzo, who was appointed Bishop of Lecce by St Paul in AD 57, and later martyred by the Roman emperor Nero. The statue was erected as thanks for deliverance from a plague in 1656, for which St Oronzo was attributed. Next to the column is an elliptical Roman amphitheatre, dating from Emperor Hadrian's time.

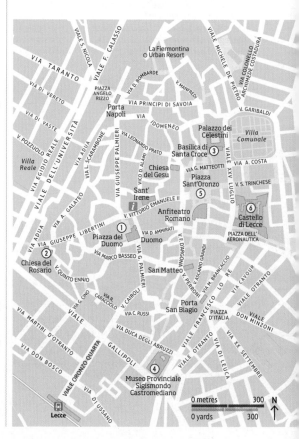

❷

PARCO NAZIONALE D'ABRUZZO, LAZIO E MOLISE

🅰 E5 🚉 Avezzano or Castel di Sangro 🚌 To Pescasseroli ⏱ Opening times vary, check website ℹ Via Colli dell'Oro, Pescasseroli; www.parcoabruzzo.it

This vast park, inaugurated in 1922, has a rich landscape of high peaks, rivers, lakes and forests, and is one of Europe's most important nature reserves. Part of a royal hunting reserve until 1877, today it provides refuge for 66 species of mammal, 52 types of reptile, amphibian and fish, and 230 species of bird, including the golden eagle and white-backed woodpecker, as well as over 2,000 varieties of flora.

Exploring the Park

The park has an extensive network of paths, and there are opportunities for horse riding, trekking and climbing. Pescasseroli is a great base from which to explore – the town has a visitor centre, good tourist facilities and a small zoological garden with animals living in the region. Other highlights of the park include Lake Barrea, a spectacular artificial lake surrounded by valleys and forests offering walking and pony trekking, and the Camosciara, a dramatic region of mountains, valleys, waterfalls and streams. The park is famous for its many dense forests – of maple, hornbeam, ash, hawthorn, cherry, wild apple and pear – which protect the once persecuted Marsican brown bears and Apennine wolves that roam the area.

WILDLIFE IN THE PARK

This great expanse of protected land offers an array of different habitats, home to an abundance of flora and fauna. The park's biodiversity is testament to careful conservation work by the Park Authority.

Apennine Chamois
This species of goat-antelope can be seen hiding in dense forests of beech and maple.

Apennine Wolves
The park guarantees protection for the Apennine wolf, and about 60 wolves survive here. The chances of seeing one, however, are fairly remote.

Marsican Brown Bear
Once hunted almost to extinction, between 80 and 100 brown bears now prowl the park. Shy and solitary, the bears tend to roam at night.

Golden Eagles
These spectacular predators may be seen near the Sangro River, and can often be observed flying over mountain peaks and ridges as they hunt for prey.

 Hikers taking a break to enjoy views of Pescasseroli from Mancino Castle ruins

←

Peaceful valley of the Camosciara mountain range

EXPERIENCE MORE

❸ Atri

🅰E4 🚉Teramo 🚌
🅦comune.atri.te.it

The prettiest in a series of small hill-towns in Abruzzo, Atri is a warren of stepped streets, alleys and passages bound by mostly brick-and-stone churches and houses. The 13th-century Duomo occupies the site of a Roman bath; the crypt was once a swimming pool, and fragments of the original mosaic floor are visible in the apse. Also in the apse is Andrea Delitio's beautiful 15th-century fresco cycle, in which he combined landscape and architecture in a variety of religious scenes from the Old and New Testaments. The cloister has views of the 15th-century brick campanile.

South of Atri is the picturesque hill-town of Penne, with its homogeneous buildings of reddish brick, which give it a wonderful, warm glow. East of Atri, Loreto Aprutino is known for *The Last Judgment* fresco (14th century) in Santa Maria in Piano.

❹ Sulmona

🅰E4 🚉L'Aquila 🚆🚌
🚺Corso Ovidio 208; www. comune.sulmona.aq.it

Famous as the home of Ovid, Sulmona is filled with ancient buildings, especially along medieval Via dell'Ospedale. The Palazzo dell'Annunziata, founded in 1320, combines Gothic and Renaissance styles. The **Museo Civico** holds a collection of local antiquities, costumes and paintings. The adjacent church of the Annunziata, with a Baroque façade, was rebuilt in the 18th century. Behind the church are 1 BC–AD 2 ruins of a Roman house.

At the end of Viale Matteotti is the cathedral of San Panfilo, built over a Roman temple. San Francesco della Scarpa, in Piazza del Carmine, has a 13th-century portal. Winding past it to the Fontana del Vecchio (1474) is an aqueduct that once fuelled local industry.

East of Sulmona is the Maiella National Park, a massif of 61 peaks and forested valleys offering walking, birdwatching, climbing and skiing.

OVID, THE LATIN POET

Born in 43 BC, Ovid was Sulmona's most illustrious inhabitant. Not much survives here to remind you of his presence, apart from a Corso Ovidio, a 20th-century statue of him in Piazza XX Settembre and, just outside the town, a ruin traditionally known as Ovid's Villa. Ovid's subjects included love (*Ars Amatoria*) and mythology (*Metamorphoses*). In AD 8 he was banished into exile on the Black Sea, the far edge of the Roman Empire, after being implicated in a scandal of adultery with Julia, the granddaughter of Emperor Augustus. Ovid died in exile in AD 17.

To the west, Cocullo hosts the May Processione dei Serpari (Festival of Snakes) in which a statue of Domenico Abate, the patron saint, is draped with serpents and carried through the town. In the 11th century he is said to have rid the area of venomous snakes.

Museo Civico

🏛Palazzo della SS Annunziata, Corso Ovidio
📞0864 21 02 16 🕐9am-1pm & 3:30-6:30pm Tue-Sun

❺ Scanno

🅰E5 🏛L'Aquila 🚌 🚺Via Napoli 21; www.comune. scanno.aq.it

Wonderfully well preserved, this medieval hill-town features alleys and narrow flights of steps, oddly shaped courtyards with small churches, and ancient mansions in whose windows women can be seen making lace or embroidering.

In the shadow of Apennine peaks and beside lovely Lago di Scanno, the town is also a favoured stop on the way to the Parco Nazionale d'Abruzzo (*p482*).

↑ Peaceful stretch of the mountain-fringed Lago di Scanno

⑥ Lanciano

 E4 ⬛ **Chieti** 🚃🚌
ℹ **Corso Roma 63; www. lanciano.eu**

Large parts of Lanciano's old nucleus remain from the Middle Ages. In the crumbling Civitanova quarter is the 13th-century church of Santa Maria Maggiore, with a magnificent 14th-century portal and a silver processional cross (1422). The Duomo stands on the remains of a Roman bridge. An underground passage links the latter to the Sanctuary of the Eucharistic Miracle, where a host and wine that turned into live flesh and blood in the 8th century are kept.

⑦ Isole Tremiti

F4 ⬛ **Foggia** 🚢 **San Nicola** ℹ **Via Emilio Perrone 17, Foggia; Via Sant'Antonio Abate 21, Monte Sant'Angelo; www.lecinqueisole.it**

The Tremiti are the Italian islands least visited by foreigners. San Domino is

the largest, with a sandy beach and coves. Julia, granddaughter of Augustus, was exiled here for adultery from AD 8 until her death in AD 28. The poet Ovid was allegedly involved.

Santa Maria a Mare, in San Nicola, is an abbey fortress founded in the 8th century. It was turned into a prison in the late 1700s, a role it maintained until 1945.

The islands of San Domino and Santa Maria a Mare are popular with Italians. The swimming is good, though the coastline of San Nicola is rocky.

⑧ Gargano Peninsula

 F5 ⬛ **Foggia** 🚃🚌
ℹ **Piazza della Libertà 1, Manfredonia; Piazza Municipio 2, Monte Sant'Angelo; www. parcogargano.gov.it**

A rocky spur jutting into the Adriatic Sea, the Gargano is dotted with coves and cliffs. Its coastal towns – Peschici, Vieste, Manfredonia and Rodi Garganico – are popular with holiday-makers. To the east lies the Foresta Umbra, a woodland of beech, oak, yew and pine, and to the north the salt lakes

🔍 HIDDEN GEM
The Grottoes of Isole Tremiti

A designated marine reserve, this group of islands is rife with grottoes, including del Bue Marino, Scoglio e del Sale, delle Rondinelle, delle Murene and delle Viole. The caves offer a glimpse into the benthic ecosystem under the deep blue Adriatic Sea. Boats can be taken from Vasto, Ortona, Vieste, Capoiale and Termoli.

of Lesina and Varano, havens for waterfowl. Plunging through the Gargano is an old pilgrim route (S272) from San Severo in the west to the shrine at Monte Sant'Angelo in the east. The first stop is San Marco in Lamis, dominated by a huge 16th-century convent. Further along, San Giovanni Rotondo is a focus for pilgrims visiting the tomb of Padre Pio (1887–1968), a beatified miracle worker. The last stop is Monte Sant'Angelo, with its grotto where the Archangel Michael is said to have appeared to the Bishop of Sipontum in 493.

9

Lucera

AE5 **A**Foggia **B** **i**Piazza Nocelli 6; www.comune. lucera.fg.it

On the northeast edge of town, once a prosperous Roman colony, are the ruins of a Roman amphitheatre. Lucera was rebuilt in the 13th century by Frederick II, who peopled it with 20,000 Sicilian Muslims. It became one of the strongest fortresses in southern Italy. Built in 1233, its magnificent castle features a fortified wall interspersed with 24 towers.

In 1300, Charles II, who killed most of Lucera's Muslim population, began the Duomo on the site of their main mosque. The soaring nave is filled with 15th- and 16th-century frescoes and carvings.

The **Museo Civico Fiorelli** has displays of episodes from throughout Lucera's history.

Museo Civico Fiorelli
A Via de Nicastri 36 **C** 0881 54 70 41 **O** 9:30am-1:30pm & 3:30-7:30pm Tue-Sun

---

10

Troia

AE5 **A**Foggia **B** **w**comune.troia.fg.it

Founded in 1017 as a Byzantine fortress against the Lombards, Troia fell to the Normans in 1066. Until Frederick II destroyed it in 1229, the town had been ruled by a succession of powerful bishops who were responsible for producing many remarkable buildings, including Troia's Duomo.

Constructed over 30 years from 1093, it blends elements of Lombard, Saracenic and Byzantine style with that of the Pisan-Romanesque. Elegant blind arcading distinguishes the Duomo's lower storey. The upper sections are characterized by

powerfully carved sculpture – projecting lions and bulls. The upper façade displays a rose window with Saracenic-style detailing.

The main entrance, with bronze doors by Oderisio da Beneventano (1119), is dominated by carved Byzantine-style capitals.

11

Trani

AF5 **A**Bari **B****B** **i**Piazza Sacra Regia Udienza II; 0883 58 88 30

In the Middle Ages, this small, whitewashed port bustled with mercantile activity and was filled with merchants and traders from Genoa, Amalfi and Pisa. It reached its peak of prosperity under Frederick II.

Today it is visited for its Norman Duomo, built mainly

↑ The magnificent bell tower of Trani's Duomo

from 1159 to 1186. It is dedicated to St Nicholas the Pilgrim, a little-remembered miracle worker (died 1094) who was canonized as an act of rivalry against the town of Bari, which possessed the bones of another, more memorable St Nicholas. The Duomo's most notable external features are its sculptures, particularly surrounding the rose window and the arched window below it, and the entrance portal with bronze doors (1175–9) by Barisano da Trani.

Next to the Duomo is the castle (1233–49) founded by Frederick II. Rebuilt in the 14th and 15th centuries, it is a well-preserved edifice with one wall dropping sheer into the sea.

 EXPERIENCE Abruzzo, Molise and Puglia

On Via Ognissanti is the Chiesa di Ognissanti, a 12th-century Templar church that was built as part of a hospital. Note the sculpture of the Annunciation in the lunette above the door.

12
Castel del Monte

A F5 **A** Località Andria, Bari **O** 10:15am-7:15pm daily (Oct-Mar: 9am-6:30pm) **C** 1 Jan, 25 Dec **W** casteldelmonte.beniculturali.it

The UNESCO World Heritage Site of Castel del Monte, built in the mid-13th century, out-classes every other castle associated with Frederick II. The emperor had broad intellectual interests, and he used his castles as hunting lodges where he could retire from court life with his falcons and books. Inside there are two floors, each with eight rib-vaulted rooms, some still lined with marble. This, and the marble mouldings on the entrance and the upper floor, as well as sophisticated lavatory arrangements, mark the castle as a palace.

13
Ruvo di Puglia

A F5 **A** Bari **FS** **I** Piazza Matteotti 31; 080 950 71 11

Once celebrated for its vases, Ruvo di Puglia's ceramics industry flourished until the 2nd century BC. The style was inspired by the striking red and black colours of Attic and Corinthian models. The **Museo Archeologico Nazionale Jatta** has a good overview.

The imposing 13th-century Cattedrale is a bold example of the Apulian-Romanesque style with a portal that blends Byzantine, Saracenic and Classical motifs.

Museo Archeologico Nazionale Jatta

◎ **A** Piazza G Bovio 35 **O** 8:30am-1:30pm daily (to 7:30pm Thu) **C** 1 Jan, 1 May, 25 Dec **W** palazzojatta.org

14
Alberobello

A G5 **A** Bari **FS** To Alberobello & Ostuni **I** Via Monte Nero 1; 080 432 28 22

Alberobello is a UNESCO World Heritage Site and the *trulli* capital, with these strange white buildings crowding the narrow streets. *Trulli* are built from limestone stacked without using mortar. Many of the stone roof tiles have mysterious symbols painted on them. The origins of *trulli* are obscure, though the name is traditionally applied to ancient round tombs found in the Roman countryside. Most of Alberobello's *trulli* are now souvenir shops or tiny cafés, though the Parrocchia Sant'Antonio di Padova, a diminutive church, is inspired by *trulli* architecture.

Did You Know?
—
Alberobello is famous for its *trulli* – strange circular whitewashed buildings with conical roofs.

↑ The typical conical roofs of Alberobello's *trulli*

⓯
Bari

🏔F5 ✈🚆🚌⛴ 🛈 Piazza
del Ferrarese 29; www.
comune.bari.it

Roman Barium was simply a
commercial centre, but the
city became the regional
capital under the Saracens in
847, and was later the seat of
the *catapan*, the Byzantine
governor of southern Italy.
Under the Normans, to
whom it fell in 1071, Bari
became a centre of maritime
significance. Today it is
Puglia's lively capital and an
important port with ferries to
and from Croatia and Greece.

The Basilica di San Nicola,
one of Puglia's first great
Norman churches (begun
1087), has a plain exterior with
a tall gabled section flanked
by towers. The Apulian-
Romanesque portal has
carving on the door jambs
and arch in Arabic, Byzantine
and Classical styles. Beyond
the choir screen is a fine 12th-
century altar canopy and an
episcopal throne (c.11th
century). The relics of St
Nicholas – patron saint of the
city – are buried in the crypt.

The late 12th-century
Apulian-Romanesque
Cattedrale is based on San
Nicola, with a dome and one
surviving tower (the other
one collapsed in 1613). The
Baroque portals on the façade
incorporate 12th-century
doorways. The interior has
been restored to its medieval
simplicity. The sacristy, built as
a baptistry, is known as the
Trulla. The crypt houses the
remains of San Sabino, Bari's
original patron saint.

The city's castle, founded
by Roger II, was adapted by
Frederick II in 1233–9. In the
vaulted hall is a collection
of plaster casts of sculpture
and architectural fragments
from various Romanesque
monuments in the region.

⓰
Ostuni

🏔G5 🚉Brindisi 🚆🚌
🛈 Corso Mazzini 8; www.
borgostuni.it

Known as the *Città Bianca*
(white city), the hill-town of
Ostuni is a beguiling tangle
of whitewashed houses,
cobbled streets and arched
alleyways. The white citadel
is traffic-free, but there are
well-signposted car parks
in the newer, lower town.

There are some lovely
palaces and churches – as
well as cafés and restaurants –
along Via della Cattedrale,
leading up to the cathedral.
Highlights include the former
Carmelite monastery of Santa
Maria Maddalena dei Pazzi
and the adjoining church of
San Vito Martire, which now
houses the **Museo di Civiltà
Preclassiche della Murgia
Meridionale**. The star exhibit
of this museum is Delia, the
28,000-year-old skeleton of
a pregnant woman – and her
foetus – discovered in a nearby
cave. The burial has been laid
out as it was found, along with
an eerie wax reconstruction
of Delia, who is thought to
have died in childbirth.

At the foot of the citadel,
Piazza della Libertà is the
focus of modern life, its bars
and cafés overlooked by a
column with Ostuni's patron,
St Oronzo, at its pinnacle.

**Museo di Civiltà
Preclassiche della
Murgia Meridionale**
🏠Via Cattedrale 15 📞0831
30 39 73 ⏰10am–1pm &
4–7pm daily (Sat: 10am–1pm;
Jul–Dec: to 7pm daily)

⓱
Taranto

🏔G6 🚆🚌 🛈 Corso
Umberto 121; www.
comune.taranto.it

Little remains of the old city
of Taras, founded by Spartans
in 708 BC. The **Museo
Archeologico Nazionale**
has artifacts that shed light
on the region's history.

Taranto was heavily
bombed in World War II and
is garlanded by factories.
The run-down but picturesque
Città Vecchia, an island
dividing the Mare Grande
from the Mare Piccolo, was the
site of the Roman citadel of
Tarentum. The city is famous
for its shellfish, which can be
bought fresh from the lively
fish market, housed in an Art
Nouveau building. Here, too, is
the Duomo, founded in 1071
and subsequently rebuilt.
The most interesting features

THE TARANTELLA

Italy's folk dance, the
tarantella grew out of
tarantism - a dancing
hysteria that appeared in
15th- to 17th-century Italy -
and was prevalent in
Galatina *(opposite)*. Victims
of the tarantula spider's
bite could supposedly cure
themselves through
frenzied dancing. The
strange ritual takes place
annually on 29 June at
celebrations in Galatina,
the only place on the
Salentine Peninsula where
tarantism has survived.

→ Alfresco dining tables overlooking Otranto's seafront

include the catacomb-like crypt, with its sarcophagi and fragments of frescoes, and the antique marble columns of the nave. Behind it is the 11th-century San Domenico Maggiore, which later gained a high double-approach Baroque staircase. The huge castle built by Frederick of Aragon (15th century) covers the eastern corner of the Città Vecchia. Now a military area, the castle can be seen on daily guided tours (free of charge).

Museo Archeologico Nazionale
 ⌖ ☖ Via Cavour 10
☎ 0994 53 86 39 ☐ Daily

---

⑱ Galatina

☖G6 ☖ Lecce ⓕⓢ🚌 ❼ Sala dell'Orologio; www. comune.galatina.le.it

An important Greek colony in the Middle Ages, this *città d'arte* (city of art) retains its Greek flavour. It is the centre of one of Puglia's chief wine-producing regions, although it is more famous for the ritual of tarantism (*see box*).

The Gothic church of Santa Caterina d'Alessandria (begun in 1384) on Piazza Orsini contains early 15th-century frescoes with scenes from the Old and New Testaments that glorify the Orsini, who were feudal lords.

---

⑲ Otranto

☖G6 ☖ Lecce ⓕⓢ🚌⛴ ❼ Piazza Castello; www. comune.otranto.le.it

Otranto was one of Republican Rome's leading ports for trade with Asia Minor and Greece, and under the Byzantines was an important toehold of the Eastern Empire in Italy. In 1070 it fell to the Normans. Turks attacked in 1480, asking its 800 inhabitants to renounce Christianity. All refused and were subsequently slaughtered. The Norman Duomo (founded 1080) on Via Duomo houses the bones of these martyrs. There is a 12th-century mosaic floor and a fine crypt.

A castle (1485–98) adds to Otranto's charm, and there are some fine beaches close by.

STAY

Hotel Palazzo Papaleo
Perfectly located hotel overlooking the sea.

☖G6 ☖ Via Rondachi 1, Otranto ⓦ hotel palazzopapaleo.com

€€€

B&B Fascino Antico
Picturesque lodging in a 19th-century hut.

☖G6 ☖ Strada Statale dei Trulli 172, Alberobello ⓦ fascino anticotrulli.com

€€€

Palazzo Baldi
Accommodation in a 16th-century building.

☖G6 ☖ Corte Baldi 2, Galatina ⓦ hotel palazzobaldi.it

€€€

Masseria Moroseta
Modernist rooms set on a 2-ha (5-acre) olive grove.

☖G6 ☖ Contrada Lamacavallo, Ostuni ⓦ masseriamoroseta.it

€€€

BASILICATA AND CALABRIA

Remote and wild, Basilicata is one of the poorest regions in Italy. It is underdeveloped and its rural areas remain largely unspoiled. Neighbouring Calabria has been immortalized in drawings by Edward Lear, who, travelling through on a donkey in 1847, was transfixed by the "horror and magnificence" of its savage landscape.

Today, these regions are distinctly separate but they share a common history and, along with Sicily and Puglia, were part of Magna Graecia. Ancient Metaponto in Basilicata was an important centre, as was Locri Epizephiri in Calabria.

After the Greeks came the Romans, followed by Basilian monks. These were members of the Greek-Byzantine church who were fleeing their territories, which had been invaded by Muslims. Their religious establishments make up a core of interesting monuments, such as the Cattolica at Stilo and Matera, where monks took refuge in caves.

Many of the historic remains are Norman, but sporadic evidence of the Swabian, Aragonese, Angevin and Spanish occupation still exists.

Nowadays, Calabria has an infamous reputation due to the 'Ndrangheta, the ferocious first cousin to the Mafia. Concerned mainly with drug trafficking, this criminal gang presents little threat to tourists.

Owing to emigration, Basilicata and Calabria are sparsely populated and have as much to offer in unspoiled countryside as in historic centres. The coastline has fine beaches, while inland are the Aspromonte and Sila mountain ranges. The remote landscape has kept change at bay. Isolated Pentedattilo, for example, preserves customs of Byzantine origin, while around San Giorgio Albanese there live close-knit communities of Albanians, descended from 15th-century refugees.

Fondi
Terracina
Gaeta
Mondragone
Castel Volturno
Giugliano
Isola d'Ischia ○Ischia
Golfo di Napoli
Isola di Capri ○Capri
Teano
CAMPANIA
Capua
Naples
Castellammare di Stabia
Sorrento
Capri
S630
A1
S87
Benevento
Maddaloni
Pratola Serra
Avellino
A30
A2
Salern
Amalfi
Battipaglia
Golfo di Salerno
Agropol
Castellabate

Tyrrhenian Sea

BASILICATA AND CALABRIA

Must See
1 Matera

Experience More
2 Melfi
3 Venosa
4 Lagopesole
5 Metaponto
6 Maratea
7 Rossano
8 Tropea
9 Stilo
10 Reggio di Calabria
11 Gerace

Aeolian Islands
Santa Marina Salina
Lipari

Capo d'Orlando
Brolo
Cefalu
Caronia
Patti
A20
Cerda
Castelbuono
SICILY
Randazzo
A19
Gangi
Valledolmo
Nicosia
Bronte

Did You Know?

Mel Gibson filmed Jerusalem scenes from *The Passion of the Christ* (2004) in Matera.

❶ MATERA

A F5 🚍📧 ℹ️ Via de Viti de Marco 9; www.matera turismo.it

Fused to a cave-ridden outcrop above a deep ravine, Matera is one of the most extraordinary cities in the south. Cave dwellings, churches, houses, stepped streets and twisting pavements form an astonishing maze of limestone. Declared a UNESCO World Heritage Site in 1993, Matera is now a thriving destination with many boutique cave hotels and excellent restaurants.

① The Sassi

The Sassi district is is made up of a labyrinth of cave dwellings on the eastern slope of Matera (the literal translation of *sassi* is "stones"). It is divided into two quarters: Sasso Caveoso, to the south, and Sasso Barisano, to the north. The *sassi* are reached by winding downhill through steep twisting alleyways. From outside the Sassi di Matera hotel, you can wander through a series of unrestored *sassi*, many of which retain stoves carved into the stone, staircases and courtyards overgrown with brambles and prickly pears.

② The Upper Town

The centre of the historic town, perched on the higher slopes of Matera above the *sassi*, is Piazza Vittorio Veneto, a

spacious square at its liveliest in the early evenings, when traffic is banned. Stroll along Via del Corso to see some lovely palazzi and churches. At the far end is the elliptical façade of Chiesa del Purgatorio, a ghoulishly decorated 17th-century church with a chequerboard of Edvard-Munch-style screaming skull and skeleton sculptures.

③ Convincinio S Antonio

A Rione Casalnuovo 📞 930 5715 07 78 🕐 Opening times vary, call ahead

These four interlinked churches were used as wine cellars in the 18th century and feature wine spouts emerging from the altar. There are great views from outside the church right over the ravine.

←

Ancient cave dwelling in Sasso Caveoso

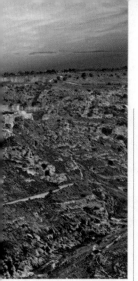

The spectacular city of Matera, a UNESCO World Heritage Site

⑤
Parco delle Chiese Rupestri

🏠 CEA, Contrada Murgia Timone 🌐 ceamatera.it

Pack a picnic and plenty of water, and explore the caves and *chiese rupestri* (rock-hewn churches) across the river on the far side of the ravine. Alternatively take one of the two daily guided hikes.

④
Madonna de Idris

🏠 Via Madonna dell'Idris
🕐 10:30am-1:30pm daily (Apr-Nov: also 2:30-7pm)
🌐 sassiweb.it

Soaring above the *sassi*, this church is carved right into the rock of conical Monte Errone. Inside are the evocative traces of medieval frescoes.

⑥
Casa Grotta di Vico Solitario

🏠 Vicinato di Vico Solitario 11 🕐 9am-6pm Mon-Sat, 9:30am-6:40pm Sun
🌐 casagrotta.it

This traditional cave dwelling has been reconstructed with the help of a family who lived here until the 1950s.

Must See

EAT

Alle Fornaci
Fish are brought in daily from the Ionian and Tyrrhenian seas to create local culinary specialities in an elegant and classy atmosphere. Try the saffron, red prawns and peppers.

🏠 Piazza Cesare Firrao 7 🕐 Mon 🌐 ristorante allefornaci.it

$$$

La Grotto nei Sassi
Eat in the intimate, vaulted stone dining room or, in warmer months, on the rooftop terrace and feast on a seafood-centred menu of regional recipes.

🏠 Via Rosario 73 🕐 Mon 🌐 ristorante sassidimatera.com

$$$

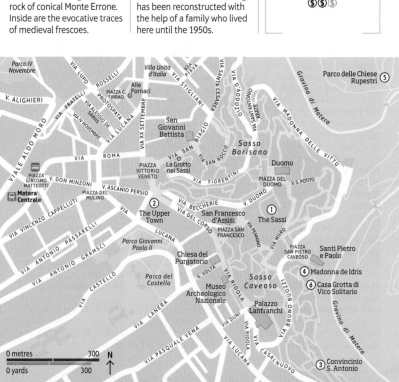

Melfi's forbidding medieval castle, set on a mound ↑

EXPERIENCE MORE

② Melfi

A F5 **ⓝ** Potenza **FS** 🚌
ⓘ Piazza Umberto I 11;
www.aptbasilicata.it

A brooding and now almost deserted medieval town, Melfi is crowned by the castle where Pope Nicholas II conducted Robert Guiscard's investiture in 1059, thus legitimizing the Normans in the south. Melfi later became the Norman capital. Here Frederick II proclaimed his *Constitutiones Augustales* (1231), which unified his kingdom as a state. In the castle is the **Museo Archeologico Nazionale del Melfese**, with its collection of Byzantine jewellery. The Duomo, off Via Vittorio Emanuele, was begun in 1155 but rebuilt in the 18th century. Only the campanile survives.

Museo Archeologico Nazionale del Melfese

 🖼️ **ⓝ** Castello di Melfi, Via Normanni **📞** 0972 23 87 26 **🕐** 2–8pm Mon, 9am–8pm Tue–Sun **🔒** 1 Jan, 25 Dec

③ Venosa

A F5 **ⓝ** Potenza **FS** 🚌
ⓘ Via Roma 22; www. comune.venosa.pz.it

Venosa was an important Roman colony around 290 BC, and remains of baths and an amphitheatre survive in the archaeological zone along Via Vittorio Emanuele. It was also the birthplace of the Latin poet Horace (65–8 BC) and the site where the Roman general Marcellus died at the hands of Hannibal in 208 BC. Marcellus' reputed tomb is in Via Melfi. For more ancient treasures, visit the **Museo Archeologico Nazionale**.

The Duomo, also on Via Vittorio Emanuele, and the huge castle in Piazza Umberto I, date from the 16th century.

An abbey complex formed by an older, possibly early Christian church (5th–6th century), La Trinità is backed by an unfinished 11th-century construction, in which five members of the Norman Hauteville family were buried.

Only the tomb of Alberada, the first wife of Robert Guiscard, has survived.

Museo Archeologico Nazionale

 ⓝ Piazza Castello **📞** 0972 360 95 **🕐** 9am–8pm Wed–Mon (from 2pm Tue)

④ Lagopesole

A F5 **ⓝ** Potenza **FS** To Lagopesole Scalo, then bus to town **🕐** Apr–Oct: 9:30am–1pm & 4–7pm daily; Nov–Mar: 9:30am–1pm & 3–5pm **🔒** 24 Dec–2 Jan **ⓦ** aptbasilicata.it

Rising dramatically on a hill, Lagopesole's castle (1242–50) was the last castle built by Frederick II. The interesting carved heads above the portal of the keep are generally said to represent Frederick Barbarossa (grandfather of Frederick II) and Barbarossa's wife, Beatrice. Inside, the royal apartments and chapel can be visited.

5

Metaponto

AF6 **A**Matera **⊟⊟**To
Metaponto **⊙**9am–30 mins
before sunset daily **⊘**Mon
am, 1 Jan, 1 May, 25 Dec
⊞Via Apollo Licio; www.
archeobasilicata.
beniculturali.it

Founded in the 7th century BC,
ancient Metaponto was once
the centre of a wealthy city-
state with a philosophical
tradition expounded by
Pythagoras, who settled
here after his expulsion from
Croton. Its sights include the
Tavole Palatine, the ruins of a
6th-century-BC Doric temple
that was probably dedicated
to the goddess Hera, which
is located near the Bradano
River bridge. The **Museo
Nazionale di Metaponto**
displays artifacts from the
site. The remains of a theatre
and a Doric Temple of Apollo
Lycius (6th century BC) are in
the Archaeological Zone.

Further south, modern
Policoro occupies what was
ancient Heracleia (founded
7th–5th century BC). Its
**Museo Nazionale della
Siritide** has finds from this
and other sites.

Museo Nazionale di Metaponto

⊛ **⊞** Via Aristea 21 **⊞** 0835
74 53 27 **⊙**9am–2pm Mon,
9am–8pm Tue–Sun **⊘**1 Jan,
1 May, 25 Dec

Museo Nazionale della Siritide

⊛ **⊞** Via Colombo 8, Policoro
⊞ 0835 97 21 54 **⊙**9am–8pm
Wed–Mon, 9am–2pm Tue
⊘1 Jan, 1 May, 25 Dec

6

Maratea

AF6 **A**Potenza **⊟⊟**
⊞Piazza del Gesù 32; 0973
87 69 08

Basilicata's tiny stretch of
Tyrrhenian coast is home to
Maratea. Its small port (Maratea
Inferiore) is beneath the old
centre (Maratea Superiore),
which straddles the flank of a
hill. From here the road climbs
Monte Biagio to a summit with
great views and a 1960s statue
of the Christ the Redeemer.

Rivello, 23 km (14 miles) to
the north, once had a largely
Greek population. Byzantine
influences can still be seen
in its churches.

7

Rossano

AF6 **A**Cosenza **⊟⊟**
⊞Piazza Steri & Lungomare
di Sant'Angelo; www.
rossanoturismo.it

This hill-town was one of the
main centres of Byzantine
civilization in Calabria. The
Museo Diocesano houses the
Codex Purpureus Rossanensis,
a rare 6th-century Greek
Gospel with silver lettering
and intricate miniatures.

The Baroque cathedral
contains the *Madonna
Achiropita* fresco, a much-
venerated Byzantine relic
of the 8th or 9th century.

On a hilltop to the
southeast is the five-domed
Greek church of San Marco
(10th century). The 12th-
century Panaghia, another
Greek church, lies just off
Via Arcivescovado.

Santa Maria del Patire,
18 km (11 miles) to the west,
is adorned with coloured
brickwork, tile and stone.

Museo Diocesano

⊛ **⊞**Palazzo Arcivescovile,
Via Arcivescovado 5 **⊞** 0983
52 52 63 **⊙**Tue–Sun

→
Peaceful
beach near
Maratea

Did You Know?

Locals believe the Madonna di Romania protects Tropea. In World War II six bombs fell on the town but none exploded.

8

Tropea

 F7 Vibo Valentia FS
 Piazza Ercole; www.tropea.biz

One of the most picturesque towns on Calabria's largely built-up Tyrrhenian coast, Tropea offers superb views of the sea and beaches. The old town hangs on to a cliffside facing a large rock, formerly an island. The rock is topped by Santa Maria dell'Isola, a former medieval Benedictine sanctuary. The cathedral at the end of Via Roma is of Norman origin, although it has been rebuilt several times. Inside is a 14th-century painting, the *Madonna di Romania*, by an unknown artist. Casa Trampo (14th century) and Palazzo Cesareo

(early 20th century) in Vicolo Manco are the most interesting of the small palaces in Tropea. The latter has a splendid balcony adorned with carvings.

Below the town are pretty beaches and a good choice of places to eat. Other seaside towns to visit are Scilla to the south and Pizzo to the north.

9

Stilo

 F7 Reggio di Calabria
  Town hall; 0964 77 60 06

A short distance from the coast, Stilo is an earthquake-damaged town clamped to the side of Monte Consolino. On a ledge looking out over the olive trees is the **Cattolica di Stilo**, which has made the town a focus of pilgrimage for lovers of Byzantine architecture. Built in the 10th century by Basilian monks, the brick building with its

 The rock of Santa Maria dell'Isola, Tropea

terracotta-tiled roof is based on a Greek cross-in-a-square plan. Four antique, mismatched marble columns divide the interior into nine sections. The capitals are placed at the base of the columns, instead of on top, to indicate the triumph of Christianity over paganism. The frescoes within, discovered in 1927, date from the 11th century.

The Cattolica dominates the town, but on Via Tommaso Campanella there is a medieval Duomo as well as the 17th-century ruins of the Convent of San Domenico, where the philosopher and Dominican friar Tommaso Campanella (1568–1639) lived. The church of San Francesco, built around 1400, has an ornate carved wooden altar and a lovely 16th-century painting of the *Madonna del Borgo* (unknown origin). Bivongi, northwest of Stilo, has two churches dedicated to St John: the Byzantine-Norman San Giovanni Theristis, and the Norman San Giovanni Vecchio.

> The capitals are placed at the base of the columns, instead of on top, to indicate the triumph of Christianity over paganism.

SHOP

Here are some of the best shops in Reggio di Calabria.

Archaeological Museum Shop
Lovely bookstore and souvenir shop.

📍 Piazza de Nava 26

Oro Argento e Mirra
Artisan goldsmiths since 1975.

📍 Corso Garibaldi 227

La Liberia Nuova Ave
The oldest independent bookstore in the city.

📍 Corso Garibaldi 206

Cattolica di Stilo

⊘ 📍 2 km (1 mile) above Stilo on Via Cattolica 📞 371 345 54 90 🕐 8am-6pm Mon-Sat (summer: to 8pm), noon-6pm Sun & pub hols

---

⑩

Reggio di Calabria

📍 F7 🚉🚌 ℹ Station; www.turismo.reggiocal.it

One reason to visit Reggio di Calabria, which was heavily rebuilt after a devastating earthquake in 1908, is the **Museo Archeologico Nazionale di Reggio Calabria**. It houses an important collection of artifacts from ancient Rhegion – a Greek city on the site of the present town – and from other Greek sites.

Chief among its treasures are two larger-than-life Greek bronze statues of warriors dredged from the sea off Riace Marina in 1972, and known as statues A and B. Statue A (460 BC) is thought to be by Phidias, the Athenian sculptor and chief exponent of the idealizing, Classical style. If true, it is a rare survivor, because his works were hitherto only known to us from Roman copies. Statue B (430 BC) has been attributed to Polyclitus. It is possible that the statues originated from an Athenian shrine at Delphi built to celebrate the victory of Marathon.

Museo Archeologico Nazionale di Reggio Calabria

⊘⊘ 📍 Piazza de Nava 26 📞 0965 81 22 55 🕐 9am-8pm Tue-Sun

---

⑪

Gerace

📍 F7 📍 Reggio di Calabria 🚌ℹ Town hall, Piazza del Tocco; www.comune.gerace.rc.it

Occupying a crag on the northeastern flank of the Aspromonte, Gerace was founded by refugees from Locri Epizephiri who fled in the 9th century to escape Saracen attack. Its defensive character is reinforced by the medieval town walls and the remains of the castle.

Apart from the slow pace of life here – where you are as likely to meet a flock of sheep in an alley as a Fiat 500 – the main attraction is Calabria's grandest Duomo. This large structure indicates the significance of Gerace at least up to the time of the Normans. Constructed around the early 12th century, rebuilt in the 13th century and restored in the 18th century, the crypt is its chief treasure. Both crypt and church are simple, adorned by a series of antique coloured marble-and-granite columns probably stolen from the site of ancient Locri Epizephiri. At the end of Via Cavour is 12th-century San Giovanello, part Byzantine and part Norman. Nearby is the Gothic church of San Francesco d'Assisi, which contains a Baroque marble altar (1615) and the Pisan-style tomb of Niccolò Ruffo (died 1372), a member of a prominent Calabrian family.

The vast site of **Locri Epizephiri**, the first Greek city to have a written code of law (660 BC), was a famous centre of the cult of Persephone. There are remains of temples, a theatre and Greek and Roman tombs. The **Museo Nazionale** displays a ground plan of the site, as well as Greek and Roman votive statues, coins and sculptural fragments.

Locri Epizephiri

📍 Southwest of Locri on the SS 106, Contrada Marasà 🕐 9am-7:30pm Tue-Sun 🌐 locriantica.it

Museo Nazionale

📍 Contrada Marasà, SS 106 📞 0964 39 00 23 🕐 Tue-Sun 🚫 1 May, 25 Dec

→

Bronze statue at Museo Archeologico Nazionale di Reggio Calabria

SICILY

On a crossroads in the Mediterranean, part of Europe and Africa, yet belonging to neither, Sicily was tramped across by half the ancient civilized world. As conquerors came and went, they left behind elements of their culture, resulting in the rich and varied mixture that typifies every aspect of Sicilian life, from language, customs and cooking to art and, most notably, architecture.

During the 6th and 5th centuries BC, there cannot have been much difference between Athens and the Greek cities of Sicily. Their ruins are among the most spectacular of the ancient Greek world. The Romans took over in the 3rd century BC, followed by the Vandals, Ostrogoths and Byzantines. Not much that is tangible has survived from the days of the Arabs, who ruled from the 9th to 11th centuries, though Palermo's Vucciria is more souk than market. The Norman era, beginning in 1061, spawned achievements such as the cathedrals of Monreale and Cefalù, while the eclecticism of that period's architecture is best seen at Santi Pietro e Paolo by Taormina.

The Sicilian Baroque of the 17th and 18th centuries is just as individual. The palaces and churches of Palermo, reflecting the elaborate ritual of the Spanish Viceregal court, tend towards extravagant display. At Noto, Ragusa, Modica, Siracusa and Catania the buildings are a useful vehicle for the Sicilians' love of ornamentation, itself a remnant from the island's early fling with the Arab world. The style is an expression of the nature of Sicilians, whose sense of pomp and pageantry is both magnificent and extreme.

Sicily is a curiosity, and the legacy of the past is redolent everywhere. They say that today there is as much Phoenician, Greek, Arabic, Norman, Spanish or French blood in Sicilian veins as there is Italian. The resulting mixture – exotic and spicy – has created a distinct culture at the foot of Italy.

Naples, Salerno,
Genoa, Cagliari

Isola
di Ustica

*Tyrrhenian
Sea*

Cagliari

Capo
Gallo

Punta
Raisi

Palermo

PALERMO ①

Carini

Capo Zafferano

Bagheria

MONREALE ②

A29

SAN VITO LO CAPO ⑦

Zingaro
Nature Reserve

Termini
Imerese

A19

S113

ERICE

Castellammare
del Golfo

Partinico

Misilmeri

S121

TRAPANI ⑥ ⑧

Paceco

Alcamo

Camporeale

Villafrati

Ciminna

SEGESTA

Calatafimi

A29d

SEGESTA ⑩

Isola
Marettimo

Isola
di Levanzo

Isola
Favignana

Trapani

Isole dello
Stagnone

S115

Tabaccaro

*Egadi
Islands*

Salemi

Roccamena

Corleone

Torto

S118

Alia

Lercara Fridd

Val di Mázara

MARSALA ⑨

Partanna

Pizzo Cangialoso
1457m △

Prizzi

S188

Castelvetrano

A29

Bisacquino

Vallelunga
Pratameno

Mazara del Vallo

S115

Belice

Menfi

Pizzo Stagnataro
1346m △

Campobello di Mazara

Caltabellotta

Burgio

Mussomeli

Capo Granitola

SELINUNTE ⑪

Sciacca

Ribera

Cianciana

Gallo d'Or

S189

Milen

Verdura

S118

S115

Platani

S189

Aragona

Capo Bianco

Raffadali

AGRIGENTO ⑬

Favara

Porto Empodocle

⑤ **VALLEY OF
THE TEMPL**

Palma di
Montechiaro

S11

↓ Pantelleria

↓ Pelagie
Islands

SICILY

Must Sees

① Palermo
② Monreale
③ Siracusa
④ Ortigia
⑤ Valley of the Temples

Experience More

⑥ Trapani
⑦ San Vito Lo Capo
⑧ Erice
⑨ Marsala
⑩ Segesta
⑪ Selinunte
⑫ Cefalù

⑬ Agrigento
⑭ Piazza Armerina
⑮ Enna
⑯ Messina
⑰ Taormina
⑱ Mount Etna
⑲ Pantalica
⑳ Catania
㉑ Scicli
㉒ Sampieri
㉓ Ragusa
㉔ Modica
㉕ Noto

↑ Palermo's bustling port surrounded by an impressive landscape

❶

PALERMO

🅰F1 ✈Punta Raisi 32 km (20 miles) W 🚆Stazione Centrale, Piazza Giulio Cesare 🚌Via Balsamo ⚓Stazione Marittima, Molo Vittorio Veneto 🛈P Castelnuovo 35; www.palermotourism.com

Vibrant, scruffy and very very noisy, Palermo sprawls chaotically around a sweeping natural harbour, dominated by the limestone bulk of Monte Pellegrino. The city was the seat of the Arab Emirate in the 10th century, and Middle Eastern influences can still be seen in the architecture of the churches and in the narrow streets and alleys of the old Arab quarter between Palazzo dei Normanni and the sea.

①
Piazza Bellini and Piazza Pretoria

Tucked behind Quattro Canti (p507), Piazza Bellini is home to three engaging churches. With its bulbous red domes, **San Cataldo** is a plain two-store cuboid perched on a bank overlooking the square. **Santa Caterina** is Palermitan Baroque at its most exuberant, every inch encrusted with coloured marble and stucco. Nearby **La Martorana**'s Baroque façade conceals an Arab-Norman core with a medieval mosaic. Adjoining

Piazza Pretoria is dominated by the 16th-century Fontana della Vergogna (Fountain of Shame), named after the immodesty of its nudes.

San Cataldo
 🕒9:30am–12:30pm & 3:30–5:30pm Mon-Sat, 9:30am–1:30pm Sun & hols

Santa Caterina
🕒9:30am–1:30pm & 3–7pm Mon-Sat, 9:30am–1:30pm Sun

La Martorana
🕒9:30am–1pm & 3:30–5:30pm Mon-Sat, 9am–1pm Sun & hols

②
Palazzo dei Normanni and Cappella Palatina

🅰Piazza Indipendenza 📞091 626 28 33 🕒8:15am–5pm Mon-Sat, 8:15am–12:15pm Sun & hols 🌐federicosecondo.org

Dominating the high ground on the western edge of the old centre, the nucleus of the present palace was built by the Arabs and enlarged for the Norman court after they conquered the city in 1072. The jewel is the dazzling Cappella Palatina, a cocktail of Byzantine, Islamic and Norman influences built by Roger II (1132–40).

↑ Pretty Cappella Palatina in Palazzo dei Normanni

③
Ballarò Market

📍 Piazza del Ballarò
🕐 7:30am-8:30pm daily

Nowhere better captures the spirit of Palermo than this fresh produce market, overlooked by the gorgeous majolica-tiled dome of Santa Maria del Carmine.

---

④
Piazza Marina

Now a busy traffic junction, Piazza Marina occupies land reclaimed from the sea in the 10th century. Nearby **Palazzo Mirto** gives a glimpse of 18th-century aristocratic life, and gives access to the old servants quarters and kitchens.

Palazzo Mirto

📍 Via Merlo 2 🕐 9am-6pm Tue-Sat, 9am-1pm Sun

⑤
Palazzo Abatellis

📍 Via Alloro 4 📞 091 623 00 11 🕐 9am-6:30pm Tue-Fri, 9am-1pm Sat & Sun

This 15th-century palazzo makes an atmospheric home for Sicily's best collection of medieval and Renaissance art. Exhibits include a collection of works by 15th-century artist Antonello da Messina.

---

⑥
San Giovanni degli Eremiti

📍 Via dei Benedettini 20
🕐 9am-7pm Mon-Sat, 9am-1:30pm Sun & hols

With its Islamic-style onion domes and filigreed windows, this deconsecrated Norman church (1132–48) was built in the grounds of a mosque.

EAT

I Cuochini

A tiny *frigittoria* founded in 1826, I Cuochini produces traditional pastries and *arancini*.

📍 Via Ruggero Settimo 68 📞 091 581 158

$ $ $

Spinnato

This *pasticceria*, with tables outside on a quiet street, is perfect for a lazy breakfast or an evening cocktail.

📍 Via Principe di Belmonte 107-115
🌐 091 749 51 04

$ $ $

⑦ Duomo

🏛 Piazza Cattedrale
🕐 7am-7pm Mon-Sat,
8am-1pm & 4-7pm Sun
⛪ For Mass 🌐 cattedrale.palermo.it

Palermo's cathedral stands on the site of an Early Christian basilica, later a mosque. Despite frequent rebuildings and alterations, elements of the original Norman building have survived, notably the arched crenellations along the walls and the beautiful interlaced arches and small columns that decorate the exterior of the apse.

⑧ Oratorio del Rosario di San Domenico

🏛 Via dei Bambinai 18 📞 091 332779 🕐 Apr-Oct: 9am-6pm Mon-Fri, 9am-3pm Sat; Nov-Mar: 9am-3pm Mon-Sat

The Oratory of San Domenico was founded at the end of the 16th century by the Society of the Holy Rosary, whose members included the artist Pietro Novelli and sculptor Giacomo Serpotta. A tumult of figures of great ladies, knights and playful *putti* form a kind of frame for statues of Christian virtues by Giacomo Serpotta and paintings representing the mysteries of the Rosary by Pietro Novelli. The altarpiece was painted by Anthony Van Dyck in 1624–8.

⑨ Vucciria

🏛 Piazza Carracciolo

Nowhere is Palermo's Arabic past more apparent than in this medieval kasbah-style market, which burrows through the ruinous Loggia district below Via Roma. The alleys are named after their professions, such as silversmiths, dyers and key-makers. Immortalized by Renato Guttuso in his painting *La Vucciria*, this is an atmospheric place to wander in the early mornings, when the fishmongers set up shop.

 HIDDEN GEM
Castello della Ziza

Beyond the centre, this country retreat *(Piazza Ziza)* was built by Arab craftsmen for Norman kings William I and William II.

↑ Corner buildings of Quattro Canti illuminated with festive lights

↑ Palermo's stately Duomo seen from across the square

Oratorio del Rosario di Santa Zita

🏠 Via Valverde 3 📞 091 843 16 05 🕐 9am-1pm Mon-Sat 🚫 Aug 15

Founded in 1590, this was one of the city's richest oratories, and it is sumptuously decorated by Giacomo Serpotta. The panel on the rear wall depicts the Battle of Lepanto, and other reliefs show scenes from the New Testament. The neighbouring 16th-century church of Santa Zita, from which the oratory takes its name, is filled with sculptures (1517–27) by Antonello Gagini.

Museo Archeologico Regionale

🏠 Piazza Olivella 24 📞 091 611 68 07 🕐 9.30am-6:30pm Tue-Sat, 9:30am-1:30pm Sun & hols

This fascinating museum has treasures from excavations across the west of the island, ranging from Phoenician sarcophagi (6th–5th centuries BC) to a fine 3rd-century-BC ram's head. There are also marvellous pieces from the temples at Selinunte, including a leonine head from the Temple of Victory and reliefs of mythological scenes, for example one showing Actaeon being attacked by dogs and Athena slaying a giant.

Catacombe dei Cappuccini

🏠 Via Cappuccini 📞 091 652 41 56/329 415 04 62 🕐 9am-12:30pm & 3-5:30pm daily 🚫 Oct-Mar: Sun pm

In Palermo's scruffy residential western suburbs are these fascinating – at least for the non-squeamish – catacombs. Over several hundred years monks here mummified the bodies of some 8,000 brothers and wealthy Palermitani.

Quattro Canti

🏠 Via Vittorio Emanuele

The busy intersection of Corso Vittorio Emanuele and Via Maqueda is marked by the Quattro Canti, or "Four Corners", an elaborate Baroque crossroads shaped by the concave façades of the four corner buildings. It dates from 1600, when the new town plan that split the old city into four quadrants was put into effect. Each façade is decorated with a fountain and statues of saints, the seasons and Spanish kings.

STAY

Principe di Villafranca

A lovely boutique art hotel full of intricate design details.

🏠 Via Giuseppina Turrisi Colonna 4 🌐 principedivillafranca.it

💲💲💲

Grand Hotel Wagner

Glamorous and elegant hotel with bags of old-world charm.

🏠 Via Riccardo Wagner 2 🌐 grandhotelwagner.it

💲💲💲

Palazzo Brunaccini

Gorgeous rooms in a converted palazzo near Ballarò market.

🏠 Piazzetta Lucrezia Brunaccini 9 🌐 palazzobrunaccini.it

💲💲💲

Grand Hotel Villa Igiea

An opulent hotel in a restored 19th-century Art Nouveau villa with marina views.

🏠 Salita Belmonte 43 🌐 sofitel.com

💲💲💲

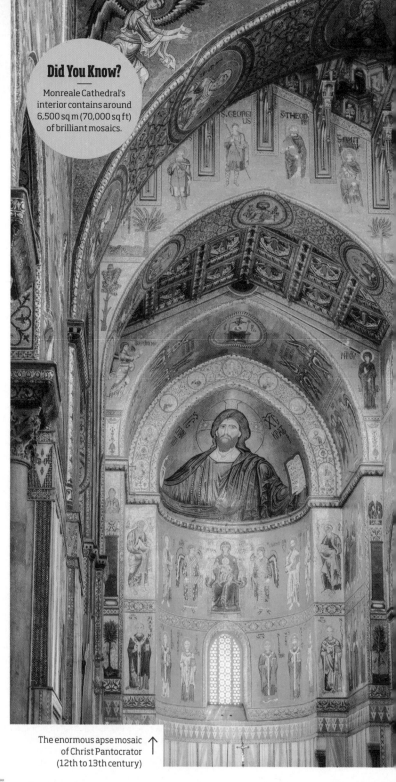

Did You Know?

Monreale Cathedral's interior contains around 6,500 sq m (70,000 sq ft) of brilliant mosaics.

The enormous apse mosaic of Christ Pantocrator (12th to 13th century) ↑

2 ⊘ ⓜ₃

MONREALE

⌂F1 **◎Piazza Guglielmo II 1** **🚌389 from Piazza Indipendenza** **◷Opening times vary, check website** **Ⓦmonrealeduomo.it**

The cathedral at Monreale sits high above the Conca d'Oro, a fertile plain overlooking Palermo. Despite its rather austere exterior, the cathedral's interior is embellished with the most extensive and significant mosaic cycle of its kind in Sicily.

Magnificently adorned, and with a splendid view of the Conca d'Oro, the Duomo at Monreale is one of the greatest sights of Norman Sicily. Founded in 1172 by the Norman King William II, it flanks a monastery of the Benedictine Order. The interior of the cathedral glitters with mosaics carried out by Sicilian and Byzantine artists – commissioned by a king who wanted to rival the power of the Archbishop of Palermo. Like Cefalù, and later Palermo, it was to serve as a royal sepulchre, housing the tombs of William I and William II.

↑ Intricately carved Norman-era columns in the cloisters

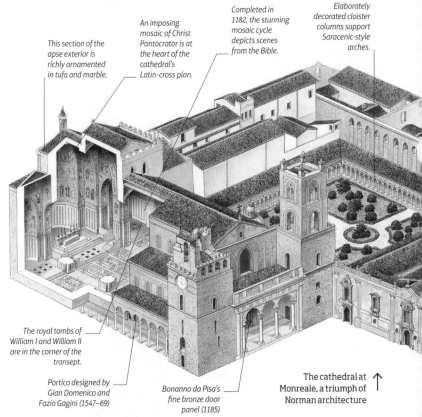

This section of the apse exterior is richly ornamented in tufa and marble.

An imposing mosaic of Christ Pantocrator is at the heart of the cathedral's Latin-cross plan.

Completed in 1182, the stunning mosaic cycle depicts scenes from the Bible.

Elaborately decorated cloister columns support Saracenic-style arches.

The royal tombs of William I and William II are in the corner of the transept.

Portico designed by Gian Domenico and Fazio Gagini (1547–69)

Bonanno da Pisa's fine bronze door panel (1185)

The cathedral at Monreale, a triumph of Norman architecture ↑

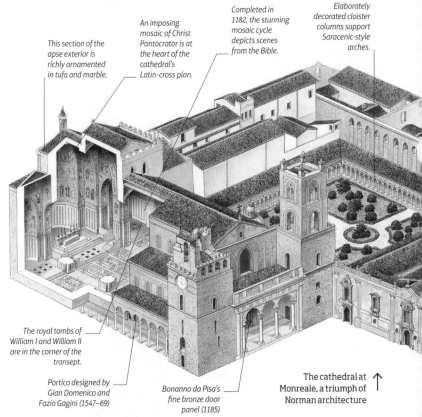

Must See

❸

SIRACUSA

Ⓐ G2 **🚊🚌 Interbus (0931 146 27 11); AST (0931 66 710)**
🚌 🛈 Via San Sebastiano 45; 0931 67 710

For three centuries, from around 500 BC, Siracusa was the most powerful city in the Mediterranean, birthplace of Archimedes and home to Pythagoras and Plato. The city's history, from prehistoric populations through to the introduction of Baroque architecture, is still clearly visible. Most of the relics of ancient Siracusa lie in the bustling mainland city, notably the Greek Theatre, the archaeological museum and the Roman catacombs.

①

The Neapolis Archaeological Zone

Ⓐ Greek Theatre and Neapolis Archaeological Zone: Viale Paradiso 14
🕘 9am-6pm Tue-Sun
🌐 indafondazione.org

The Neapolis Archaeological Zone was established in 1955 with the aim of grouping the antiquities of Siracusa within one site, for an uninterrupted tour of the city's remote past.

Roman Amphitheatre and Altar of Hieron II

Built during the early years of the Roman Empire, the amphitheatre, with an outer diameter of 140 by 119 m (459 by 390 ft), is only slightly smaller than the Arena in Verona (p108). Beneath the tiers were corridors through which the gladiators and wild beasts entered the arena.

Beyond are the massive foundations of the Altar of Hieron II. Dedicated to Zeus, it was used for public sacrifices in which as many as 400 bulls were put to death at one time.

The Greek Theatre

Built in the 5th century BC, this is one of the most important examples of ancient theatre architecture anywhere. Throughout May and June the theatre still hosts an annual festival of Greek drama.

Latomie

A huge hollow separates the theatre area and the southern section of the site. This is the area of the Latomie – stone quarries – from which the architects of ancient Siracusa extracted millions of cubic metres of stone for building. The enormous caves carved out by the quarries were used as prisons. The Ear of Dionysius (Orecchio di Dioniso) is one of the most impressive. The artist Caravaggio – who had himself recently escaped from prison in Malta – reputedly coined the cave's nickname when taken to see the quarries here.

Demeter and seated Kore statue, Museo Archeologico Regionale

← View from the top of the vast Greek Amphitheatre of Siracusa

southeast. Highlights include reconstructions of ancient Greek temples, the fossilized skeletons of two indigenous Sicilian dwarf elephants and various sculptures, including the *Venus Landolina*, a Roman copy of a Greek statue showing Venus emerging from the sea.

↑ Church above the Catacombs of San Giovanni Evangelista

② Museo Archeologico Regionale

⌂ Via Teocrito 66 ☎ 0931 48 95 11 🕐 Tue–Sat 9am–6pm, Sun 9am–1pm

Sicily's finest archaeological collection is a fabulous showcase of antiquities from Greek and Roman Siracusa, Megara Hyblaea, Thapsos and the Greek colonies of Sicily's

③ Catacombs of San Giovanni Evangelista

⌂ Via San Giovanni alle Catacombe ☎ 0931 64 694 🕐 Daily (Apr–Oct: 9:30am–noon, 2:30–4:30pm; May–Jun: 9:30am–1pm & 2:30–5:30pm; Jul–Aug: 9:30am–1:30pm & 2:30–6pm)

This underground complex, dating to the 4th century AD, housed hundreds of *loculi*, or rooms, used to bury the followers of the new Christian religion in Roman times. The main gallery of the catacombs leads to a series of chapels.

④ Castello Eurialo

⌂ Frazione Belvedere, 8 km (5 miles) from Siracusa ☎ 0931 71 17 73 🕐 9am–5pm Mon–Sat (to 7pm summer), 8am–2pm Sun & hols

On a hill overlooking the city, this castle is an impressive work of ancient Greek military architecture. It was built by Dionysius the Elder in 402 BC to defend Siracusa against attack. The fortress was protected by two rock-cut moats, a tower and a keep.

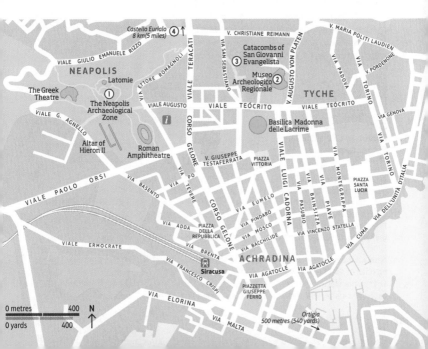

↑ The Piazza del Duomo and Duomo illuminated in the evening

❹

ORTIGIA

🅰️ G2 🚂🚌 Interbus (0931 14 62 711); AST (0931 66 710)
ℹ️ Via Maestranza 33; 0931 46 42 55

Traces of Siracusa's glorious past are everywhere in its historic centre, Ortigia, an offshore island where Baroque buildings of mellow golden sandstone twist and turn along a labyrinth of narrow medieval streets lined with pavement cafés, restaurants and stylish little shops. Intersperse sightseeing with lunch in the market, take a swim in one of the miniature lidos along Lungomare Levante, or enjoy a predinner drink while watching the sun set over the Porto Grande.

①

Duomo

🅰️ Piazza del Duomo 4
📞 0931 64 694 🕐 7:30am-8pm daily

Siracusa's Duomo is an ancient Greek temple that was converted into a church sometime during the 6th century. Twelve of the Doric temple's fluted columns are embedded in the Duomo's battlemented Norman wall, while inside, the nave was formed by hacking eight arches in the cella walls. The Norman façade was destroyed in the earthquake

of 1693 and replaced with the flamboyant Baroque edifice that now dominates the piazza.

---

②

Piazza del Duomo

Piazza Duomo is Sicily's most magnificent piazza, an immense theatrical space free of traffic, except for the occasional wedding car. It is gorgeous at any time of day, but perhaps most magical at night when its pavement gleams like silk and the Baroque façades that surround it are illuminated.

③

Santa Lucia alla Badia

🅰️ Via Pompeo Picherali
🕐 11am-2pm Tue-Sun

The façade of Santa Lucia alla Badia, with its barley-sugar twist columns and intricate stonework, is one of Ortigia's prettiest. The church is home of one of Siracusa's most prized works of art, *The Burial of Santa Lucia* by Caravaggio. The canvas was not designed for this church but for the Church of Santa Lucia across in the Borgata, the location to the saint's martyrdom. Bathed in shafts of sunlight, dwarfed by stark, bare plaster walls, two gravediggers brace themselves to lower the corpse of the saint into her tomb, watched by a bishop and a group of mourners.

④

Temple of Apollo

🅰️ Largo XXV Luglio

The ruins of the oldest temple in Magna Graecia were discovered in 1860 inside an old Spanish barracks. Built in the early 6th century BC, the temple is huge – 58 m by 24 m

EAT

Fratelli Burgio

Siracusa's best delicatessen has a simple outdoor restaurant among the bustle of the market, where guests can feast on platters of gourmet cheeses, hams and salamis sourced from all over Italy, along with their own cured olives, *caponata*, sun-dried tomatoes and other delectable conserves.

🏠 Piazza Cesare Battisti 4 🕒 Sun
🌐 fratelliburgio.com

$ⓢ ⓢ ⓢ$

Siracusa 500 metres (540 yards)

0 metres 400
0 yards 400
N ↑

(190 ft by 79 ft) – and over the centuries has served as a Byzantine church, a mosque and a military stronghold. Visiting in the 18th century, the French writer Vivant Denon reported finding one of the columns embedded in the wall of a bedroom of a house on the adjacent Via Resalibera. To make more room, the owner had hacked away part of the stone.

⑤
Fonte Aretusa

🏠 Largo Aretusa

Surrounded by papyrus plants and inhabited by a colony of ducks and bream, this fountain is fed by a freshwater spring that bubbles up under the sea. It is the origin of the myth of the nymph Arethusa, who escaped the advances of the river god Alpheios by turning into the spring, which disappeared beneath the Ionian sea and re-emerged here.

SWIMMING SPOTS IN ORTIGIA

The most popular place to swim in Ortigia is the big rock at Forte Vigliena (commonly known as "Lo Scoglio", or "the rock") – during the summer the local council "extends" it by erecting a platform. There is also a small beach at Cala Rossa (the foot of Via Roma). There are two lidos in Ortigia, one on the Lungomare Levante (at the foot of Via Maestranze), the other below the Fonte Aretusa.

⑥
Palazzo Bellomo: Galleria d'Arte Regionale

🏠 Via Capodieci 14 📞 0931 69511 🕒 9am-7pm Tue-Sat, 9am-1pm Sun

Palazzo Bellomo is a sprawling 13th-century building, whose austere, minimalist façade dates from a time when Sicily was part of the Holy Roman Empire. The palace now houses a regional art museum. A highlight of the collection is Antonello da Messina's *Annunciation*, painted for a church in Palazzolo Acreide, with the Hyblaean mountains visible through the windows behind the angel.

Temple of Concord, with a statue by Igor Mitoraj in the foreground ↑

5

VALLEY OF THE TEMPLES

⟁F2 **⌂Agrigento** **◷8:30am–7pm daily (ruins); 9am–7:30pm Tue–Sat, 9am–1:30pm Mon, Sun & pub hols (Museo Archeologico)** **☎0922 62 16 11** **ⓦparcodeitempli.net**

Straddling a low ridge to the south of Agrigento, the Valley of the Temples (Valle dei Templi) is one of the most impressive complexes of ancient Greek buildings outside Greece and a prime example of the magnificence of Magna Graecia.

The Valley of the Temples was once at the heart of the ancient city of Akragas. Founded in 581 BC by colonists from Gela, Akragas was one of Sicily's richest and most powerful cities – visitors reported that its citizens had ivory furniture, abundant silver and gold, and even made elaborate tombs for their pets. The city was especially well known for breeding horses, which consistently won the Olympic Games. After being besieged by the Carthaginians in 406 BC, Akragas was taken by the Romans in 261 BC, renamed Agrigentum, and remained in Roman control until the fall of the Empire. Today, you can explore the ruins of nine major temples, a series of minor shrines and a fascinating archaeology museum on the site.

Museo Archeologico

◄ The Archaeological Museum was opened to the public in 1967. The 13 rooms display objects ranging from prehistoric times to the early Christian period, but the emphasis is on Greek and Roman finds such as vases, statues and sarcophagi. There is also a Telamon (pillar in the form of a male statue) from the Temple of Olympian Zeus.

Temple of Olympian Zeus

Only fragmentary ruins remain of this 5th-century-BC temple – the largest Doric temple ever built. It was once supported by 38 giant Telamons, one of which is now on display in the Museo Archeologico.

Temple of Concord

With its 34 columns, this is one of the best-preserved Doric temples in the world, partly thanks to alterations made in the 4th century, when it became a Christian basilica. It was restored to its original Classical form in 1748.

Temple of Hera

▶ Relatively well-preserved, this 5th-century-BC temple was restored in Roman times. There are 25 of the original 34 columns still standing. Steps lead up to an altar where animals were sacrificed to the goddess Hera, known by the Romans as Juno.

Temple of Heracles

◄ These eight columns belonged to the oldest temple dedicated to Heracles, worshipped by both the Greeks and the Romans (as Hercules). The archaic 6th-century-BC Doric structure has an elongated rectangular plan.

EARLY CHRISTIAN CATACOMBS

The Valley features early Christian ruins as well as Magna Graecian monuments. Ipogei of Villa Igea (also known as the Grotta di Frangipane), between the Temple of Heracles and the Temple of Concord, were cut out of the rock to house the bodies of the first Christians here. A series of niches, closed off by stone slabs, alternated with small chapels that still bear traces of wall paintings.

Temple of Castor and Pollux

▶ This temple's four surviving columns, a symbol of the Valley of the Temples, were restored in the 19th century.

Kolymbetra

From the Greek for "pool", this sunken garden with a stream running through it formed part of the city's irrigation system.

EXPERIENCE MORE

❻
Trapani

ⒶE1 🚉🚌⛴ **𝒊** Via Torrearsa 69; www.distrettosicilia occidentale.it

Old Trapani occupies a narrow peninsula. The best buildings in this lively quarter are the Cathedral of San Lorenzo (1635) and the Chiesa del Collegio dei Gesuiti (c.1614–40). The façades of both churches reflect the ebullience of west Sicilian Baroque architecture.

The 17th-century Purgatorio on Via San Francesco d'Assisi contains 18th-century *Misteri* – realistic, life-sized wooden statues used in the annual Good Friday procession. Santa Maria del Gesù on Via Sant'Agostino houses the *Madonna degli Angeli* by Andrea della Robbia (1435–1525) and Antonello Gagini's canopy (1521).

The **Museo Pepoli** displays local antiquities such as coral objects and Christmas crib figures (*presepi*). Next to the museum, the Santuario di Maria Santissima Annunziata contains the *Madonna di Trapani*, a statue revered by fishermen and sailors for its legendary miraculous powers.

Museo Pepoli

✍ 🄰 Via Conte Agostino Pepoli 200 📞 0923 55 32 69 ⏰ 9am–1:30pm & 2–7:30pm Tue–Sat (am only Sun & hols)

❼
San Vito Lo Capo

ⒶE1 🄰 Trapani 🚌 🌐 sanvitolocapoweb. co.uk

A popular holiday resort set on the magnificent Golfo di Castellammare, San Vito Lo Capo is a lively place with one of the finest sandy beaches in Sicily. The focus of life is

pedestrianized Via Savoia, lined with shops and restaurants and the main scene of the evening *passeggiata*. Another highlight is the promenade backing the sweeping crescent of white sand that stretches east of town. A 10-minute walk beyond the harbour is a lighthouse perched on a windswept cape. Beyond there are great views across the entire gulf from the cliffs, although in hot weather you may prefer to take in the coast from one of the many boat trips operating from the harbour.

Just 12 km (7 miles) south of San Vito, the **Zingaro Nature Reserve** is a pristine 7-km (4-mile) stretch of coastline with tiny white pebble bays backed by steep mountains. Home to the rare Bonelli's eagle and some 600 species of plant, it is a fantastic place for a day's hiking. There are two main paths, the upper Sentiero Alto and the lower Sentiero Basso, which keeps close to the shore, with access to little coves. There are no shops or facilities here, so bring food and plenty of water.

Zingaro Nature Reserve

✍ 🄰 San Vito Lo Capo 🚌 From Castellammare del Golfo 🌐 riservazingaro.it

↑ Coastline of the Zingaro Nature Reserve

 TOP 3 **ZINGARO RESERVE DIVES**

Capua Wreck, Coast of Scopello
ⒶF1

During WWII, a British cargo ship carrying arms for Italian troops sank. Mysteries still linger, making this 38-m (125-ft) dive extra intriguing.

Grotta dell'Acqua Dolce, Uzzo Bay
ⒶE1

For more experienced divers, this 60-m (197-ft) deep chamber of glassy, fresh water is alive with marine life.

Grotta del Camino, Park Entrance
ⒶF1

The cave has two accesses: one at 18 m (59 ft) and the other at 35m (115 ft). A rock wall partitions the cavity, home to a troupe of fascinating red- and white-striped shrimp.

INSIDER TIP
Couscous Festival

San Vito Lo Capo's annual Couscous Festival is held in late September, with a smaller preview event in early June. Both include free tastings of dozens of different kinds of couscous, with concerts on the main Piazza Santuario and a great fireworks display on the last night at midnight.

8

Erice

A E1 **A** Trapani
i Piazza della Loggia 3;
0923 50 21 11

Poised on a crag overlooking Trapani, the town of Erice was once the seat of the cult of the fertility goddess Venus Erycina. Her temple stood on the present site of the Norman castle (Castello di Venere), beyond the public gardens. On a clear day, you can see all the way to Tunisia from the castle. The ancient town of Eryx was renamed Gebel-Hamed by the Arabs, Monte San Giuliano by the Normans and, finally, Erice in 1934 by Mussolini.

The Duomo (14th century) has a battlemented campanile and a 15th-century porch. Inside is a *Madonna and Child* (c.1469), attributed to either Francesco Laurana or Domenico Gagini. The deconsecrated 13th-century San Giovanni Battista on Viale Nunzio Nasi (now a hotel) contains Antonello Gagini's *St John the Evangelist* (1531) and Antonino Gagini's *St John the Baptist* (1539). In the **Museo Cordici** is Antonello Gagini's *Annunciation* (1525).

Museo Cordici

A Piazza Umberto I **C** 346 577 35 50 **O** Opening times vary, call ahead

9

Marsala

A E2 **A** Trapani
i Via XI Maggio 100; www. consorziovinomarsala.it

The port of Marsala is the home of a thick, strong, sweet wine that has been in production here since the 18th century. A former wine warehouse is now the **Museo Archeologico Baglio Anselmi**, housing important Phoenician artifacts.

The ruins of Lilybaeum are another attraction. Founded in 397 BC, this outpost of the Phoenician Empire was peopled by the survivors of the massacre at Mozia (ancient Motya) – the island used by the Phoenicians as a commercial centre. Best of all are the reconstructed remains of a Punic ship thought to have been active in the First Punic War (263–241 BC). The **Museo di Mozia** contains a remarkable early 5th-century-BC statue of a Greek youth.

The Duomo, begun in the 17th century, is full of sculptural works by members of the Gagini family. The small **Museo degli Arazzi**, behind the Duomo, contains several magnificent 16th-century Brussels tapestries.

Museo Archeologico Baglio Anselmi

A Lungomare Boeo 30 **C** 0923 95 25 35 **O** Tue-Sun (am only Tue & Sun)

Museo di Mozia

A Isola di Mozia (San Pantaleo) **C** 0923 71 25 98 **O** Daily

Museo degli Arazzi

A Via Garafa 57 **C** 0923 71 13 27 **O** Tue-Sun

The dramatic location of Erice's Castello di Venere

SICILIAN ISLANDS

From the dramatic volcanic islands of the Aeolian archipelago to the divers' paradise of Ustica, each of the minor islands surrounding Sicily has its own distinctive character. The best times to visit are spring and autumn, when you can experience island life without the summer hordes, yet with warm seas, balmy evenings and hotels, bars and restaurants still open.

Aeolian Islands

Climb Stromboli and see it erupting at night, take a boat trip around the islets off Panarea, or wallow in the sulphurous mudbaths of Vulcano. You can follow the old mule tracks of Filicudi, or laze on the beach at Pecorini Mare, where donkeys are the only form of transport.

Ustica

Dive or snorkel in Ustica's pristine waters, protected by a marine reserve, or follow the coastal footpath that circles the entire island. In the evening, sample local fish and locally grown lentils in one of the port's trattorias.

Egadi Islands

Cycle Favignana's network of unpaved roads, stopping for swims at Cala Azzurra and Cala Rossa. Take a boat trip to see prehistoric cave engravings on the island of Levanzo, or hike the solitary paths of spectacular Marettimo.

Pantelleria

Swim in the volcanic lake known as Specchio di Venere, and discover the rocky bays and hot springs along the coast. Follow the walking trail from the crumbling village of Siba to a natural outdoor sauna, or sample local dessert wines in the island's vineyards.

Pelagie Islands

Laze on the gorgeous sandy beach of Lampedusa's Isola dei Conigli, or opt for the brightly coloured houses, little black beaches and silence of remote Linosa.

① Dramatic eruption of the Stromboli volcano.

② Diving amid shoals of fish in the waters around Ustica.

③ The marina at Favignana.

④ Picking grapes in Pantelleria for the island's sweet wine.

⑤ Craggy Isola dei Conigli.

Monumental Doric columns at a Greek temple in Selinunte

 10

Segesta

F1 **Trapani** **From Trapani & Palermo** **0924 95 05 00** **10am-1pm Mon, Wed & Fri (also 4-6pm Wed)**

According to legend, the ancient town of Segesta – still largely unexcavated – was founded by Trojan followers of Aeneas. It presents one of the most spectacular sights on the island: a massive unfinished temple stranded on a remote hillside. Its construction started between 426 and 416 BC, and it was left incomplete following the devastation of Selinunte by the Carthaginians in 409 BC. Nearby, close to the summit of Monte Barbaro, the ruins of an ancient theatre (3rd century BC) can be visited. Summer concerts are now held here.

 11

Selinunte

F2 **Trapani** **0924 462 77** **Castelvetrano then bus** **9am-6pm daily**

Founded in 651 BC, Selinunte became one of the great cities of Magna Graecia – the part of southern Italy that was colonized by ancient Greece – and its toppled ruins are among Sicily's most important historic sites. Its ancient name, Selinus, derives from the wild celery that still grows here. The city was an important port, and its wall defences can still be seen around the Acropolis. The Carthaginians, under Hannibal, completely destroyed the city in 409 BC in a battle famous for its epic and savage proportions.

While the city itself has virtually disappeared, eight of its temples (each named after

Did You Know?

Stromboli has been erupting continuously for more than 20,000 years.

a letter of the alphabet) are distinguishable, particularly the so-called Eastern Temples (E, F and G). Of these, the columns of huge Doric Temple E (490–480 BC) have been partially re-erected. Temple F (c.560–540 BC) is in ruins. Temple G (late 6th century BC), which had 17 massive side columns, was one of the greatest Greek temples ever built.

Higher on the Acropolis lie the remains of Temples A, B, C, D and O. Metope sculpture from Temple C (early 6th century), originally located on the frieze between the triglyphs, can be seen in the Museo Archeologico Regionale in Palermo (p507), along with other artifacts excavated here. A small museum on site houses less important finds, as does one in Castelvetrano, 14 km (9 miles) north of Selinunte. The ancient city is still being excavated; its North Gate entrance is well preserved, and further north there is also a necropolis.

12

Cefalù

F1 **Palermo** **Corso Ruggero 77; www. comune.cefalu.pa.it**

This pretty seaside town is dominated by a huge rock known as La Rocca – once the site of a Temple of Diana – and by one of the finest Norman cathedrals in Sicily. Begun in 1131 by Roger II, the Duomo was intended as the main religious seat in Sicily. Though it failed to fulfil this function, the building's magnificence has never been eclipsed. Its splendid mosaics (1148), which feature an image of Christ Pantocrator in the apse, are remarkable and often celebrated as purely Byzantine works of art on Sicilian soil.

The **Museo Mandralisca** houses a fine *Portrait of a Man* (c.1465) by Antonello da Messina and a collection of coins, ceramics, vases and minerals.

Museo Mandralisca

Via Mandralisca **0921 42 15 47** **9am-7pm daily (Aug: until 11pm)** **12:30-3:30pm Sun & hols**

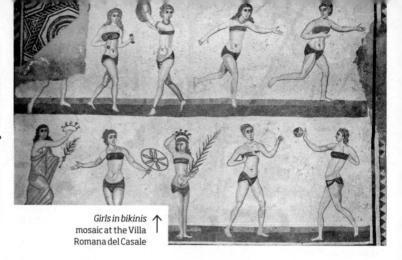

Girls in bikinis mosaic at the Villa Romana del Casale ↑

⑬

Agrigento

ⒶF2 🚉🚌🚢 **🛈Porto Empedocle 73 & Piazzale Aldo Moro; www.comune. agrigento.it**

Modern Agrigento occupies the site of Akragas, an important city of the ancient Greek world. Founded by Daedalus, according to legend, it was famed for the luxurious lifestyle of its inhabitants, and was a great power and rival to Siracusa. In 406 BC it fell to the Carthaginians, who sacked and burned it.

The historic core of the city, with its medieval streets, focuses on the Via Atenea. Santo Spirito (13th century) houses stuccoes by Giacomo

 Greek vase in the Museo Regionale Archeologico in Agrigento

Serpotta (1695). Santa Maria dei Greci was built on the remains of a 5th-century-BC temple – see the flattened columns in the nave. The Duomo, founded in the 14th century and altered in the 16th and 17th centuries, exhibits a unique mixture of Arab, Norman and Catalan detailing.

The chief reason to visit Agrigento is to see the archaeological zone known as the Valley of the Temples (p514). The **Museo Regionale Archeologico** houses an interesting display of artifacts from the temples and the city, including a collection of vases, coins and Greek and Roman sculpture.

Museo Regionale Archeologico

♿ 🏠Contrada San Nicola 12
🕐8:30am–7pm daily
🌐parcovalledeitempli.it

⑭

Piazza Armerina

ⒶF2 🏠**Enna** 🚌
🛈Via F Guccio 24b; www. piazzaarmerina.org

This active town is half medieval and half Baroque. The 17th-century Duomo, at its highest point, is the most interesting of the Baroque buildings.

🔺 GREAT VIEW
Scala dei Turchi

Named one of the Seven Wonders of Italy, these white marl cliffs are the result of centuries of erosion. Folklore tells of marauding Saracens and the healing powers of the staircase's marl – a chalk-like mixture of mud and silt.

In August, the lively Palio dei Normanni festival attracts many visitors, but the star sights are the mosaics in the UNESCO-listed **Villa Romana del Casale**, 5 km (3 miles) southwest of the town.

It is thought that this huge, sumptuous villa, with its public halls, private quarters, baths and courtyards, once belonged to Maximianus Herculeus, Diocletian's co-emperor, from AD 286 to 305. His son and successor, Maxentius, probably carried on its decoration, with Constantine taking over on Maxentius's death in 312.

Although little remains of the building fabric, the floors

→

Impressive white cliffs of the Scala dei Turchi, near Agrigento

have some of the finest surviving mosaics from Roman antiquity. Highlights include a circus scene showing a chariot race, ten female athletes dressed in bikinis and a 60-m- (197-ft-) long hunting scene featuring tigers, ostriches, elephants and a rhino being trapped and transported to games at the Colosseum.

Villa Romana del Casale

⊚ ⌂ Contrada Casale █ 0935 68 00 36 ⊙ Daily; May–Oct: 9am–6pm (Jul–Aug: to 11pm Fri & Sun); Nov–Aug: 9am–4pm

---

Enna

🅐 F2 🅵🅢🆎 🅘 Via Roma 441; www.culturasicilia.it

Impregnable on a crag above a fertile landscape where Persephone, mythological daughter of Demeter, once played, Sicily's highest town (942 m/3,090 ft) has always been coveted by successive invaders. The seat of the Cult of Demeter (goddess of fertility) was at Enna. Her temple stood on the Rocca Cerere, not far from the huge Castello di Lombardia (13th century) built by Frederick II.

Most sights are clustered in the old town, among the ancient streets that open out of the Via Roma. The church of San Francesco has a 16th-century tower. Piazza Crispi, with its fine views to nearby Calascibetta, is dominated by a copy of Bernini's *Rape of Persephone*. The 14th-century Duomo, altered in later centuries, contains parts of Demeter's temple, an arch of which is still visible in the exterior of the apse. Its façade is rich in Gothic decorations. Inside, don't miss the original wooden ceiling.

The **Museo Varisano** has exhibits on the area's history, from the Neolithic to Roman periods. Standing outside the centre, the octagonal Torre di Federico II (13th century) is a former watchtower.

The ancient hill-town of Nicosia, northeast of Enna,

> **Founded by Daedalus, according to legend, it was famed for the luxurious lifestyle of its inhabitants, and was a great power and rival to Siracusa.**

was damaged in the 1967 earthquake, but still contains a smattering of churches. San Nicola, built in the 14th century, has a magnificent, carved entrance portal. Inside there is a much-venerated wooden crucifix (17th century) by Fra Umile di Petralia. Santa Maria Maggiore houses a 16th-century marble polyptych by Antonello Gagini and a throne reputedly used by Charles V in 1535. Further east is Troina. It was captured in 1062 by the Normans, whose work survives in the Chiesa Matrice.

Museo Varisano

⌂ Piazza Mazzini █ 0935 50 76 304 ⊙ 9am–7pm Mon–Sat

Did You Know?

Many scenes from the three *Godfather* movies were filmed in the hill-towns of Savoca and Forza d'Agrò *(p36)*.

16
Messina

G1 FS 🚌 🚆 ℹ️ Piazza Palazzo Satellite; www. comunemessina.gov.it

Messina has been the victim of earthquakes and World War II bombing. The **Museo Regionale** houses treasures including works by Antonello da Messina and Caravaggio. Santissima Annunziata dei Catalani in Piazza Catalani displays the eclecticism typical of 12th-century Norman architecture, with rich decoration. To visit the church, ask at the tourist office.

Outside, G A Montorsoli's Fontana d'Orione (1547) is the finest fountain of its kind from 16th-century Sicily. His Fontana di Nettuno (1557) celebrates Messina's foundation and position in the world as a principal commercial port.

↓ The City of Messina with mountains beyond

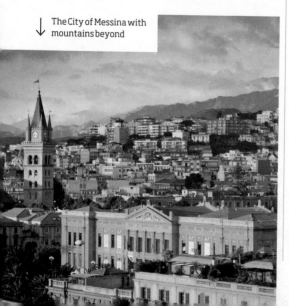

Museo Regionale

⌖ 🏛 Via della Libertà 465 ☎ 090 36 12 92/93 🕒 9am–7pm Tue–Sat, 9am–1pm Sun & hols

17
Taormina

G2 🏛 Messina FS 🚌 ℹ️ Palazzo Corvaja, Piazza Santa Caterina; 0942 232 43

Splendidly situated, Taormina is Sicily's best-known resort. It retains an air of exclusivity while being on the tourist trail, with sandy beaches and a wide range of restaurants and hotels.

The most illustrious relic of the past is the theatre. Begun in the 3rd century BC by the Greeks, it was subsequently rebuilt by the Romans. Among other Classical remains are the ruins of the odeon (for musical performances) and the *naumachia* (an artificial lake for mock-battles). On Piazza Vittorio Emanuele (site of the Roman Forum), Palazzo Corvaja (14th century) was built using stone from a temple that once stood here. The 13th-century Duomo (renovated in 1636) is a fortress-like building.

Taormina's main beach, Mazzarò, boasts crystal-clear waters and is easily reached from the town. South of Taormina at Capo Schisò are the ruins of ancient Naxos. To the west is Gole dell'Alcantara, a 20-m- (66-ft-) deep gorge of basalt rock, a river and waterfalls.

18
Mount Etna

G2 🏛 Catania FS Linguaglossa or Randazzo; Circumetnea railway from Catania to Riposto 🚌 To Nicolosi ☎ 095 791 47 55 (to hire a guide) ℹ️ Piazza Vittorio Emanuele 32, Nicolosi; www.parcoetna.ct.it

At 3,370 m (11,050 ft), Mount Etna is Europe's highest and most active volcano. It was thought by the Romans to have been the forge of Vulcan, the god of fire. The climb to the summit should be tackled only with an experienced guide. The Circumetnea railway runs around the base of the volcano, offering a good alternative to hiking and fantastic views.

←

The desert-like landscape on Mount Etna, the most active volcano in Europe

⑲ Pantalica

 G2 🏠 Siracusa
🚌 From Siracusa to Sortino, then 5-km (3-mile) walk to entrance (partial access), or bus from Siracusa to Ferla, then 10-km (6-mile) walk to entrance
🌐 comune.ferla.sr.it

Remote in the desolate Monti Iblei and overlooking the River Anapo is the prehistoric necropolis of Pantalica, a pleasant place to walk and picnic. The dead of a large, unexcavated village (occupied from the 13th to 8th centuries BC) were buried here in cave-like tombs cut into the rock. More than 5,000 of these tombs were arranged in tiers with a single flat stone sealing each opening.

The inhabitants of Pantalica are thought to have come from coastal Thapsos, which was abandoned after raids by warlike tribes from mainland Italy. The site was re-inhabited during the Byzantine period, when some of the tombs were made into cave dwellings and chapels. Artifacts from the necropolis are now on display in Siracusa's Museo Archeologico Regionale.

⑳ Catania

 G2 ✈ FS 🚌 ℹ Via Cimarosa 10; www.apt-catania.com

Mount Etna looms high over Catania. A volcanic eruption in 1693 completely destroyed the city, and its centre was entirely reconstructed from Etna lava – even the streets and piazzas are paved with lava. The 18th-century rebuilding created imposing Baroque edifices, set on broad, straight streets and unevenly shaped squares, a precaution for earthquakes. Today it is a big, bustling and rather austere city, with a compact historic centre.

Via Etnea slices through Catania, with Etna rising at one end. At the other end stands Piazza Duomo, a large pedestrianized space with a lava monument of an elephant (Catania's emblem) in its centre. Black lava buildings trimmed with white limestone dominate: the Duomo's façade incorporates columns filched from the city's Roman amphitheatre (still visible 500 m/500 yd away on Piazza Stesicoro), while inside is the elaborately decorated chapel of the city's patron saint, Agatha, whose statue and relics are paraded through the city during the Festa di Sant'Agata (3–5 February). At the far end of the piazza, steps lead down to the Pescheria, where Catania's exuberant morning fish, fruit and vegetable market is held.

A wander along Via dei Crocifissi leads past the best of the city's black-and-white Baroque buildings. Back on Piazza Duomo, bus 1 or 4 goes to the train station, beyond which, housed in the former sulphur works of Le Ciminiere, is a superb arts complex.

↑ Market stalls in front of a Baroque church in Catania

EXPERIENCE Sicily

Scicli

🅰G2 🄰Ragusa ✈🚆🚌 ℹ
InfoPoint, Passatempo; 366
303 3952

Scicli is an enchanting place
full of exuberant churches and
palaces, many of which appear
in the *Inspector Montalbano* TV
series. Fans of the programme
can visit the Municipio, or town
hall (filmed as Montalbano's
police station). The church
of San Bartolomeo has a
Baroque façade framed by a
backdrop of limestone crags.
Other must sees are Palazzo
Beneventano, its balconies
supported by snarling
Baroque monsters, and the
church of San Giovanni. The
latter is home to the *Cristo
di Burgos*, an unsettling
17th-century Spanish
portrait of Christ wearing
what appears to be a dirndl
skirt (it is, in fact, his shroud).

22
Sampieri

🅰G2 🄰Ragusa 🚆🚌

Sampieri is a diminutive
summer resort at the head
of a 3-km (2-mile) sweep of
fine sandy dunes. Unlike many
coastal villages, it retains a
grid of simple, cubic fishermen's houses built of the
same vanilla-hued limestone
as the cobbles of its narrow
streets. There are two lidos
and a handful of places to
eat and drink in the summer.

BAROQUE TOWNS OF THE VAL DI NOTO

In 1693 a devastating earthquake destroyed the entire
southeast corner of Sicily. At the time, Sicily was under
the rule of the Spanish Bourbons, and the architecture
favoured was flamboyant, bold and extravagant. Many
of the towns were rebuilt in this style and, as a result,
this beautiful region of dramatic limestone gorges,
flower-filled meadows and long sandy beaches is
peppered with glorious Baroque towns. Now designated
World Heritage Sites by UNESCO, Noto, Ragusa, Modica
and Scicli are the most famous, but there are also some
wonderful smaller towns to discover, such as Ispica,
Chiaramonte Gulfi and Militello Val di Catania.

23
Ragusa

🅰G2 ✈🚆🚌 ℹPiazza San
Giovanni, Ragusa
Superiore; www.comune.
ragusa.gov.it

A UNESCO World Heritage
Site, Ragusa is divided into
two by a dramatic gorge.
Ibla, the original settlement
on a rocky crest, was rebuilt
in Baroque style after the
1693 earthquake but retains
its wiggly medieval street
plan. The upper town, Ragusa
Superiore, was founded on
the plain above the gorge
after the earthquake.
 In Ibla, the three-tiered
Baroque façade of the Duomo
di San Giorgio, designed by
Rosario Gagliardi, stands atop
a voluptuous flight of steps.
On Via Orfanotrofio, to the
left of San Giuseppe, is the
exquisite church of San
Francesco all'Immacolata,
which incorporates the
Gothic portal of Palazzo

Chiaramonte, a nobleman's
palace destroyed in the
earthquake. From here
zigzag back through Ibla
to the church of Santa Maria
della Scala, which presides
over the steps linking Ibla
with Ragusa Superiore. The
main target in the newer town
is the **Museo Archeologico
Ibleo**, which has a splendid
collection of prehistoric,
Greek and Roman artifacts
unearthed in the region.

Museo Archeologico Ibleo
Ⓢ 🄰Via Natalelli 11
🄲9am–6:30pm Mon–Sat

24
Modica

🅰G2 🄰Ragusa 🚆🚌
ℹCorso Umberto I 1431;
0932 904444

The historic centre of
Modica – a town famous for
its chocolate – spills down the
opposing slopes of a ravine.
Sweeping between the ornate
façades of Baroque palazzos,
Corso Umberto is the focus of
local life, full of restaurants,
shops, delicatessens and cafés.
 If you want to find out
about Modica's chocolate,
which is made to an Aztec
recipe brought to Sicily by

←

Ragusa Ibla, the town's
original core, situated on
a rocky crag

EAT

Here are some of the best restaurants in Ragusa Ibla.

Locanda Don Serafino
Set in a cave-cum-wine cellar, this restaurant offers traditional dishes.

 Via Avvocato G Ottaviano locanda donserafino.it

€€€

Ristorante Duomo
Regarded as the best restaurant in Sicily. The menu is tirelessly innovative.

 Via Capitano Bocchieri 31 cicciosultano.it

€€€

I Banchi
A restaurant, café and deli; perfect for lunch.

 Via Orfanotrofio ibanchiragusa.it

€€€

Trattoria la Bettola
Try the pork braised in wine and herbs at this family-run trattoria.

 Largo Kamarina 0932 653 377

€€€

Spanish *conquistadores*, head to the historic chocolatier Bonajuto. It offers free tastings, but it's also worth trying a hot chocolate spiked with chilli or cinnamon, or even a savoury meat-and-chocolate pastry (*impanata*) at the Caffé dell'Arte.

The real pleasure of Modica lies in exploring the steep labyrinth of streets on either side of the ravine, while the architectural jewel of the town is the Duomo di San Giorgio, spectacularly sited at the head of a theatrical 250-step Baroque stairway. The magnificent elliptical façade and belfry are attributed to Rosario Gagliardi.

25
Noto

G2 Siracusa FS
Piazza XVI Maggio;
www.comune.noto.sr.it

All that was left of Noto following the 1693 earthquake was "a mountain of abandoned rocks", according to Giuseppe Lanza, who was given the job of rebuilding it. He decided to create a new town from scratch, 16 km (10 miles) away, and the people of Noto were furious – they had begun to rebuild the old town (Noto

↑ Splendid example of a Sicilian Baroque church in the town of Modica

Antica) among the ruins. Rebuilt in Baroque style out of apricot-hued limestone, the new Noto was revolutionary, divided into an upper town for the people, and a monumental lower town, its broad avenues lined with political and religious buildings.

To see the best of the town, walk along the main street, Corso Vittorio Emanuele, passing through the imposing Porta Reale. On the left is the church of Santa Chiara, built on an unusual elliptical plan, and beyond, the theatrical central square, Piazza Municipio, where a magnificent flight of steps rises to the muscular Baroque Duomo, its interior serene and flooded with light from the rebuilt dome. Opposite the Duomo is the elegant Palazzo Ducezio, Noto's town hall. Walk alongside the Duomo to Palazzo Trigona, with its curvaceous balconies, where steps lead up past more fine Baroque buildings to Noto Alta, the upper town, and the church of Santa Maria di Gesù (rarely open to the public), from where there are views of the surrounding countryside.

Snorkellers at Porto Giunco beach in Villasimius, near Cagliari

SARDINIA

In his travelogue *Sea and Sardinia*, D H Lawrence wrote that Sardinia was "left outside of time and history". Indeed, the march of time been slow here, and traditions from ancient Europe have survived – the legacy of invasion by Phoenicians, Carthaginians, Romans, Arabs, Byzantines, Spaniards and Savoyards. These traditions are displayed in Sardinia's many festivals – some soberly Christian, others with pagan roots. Several different dialects and languages are spoken in Sardinia. Catalan can be heard in Alghero, and on the island of San Pietro there is a Ligurian dialect. In the south, the traditional influences are Spanish, while conservative native strains of people and language survive in the Gennargentu mountains. Peopled by shepherds in isolated communities, this region is so impenetrable that invaders have never bothered it.

Of particular interest are the prehistoric nuraghic castles, villages, temples and tombs dotted around the countryside – most notably around Barumini, north of Cagliari, and in the Valle dei Nuraghi, south of Sassari. The *nuraghi* were built by a people whose origins constitute one of the Mediterranean's great mysteries.

Sassari, Oristano, Alghero and Olbia are all centres of areas marked by their individuality. Some remarkable Pisan-Romanesque churches are located around Sassari and here, too, dialects reveal close links with the languages of Tuscany. Olbia is a boom town made rich by tourism and the proximity of the jet-setting Costa Smeralda. Sober Nuoro with its province in the shadow of the Gennargentu mountains, by contrast, offers dramatic scenery and a rich literary heritage.

Genoa,
Marseille, Barcelona

Isola Asinara

*Golfo
dell' Asinara*

Fornelli

Stintino

Castelsardo

S200

Porto Torres

Sorso

Palmadula

La Nurra

S131

Osilo

*Capo dell'
Argentiera*

SASSARI ❷

Ploaghe

Olmedo

**Alghero-
Fertilia**

Mannu

Ardara

*Grotta di
Nettuno*

Ittiri

S131

❸

Torralba

ALGHERO

S292

*Valle de
Nuraghe*

Monteleone Rocca Doria

*Mediterranean
Sea*

Montresta

Bonorva

Capo Marargiu

❹ **BOSA**

S129b

Bosa Marina

Macomer

Cuglieri

*Monte Ferru
1050m*

Ghilarz

Capo Mannu

S292

Riola Sardo

Fordongianus

Stagno di Cabras

Crabas

ORISTANO ❼

Simaxis

Santa Giusta

Usellu

Arborea

S131

Ales

*Capo della
Frasca*

Terralba

Uras

S126

Pardu Atzei

Sardara

Campidano

Guspini

Villacidro

Capo Pecora

*Monte Linas
1236m*

Buggerru

Masua

S126

Vallermosa

Iglesias

S130

Siliqua

Gonnesa

Portoscuso

Narcao

Carbonia

*Isola di
San Pietro*

Calasetta

*Monte Caravius
1116m*

Santad

Sant'Antioco

S195

SANT'ANTIOCO ❽

Porto Botte

*Golfo di
Palmas*

Teulada

Capo Teulada

SARDINIA

Experience

EXPERIENCE

❶

The Maddalena Archipelago and Costa Smeralda

🅐B5 🅐Sassari 🆑🚢Olbia 🚌Porto Cervo 🅘AAST La Maddalena, P Barone de Genesis & AAST Palau, Via Nazionale 94; www. sardegnaturismo.it

The islands of the Arcipelago della Maddalena have white sandy beaches and turquoise waters. Linked with Palau, on the mainland, by ferry, the only settlement of any size is La Maddalena, on the Isola Maddalena island. A causeway runs across the sea to the island of Caprera, the home and final resting place of revolutionary hero Giuseppe Garibaldi (1807–82). The **Compendio Garibaldino** is a small museum in his former home. The archipelago's smaller islands can be accessed only by boat.

Southeast of Palau, stretching from the Golfo di Arzachena to the Golfo di Cugnana, the Costa Smeralda was developed in the 1950s by a consortium of magnates headed by the Aga Khan. One of the world's most exclusive holiday playgrounds, it is kept immaculate by strict controls. Its boutiques, restaurants, clubs and luxury hotels cater

for the seriously rich, like billionaires, crowned heads and pop stars.

Compendio Garibaldino
🅐Forte Arbuticci, Caprera
🕗8:30am-7:30pm Mon-Sat
🌐compendiogaribaldino.it

❷

Sassari

🅐A5 ✈🆑🚌 🅘Palazzo di Città, Via Sebastiano Satta 13; www.comune. sassari.it

Founded by Genoese and Pisan merchants in the 13th century, Sassari has a tight, church-filled medieval quarter around the Duomo (11th-century, with later additions). To the north is the huge Fonte Rosello, a late Renaissance fountain. The **Museo Archeologico Nazionale "GA Sanna"** is a good starting point for investigating the region's nuraghic history.

To the southeast along the S131 is the Pisan-Romanesque church of Santissima Trinità di Saccargia (1116), with the only extant 13th-century fresco cycle in Sardinia. Further on is the 12th-century church of San Michele di Salvenero, and at Ardara the basalt-built Romanesque Santa Maria del Regno, or "Black Cathedral".

↑ Pristine landscape and turquoise waters along the Costa Smeralda

Museo Archeologico Nazionale "GA Sanna"
⊛ 🅐Via Roma 64 📞079 27 22 03 🕗9am-8pm Tue-Sat & 1st Sun of month

❸

Alghero

🅐A5 🅐Sassari ✈🆑🚌 🚢 🅘Largo San Francesco; www.comune.alghero.ss.it

Founded in the 12th century, and taken from the Genoese Dorias by the Aragonese in 1353, Alghero was peopled by settlers from Barcelona and Valencia. Its original occupants – Ligurians and Sardinians – were expelled with such thoroughness that today the Catalan language and culture is enjoying a revival and the look of the old town is consistently Spanish.

Filled with labyrinthine alleys and cobbled streets, the lively port of old Alghero is flanked by battlemented walls and defensive towers on all but the landward section. Facing the Giardino Pubblico is the massive 16th-century Torre di Porta Terra, also known as the Jewish Tower after its builders. The 16th-century Duomo at the bottom of Via Umberto is predominantly Catalan-Gothic

NURAGHI IN SARDINIA

There are 7,000 or so *nuraghi* dotted around Sardinia. Dating from 1800 to 300 BC, these truncated cone structures were built from huge basalt blocks without any bonding. Little is known about the identity of the nuraghic people. They must have possessed remarkable engineering skills, but appear to have left no written record.

with an Aragonese portal. Off Via Carlo Alberto, San Francesco (14th century) has a pretty cloister and octagonal campanile towering over Alghero, and Baroque San Michele has a bright tiled dome. On Via Principe Umberto is the Casa Doria, the house where the pre-Hispanic rulers of Alghero lived. It has a beautiful Renaissance portal and Gothic-arched window.

Take a boat trip to the spectacular Grotta di Nettuno, a deep natural cave round the point of Capo Caccia, or the nearby Grotta Verde.

Bosa

**⚠A5-A6 ⚑Nuoro FS⛴
ℹ️Località Isola Rossa, Bosa Marina; 0785 37 55 50**

Bosa is a small, picturesque seaside town at the mouth of Sardinia's only navigable river, the Temo. The historic Sa Costa district struggles up the side of a low hill capped by the Castello di Serravalle, built in 1122 by the Malaspina family. The narrow passages and alleys here have changed little since the Middle Ages. By the Temo are Sas Conzas, the former tanneries, dyers' houses and workshops.

Languishing on the riverside, the cosmopolitan Sa Piatta district houses the Aragonese-Gothic Duomo (15th century)

and Romanesque San Pietro Extramuros (11th century), with a Gothic façade added in the 13th century.

Nuoro

⚠B5 FS⛴ ℹ️Piazza Mameli; www.comune. nuoro.it

This town, in a spectacular setting beneath Monte Ortobene and the dramatic Supramonte, was the home of Grazia Deledda, who won the Nobel Prize for Literature in 1926 for her portrayal of the communities around her. A collection of ethnic items, such as traditional Sardinian costumes and jewellery, can be seen in the excellent **Museo Etnografico Sardo**.

Nuoro is on the edge of the Barbagia region, which has isolated villages of shepherds who have never experienced the hand of any overlord, so impenetrable are the Gennargentu mountains. This region was known to the Romans as Barbaria, an area they were never able to subdue. In Orgosolo, you may see wall murals calling for Sardinia's independence.

Museo Etnografico Sardo
⊗ 🏛Via Mereu 56 🕐10am–1pm & 3-7pm Tue-Sun (Mar-Sep: to 8pm) 🌐isre sardegna.it

---

STAY

Villas Las Tronas
This palatial hotel has scenic views, gardens, indoor and outdoor pools, and a Turkish bath. Offering genteel, old-style elegance, it is open all year round.

⚠A5 🏛Lungomare Valencia 1, Alghero 🌐hotelvillalastronas.it

€€€

Hotel Cala Di Volpe
This tranquil resort overlooks the turquoise waters of the Costa Smeralda. The hotel's design is inspired by traditional Sardinian craftsmanship.

⚠B5 🏛Loc Cala di Volpe, Porto Cervo 🌐caladivolpe.com

€€€

Valle dell'Erica Resort Thalasso & Spa
Looking on to the Maddalena archipelago, this family-friendly resort has four swimming pools and a spa with a hammam.

⚠B5 🏛Loc Valle dell'Erica, Santa Teresa Gallura 🌐hotel valledellerica.com

€€€

TOP 5 BEACHES IN SARDINIA

Cala Granara, Isole della Maddalena
B5

A crescent of silvery sand in a sheltered turquoise cove backed by maquis.

Cala Goloritzé, nr Baunei, Orotzei
B5

At the foot of a ravine, This tiny white-sand beach is a great place for snorkelling.

Cala Gonone, Orotzei
B5

This picturesque bay includes several gorgeous beaches reached by footpath.

Sinis Peninsula, Oristano
A6

A series of exquisite beaches of glistening white quartz sand.

Costa Rei, Sarrabus
B6

The beaches of Costa Rei have fabulous turquoise waters and soft, white-gold sands.

6 Cala Gonone

99 X9 **Nuoro**
Pro Loco, Viale Bue Marino; 0784 936 96
from Dorgali to grottoes
347 720 96 96

East of Nuoro, between the sea and the mountains, is the hamlet of Cala Gonone – a bustling seaside resort and fishing port, with magnificent beaches. Along the unspoiled coast are the isolated coves of Cala Luna, linked with Cala Gonone by a well-marked 2-hour trail, and Cala Sisine. The famous Grotta del Bue Marino, adorned with weird rock formations, can only be reached by boat.

---

7 Oristano

A6 **Cagliari** **FS**
Pro Loco, Via Ciutadella de Menorca 14; 0783 706 21

The province of Oristano corresponds roughly with historical Arborea, over which Eleonora of Arborea ruled in the late 14th century. She is commemorated by an 18th-century statue in Piazza Eleonora. On Corso Vittorio Emanuele is the 16th-century Casa di Eleonora, and nearby the **Antiquarium Arborense**, which has Neolithic, nuraghic, Punic and Roman artifacts. The Torre di San Cristoforo (1291) in Piazza Roma once formed part of Oristano's fortifications. The Duomo (13th century) was later rebuilt in the Baroque style. More interesting are the churches of Santa Chiara (1343) on Via Garibaldi and 14th-century San Martino on Via Cagliari.

The 12th-century Pisan-Romanesque Cathedral at Santa Giusta has columns probably taken from Tharros, an 8th-century-BC Punic settlement, 20 km (12 miles) west of Oristano on the Sinis Peninsula.

Antiquarium Arborense
Piazza Corrias
0783 79 12 62 **Daily**
2–3pm Sat & Sun

↑ The island of Sant' Antioco, seen from the lagoon

8

Sant'Antioco

🅰A6 🚗Cagliari 🚊🚌 🛈Pro Loco, Piazza Repubblica 41; 0781 84 05 92

The main town on this tiny island is Sant'Antioco, once a Phoenician port and an important Roman base. Proof of almost continuous occupation is clear from the **catacombs**, a Phoenician burial place later used by Christians, under the basilica of Sant'Antioco Martire (12th century). The **Museo**

Pastel-coloured buildings in Cagliari's old town

Archeologico has Phoenician artifacts. The Punic Tophet (sanctuary of the goddess Tanit) and the necropolis are located nearby.

Catacombs

⊛⊛ 🏠Piazza Parrocchia 22 📞0781 92 18 87 🕑9am-noon & 3:30-5:15pm Mon-Sat (to 8pm Sat), 11am-noon & 3:30-6pm Sun & hols

Museo Archeologico

⊛⊛ 🏠Via Sabatino Moscati 📞0781 821 05 🕑9am-7pm daily 🚫1 Jan, Easter, 25, 26 Dec (& Tophet & necropolis)

9

Cagliari

🅰B6 ✈🚊🚌🚢 🛈Via Roma 145; www.cagliari turismo.it

The capital of Sardinia, Cagliari was occupied by the Phoenicians, Carthaginians and Romans, and extensive ruins of the Phoenician city of Nora lie to the southwest. A 2nd-century amphitheatre survives from the Roman era, cut from rock. Discover the town's earlier history in the **Cittadella dei Musei**, which houses several museums, including the Museo Archeologico Nazionale. The nuraghic items are the most interesting in the collection. Also in the Cittadella dei Musei is the Pinacoteca, an art gallery.

The old core of Cagliari has an appealing North African character. In the high Castello district, the Romans and, later, Pisans built defences. The gracious Bastione San Remy on Piazza Costituzione offers magnificent views over the city and surrounding countryside. The Duomo is a 20th-century rehash of a Romanesque building.

Flanking the entrance are two 12th-century pulpits originally destined for Pisa's cathedral.

Nearby is the Pisan tower Torre San Pancrazio (14th century). Down in Stampace quarter, Piazza Yenne is the lively centre of old Cagliari. In Piazza San Cosimo, the 6th-century church of San Saturnino is a rare monument to Byzantine occupation.

Cittadella dei Musei

⊛ 🏠Piazza Arsenale 📞070 675 76 27 🕑9am-8pm Tue-Sun

EAT

Here are some of the best restaurants in Cagliari.

Antico Caffè 1855
Landmark bistro with a terrace over the square.

🏠Piazza Costituzione 10/11 📞070 65 82 06

€€€

Dal Corsaro
Classic cooking by an expert chef.

🏠Viale Regina Margherita 28 📞070 66 43 18

€€€

Stella Marina di Montecristo
Simple seafood osteria.

🏠Via Sardegna 140 📞347 578 89 64

€€€

Su Cumbidu
A range of traditional Sardinian dishes.

🏠Via Napoli 13 📞070 67 07 12

€€€

NEED TO KNOW

Via della Conciliazione and St Peter's, Rome

BEFORE YOU GO

Forward planning is essential to any successful trip. Be prepared for all eventualities by considering the following points before you travel.

AT A GLANCE

CURRENCY
Euro (EUR)

AVERAGE DAILY SPEND

SAVE	SPEND	SPLURGE
€50	€100	€200+

BOTTLED WATER	COFFEE	BEER	DINNER FOR TWO
€1.30	€1	€5	€60

ESSENTIAL PHRASES

Hello	Buongiorno
Goodbye	Arrivederci
Please	Per favore
Thank you	Grazie
Do you speak English?	Parla inglese?
I don't understand	Non ho capito

ELECTRICITY SUPPLY

Power sockets are type F and L, fitting two- and three- pronged plugs. Standard voltage is 220-230v.

Passports and Visas

EU nationals and citizens of the UK, US, Canada, Australia and New Zealand do not need visas for stays of up to three months. Consult your nearest Italian embassy or check the **Polizia di Stato** website if you are travelling from outside these areas.
Polizia di Stato
w poliziadistato.it

Travel Safety Advice

Visitors can get up-to-date travel safety information from the UK Foreign and Commonwealth Office, the US State Department, and the Australian Department of Foreign Affairs and Trade.
AUS
w smartraveller.gov.au
UK
w gov.uk/foreign-travel-advice
US
w travel.state.gov

Customs Information

An individual is permitted to carry the following within the EU for personal use; If travelling outside the EU limits vary so check restrictions before departing.

Tobacco products 800 cigarettes, 400 cigarillos, 200 cigars or 1 kg of smoking tobacco.

Alcohol 10 litres of alcoholic beverages above 22% strength, 20 litres of alcoholic beverages below 22% strength, 90 litres of wine (60 litres of which can be sparkling wine) and 110 litres of beer.

Cash If you plan to enter or leave the EU with €10,000 or more in cash (or equivalent in other currencies) you must declare it to the customs authorities prior to departure.

Insurance

It is wise to take out an insurance policy covering theft, loss of belongings, medical problems, cancellation and delays.

Emergency medical care in Italy is free for all EU and Australian citizens. EU citizens should ensure they have an **EHIC** (European Health Insurance Card) and Australians should be registered to **Medicare** to receive this benefit.

Visitors from outside these areas must arrange their own private medical insurance before arriving in Italy.

EHIC

 gov.uk/european-health-insurance-card

Medicare

 humanservices.gov.au/individuals/medicare

Vaccinations

No inoculations are needed for Italy, but bring mosquito repellent, especially if you are travelling during the summer months.

Money

Most establishments accept major credit, debit and pre-paid currency cards, but carry cash for smaller items, such as coffee, *gelato* and pizza-by-the-slice.

Northern Italy is generally more expensive than the south. This is due to an historical wealth disparity that dates back to Italy's unification in 1871. Nowadays, affluent cities in the north benefit from a healthy economy, whilst southern cities such as Naples and Palermo suffer from high unemployment rates and a low GDP.

Booking Accommodation

In the summer months accommodation is snapped up fast, and prices are often inflated. In some cities you will be charged a city tax on top of the price for the room (usually a few euro per person per night).

Under Italian law, hotels are required to register guests at police headquarters and issue a receipt of payment *(ricevuta fiscale)*, which you must keep until you leave Italy.

Travellers with Specific Needs

Italy's historic towns and cities are ill-equipped for disabled access. Many buildings do not have wheelchair access or lifts.

In Milan **AIAS** and in Rome **CO.IN**. **Sociale** and **Rome and Italy** provide information and general assistance for disabled travellers. Trenitalia *(p538)* can arrange special reservations and assistance at stations.

AIAS

 aiasmilano.it

CO.IN.Sociale

 coinsociale.it

Rome and Italy

 romeanditaly.com

Language

Italian is the official language, but there are also many regional languages spoken, such as Friulian, Piedmontese, Sardinian and Sicilian.

The level of English and other foreign languages spoken can be limited, particularly in rural areas, but locals appreciate visitors' efforts to speak Italian, even if only a few words.

Closures

Lunchtime Most churches and small businesses close for a few hours in the afternoon.

Monday Museums and some restaurants and cafés close for the day.

Sunday Restaurants usually close for lunch. Churches and cathedrals forbid tourists from visiting during Mass and public transport runs a reduced service.

Public holidays Shops, churches and museums and some restaurants either close early or for the entire day.

PUBLIC HOLIDAYS 2019	
1 Jan	New Year's Day
6 Jan	Epiphany
21 Apr	Easter Sunday
22 Apr	Easter Monday
25 Apr	Liberation Day
1 May	Labour Day
2 Jun	Republic Day
15 Aug	Ferragosto
1 Nov	All Saints' Day
8 Dec	Feast of the Immaculate Conception
25 Dec	Christmas Day
26 Dec	St Stephen's Day

GETTING AROUND

Whether you are visiting for a short city break or rural country retreat, discover how best to reach your destination and travel like a pro.

AT A GLANCE

PUBLIC TRANSPORT COSTS

MILAN

€1.50

One-way
Bus, tram & metro

ROME

€1.50

One-way
Bus, tram & metro

FLORENCE

€1.20

One-way
Bus & tram

SPEED LIMIT

MOTORWAY

130 kmph
(80 mph)

DUAL CARRIAGEWAY

100 kmph
(60 mph)

NATIONAL ROADS

80 kmph
(50 mph)

URBAN AREAS

50 kmph
(30 mph)

Arriving by Air

Rome's Leonardo da Vinci (Fiumicino) and Milan's Malpensa are the main airports for long-haul flights into Italy.

European budget airlines fly to cities across Italy year round at very reasonable prices. They also offer very good rates on internal flights within the country – ideal if you want to cover multiple destinations in one trip .

For information on getting to and from Italy's main airports, see the table opposite.

Train Travel

International Train Travel

Regular high-speed international trains connect Italy to the main towns and cities in Austria, Germany, France and Eastern Europe. Reservations for these services are essential and tickets are booked up quickly.

You can buy tickets and passes for multiple international journeys via **Eurail** or **Interrail**, however you may still need to pay an additional reservation fee depending on which rail service you travel with. Always check that your pass is valid before boarding.

Eurail
W eurail.com
Interrail
W interrail.eu

Domestic Train Travel

Trenitalia is the main operator in Italy. Tickets can be bought online, but there are only a fixed number available so book ahead.

Italo Treno (NTV) and Trenitalia (FS) offer a high-speed service between major train stations throughout Italy. Book in advance to ensure a good price; reservations are essential.

Train tickets must be validated before boarding by stamping them in machines at the entrance to platforms. Heavy fines are levied if you are caught with an unvalidated ticket.

Italo Treno
W italotreno.it
Trenitalia
W trenitalia.com

GETTING TO AND FROM THE AIRPORT

Airport	Distance to City	Taxi Fare	Public Transport	Journey Time
Bergamo (Orio al Serio)	6 km (4 miles)	€18	bus	25 mins
Florence (Amerigo Vespucci)	4 km (3 miles)	€22	bus	20 mins
Milan (Linate)	10 km (6 miles)	€20	bus	20 mins
Milan (Malpensa)	50 km (31 miles)	€95	train (FS)	1 hour
Naples (Capodichino)	7 km (4 miles)	€25	bus	30 mins
Palermo (Falcone-Borsellino)	31 km (20 miles)	€45	bus	50 mins
Pisa (Galileo Galilei)	2 km (1 mile)	€10	train (FS)	10 mins
Rome (Fiumicino)	35 km (22 miles)	€48	train (FS)	30 mins
Rome (Ciampino)	15 km (9 miles)	€30	bus	45 mins
Turin (Torino-Caselle)	18 km (11 miles)	€30	train (GTT)	30 mins
Venice (Marco Polo)	13 km (8 miles)	€35	bus	20 mins
Venice (Treviso)	41 km (25 miles)	€75	bus	1 hour 10 mins
Verona (Villafranca)	10 km (6 miles)	€25	bus	15 mins

RAIL JOURNEY PLANNER

This map is a handy reference for intercity travel on Italy's major train routes. Journey times given below are for the fastest available service on each route.

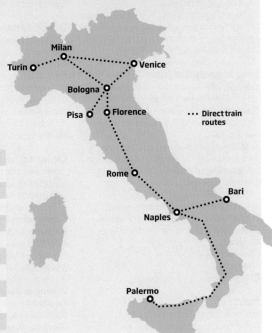

••• Direct train routes

Milan to Bologna	1 hr
Milan to Turin	1 hr
Milan to Florence	2 hrs
Milan to Rome	3 hrs
Rome to Florence	1.5 hrs
Rome to Naples	1 hr
Pisa to Florence	1 hr
Naples to Bari	4 hrs
Naples to Palermo	10 hrs
Venice to Milan	2.5 hrs
Venice to Bologna	1.5 hrs

Public Transport

Most cities operate multiple public transport services comprising buses, trams, metro and in the case of Venice, boats. It is worth noting that many historic centres are relatively compact and can easily be covered on foot.

Public Transport Operators
Florence: ATAF
W ataf.net
Rome: ATAC
W atac.roma.it
Milan: ATM
W atm.it
Venice: Venezia Unica
W veneziaunica.it

Buses and Trams
Tickets (biglietti) are available from kiosks, stations, bars, and newsstands. A single ticket is normally valid on all modes of public transport, including metro if avalable, and transfers for a designated amount of time (usually around one hour).

Some operators accept contactless payments or smart cards rather than traditional paper tickets. It is always best to check the website of the local transport company before travelling.

Discounted tickets bought in bulk (un blocchetto or un carnet), or day- or week-long visitor's tickets and passes, are usually better value than paying as you go.

Tickets for public transport must be validated at the time of boarding. Validation machines are usually placed in the entrance hall at metro stations and on board buses and trams.

Long Distance Bus Travel
Eurolines offers a variety of coach routes to various destinations in Italy from other European cities. Fares are very reasonable, with discounts available for students, children and seniors.

SITA offer reasonably priced coach travel throughout Italy. You can usually buy tickets on board for long-haul buses (pullman or corriera) between towns and cities.

Services often depart from outside main railway stations or from a town's main piazza. In rural areas, check bus stops for timetables and the details of local transport companies.
Eurolines
W eurolines.eu
SITA
W sitabus.it

Metro
Italy's major cities have a metro system (la metropolitana, or la metro for short), with the exception of Florence and other historic cities.

Milan, Naples and Rome are the largest with multiple lines, whilst Brescia, Catania, Genoa, and Turin have only one line.

For transport information about a specific town or city, consult the relevant public transport operator.

Taxis
Taxis are not hailed; take one at an official taxi stand (usually found at the station, main piazza or close to key tourist sights), or reserve one by phone. When you order a taxi by phone, the meter will run from your call.

Only accept rides in licensed, metered taxis. In Rome, official taxis are white, have a "taxi" sign on the roof and their official taxi licence number on the doors.

Extra charges are added for each piece of luggage placed in the boot, for rides between 10pm and 7am, on Sundays and public holidays, and for journeys to and from airports.

Taxi apps such as UBER (black service only) also operate in most major towns and cities.

Driving

One of the best ways to explore Italy is by car. However, it can also be a hair-raising experience. Italians have a reputation for driving erratically; this is particularly true in the south. Make sure you are familiar with the rules of the road and have all the necessary documentation, as traffic police (carabinieri) carry out routine checks.

Driving to Italy
Italy is easily reachable from other European countries via E-roads, the International European Road Network connecting major roads across national borders within Europe, or by national (N) and secondary (SS) roads from neighbouring France, Switzerland, Austria and Slovenia.

Vehicles may also be transported into the country by ferry or rail.

Car Rental
To rent a car in Italy you must be over 21 and have held a valid driver's licence for at least a year.

Driving licences issued by any of the EU member states are valid throughout the European Union, including Italy. If visiting from outside the EU, you may need to apply for an International Driving Permit (IDP). Check with your local automobile association.

Driving in Italy
If you bring your own foreign-registered car into the country, you must carry a Green Card, the vehicle's registration documents and a valid driver's licence with you when driving.

Main towns and cities often enforce a Limited Traffic Zone (**ZTL**). To avoid fines, consult the **Urban Access Regulations in Europe** website.

Tolls are payable on most motorways (*autostrade*), and payment is made at the end of the journey in either cash, credit card or pre-paid magnetic VIA cards, available from tobacconists and the **ACI** (Automobile Club d'Italia). Avoid tolls by using the national roads (*strade nazionali*), or secondary state roads (*strade statali*). Although less direct, they are often more scenic, allowing you to stop at viewpoints, towns and places of interest en route.

Roads known as white roads (*strade bianche*) have only a gravel surface. These are often narrow and steep, but are usually passable to cars. Always check your route before travelling.

ACI
W aci.it

ZTL and Urban Access Regulations in Europe
W urbanaccessregulations.eu

Rules of the Road
Drive on the right, use the left lane only for passing, and yield to traffic from the right.

Seat belts are required for all passengers in the front and back, and heavy fines are levied for using a mobile phone while driving. A strict drink-drive limit (*p542*) is enforced.

During the day dipped headlights are compulsory when you are driving on motorways, dual carriageways and on all out-of-town roads.

A red warning triangle, spare tyre and fluorescent vests must be carried at all times, for use in the event of an emergency.

In the event of an accident or breakdown switch on your hazard warning lights and place a warning triangle 50m (55 yd) behind your vehicle. For breakdowns call the ACI emergency number (116) or the emergency services (112 or 113). The ACI will tow any foreign-registered vehicle to the nearest ACI-affiliated garage free of charge.

Hitchhiking

Hitchhiking, or *autostop*, is illegal on motorways, but in more rural areas it is a common way for tourists and backpackers to get around on a budget. Always consider your own safety before entering an unknown vehicle.

Bicycle and Scooter Hire

Public bicycle sharing systems are available in most major cities, such as **BikeMi** in Milan and **[TO]BIKE** in Turin. You can rent bicycles, motorcycles and scooters hourly or by the day. You may have to leave your passport with the rental shop as a deposit, and you must have a valid licence to hire a scooter or motorcycle. Italian drivers are infamous for their blasé attitude to road safety, so only take to the roads if you are a confident cyclist or motorcyclist.

BikeMi
W bikemi.com

[TO]BIKE
W tobike.it

Boats and Ferries

The Italian islands are linked by sea to the mainland by regular ferry services including car ferries and hydrofoils.

The main Italian ports that serve the large islands of Sicily and Sardinia in the south are Genoa, Livorno, Civitavecchia, Fiumicino, Naples and Villa San Giovanni.

Ferry services are more frequent and reliable in summer, but book in advance to travel in July or August, especially if taking a vehicle.

The following international ferries run regular services to Italy's main ports from Spain, France, Corsica, Malta, Tunisia, Morocco, Slovenia, Croatia, and Greece:

Emilia Romagna Lines
W directferries.it/emilia_romagna_lines.htm

Gnv Grandi Navi Veloci
W gnv.it

Grimaldi Line
W grimaldi-ferries.com

Snav
W snav.it

TRAVEL IN VENICE

Venice has a unique transport network made up of the following vehicles:

Gondolas

A luxury form of transport. Before boarding, check the official tariffs and agree a price with the gondolier.

Traghetti

These gondola ferries cross the Grand Canal at seven different points. To find traghetti stops, look out for yellow street signs featuring a gondola.

Vaporetti

These large boats connect numerous ports across Venice and are the cheapest and most efficient way to travel. Smaller boats called Motoscafi and larger boats called Motonave also service the Vaporetti route.

Watertaxis

The fastest and most practical means of getting around in Venice. Beware of extra charges for transporting luggage, waiting, night service and call-out fees.

PRACTICAL
INFORMATION

A little local know-how goes a long way in Italy. Here you will find all the essential advice and information you will need during your stay.

AT A GLANCE

EMERGENCY NUMBERS

EMERGENCY OPERATOR	POLICE
113	**112**

AMBULANCE	FIRE SERVICE
118	**115**

TIME ZONE
CET/CEST
Central European
Summer Time
(CEST) runs
31 Mar–27 Oct 2019

TAP WATER
Unless stated
otherwise, tap
water in Italy
is safe to drink.

TIPPING

Waiter	Not expected
Hotel Porter	€1 a bag
Housekeeping	€1 a day
Concierge	€1–2
Taxi Driver	Not expected

Personal Security

Bag-snatching scooter drivers are a problem in some Italian cities, so hold bags on the inside of the pavement where possible.

Be wary of pickpockets on public transport and in crowded city centres.

If you have anything stolen, report the crime within 24 hours to the nearest police station and take ID with you. If you need to make an insurance claim, get a copy of the crime report *(denuncia)*. Contact your embassy if you have your passport stolen, or in the event of a serious crime or accident.

Health

Seek medicinal supplies and advice for minor ailments from pharmacies *(farmacia)*. You can find details of the nearest 24-hour service on all pharmacy doors.

Emergency medical care in Italy is free for all EU and Australian citizens *(p537)*. If you have an EHIC card, be sure to present this as soon as possible. You may have to pay after treatment and reclaim the money later.

For visitors from outside the EU and Australia, payment of medical expenses is the patient's responsibility. As such it is important to arrange comprehensive medical insurance.

Smoking, Alcohol and Drugs

Smoking is banned in enclosed public places. and the possession of illegal drugs is prohibited and could result in a prison sentence.

Italy has a strict limit of 0.05 per cent BAC (blood alcohol content) for drivers. This means that you cannot drink more than a small beer or a small glass of wine if you plan to drive. For drivers with less than three years' driving experience the limit is 0.

ID

By law you must carry identification at all times in Italy. A photocopy of your passport photo page (and visa if applicable) should suffice.

If you are stopped by the police you may be asked to present the original document within 12 hours.

Local Customs

In some towns and cities you can be fined for dropping litter, sitting on monument steps, or eating or drinking outside churches, historic monuments and public buildings. It is an offence to swim or bathe in public fountains.

Illegal traders operate on the streets of all major Italian cities; avoid buying from them as you could be fined by the local police.

LGBT Safety

Homosexuality is legal and widely accepted in Italy, particularly in cosmopolitan cities such as Rome and Milan. However, smaller towns and rural areas are often traditional in their views, and overt displays of affection may receive a negative response from locals.

Visiting Churches and Cathedrals

Strict dress codes apply: cover your torso and upper arms, and ensure shorts and skirts cover your knees. Shoes must be worn.

Mobile Phones and Wi-Fi

Wi-Fi is generally widely available throughout Italy, and cafés and restaurants will usually give you the password for their Wi-Fi on the condition that you make a purchase.

Visitors travelling to Italy with EU tariffs are able to use their devices abroad without being affected by roaming charges. Users will be charged the same rates for data, SMS and voice calls as they would pay at home.

Post

Stamps (*francobolli*) are sold in kiosks and tobacconists (*tabacchi*).

The Vatican City and San Marino have their own post systems and stamps. Only letters bearing San Marino or Vatican stamps can be posted in San Marino and Vatican postboxes. Italian post is notorious for its unreliability.

Letters and postcards can take anything between four days and two weeks to arrive, depending on the destination.

Taxes and Refunds

VAT (called IVA in Italy) is usually 22%, with a reduced rate of 4–10% on some items. Non-EU citizens can claim an IVA rebate subject to certain conditions.

It is easier to claim before you buy (you will need to show your passport to the shop assistant and complete a form). If claiming retrospectively, present a customs officer with your purchases and receipts at the airport. Receipts will be stamped and sent back to the vendor to issue a refund.

Discount Cards

Many cities offer a visitor's pass or discount card for exhibitions, events and museum entry. Some even cover the cost of public transport for the duration of your stay. These are not free, so consider carefully how many of the offers you are likely to take advantage of before purchasing a card.

For a full list of the discount cards available across Italy, visit the ENIT website (*below*). The following offer some of the best deals:

Campania Artecard
W campaniartecard.it
Firenze Card
W firenzecard.it
Roma Pass
W romapass.it

WEBSITES AND APPS

ENIT
Check out Itay's national tourist board website at www.italia.it
Pronto Treno
A useful app for buying tickets and checking journey times.
Navigazione Laghi
This app displays ferry times and routes for lakes Como, Garda and Maggiore.
WiFi°Italia°
This app allows you to connect to free Wi-Fi hotspots throughout Italy.

INDEX

Page numbers in **bold** type refer to main entries

Index

Index

PHRASE BOOK

IN EMERGENCY

Help!	Aiuto!	eye-*yoo*-toh
Stop!	Ferma!	fair-*mah*
Call a doctor	Chiama un medico	kee-*ah*-mah oon meh-dee-koh
Call an ambulance	Chiama un' ambulanza	kee-*ah*-mah oon am-boo-*lan*-tsa
Call the police	Chiama la polizia	kee-*ah*-mah la pol-ee-*tsee*-ah
Call the fire brigade	Chiama i pompieri	kee-*ah*-mah ee pom-*pee*-air-ee
Where is the telephone?	Dov'è il telefono?	dov-*eh*el teh-*leh*-foh-noh?
The nearest hospital?	L'ospedale più vicino?	loss-peh-*dah*-leh pee-*oo*vee-*chee*-noh?

COMMUNICATION ESSENTIALS

Yes/No	Sì/No	*see*/noh
Please	Per favore	pair fah-*vor*-eh
Thank you	Grazie	*grah*-tsee-eh
Excuse me	Mi scusi	mee *skoo*-zee
Hello	Buon giorno	bwon *jor*-noh
Goodbye	Arrivederci	ah-ree-veh-*dair*-chee
Good evening	Buona sera	*bwon*-ah *sair*-ah
morning	la mattina	lah mah-*tee*-nah
afternoon	il pomeriggio	eel poh-meh-*ree*-joh
evening	la sera	lah *sair*-ah
yesterday	ieri	ee-*air*-ee
today	oggi	*oh*-jee
tomorrow	domani	doh-*mah*-nee
here	qui	*kwee*
there	la	*lah*
What?	Quale?	*kwah*-leh?
When?	Quando?	*kwan*-doh?
Why?	Perchè?	pair-*keh*?
Where?	Dove?	*doh*-veh

USEFUL PHRASES

How are you?	Come sta?	*koh*-meh stah?
Very well, thank you.	Molto bene, grazie	*moll*-toh *beh*-neh, *grah*-tsee-eh
Pleased to meet you.	Piacere di conoscerla.	pee-ah-*chair*-eh dee coh-*noh*-shair-lah
See you soon.	A più tardi.	ah pee-oo *tar*-dee
That's fine.	Va bene.	va *beh*-neh
Where is/are ...?	Dov'è/Dove sono ...?	dov-*eh*/doveh*soh* noh?
How long does it take to get to ...?	Quanto tempo ci vuole per andare a ...?	*kwan*-toh tem-poh chee voo-*oh*-leh pair an-*dar*-eh ah...?
How do I get to ...?	Come faccio per arrivare a ...?	*koh*-meh fah*-choh pair arri-var-eh ah...?
Do you speak English?	Parla inglese?	*par*-lah een-*gleh*-zeh?
I don't understand.	Non capisco.	non ka-pee-skoh
Could you speak more slowly, please?	Può parlare più lentamente, per favore?	pwoh par-*lah*-reh pee-oo len-ta-men-*teh* pair fah-*vor*-eh?
I'm sorry.	Mi dispiace.	mee dee-spee-*ah*-cheh

USEFUL WORDS

big	grande	*gran*-deh
small	piccolo	*pee*-koh-loh
hot	caldo	*kal*-doh
cold	freddo	*fred*-doh
good	buono	*bwoh*-noh
bad	cattivo	kat-*tee*-voh
enough	basta	*bas*-tah
well	bene	*beh*-neh
open	aperto	ah-*pair*-toh
closed	chiuso	kee-*oo*-zoh
left	a sinistra	ah see-nee-strah
right	a destra	ah *dess*-trah
straight on	sempre dritto	*sem*-preh *dree*-toh
near	vicino	vee-*chee*-noh
far	lontano	lon-*tah*-noh
up	su	*soo*
down	giù	*joo*
early	presto	*press*-toh
late	tardi	*tar*-dee
entrance	entrata	en-*trah*-tah
exit	uscita	oo-*shee*-ta
toilet	il gabinetto	eel gah-bee-*net*-toh
free, unoccupied	libero	*lee*-bair-oh
free, no charge	gratuito	*grah*-too-ee-toh

MAKING A TELEPHONE CALL

I'd like to place a long-distance call.	Vorrei fare una interurbana.	vor-*ray* far-eh oona in-tair-oor-*bah*-nah.
I'd like to make a reverse-charge call.	Vorrei fare una telefonata a carico del destinatario.	vor-*ray* far-eh oona teh-leh-*fon*-ah-tah ah kar-ee-koh dell dess-tee-nah-*tar*-ree-oh.
I'll try again later.	Ritelefono più tardi.	ree-teh-*leh*-foh-noh pee-oo *tar*-dee.
Can I leave a message?	Posso lasciare un messaggio?	*poss*-oh lash-*ah*-reh oon mess-*sah*-joh?
Hold on	Un attimo, per favore	oon *ah*-tee-moh, pair fah-*vor*-eh
Could you speak up a little please?	Può parlare più forte, per favore?	pwoh par-*lah*-reh pee-oo for-teh, pair fah-*vor*-eh?
local call	la telefonata locale	lah teh-leh-fon-*ah*-ta loh-*kah*-leh

SHOPPING

How much does this cost?	Quant'è, per favore?	kwan-*teh*, pair fah-*vor*-eh?
I would like ...	Vorrei ...	vor-*ray*...
Do you have ...?	Avete ...?	ah-*veh*-teh...?
I'm just looking.	Sto soltanto guardando	stoh sol-tan-toh gwar-*dan*-doh
Do you take credit cards?	Accettate carte di credito?	ah-chet-tah-teh *kar*-teh dee creh-dee-toh?
What time do you open/close?	A che ora apre/ chiude?	ah keh or-ah *ah*-preh/kee-*oo*-deh?
this one	questo	*kweh*-stoh
that one	quello	*kwell*-oh
expensive	caro	*kar*-oh
cheap	a buon prezzo	ah bwon *pret*-soh
size, clothes	la taglia	lah *tah*-lee-ah
size, shoes	il numero	eel*noo*-mair-oh
white	bianco	bee-*ang*-koh
black	nero	*neh*-roh
red	rosso	*ross*-oh
yellow	giallo	*jal*-loh
green	verde	*vair*-deh
blue	blu	*bloo*
brown	marrone	mar-*roh*-neh

TYPES OF SHOP

antique dealer	l'antiquario	lan-tee-*kwah*-ree-oh
bakery	la panetteria	lahpah-net-tair-ee-ah
bank	la banca	lah *bang*-kah
bookshop	la libreria	lah lee-breh-*ree*-ah
butcher's	la macelleria	lah mah-chell-eh-*ree*-ah
cake shop	la pasticceria	lahpas-tee-chair-ee-ah
chemist's	la farmacia	lah far-mah-*chee*-ah
department store	il grande magazzino	eel *gran*-deh mag-gad-*zee*-noh
delicatessen	la salumeria	lah sah-loo-meh-*ree*-ah
fishmonger's	la pescheria	lah pess-keh-*ree*-ah
florist	il fioraio	eel fee-or-*eye*-oh
greengrocer	il fruttivendolo	eel froo-tee-*ven*-doh-loh
grocery	alimentari	ah-lee-men-*tah*-ree
hairdresser	il parrucchiere	eel par-oo-kee-*air*-eh
ice cream parlour	la gelateria	lah jel-lah-tair-*ree*-ah
market	il mercato	eel mair-*kah*-toh
news-stand	l'edicola	leh-*dee*-koh-lah
post office	l'ufficio postale	loo-*fee*-choh pos-*tah*-leh
shoe shop	il negozio di scarpe	eel neh-*goh*-tsioh dee *skar*-peh
supermarket	il supermercato	eel su-pair-mair-*kah*-toh
tobacconist	il tabaccaio	eel tah-bak-*eye*-oh
travel agency	l'agenzia di viaggi	lah-jen-*tsee*-ah dee vee-*ad*-jee

SIGHTSEEING

art gallery	la pinacoteca	lahpeena-koh-*teh*-kah
bus stop	la fermata dell'autobus	lah fair-*mah*-tah dell ow-toh-booss
church	la chiesa	lah kee-*eh*-zah
	la basilica	lah bah-*seel*-i-kah
garden	il giardino	eel jar-*dee*-no
library	la biblioteca	lah beeb-lee-oh-*teh*-kah
museum	il museo	eel moo-*zeh*-oh
railway station	la stazione	lah stah-tsee-*oh*-neh

| tourist information | l'ufficio turistico | loo-fee-choh too-ree-stee-koh |
| closed for the public holiday | chiuso per la festa | kee-oo-zoh pair lah fess-tah |

STAYING IN A HOTEL

Do you have any vacant rooms?	Avete camere libere?	ah-veh-teh kah-mair-eh lee-bair-eh?
double room	una camera doppia	oona kah-mair-ah doh-pee-ah
with double bed	con letto matrimoniale	kon let-toh mah-tree-moh-nee-ah-leh
twin room	una camera con due letti	oona kah-mair-ah kon doo-eh let-tee
single room	una camera singola	oona kah-mair-ah sing-goh-lah
room with a bath, shower	una camera con bagno, con doccia	oona kah-mair-ah kon ban-yoh, kon dot-chah
porter	il facchino	eel fah-kee-noh
key	la chiave	lah kee-ah-veh
I have a reservation.	Ho fatto una prenotazione.	oh fat-toh oona preh-noh-tah-tsee-oh-neh

EATING OUT

Have you got a table for ...?	Avete un tavolo per ...?	ah-veh-teh oon tah-voh-loh pair ...?
I'd like to reserve a table.	Vorrei riservare un tavolo.	vor-ray ree-sair-vah-reh oon tah-voh-loh
breakfast	colazione	koh-lah-tsee-oh-neh
lunch	pranzo	pran-tsoh
dinner	cena	cheh-nah
The bill, please.	Il conto, per favore.	eel kon-toh pair fah-vor-eh
I am a vegetarian.	Sono vegetariano/a.	sono veh-jeh-tar-ee-ah-noh/nah
waitress	cameriera	kah-mair-ee-air-ah
waiter	cameriere	kah-mair-ee-air-eh
fixed price menu	il menù a prezzo fisso	eel meh-noo ah pret-soh fee-soh
dish of the day	piatto del giorno	pee-ah-toh dell jor-no
starter	antipasto	an-tee-pass-toh
first course	il primo	eel pree-moh
main course	il secondo	eel seh-kon-doh
vegetables	il contorno	eel kon-tor-noh
dessert	il dolce	eel doll-che
cover charge	il coperto	eel koh-pair-toh
wine list	la lista dei vini	lah lee-stah day vee-nee
rare	al sangue	al sang-gweh
medium	a puntino	a poon-tee-noh
well done	ben cotto	ben kot-toh
glass	il bicchiere	eel bee-kee-air-eh
bottle	la bottiglia	lah bot-teel-yah
knife	il coltello	eel kol-tell-oh
fork	la forchetta	lah for-ket-tah
spoon	il cucchiaio	eel koo-kee-eye-oh

MENU DECODER

apple	la mela	lah meh-lah
artichoke	il carciofo	eel kar-choff-oh
aubergine	la melanzana	lah meh-lan-tsah-nah
baked	al forno	al for-noh
beans	i fagioli	ee fah-joh-lee
beef	il manzo	eel man-tsoh
beer	la birra	lah beer-rah
boiled	lesso	less-oh
bread	il pane	eel pah-neh
broth	il brodo	eel broh-doh
butter	il burro	eel boor-oh
cake	la torta	lah tor-tah
cheese	il formaggio	eel for-mad-joh
chicken	il pollo	eel poll-oh
chips	patatine fritte	pah-tah-teen-eh free-teh
baby clams	le vongole	leh von-goh-leh
coffee	il caffè	eel kah-feh
courgettes	gli zucchini	lyee dzoo-kee-nee
dry	secco	sek-koh
duck	l'anatra	lah-nah-trah
egg	l'uovo	loo-oh-voh
fish	il pesce	eel pesh-eh
fresh fruit	frutta fresca	froo-tah fress-kah
garlic	l'aglio	lahl-yoh
grapes	l'uva	loo-vah
grilled	alla griglia	ah-lah greel-yah
ham	il prosciutto	eel pro-shoo-toh
cooked/cured	cotto/crudo	kot-toh/kroo-doh
ice cream	il gelato	eel jel-lah-toh
lamb	l'abbacchio	lah-back-kee-oh
lobster	l'aragosta	lah-rah-goss-tah
meat	la carne	la kar-neh
milk	il latte	eel laht-teh
mineral water fizzy/still	l'acqua minerale gasata/naturale	lah-kwah mee-nair-ah-leh gah-zah-tah/nah-too-rah-leh
mushrooms	i funghi	ee foon-gee
oil	l'olio	loll-yoh
olive	l'oliva	loh-lee-vah
onion	la cipolla	lah chee-poll-ah
orange	l'arancia	lah-ran-chah
orange/lemon juice	succo d'arancia/ di limone	soo-kohdah-ran-chah/ dee lee-moh-neh
peach	la pesca	lah pess-kah
pepper	il pepe	eel peh-peh
pork	carne di maiale	kar-neh dee mah-yah-leh
potatoes	le patate	leh pah-tah-teh
prawns	i gamberi	ee gam-bair-ee
rice	il riso	eel ree-zoh
roast	arrosto	ar-ross-toh
roll	il panino	eel pah-nee-noh
salad	l'insalata	leen-sah-lah-tah
salt	il sale	eel sah-leh
sausage	la salsiccia	lah sal-see-chah
seafood	frutti di mare	froo-teedee mah-reh
soup	la zuppa, la minestra	lah tsoo-pah, lah mee-ness-trah
steak	la bistecca	lah bee-stek-kah
strawberries	le fragole	leh frah-goh-leh
sugar	lo zucchero	loh zoo-kair-oh
tea	il tè	eel teh
herb tea	la tisana	lah tee-zah-nah
tomato	il pomodoro	eel poh-moh-dor-oh
tuna	il tonno	eel ton-noh
veal	il vitello	eel vee-tell-oh
vegetables	i legumi	ee leh-goo-mee
vinegar	l'aceto	lah-cheh-toh
water	l'acqua	lah-kwah
red wine	vino rosso	vee-noh ross-oh
white wine	vino bianco	vee-noh bee-ang-koh

NUMBERS

1	uno	oo-noh
2	due	doo-eh
3	tre	treh
4	quattro	kwat-roh
5	cinque	ching-kweh
6	sei	say-ee
7	sette	set-teh
8	otto	ot-toh
9	nove	noh-veh
10	dieci	dee-eh-chee
11	undici	oon-dee-chee
12	dodici	doh-dee-chee
13	tredici	treh-dee-chee
14	quattordici	kwat-tor-dee-chee
15	quindici	kwin-dee-chee
16	sedici	say-dee-chee
17	diciassette	dee-chah-set-teh
18	diciotto	dee-chot-toh
19	diciannove	dee-chah-noh-veh
20	venti	ven-tee
30	trenta	tren-tah
40	quaranta	kwah-ran-tah
50	cinquanta	ching-kwan-tah
60	sessanta	sess-an-tah
70	settanta	set-tan-tah
80	ottanta	ot-tan-tah
90	novanta	noh-van-tah
100	cento	chen-toh
1,000	mille	mee-leh
2,000	duemila	doo-eh mee-lah
5,000	cinquemila	ching-kweh mee-lah
1,000,000	un milione	oon meel-yoh-neh

TIME

one minute	un minuto	oon mee-noo-toh
one hour	un'ora	oon or-ah
half an hour	mezz'ora	medz-or-ah
a day	un giorno	oon jor-noh
a week	una settimana	oona set-tee-mah-nah
Monday	lunedì	loo-neh-dee
Tuesday	martedì	mar-teh-dee
Wednesday	mercoledì	mair-koh-leh-dee
Thursday	giovedì	joh-veh-dee
Friday	venerdì	ven-air-dee
Saturday	sabato	sah-bah-toh
Sunday	domenica	doh-meh-nee-kah

ACKNOWLEDGMENTS

DK Travel would like to thank the following people whose help and assistance contributed to the preparation of this book

Karissa Adams, Adam Brackenbury, Elizabeth Byrne, James Davis, Sarah Dennis, Matt Dobbin, Bridget Fuller, Pauline Giacomelli-Harris, Meryl Halls, George Hamilton-Jones, Catherine Hetherington, Debbie James, Tom Morse, Chris Rushby, Mike Sansbury

Cartographic Data Lovell Johns Ltd

PICTURE CREDITS

The publisher would like to thank the following for their kind permission to reproduce their photographs:

Key: a-above; b-below/bottom; c-centre; f-far; l-left; r-right; t-top

10 Corso Como: 146tl.

123RF.com: Boris Breytman 307t; gonewiththewind 138-9b, 140bl; Yulia Grogoryeva 66tl; itsajoop 328tc; Olena Kachmar 397b; manjik 288t; marcovarro 339br; Valerio Mei 29cl, 324b; Yana Menshchikova 274cra; mikolaj64 473tr; Christian Mueller 336cl; Luca Pescucci 341cl; alex postovski 339tr; Davide Ferdinando Precone 193tl; Roman Smirnov 126tl; Ekaterina Spirina 486tr; Vaclav Volrab 137bl.

4Corners: Marco Arduino 6-7b; Matteo Carassale 341tr; SIME / Paolo Giocoso 504br.

500px: David Juan 14-5b; Carlo Murenu 447bl, 526-7; Gabi Rusu 250bl.

Alamy Stock Photo: AF archive 275tl age fotostock 66-7b, 365br; AGF Srl 150br, 152-3t, 188-9t, 430bc; Ambrosiniv 347c; Artexplorer 339cl; avphotosales / Lorenzo Quinn *Support* 2017 Venice Biennale 35tr; Awakening / Simone Padovani 64-5b; Azoor Photo 305tl; Bailey-Cooper Photography 13br; Stuart Black 13tHolger Burmeister 232b; Giuseppe Cammino 235tr; Nattee Chalermtiragool 276t; Loetscher Chlaus 172crb; Chromorange / Lynne Otter 109cr; Classic Image 42bc, 242cl; Sorin Colac 346t; Davide D'Amico 521b; Luis Dafos 259bc; Ian Dagnall 348-9, 349cra; massimo danza 234tl; De Agostini / M. Leigheb 518br; Martin A. Doe 515cb; saturno dona' 336cr; Adam Eastland 281tr, 290bl; FC_Italy 109cra; Paul Fearn 85tr; Kirk Fisher 347crb; Florilegius 45bc; Nicola Forenza 273; Funky Stock - Paul Williams 381t; Jeff Gilbert 160bl; GL Archive 258cb; Susana Guzman 277br; Dennis Hallinan 294tl; Andrew Hasson 354t; Gary Hebding Jr. 291t; Hemis 152br, 237t, 340-1b, 430tc, / Jean-Pierre Degas 19cla, / Francis Leroy 456t, / Jacques Sierpinski 518crb; John Heseltine 41bl; Peter Horree 289clb; Jiri Hubatka 179tl, 179br; imageBROKER 20-1b, 186tl, 259bl, 447t, 500-1, / Katja Kreder 530b; Interfoto 43bc; Alexander Karelin 272cla; John Kellerman 272cl, 343ca; Kiefer 352br; Art Kowalsky 351tr; Raimund Kutter 328bl; Lanmas 260clb; Lifestyle pictures 242clb; ; Angelo Fausto Lo Buglio 188bl; Luca Antonio Lorenzelli 141t; Lphoto 351cr; Cedric Maes 453tc; angel manzano 435tr; Marka 147br, 452-3b; Stefano Politi Markovina 134bc; Martin Thomas Photography 114; mauritius images GmbH 289fcrb; Valerio Mei 18cla, 236b; Andrew Michael 295; Mikel Bilbao Gorostiaga- Travels 288br; Hercules Milas 81tr, 86-7t, 230br; Julian Money-Kyrle 520t; muART 40br; MuseoPics - Paul Williams 342crb, 499br; National Geographic Creative 405; Olivia Nitaji 161t; North

Wind Picture Archives 45cr; B.O'Kane 75cr; Pacific Press/ Leo Claudio De Petris 235br; Panther Media GmbH 20tl; Photononstop 483cr; PhotoStock-Israel 34tl; J. Pie 244cra; Prisma Archivo 72fcrb; QEDimages 136tl; Andrea Raffin 148crb; M Ramírez 315cr; Realy Easy Star / Luca Scamporlino 15t, / Toni Spagone 518cr; REDA &CO srl 36-7t, 157c; John Rees 248clb; robertharding 233cb, 304clb; Giorgio Rossi 68-9t; Alexandre Rotenberg 147cl; Sagaphoto.com / Stephane Gautier 232cra; marco scataglini 360br; Scenics & Science 111t; Peter Scholey 515ca; Andrea Spinelli 40cl; Marina Spironetti 21tr; Wojciech Stróżyk 385; Krystyna Szulecka 248br; TravelCollection 237bl; Travelwide 14t; Trigger Image 25br; Viennaslide 81bl; WaterFrame 518cra; WENN UK 154bl; World History Archive 236tr.

Armani/Silos Museum/Giorgio Armani: Davide Lovatti 159bl.

AWL Images: Marco Bottigelli 219t, 320-1; ClickAlps 371tl, 445t, 462-3; Matteo Colombo 2-3, 39clb; Christian Handl 308t; Francesco Iacobelli 221t, 414-5, 446t, 490-1; Maurizio Rellini 4, 48-9, 258t; Mark Sykes 386br.

Bridgeman Images: Basilica San Francesco, Arezzo / Piero della Francesca *The Verification of the True Cross, The Victory of Heraclius and the Execution of Chosroes in 628 AD* (c.1415-92) 384bc; Gabinetto Comunale delle Stampe, Rome, Italy / De Agostini Picture Library / A. Dagli Orti 258clb.

Cortina Adrenalin Center: 133crb.

Depositphotos Inc: Bertl123 94t; borisb17 305cra; diabolique04 408tl; Ody1988 109tr; scorton 220cb, 400-1; scrisman 212t; siculodoc 116br; tan4ikk 304b.

Dorling Kindersley: Nigel Hicks 327tr; Mockford and Bonetti 280b, / MAXXI 316t.

Dreamstime.com: Adrea 522-3t; Akulamatiau 209b; Alfiofer 455br; Alkan2011 30-1t; Amoklv 470tc; Giuseppe Anello 523br; Antonel 67br; Piotr Antonów 41tl; Anyaivanova 81tl, 317b; Stefano Armaroli 433tr; Roberto Atzeni 21br; Kushnirov Avraham 166br; Frank Bach 43tl; Andrea Bacuzzi 40bl; Claudio Balducelli 41cl; Barmalini 331tr; Bbeckphoto 25c; Gordon Bell 363; Yulia Belousova 467b; Alexey Belyaev 290tr; Benkrut 310bl; Alexander Bezmolitvennyy 15cr; Blitzkoenig 357bl, 381br, 515cr; Bographics 468clb; Boris Breytman 252bl; Theodor Bunica 390bl; Callistemon3 41br; Duncan Campbell 407cla; Marco Dal Canto 398b; Francesco Carniani 191cra; Stefano Carocci 311tl; Adriano Castelli 41cra; Ana Del Castillo 110bl; Joaquin Ossorio Castillo 171tl; Ekaterina Chernenko 68br; Christophefaugere 101tl; Claudiodivizia 151tl, 191tr; Mike Clegg 99t; Sorin Colac 307bc; Claudio Giovanni Colombo 39b; Andrea Comari 50-51; Copora 62cr; Cosmin - Constantin Sava 22-3t; Alessandro Cristiano 191cr, 197cra; Daliu80 246-7tl, 389t; Dogofg 147tr; Dennis Dolken 234-5b; Dreamfotografs 37crb; Eddygaleotti 513bl; Emicristea 74-5b, 279bl, 296-7b; Enzodebe 115cl, 422cla; Ermess 390tl, 409bl, 410-1b, 412t, 437b; F11photo 62t; Fedecandoniphoto 233t; Prochasson Frederic 226c, 238-9; Freesurf69 31cla; Filip Fuxa 386-7t; Giovanni Gagliardi 498t; Veronika Galkina 355b; Markus Gann 418-9t; Gianluigibec 467cl, 532-3b; Ruslan Gilmanshin 242cla; Giorgiobonalumi 174t; Giuseppemasci 436tl, 481tr; Viktor Gladkov 161bc; Rostislav Glinsky 198b; Golasza 489t; GoneWithTheWind 31crb, 487b; Kaspars Grinvalds 67cl; Marco Guidi 388bl; Sven Hansche 112t; Eliane Haykal 87br; Francesco Riccardo Iacomino 8cl; Ilongplay 392bl; Inavanhateren 133cla; Gabriela Insuratelu 474bl; Iryna1 374t; Mihail Ivanov 98b; Ivansmuk 120bl; Wieslaw Jarek 112bc, 298br; Javarman 94bl; Jorisvo 431clb; Thomas Jurkowski 154-155; Kasto80 127crb,

191br; Sergii Kolesnyk 12-3b, 356t; Nikolai Korzhov 134t; Krivinis 512t; Lachris77 40tr; Laudibi 457r; Ethan Le 19tr; Lejoch 391tr; Leochen66 410tc; Lindom 98tr; Markos Loizou 186-7b; Loren Image 135tc; Luca Lorenzelli 32-3t, 140tc, 194t, 195tr; Luxerendering 306b; Mirko Macari 191crb; Madrabothair 370tr; Roberto Maggioni 195br; Marcorubino 517br; Marinv 254tc, 254-5; Alberto Masnovo 28-8b; Ewa Mazur 138tl; Aliaksandr Mazurkevich 8clb; Antony Mcaulay 242cr; Mfron 522bl; Giulio Mignani 38-9b; Milacroft 511tr; Hercules Milas 75bl; Minnystock 70b, 176-177b, 213b, 370-1c, 404cra, 432t; Martin Molcan 372-3t, 524bl, 530-1t; Luciano Mortula 30-1b; Sergey Mostovoy 172-3t; Roland Nagy 82-3t; Nejron 260crb; Neneo 32tc, 47br; Corina Daniela Obertas 384cra; Andrey Omelyanchuk 77t, 77cra, 244-5b; Dmitry Ometsinsky 92tl; Michelangelo Oprandi 38tl; Anna Pakutina 376cra; Ralph Paprzycki 109tl; Pavlinec 519tr; Roberto Pecci 533tl; Valery Pechinsky 13cr; William Perry 72crb, 247tr, 286bl; Perseomedusa 193br; Sergey Peterman 39br; Photogolfer 22bl, 289bl, 292-3, 456bl; Enrico Della Pietra 318, 466bl, 446cra, 496-7t; Beatrice Preve 158t; Progosu81 483tr; Dzianis Rabtsevich 466-7t; Rigmanyi 382t; M. Rohana 375br; Valerio Rosati 264bl, 319br; Rosshelen 221bl, 424-5; Rudi1976 55t, 102-3, 420-1t; Rusel1981 252t; Marco Saracco 166-7t, 190-1t, 407t; Sborisov 372bl; Scaliger 39tr, 78-9b, 84b, 93cl, 93b, 148bl, 150-1t, 251tl, 308br, 458-9b; Schlenger86 132b; Uta Scholl 65cl; Jozef Sedmak 65br, 81cr, 97t, 253br, 278bc; Olena Serditova 108t; Sikeyplus 189cr; Serghei Starus 169br; Cellai Stefano 40cr, 41tr; Stefanocar75 198tc; Stevanzz 377, 391b, 393tr, 399t; Kanokrat Tawokhat 452cra; Tcantlon 471bl; Theripper 483cra; Thevirex 525t; Timedreamer 338-9b, 353tl; Tomas1111 8-9b; Anibal Trejo 347br; Lev Tsimbler 276crb; Tupungato 262tl; Mirco Vacca 32bl; Gian Marco Valente 434bl; Stefano Valeri 299t, 330tl; Vdvtut 266bc; Alvaro German Vilela 461br; Mirko Vitali 187tr; Volodymyr Vyshnivetskyy 378t; Wallaceweeks 350-1; Hilda Weges 62t; Xantana 196-7b, 211t; Xbrchx 168t; Catalina Zaharescu Tiensuu 233cl; Natalia Zakharova 111tr; Andreas Zerndl 504t, 508; Znm 291cr; Zoomzoom 17tr.

Fondazione Musei Civici di Venezia: 70clb, 79tr, / Palazzo Ducale - Sala dell'Anticollegio / Paolo Caliari detto il Veronese *Il ratto di Europa* (1576 – 1580) 78cla.

Getty Images: AFP / Marco Bertorello 35br, / Vincenzo Pinto 235cl, / Alberto Pizzoli 47tr, 344bl; AGF 206-7b; Alinari Archives 315tc; Ayhan Altun 365tl; alxpin 431bl; Jon Arnold 64tl; Rob Atkins 44tl; Atlantide Phototravel 71cra, / Igor Mitoraj © ADAGP, Paris and DACS, London 2018 *Ikaro crashed* 514-5; Andrew Bain 483crb; Salvator Barki 429bc; Lutz Bongarts 47bl; Marco Bottigelli 54c, 56cb, 58-9, 162-3; Thekla Clark 338tl; Corbis / Stefano Montesi 314-5b, / Steve Schapiro 37cla; Pietro D'aprano 236cla; Luis Davilla 445bl, 476-7; De Agostini 21cl, 72cb, / Biblioteca Ambrosiana 260bc, / G. Cigolini 439br, / G. Dagli Orti 510br, / G. Nimatallah 23cla, 520bl, / L. Romano 488bl, / V. Pirozzi 315clb; Sofie Delauw 26-7t; Dosfotos 242bl; Norbert Eisele-Hein 133tr; EyeEm /Jerry Hoekstra 515br, / Devis Marchetto 516tr, /Antonio Sangermano 428t; EyesWideOpen 34-5b; Fine Art 345br; Mark Harris 23b; Heritage Images 45tr, 297tc, Fine Art Images 153cr; Francesco Riccardo Iacomino 440-1; Italian School 44bc; Jumping Rocks 299bl; Omar Kamel 484-5t; Dmitri Kessel 289crb; Keystone-France 46br, 47cra; Leemage 159tc, / Photo Josse 46-7t; Brian LoPiccolo 274-5b; Mondadori Portfolio 95br, 151br, 345cr; Flavia Morlachetti 340tl; Popperfoto / Bob Thomas 46bl; Andrea Pucci 326tl; Vittoriano Rastelli 293br; REDA&CO 106crb; Maurice Rougemont 341bpr; Slow Images 230cl; Ekaterina Smirnova 88bc; soblue.weina@gmail.com 344-5t; Sylvain Sonnet 69cla; Laszlo Szirtesi 261; ullstein bild Dtl. 46tl, 453cra; Universal Images Group Editorial 72clb, 294br; Guy Vanderelst 518tr; Eric Vandeville

248cr; Venturelli 35cl; Elisabetta A. Villa 37tr; Tim E White 237c; Gary Yeowell 219bl, 332-3cl.

Glass Hostaria: Giovanna Di Lisciandro 244tl.

iStockphoto.com: agustavop 73; aizram18 331br; AlexPro9500 26tl; Alfaproxima 124b; alle12 184crb; Alphotographic 72cra; ArtMarie 444c, 448-9, 455t; bdsklo 207tr; belenox 230t; benedek 266-7t; bennymarty 218c, 222-3; binabina 171cla; bluejayphoto 28tl, 116t; boggy22 43cla; borchee 342-3t; Francesco Cantone 263br; chang 12clb; Charles03 178b; ChiccoDodiFC 125tr; Creativaimage 29tr; dade80 419tr; deimagine 148br; edella 469; Ekspansio 395tr; ermess 494-5t; eugenesergeev 33b; EunikaSopotnicka 480t; Eva-Katalin 534-5; Fabrizio_Esposito 26cra; fazon1 227bl, 268-9; Flory 43br; FooTToo 438-9t; frankix 383t; gaffera 397cr; gameover2012 127b; Javier GarcÂa Blanco 62br; Garsya 204-5t; georgeclerk 12ca, 287cla; Giacomomo 122-3b; Gim42 144clb; GitoTrevisan 106t, 120-1t; Givaga 89b; holgs 18tl; InnaFelker 371tr; ipag 56tl, 142-3; Jag_cz 370tl; KavalenkavaVolha 259clb; kenex 539tl; Uğur Keskin 17cla; Kisa_Markiza 187br; Anna Kolesnikova 536bl; kurmyshov 244cr; Ladiras 175br; lillisphotography 275cr; lkonya 16-7t; Mableen 184t; mammuth 118-9b; MatteoCozzi 460; Maudib 220tl, 366-7; mikolajn 472t, 475t; mrtom-uk 29br; NAPA74 18-9t; narvikk 25tr; Nastasic 277bc; nejdetduzen 260cla; nicolamargaret 16-7cra; NiseriN 214-5; oreundici 187cl; pabloborca 276bl; peeterv 506b; piola666 40tl, 327b; QQ7 57bl, 200-201; Remedios 55bl, 128-129; repistu 360-1t; rez-art 27crb; ribeiroantonio 24tl; RolfSt 119cr; RomanBabakin 18-9cra; ROMAOSLO 228cb, 248cra, 278t, 300-1, 506-7t; RossHelen 16tl, 26b; sandrixroma 265tr; Marco Saracco 199t; SerrNovik 336t; Shaiith 396t; sphraner 123tr; spooh 325tr; StevanZZ 208t; TatyanaGl 287cr; tomazl 15br; TommasoT 106bl; TommL 146-7b; treeffe 422-3b; tunart 72cl; ultramarinfoto 132-3t; undefined undefined 27cl; ValerioMei 482-3b; ventdusud 24-5b, 148-9; WE-KWEK 246br; Wicki58 106cr; Waler Zerla 406b; Zolga_F 67tr; zorazhuang 243t; ZU_09 277clb, 287tc.

Museo MADRE, Naples: 454bl.

Museo Poldi Pezzoli, Milan: /Walter Gumiero 156br; / Piero del Pollaiolo *Portrait of a Young Woman* 156tl.

Museo Teatrale alla Scala: 157t.

Picfair.com: Turzo Almerindo 494bc.

Rex by Shutterstock: Kobal / Merchant Ivory / Goldcrest 36bl.

Robert Harding Picture Library: Neale Clark 228tl, 282-3; Marco Cristofori 229, 312-3; Christian Goupi 468br; Ben Pipe 65tr; Ingolf Pompe 184cl, 184cr; Matthew Williams-Ellis 509cla, 510-1t; Walter Zerla 57t, 180-1.

Photo Scala, Florence: DeAgostini Picture Library 155cr; courtesy of the Ministero Beni e Att. Culturali e del Turismo 384cl, 384clb, 384cb, 384bl; Mauro Ranzani 155clb, 171br.

SuperStock: 4X5 Collection 115cb, 115br; age footstock / Marco Brivio 90cl, 171cra, ; Funkystockk 230cr, 452bl; / Phil Robinson 42bl, / Ivan Vdovin 192bl; AGF photo / Smith Mark Edward 90-1b; The Art Archive 46cr; Peter Barritt 88tr; ClickAlps / Mauritius 497br; DeAgostini 42t, 43tr, 45cra, 349br; Hemis / Bertrand Rieger 210bl; Iberfoto 44-5t, 45br; imageBROKER / Barbara Boensch 379bl, / Christian Handl 484bl, / Raimund Kutter 329t, / Michael Nitzschke 358-9b; Prisma / van der Meer Rene 399br; Quint & Lox Limited 44br.

Front flap: 500px: Carlo Murenu cra; AWL Images: Francesco Iacobelli bl; Dreamstime.com Tomas1111 cb; Getty Images: Marco Bottigelli t; iStockphoto.com: cla; Picfair.com: monti br.

Sheet map cover: Picfair.com: monti.

Cover images:
Front and spine: Picfair.com: monti.
Back: Dreamstime.com: Francesco Riccardo Iacomino cl; iStockphoto.com: ipag c, QQ7 tr; Picfair.com: monti b.

For further information see: www.dkimages.com

Penguin Random House

Main Contributors Ros Belford, Paul Duncan, Tim Jepson, Andrew Gumbel, Christopher Catling, Sam Cole

Senior Editor Alison McGill

Senior Designer Laura O'Brien

Project Editor Sophie Adam

Project Art Editors Bess Daly, Tania Gomes, Ben Hinks, Stuti Tiwari Bhatia, Bharti Karakoti, Priyanka Thakur, Vinita Venugopal

Factcheckers Toni DeBella, Daniel Mosseri, Marcella Simone

Editors Lucy Sienkowska, Danielle Watt, Freddie Marriage, Sands Publishing Ltd

Proofreader Samantha Cook

Indexer Zoe Ross

Senior Picture Researcher Ellen Root

Picture Research Lucy Sienkowska, Mark Thomas

Illustrators Stephen Conlin, Donati Giudici Associati srl, Stephen Gyapay, Roger Hutchins, Maltings Partnership, Simon Roulstone, Paul Weston, John Woodcock, Andrea Corbella, Richard Draper, Kevin Jones Associates, Chris Orr and Associates, Robbie Polley, Simon Roulstone, Martin Woodward

Senior Cartographic Editor Casper Morris

Cartography Mohammad Hassan, Suresh Kumar, Simonetta Giori

Jacket Designers Maxine Pedliham, Bess Daly

Jacket Picture Research Susie Peachey

Senior DTP Designer Jason Little

DTP Coordinator George Nimmo

Senior Producer Stephanie McConnell

Managing Editor Rachel Fox

Art Director Maxine Pedliham

Publishing Director Georgina Dee

First American edition 1996
Published in the United States by DK Publishing, 345 Hudson Street, New York, New York 10014.

Copyright 1996, 2018 © Dorling Kindersley Limited, London

A Penguin Random House Company

18 19 20 21 10 9 8 7 6 5 4 3 2 1

All rights reserved.

Without limiting the rights under copyright reserved above, no part of this publication may be reproduced, stored in or introduced into a retrieval system, or transmitted, in any form, or by any means (electronic, mechanical, photocopying, recording, or otherwise), without the prior written permission of both the copyright owner and the above publisher of this book.

Published in Great Britain by Dorling Kindersley Limited.

A catalog record for this book is available from the Library of Congress.

ISSN: 1542-1554
ISBN: 978-1-4654-7158-1

Throughout this book, floors are referred to in accordance with European usage; i.e., the "first floor" is the floor above ground level.

Printed and bound in China

www.dk.com

MIX
Paper from responsible sources
FSC™ C018179
www.fsc.org

The information in this DK Eyewitness Travel Guide is checked regularly.

Every effort has been made to ensure that this book is as up-to-date as possible at the time of going to press. Some details, however, such as telephone numbers, opening hours, prices, gallery hanging arrangements and travel information, are liable to change. The publishers cannot accept responsibility for any consequences arising from the use of this book, nor for any material on third party websites, and cannot guarantee that any website address in this book will be a suitable source of travel information. We value the views and suggestions of our readers very highly. Please write to: Publisher, DK Eyewitness Travel Guides, Dorling Kindersley, 80 Strand, London, WC2R 0RL, UK, or email: travelguides@dk.com